THE ORIGINS OF NATIONAL INTERESTS

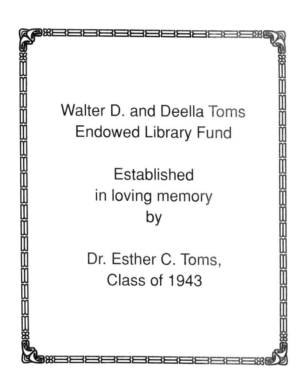

CASS SERIES ON SECURITY STUDIES
ISSN 1363-2329

General Editor
Benjamin Frankel

This series explores both the traditional and emerging themes of international security, offering theoretical and historical examinations of the contexts, sources, causes, dynamics, uses, ramifications and outcomes of conflict and war.

The Origins of National Interests
edited by Glenn Chafetz, Michael Spirtas and Benjamin Frankel

Roots of Realism
edited by Benjamin Frankel

Realism: Restatements and Renewal
edited by Benjamin Frankel

The Origins of National Interests

Editors

Glenn Chafetz
Michael Spirtas
Benjamin Frankel

FRANK CASS
LONDON • PORTLAND, OR

First published in 1999 in Great Britain by
FRANK CASS PUBLISHERS
Newbury House, 900 Eastern Avenue, London IG2 7HH

and in the United States of America by
FRANK CASS PUBLISHERS
c/o ISBS, 5804 N.E. Hassalo Street
Portland, Oregon 97213-3644

Website www.frankcass.com

Copyright © 1999 Frank Cass & Co. Ltd.

British Library Cataloguing in Publication Data

The origins of national interests. – (Cass series on
security studies; v.3)
1. Nationalism – Philosophy 2. Sovereignty – Philosophy
3. Nationalism – Cross-cultural studies 4. Sovereignty –
Cross-cultural studies
I. Chafetz, Glenn II. Spirtas, Michael III. Frankel, Benjamin, 1949–
320.5'4'01

ISBN 0 7146 4985 6 (cloth)
ISBN 0 7146 8048 6 (paper)
ISSN 1363 2329

Library of Congress Cataloging-in-Publication Data

The origins of national interests / edited by Glenn Chafetz,
Michael Spirtas, and Benjamin Frankel.
    p. cm. — (Cass series on security studies, 1363-2329)
  Includes bibliographical references and index.
  ISBN 0-7146-4985-6 (hard)
  ISBN 0-7146-8048-6 (pbk.)
    1. International relations. 2. Nationalism. 3. World politics. I.
Chafetz, Glenn R. II. Spirtas, Michael. III. Frankel, Benjamin,
1949- IV. Series.
  JZ1316 .075 1999
  327.1—dc21   99-38155
                                                           CIP

This group of studies first appeared in a special issue of *Security Studies* (ISSN 0963 6412),
Vol.8, No.2/3 (Winter 1998/99–Spring, 1999) published by Frank Cass and Co. Ltd.

Printed in Great Britain by Anthony Rowe Ltd., Chippenham, Wiltshire

CONTENTS

INTRODUCTION: TRACING THE INFLUENCE OF IDENTITY ON FOREIGN POLICY

GLENN CHAFETZ, MICHAEL SPIRTAS, AND BENJAMIN FRANKEL

The concept of "identity" has gained increasing currency in international relations scholarship. Two flaws, however, have so far hobbled identity scholarship. First, it offers too many vague and imprecise definitions—which means that it offers none—of the concept that stands at its very core; second, most of this scholarship does not go much beyond the mere assertion that identity is important, and that, somehow, in one way or another, it plays a role in how states define and pursue their national interests. These flaws have allowed critics to argue that the identity school offered little that was startling or new; that international relations scholars had already taken account of the fact that ideas mattered in shaping and implementing policy;[1] and that norms and institutions offered explanations similar to those drawn from identity, but without relying on vague terms and causal links which were vaguer yet.

Before we can determine whether the appeal to identity is helpful in understanding state behavior, we should correct these debilitating flaws. First, we should offer clear definitions of identity and the concepts surrounding the term; second, we should demonstrate, in a clear and precise way which can be tested, the causal link between identity and the behavior of states.

The authors whose articles are gathered in this volume have taken up this challenge. In doing so, they have assumed the risks that attend new work: their conceptualization of the concept of identity and the

Glenn Chafetz is a policy planner in the Bureau of Political-Military Affairs at the Department of State; Michael Spirtas is a fellow at the Center for National Policy and research fellow at U.S. CREST; Benjamin Frankel is editor of *Security Studies*.

---

1. Jack Snyder, *The Ideology of the Offensive: Military Decision Making and the Disasters of 1914* (Ithaca: Cornell University Press, 1984); Jack Snyder, *Myth of Empire: Domestic Politics and International Ambition* (Ithaca: Cornell University Press, 1991); Stephen Van Evera, "The Cult of the Offensive and the Origins of the First World War," *International Security* 9, no. 1 (summer 1984) 58–107; Peter Haas, *Saving the Mediterranean* (New York: Columbia University Press, 1990); Martha Finnemore, *National Interests in International Society* (Ithaca: Cornell University Press, 1996).

manner in which they operationalize it may be questioned, or they may be proven wrong on empirical grounds. These risks, however, are necessary if identity is to become a useful social-scientific concept and if it is to make a meaningful contribution to our understanding of politics among nations. Some of the authors differ over conceptualizing identity, but we, the editors, borrowing from common usage, have chosen to define identity as the state of being similar to some actors and different from others in a particular circumstance. Identity involves the creation of boundaries that separate self and other. The process of boundary creation has significant consequences for many disciplines, and world politics is no exception.

WHAT IS IDENTITY IN THE CONTEXT OF INTERNATIONAL POLITICS?

THE APPROACH we (the editors, but not all of the authors in the volume) take is essentially a psychological one. Definitions within psychology vary, but most hold that each actor possesses a self-concept that is made up of discrete category or chosen group memberships (including political affiliation, religion, nationality, and ideology). The actor represents each category membership as a social identity. The identity is a mental construct that both describes and prescribes how the actor should think, feel, evaluate, and, ultimately, behave in group-relevant situations.[2]

Cognitively, identities help individuals cope with complex, demanding situations. Identities are self-schemas, mental representations that allow individuals to overcome the inherent deficits in short-term memory and other information-processing capacity by organizing an otherwise overwhelming amount of incoming stimuli into categories based on prior experience.[3] Self-schemas are tools for managing and organizing information about oneself and the self's relationship to the

2. John C. Turner, "Social Categorization and the Self-Concept: A Social Cognitive Theory of Group Behavior," in *Advances in Group Processes*, vol. 2, ed. Edward J. Lawler (Greenwich, Conn.: JAI Press, 1985), 80.

3. Susan T. Fiske and Shelley E. Taylor, *Social Cognition*. 2nd ed. (New York: McGraw Hill, 1991); Yuen F. Khong, *Analogies at War: Korea, Munich, Dien Bien Phu, and the Vietnam Decisions of 1965* (Princeton: Princeton University Press, 1992); Deborah Welch Larson, "The Role of Belief Systems and Schemas in Foreign Policy Decision-Making," *Political Psychology* (15 March 1994): 17–33; and Richard E. Nisbett and Lee Ross, *Social Inference: Strategies and Shortcomings of Social Judgment* (Englewood-Cliffs, N.J.: Prentice-Hall, 1980).

environment.[4] An identity, then, is the mechanism that provides individuals with a sense of self and the means for comprehending the relationship of the self to the external environment. Identity is an inherent part of cognition, and it makes life more predictable and less inchoate, inexplicable, and random by giving actors more of a sense of how their behavior will affect others' behavior toward them.[5]

Identity is not strictly cognitive, however. The cognitive function is accompanied by evaluative and emotional functions that operate simultaneously. At the same time that actors perceive and make predictions about themselves based on social stimuli, identities evaluate what these stimuli imply about the actors' worth and provide emotional input.[6] As an example, an actor will likely categorize the destruction of its military by an adversary as a defeat. This act will probably also evoke humiliation and shame and anger, and an assessment of diminished self-worth.[7]

In addition to the psychological components, identities comprise social and nonsocial elements. They are social because individuals share identities, or identify with others, in groups. Because individuals belong to multiple groups, identity is not unitary. Multiple groups mean multiple identities, as Bruce Cronin and Rodney Bruce Hall show.[8] Moreover, because groups overlap, we can speak not only of individual identities, but group identities as well. These identities, in turn, can be altered by and through interaction to create larger or smaller group identities.[9] Accordingly, positive group identification makes Gascons, Normans, and Corsicans into French (in certain social settings); posi-

4. Fiske and Taylor, *Social Cognition* 180–204.

5. Ibid., 100–138.

6. John A. Bargh, "The Automaticity of Everyday Life," in *Advances in Social Cognition* , ed. R. S. Wyer Jr. (Mahwah, N.J: Erlbaum, 1996); and John A. Bargh and Kimberly Barndollar, "Automaticity in Action: The Unconscious as Repository of Chronic Goals and Motives," in *The Psychology of Action: Linking Cognition and Motivation to Behavior*, ed. Peter M. Gollwitzer and John A. Bargh (New York: Guilford, 1996.

7. Robert E. Harkavy, "Defeat, National Humiliation, and the Revenge Motif in International Politics" (paper presented at the Annual Scientific Meeting of the International Society of Political Psychology, Vancouver, British Columbia 1995).

8. Rodney Bruce Hall, "Territorial and National Sovereigns: Sovereign Identity and Consequences for Security Policy," *Security Studies* 8, nos. 2/3 (winter 1998/99–spring 1999): 145–97; Bruce Cronin, "From Balance to Community: Transnational Identity and Political Integration," *Security Studies* 8, nos. 2/3 (winter 1998/99–spring 1999): 270–301.

9. Samuel Gaertner, et al., "The Common Ingroup Identity Model," in *European Review of Social Psychology* 4, ed. Wolfgang Stroebe and Miles Hewstone (New York: Wiley, 1993), 1–26.

tive group identification also makes the United States, Italy, France, Germany, and others into an entity often called "the West." Negative identification made Czechoslovakia into the Czech Republic and Slovakia, and threatens the integrity of Canada, Russia, and Great Britain.

Identification refers to the importance or intensity of an identity. Identification exists along a continuum from absolutely negative to absolutely positive. Absolutely negative describes a zero-sum conflict situation. Absolutely positive identification describes some family relationships and the bonds between soldiers during combat.[10] On the other end of the continuum, the lack of identification indicates the absence of any perceived relationship, and no identity exists.

The authors in this volume show that identities change. Actor A can have, among its identities, "adversary of actor B." Over time that identity may become "friend of actor B." In that case we say that A's level of negative identification with B decreased and the level of positive identification increased. The process by which identities change is social interaction. Through social interaction, actors create values, norms, beliefs, role conceptions, attitudes, stereotypes, and other cognitive, affective, and motivational phenomena which become embodied in and, as a consequence, change the actor's psychology.[11] Over time actors internalize those constructs which prove psychologically rewarding (this includes material benefits such as security and welfare). The level of the perceived reward, and the duration over which the actor perceives the reward as forthcoming, affect the strength and durability of the internalized values, beliefs, and attitudes.[12] The dynamic nature of identity holds significant theoretical and political implications. Most importantly, it invalidates the common claims that a given community (for example, "the West," "Palestine," or "Yugoslavia") are "unnatural" or "artificial." These claims are operationally irrelevant and methodologically intractable. They are operationally irrelevant because all political communities, whether "natural" or "invented,"

---

10. Kristen Renwick Monroe, "Psychology and Rational Actor Theory," *Political Psychology* 16 (March 1995): 1–21.

11. Turner, "Social Categorization," 80.

12. Michael A Hogg, Deborah J. Terry, and Katherine M. White, "A Tale of Two Theories: A Critical Comparison of Identity Theory with Social Identity Theory," *Social Psychology Quarterly* 58 (December 1995): 259–62; Turner, "Social Categorization."

have political consequences. They are methodologically intractable because they are not based on independent or measurable criteria.[13]

The dynamic and social nature of identities does not, however, imply infinite malleability. First, identities contain nonsocial elements. Physical and other characteristics such as size, race, and language, which strongly resist change, often provide specific identity cues to actors which affect the perceptions of both the actor toward others and others toward the actor.[14] Similarly, material factors can shape how states (more properly, those that act in the name of states) perceive their relationships with other states.[15] These include size, race, ethnicity, geography, and the traditions and values by which other states govern themselves. Nevertheless, without the experience of social interaction, such attributes have no meaning. Race has no significance as a social category without the experience of colonialism, slavery, or discrimination. Economic strength, culture, and ideology lack significance in the international context without international interaction. Without histories of hostility or friendship, states lack the experiential basis for developing images of what kind of states are more likely to be friendly and what kind are likely to be adversarial.[16]

In addition, we may infer that identities, despite their susceptibility to social molding, are relatively stable because identities are a kind of schema and schemas, in turn, must resist easy change. This perseverance effect, well known in cognitive psychology, occurs because a schema increases cognitive efficiency by focusing attention on information that is consistent with previous categorizations of the schema topic. Information inconsistent with the schemas that decisionmakers have developed to understand their environment, including themselves, will likely go unnoticed or cause stress. Accordingly, individuals tend to bypass or distort discrepant information in order to make it fit into previously held conceptions or to avoid stress.[17] Schemas must

13. Rasma Karklins, *Ethnopolitics and Transition to Democracy: The Collapse of the USSR and Latvia* (Baltimore: Johns Hopkins University Press, 1994); Russell Hardin, *One For All: The Logic of Group Conflict* (Princeton: Princeton University Press, 1995).

14. Fiske and Taylor, *Social Cognition*, 145–52.

15. See Michael Spirtas, "French Twist: French and British NATO Policies from 1949 to 1966," *Security Studies* 8, nos. 2/3 (winter 1998/99–spring 1999): 302–46.

16. Richard K. Herrmann and Michael P. Fischerkeller, "Beyond the Enemy Image," *International Organization* 49, no. 3 (summer 1995): 415–50; Alexander Wendt, "Anarchy is What States Make of It: The Social Construction of Power Politics," *International Organization* 42, no. 2 (Spring 1994): 391–425.

17. Fiske and Taylor, *Social Cognition*; Larson, "The Role of Belief Systems and Schemas in Foreign Policy Decision-Making," 149–52; Yaacov Y. I. Vertzberger, *The*

thus be subjected to masses of inconsistent information before they are replaced or altered. The self-schema, which is the cognitive basis for identity, is the most highly resistant of all schemas because a stable self-concept is so important to an actor's stability and well-being.[18]

The main implication of this resistance is that international actors tend to change their concepts about their roles only reluctantly and with difficulty. Two factors impede change, each arising from identity defense mechanisms. First, as noted above, at the individual level, the need for predictability and consistency, which leads to identity formation in the first place, inhibits the ability to perceive and cope with stimuli inconsistent with one's sense of self. At the group level, neither government bureaucracies nor society at large can function without a minimal level of stability of expectations.[19] It is probably for this reason that political communities develop powerful myths and institutions designed to enhance and defend their roles and to foster citizen identification with those roles.[20]

The importance of a given identity to an actor depends on two factors: the relevance of the situation salience and the overall psychological significance of the identity centrality. Salience, in turn, depends on the accessibility and fit of the identity to a social setting and the centrality and value of a given identity to the person's self-concept.[21] Centrality has two components. First, the centrality of a given identity is, in part, a simple function of the number of identities in an actor's self-

---

World In Their Minds: Information Processing, Cognition, and Perception in Foreign Policy Decisionmaking (Stanford: Stanford University Press, 1990), 147–93; Renee Weber, and Jennifer Crocker, "Cognitive Processes in the Revision of Stereotypic Beliefs, *Journal of Personality and Social Psychology* 45, no. 5 (November 1983): 961–67.

18. Vertzberger, *World in Their Minds,* 190.

19. Hedley Bull, *The Anarchical Society* (Oxford: Oxford University Press, 1977), 3–52; Mary Douglas, *How Institutions Think* (Syracuse: Syracuse University Press, 1986).

20. Even when elites try to modify the relationship of their country to the external environment, domestic forces hostile to any alteration in the status quo resist. Ideologically oriented schemas molded by previous rhetoric about the state's place in the world may resist change. James G. Richter, "Perpetuating the Cold War," *Political Science Quarterly* 107, no. 2 (summer 1992): 271–301. Moreover, in an interdependent environment, any alteration in foreign political commitments also entails alienating domestic constituencies that may have powerful interests in maintaining the status quo in relations with allies and adversaries. See Peter F. Cowhey, "Domestic Institutions and International Commitments," *International Organization* 47, no. 2 (spring 1993): 299–326. These interests may be based on ethnic, cultural, ideological, racial, commercial, or some other kind of connections. They may be limited and instrumental, and therefore transitory, or they may be psychologically internalized and thus relatively stable.

21. Fiske and Taylor, *Social Cognition,* 142–79; Penelope Oakes, "The Salience of Social Categories," in *Rediscovering the Social Group: A Self-Categorization Theory,* ed. John C. Turner, et al. (New York: Basil Blackwell, 1987).

concept. An actor is more likely to attach greater value to a given identity if that identity is one out of a few instead of one out of many. In addition, an identity's centrality depends on an actor's subjective understanding of how cognitively and affectively rewarding it has been for the actor in the past.[22]

Social settings may be area or issue specific. Individuals, for example, maintain different identities depending on whether the social setting is the home, work, neighborhood, town, country, or world. One may be Welsh in Britain, British in Europe, European in the West, and Western in the Third World. The social setting often cues identities. The history of NATO is full of examples of alliance cohesion in the North Atlantic area but neutrality on out-of-area issues.[23]

Group cohesion often increases in response to external threats but such threats, by themselves, are not necessary for cohesion to persist. The American colonies prior to the Constitution and the Inter-German alliance before unification are cases in point. The implication for international relations theory and our authors is clear: groups of states require neither the external threat, as posited by neorealism, nor the institutional tasks, as predicted by institutionalism, to exist as distinctive collectivities.

The question, then, is: if threats or other tasks are not always necessary, what else can account for the voluntary formation or degradation of collectivities? The authors in this volume, consistent with their predictions, find that change usually occurs slowly as a result of repeated interactions. Relatively rapid, traumatic events can lead an individual or collective entity to add new identities, or reorder the salience of existing ones.[24] States suddenly thrust into new roles or new environments may radically reorder their priorities. Such sudden policy changes, however, are rare.[25] A greater appreciation for identity can help explain state policies.

22. Patricia W. Linville, "Self-Complexity and Affective Extremity: Don't Put All Your Eggs in One Cognitive Basket," *Social Cognition* 3 (spring 1985): 94–120.

23. Douglas Stuart and William Tow, *The Limits of Alliance: NATO Out-of-Area Problems since 1949* (Baltimore: Johns Hopkins University Press, 1990).

24. Irving L. Janis and Leon Mann, *Decision Making: A Psychological Analysis of Conflict, Choice, and Commitment* (New York: Free Press, 1977), 107–33; Linville, "Self-Complexity and Affective Extremity," 94–120; and Linville, "Self-Complexity as a Cognitive Buffer Against Related Depression and Illness." *Journal of Personality and Social Psychology* 52 (April 1987): 663–76.

25. K. J. Holsti, *Why Nations Realign* (London: Allen & Unwin, 1982).

WHAT DOES IDENTITY ADD TO THE STUDY OF INTERNATIONAL POLITICS?

WE OFFER two principal justifications for a book on identity and international politics. First, the narrowly rationalist approaches that dominate the field of international relations usually assume interests and preferences, rather than try to explain these interests and preferences. Most observers would grant that realist, expected utility, and institutionalist theories have expanded our understanding and clarified our thinking on the international system and foreign policy, but when these approaches take actor identities as given, they leave a large hole in our understanding of war, cooperation, alliances, and foreign policy decision making.

The second main reason for this project stems from the disparate nature of the identity agenda itself. First, the work being done encompasses a variety of different theoretical approaches. The separate development of these identity research programs reflects, in part, the multidisciplinary nature of identity as a subject. These different disciplines examine different actors and systems, and use different methodologies to do so, but all share an interest in how a given actor—be it a cell, a person, or a group of people—distinguishes self from other in a larger social environment, and in different contexts. All assume that this process of distinction holds significant implications for that actor's behavior. By gathering representatives from some of these approaches together in one volume, we allow for the possibility of cross-fertilization among approaches. We also make it possible for the reader to compare among approaches to see which offers the best way to explain state behavior.

ADDRESSING CRITICS

THIS VOLUME will be attacked by those who argue that the concept of identity is too complex to be defined, and those who argue that the conceptualizations of identity used here carry a danger of false precision. If these attacks are correct, we face the possibility that identity is too murky, and too susceptible to manipulation by researchers seeking to confirm their hypotheses, to be used to explain state policy. The difficulty of the task and the possibility of failure, however, should not deter efforts to define and examine what so many students have come to believe to be an important force in international politics. International relations scholars use a host of complex concepts, some of which have been the subject of long and exhaustive debates over their proper definitions. The concept of power, for example, a concept central to a field that tries to explain and understand politics, has been subjected to years of inconclusive debate.[26] The concept of identity, if it is difficult to approach, deserves similar effort and attention from social scientists. If we fail, it should be as a result of the difficulty of the task before us, not because of an unwillingness to dirty our hands or risk failure.

IDENTITY AND INTEREST

SCHOLARS skeptical of the concept of identity argue that it adds little to our understanding of state policy, and that we are better served by the concept of interest. Indeed, many international relations scholars turn to the concept of national interest to explain why states follow particular foreign policies. The concept of national interest is often a contentious subject, owing to constant bickering over its definition in specific instances. Great and small issues feature debates over national interest. Was it in the U.S. national interest, for example, to enter into the First World War? Fight in Vietnam? Debates over national interest are not limited to military issues, but pervade all areas of foreign policy. Is it in the U.S. national interest to admit China into the World Trade Organization (WTO) ? To support the International Monetary Fund (IMF)?

Realists have long championed the concept of national interest, inspired by Hans Morgenthau's dictum that states pursue the national interest in terms of power.[27] Neorealists argue that states are functionally similar, responding to the inducements and constraints of the international environment to guarantee their survival.[28] Stephen Krasner, another realist, has made the most persistent attempt to prove the existence of a national interest.[29] Krasner traces several episodes of U.S. for-

---

26. David A. Baldwin, *Paradoxes of Power* (London: Basil Blackwell, 1989); Peter Bachrach and Morton S. Baratz, "The Two Faces of Power," *American Political Science Review* 56 (1962); Stephen Lukes, *Power: A Radical View* (London: Macmillan, 1974).

27. Hans J. Morgenthau, *Politics Among Nations: The Struggle for Power and Peace,* 5th ed. (New York: Knopf, 1973).

28. Kenneth N. Waltz, *Theory of International Politics* (New York: Addison Wesley, 1979).

29. Stephen Krasner, *Defending the National Interest: Raw Materials Investments and U.S. Foreign Policy* (Princeton: Princeton University Press, 1978).

eign policy in an effort to show that even the United States, a weak state by many standards owing to its divided government, was able to conceive of and carry out policies consistent with its national interest.

The problem with the concept of national interest lies in its circular nature. Realists, reviewing past state policies, may declare these policies to have been in the national interest because they were executed by the state. For the concept of national interest to mean something, realists and other proponents must be able to derive its existence independently of outcomes.

The same criticism applies to the concept of identity, and one of the goals of this volume is to show various ways in which identity may be conceived of and measured. We raise the criticisms of national interest not to dismiss the concept, which is useful, but to remind critics of identity that identity is not the only contested concept in the field. Moreover, identity and interest intermingle.[30] If national interest were determined solely by material factors, then states possessing similar attributes placed in similar situations would act similarly. The cases examined in this book do not confirm this expectation.[31] By highlighting some of the problems with using an exclusively materially based conception of national interest, these essays suggest the benefit of incorporating identity to explain the full variety of state behavior evident in the international sphere. We can not know what we want if we do not know who we are. This insight holds for foreign policy as much as it does for personal preferences.[32]

In addition to these benefits, paying attention to identity will be particularly beneficial to observers of current international events. Two major powers in the international system, Germany and Japan, show an unprecedented aversion to military intervention.[33] This shift is not understandable from the position of these two powerful states in the power structure. Likewise, even the most powerful state in the system,

30. Mlada Bukovansky, "American identity and neutral rights from independence to the War of 1812," *International Organization* 51, no. 2 (spring 1997): 210.

31. Mary N. Hampton, "NATO, Germany, and the United States: Creating Positive Identity in Trans-Atlantia," *Security Studies* 8, nos. 2/3 (winter 1998/99–spring 1999): 235–69.

32. David Campbell, *Writing Security: United States Foreign Policy and the Politics of Identity* (Minneapolis: University of Minnesota Press, 1992).

33. Germany's intervention in Kosovo is unprecedented, and the Germans are engaging in it quite gingerly. On Germany and Japan, see Thomas U. Berger, *Cultures of Antimilitarism: National Security in Germany and Japan* (Baltimore: Johns Hopkins University Press, 1998); and John S. Duffield, *World Power Forsaken: Political Culture, International Institutions, and German Security Policy after Unification* (Stanford: Stanford University Press, 1998).

the United States, has shown a distaste for unilateral military action, seeking to achieve international consensus on such major issues as the war against Iraq and the subsequent sanctions regime against it; achieving peace in the former Yugoslavia; and maintaining stability in East Asia and Russia. Considering identity in addition to other nonmaterial factors such as norms can help better explain today's world.

NORMS AND IDENTITY

Acknowledging the importance of norms brings us to another argument raised against the current wave of identity approaches: that these approaches use identity as an "error" term consisting of various adopted norms and institutions.[34] To be sure, current interest in identity has attracted a wide range of approaches, some of which will have more long-term merit than others. Nevertheless, interest in identity is more than a passing fad. To agree that norms can influence identities (and vice versa) does not mean that identities are reducible to norms. Indeed, states adopting particular identities are more likely to conform to some norms over others. If anything, identity can be used to show how states with particular historical and cultural backgrounds adopt a particular norm. One may argue, for example, that Germany's experience following the disastrous Third Reich has left it with a powerful inhibition against military intervention abroad. Military nonintervention may be considered a norm, but without recourse to German identity and the reasons for its formation it is unclear why the Germans would adopt this norm over other norms—such as military intervention to prevent human rights violations or genocide—or military intervention for territorial gain. Even as Germany intervenes in Kosovo to aid the Albanian refugees, the ruling coalition in Germany is bitterly divided over the issue, with its most liberal element, the Greens, raising persistent objections to it.

TAKING STOCK

The academic exploration of the origins and consequences of identity ranges across the humanities, and social and biological sciences, as well as law and business. Within the social sciences, as Paul

---

34. We are grateful to Martha Finnemore for pointing out this argument.

Kowert notes, anthropology, sociology, psychology, and political science have investigated the concept from sometimes clashing, sometimes complementary, and often unrelated perspectives.[35]

In political science, the subject has earned attention from all subfields, though probably the best known involve inquiries about the impact of party identification on voting, the causes and remedies for ethnic conflict within and across national boundaries, and the making of nations.[36] In international relations, relatively little has been devoted to the nature, causes, and consequences of state identities in the international system.[37] Even fewer works have gone beyond explication and literature review into historically informed empirical analysis.[38] This is where our effort belongs.

All of the approaches to political identity, with the exception of some studies of nationalism, are constructivist in that they hold that actor identities, whether individual, subnational, national, or supranational, are affected by social interactions. In contrast, primordialists hold that these identities are given and immutable. Constructivism is a broad and varied approach, including both critical theorists and postmodernists and positivists.[39] There are finer divisions (for example, social identity theory, image theory, and role theory. Some expressly

35. See Paul Kowert, "National Identity: Inside and Out," *Security Studies* 8, nos. 2/3 (winter 1998/99–spring 1999): 1–34, esp. n. 15. One of the best known works proposing a "primordial" view of identity is anthropologist Clifford Geertz's *The Interpretation of Cultures: Selected Essays* (New York: Basic Books, 1973). This primordialist view is currently out of favor, and not embraced by any of the contributors to this volume.

36. Donald L. Horowitz, *Ethnic Groups in Conflict* (Berkeley: University of California Press, 1985); Michael E. Brown, Owen R. Coté Jr., Sean M. Lynn-Jones, and Steven E. Miller, eds., *Nationalism and Ethnic Conflict* (Cambridge: Massachusetts, 1997); and Charles Tilly, ed. *The Formation of National States in Western Europe* (Princeton: Princeton University Press, 1975).

37. See Michael Barnett, "Institutions, Roles, and Disorder: The Case of the Arab States System," *International Studies Quarterly* 37, no. 3 (September 1993): 271–96; Alexander Wendt, "Anarchy Is What States Make of It: The Social Construction of Power Politics," *International Organization* 42, no. 2 (spring 1992): 391–425; Wendt, "Collective Identity Formation and the International State," *American Political Science Review* 88, no. 2 (June 1994): 384–96; and Jonathan Mercer, "Anarchy and Identity," *International Organization*, 49, no. 2 (spring 1995): 229–52.

38. See Glenn Chafetz, "The Political Psychology of the Nuclear Nonproliferation Regime," *Journal of Politics* 57, no. 3 (August 1995): 743–75; and Peter J. Katzenstein, ed. 1996, *The Culture of National Security: Norms and Identity in World Politics* (New York: Columbia University Press, 1996).

39. One of the best known examples of the postmodern approach is David Campbell, *Writing Security: United States Foreign Policy and the Politics of Identity* (Minneapolis: University of Minnesota Press, 1992). Positivist constructivist approaches include Wendt, "Collective Identity Formation and the International State."

materialist takes on the problem include real interest theory).[40] Finally, traditional theories of nationalism and ethnic conflict consciously and unconsciously overlap some of the previously noted approaches.[41]

Where do the articles in our volume fit? In trying to refine a slippery and difficult concept, Kowert finds it useful to distinguish between internal and external treatments of identity. The former focuses on the internal cohesion of actors, whereas the latter addresses the place that actors occupy in their environments. These overlap in important ways, and with important consequences, including the tendency of some actors to create or exploit animosities with others to strengthen and make more coherent what they perceive to be their shaky selves. Immigration is another place where the internal and external dimensions of identity overlap. In the broadly constructivist "Immigration and Politics of Security," Roxanne Lynn Doty examines this overlap to show how immigration becomes a security interest for states.[42] Using the U.S. response to the Haitian immigration in the early 1990s, she finds that "securitization" can follow three distinct logics for any given state facing immigration: (1) the classical security logic in which the state responds to a violation of borders; (2) the societal security logic in which the state finds the immigration threatening to its identity; and (3) the radical pluralist logic in which the state sees no threat to its security, only a challenge in providing for the welfare of the immigrants.

David Cheshier and Cori Dauber use argumentation theory and the concept of the public sphere.[43] The concept of the public sphere refers to real and metaphoric places where political actors argue, negotiate, and discuss, including the media, the internet, diplomacy, and other means of communication. Chesier and Dauber examine the implicit

40. Materialist approaches include Russell Hardin, *One For All: The Logic of Group Conflict* (Princeton: Princeton University Press, 1995; and David Laitin, *Identity in Formation* (Ithaca: Cornell University Press, 1998). The label "real interest theory" comes from H. D. Forbes, *Commerce, Culture, and the Contact Hypothesis* (New Haven: Yale University Press, 1997). Though interested in the broader question of ethnic conflict Forbes presents a linguistic model of ethnic conflict as distinct from social identity theory and real interest theory.

41. See the work of Anthony Smith, including his "National Identity and the Idea of European Unity," *International Affairs*, no. 68 (1992): 55–76. See also Geoff Eley and Ronald Grigor Suny, eds., *Becoming National* (Oxford: Oxford University Press, 1998).

42. Roxanne Lynn Doty, "Immigration and the Politics of Security," *Security Studies* 8, nos. 2/3 (winter 1998/99–spring 1999): 71–93.

43. David M. Cheshier and Cori E. Dauber, "The Place and Power of Civic Space: Reading Globalization and Social Geography Through the Lens of Civilizational Conflict," *Security Studies* 8, nos. 2/3 (winter 1998/99–spring 1999): 35–70.

and explicit identity claims made by Samuel Huntington in his essay "The Clash of Civilizations." Cheshire and Dauber find little logical or empirical support for Huntington's claim that fault lines created by historically fixed, religiously based civilizations are more likely to shut down the public argument and produce major wars than other identity borders.

Marc Lynch's explanation also involves the public sphere. He explains Jordan's international twists and turns during the 1990s, first supporting and then turning away from Iraq, as a function of publicly contested identity.[44] The Jordanian-Israeli peace treaty provoked a crisis that led the public and the state to grapple with questions about the nature of Jordan's international identity: Was it an international pariah and supporter of Iraq, or a respected member of the u.s.-dominated international community but traitor to solidarity with Iraq? Differences in the answer led to fissures in the state-society relationship.

Both Rodney Bruce Hall and Bruce Cronin point out deficiencies in purely structural models of state behavior in nineteenth-century Europe.[45] Hall addresses the relationship among sovereignty, identity, and the national interest. He finds that the behavior of state actors, particularly France and Germany, varied according to their transitions from territorial-sovereign identity to a national-sovereign identity. Cronin, using assumptions and hypotheses drawn from both social identity theory and symbolic interactionism, examines the conditions under which a group of independent states transform themselves into a single actor. He shows why Italy transformed from a competitive balance-of-power system into "an amalgamated security community."

Moving from the nineteenth-century to the end of the twentieth-century, three of the contributors, Colin Kahl, Mary Hampton, and Frank Schimmelfennig, examine the puzzle presented by European behavior at the end of the cold war.[46] Though not specifically addressed to NATO, Kahl's analysis of the liberal democratic peace has

44. Marc Lynch, "Abandoning Iraq: Jordan's Alliances and the Politics of State Identity," *Security Studies* 8, nos. 2/3 (winter 1998/99–spring 1999): 347–88.
45. Hall, "Territorial and National Sovereigns: Sovereign Identity and Consequences for Security Policy"; Cronin, "From Balance to Community: Transnational Identity and Political Integration."
46. Hampton, "NATO, Germany, and the United States: Creating Positive Identity in Trans-Atlantia"; Colin H. Kahl, "Constructing a Separate Peace: Constructivism, Collective Liberal Identity, and Democratic Peace," *Security Studies* 8, nos. 2/3 (winter 1998/99–spring 1999): 94–144; Frank Schimmelfennig, "NATO Enlargement: A Constructivist Explanation," *Security Studies* 8, nos. 2/3 (winter 1998/99–spring 1999): 198–234.

clear implications. Kahl argues that the institutional and ideational explanations of the democratic peace can be improved by grounding them in constructivist theory. He shows that a collective liberal identity leads to a definition of state interests that facilitate cooperation and a tendency to ally.

The implications of this for NATO are obvious, and are the subject of Hampton's and Schimmelfennig's contributions. Hampton asks why NATO continues to exist. Shimmelfennig asks why it expanded the way it did. The constructivist assumption that interaction between actors affects their identity and influences the formulation of their interests is translated into the hypothesis that decades of cooperation in NATO changed the identities, and, therefore, the interests of the organization's members. Hampton focuses on Germany and the United States, particularly on their shared historical memory and ideas about military security. NATO members now value their alliance for its own sake, as opposed to any instrumental purpose it may serve. Questions about the purpose of NATO are as irrelevant as questions about the purpose of Italy or the World Cup football tournament.

Schimmelfennig sees NATO expansion as international socialization. He takes as a starting point NATO members' view that NATO, as a good in itself, should expand its benefits of liberal democracy and multilateralism to others in order to expand the zone of its stable peace.[47] While applicants from central-eastern Europe had different reasons for wanting to join, including a hedge against a future threat from Russia, the three countries invited into NATO in the initial round of expansion—Poland, Hungary, and the Czech Republic—were chosen because they were more advanced than other applicants in internalizing community values.

In another essay that examines identity and NATO, Michael Spirtas draws from social psychology to measure identity and uses it to compare British and French policies toward the alliance from 1949 to 1966.[48] During this period the two states held similar positions in the international hierarchy, but pursued strikingly different policies. One would expect that the British, whose security was bolstered by the English channel, would be more critical of alliance policy and less willing to cooperate in alliance councils than the French, who have suffered repeated invasions. Their policies, however, defy expectations—

47. On this, see Kahl, "Constructing a Separate Peace."
48. Spirtas, "French Twist: French and British NATO Policies from 1949 to 1966."

the French became increasingly distant from the alliance, eventually dropping out of the integrated military command of NATO—providing an opportunity for innovative explanations of their behavior.

LOOKING AHEAD

The readers of this volume will judge whether the essays that follow live up to our claims and expectations; the community of international relations scholars as a whole will determine whether work on identity has made—can make—a lasting contribution to scholarship. We, the editors, believe that what follows is some of the best writing applying the concept of identity to foreign policy. We have chosen to order the essays according to the specificity with which they consider the link between identity and state policy, moving from the general to the specific. We chose this plan for the book for a reason: we believe it is a useful model for future work which takes identity seriously as a factor influencing states' foreign policies.

We began by noting that critics charge that much of the identity scholarship has remained too vague, seemingly reluctant to engage in the empirical spadework necessary for the growth and development of new approaches and theories. These charges have merit regardless of the motives of those who make them. Theories may be judged to be more elegant or less elegant based on their internal logic and parsimony; to be worthy of the name, however, they must be tested on empirical grounds, or be regarded as mere curiosity. In the following pages the contributors to this volume subject identity to the only test that matters.

NATIONAL IDENTITY: INSIDE AND OUT

PAUL A. KOWERT

NATIONAL SECURITY depends on national identity. Two claims are often advanced in support of this simple proposition. One is that internal cohesion facilitates orderly and efficient responses to external threats. This form of identity might be called patriotism or a sense of national purpose, yet efforts to promote national cohesion have also produced much insecurity, leading to violence deployed along ethnic, religious, linguistic and a variety of other fault lines. When national identity breaks down, this too has implications for international relations: civil wars, spin-off crises, changing alliance patterns, the dissolution of existing states, and the constitution of new ones. It is easy to recognize the importance of such identity politics in international relations.

Identity is also said to be important for a second reason: a state must distinguish its "friends" from its "enemies." Structural realists maintain, of course, that other states are always (at least potentially) enemies, that international friendship is fleeting, and that such anthropomorphism misleads and obscures more than it reveals. Neoliberals, on the other hand, find greater merit in distinguishing among states. Democracies, they expect, will behave differently than other states, and free-riders differently than the "good citizens" of a nascent international community. Such distinctions, while clearly not eternal, are presumed by many neoliberals to have enough stability to guide foreign policy (and scholarship).

The "constructivist turn in international relations theory" brings this debate into sharper relief by challenging the rationalist individual-

Paul A. Kowert is assistant professor of international relations at Florida International University.

I am grateful to Emanuel Adler, John Clark, Richard Herrmann, Jeffrey Legro, Henry Nau, Nicholas Onuf, Nina Tannenwald, Katja Weber, participants in the Miami IR Group from Florida International University and the University of Miami, and two anonymous reviewers of *Security Studies* for their comments and advice. I am also indebted to Dina Evans and Kamila Valkova for their research assistance, and to Kei Karasawa and Makoto Kobayashi of Ritsumeikan University in Kyoto, Japan, the Social Science Research Council, and the Japan Society for the Promotion of Science (grant P97272) for their support of this research.

ism on which neorealists and neoliberals alike have relied.[1] Rationalist theories explain how actors should choose (parametric theories) or how they should bargain (strategic theories).[2] They offer answers to some important questions about when states should cooperate and when they might be expected to fight. Yet they say nothing about who the actors are or how their interests were constituted. Although neoliberals may expect to find greater diversity in the goals of states than do neorealists, neither approach offers a theory of preferences. Justifiably reluctant to proclaim certain goals or values as themselves rational, most rationalists fall back instead on assumed or revealed preferences.[3] Constructivists urge attention to this problem, going beyond theories of structural limits in an effort to account for the purposes and worldviews that shape national behavior. They argue that how states (usually, that is to say, their leaders) see themselves and other states is central to understanding what states actually do.[4] To put this another way, constructivists insist on the importance of agents as well as structures.[5] Even had the end of the cold war not intensified ethnic conflicts

1. Jeffrey Checkel, "The Constructivist Turn in International Relations Theory," *World Politics* 50, no. 2 (January 1998): 324–48. Recent discussion and criticism of rationalist individualism in contemporary international relations scholarship includes: Jeffrey W. Legro, "Culture and Preferences in the International Cooperation Two-Step," *American Political Science Review* 90, no. 1 (March 1996): 118–37; Alexander Wendt, "Collective Identity Formation and the International State," *American Political Science Review* 88, no. 2 (June 1994): 384–96; and Albert S. Yee, "Thick Rationality and the Missing 'Brute Fact': The Limits of Rationalist Incorporations of Norms and Ideas," *Journal of Politics* 59, no. 4 (fall 1997): 1001–39.

2. Jon Elster, *Rational Choice* (New York: New York University Press, 1986), 7.

3. Some might venture the possibility that certain goals (or certain kinds of nation state) are more fit in evolutionary terms. Yet with rare exceptions—perhaps the abrupt collapse of many communist states at the end of the 1980s is one—it is not obvious that there is enough turnover among states for evolution on this grand scale to have had much of a chance to work. Moreover, even if evolution has more powerful effects on the forms and preferences of states than it appears, this is usually thought (as in Waltzian neorealism) to contribute to isomorphism (all states seek security). It is far less clear how this might contribute to a theory of differences among states. For recent explorations of evolutionary dynamics in international relations, see Takashi Inoguchi, *Sekai Hendo no Mikata* (The standpoint of global change) (Tokyo: Chikuma Shobo, 1994); and George Modelski et al., "Special Issue: Evolutionary Paradigms in the Social Sciences," *International Studies Quarterly* 40, no. 3 (September 1996): 315–431.

4. Peter J. Katzenstein, ed., *The Culture of National Security: Norms and Identity in World Politics* (New York: Columbia University Press, 1996); Audie Klotz, *Norms in International Politics: The Struggle against Apartheid* (Ithaca: Cornell University Press, 1995); Vendulka Kubálková, Nicholas G. Onuf, and Paul Kowert, eds., *International Relations in a Constructed World* (Armonk: M. E. Sharpe, 1998).

5. David Dessler, "What's at Stake in the Agent-Structure Debate," *International Organization* 43, no. 3 (summer 1989): 441–74; Nicholas Onuf, *World of Our Making: Rules and Rule in Social Theory and International Relations* (Columbia: University of South Carolina Press, 1989); and Alexander Wendt, "The Agent-Structure Problem in

within states (or what were formerly states) and relaxed the ideological blinders through which states had long viewed each other, therefore, the constructivist turn would lead one to regard national identity as central to disputes in international relations.[6]

Its importance notwithstanding, the field of international relations in general (and of security studies in particular) rarely avails itself of the rich lexicon of national identity. Nation-states are assumed to exist as discrete political actors, more or less since the Peace of Westphalia, and to seek wealth and power or, in more Spartan formulations, merely survival. One can scarcely fail to notice the disjuncture between the utterly homogeneous nation-state "actors" that populate international relations theory and the evident variety of real nation-states. Abstraction away from the messiness of apparent differences among juridically equivalent sovereign states has been the name of most theoretical games.

Quite apart from any benefits to be gained by this parsimony, there are other reasons to hesitate before complicating matters by introducing taxonomies of nation-states. Once one is prepared to distinguish among types of nation, for example, it may seem a short step to distinguishing among types of people as well. People differ in many ways, but there is surely some virtue in the democratic project of ignoring differences in taste, desires, abilities, language, culture, history, and so on—of postulating citizens, that is, rather than members of distinctive groups. By extension, it may reflect (and serve) the purposes of neo-Kantian internationalism to adopt the same attitude toward nation-states, differentiating only between those that are democratic (a condition of good international citizenship) and those that are not.

International Relations Theory," *International Organization* 41, no. 3 (summer 1987): 335–70. Checkel complains, with some justification, that constructivists have in practice said more about structures than about agents.

6. Yosef Lapid and Friedrich Kratochwil, eds., *The Return of Culture and Identity in IR Theory* (Boulder: Lynne Rienner, 1996). Lapid and Kratochwil make plain that the relevance of culture and identity is renewed—part of a cycle of fluctuating interest, perhaps, but certainly not novel. Some go further still in arguing the importance of identity politics. David Campbell, for one, argues that the state justifies its existence, and that of the nation-state system, only by reproducing the insecurity that forms its raison d'étre. To do so, it invokes a variety of metaphors (a quasimedical discourse on the "body politic," for example, or religious themes of good and evil) to reinforce the boundary between internal and external. The state, and the practice of "securing" it, thus rely on this basic distinction of identity. See Campbell, *Writing Security: United States Foreign Policy and the Politics of Identity* (Minneapolis: University of Minnesota Press, 1992); and R. B. J. Walker, *Inside/Outside: International Relations and Political Theory* (Cambridge: Cambridge University Press, 1993).

There is yet another reason to approach the Pandora's box of national identity with trepidation: national identity is a notoriously slippery concept, on a par with the much maligned political culture.[7] Even those otherwise prepared to make distinctions among national identities might well balk at the sheer implausibility of devising acceptable definitions. In a recent study of Chinese national identity, for example, Lowell Dittmer and Samuel Kim complain from the outset about the paucity of "efforts at conceptual refinement" and the lack of precision with which national identity is usually treated.[8] The related issue of nationalism, Benedict Anderson notes, "has never produced its own grand thinkers."[9] Perhaps, if it had, their work would help to anchor the concept, for the problem is not that national identity has been ignored but rather that scholars mean so many different things by the term. For some it is an ideology, for others a social movement, and for others mere awareness that binds people together. Some tie it closely to the state, while others fix their sights on some quality imputed to the nation (ethnicity, culture, language, and so on). For some, the very notion of national identity is quintessentially modern; for others, the term expresses an ancient heritage.

This essay is an "effort at conceptual refinement" and, beyond that, an effort to outline some of the uses to which theories of national identity can be put. It argues for a basic distinction among approaches to national identity. This distinction—between internal and external accounts of national identity—is intended not only to reduce some of the present confusion and argumentative repetitiveness, but also to clarify the ways different theories of national identity can usefully address the problems outlined above. "Internal identity" describes the cohesion or uniformity of the nation-state's parts and, in particular, the way such cohesion manifests itself in loyalty to the nation-state. "External identity" refers to a nation-state's distinctiveness, as compared with other

7. For many of the same reasons that identity has gained new prominence, in fact, political culture is also enjoying renewed attention in comparative politics and international relations. In addition to Katzenstein, *The Culture of National Security*, see also Larry Diamond, ed., *Political Culture and Democracy in Developing Countries* (Boulder: Lynne Rienner, 1994); Robert D. Putnam, with Robert Leonardi and Raffaella Y. Nanetti, *Making Democracy Work: Civic Traditions in Modern Italy* (Princeton: Princeton University Press, 1993); and Stephen Welch, *The Concept of Political Culture* (New York: St. Martin's Press, 1993).

8. Lowell Dittmer and Samuel S. Kim, eds., *China's Quest for National Identity* (Ithaca: Cornell University Press, 1993), 1.

9. Benedict Anderson, *Imagined Communities: Reflections on the Origin and Spread of Nationalism* (London: Verso, 1983), 5.

nation-states. Erik Erikson remarked on this difference in approaches when he pointed out that identity "connotes both a persistent sameness within oneself (self-sameness) and a persistent sharing of some kind of essential character with others."[10] To say that a group of people has a particular identity is to suggest both that they share certain qualities and also that these qualities somehow set them apart from others. Likewise, national identity may refer either to internal coherence or to external distinctiveness. These two faces of identity are sometimes blurred together. Yet they have given rise to very different sorts of theories, and they cannot be put to the same use by students of international relations.

This distinction between approaches to studying national identity recalls the well-worn analytical divide between nation and state. Ted Robert Gurr and Barbara Harff emphasize the difference when they complain that "maps that show the world neatly divided into countries, each with its own boundaries and territory, convey a misleading image of people's political identities."[11] Indeed, the twin institutions of nation and state have never overlapped reliably in most parts of the world, and they appear increasingly disjointed, even as each has come under attack from above and below. Larger regional organizations, transnational religious, cultural, and humanitarian groups, and multinational financial and business conglomerates have taken on many of the functions (even military functions) once performed by state. They often command allegiance, moreover, that was formerly given to the nation. At the same time, domestic subgroups challenge state authority and national sentiment from below on almost every continent. Increasingly, ethnic loyalty, religious loyalty, and even brand loyalty supplant

10. Erik Erikson, "The Problem of Ego Identity," in *Identity and Anxiety*, ed. Maurice R. Stein, Arthur J. Vidich, and David M. White (Glencoe, IL: Free Press, 1960), 30; quoted in Dittmer and Kim, *China's Quest for National Identity*, 4. In a recent article on collective identity formation, Alexander Wendt offers a similar distinction between corporate and social identities. He defines corporate identities as the "intrinsic, self-organizing qualities that constitute actor individuality," whereas social identities are "sets of meanings that an actor attributes to itself while taking the perspective of others" (Wendt, "Collective Identity Formation and the International State," 385). Anthony Smith also offers a related, but slightly different, distinction between the internal and external functions of national identity in *National Identity* (Reno: University of Nevada Press, 1991), 15–17.

11. Ted Robert Gurr and Barbara Harff, *Ethnic Conflict in World Politics* (Boulder: Westview, 1994), 1. For an interesting discussion of politics among nations, but not nation-states, see Neta C. Crawford, "A Security Regime Among Democracies: Cooperation Among Iroquois Nations," *International Organization* 48, no. 3 (summer 1994): 345–85.

loyalty to the nation-state.[12] In the wake of these transformations, nation and state appear more free than ever to drift apart.

Yet the distinction between internal and external accounts of national identity is not so obvious, nor so closely tied to nation and state respectively, as it might seem. The nation and the state depend heavily on each other as institutional forms. The external meaning of the state—its juridical independence from other states, encapsulated in the notion of self-determination—has always been (and remains) a driving force behind nationalist movements. As Anthony Smith has observed, "it is the very political configuration of states into wider regional systems that helps to entrench the power of the nation and fan the flames of nationalism everywhere."[13] Not only does the idea of the state help to legitimize national peoples, but conversely the presumptive (whether actual or not) existence of a nation has always been the rationale of the state as a distinct form of large-scale social organization. The Leviathan needs a people since, in principle at least, it is the people. So long as the nation-state remains the defining actor in international relations, then, investigations of national identity must reckon with both the nation and the state.[14] While it is often useful to distinguish between the two, the following discussion will concern itself more with the way people (both leaders and citizens) commonly use, and conflate, the terms in their efforts to make sense of national identity. Willingness to blur the distinction between nation and state is central to the phenomenon of national identity.

The distinction between internal and external approaches to national identity depends more on a difference in perspective than on the difference between nation and state. To ascribe identity to the nation-state (or nation or state independently) is to suggest two different things: (1) that the nation-state is a sufficiently coherent entity that it is meaningful to treat it as an agent (internal identity); and (2) that it is

12. For a compelling vision of these trends, see Benjamin R. Barber, *Jihad vs. McWorld: How Globalism and Tribalism are Reshaping the World* (New York: Ballantine, 1995).

13. Smith, *National Identity*, 169.

14. Walker Connor estimated, in the 1970s, that less than 10 percent of states were truly nation-states. He joins Gurr and Harff in complaining about the casual conflation of the terms nation and state. See Walker Connor, "Nation-Building or Nation-Destroying?" *World Politics* 24, no. 3 (April 1972): 319–55; and Connor, "A Nation is a Nation, is a State, is an Ethnic Group, is a...," *Ethnic and Racial Studies* 1, no. 4 (October 1978): 378–400. The distinction might be maintained for analytical purposes, but in common parlance it is a lost cause. The United Nations, to take an obvious example, is an organization of states, and the term *international* likewise ordinarily refers to relations among states.

somehow distinct from other nation-states, with different interests, purposes, preferences, and so on (external identity). Whether one adopts an inward- or outward-looking approach to identity depends not on discerning the correct way to understand the nation-state but rather on theoretical purpose. The following two sections will explore the uses to which each approach can be put. To put it simply, theories of internal coherence tell us whether or not (or to what extent) a state is able to act coherently (as a unitary actor). Theories of external distinctiveness, on the other hand, tell us something about whether a given state might want to act differently from other states.

INTERNAL COHERENCE

IF NATIONAL identity is defined as similarity among individuals, manifest in their shared identification with the nation-state, then the field of international relations has contributed relatively little to an understanding of it. Perhaps this is unsurprising. As the field developed during (and partly because of) the cold war, its most prominent theorists took the internal coherence of the nation-state for granted. Most contributions to an internal account of national identity have come instead from the fields of psychology, anthropology, sociology, and comparative politics.[15] Yet the coherence of the nation-state is a permissive condition of international relations (both the academic discipline and its subject matter). Broadly speaking, the nation-state's internal coherence has been explained in three different ways: (1) it satisfies the needs of individuals; (2) it satisfies the needs of powerful social groups; and (3) it is the culmination of larger social processes that neither individuals nor groups can control. This section will consider each of these approaches in turn.

---

15. For helpful overviews of some of the extensive literatures on national identity as group cohesion and loyalty, see: Daniel Druckman, "Nationalism, Patriotism, and Group Loyalty: A Social Psychological Perspective," *Mershon International Studies Review* 38, no. 1 (April 1994): 43–68; R. Alan Hedley, "Identity: Sense of Self and Nation," *Canadian Review of Sociology and Anthropology* 31, no. 2 (May 1994): 200–14; Robert Miles, "Recent Marxist Theories of Nationalism and the Issue of Racism," *British Journal of Sociology* 38, no. 1 (March 1987): 24–43; Iver B. Neumann, "Identity and Security," *Journal of Peace Research* 29, no. 2 (May 1992): 221–26; Gail Stokes, "Cognition, Consciousness, and Nationalism," *Ethnic Groups* 10, no. 1–3 (August 1993): 27–42; and Arthur N. Waldron, "Theories of Nationalism and Historical Explanation," *World Politics* 37, no. 3 (April 1985): 416–33.

When an effort to explain national cohesion begins by considering individual needs, the danger is that one might end up with a theory of individual identity instead. The burden on such "individualist" arguments is great, therefore, to make plain the logic by which individual desires lead to national cohesion, and not merely to some personal sense of citizenship. In a recent study of the relationship between personal identity and national identity, William Bloom set for himself just this task: "to examine the possibility of a psychological theory—identification theory—giving the mass national population of a state...a theoretically coherent status."[16] Identification theory, for Bloom, derives from personality theory and holds that "every individual possesses an inherent drive to internalize—to identify with—the behavior, mores and attitudes of significant figures in her or his social environment; that is people actively seek identity." Identification "is a psychological dynamic that is biologically derived."[17] People are naturally social animals because all people share a personal need for security and well-being that they can satisfy only in the presence of others.

Bloom is not the first to comment on the apparent relevance of such needs to nationalist sentiment and behavior. Harold Lasswell argued at length that civic education must temper the need to belong with tolerance for difference in order for the democratic national form to flourish.[18] Theodor Adorno and his colleagues attributed to the same needs—intensified by the ego-bruising effects of interwar political humiliation and economic collapse—an "authoritarian personality" that sustained German nationalism and ethnocentrism.[19] Many contemporary historians and anthropologists also speak of national character in individualist terms that emphasize personal needs. Rupert Wilkinson, for example, defines national identity simply as "those traits of individual personality and attitude that the population shows more frequently or in different ways than other, compared populations do."[20]

16. William Bloom, *Personal Identity, National Identity, and International Relations* (Cambridge: Cambridge University Press, 1990), 2.

17. Bloom, *Personal Identity, National Identity, and International Relations*, 23, 33.

18. Harold Lasswell, *Psychopathology and Politics* (Chicago: University of Chicago Press, 1930); and Lasswell, *World Politics and Personal Insecurity* (New York: McGraw-Hill, 1935).

19. Theodor W. Adorno, Else Frenkel-Brunswik, Daniel J. Levinson, and R. Nevitt Sanford, *The Authoritarian Personality* (New York: Harper, 1950). Similar claims were advanced earlier in Erich Fromm, *Escape from Freedom* (New York: Farrar & Rhinehart, 1941).

20. Rupert Wilkinson, *The Pursuit of American Character* (New York: Harper and Row, 1988), 3.

Margaret Mead, Geoffrey Gorer, and Erik Erikson have all stressed the contribution of child-rearing practices to a nation's "modal personality."[21] These works mean by national identity a kind of psychic unity that stems from shared needs and from the extent to which they are met in a given environment.

Yet even where such anthropological studies succeed in uncovering a modal national personality, does this give the nation itself "a theoretically coherent status" as Bloom suggests? Asserting that similar needs bring citizens together assumes what still must be explained. Why should similarities of individual character have the effect of drawing citizens together when familiarity is as often said to breed contempt as comfort? Other questions remain as well. Are some shared needs more likely to produce national cohesion than others and, if so, which ones? Why should shared personal needs give rise to the nation-state rather than, say, to an international labor movement, religious affiliation, ethnic identification, or some other form of belonging? The likely answer to this last question is that only needs produced and shared on a specifically national scale will generate national cohesion. This answer has the effect, however, of directing attention away from individuals and toward the social groups and larger forces that shape these needs.

The state itself is a clear beneficiary of such needs, with an evident interest in manipulating national cohesiveness. To secure its capacity to make war, and by the very act of exercising this capacity, the state creates and renews bonds among its citizens. In his uncompleted multivolume study of French identity, for example, Fernand Braudel concludes that just such strategic needs gradually and inevitably drew together the highly diverse regions and inhabitants of France. By the eighteenth century,

> there was not a French river of any size that did not ship or float the timber and masts necessary for the navy....[T]here was no province, however remote from the frontier, which did not contribute its share of recruits or its part toward the upkeep of the army—even

21. Margaret Mead, *And Keep Your Powder Dry: An Anthropologist Looks at America* (New York: Morrow, 1942); Geoffrey Gorer, *The American People: A Study in National Character* (New York: Norton, 1948); Gorer, *The People of Great Russia: A Psychological Study* (New York: Chanticleer Press, 1950); Gorer, *Exploring English Character* (London: Criterion Books, 1955); and Erik Erikson, *Childhood and Society* (New York: Norton, 1950). Other postwar anthropological studies that treat national character as modal personality include: Christopher Lasch, *The Culture of Narcissism: American Life in an Age of Diminishing Expectations* (New York: Norton, 1979); and David Riesman, Reuel Denney, and Nathan Glazer, *The Lonely Crowd: A Study of the Changing American Character* (New Haven: Yale University Press, 1950).

the Berry and the Limousin, even the Auverne, the Velay or the Bourbonnais. There was no province that did not resound to the annual tramp of troops on the move, or that was exempt from the burden—there was no other word for it—of billeting infantry and cavalry.[22]

For Braudel, as for Charles Tilly and Eugen Weber, French identity did not arise spontaneously from the needs of the French people themselves to belong to a larger and more glorious whole. Relatively few of them, particularly south of the Garonne, even spoke French. Rather, French cohesiveness was manufactured, they argue, by those in a position to do so because it served their interests. The French language was nothing other than the "language of power."[23]

Of course, the state is not the only agent of national unification. Indeed, as the millennium draws to a close, the state itself seems increasingly removed from nationalist movements and, in many parts of the world, it is more and more imperiled by them. Instead, other groups—Anthony Smith calls them "demotic ethnies"—have taken the lead in promoting national identities that rarely correspond perfectly to state borders.[24] The groundwork for Israel's national cohesion, to take an obvious example, was laid long before the inception of the Israeli state. Religious organization has been an especially powerful alternative to state-led efforts at national unification, and so it remains, as the experience of Irish Catholics, Indian Sikhs, and Iranian Shiites suggests.

Whatever the institutional advantages of national religious movements, other kinds of social groups have also found reason to propound nationalism. Smith argues that aristocratic and intellectual elites generally play a critical role, for their own reasons, in rediscovering elements of a mythic national past, venerating its heroes, and promot-

---

22. Fernand Braudel, *The Identity of France: History and Environment*, vol. 1, trans. Siân Reynolds (New York: Harper & Row, 1986), 373, 374. Braudel's definition of national identity is clearly internal. As he puts it, "national identity necessarily implies a degree of national unity, of which it is in some sense the reflection, the transposition and the condition" (Braudel, *The Identity of France*, 23). Much of Volume 1 is given over, in fact, to descriptions of wide regional variations within France—thus, to establishing the absence of any particularly French identity before one was painstakingly constructed.

23. Braudel, *The Identity of France*, 375. See also Charles Tilly, ed., *The Formation of National States in Western Europe* (Princeton: Princeton University Press, 1975); and Eugen Weber, *Peasants into Frenchmen: The Modernization of Rural France, 1870–1914* (Stanford: Stanford University Press, 1976).

24. Smith, *National Identity*, 53, 61.

ing patriotic renewal.[25] The Meiji elites who overthrew the Tokugawa shogunate in 1868 were driven, by Japan's apparent economic and strategic disadvantage, to catch up with the West. To do so, however, they needed to replace local economies with a national one, and restoring the emperor while breaking down local allegiances was critical. To take another example, Mobutu's efforts (and Lumumba's before him) to promote a coherent Zairian identity were motivated in no small part by the importance of keeping mineral-rich Katanga within the country. In nearby Rwanda as well, the administrative rubble of Belgian colonialism gave rise to domestic groups prepared to assert quasinational interests where none had existed before.[26]

It is surely possible to describe many other motives that domestic groups may have for promoting particular forms of national unity. In many cases—not only Rwanda, but also in the former Yugoslavia and the former Soviet states as well, to take other recent examples—the unity sought has not included every group within the state's border. Some were systematically disenfranchised, some even systematically killed. Precisely because it is so easy, especially after the fact, to identify segments of society that benefit from nationalist movements, such explanations of national identity are not particularly satisfying. As Smith observes, "the social composition of nationalist movements, viewed comparatively, is both cross-class and highly variable depending on the historical juncture and the phase of the movement."[27] Powerful social groups have many and varied needs. It is almost always possible to identify some that benefit from unity movements, but doing so is more an exercise in description than in explanation.[28]

---

25. Smith suggests that these interests were less often in attaining power—which, at any rate, the intellectual authors of nationalist movements rarely achieved—than in resolving their own personal identity crises. This is an interesting, albeit apparently *ad hoc,* variation on the individualist arguments discussed previously. See Anthony Smith, *National Identity,* 95–96. Others who stress the role of the intelligentsia include: Leonard O'Boyle, "The Problem of an Excess of Educated Men in Western Europe, 1800–1850," *Journal of Modern History* 42, no. 4 (December 1970): 471–95; and Miroslav Hroch, *Social Preconditions of National Revival in Europe: A Comparative Analysis of the Social Composition of Patriotic Groups among the Smaller European Nations* (Cambridge: Cambridge University Press, 1985).

26. Catharine Newbury, *The Cohesion of Oppression: Clientship and Ethnicity in Rwanda, 1860–1960* (New York: Columbia University Press, 1988); Rene Lemarchand, *Rwanda and Burundi* (New York: Praeger, 1970).

27. Smith, *National Identity,* 120.

28. The history of nationalism is really a history of competing nationalisms rather than an inevitable march toward the unity of nation and state. Even where such unity exists, it can come unravelled. Barber argues, in *Jihad vs. McWorld,* that it is doing so on every continent. Even the United States, which could make a better claim than

Many of the most prominent theorists of nationalism consequently look to larger social processes in an effort to explain the needs of both individuals and groups. In his well-known address at the Sorbonne in 1882, Ernest Renan held nations to be "something fairly new in history."[29] More than a few scholars of nationalism have joined Renan in proclaiming the nation (and thus national identity) a distinctly modern form, neither the inevitable result of deep-seated human needs nor the product of ancient antagonisms and loyalties. In one of the classics on the topic, Ernst Gellner links nationalism directly to the roughly contemporaneous impact of two modern revolutions: the transformation of subject into citizen and the emergence of industrial capitalism. The combined effects of what Gellner calls the "tidal wave of modernization" created two distinct paths to nationalism. On one hand, in the larger and more economically advanced states, economies of scale and the need for an educated, mass labor force produced a functional imperative for nationalist unification. At the same time, smaller and less advanced regions could hardly fail to become aware of their own increasing vulnerability. In this awareness, too, nationalism sentiment was born.[30]

Others, Karl Deutsch and Benedict Anderson chief among them, have placed greater emphasis on revolutions in communication than in

---

many other multiethnic states to having forged its own distinctive national identity, is witnessing a resurgence of ethnic identification according to Arthur Schlesinger Jr., *The Disuniting of America* (New York: Norton, 1991).

29. Ernest Renan, "Qu'est-ce qu'une nation?" *Oeuvres Complètes*, vol. 1 (Paris: 1947–61), 887–907; Martin Thom's translation is reprinted in *Becoming National*, ed. Geoff Eley and Ronald Grigor Suny (New York: Oxford University Press, 1996), 42–55 (see p. 43 for the quoted excerpt). The pseudo-debate over the historical novelty of nationalism depends largely on how one is prepared to define the term. Those who trace the lineage of nationalist sentiment further into the past also tend to define the term more broadly. See Prasenjit Duara, *Rescuing History from the Nation: Questioning Narratives of Modern China* (Chicago: University of Chicago Press, 1995).

30. Ernst Gellner, *Nations and Nationalism* (Ithaca: Cornell University Press, 1983). On this distinction between nationalism in small and large states, see also Tom Nairn, *The Break-Up of Britain: Crisis and Neo-Nationalism* (London: Verso, 1977); and Hroch, *Social Preconditions of National Revival in Europe*. Erich Fromm also argued that modern, industrial society "could not have attained its ends had it not harnessed the energy of free men for work in an unprecedented degree....The *necessity* for work, for punctuality and orderliness had to be transformed into a *drive* for these qualities. This means that society had to produce such a social character in which these strivings were inherent" (Erich Fromm, "Psychoanalytic Characterology and Its Application to the Understanding of Culture," in *Culture and Personality*, ed. S. Stansfeld Sargent and Marian W. Smith [New York: Wenner-Gren Foundation, 1949], 5–6); for a related argument, see E. P. Thompson, "Time, Work-Discipline, and Industrial Capitalism," in *Essays in Social History*, ed. Michael W. Flinn and T. Christopher Smout (Oxford: Clarendon Press, 1974), 39–77.

commerce. For Deutsch, as for Gellner, nationalism is functional. Yet, by reducing social fragmentation, it serves the function of facilitating the transmission of knowledge, or "complementarity," as he termed it.[31] Anderson's account also resembles Gellner's in that both are linked to the emergence of national economies of scale under capitalism. For Anderson, however, the vital link between capitalism and nationalism was the printing press and the consequent emergence of national print-languages. "Print-capitalism gave a new fixity to language, which in the long run helped to build that image of antiquity so central to the subjective idea of the nation."[32] For the first time, not only elites but other social strata shared common idioms, expressed and transmitted in a common print vernacular.[33]

A different case for the modern character of nationalism has been made by some feminist theorists who, like Weber, see the state as part of the administrative triumph of modern rationalism. They argue that rationality, the state, and the demarcation of public (state) and private (national) spheres of activity are notoriously gendered constructs.[34] The public domain of the state itself is commonly masculinized (*liberté, egalité, fraternité*), while its power is deployed to protect a feminized (mother) country. Iraq did not simply attack but, as western newspapers widely proclaimed, "raped" Kuwait.[35] Nationalist distinctions between self and other partly depend, it would seem, on the gen-

31. Karl Deutsch, *Nationalism and Social Communication: An Inquiry into the Foundations of Nationality* (Cambridge: MIT Press, 1966). Deutsch's view of nationalism is more sanguine than most, and is heavily influenced by research on cybernetics and systems theory.

32. Anderson, *Imagined Communities*, 44.

33. Hugh Seton-Watson also emphasizes the importance of denser networks of communication and vernacular literatures, but primarily in what he calls "old nations." Like Gellner, he distinguishes between these and newer, often smaller nations in which, he argues, the intelligentsia played a crucial role in promoting nationalism on the model of the older nations. See Hugh Seton-Watson, *Nations and States: An Enquiry into the Origins of Nations and the Politics of Nationalism* (Boulder: Westview, 1977), 5.

34. Louise M. Antony and Charlotte Witt, *A Mind of One's Own: Feminist Essays on Reason and Objectivity* (Boulder: Westview, 1993); Sandra Harding, *The Science Question in Feminism* (Ithaca: Cornell University Press, 1986); Sabina Lovibond, "Feminism and the 'Crisis of Rationality'," *New Left Review* no. 207 (September/October 1994): 72–86; Susan M. Okin, *Women in Western Political Thought* (Princeton: Princeton University Press, 1979); and Phyllis Rooney, "Recent Work in Feminist Discussions of Reason," *American Philosophical Quarterly* 31, no. 1 (January 1994): 1–21.

35. See also Renata Salecl's discussion of Serbian portrayals of Albanians as "rapists of the Serbian nation," in Salecl, "National Identity and Socialist Moral Majority," in Eley and Suny, *Becoming National*, 418–24.

dered symbolism of home and hearth, of defending the honor of na-
tion-as-woman.[36]

What the various arguments attributing nationalism to modern social processes do well is to explain why agents' needs give rise to specifically nationalist sentiment rather than to some other expression of
group cohesion. The modern acceptance of national (internal) identity
might even appear overdetermined were it not so frequently and obviously contested. Yet the easy conflation of nation and state (which, as
argued earlier, is routine in popular formulations of national identity)
often rests on a tense compromise between the desire for more local
forms of control and the apparent need for more centralized management of regional and global problems. Some claim that the success of
national identity is now limited by our passage into a "postmodern"
era, characterized by a fragmentation of identity and a loss of faith in
centralized bureaucratic rationalism.[37] Even so, one might legitimately
wonder, if the nation-state is (or was) such a central institution of
modernity and so functionally useful a construct as many of the scholars cited above argue, why national identity has not been more successful and why it faces so many contemporary challenges.

One way to answer this query is to point out that powerful groups
(and individuals) have always contested unifying ideologies for their
own   reasons.   Perhaps,   as   Anthony   Richmond   has   argued,
"postindustrial" communication technologies have enhanced their ability to promote locally specific forms of identity (ethnic, cultural, religious, and so on).[38] This reverses the claims of low-level identity theories, which stressed individual and group needs for cohesion. The intellectuals who Smith says played a critical role in promoting nationalism
are now also seemingly more able than ever, sometimes as anti-
intellectuals, to challenge the national form. Renata Salecl's interesting
discussion of Serbian populism emphasizes the ways, to take one example, that the true Serb is portrayed as the antithesis of the "effete"

36. Anne McClintock, "'No Longer in a Future Heaven': Nationalism, Gender, and
Race," in Eley and Suny, Becoming National, 260–84; V. Spike Peterson, "The Politics
of Identity and Gendered Nationalism," in Foreign Policy Analysis: Continuity and
Change in Its Second Generation, ed. Laura Neak, Jeanne A. K. Hey, and Patrick Haney
(Englewood Cliffs: Prentice Hall, 1995), 167–86; and Nira Yuval-Davis and Floya
Anthias, Women-Nation-State (London: Macmillan, 1989).

37. For a helpful discussion, see Anthony Giddens, Modernity and Self-Identity: Self
and Society in the Late Modern Age (Oxford: Polity Press, 1991), esp. 10–34. Giddens's
own view is that such fragmentation is part of late modernity itself.

38. Anthony Richmond, "Ethnic Nationalism and Postindustrialism," Ethnic and
Racial Studies 7, no. 1 (January 1984): 4–18; see also Barber, Jihad vs. McWorld.

and "morally corrupt" bureaucrat. Real Serbs are men, it appears, but bureaucrats are neither.[39] By appealing to the tension between state and society, this is both an antinational message and, at the same time, an effort to promote a different, ethnically specific nationalism. Despite various forms of corporatist compromise in industrialized economies, not only "real Serbs" but a wide variety of business interests have resisted prevailing national identities. As Barber's *Jihad vs. McWorld* suggests, such resistance can occur on a large scale. As it challenges national authority, McWorld challenges national identity too.

Especially interesting is the way such observations draw together strands of the various internal accounts of national identity described above. Few discussions of internal identity have sought to integrate different levels of analysis in their arguments. Psychological studies of individual needs rarely place the evolution of these needs in a wider social context, and the needs of groups are likewise often treated as intrinsic or primordial.[40] Those who focus on the evolution of social context, on the other hand, rarely elaborate the way functional necessity is translated into perceived need. The virtue of Richmond's (and Barber's) argument is its recognition of the way changing structures of communication, emphasized by Deutsch and Anderson, enhance the power of agents to promote alternative forms of identity. By considering the relationship between patriarchal symbols and the success of ethno-nationalist movements, Salecl also helps to uncover links among low- and high-level explanations.

These few examples notwithstanding, internal discussions of national identity have had greater success at suggesting explanations for the emergence of identity than at evaluating the relative merits of these explanations, at exploring connections among them, or at theorizing their limits. Even improved theories of internal identity, however, cannot answer the other main question of national identity: which, among the wide variety of possible national identities, will a particular

39. Salecl, "National Identity and Socialist Moral Majority."

40. The distinction between essential or primordial conceptions of identity and manufactured or imagined identities is not uncommon, particularly among students of ethnic, religious, and cultural politics. See, for example, John Clark, "Ethno-Regionalism in Zaire: Roots, Manifestations and Meaning," *Journal of African Policy Studies* 1, no. 2 (1995): 23–45; Clifford Geertz, ed., *Old Societies and New States* (Glencoe, Ill.: Free Press, 1963); David Laitin, *Hegemony and Culture: Politics and Religious Change among the Yoruba* (Chicago: University of Chicago Press, 1986); Joseph Rothschild, *Ethnopolitics: A Conceptual Framework* (New York: Columbia University Press, 1981); and John F. Stack, ed., *The Primordial Challenge: Ethnicity in the Contemporary World* (New York: Greenwood, 1986).

national people adopt? Also, what kinds of identities will they ascribe to others? Internal theories hold that people need identities (perhaps even national identities), but they predict nothing about the particular content of national identity.

EXTERNAL DISTINCTIVENESS

THE CENTRAL analytical problem for internal theories is whether the nation-state is a sufficiently coherent form of large-scale social organization that it can be treated as an agent in world politics. The central problem for external theories, on the other hand, is how such agents might be expected to behave. External theories of national identity are explanations of the distinctive qualities, interests, and ambitions of particular nation-states. As in the preceding discussion of internal theories, this definition of an external theory of national identity does not insist on separating nation from state. Of course the two are analytically distinct, but when people ask whether Russia will again embrace authoritarianism, whether China will emerge as a new superpower, or whether the United States has lost direction after the end of the cold war, they refer to some combination of nation and state. That none of these really is a nation-state is, apparently, not a great impediment to perceiving them as such. Precisely the point of a theory of external identity is to explain nation-states as people see them, and not merely as neat analytical abstractions.

Perceptions of qualitative difference among nation-states are not usually given ontological status in international relations scholarship. International relations theory, unlike public discourse, ordinarily treats nation-states as functionally interchangeable. Certainly there are differences among them, but usually only in degree (relative power, size, or economic competitivity, for example). Differences in kind are acknowledged rarely—the division between democracies and nondemocracies is one example—and they tend to be only such general (rather than fine or specific) distinctions. Even when differences are observed, moreover, the materialist bent of much scholarship suggests that perceptions are less important than "reality."

Theories of external identity, however, can scarcely afford to ignore perception. As Benedict Anderson cogently observed of internal identity, national communities must be "*imagined* because the members of even the smallest nation will never know most of their fellow-members, meet them, or even hear of them, yet in the minds of each lives the image of their communion."[41] So it is with external identity as well. Even in the case of the widely observed distinction between democracies and nondemocracies, what separates one from the other (voting rights? multiparty elections? various civil liberties?) is a matter of perception and debate.[42]

As with internal theories, therefore, some accounts of external national identity have been linked explicitly to psychological theory. In contrast to earlier research that attributed group identities to conditions of conflict or cooperation among groups, the present consensus among social psychologists is that the mere perception of social categories is sufficient to prompt discriminatory identification.[43] Numerous experiments in both laboratory and natural settings show that individuals will give preferential treatment to members of their own group (that is, in-group) over members of other groups (out-groups), even when the standard for categorization is meaningless (when groups are distinguished by eye color, for example, or by the color of name badges).[44] Not only are out-groups typically evaluated negatively, but they are also generally assumed to be more homogeneous than in-groups (an observation that explains why theories based on these experiments say more about external than internal identity). To explain these biases, cognitive variants of "social identity theory" (SIT) hold

41. Anderson, *Imagined Communities*, 6.

42. See Robert Dahl, *Polyarchy: Participation and Opposition* (New Haven: Yale University Press, 1971); Michael Doyle, "Kant, Liberal Legacies, and Foreign Affairs, Part 1," *Philosophy and Public Affairs* 12, no. 3 (summer 1983): 205–35; Alex Inkeles, ed., *On Measuring Democracy: Its Consequences and Concomitants* (New Brunswick, NJ: Transaction Books, 1991).

43. Muzafer Sherif and his colleagues, who pioneered research on intergroup bias, assumed that such biases were caused by actual conflicts. In a classic experiment, also notable for the ethical issues it raises, Sherif divided boys attending a summer camp into two groups and gave them first competing and then superordinate goals. He succeeded in producing considerable animosity among the boys, sufficient to destroy previously existing friendships. See Muzafer Sherif et al., *Intergroup Conflict and Cooperation: The Robbers Cave Experiment* (Norman: University of Oklahoma Book Exchange, 1961); Muzafer Sherif, *In Common Predicament: Social Psychology of Intergroup Conflict and Cooperation* (Boston: Houghton Mifflin, 1966); and Muzafer Sherif, *Group Conflict and Cooperation: Their Social Psychology* (London: Routledge and Kegan Paul, 1966).

44. See, for example, the experimental results reported in Henry Tajfel, Michael Billig, R. P. Bundy, and Claude Flament, "Social Categorization and Intergroup Behavior," *European Journal of Social Psychology* 1, no. 2 (1971): 149–78; see also Henry Tajfel, ed., *Differentiation Between Social Groups: Studies in the Social Psychology of Intergroup Relations* (London: Academic Press, 1978). Tajfel's description of this finding as the "minimal group paradigm" reflects his assessment that the mere perception of difference, regardless of whether ego is actually at stake, is sufficient to prompt discriminatory social identification.

that mental efficiency is the functional cause of social stereotyping.[45] Because individuals have limited cognitive resources to devote to the task of locating themselves and others in a web of partly overlapping social categories, they must make use of simplifying assumptions. This necessity, cognitive theorists argue, leads individuals to exaggerate their initial assumptions and impressions of others.[46] Yet some psychologists argue that mental efficiency alone is not sufficient to explain the emotional content of in-group and out-group identities. Drawing on motivational psychology, for example, Marilyn Brewer has suggested that two competing imperatives—distinctiveness and belonging—shape identity.[47] Whereas stereotypes are simply efficient storage devices according to cognitive theorists, for motivational theorists like Brewer stereotypes satisfy needs.

In neither case, however, does SIT say much about the content of identity stereotypes. Its recent application to international relations shares this problem. Jonathan Mercer argues, for example, that SIT predicts egocentric national images and thus an international society in the image of realism.[48] States, he suggests, can be expected to fear each other and consequently to prepare for the worst. The value of the link SIT provides between structural realism and expectations about foreign policy should not be underestimated. It is a plausible psychological foundation for the national egocentrism that structural realism itself falls short of explaining (other than by the slow process of natural se-

45. General discussions of SIT include Michael Billig and Henry Tajfel, "Social Categorization and Similarity in Intergroup Behavior," *European Journal of Social Psychology* 3, no. 1 (1973): 27–52; Michael Hogg and Dominic Abrams, *Social Identifications: A Social Psychology of Intergroup Relations and Group Processes* (New York: Routledge, 1988); Henry Tajfel, *Human Groups and Social Categories: Studies in Social Psychology* (Cambridge: Cambridge University Press, 1981); and Stephen Worchel and William G. Austin, eds., *Psychology of Intergroup Relations* (Chicago: Nelson-Hall, 1986).

46. See chap. 4, "The Importance of Exaggerating," in Henry Tajfel, *Human Groups and Social Categories*, 62–89, in which Tajfel summarizes a good deal of evidence for the "cognitive miser" explanation of SIT. Also see John Turner, "Toward a Cognitive Redefinition of the Social Group," in *Social Identity and Intergroup Relations*, ed. Henry Tajfel (Cambridge: Cambridge University Press, 1982), 15–40.

47. Marilyn Brewer, "The Social Self: On Being the Same and Different at the Same Time," *Personality and Social Psychology Bulletin* 17, no. 5 (October 1991): 475–82; and Brewer, "The Role of Distinctiveness in Social Identity and Group Behavior," in *Group Motivation: Social Psychological Perspectives*, ed. Michael Hogg and Dominic Abrams (London: Harvester Wheatsheaf, 1993), 1–16.

48. Jonathan Mercer, "Anarchy and Identity," *International Organization* 49, no. 2 (spring 1995): 229–52; also see Glenn Chafetz, "The Political Psychology of the Nuclear Nonproliferation Regime," *Journal of Politics* 57, no. 3 (August 1995): 743–75; and Paul Kowert, "Agent versus Structure in the Construction of National Identity," in Kubálková, Onuf, and Kowert, *International Relations in a Constructed World*, 101–22.

lection). Yet much finer distinctions among nation-states than that between self and other are often made, and SIT says little about these.

The famous nineteenth-century German historian Leopold von Ranke claimed that "every nation has been endowed by god with its own special character, and the course of history was marked by 'each nation's independent development of its own specific character in the manner ordained by god'."[49] Descriptive efforts to uncover these national differences proliferated in the nineteenth century and remained popular in the first half of the twentieth. Tocqueville's *Democracy in America* is one of the more sophisticated examples of this genre, but many others have sought, sometimes crudely, to capture the essential distinctions among nations.[50] Two years after the first part of *Democracy in America* was published, Francis Grund repeated the undertaking for a British audience. Although he believed that "Americans, in general, have fewer prejudices, than any nation in Europe, and possess, therefore, less of a national character," he nevertheless proceeded, in two volumes, to generalize extensively about this character.[51] A later British effort at self-description evidently took Grund's claim to heart, missing few opportunities to explore the author's own prejudices:

> The English are a virile race. They are men first and foremost and
> have the dominance, the masculinity and the strength of the male.
> With the Mediterranean the female is apt to dominate and the tone
> of the race is feminine, whereas the essential maleness of the Asiatic
> is enhanced by the accident of Nordic supremacy.[52]

Although these observations may strike today's ear as absurd in their patent racial and sexual essentialism, this is far from a unique example of prewar writing on national identity.[53]

49. Hagen Schulze, *States, Nations and Nationalism: From the Middle Ages to the Present*, trans. William E. Yuill (Oxford: Blackwell, 1996), 164; Schulze cites Leopold von Ranke, "Zur Geschichte Deutschlands und Frankreichs im 19. Jahrhundert," in Alfred Dove, *Sämtliche Werke*, vol. 49–50 (Leipzig: Duncker and Humblot, 1887), 78.

50. Robert Nisbet points out that "*Democracy in America* was conceived by its author in an age rich in reification. Typologies, entelechies, ideal types, and abstractions of all kinds flourished during Tocqueville's life" (Nisbet, "Tocqueville's Ideal Types," in *Reconsidering Tocqueville's Democracy in America*, ed. Abraham Eisenstadt [New Brunswick: Rutgers University Press, 1988], 171).

51. Francis J. Grund, *The Americans in Their Moral, Social, and Political Relations* (London: Longman, Rees, Orme, Brown, Green, & Longman, 1837), 262.

52. Robert N. Bradley, *Racial Origins of English Character* (1926; London: Kennikat Press, 1971), 139.

53. The United States, in particular, has been the subject of an extensive collection of national character studies whose growth shows little sign of abatement. See, for example, Thomas L. Hartshorne, *The Distorted Image: Changing Conceptions of the*

Nor are such propositions quite as rare today as one might expect. In a recent interview conducted by Fareed Zakaria, Lee Kuan Yew (Singapore's prime minister from 1959 to 1990) argued that "Asian societies are unlike Western ones. The fundamental difference between Western concepts of society and East Asian concepts...is that Eastern societies believe that the individual exists in the context of his family."[54] Lee is speaking of the essential character of groups other than the nation-state, but he believes that these cultural differences directly inform national differences. Lee makes the essentialism of his argument even more explicit in another statement.

> Groups of people develop different characteristics when they have evolved for thousands of years separately. Genetics and history interact. The Native American Indian is genetically of the same stock as the Mongoloids of East Asia—the Chinese, the Koreans and the Japanese. One group, however, got cut off after the Bering Straits melted away....The two groups may share certain characteristics, for instance if you measure the shape of their skulls and so on, but if you start testing them you find that they are different, most particularly in their neurological development, and their cultural values. Now if you gloss over these kinds of issues because it is politically incorrect to study them, then you have laid a land mine for yourself.[55]

The problem, however, is not just political correctness. As Zakaria asks: "If culture is destiny, what explains a culture's failure in one era and success in another?"[56]

Such accounts can scarcely be called theories and are ill-suited for answering such questions. They treat national identity as the essential character of a nation, readily understandable to the casual observer or perhaps revealed by that nation's historical behavior. At best, they uncover certain historical continuities in national characteristics and, at worst, they are unfounded assumptions that may say more about their authors than their subject matter. In either case, they are purely descriptive. They generate no clear expectations about the duration of

---

American Character Since Turner (Cleveland: Case Western Reserve University Press, 1968); Ralph Barton Perry, Characteristically American (Ann Arbor: University of Michigan, 1949); Wilkinson, The Pursuit of American Character; and Rupert Wilkinson, ed., American Social Character: Modern Interpretations (New York: Icon, 1992).

54. Lee Kuan Yew, quoted in Fareed Zakaria, "Culture Is Destiny: A Conversation with Lee Kuan Yew," Foreign Affairs 73, no. 2 (March/April 1994): 113.

55. Lee, quoted in Zakaria, "Culture Is Destiny," 117.

56. Zakaria, "Culture Is Destiny," 125.

particular identities or the direction in which they might change. This is what Jeffrey Legro has called the rationalist "two-step," but in a slightly different guise, substituting "identity" for "preferences."[57] These essentialist accounts infer identity from behavior over time, and then explain the latter as a product of the former.

Perhaps seeking a way out of this circularity, others have linked identity to place rather than time. F. J. Turner's classic study of the American frontier attributes American national identity, for example, to seemingly endless possibilities for westward expansion.[58] When these possibilities did threaten to end a century ago, Americans "pioneered" the development of national parks to preserve something of a frontier where they could still enjoy salubrious and formative encounters with "nature." As Daniel Deudney has put it, "by ritually reenacting in 'recreational' activities the disciplining encounter with the wilds, its character-building value could be preserved, even improved....What unites John Muir and Theodore Roosevelt is that the encounter with nature is to build character."[59] Yet tracing national identity to a particular setting—and it is, after all, not just any "natural" place but their own country that good citizens must love—is only a very short step beyond description. A good descriptive account of national identity has its uses, but it is not a theory. Attributing national identity to history or geography does not explain why such attributions seem plausible, and it says little about how identity might change (other than, presumably, that change is unlikely).

A more flexible alternative to grounding national identity in time or space is to treat it as a perception of political, economic, or cultural differences that are neither historically nor geographically inevitable. Alexander Wendt takes this approach in seeking to show that the political and economic interaction of states themselves can generate both cooperative and conflictual national identities.[60] It is a staple of neorealist thought, after all, that the international system socializes actors within it. If survival is the bottom line, as neorealists argue, then states

57. Legro, "Culture and Preferences in the International Cooperation Two-Step."

58. Frederick Jackson Turner, *The Frontier in American History* (New York: Holt, 1920).

59. Daniel Deudney, "Ground Identity: Nature, Place, and Space in Nationalism," in Lapid and Kratochwil, *The Return of Culture and Identity in IR Theory*, 139. See also Roderick Nash, *Wilderness and the American Mind* (New Haven: Yale University Press, 1982); and, more generally on space and national identity, John Agnew, *Place and Politics: The Geographical Mediation of State and Society* (Boston: Allen and Unwin, 1987).

60. Wendt, "Collective Identity Formation and the International State."

are socialized to be self-regarding and to consider others at least potentially as threats.[61] Yet even within these constraints, states can also share interests: others are potentially allies as well as enemies.[62] Wendt thus observes that "British nuclear capabilities were a very different social fact for the United States from Soviet nuclear capabilities."[63] American indifference to British nuclear forces notwithstanding, states must also take the capabilities of other nation-states seriously. Although the international distribution of national capabilities is the cornerstone of Waltz's (and many other) theories of the international system, Waltz does not explore the ways differences in capability might further socialize nation-states.[64] After all, national leaders often base their assessments of another state's "intentions" on its capabilities.[65] Even constructivists, such as Wendt, might reasonably conclude that "material capabilities may be part of the problem in a conflict, inhibiting the emergence of positive identifications."[66]

Neoliberals also emphasize capabilities. Hegemonic stability theory begins, for example, with an assumption of hierarchy.[67] Regardless of the sources of this hierarchy—and there are many, including differences in the size of national economies, in resource endowments, in position within the international division of labor, in national investment strategies, and so on—differences in capability are once again likely to affect the way national leaders infer other states' intentions. In one of the few attempts to link these differences to national strategies, David Lake distinguishes between six categories of nations, ar-

61. As Waltz puts it, "a self-help system is one in which those who do not help themselves, or who do so less effectively than others, will fail to prosper, will lay themselves open to dangers, will suffer" (Kenneth N. Waltz, *Theory of International Politics* [New York: Random House, 1979], 118).

62. Alexander Wendt, "Anarchy is What States Make of It: The Social Construction of Power Politics," *International Organization* 46, no. 2 (spring 1992): 395–421.

63. Wendt, "Collective Identity Formation and the International State," 389.

64. Stephen Walt responded to Waltz's argument by arguing that states are more likely to balance against threat than against capabilities (that is, power). Walt thus directs our attention, once again, to the orientation (ally/enemy) of other states. Certainly he would not deny, however, that capabilities are also important. See Walt, *The Origins of Alliances* (Ithaca: Cornell University Press, 1987).

65. See Robert Jervis, "Cooperation Under the Security Dilemma," *World Politics* 30, no. 2 (January 1978): 167–214.

66. Wendt, "Collective Identity Formation and the International State," 389.

67. For basic statements of hegemonic stability theory, see Robert Gilpin, *U.S. Power and the Multinational Corporation: The Political Economy of Foreign Direct Investment* (New York: Basic, 1975); Charles P. Kindleberger, *The World in Depression, 1929–1939* (Berkeley: University of California Press, 1973); and Stephen D. Krasner, "State Power and the Structure of International Trade," *World Politics* 28, no. 3 (April 1976): 317–47.

rayed along the two dimensions of relative size and relative productivity: imperial leader, hegemonic leader, spoiler, supporter, protectionist free rider, and liberal free rider.[68] He suggests, for example, that large and productive nations will be seen as hegemonic leaders, whereas large but less productive nations will be seen as imperial leaders. The latter will presumably lead more by coercion than example, seeking to share the burdens of regime management.

Emphasizing absolute rather than relative gains, neoliberals would add that for all of these states, contra Waltz, national survival is rarely at stake. As Paul Krugman bluntly put it in a recent article on national competitiveness, "when we say that a corporation is uncompetitive, we mean that its market position is unsustainable—that unless it improves its performance, it will cease to exist. Countries, on the other hand, do not go out of business."[69] Russian communists might demur, and Krugman's assertion flies in the face of the widespread belief that the twenty-first century will bring an era of economic competition in which states that fail to prepare have much to lose. This debate pits the "rise of the trading state" against the expectation that relative gains and power politics will remain fundamental in international politics.[70] Whether Krugman or Waltz is ultimately correct, however, the mere existence of such debates indicates a potential for external national identities beyond those dictated by military threat and opportunity.

In one of the few attempts to integrate hypotheses about the political and economic relationships among nations into a theory of external national identity, Richard Cottam and his colleagues have argued that three judgments about other states are important: threat or opportunity, relative capability, and cultural distance. Richard Herrmann later refined the typology of perceptions to yield a 3x3x3 classification scheme and twenty-seven consequent national identity types.[71] Draw-

68. David Lake, "Beneath the Commerce of Nations: A Theory of International Economic Structures," *International Studies Quarterly* 28, no. 2 (June 1984): 143–70.

69. Paul Krugman, "Competitiveness: A Dangerous Obsession," *Foreign Affairs* 73, no. 2 (March/April 1994): 31.

70. Joseph Grieco, "Anarchy and the Limits of Cooperation: A Realist Critique of the Newest Liberal Institutionalism," *International Organization* 42, no. 3 (summer 1988): 485–507; Richard Rosecrance, *The Rise of the Trading State: Commerce and Conquest in the Modern World* (New York: Basic Books, 1986). A more direct response to Krugman is Clyde Prestowitz, Lester Thurow, Rudolf Sharping, Stephen Cohen, and Benn Steil, "The Fight over Competitiveness: A Zero-Sum Debate?" *Foreign Affairs* 73, no. 4 (July/August 1994): 186–97.

71. Cottam and Herrmann view these national role conceptions as "perceptual ideal types." They are ideal forms of the identities leaders are expected to ascribe to other nations. See Richard Cottam, *Foreign Policy Motivation: A General Theory and a Case*

ing on Festinger's theory of cognitive dissonance and Heider's balance theory, Cottam and Herrmann go on to argue that not all combinations of threat, capability, and cultural distance make sense.[72] Many would produce cognitive dissonance or "imbalance." Cottam and Herrmann would not expect a nation that policymakers consider to have inferior capabilities and an "inferior culture," for example, to be seen as particularly threatening. Herrmann and Fischerkeller have thus recently argued for five primary ideal types that span both military and economic issues: enemy, ally, degenerate, imperialist, and colony.[73]

Table 1

SELECTED EXAMPLES OF NATIONAL ROLE IMAGES

National role image	Threat/opportunity	National capability
Enemy*†	Threat	Comparable
Ally*†	Opportunity	Comparable
Degenerate†	Opportunity	Declining
Imperialist*†	Threat	Superior
Colony ("good")*†	Opportunity	Inferior
Colony ("bad")†	Threat	Inferior

* Richard Cottam, *Foreign Policy Motivation* (Pittsburgh: University of Pittsburgh Press, 1977).
† Richard Herrmann and Michael P. Fischerkeller, "Beyond the Enemy Image and Spiral Model," *International Organization* 49, no. 3 (summer 1995): 415–50.

The distinction between threat and opportunity in Cottam and Herrmann's work corresponds to the dimension of identity generated

---

Study (Pittsburgh: University of Pittsburgh Press, 1977); Richard K. Herrmann, *Perceptions and Behavior in Soviet Foreign Policy* (Pittsburgh, University of Pittsburgh Press, 1985); and Richard K. Herrmann, "The Power of Perceptions in Foreign-Policy Decision Making: Do Views of the Soviet Union Determine the Policy Choices of American Leaders?" *American Journal of Political Science* 30, no. 4 (November 1986): 841–75.

72. Leon Festinger, *A Theory of Cognitive Dissonance* (Stanford: Stanford University Press, 1966); and Fritz Heider, *The Psychology of Interpersonal Relations* (New York: Wiley, 1958).

73. Richard Herrmann and Michael P. Fischerkeller, "Beyond the Enemy Image and Spiral Model: Cognitive-Strategic Research After the Cold War," *International Organization* 49, no. 3 (summer 1995): 415–50. Cottam also argued for five ideal types: enemy, complex, allied, imperial, and colonial (Cottam, *Foreign Policy Motivation*, 62–73).

by what neorealists and neoliberals alike consider to be the high stakes of international politics (though they differ on how high the stakes really are). For neorealists, the anarchical system means that threats must be taken seriously and opportunities can be exploited. For neoliberals (and some neo-Marxists), the pursuit of wealth produces similar concerns. Cottam and Herrmann's other distinctions range from superior to inferior capabilities and from superior to inferior cultural development. Because these two dimensions covary in all of the images Cottam and his successors consider to be important, they might conceivably be collapsed into a single dimension, which corresponds to differences in relative national capabilities, also discussed above.[74]

Table 1 summarizes the national role images or identities described by Cottam and elaborated by Herrmann and Fischerkeller. Enemy and ally, which are undoubtedly the most widely discussed external identities in the general literature on international relations, derive their meaning primarily from concern with military capabilities.[75] They are distinguished by whether these capabilities represent a threat or an opportunity. Both of these images, moreover, assume relatively high capabilities. A third image, the degenerate, has low (or declining) capabilities and presents a military opportunity for domination. Imperialist and colony, on the other hand, derive from a greater concern with economic capabilities.[76] The imperialist state is "interested in maintaining the colony as a source of raw materials, a locus for investments, and a market for its manufactured products and culture."[77] The colony is seen as the target of such ambitions. Imperialists are thus economic

---

74. It should be no surprise that these two dimensions covary given the balance/consistency theory that is Cottam's theoretical point of departure. In the long run, one might expect a "superior" culture to produce superior capabilities.

75. See David P. Barash and Judith Eve Lipton, *The Caveman and the Bomb* (New York: McGraw-Hill, 1985); Urie Bronfenbrenner, "The Mirror-Image in Soviet-American Relations: A Social Psychologist's Report," *Journal of Social Issues* 17, no. 3 (1961): 45–56; Brett Silverstein, "Enemy Images: The Psychology of U.S. Attitudes and Cognitions Regarding the Soviet Union," *American Psychologist* 44, no. 6 (June 1989): 903–13; and Ralph K. White, *Fearful Warriors: A Psychological Profile of U.S.-Soviet Relations* (New York: Free Press, 1984).

76. Herrmann and Fischerkeller use the terms *imperialist* and *colony* in a different (and clearer) way than does Cottam. For Cottam, the "imperial" image is the way a superior power might view an inferior one. The image itself is, therefore, of a "colony," as Herrmann and Fischerkeller rightly label it. Similarly, Cottam's "colonial" image refers to the way a subordinate power might see an aggressive, stronger nation—an "imperialist." See Cottam, *Foreign Policy Motivation*, 63; Herrmann and Fischerkeller, "Beyond the Enemy Image and Spiral Model," 428–31.

77. Herrmann and Fischerkeller, "Beyond the Enemy Image and Spiral Model," 428 (Table 1).

threats of high capability; colonies represent economic opportunities with low independent capabilities. With the colony image, however, Herrmann and Fischerkeller muddy the water somewhat by distinguishing between "good forces" and "bad forces" in colonies. The good forces version casts the colony in the image of a child, to be "instructed" by the imperial power. The bad forces version has military overtones, describing an extremist, demagogic, deceptive, or terrorist state, and thus represents a threat rather than an opportunity. Such a state might also be labeled (indeed, it is by many American elites) a rogue or backlash state.[78]

It is undoubtedly easier to articulate a typology of national images than to show that national leaders (or citizens) actually apply it to other nations. Through careful historical analysis, Cottam has demonstrated that his categories account well for British views of Egypt from 1876 to 1956. He also finds support for these images in British leaders' views, at certain junctures, of the United States, Russia/USSR, Germany, Austria-Hungary, France, and the Ottoman Empire. Herrmann finds that roughly the same set of potential identities accounts for Soviet views of Afghanistan and for U.S., Soviet, Iranian, and Iraqi views of each other.[79] A series of experimental studies found, moreover, that college students who read descriptions of the enemy, degenerate, ally, and colony images made deductions about threat/opportunity and capabilities in accordance with the predictions of Cottam's theory.[80] The body of research generated by Cottam and those who have adopted his

---

78. See, for example, Anthony Lake, "Confronting Backlash States," *Foreign Affairs* 73, no. 2 (March/April 1994): 45–55; and the report of the U.S. House Committee on Foreign Affairs, Subcommittee on International Security, International Organizations, and Human Rights, on "U.S. Security Policy toward Rogue Regimes," 103rd Congress, First Session, 28 July and 14 September 1993. See also Michael Klare, *Rogue States and Nuclear Outlaws: America's Search for a New Foreign Policy* (New York: Bill and Wang, 1995).

79. Cottam, *Foreign Policy Motivation*, 151–310; Herrmann, *Perceptions and Behavior in Soviet Foreign Policy*; Herrmann, "The Power of Perceptions in Foreign-Policy Decision Making"; Richard K. Herrmann, "The Role of Iran in Soviet Perceptions and Policy," in *Neither East Nor West*, ed. Nikki Keddie and Mark Gasiorowski (New Haven: Yale University Press, 1990), 63–99; Richard K. Herrmann, "The Soviet Decision to Withdraw from Afghanistan: Changing Strategic and Regional Images," in *Dominoes and Bandwagons: Strategic Beliefs and Great Power Competition in the Eurasian Rimland*, ed. Robert Jervis and Jack Snyder (New York: Oxford University Press, 1991), 220–49; and Herrmann and Fischerkeller, "Beyond the Enemy Image and Spiral Model."

80. Richard K. Herrmann, James F. Voss, Tonya Y. E. Schooler, and Joseph Ciarrochi, "Images in International Relations: An Experimental Test of Cognitive Schemata," *International Studies Quarterly* 41, no. 3 (September 1997): 403–33.

approach thus provides some general empirical support for their structural categories of national identity.[81]

Many other students of nationalism and foreign policy have described similar categories even though they did not adopt Cottam's framework. Edward Said's well-known study of orientalism describes British, French, and American attitudes toward the East that evoke the degenerate (and, more recently, the bad forces colony) image. For Said, Chateaubriand's account of his "literary pilgrimage" to the Holy Land perfectly encapsulates the western image of the Oriental Arab as a "civilized man fallen again into a savage state."[82] Taking a more quantitative approach, Kal Holsti identifies no fewer than seventeen different national role conceptions in a content analysis of speeches by the leaders of seventy-one states.[83] These are "self"-descriptions (of a leader's own state), but many of them describe roles that make sense only as responses to other states characterized by one of the national identities discussed above. Holsti's "protectee" category, for example, perfectly describes a state's orientation toward another, "protector" state or superior "ally." Similarly, "anti-imperialist agent" describes a relationship with an "imperialist."

Table 2 lists the national role conceptions (self) in Holsti's typology and their counterparts among images of (other) national identity. All of Cottam and Herrmann's categories are represented. Unsurprisingly, most of the self-descriptions that fail to correspond to one of these other-identities are those that emphasize independence from other nations. Stephen Walker has argued, more recently, that Holsti's original

---

81. See also Shannon Lindsey Blanton, "Images in Conflict: The Case of Ronald Reagan and El Salvador," *International Studies Quarterly* 40, no. 1 (March 1996): 23–44; Martha Cottam, "The Carter Administration's Policy Toward Nicaragua: Images, Goals and Tactics," *Political Science Quarterly* 107, no. 1 (spring 1992): 123–46; Keith L. Shimko, *Images and Arms Control: Perceptions of the Soviet Union in the Reagan Administration* (Ann Arbor: University of Michigan Press, 1991); and Keith L. Shimko, "Reagan on the Soviet Union and the Nature of International Conflict," *Political Psychology* 13, no. 3 (September 1992): 353–77.

82. Edward W. Said, *Orientalism* (New York: Vintage, 1979), 171; Said cites François-René de Chateaubriand, *Oeuvres Romanesques et Voyages*, ed. Maurice Regard (Paris: Gallimard, 1969), vol. 2. The British and French views of the Orient, as Said describes them, correspond closely to the degenerate or client image. The American view, however, treats Middle Eastern nations more often as opportunities for economic exploitation—that is, as colonies (primarily suppliers of oil)—or as rogue (terrorist) states; see Said, "The Latest Phase," in *Orientalism*, 284–328. Common to all of these images is the Orient's positioning as inferior to the Occident. See also Edward W. Said, *Culture and Imperialism* (New York: Knopf, 1993), for an extension of Said's views on national images.

83. Kal J. Holsti, "National Role Conceptions in the Study of Foreign Policy," *International Studies Quarterly* 14, no. 3 (September 1970): 233–309.

typology is also consistent with a simplified typology developed as part
of the CREON (Comparative Research on the Events of Nations) project

Table 2

HOLSTI'S NATIONAL ROLE CONCEPTIONS AND THEIR
COUNTERPARTS AMONG NATIONAL IMAGES OF OTHER

National role (self) conception	Images of other nations
Bastion of the revolution/liberator	Enemy
Regional leader	Colony (good forces)
Regional protector	Colony (good forces)
Active independent	
Liberator/supporter	Colony (bad forces)
Anti-imperialist agent	Imperialist
Defender of the faith	Degenerate
Mediator/integrator	
Regional collaborator	Ally
Developer	Colony (good forces)
Bridge	
Faithful ally	Ally
Independent	
Example	Colony (good forces)
Internal development	
Isolate	Degenerate
Protectee	Ally

See Kal J. Holsti, "National Role Conceptions in the Study of Foreign Policy," *International Studies Quarterly* 14, no. 3 (September 1970): 233–309.

at the Ohio State University.[84] The CREON model identifies five basic
role conceptions: consumer, producer, belligerent, facilitator, and pro-

84. Stephen Walker, "Role Theory and the Origins of Foreign Policy," in *New Directions in the Study of Foreign Policy*, ed. Charles F. Hermann, Charles Kegley, and James Rosenau (Boston: Unwin Hyman, 1987), 269–84. On the CREON model and national roles, see also Stephen Walker, ed., *Role Theory and Foreign Policy Analysis* (Durham: Duke University Press, 1987). For a description of the CREON dataset, see

vocateur. These self-images appear to correspond, respectively, to images of the other as: imperialist, colony, enemy, ally, and again enemy (or perhaps degenerate).

There is good support, then, for Wendt's basic claim that the international system is not so restrictive in its socializing effects as some have imagined. Other states are thought of in a variety of ways by national leaders. One might object that the images of other states outlined by Cottam and Herrmann, and Lake for that matter, are not really the same thing as identity. They consider only how other nations are perceived, not necessarily their "true identity" or how they see themselves. This objection suggests that a true identity must be an essential one, perhaps linked through culture to history or geography after all, rather than a manufactured perception. It runs directly counter to Wendt's appeal to international relations scholars "to construct measures of state identity and interest capable of sustaining inferences about change."[85] Inasmuch as self and other are always to some extent mutually referential—a point reinforced by Holsti's study of national role conceptions—there is little reason to preserve an analytical purism that insists on treating self in a vacuum. Self and other are practically and theoretically connected. In other words, perceptions of other reveal something about self. Exploring these linkages would be a valuable contribution to identity theory, but it would be difficult to achieve while adhering to a conception of national identity as some essential form of national character.

PROSPECTS FOR THEORY

IF THERE IS any agreement among the wide variety of theories and scholars discussed here, it is that the term "national identity" is in great need of refinement. Essays such as this one can only go so far toward that end: ultimately, the way national identity is defined depends on the uses to which it is put. The distinction argued here—between internal and external identity—is thus an effort to clarify two distinct ways that a theory of national identity can be used in international relations.

Charles F. Hermann, Maurice East, Margaret G. Hermann, Barbara Salmore, and Stephen Salmore, *CREON: A Foreign Events Data Set* (Beverly Hills: Sage Professional Papers Series, 1973).

85. Wendt, "Collective Identity Formation and the International State," 391.

Internal theories of identity address the debate over the ontological status of the nation-state as an agent in international politics. Most of this debate has been conducted in overly dichotomous terms. Some argue that "the nation-state as agent" remains a good assumption, that nation-states are jealous of their power and privilege, and that there is still every reason to treat them as the defining actors in international politics (even if other kinds of actor have proliferated). Against this position are those who suspect that the era of nation-building is over, who find the state anachronistic, and who look to refocus attention on other agents—either smaller (domestic interest groups), larger (international organizations), or simply different (corporate and cultural transnational organizations). David Held is one of many in the latter camp who argue for "creating a politics beyond the sovereign nation state—a new international politics for new times."[86]

Explicit theorization of internal identity presents a way out of this essentially fruitless debate over the conceptual utility of the nation-state by recasting it in terms of degree rather than of kind. The challenge to scholars of international relations is more to grapple with how the nation-state is being contested than simply, as Held implies, to recognize or devise new ontological constructs beyond the nation-state. There is undoubtedly a great deal more that theorists of internal identity could say about the nation-state's ongoing evolution.

More research on internal identity has been backward-looking, attuned to the question of how the nation-state emerged, than forward-looking. Yet Wendt's injunction to formulate accounts of identity "capable of sustaining inferences about change" applies here as well. If national identity serves various economic, cultural, political, and communicative functions, then the obvious question is whether—and, if so, how—those functions are changing. There is no shortage of banal assertions that the end of the cold war, or the arrival of a "new world order," means that we should recast issues of security and prosperity in other-than-national terms. Yet few have systematically explored challenges to the functional implications of modernity for national identity (such as those described by Deutsch and Gellner). Postmodernists sometimes claim to do so, but their frequently antitheoretical, antipositivist, or simply antifoundational stance imposes its own limits on the

---

86. David Held, "The Decline of the Nation State," in Eley and Suny, *Becoming National*, 416. See also Jens Bartleson, *A Genealogy of Sovereignty* (Cambridge: Cambridge University Press, 1995), 237–48.

appeal of their analysis.[87] Many important questions thus remain barely addressed (much less answered). Do modern economies of scale require the internationalization of cultural and corporate symbols, paving the way for supranational "postmodern" identities? Can this process be countered by those social groups who stand to lose, economically or politically, from transferring authority and identity to higher (more inclusive) levels?[88] What, for that matter, are the limits on the integration of political authority?

As the demise of some nation-states and threats to the viability of others capture headlines, answering questions such as these is an important use to which theories of internal identity can be put. So long as the nation-state has some ontological standing, however, a second problem will remain that internal theories do not address: what do nation-states want? Contemporary international relations theory addresses this almost exclusively in one of two ways: either simplistically (assuming that all states pursue roughly the same things) or systemically (arguing that the international system socializes states to pursue the same things). This is not much of a choice. Beyond it, most scholars fall back on revealed preferences.

Repeated calls for a theory of national preferences—one that recognizes differences as well as similarities in national objectives—have generated few results. Yet this is precisely what a theory of external identity can contribute. To do so, it must be a theory of national (nation-state) preferences, and not of organizational or individual preferences writ large. Moreover, it must not entangle actor preferences and behavior, explaining each as a consequence of the other (as historically oriented discussions of national character, for example, often do). The more dynamic theories of external identity—those that treat identity as

87. For a sympathetic discussion of these aspects of postmodernism, see Pauline Marie Rosenau, *Post-Modernism and the Social Sciences: Insights, Inroads, and Intrusions* (Princeton: Princeton University Press, 1992). Also see Zygmunt Bauman, *Legislators and Interpreters: Modernity, Post-Modernity and Intellectuals* (Ithaca: Cornell University Press, 1987); David Harvey, *The Condition of Postmodernity: An Enquiry into the Origins of Cultural Change* (Cambridge: Basil Blackwell, 1989); and Henry S. Kariel, *The Desperate Politics of Postmodernism* (Amherst: University of Massachusetts Press, 1989). One prominent application of postmodernism to the problem of sovereignty is Richard Ashley and R. B. J. Walker, "Reading Dissidence/Writing the Discipline: Crisis and the Question of Sovereignty in International Studies," *International Studies Quarterly* 34, no. 3 (September 1990): 367–416.

88. Barber's pithy formulation, "Jihad vs. McWorld," poses this question neatly but provides little in the way of an answer. Both of these trends, as Barber explains in detail, threaten democracy, yet the general tone of his analysis is that no one is willing or able to do much about it. See Barber, *Jihad vs. McWorld*.

a manufactured perception rather than a geographically or historically given character—seem especially promising.[89] They help to explain what theories that ignore perceived differences among nation-states cannot: why national leaders devote considerable time and energy both to projecting a desirable national image and to discerning the nature of other states. Are "they" more likely, for example, to be good trading partners or free riders? On a more basic level, are they allies or enemies in an emergency?

Neorealists say that these questions are meaningless. Constructivists, on the other hand, say that perceptions of identity are essential. Yet perhaps constructivists are promising more than they can deliver. Unless they too mean to provide only descriptive accounts of national behavior, then constructivists are committing themselves to a theory of foreign policy based on an account of identity (or of social norms).[90] It remains far from certain whether perceptual theories of national identity can provide a reliable guide to other states' behavior.

The improbability of a perfect or complete theory of foreign policy, however, does not mean that theory is impossible. One way around this problem is to investigate what perceptions of other say about self. The apparent correspondence of Holsti's national role self-conceptions to the Cottam and Herrmann typology of other-images suggests that further exploration of this link might be fruitful. In an extension of this logic, Herrmann and Fischerkeller have recently sought to connect a typology of national images to specific foreign policies by developing extended, multilevel scripts for each type of national image. Facing a state identified as "enemy," for example, they expect national leaders to apply a containment script. The containment script prescribes general goals such as deterrence and alliance-building, more concrete objectives such as the development of "assured destruction" capability and alliance integration, and specific policy tracks such as the deployment of various weapons systems and the pursuit of joint political and eco-

89. Structural theories of external identity such as Cottam's are dynamic: they expect changes in international "position" to lead to changes in identity. This provides a good illustration of Ruggie's complaint that Waltz overemphasizes the static character of systems theory. See John G. Ruggie, "Continuity and Transformation in the World Polity: Toward a Neorealist Synthesis," *World Politics* 35, no. 2 (January 1983): 261–85.

90. Most constructivists consider identity and social norms to be closely related. The latter may be thought of, for example, as behavioral prescriptions appropriate to given identities. See, for example, Martha Finnemore, *National Interests in International Society* (Ithaca: Cornell University Press, 1996); Katzenstein, *The Culture of National Security*; and Klotz, *Norms in International Relations*.

nomic planning with allies.[91] In this way, Herrmann and Fischerkeller relate leaders' perceptions of other-identity to these leaders' own behavior. Their multilevel approach to behavioral scripts also receives some support from Hurwitz's and Peffley's hierarchical model of foreign-policy belief systems, which finds longitudinal stability in the relationship between leaders' core values and the specific policy attitudes of these leaders.[92]

In an effort to promote conceptual clarity, this essay has discussed internal and external theories of identity, and the uses to which they can be put, in mutually exclusive terms. A final, important issue thus remains: the relationship between the two. It takes little effort to imagine that an important connection exists. In saying how one's own nation-state differs from others, external identities are powerful ideological tools for the promotion of internal identities. Conversely, without internal coherence, external identities are meaningless descriptions of nonexistent entities. The cold war commonplace that external enemies help to suppress internal dissent is one recognition of this relationship, as is, perhaps, Gellner's claim that the sheer power of Europe's early industrial giants created a threat that gave rise to nationalism in smaller industrial late-comers.[93] Beyond recognizing that some connection exists, what do external and internal theories have to say to each other?

The relationship between them is not straightforward. So far in the history of international relations, there have always been external threats while, certainly, nation-states have not always displayed internal cohesion. This is one more area in which attention to social construction could help. Some scholars may know threats when they see

---

91. Herrmann and Fischerkeller, "Beyond the Enemy Image and Spiral Model." Like Herrmann and Fischerkeller, James Rosenau also predicted (in the 1960s) that certain foreign policies or behaviors would result from the interaction of specific types of states. For empirical tests of Rosenau's propositions, see the essays in James Rosenau, ed., *Comparing Foreign Policies: Theories, Findings, and Methods* (New York: Wiley, 1974) by James E. Harf, David G. Hoovler; and Thomas E. James, "Systemic and External Attributes in Foreign Policy Analysis," 235–49; James Rosenau and Gary D. Hoggard, "Foreign Policy Behavior in Dyadic Relationships," 117–49; and Stephen Salmore and Donald Munton, "An Empirically Based Typology of Foreign Policy Behaviors," 329–52.

92. Jon Hurwitz and Mark Peffley, "How Are Foreign Policy Attitudes Structured? A Hierarchical Model," *American Political Science Review* 81, no. 4 (December 1987): 1100–20; Jon Hurwitz and Mark Peffley, "Public Images of the Soviet Union: The Impact on Foreign Policy Attitudes," *Journal of Politics* 52, no. 1 (February 1990): 3–28; and Jon Hurwitz, Mark Peffley, and Mitchell Seligson, "Foreign Policy Belief Systems in Comparative Perspective: The United States and Costa Rica," *International Studies Quarterly* 37, no. 3 (September 1993): 245–70.

93. Gellner, *Nations and Nationalism.*

them, but it seems clear enough that threat is not an objective matter, as Wendt's example of American attitudes about British nuclear weapons suggests. Perhaps some kinds of threat lead more readily to internal cohesion than others. Some threats, for that matter, may even undermine the internal identity of nation-states. Inspired by Mitrany's functionalist regionalism, many expect the modern litany of global threats (to health, safety, the environment, and so on) to inspire global identities as well.[94] Yet another distinction of external identity, between democracy and nondemocracy, has different implications for internal identity. Democratic rights remain attached more to national citizenship than to other forms of identity, providing a functional incentive to sustain the nation-state as a form of internal identification.

Whatever the long-term prospects of the nation-state, the problem of identity will remain central to research on global governance and security. Identity tells us who is being governed or secured. It is impossible to conceive of either without making assumptions about identity. In international relations, scholars have thus assumed a world of nation-states with (assumed) common preferences. These have been fertile assumptions. One cannot challenge or defend them, however, without a theory of identity.

94. David Mitrany, *A Working Peace System: An Argument for the Functional Development of International Organizations* (London: Royal Institute of International Affairs, 1944). Also see Ernst Haas, *The Uniting of Europe: Political, Social, and Economic Forces* (Stanford: Stanford University Press, 1958); and Ernst Haas, *Beyond the Nation State: Functionalism and Inter-National Organization* (Stanford: Stanford University Press, 1964).

THE PLACE AND POWER OF CIVIC SPACE:

READING GLOBALIZATION AND SOCIAL GEOGRAPHY THROUGH THE LENS OF CIVILIZATIONAL CONFLICT

DAVID M. CHESHIER AND CORI E. DAUBER

THE END OF THE cold war dealt a sustained blow to traditional international relations paradigms. (Neo)realists, primordialists, globalists, and constructivists have rushed in to make sense of the new and troubling geopolitical terrain. Now is thus an opportune moment for scholars of public argument to introduce a perspective centered on issues of culture, public controversy and identity. Such a framework explicitly explores the possibility of public deliberation under circumstances of geopolitical stress, and brings to bear a disciplinary commitment to the idea that strong and progressive societies can only exist when they enable open and healthy public debate, a civic space where citizens are meaningfully heard. When this space shuts down, occluded like an artery slowly closing, conflicts between ethnic groups move closer and closer to physical violence. A new orientation to international conflict is all the more important given that, to date, no consensus has emerged, partly because of the apparent perception that existing alternatives mark out incommensurable ground.

The absence of a dominant paradigm for explaining the post–cold war world explains recent efforts to articulate a coherent worldview for American foreign policy. We argue for a conceptualization of international relations rooted not in realpolitik but in public argument, not in power and ethnicity as pregiven but as made salient through processes of persuasion and deliberation, where culture and identity are given particular force in struggles for political influence.

Samuel Huntington's recent "clash-of-civilizations" hypothesis has provoked a great deal of attention. We use his provocative thesis, and

David M. Cheshier is assistant professor in the Department of Communication, Georgia State University; Cori E. Dauber is associate professor in the Department of Communication Studies, University of North Carolina.

We wish to thank Robert Newman, Ralph Levering, Lawrence Grossberg, V. William Balthrop, Carol Winkler, and the anonymous reviewers of *Security Studies* for their helpful comments.

the debate over it, as a point of departure in laying out a contrasting view of the geopolitical scene.[1] Using Huntington in this way may seem curious, given the ready willingness of so many international relations theorists to downplay and attack his argument. The steady emergence of a cottage industry commenting on the clash of civilizations,[2] however, signals concerns that belie the easy dismissals. While few in the academic community are prepared to defend Huntington, such disturbing evidence mounts with every day's coverage of such conflicts as those between the United States and Iraq, Iran, and China that the public, if not foreign policy decisionmakers, remain open to the civilizational framework and its pessimistic implications for inter-civilizational peace. There seems to be a fear, deriving perhaps from the simple elegance of Huntington's position, that the clash of civilizations hypothesis will gain adherents, or at least influence, outside academe. Thus, while the debate is increasingly stacked against Huntington, the "Clash of Civilizations" has touched raw nerves, making it a fertile site from which to approach the study of post–cold war identity and culture.

Huntington's argument is easily described and already familiar, an attempt to help decisionmakers come to terms with the explosive potentialities of ethnic and nationalistic conflicts.[3] The terrain of global geopolitics, says Huntington, consists of a playing-field of vast and ancient civilizations. While conflicts can and do erupt within civilizations, those are not likely to escalate. Rather, it is cross-civilizational war that maximally threatens global stability, and which must therefore be contained as quickly as possible.

---

1. See David A. Welch, "The 'Clash of Civilizations' Thesis as an Argument and as a Phenomenon," *Security Studies* 6, no. 4 (summer 1997): 197–216. Huntington's argument appeared originally in *Foreign Affairs* 72, no. 3 (summer 1997): 197–216, as "The Clash of Civilizations?" The book-length version is Samuel P. Huntington, *The Clash of Civilizations and the Remaking of World Order* (New York: Simon and Schuster, 1996).

2. Welch, "Clash Thesis," 198.

3. Cf., Daniel Patrick Moynihan, *Pandaemonium: Ethnicity in International Politics* (Oxford: Oxford University Press, 1993); Zbigniew K. Brzezinski, *Out of Control: Global Turmoil on the Eve of the Twenty-First Century* (New York: Scribner's, 1993). Both are cited by Huntington, and he distances himself from the arguments of both. A more nuanced version of Huntington's argument (and it is better for the nuance) is Benjamin R. Barber, *Jihad vs. McWorld: How Globalism and Tribalism Are Reshaping the World* (New York: Ballantine, 1996).

This view has attracted much criticism. Many judge Huntington's conception of culture to be simplistic and reductionist. Others find nothing new, simply a replay of historical versions of realism translated into the new vernacular of the post–cold war era. For us, Huntington's argument that cross-civilizational conflicts should be of most concern, that the world is best conceptualized as a small and irreducible set of ancient and stable civilizations, and that war conducted within civilizations should absorb less of our diplomatic energies than those crossing civilizational lines, is a disturbing one, out of tune with intracivilizational bloodletting worldwide. His work would have us pay little attention to several recent conflicts of appalling ferocity.

Rather than simply add to the growing list of critiques, we aim to use Huntington as the starting point for focused attention on the dynamics of civic space. Here, however, is a curiosity: despite the presumed differences characteristic of work done by constructivists, primordialists, neorealists and globalists, all begin with the shared assumption that ethnic fracturing within societies has the effect of shutting down civic space.[4] Some event must trigger violence where it has not existed before. Whether violence results from primordial differences or culturally constructed ones, some event triggers a jump from peaceable community to ethnic cleansing. Where such a jump occurs, all schools seem to agree, the transition to war is invariably marked by a closing down of the shared ability to negotiate competing interests.

Everyone (primordialists, constructivists, and so on) despairs of this outcome, although there are varying interpretations, if not great skepticism, about the extent to which the chaos resulting from civic shutdown can be averted by the cultivation of deliberative political practices. The functioning of public argument, however, especially within societies under stress, barely appears in Huntington's recent work. Societies are the building-blocks of civilizations, yet the fact of civilizational differences is taken by Huntington as more important than their specifics, and civilization becomes the black box at the heart of the clash-of-civilizations hypothesis. Lacking a consideration of the way civilizations differ, however, solutions to conflict that can preempt or

---

4. Much of the debate we describe here is referenced and extended in a recently published *International Studies* reader. See Michael E. Brown, Owen Coté Jr., Sean M. Lynn-Jones, and Steven Miller, eds., *Nationalism and Ethnic Conflict* (Cambridge, Mass.: MIT Press, 1997). For another approach to integrating cultural analysis and international relations work, see Marco Verweij, "Cultural Theory and the Study of International Relations," *Millennium: Journal of International Studies* 24, no. 1 (spring 1995): 87–111.

avert violence will be hard to discover. Even as Huntington places civilization at the heart of his theory, he thus underplays the role civilization plays in our lived experiences.

Thus, while other reviews have focused on explicit flaws in Huntington's analysis, we prefer to focus on what is absent or dismissed there. Consider Huntington's rejection of the now vast literature on "globalization." He reduces the concept to the idea that "the spread of Western consumption patterns and popular culture around the world is creating a universal civilization." Having caricatured globalization, he then pronounces it "neither profound nor relevant." "Cultural fads," as he belittles them, are "either techniques lacking in significant cultural consequences or fads that come and go without altering the underlying culture of the recipient civilization." Moving from McDonald's to Murdoch, to name only two possible emblems of essentially planetary forms of mass mediation, Huntington is only able to theorize global communications as an affront easily denounced by local demagogues, used by them "to rally their publics to preserve the survival and integrity of their indigenous culture."[5] His conclusion is hardly surprising, given his assertion that none of the arguments that "a universal culture or civilization is now emerging…withstands even passing scrutiny."[6]

We find such a diagnosis seriously oversimplified (as elaborated later, we argue that it attacks a straw person—monolithic and imperialistic global culture) and we want to use Huntington as a starting point for a dialogue that brings newer work in argumentation theory, cultural studies and globalization into conversation with the more traditional conceptions of culture employed by *The Clash of Civilizations*, in a manner we hope contributes to the growing intellectual controversy in international relations studies between realism and its more critical adversaries.[7] Much of the "critical turn" work in international relations has been seen as advocating a strong version of social constructivism, where the material conditions that enable struggle are reducible to

5. Huntington, *The Clash of Civilizations*, 58–59.

6. Samuel P. Huntington, "'If Not Civilizations, What?' Paradigms of the Post-Cold War World," in *Samuel P. Huntington's The Clash of Civilizations? The Debate* (New York: Council on Foreign Relations, 1996), 63 (hereafter, *Huntington: The Debate*).

7. In some respects we seek to respond to Ole Woever's call for "new images" that break out of the "three paradigms" and "inter-paradigm" models which continue to shape international relations scholarship. Ole Woever, "The Rise and Fall of the Inter-Paradigm Debate," in *International Theory: Positivism and Beyond*, ed. Steve Smith, Ken Booth, and Marysia Zalewski (Cambridge: Cambridge University Press, 1996), 149–85.

"text" and "performance," a move which implies that all of life is talk and its reception, and all of identity is role playing.[8] Framed in those terms, the hostility of recent exchanges is not surprising, since often such a critique of "critical" international relations studies reduces to caricature.

Our position employs a vocabulary derived from work in the study of public argument. The perspective we describe and defend is sensitive both to the power of language and to its embeddedness in the material conditions of history, culture, power, nationhood, economics, and ethnicity. As recently put by Beer and Hariman, from within the perspective of public argument studies (they call it a "rhetorical perspective") "one takes words seriously, but not for their own sake alone. The emphasis is on discourse—with a corresponding wariness of the conventional distinctions between speech and action, language and reality—yet this interest is in the effect the discourse has on conduct."[9] By analyzing events as concretely grounded in the historical record, yet nonetheless subject to transformed interpretations over time through processes of persuasion and deliberation, scholars of public argument, we argue, sidestep the reductionism of both some current work in critical international relations (which invariably sees "discourse" trumping "force") and the type of work exemplified by Huntington (which invariably sees the opposite).[10] Put plainly, our

8. It is difficult to find scholars who defend this strong version of ethnicity. Perhaps the closest is R. Paul Shaw and Yuwa Wong's, *The Genetic Seeds of Warfare: Evolution, Nationalism, and Patriotism* (Boston: Unwin Hyman, 1989). We would distinguish our work from what is generally referred to in classical international relations as "constructivism." As several essays in this issue make clear, often quite explicitly, constructivism is an attempt to marry the benefits of an interpretivist methodology with the overarching goals of social science as traditionally understood. We are not convinced the circle can be squared. As Kahl makes clear, such efforts stake out ontological and not epistemological ground (Colin H. Kahl, "Constructing a Separate Peace: Constructivism, Collective Liberal Identity, and Democratic Peace," *Security Studies* 8, nos. 2/3 [winter 1998/99–spring 1999]: 94–144). By contrast, symbolic interactionism, a theoretical framework which grounds our work, fits more comfortably with the latter than the former.

9. Francis A. Beer and Robert Hariman, eds., *Post-Realism: The Rhetorical Turn in International Relations* (East Lansing: Michigan State University Press, 1996), 11.

10. The work we describe here is interdisciplinary, reflecting contributions made by argumentation and communication theorists, but also by scholars of political theory and sociology. In several fields, work on public argument and its status is focused on the valuable notions of "civic space" and "public spheres." Elsewhere, it advances age-old arguments about the status of rhetorical (persuasive) claims. Still other fields do work on the nature of "public argument" when they assess the potency of political action conducted by new social movements. For examples of work we place under the umbrella term "public argument," see: Charles Arthur Willard, *Liberalism and the Problem of Knowledge: A New Rhetoric for Modern Democracy* (Chicago: University of

contention is that global politics will neither be wholly determined by force structures, geography, economic might, blood, race or religion, nor by our patterns of talking about them. Rather, the political scene in any polity will be shaped by complex interactions between public arguers, where the realities of geopolitics and culture will shape both arguer and audience and in turn be made the topoi and evidence of their claims. Culture is not the immutable basis of civilizational conflict; it is simultaneously the product and precondition for these interactions, from which will be abstracted contesting visions for the future and, conversely, the bases for civilizational conflict.

To advance this position, and to outline some of its implications for international relations work, we concentrate on the idea of "civic space" as opening up points of theoretical opposition to the geopolitical vision offered by Huntington and even many of his critics. "Civic" takes us to notions of citizenship and its possibilities given the phenomena of globalization and nationalism (often refracted through ethnic difference), both of which transform and potentially subvert the possibilities for meaningful violence-averting deliberation. "Space" as a discursive construction brings to the forefront the idea of tangible and material places for such deliberation, and introduces social geographical theorization as central to the project of conceptualizing citizenship. Finally, we argue that civic space can illuminate some blindspots in Huntington's essay, and make some suggestions for how international relations work might usefully proceed given our position.

Chicago Press, 1996); Edward Schiappa, ed., *Warranting Assent: Case Studies in Argument Evaluation* (Albany: SUNY Press, 1995); James Crosswhite, *The Rhetoric of Reason: Writing and the Attractions of Argument* (Madison: University of Wisconsin Press, 1996); Sally A. Jackson, ed., *Argumentation and Values: Proceedings of the Ninth, SCA/AFA Conference on Argumentation* (Annandale, Va.: Speech Communication Assoc., 1995); Thomas B. Farrell, *Norms of Rhetorical Culture* (New Haven: Yale University Press, 1993); John S. Nelson, Allan Megill, and Donald N. McCloskey, eds., *The Rhetoric of the Human Sciences: Language and Argument in Scholarship and Public Affairs* (Madison: University of Wisconsin Press, 1987). Some of the new work on public deliberation is also relevant. Cf., Susan Bickford, *The Dissonance of Democracy: Listening, Conflict, and Citizenship* (Ithaca: Cornell University Press, 1996); Simone Chambers, *Reasonable Democracy: Jürgen Habermas and the Politics of Discourse* (Ithaca: Cornell University Press, 1996); James S. Fishkin, *Democracy and Deliberation: New Directions for Democratic Reform* (New Haven: Yale University Press, 1991); Amy Guttmann and Dennis F. Thompson, *Democracy and Disagreement: Why Moral Conflict Cannot be Avoided in Politics, and What Should Be Done About It* (Cambridge: Harvard University Press, 1996). For work that connects these issues directly to the study of international relations, see: Cori E. Dauber, *Cold War Analytical Structures and the Post Post-War World: A Critique of Deterrence Theory* (Westport, Conn.: Praeger, 1993); Beer and Hariman, *Post-Realism:The Rhetorical Turn in International Relations.*

CIVIC SPACE: DELIBERATION AND ITS POSSIBILITIES
GIVEN TRIBE, NATION, GLOBE

CRITICS OF civilizational hypotheses point to ambiguity in the term "culture" as revealing conceptual failings, but the fact that "culture" and its meaning are so endlessly debated may evidence not its failure as a theoretical category but its centrality. The question is not whether culture (however defined) powerfully shapes national self-identity (and thus the possibilities for conflict), but how varying categories of culture come to dominate particular situations. What is it about nationality, for example, that makes it an abiding and effective commonplace in political processes of persuasion? Why does ethnic and religious difference do such effective demagogic work, while linguistic and economic differences have produced a much more mixed track-record? How powerful, by contrast, will globalization be as the basis of argument and counterargument?

In this regard, the disputes between primordialism and constructivism are particularly interesting. Many have noted how these approaches apparently form two diametrically opposed theories of nationalistic phenomena. Several proposals have been advanced to bridge the divide. Majstorovic's is a commonsensical view that notes how "ethnic identity is malleable, but not infinitely malleable, and that an ethnonational identity cannot be completely imagined without something to stimulate the imagination."[11] For Majstorovic, what unites the two conceptions is an understanding of how history, myth, and memory constrain attempts to construct nationalist identity. As he puts it, "identity is not produced upon a blank slate, and ethnic groups do not suffer from historical Alzheimer's disease. There is historical clay that needs to be reshaped, and the shape of the clay in a previous epoch lends a constraining factor to the political elites in a subsequent historical juncture."[12]

Such a view advances the primordialism/constructivism debate, but it has two important shortcomings. An overemphasis on the constraints of history and memory tends to underestimate how profoundly history and memory can be (and are) shaped by processes of public deliberation. The point is not that leaders can infinitely shape the historical record. Majstorovic is right when he notes that "ethnic

---

11. Steven Majstorovic, "Ancient Hatreds or Elite Manipulation: Memory and Politics in the Former Yugoslavia," *World Affairs* 15, no. 4 (spring 1997): 173.
12. Ibid.

entrepreneurs have to confront the reality of shared historical experience, and the emotional symbols available for political manipulation cannot just be invented out of thin air but must have socio-historical resonance." There is nonetheless an enormous degree of operating freedom for eloquent politicians. History, however "mythic,"[13] is an important argumentative resource, a well into which people can dip in order to generate persuasive argument strategies.

The second shortcoming follows from this: an overemphasis on history's constraining power tends to unduly downplay the possibilities of oppositional politics. History abounds with instances where even the most horrific circumstances have nevertheless yielded powerful oppositional narratives suitable for mobilizing whole societies. The humiliating defeat of the South in America's Civil War generated an entire worldview centered around episodes of chivalry, honor and victimage (which emerged out of representations of the "Lost Cause"), which continues to play out in our nation's contemporary politics. If such oppositional mythologies can emerge out of a war as well documented as America's, one can only imagine the argumentative possibilities on all sides enabled by more distant events, where much less documentary evidence remains. Indeed, a "good" example operates today, as the Serbian loss in the Battle of Kosovo, six hundred years ago, continues to work as a central theme in political arguments used to mobilize the nation. Again, the point is not the infinite malleability of historical evidence, but an acknowledgement of the multisided argumentative topoi generated by any broad social struggle centered on power claims and a genuine contest of interests.[14]

Majstorovic emphasizes the constraints imposed by history and memory, while we stress the possibilities for endless public deliberation they create. He would emphasize how the potential for such arguments is narrowed over time, while we stress the opposite, for as

13. In using this term we do not mean to imply a contrast between historical myths and objectively accurate representations of "what actually happened" (which are not possible), but rather to argue that some historical accounts can come to play a mythic role one way or the other.

14. Majstorovic, perhaps inadvertently, provides some evidence for such a view in the context of his evaluation of the situation in the former Yugoslavia. One of his examples is "the issue of Serbian dominance," which "is hotly debated between Serbs and Croats. While Croats refer to Serbian dominance, Serbs refer to Croat obstructionism. The debate has no resolution" ("Ancient Hatreds," 175). Surely Majstorovic means that, historically speaking, the debate has no resolution. Of course, it also has no resolution within the political debates of Serb and Croat culture. Why? Because one can make a credible case either way for audiences predisposed to believe either way. We think this circumstance typical in the context of ethnic and nationalistic controversy.

history recedes and as hard evidence founded upon historical testimony and pure bloodlines is replaced with the softer evidence of scattered memory and mixed lineage, oppositional argument is empowered, not debilitated.[15]

Huntington's position is different from Majstorovic's. He handles the nationalism problem (formerly dealt with in the literatures on nation-states) by abstracting it to the more general level of civilization, a term of art that manages simultaneously to capture both the ongoing power of ethnicity, culture, and national history, and the fragile manner by which state groupings can be theorized as cultural abstractions. The debate over *The Clash of Civilizations* points to some interesting affiliations and linkages between approaches normally considered incommensurate—primordialism, constructivism, and globalism—which we argue can productively shift attention to the issue of civic space.

The major primordialist claim, of course, is contained in the word, which names the view that ethnic/national loyalty is literally primordial: arising out of blood, tangibly embodied in immutable characteristics like skin tone and eye color. Within such a worldview, civilization not only matters, it may be all that matters. Civilizations, once galvanized by nationalist ideology, become juggernauts not easily stopped. Ethnicity may not play a great role in everyday public life, or even be thought salient to a culture's existence, right up to the point where group members believe themselves (or their ethnic brethren) threatened. Oppositional actions are likely to be interpreted as threatening even if only ambiguously so, because group membership and identity formation evoke a certain overpowering defensiveness. When opportunities for communal self-identification are made clear by external threat (or by domestic redefinition of otherwise nonthreatening activity into perceived threats), cultures revert to thinking primordially, through the lens of their shared birthright. Conflict, once the lens of ethnicity is snapped firmly in place, cannot be "uninterpreted" and little or no ambiguity exists when sides are taken and defended. Once

---

15. Some examples of where Majstorovic makes the limiting case with which we disagree: "Ethnonational identity is continually reformulated in an iterative process in which memory and myth shape and *limit* the boundaries of social construction" (ibid., 171). Later, speaking of the Serbs in particular, "the parameters of construction and reconstruction become *narrower* with each historical iteration of identity reinforcement, or primordialization" (ibid., 173). Emphasis ours.

begun such conflicts can only produce one of three outcomes: total victory, total defeat, or the cold peace produced by total exhaustion.[16]

Social constructivism is often defended as primordialism's opposite. Following the lead of symbolic interactionism, its advocates tend to argue that ethnic, national, and civilizational loyalties are fundamentally constructed. Skin color and ethnic heritage may be immutable, but the meaning ascribed to such characteristics is fluid, social, not pregiven but constituted through talk. Culture matters (in this view) because it is the pregiven social force that constructs identity. Once identities are seen as real (as individuals are literally "talked into"— interpellated into—social roles), they are worth dying to defend, no less than nation in a primordialist's worldview. (If primordialism's argument is that identity has power "all the way up," constructivists would say language exerts its force "all the way down.") In the eyes of many constructivists, the primordialists and Huntington are both guilty of "essentializing," of seeing people as consisting of unchanging and pregiven characteristics.[17] The truth of the charge is less important to us than the fact that the two theories can be seen to interlock like pieces of a jigsaw puzzle, each addressing a different part of the problem.

16. This comes very close to Huntington's view. Huntington, *The Clash of Civilizations*, 266, 291, passim. Van Evera, although not a primordialist, articulates in more detail the mental processes which produce this result. Stephen Van Evera, "Hypothesis on Nationalism and War," in Brown et al., *Nationalism and Ethnic Conflict*, 26–60.

17. Huntington has insisted that his view of cultures is not determined. Cf., Samuel P. Huntington, "Clashing On: Reply to Hassner," *The National Interest*, no. 48 (summer 1997): 110. There Huntington dismisses as "false" the charge that he is a "cultural determinist," as he has on many other occasions. In *The Clash of Civilizations* he does passingly note that "cultures can change" (29). Despite these protestations, Huntington puts forward in all other relevant respects a view of culture that emphasizes its unchanging essential nature. He depicts the rate of possible cultural change as very slow. One of his basic theses is that efforts to have societies move from one civilizational category to another are unsuccessful (20). Of the theories of cultural change to which he points, all end up confirming his view that modernization will only produce localistic backlashes, which of course reinforces existing cultural categories (72–78). This one-way relationship he names the "democracy paradox" (which, generalized, argues that external attempts to sustain Western institutions will [mainly?] encourage nativism)(94). His view that "culture almost always follows power" (91) implies that, because they are backed by force, cultural formations are likely to change only slowly, if at all (and then only in response to civilizational collapse). He is dismissive of the idea that globalization will produce cultural changes. He argues that alternative forces which might constrain or direct cultures in other directions are weakening (128). While conditions for civilizational change are offered, we are quickly reminded that they have never worked (139). Only severe traumas like war (he says it won't likely happen) and also economic growth can change cultures. The latter, he reminds us, however, is itself rooted in cultural particularities (226). Huntington's policy prescriptions also invariably shy away from urging cultural transformation, except in the "thinnest" sense. Can fault-line wars end? Yes and no, but mainly no under present circumstances: "fault line conflicts are interminable" (291).

Primordialism offers an explanation for *why* ethnic, national, cultural disputes begin—as does Huntington, for that matter—while constructivism offers a description of *how* such disputes begin. We might square the apparent incommensurability circle by noting that we need some version of both to fully account for conflict in these times.

Globalization theorists also plainly believe in the importance of culture and civilization. Their focus, however, is on sites where civilizations brush against one another and, by their interaction, cross-pollinate. In such a view, the current situation pits forces of homogenizing globalization against centripetal forces of fragmenting localism. This is the version of globalization that Huntington dismisses, because (in his view) it overemphasizes the influence of American popular culture, ascribing to it a world-changing power it does not possess. As we have argued, this dismissal is too quick since it makes the mistake of treating culture as mere epiphenomena, when actually over time cultural influence is likely to redirect national energies.

Nonetheless, globalization theorists must more adequately deal with micronationalism. Conceding that localism exists in dynamic tension with globalism is probably true, but it does not take us far in the direction of conceptualizing how conflicts between groups start or how they might be averted by creative diplomatic engagement. If fundamentalist groups are energized by their resistance to a perceived all-encompassing and corrupting global secular culture, how does that explain disputes among different nationalities on the periphery? If, for example, Third World traditionalists resist Western culture as overly secular, disrespectful, and threatening (a characterization Huntington adopts), that fact still fails to explain why or how marginalized Third World groups edge into conflict with one another rather than aligning against the West. Beyond waiting for globalism eventually to triumph, what solutions do theorists of globalization offer?

If all three positions agree on the centrality of culture (even as they differently conceive of its constitution and influence in world affairs), to what extent do they agree on whether civilizational divides conducive to war can be overcome? Is there a way to back away from conflict? Can political programs be offered in the context of increasingly salient cultural differences strong enough to forge a peace created and sustained out of civic procedure? How that question plays out in the disputes among primordialists, globalists, and constructivists, not to mention Huntington, is fascinating.

For Huntington, the answer is clearly no. If civilizational affiliation could be overcome on more than a short-term basis, there would hardly be a need for a theory explaining *The Clash of Civilizations* between them. Two curiosities arise here. First, Huntington ends up defending a position of tremendous relativism. While normally it is constructivists (seeing culture as fluid) who stand accused of relativism, here it is Huntington's turn. If civilizations are relatively immutable (in the sense that they change only very slowly), and if, as Huntington argues, our top priority must be to maintain stability in the system and avert conflict which crosses civilizational lines, then we are primarily stuck in a world of "live and let live." One cannot read Huntington and avoid such a conclusion.[18]

To illustrate the point, recall the episode several years ago which placed Singapore at the center of an American argument over whether the West should presume its values regarding political freedom carry universal force. The debate was fueled, of course, by the notoriety of the Michael Faye caning incident, and the much discussed presidential address by Wee Kim Wee (January 1989) that explicitly argued for the uniqueness of Eastern values and human rights, based on civilizational difference. If Huntington is right (he cites this episode to prove how the assertion of local values follows hard power),[19] then not only does American policy lack any vantage from which to assert the priority of one human rights approach as preferable to another, but we must also accede to inaction even if we believe our values are superior. To do otherwise would trigger conflict of the most dangerous type (intercivilizational), meaning that the "need" to impose our values on Eastern nations by leveraging our influence to improve certain nation's treatment of their own citizens is invariably trumped by the (very real) need to avoid risking escalation of such a dangerous conflict.[20]

The primordialists have, on this issue, cast their lot with Huntington, and in language far stronger even than his strong closing words. Whether civilizational value assertions are right or wrong is irrelevant. Cultures, nations, civilizations are different because they are. Since dif-

---

18. Contrast Huntington's brand of cultural relativism with Doty's call, in this issue, for a conception of human security that would enable the "deterritorialization of identity, security, justice, and human rights" (Roxanne Doty, "Immigration and the Politics of Security," *Security Studies* 8, nos. 2/3 [winter 1998/99–spring 199]: 82).

19. "Cultural assertion follows material success; hard power generates soft power" (Huntington, *The Clash of Civilizations*, 109).

20. Of course this is precisely Huntington's warning in the last chapter. Ibid., 310–11.

ferences are hard-wired, and reflect simply disparate levels of power, there is little point or promise in instigating conflict over them.

To such a critique Huntington responds that he advocates not a total abdication of human rights promotion, but rather a more tactically careful attempt to build international consensus on the illegitimacy of a certain minimal list of indefensible acts (these presumably include such behaviors as torture and genocide). He concedes that such advice will likely produce only a "thin" universal conceptualization of the universal good, but accepts the outcome as inevitable in a world of slipping American hegemony. We return to this recommendation and its shortcomings at the essay's close.

The constructivists and the globalists, by contrast, insist culture and race and nationality can be overcome, as each arises out of socially constructed realities. Thus when conflict erupts along civilizational fault lines, we are (both would say) not doomed to see it play out to the bitter end. Understanding the constructed nature of identities helps us insist on their fluidity, and potentially to deflate conflict before it goes too far. That answer, however, is hardly satisfying either, in part because it offers so little practical guidance to post–cold war policy-makers. That national identities are constructed from particular inter-pretations of historical myths does not make them any less real. By the time ethnic conflict has broken out, the stage has certainly passed where simply manipulating the way the parties talk about one another or teach history can have even the slightest impact. By that point, the social constructedness of identities is irrelevant because people behave under duress as if their identities are primordially unchangeable.

It is in this sense we spoke earlier in arguing for a "both/and" accep-tance of the insights of primordialism and constructivism, despite their obvious disagreements. One might say that both theories contain some truth about civilizational formations, but that they speak to different moments in time. Constructivism may account best for a nation's so-cialization processes, and for the possibilities (over time) of changes in self-identity. Primordialism may best account for how nations (and their subgroups) react when under the stresses of external attack.

Faced with such views, it should not surprise us that a scholar like Huntington, mainly concerned to advise policymakers who are dealing with conflict at these later and more intractable points in time, should be so dismissive of globalism's claims to (over time) subsume difference within a broader and more peaceful framework. Such a dismissal is also understandable given the circumstances which gave rise to the globalization hypothesis. For scholars of mass communication, the globalization debate became a serious disciplinary concern with Herbert Schiller's famous 1969 assertion that the "cultural homogenization that has been under way for years threatens to overtake the globe,"[21] a point of view which gave rise to a strong "cultural imperialism" hypothesis. Schiller went so far as to advocate an almost complete severance between the cultural systems of the North and South, so that indigenous cultural forms could continue to operate untainted by the glittering productions of industrial capitalism. The extremes which this theory reached in the 1970s, which included the idea that local cultures around the world would be completely obliterated by "Dallas" and "Dynasty," may continue to condition Huntington's largely skeptical alternative viewpoint.

Even Schiller, however, was toning down his case against American cultural imperialism, and soon after his *Mass Communication and American Empire* he had adjusted his conceptions to fit within the more easily defended world-systems theory then prevalent.[22] The resilience of local cultures, even as inundated by "trash TV" from the United States, has produced more sophisticated renditions of the complex relationship than earlier accounts of center and periphery articulated. The mass audience and its variegated ability to ignore and consume texts in specific ways that protect local traditions has increasingly been the focus of critical attention.[23] As the international coverage of the Gulf war proved once again, "the same visual images transmitted simultaneously into living rooms across the globe can trigger opposing perceptions."[24]

Most who write about globalization tend to see it as diffusing potential intercultural conflict by providing a stock of universal experiences, even while they also acknowledge the potential for isolation and backlash. Huntington seems only able to see the latter. Because he seems particularly persuaded that communities only emerge by identifying enemies, he repeatedly asserts the potential of globalizing institutions to fire conflict, where local leaders will use "outsider" economic and

21. Herbert I. Schiller, *Mass Communication and American Empire* (New York: A. M. Kelley, 1969), 112.

22. This broadened perspective is evident in Schiller's *Communication and Cultural Domination* (New York: International Arts and Sciences Press, 1976).

23. Cf., Ien Ang, *Watching Dallas: Soap Opera and the Melodramatic Imagination* (London: Methuen, 1985).

24. Kishore Mahbubani, "The Dangers of Decadence: What the Rest Can Teach the West," in *Huntington: The Debate*, 37.

cultural forces to cohere oppositional political movements.[25] Clearly there are powerful forces which will operate along these lines, and there is some truth in Huntington's insight that national leaders will likely grab cultural arguments to rally their people toward greater glory (or at least toward a higher standard of living), if only because those weapons lie closest at hand and reflect latent psychological preferences for kinship. After all, this is precisely what Tudjman and Milosevic did.[26]

The beneficial effects of globalism, however, cannot and should not be underestimated. Indeed, one need not agree with Robert Bentley's utopian conclusion that "instant information, economic interdependence and the appeal of individual freedom" felled the Soviet Union to see the power of those forces nonetheless.[27] The very mixed record of globalizing forces in China and Eastern Europe evidence the benefits and perils simultaneously. Press coverage of Tiananmen made clear the possible benefits of global interconnectedness, as students employed fax machines and email to stay in touch with supporters in the West and to receive information on the way the Democracy Movement was being perceived and represented there, and (some argue) to adjust strategies accordingly. Tiananmen revealed globalism's ugly downside as well. Few will defend the premise that faxes and the internet brought down the Berlin Wall. It is undeniable, however, that these forces helped both to build momentum for reform in the eastern states and former Soviet republics, and to accelerate the dynamics of realignment.

Globalism can also be seen as contributing to a phenomenon some say has existed since the first European colonies were established in the New World: creolization. Civilizations are often portrayed (and certainly Huntington is guilty of this) as relatively static. Many existing cultures, however, have roots in several civilizations. To take but one example, consider the Caribbean community: rather than coherently

25. Here Huntington echoes David Campbell, one of the most prominent international relations scholars doing poststructuralist work, and an avowed deconstructionist. For Campbell threat construction is the process which enables identity formation, since a clear idea of who threatens us is a precondition to forming our ideas of who we are. David Campbell, *Writing Security: United States Foreign Policy and the Politics of Identity* (Minneapolis: University of Minnesota Press, 1992).

26. See Beverly Crawford and Ronnie Lipschutz, "Discourses of War: Security and the Case of Yugoslavia," in *Critical Security Studies*, ed. Keith Krause and Michael Williams (Minneapolis: University of Minnesota Press, Borderlines volume 8, 1997), 149–86.

27. Bartley, "Case for Optimism," 43.

reflective of their status as former colonies, they are more accurately described as the ultimate in Creole culture.[28]

Huntington insists that nations do not simply bounce off each other like billiard balls.[29] Neither, of course, do cultures. They interact, and their interactions reverberate through both. As just one example, Huntington mocks those concerned about the so-called coca-colonization produced by American cultural hegemony. He appears to be basing this dismissiveness on a general sense that the kind of popular and mass culture represented by McDonald's or "Jurassic Park" cannot have "real" effects on hardy preexisting civilizations of ancient heritage. Yet American mass culture is of tremendous concern for Europe—while Huntington may lump the United States and Canada in with Western Europe ("the West"), that is clearly not the attitude taken by many Europeans. It was the French, not marginalized Third World countries, who established bureaucracies to punish instances of American slang contaminating "purer" forms of the French language.[30] Substantial work now illustrates how the rise of an international "youth" culture, consisting of a hybridization of cultural artifacts, attitudes, and postures from around the world, holds transformative potential as youth cohorts rise to political and economic prominence in their societies.[31] To a greater or lesser extent, all of the world's civilizations are now creolized.[32]

David Welch and others are right to argue that the variable most predictive of the source of conflict is identification of the most influential institution in a society. As he puts it, "when churches played a significant role in European politics, conflict often followed religious lines....As monarchy lost its ability to legitimize political authority, the main fault lines of world politics began to reflect contending ideologies."[33] There is a degree of circularity in such a claim.[34] Taking it at

---

28. Huntington, *The Clash of Civilizations*, 131.

29. Huntington, "Clashing On," 110.

30. More ironic may be Pells's comment in a recent edition of *Lingua Franca*. He pointed out that "if the Champs-Elysees hasn't been quite the same since McDonald's arrived, neither has McDonald's. There's Perrier and beer on the menu; the salad dressing has more mustard and less sugar than usual; and, as John Travolta's character in *Pulp Fiction* reports, the Big Mac is a 'Royale with cheese'." Quoted. by Adam Shatz, *Lingua Franca* 7, no. 5 (June/July 1997): 23.

31. Cf., Lawrence Grossberg, *Dancing in Spite of Myself: Essays on Popular Culture* (Durham: Duke University Press, 1997).

32. Including, as Benedict R. O'G. Anderson discusses at length, the cultures and civilizations of Latin America. See *Imagined Communities: Reflections on the Origin and Spread of Nationalism* (London: Verso, 1983).

33. Welch, "Clash Thesis," 14.

face value, however, we might productively ask whether the abidingly strong international institutions of global capital, and their often total control over nation-state policy formulation, portend particular kinds of conflict in the future.[35]

Changes in the nature of global capital, and its attendant networks of global communication and distribution, have multidirectional influences. Placing a focus on this phenomenon is one of the great strengths of the globalization literature. Technological changes in the processes of industrial production and dissemination have also simultaneously connected distant lands and localized marketing and market niche filling, and have done so simultaneously. The increasingly exploited potential for market segmentation, which paradoxically depends on massive scales of economy, has produced unprecedented product adaptation and particularized campaign promotions. Transnational corporations both subvert and pander to local cultures, all at the same time.

In contrast to this subtle process of cultural transformation, local enemy-identifying demagoguery is often received as quite hackneyed and unpersuasive, if not backward. While the influence of small but empowered revolutionary groups should not be underestimated, it has proved extraordinarily difficult for such groups to retain coherent authority once in power, except under conditions of radical geographical (Cuba) or ideologically alienating (North Korea and Libya) isolation, the latter of which is, at least potentially, subject to subversion by globalizing forces. Unless revolutionary/fundamentalist leaderships exhibit basic operational pragmatism as they govern complex societies, they risk fragmenting their base and losing popular support by enacting ongoing purity campaigns. There is some evidence that this process is underway today in Iran.[36]

Given this, should we be surprised that some of the gravest threats to global integration have reflected the stress points of global systems of production? The extraordinary attention given to the transfer of political control of Hong Kong from Britain to China, the clashes among EU members over the Common Agricultural Policy, the manner by which the argument over NATO expansion has been transmuted from security to economic concerns (that is, the cost to present alliance

---

34. After all, how does one identify the strongest institution except by, after the fact, determining who shaped the nature of the major conflicts of the period?

35. Cf., Susan Strange, *The Retreat of the State: The Diffusion of Power in the World Economy* (Cambridge: Cambridge University Press, 1996).

36. Cf., Carroll Bogert, "Mullah Melee," *New Republic*, 19 January 1998, 12–15.

contributors of securing new and less wealthy members), and continuing controversies over free trade and intellectual property all demonstrate this change. It is increasingly easy to find evidence that today's citizen customer wants "Sony, not soil."[37]

These changes are not all or perhaps even principally economic in nature and, as such, one cannot predict all of the world's coming conflicts simply through the old lens of Marxist political economy. For globalism is a profoundly cultural, as well as economic, phenomenon. Thus the conflicts over whether Rupert Murdoch is to be permitted to beam BBC broadcasts into China, debates in the United States about the effect of TV and movie violence, and arguments over the rightful future of Radio Free Europe and Radio Marti may have consequences as abiding as the more formal and institutional changes wrought by economic transformation and the collapse of anticapitalist sentiment worldwide.

The reason is not simply that identity matters, as Welch rightly insists,[38] but that processes of cultural globalization are subtly but profoundly changing our perceived self-identities. Identity is not a given, and like our values and attitudes it does not appear ex nihilio or in our genes, but emerges as the outcome of ongoing socialization and collective patterns of persuasion. As our circle of experiences (and therefore influences) is broadened by global mass mediation, and made common thanks to international distribution networks, our identities will invariably drift more closely together. A growing stock of common experiences will, over time, cause the Budapest merchant to see things in a light very similar to a logger in the Amazon, not because they will feel a sense of particular responsibility for each other but because they will have shared experiences and lived traditions.

Opinion on the question of the staying power of these increasingly shared worldwide cultural experiences is decidedly mixed. Ajami has argued that India's "resourceful middle class partakes of global culture and norms," and, having tasted the fruit of the tree of knowledge, will not "cede all this for a political kingdom of political purity."[39] Others, like Benjamin Barber, see globalism eventually trumping forces of localism, but only over a very long time frame indeed, leaving a dangerous and unpredictable transition period for the foreseeable future.[40] Still others might concede the perennial power of global economic

37. Kenichi Ohmae, cited in Ajami, "Summoning," in *Huntington: The Debate*, 30.
38. Welch, "Clash Thesis," 23–24.
39. Ajami, "Summoning," 28.
40. Barber, *Jihad vs. McWorld*, 12.

forces, but note that their historical inevitability has never lasted long against the seductive powers of nationalism and fundamentalism.[41]

CIVIC *SPACE*: THE SOCIAL GEOGRAPHY OF DELIBERATION

> "The global" appears to have become the dimension in which power is theorized, the plane in which a new social topography is mapped and the trajectory along which the specificity of the contemporary is described. We must, however, be careful to distinguish between the historical question of whether there are different forms of globalization and the theoretical question of how to describe such forms. In both of these registers, the question of globalization raises a number of crucial issues for cultural studies and simultaneously it poses some serious problems. It demands that cultural studies consider questions of space, spatial relations and the spatiality of power.[42]

THE PREVIOUS section dealt with "civic space" as a metaphor for the discursively constructed place where the body politic operates, and where nation and race are made salient. It was, therefore, primarily concerned with the causes and consequences of conflict within societies containing members representing widely divergent values. There are larger assumptions, however, which underlie notions of space in a global context, as the place or the stage on which intercivilizational conflict plays out, and these must be more fully theorized if deliberation is to be understood in the context of fundamental difference. Here, then, we focus on arguments about conflict between existing political units exercising sovereignty over specific territory—states, in

41. Ajami inadvertently undermines the most confident case for the staying power of globalism over fundamentalism when he cites Braudel's diagnosis of the sixteenth century, when, despite strong institutionalized religion (quoting Braudel), "men passed to and fro, indifferent to frontiers, states and creeds." Ajami's use of the argument undermines the claims of many present-day globalists who derive their optimism from the unique instantiation of global economic and cultural forces observable in "postmodernity" (Ajami, "Summoning," 31). Of course, one might reply that the trade liberalization started in the sixteenth century eventually fully flowered into Enlightenment cosmopolitanism and exit from the West's Dark Ages.

42. Lawrence Grossberg "The Space of Culture, The Power of Space," in *The Post-Colonial Question: Common Skies, Divided Horizons*, ed. Lain Chambers and Lidia Curti (New York: Routledge, 1996), 172.

other words, as they serve as core and periphery of Huntington's civilizations.[43]

Contested spaces are not "just there," and they are not simply the neutral sites of human exchange. While all spaces have a certain and obvious materiality (a concreteness, reflected partially in the resources they contain) which must be taken seriously, space has a more powerful presence in human affairs than its mere materiality would suggest. (If this were not so we would not face a history so littered with bloody conflicts fought over land devoid of resources, unminable, arid, extreme and often inhospitable, land offering no benefit to its owner other than an ability to occupy "homeland.") This discursive "supplement" is easy to understand, but so commonsensical that often our presumptive inclination to quantify and value space causes it to recede in our analysis. Our conceptions of contested spaces thus become naturalized; that is, we begin to see the value of spaces (or lack thereof) as self-evident, pregiven as part of the natural world and simply a background feature of the "way things are." We can be too easily blinded to the fact that, while geographical spaces may naturally exist, the meanings we invest in such spaces are not natural at all, but socially constructed. Keith and Pile speak to this when they insist that "space cannot be dealt with as if it were merely a passive, abstract arena."[44] Space must be interpreted, invested with particular meaning, and it is to those meanings people respond, as much or more than to the concrete, material reality they see before them, or feel beneath their feet.

Huntington's argument rests on assumptions about space that can be productively problematized. The centrality of space (or, more accurately, of certain assumptions about space) to Huntington's thesis should be immediately obvious, and for that reason a focus on Huntington permits us to introduce claims in a less abstract fashion. He begins, for example, with the working assumption that the civilizations he identifies can be separately treated because each civilization can be linked with mappable territory. There are, of course, global diasporas.

---

43. Much work has recently been done within cultural studies on how conceptions of space function, on the way differing assumptions about space underlie various aspects of our daily lives. See, for example, Edward W. Soja, *Postmodern Geographies: The Reassertion of Space in Critical Social Theory* (New York: Verso, 1990). Particularly elegant work has been done in "critical geopolitics," much of it published by the University of Minnesota Press. See esp. Gearoid O' Tuathail, *Critical Geopolitics*, Borderlines vol. 6 (Minneapolis: University of Minnesota Press, 1996).

44. "Introduction: The Politics of Place," in *Place and the Politics of Identity*, ed. Michael Keith and Steven Pile (New York: Routledge, 1993), 2.

Indeed, for civilizations defined by Huntington via reference to religion, one easily finds cocongregants living amidst alien civilizations, who may never have seen the "Motherland." While Huntington has rather little to say about these émigrés, civilizations are for him grounded in land, their contours determined by territory, demographics and history. Which civilization is dominant where? Who exerts political control there? Who makes plausible historical claims to govern? All these questions can be productively spatialized, mapped out to facilitate historical claims and understanding. If civilizations lack identifiable territories, Huntington loses his argument, since differing points of view would otherwise invariably intermingle over time, unrooted and always in motion, finally quieting the urgency of struggle.

Thus, the first explicitly spatial assumption made by Huntington is that space and its distribution (who lives where) are historically natural. The territorial locations and boundaries for each civilization are knowable. Their locations and limits can be represented in maps.[45] While it is a truism to notice the "map is not the territory," it is still theoretically important that all implications of such an insight be fully understood. Because no map can function as a flawless representation of the space it represents, if only because of the constraints involved in translating from three dimensions to two (and because a map as detailed as reality would overwhelm us with trivial information), mapmakers engage in creative acts of decision making as they decide what to include and what to leave out. The unavoidable need to be selective makes mapmaking, in virtually every instance, a political act.

When abstracted to the realm of international affairs, such decisions have political, as well as aesthetic, import. Surface mapmaking is almost always a thoroughly political act, and as a result maps constitute a form of argument. The lines which form the contours of Huntington's maps make assumptions about who lives where, and whether peoples are living within proper civilizational lines. Lewis and Wigen argue that such assumptions must be understood "not merely as naive...but often as instruments of ideological power."[46] Indeed, mapping "is representation—creation as much as discovery."[47]

45. Huntington, *The Clash of Civilizations*, 26–27.

46. Martin W. Lewis and Karen E. Wigen, *The Myth of Continents: A Critique of Metageography* (Berkeley: University of California Press, 1997), xiii.

47. Kennan Ferguson, "Unmapping and Remapping the World: Foreign Policy as Aesthetic Practice," in *Challenging Boundaries: Global Flows, Territorial Identities*, Borderlines vol. 2, ed. Michael J. Shapiro and Hayward R. Alker (Minneapolis: University of Minnesota Press, 1996), 177.

Huntington is not, of course, entirely unreflective about this fact. In initially describing his paradigmatic perspective on civilizational conflict, he explicitly invokes the mapmaking metaphor. He understands that paradigms leave information out, and that they do so to serve interests. "In short," he writes, "we need a map that both portrays reality and simplifies reality in a way that best serves our purposes."[48]

Viewing space as natural, easily and accurately representable on a map, however, ends up reproducing a "jigsaw puzzle" view of the world. The metaphor is Lewis and Wigen's, who explain:

> By a jigsaw puzzle view of the world, we mean the expectation that a proper map will always show a set of sharply bounded units that fit together with no overlap and no unclaimed territory. The paradigm for such a picture may well be the map of American states which is taught to every American child....Implicated in this jigsaw-puzzle image are two further expectations: (1) that the discrete pieces thus delineated are fully comparable and can be abstracted from their contexts for analytical purposes, and (2) that the world order thus described is essentially stable.[49]

There is little question this accurately describes how Huntington uses maps to illustrate his points.[50] Indeed, he explicitly uses naturalizing metaphors to stress the inevitability of civilizational conflict (divided countries are "cleft countries," civilizations are divided along "fault lines"). The theoretically interesting issue is, then, so what? How can recognizing the infusion of territorially spatial representation in Huntington help us determine the usefulness and adequacy of the clash-of-civilizations hypothesis?

One point to be made is this: jigsaw-puzzle pieces have sharp edges. They fit neatly and cleanly one against the other. Huntington understands this is not the case of real world geopolitics. Civilizational representatives are intermingled, entire populations are on the "wrong" side of the line, and refugee movements further cloud the picture. As

---

48. Huntington, *The Clash of Civilizations*, 31.
49. Lewis and Wigen, *The Myth of Continents*, 11.
50. If there is any doubt on this point, one need look no further than pp. 22–27 in the text (Huntington, *The Clash of Civilizations*). Frank Schimmelfennig's essay in this issue, as one example, proves that collective identity can easily transcend spatial constraints of the nation-state. Clearly Huntington's analysis of "the West" would be compatible with Schimmelfennig's assessment. The difference is that Huntington does not leave room for the kind of "socialization" or "internalization" that Schimmelfennig's work describes, which we take to support our argument that even civilizations are clearly mutable.

the messiness of reality is reduced (clarified) to produce an elegant model, however, clean lines suddenly emerge. Consider the map he chooses to represent the "cleft country" phenonemon (166), a representation of Ukraine. The contrasting shading draws clean and sharp lines which purport to show Ukraine as neatly divided. It is only upon closer scrutiny, at which point electoral figures come into focus as the basis for the line, that one discovers the ambiguities of such a construction. The differences of far east and west blur into closer differentials at the country's center. Yet Kiev, Cherkasy, Vinnytsia, and Khmelnytsk are visually treated as incommensurably different from Poltava, Kirovohrad, and Mykolaiv, based on electoral results (Kuchma versus Kravchuk) which create visual information sharper by far than the geopolitical realities would reveal given other representations.

If paradigms inevitably suffer from oversimplification, and if, in this case, the mapmaker has provided us with the information relevant to second-guess his demarcations, then of what import are these facts? One profound consequence is that, although lines will never perfectly represent the way things are, they too easily take on a certain normative power, and soon come to represent how things ought to be.

This manner by which maps glide from functioning descriptively to normatively conceals fundamentally political choices, and often insidiously so. The choices that drive a map's construction tell an observer what to see and what to ignore. A map with sharp edges signals the importance and irreducible givenness of national borders, and suggests a geopolitical interest in their preservation. They identify the pressure points of intercivilizational conflict, and (for Huntington) tell us which conflicts are more or less dangerous to global stability. The image transmutes from one of sharp lines to one of sharp wire and checkpoints. A worldview that treats borders as pregiven, as the inevitable markers of civilizational conflict, erases the important complexities of cross-border influences (both of people and culture), and the positive and negative consequences that follow for diplomatic practice. The image is therefore one that stresses division, not engagement.

As cultural studies scholars are increasingly arguing, however, border spaces are precisely where the action is. Borders are where civilizations rub up against each another. Huntington sees this as an inevitable source of friction, thereby missing that such interactions can also be the site of tremendous cross-pollinization and opportunity. James Rosenau, in one of many recent detailed efforts to concentrate on what happens at borders instead of between or inside them, makes this argument (for Rosenau those sites where peoples, cultures, and states come into contact merit a capital letter):

> [T]he Frontier is a *terra incognita* that sometimes takes the form of a market, sometimes appears as a civil society, sometimes resembles a legislative chamber, periodically is a crowded townsquare, occasionally a battlefield, increasingly is traversed by an information highway, and usually looks like a several-ring circus in which all these—and many other—activities are unfolding simultaneously. Given this diversity, it is not so much a single frontier as a host of diverse frontiers...in which background often becomes foreground, time becomes disjointed, nonlinear patterns predominate, organizations bifurcate, societies implode, regions unify, markets overlap, and politics swirl about issues of identity, territoriality, and the interface between long-established patterns and emergent orientations. As different issues widen or narrow the Frontier, moreover, so do corresponding shifts occur in the distinction beween "us" and "them" or—to use a less combative distinction—between self and other.[51]

Robert Kaplan's recent work, part travelogue and part disposition on the progress (or lack thereof) of globalization, offers important empirical if anecdotal evidence of this very process.[52]

This mapping of the world's civilizations also colors Huntington's reaction to immigrants and refugees. In a general sense, Huntington treats the movement of people as not dissimilar from the movement of armies.[53] Given such movements, how do we know where to draw borderlines? By determining where members of a given civilization (most of them anyway) live, and where they have historic claims. People who move from the territory associated with their civilizational membership to the heart of another civilization mess up the map, and pose "challenges" to international decisionmakers. They are in the wrong place (all the time), and this can only produce conflict.

Such a vision of the relationship between space and persons approaches an expression of the desire to retain the purity of one's own civilization, and for that matter of all the others. People belong where they belong and no good can come from their wandering around, es-

51. James N. Rosenau, *Along the Domestic-Foreign Frontier: Exploring Governance in a Turbulent World* (New York: Cambridge University Press, 1997), 6–7.

52. Robert D. Kaplan, *The Ends of the Earth: A Journey to the Frontiers of Anarchy* (New York: Vintage, 1996).

53. "Nineteenth-century Europeans were, however, the master race at demographic invasion" (Huntington, *The Clash of Civilizations*, 198).

pecially if they are roaming in groups, thereby risking intercivilizational conflict. On this point Huntington is most explicit when he argues against the expansion of NATO and other "Western organizations" to Orthodox Christian and Islamic nations. Literally arguing from a map (159), he writes approvingly of the emerging EU consensus decision to extend membership only to states "culturally Western."[54]

The same impulse to draw dividing lines may also predispose Huntington away from proposals that would strengthen institutional settings where strangers from different civilizations can come together. In a jigsaw-puzzle world, there is no neutral ground, no realm not underwritten by intractable territorial possessiveness. In such a world there is no place for deliberation or compromise, only the ugly idea of "bloody borders." Indeed, Huntington does not address the wide range of transnational issues and organizations that are already putting demands on the loyalties of millions.[55]

If Huntington's first set of assumptions about space involve its "naturalness," the second has to do with the immutability of spatial markers. Jigsaw-puzzle pieces do not overlap: each piece is stable, and the whole point of the game is that each piece fits one and only one spot on the board, thus making the pieces' spaces and places incommensurate. In one obvious sense the metaphor works, since different spaces forever occupy unique locations. Not even the most radical of relativists can get around this fact. Borderlines, however, are different altogether, and how borders are drawn is what matters when human civilization is at issue.

It is a short step from the immutability of borders to the immutability of civilizational affiliation. As Huntington put it, "in the former Soviet Union, communists can become democrats, the rich can become poor and the poor rich, but Russians cannot become Estonians and Azeris cannot become Armenians....In conflicts between civilizations, the question is 'what are you?' That is a given that cannot be changed."[56] Extending his logic, we are also led to conclude this would be so regarding civilizational background. A woman can live in France for thirty years, but if she was born Algerian, then her civilizational

54. Huntington, *The Clash of Civilizations*, 158–62.
55. See Rosenau, *Frontier*, especially 63. Here Rosenau describes existing transnational pulls, but the entire book can be productively read as a comprehensive articulation of this argument and its implications.
56. Huntington, "The Clash of Civilizations?" in *Huntington: The Debate*, 5. Obviously, critical race theorists would disagree with this conclusion.

affiliation is not Western.[57] Such a conclusion is not changed by Huntington's argument that civilizations are rooted in religion.[58] While one might imagine that one's religon is extremely mutable (after all, of what meaning is the "conversion experience" otherwise?), Huntington's representation fixes religious affiliation to specific civilizations and hence to mapped territories, and to particular spaces. Immigrants, remember, are out of place. Huntington weaves a spatially confined, geographic metanarrative, a master story that ties peoples to their place, that literally puts them *in* their place. He is explicit on this issue, as revealed in the strong cautionary tone of his final warnings against multiculturalism. Thus all space is territory and all territory is someone's Motherland.

In an important sense, then, despite Huntington's emphasis on the particularities of Islamic civilization, the differences between civilizations are ultimately irrelevant to the the clash-of-civilizations hypothesis, subordinated finally to the fact of difference and unchangeable contiguity (facts which give rise to his concerns about intercivilizational clashes). Intercivilizational conflict invariably trumps intracivilizational conflict. As Ferguson argues,

> rather than recognizing cultural landscapes as enabling new possibilities for understanding the world as political, Huntington wants to remap the world along the old configurations of "nation-states"....Culture as a code of mapping is depoliticized. Cultures cease to exist as a practice of lives, with all the plurality, ambiguity, and wonder that life entails, and instead become no more than a positivist descriptive category. Hence a clear and disturbing complicity between academic and bureaucratic discourses to simplify

57. Huntington specifically argues that "Western culture is challenged by groups within Western societies. Once such challenge comes from immigrants from other civilizations who reject assimilation and continue to adhere to and to propagate the values, customs, and cultures of their home societies. This phenomenon is most notable among Muslims in Europe....In Europe, Western civilization could also be undermined by the weakening of its central component, Christianity" (304–5). Huntington concedes this is a long-term threat. Nevertheless, Islamic civilization is defined by religous affiliation. Thus, no matter how Westernized an immigrant—or his children—the refusal to convert is enough to justify the stigma earned by having "refused assimilation," and the subsequent judgment that such persons are not simply civilizational interlopers but very real threats to Western civilization.

58. Huntington, *The Clash of Civilizations*, 47–48. For a typical example, see his discussion of Swedish culture as being rooted in Lutheranism despite the typically areligous contemporary lifestyle of the Swedes (305).

and flatten culture, to make ethnographic differences serve only as the ideograph of geopolitical mapping.[59]

It is true that most people of a particular shared background live together (undoubtedly this is one reason we use the term "back-*ground*"). Most will share certain characteristics, live in roughly predictable and mappable areas, and will probably not acquire the characteristics of people living in other territories over their lifetimes. For most, civilizational characteristics are relatively stable and immutable. The exceptions to these generalizations, however, matter profoundly, because "immutable" and "relatively immutable" are not the same, and have very different implications for geopolitical practice. Reinforcing the notion that dividing lines between civilizations are bright makes it easy to treat them forever as such, and harder, in the end, to traverse them, to appropriate the benefits of cultural intermixture and diversity.

IMPLICATIONS FOR INTERNATIONAL RELATIONS WORK

W HAT DIFFERENCE does it make if globalization and borderlines exert a more subtle influence than that envisioned by Samuel Huntington? More to the point, what different foreign policy advice follows from the conceptions of civic space defended here?

If culture and cultural differences are the antecedents of public arguments out of which emerge conflict, can policymakers adjust the terrain to disadvantage certain polarizing claims? Or must they simply rely on emerging counterweights like globalization eventually to overwhelm tribal claims? On this point Huntington is rather clearly a pessimist. Although he believes cultural/civilizational conflicts can be managed peacefully, he seems to hold little stock in the idea that such peace will result from patterns of persuasion. If, however, the ideological contest between communism and liberal capitalism was able to subordinate ethnic conflict for so long, what is the basis for pessimism regarding other ideas conducive to global community or, at least, some form of tolerance?[60]

59. Ferguson, "Unmapping and Remapping," 172.
60. Some will undoubtedly find such a question absurd. After all, there is an apparent popular and academic consensus that ethnicity was not subordinated at all by the cold war. In fact, some defend the view that the cultural containment of ethnicity in places like Yugoslavia only created a pressure-cooker effect, magnifying ethnic bonds and worsening the eventual explosions. Cf., Sabrina P. Ramet, *Nationalism and Federalism in Yugoslavia, 1962–1991*, 2nd ed. (Bloomington: Indiana University Press, 1992).

One such potential (and much discussed) ideological structure is "citizenship." Readers of this journal know well the quickly proliferating literature now dedicated to such concepts as "democracy promotion," the creation and encouragement of "civic spaces and associations," "civil society," and "community formation." The theoretical promotion of citizenship strikes some as an absurdity, given its historic conceptualization as derived from the nation-state system, which most attack as withering in influence,[61] and the apparent impossibility of inducing a real sense of "global citizenship."

Of the many difficulties one faces in trying to induce such a sense of civic life, several seem intractable. There is the difficulty of inducing meaningful participation given communication technologies that still privilege spectatorship over active engagement in the political give and take. Then there is the problem of producing a citizenry literate (competent) enough to take advantage of representation opportunities when made available.[62] To some extent, each of these challenges centers on the possibility of carving out and sustaining vital civic spaces, what Jürgen Habermas and others have termed "public spheres," where open and politically meaningful dialogue can occur undistorted by the relative privilege of the participants.[63]

Globalization has transforming effects on security policy that go beyond the internal dynamics of societies struggling to reconcile tradition and modernity. For instance, the information age is much applauded for its liberating effects, but it has effects more insidious as well. As Bartley puts it, mentioning only one, "in an information age, dominated by people-to-people contacts," a nation's foreign policy will

---

How can one know, however, that the historical alternative would have been less severe, especially given the highly amplified ethnic polarization that preceded the aftermath of the Second World War? If it is reasonable to see in the last decade's fratricidal Balkan conflicts evidence of pent-up ethnic tension, surely it is also reasonable to find in the fifty years prior to that (forty or so of them under Tito, nearly ten thereafter before ethnic conflict erupted with full force) evidence that the worst effects of ethnic conflict can be successfully managed without genocide or other social control grotesqueries.

61. Huntington among them. Huntington, *The Clash of Civilizations*, 35. Of course the collapse of national sovereignty is a major theme in the critical international relations literature. Cf., Jens Bartelson, *A Genealogy of Sovereignty* (Cambridge: Cambridge University Press, 1995).

62. One recent work argues that this need is rapidly being met. See James Rosenau, *Frontier*, 58–61.

63. Cf., Jürgen Habermas, *The Structural Transformation of the Public Sphere*, trans. Thomas McCarthy (Cambridge: MIT Press, 1989); Craig J. Calhoun, ed., *Habermas and the Public Sphere* (Cambridge: MIT Press, 1992).

shift in the direction of the "moralistic, Wilsonian pole."[64] Bartley welcomes such a change, but agents of American global policy are already struggling to cope with the downsides produced out of the combination of compassion fatigue and bloodlust, both a result of global media coverage of disaster and chaos, and both seen, for example, in the outcome of America's failed Somalian intervention.[65] The same compression of space and time characteristic of politics in the information age which causes Huntington to despair of civilizations thrown together in conflict also compresses institutional procedures for conflict resolution. In the same way that global communication throws fundamentalists on the defensive, it can also throw coherent and pragmatic policy making on the defensive as well.

Huntington resists making policy on grounds that acknowledge the possibility of cultural changes, since he sees in it a necessary and retrograde assertion of ugly American hegemony. He derives such a warning from the view that cultures can only be sustained by force. As he puts it:

> The link between power and culture is almost univerally ignored by those who argue that a universal civilization is and should be emerging as well as by those who argue that Westernization is a prerequisite to modernization. They refuse to recognize that the logic of their argument requires them to support the expansion and consolidation of Western domination of the world, and that if other societies are left free to shape their own destinies they reinvigorate old creeds, habits, and practices which, according to the universalists, are inimical to progress.[66]

A major drawback of this claim (and it is typical of those who caricature "democracy promotion") is how it conflates American efforts to promote, say, institutions of self-government and public deliberation with nastier and more brutish attempts to impose Western values on the "rest" of the world. From such a premise it requires only a small additional step to reject efforts to bring diplomatic practice to a greater level of tactical and strategic awareness of how globalization shapes geopolitics. It is not hard to see how one who believes that "the civili-

---

64. Bartley, "Case for Optimism," 45.

65. The so-called CNN effect has been much discussed in the globalization literature. For one often-cited analysis of how media coverage shapes international relations, see Johanna Neuman, *Lights, Camera, War: Is Media Technology Driving International Politics?* (New York: St. Martin's, 1996).

66. Huntington, *The Clash of Civilizations*, 92.

zational 'us' and the extracivilizational 'them' is a constant in human history," would tend to dismiss proposals to create a deliberative dialogue between strangers from strange lands.[67]

Nonetheless, such an attempt is tentatively defended by Huntington when he closes by arguing for the emergence of "thin" universal norms which will outlaw (at a minimum) the most eggregious of human rights violations. He cites Singapore's quite public effort to identify its "Shared Values" as illustrative of how very different civilizations might reach a common ground broad enough to justify concerted action in certain presently contested areas without inducing conflict.[68]

The irony in Huntington's concession to human rights promotion is that by opening the door ever so slightly to the possibility of cross-civilizational action he arguably opens it all the way, or at least permits such an opening.[69] A major part of the globalization hypothesis is taken with the thinness or thickness of universal norms. Globalization is the very influence which is presently converting these thin areas of agreement into broader ones. If Huntington is right that global mass mediation is strong enough to empower kinship alliances (a factor which he cites to evidence the destructiveness of globalization,[70]) then there is also some truth in the globalization premise that global systems of communication also arouse fellow feeling in the face of atrocity and abuse which can arouse peacemaking activity and a strengthening of moderate political forces as a counter to destructiveness.[71]

---

67. Ibid., 129. In fact, Huntington dismisses this possibility out of hand: "Differences in secular ideology between Marxist-Leninist and liberal democracies can at least be debated if not resolved. Differences in material interest can be negotiated and often settled by compromise in a way cultural issues cannot. Hindus and Muslims are unlikely to resolve the issue of whether a temple or a mosque should be built at Ayodhya by building both, or neither, or a syncretic building that is both a mosque and a temple....Cultural questions like these involve a yes or no, zero-sum choice" (Huntington, The Clash of Civilizations, 130).

68. Huntington, The Clash of Civilizations, 319. It is not entirely clear how this view departs from American policy since Nixon (with some Carter-era exceptions), which has mainly answered (for instance) Asian claims to cultural specificity (and Soviet ones before that) with appeals to universal instruments signed by all of the major powers, and embodied in United Nations charter law. The East has, of course, replied by arguing against the coerciveness with which these instruments were enacted as charter law.

69. That Huntington intends to open a narrow door is evidenced by his earlier rejection of the very same "thin" conceptions of rights he advocates at the book's close. The very theorization he later endorses is dismissed (at p. 56) as "both profound and profoundly important, but it is also neither new nor relevant."

70. Huntington, The Clash of Civilizations, 254.

71. Van Evera is more optimistic about the prospects for universalist conceptions to stabilize nationalistic conflict. Van Evera, "Hypothesis on Nationalism and War," 31, 57–59.

The possibility of expanded universal norms of behavior, however, does not go far enough, or offer with sufficient specificity a set of guidelines for American conduct in the world. How might a hegemonic power, even one arguably in decline, act to open up the possibilities for global dispute resolution and intercivilizational confidence-building, without inviting local demagogues to rail against "imperialism" and core civilizational states constructed as oppositional to the West to fight? How are such policies to be credibly undertaken without entailing responsibilities to intervene in their defense, everywhere and under all circumstances?

Several possibilities present themselves, all of which seem to be downplayed in Huntington's prescriptions for American policy. First, there is a continuing urgency to sustain efforts to strengthen global mechanisms of economic and cultural interaction, since such ties can create powerful motivations in favor of civilizational interaction, which, when instantiated as a part of internal debates over national direction are likely to help offset more demagogic appeals to racial or religious particularity. Obviously such initiatives cannot successfully be undertaken in a manner that coercively imposes the conditions for expanded interaction on others, or acts insensitively to areas of national self-identity. Such measures are likely to proceed in fits and starts, more quickly in periods of high overall rates of international economic growth, more slowly in times of resource constraints. As the fledgling but inexorable expansion of such international efforts as the World Trade Organization and its dispute resolution mechanisms, and the often-apparently derailed but slowly expanding realm of United Nations peacekeeping and humanitarianism illustrate, steps forward might be preservable even in times when strong backlash undercurrents must be navigated.[72] Discussing the most intractable conflict situations, when ethnic conflict erupts within particular nations, Brown and de Jonge Oudraat conclude that while "the problems posed by internal conflict are formidable, options for international action do exist."[73] If economic opportunities are expanded, there is some hope that international struggles can be peacefully mediated as nations from

---

72. For further elaboration of this point, see Michael E. Brown and Chantal de Jonge Oudraat, "Internal Conflict and International Action: An Overview," in Brown et al., *Nationalism and Ethnic Conflict*, 235-64.

73. Ibid., 235.

different religious perspectives learn to tolerate others, if only out of self-interest.[74]

Second, American policy might endeavor to more aggressively assist civilizational efforts to expand spaces for public deliberation within their own spheres of influence. Again, such efforts cannot simply be exported (as opponents of "democracy promotion" rightly insist). When opportunities arise, however, for national or international agents to support the formation of civic spheres, as now appears to be the case in Eastern Europe, we act imprudently if we ignore the opportunities of the moment. The successful record of similar efforts when undertaken by the private sector (for instance, the manner by which international labor and religious organizations sustained forums for deliberation and political organizing in Eastern Europe, whose success in nations like Poland many credit with speeding the collapse of the Soviet empire) imply that such efforts need not run aground when confronted by local opposition. Such measures might work to expand (where possible) labor unions and grassroots movements, or (more broadly) to expand confidence-building regimes.[75]

Third, ongoing attention should be given to expanding efforts to address the causes of intercivilizational conflict, whether within single states or between several different states. Huntington is right that, once engaged, conflicts can be difficult to defuse, if only because leaders will emerge whose political fortunes closely mirror their ability to keep domestic audiences whipped up. If civic spaces are to be nurtured and preserved, they must be especially encouraged during times of relative quiet. As Brown and de Jonge Oudraat note, "long-term efforts to address the permissive conditions of internal conflicts are relatively low-risk undertakings, but they tend to be neglected by policymakers in national capitals and international organizations who are inevitably preoccupied with the crisis du jour."[76]

Many would agree that under conditions of extreme duress (struggles over resources, territory or power) talk is too often the first casualty.

---

74. Marc Lynch's work in this issue illustrates how symbolic affiliations and identifications can supercede realist considerations—a claim also demonstrated by the widespread support in Pakistan for the recent testing of several nuclear devices, despite the knowledge that the tests will result in automatic and potentially devastating economic sanctions.

75. Cf., Joanna Spear, "Arms Limitations, Confidence-Building Measures, and Internal Conflicts," in *The International Dimensions of Internal Conflict*, ed. Michael E. Brown (Cambridge: MIT Press, 1996), 377–410.

76. Brown and de Jonge Oudraat, "Internal Conflict," 252.

At root, however, all of these objections rely on a theory of social interaction which overestimates the practical difficulties of reinstating dialogue, and which thoroughly pervades Huntington's analysis of the global situation.[77] We might call this theory "threat construction," or refer to it (as does Huntington) as "distinctiveness theory."[78] The idea is simply that civilizations define themselves in oppositional terms, and by contrast to others. What we do, what values we embrace, are not only different from those embraced by others, but they are of necessity better, "theirs" worse. If a pale complexion is good, then a dark one must be bad.

Such views are strongly grounded in the work of many disciplines. Scholars of communication often follow the lead of the literary critic Kenneth Burke, who argued that constructed hierarchies of difference are grounded in language itself (since, for example, one can only define the term good by reference to its opposite: evil), and often concretize human interaction as a result of such linguistic polarities. Distinctiveness theory, which comes out of social psychological work, notes how individuals create their own self-identity by looking for differences that mark them as separate or distinctive from others. Cultural studies scholars (including those like Edward Said, influential as a theorist of intercultural difference) emphasize how distance and incommensurable value claims exaggerate difference, and are over time transmuted into mythical constructions of otherness which both form identity and spark imperialism.[79]

---

77. Huntington returns to this argument again and again. At some points he grounds his view in the idea of intercultural fear: "Publics and statesmen are less likely to see threats emerging from people they feel they understand and can trust because of shared language, religion, values, institutions, and culture. They are much more likely to see threats coming from states whose societies have different cultures and hence which they do not understand and feel they cannot trust" (34). Distinctiveness theory is specifically cited (67). At other points it arises as an innate feature of human existence: "Identity at any level—personal, tribal, racial, civilizational—can only be defined in relation to an 'other,' a different person, tribe, race, or civilization....The civilizational 'us' and the extracivilizational 'them' is a constant in human history" (129). He adds, "It is human to hate. For self-definition and motivation people need enemies: competitors in business, rivals in achievement, opponents in politics. They naturally distrust and see as threats those who are different and have the capability to harm them" (130). Elsewhere the implication is less of innate difference-making, and the suggestion is that political leaders will distort realities to advance their agendas. He cites, for example, how the United States creates threats by use of official language that defines others as "rogues" and "outlaws" (216). All of these factors produce a "hate dynamic" virtually impossible to close down (266).

78. Ibid., 67.

79. Said's groundbreaking work, *Orientalism*, is premised on precisely this argument. Edward W. Said, *Orientalism* (New York: Vintage, 1978). While a foundational

Our difficulty with these appropriations is the implication that enemy-making has a certain inevitability, that we are doomed (either by virtue of our humanness or our susceptibility to demagoguery) to escalate and accentuate our differences to the point of invariable conflict. The fact that many intercivilizational arguments devolve into genuine hatreds does not warrant the view that such devolution is a certainty of human interaction. The certainty-of-hatred argument is so commonly cited, and such an easy extrapolation from well-known features of identity formation, that it can be hard to see how it could be otherwise. If, however, identity-formation invariably generates hatred that exhibits itself in extremes of threat construction, then one might ask why the civilizations of the world have not been in constant warfare from the dawn of time. It is no answer to cite the neverendingly sporadic nature of outbreaking war. If we are hardwired to hate, war should never cease except by function of our exhaustion or our extermination, nor should there be any historical evidence of crosscivilizational alliances.

More importantly, to say cultures define themselves by contrast to (an)other is not necessarily to determine that such definitions will be ugly or hateful, or even made by reference to other civilizations at all. The self-definition alternatives are simply not exhausted by naming today's major civilizations. A tribe or group might define itself by reference not to another presently existing civilization, but by opposition to its own past (a process being worked out, albeit painfully, in modern Germany, Russia, South Africa, and Japan). Or it might define itself by comparison to some otherworldly standard (to God's Law, for instance, or to some normative or idealized theory of self-government). Or it might engage in an internal debate whose point is to borrow the best ideas from each of the alternatives, so as to facilitate greater national success.

Obviously, all of these alternatives can be redirected, accomplishing the same endpoint of hate-motivated conflict. Our point is not to diminish the ease with which national leaders can slip into rhetorics of xenophobia when they find it convenient or inspirational. As strong as the evidence of twentieth-century wars is, however, it does not justify

---

text in what now goes by the name "postcolonialism" or "postcolonial studies," Said is not without his critics. For a detailed analysis of Said and the responses to his work since its publication in 1978, see Bart J. Moore-Gilbert, *Postcolonial Theory: Contexts, Practices, Politics* (New York: Verso, 1997). For an analysis of how international relations scholarship on nationalism perpetuates otherness, see Partha Chatterjee, *Nationalist Thought and the Colonial World: A Derivative Discourse?* (London: Zed, 1986).

so pessimistic a conclusion as that reached by many (neo)realists, who throw up their hands at the inevitability of it all, and argue for accommodation to what must be.

As international economic and mass mediation forces become more pervasive, they will condense spaces and differences. In time there is reason to believe that efforts to promulgate institutions of intercivilizational dialogue, spaces for public argument where representatives of estranged cultures can argue their respective cases, might increasingly bridge differences as the stock of universally shared experiences grows. If one accepts the part of the globalist thesis arguing that the entire planetary population will gradually drift toward a shared stock of experiences, then even religious difference might not be inconquerable.

Theorists of civic space and public argument understand well the difficulties encountered by efforts to establish and nurture procedures for deliberation. Following the English-language publication of Jürgen Habermas's *Structural Transformation of the Public Sphere* (which argued that institutions of deliberation briefly flowered but were then disabled by the rise of state capitalism), social theorists have argued for and against the proposition that so-called public spheres can function in the face of civilizational difference, at least without repressing those differences in the name of manufactured consensus. As we have noted, however, nationalism is made salient through discourses that have their power in public spaces and through the mechanisms of public argument. As Craig Calhoun has put it, nationalism, as a "discourse, marks nearly every political public sphere in the contemporary world as an inescapable, if often unconscious, rhetoric of identity-formation, delimitation, and self-constitution. Nations are discursively constituted subjects, even if the rhetoric of their constitution is one that claims primordiality or creation in the distant, seemingly prediscursive, past. It is only as nationalist discourse becomes institutionalized in a public sphere that 'nation' or 'people' are constituted as such."[80]

This is, therefore, no call for naiveté in American foreign policy; nor do we issue here an appeal for the idea that simple communication can solve all conflicts. Even as we concede the intractability of civilizational affiliation, however, it seems prudent to take advantage of the potential benefits of globalization, and not simply to despair of its negative repercussions. If any possibility exists that such mechanisms

80. Craig Calhoun, "Nationalism and the Public Sphere," in *Public and Private in Thought and Practice: Perspectives on a Grand Dichotomy*, ed. Jeff Weintraub and Krishan Kumar (Chicago: University of Chicago Press, 1997), 91.

might be strengthened and made more successful, the obligation to add such instruments to the nation's arsenal of policy-making tools seems not only prudent, but morally advisable as well. As Ken Booth has recently argued, "this is why the growth of civil society is so important for security, cooperation, and development....To attempt to do less is to commit ourselves as university teachers and researchers to being clerks of the powerful, the priests of necessity (rather than architects of possibility), and fatalists about the geography of meaning."[81]

81. Ken Booth, "Security and Self: Reflections of a Fallen Realist," in *Critical Security Studies: Concepts and Cases*, ed. Keith Krause and Michael C. Williams (Minneapolis: University of Minnesota Press, 1997), 115.

IMMIGRATION AND THE POLITICS OF SECURITY

ROXANNE LYNN DOTY

N EMERGING consensus across a wide array of academic and policy-making arenas seems to be developing regarding the movement of peoples across national borders. This consensus suggests that such movements be regarded as a security issue. A 1993 report to the Trilateral Commission, for example, suggests that growing migration pressure occurring at a time of increasing interdependence makes international migration a critical concern for peace and stability in the post–cold war era. At a recent academic conference entitled "Global Security Beyond 2000," one of the major areas of focus was immigration.[1] It was suggested that "migration is increasingly perceived as a potential threat to the security and well-being of the industrialized states of the West."[2] This emerging consensus takes place amidst increasing calls to rethink the concept of security itself. While laudable and arguably overdue, calls to rethink security do not necessarily result in a fundamental change in the conceptualization of security or in a rethinking of the kinds of policies that are appropriate to address the post–cold war security concerns. In contrast, rethinking security can lead to the "securitization" of new realms of activity such as environmental, social, economic, and demographic issues. "Securitization" refers to a process through which the definition and understanding of a particular phenomenon, its consequences, and the policies/courses of action deemed appropriate to address the issue are subjected to a particular logic.[3] The kind of logic that drives securitiza-

Roxanne Lynn Doty is associate professor of political science at the Arizona State University.

An earlier version of this paper was presented at the annual meeting of the International Studies Association, 17–21 March 1998, Minneapolis, Minnesota. I would especially like to thank Jutta Weldes for her helpful comments as well as the members of the audience. I would also like to thank the anonoymous reviewers for *Security Studies* for their comments and suggestions.

1. *Global Security Beyond 2000*, Executive Summary (Pittsburgh: Pittsburgh: University of Pittsburgh, Center for West European Studies, November 1995), 2–3.
2. Ibid., 9.
3. Ole Waever,"Securitization and Desecuritization," in *On Security*, ed. Ronnie D. Lipschutz (New York: Columbia University Press, 1995), 54–58, defines securitization

tion of an issue leads to certain kinds of politics which are associated with particular realms of policy options. This has important implications for the way that issue will be dealt with. The issues of immigration, especially undocumented immigration, and refugee movements are prominent among those being securitized today. This article examines three ways that security can be understood and the political implications of each. In outlining these three modes of securitization, I examine how immigration, as a security threat, is understood in each mode. Each of these modes is driven by a logic and is associated with a particular type of politics that gives rise to certain policy possibilities. Each is also intimately linked with an understanding of self and other and their relationship to one another. An important question that arises concerns the relationship between the three kinds of security. The issue of immigration can illuminate this relationship. I argue that while all three modes can be found in immigration discourses, two dominate and function as constraints on the creation of a type of politics that would go beyond one that relies upon an oppositional understanding of self and other. An empirical examination of U.S. policy and discourse regarding Haitian immigration into the United States during the period of circa 1991–94 illustrates this argument and suggests that more than one understanding of security may be operative in any particular case and that there is no single logic to security. My purpose here is not to use Haiti to prove or disprove one mode of securitization over another. Rather, my purpose is to use Haiti to illustrate the complexity and multidimensionality of security and to suggest that a one-dimensional understanding is inadequate in terms of both scholarship and policy.

THE POLITICS OF SECURITIZATION

THE TERM securitization suggests that issues are not inherently security issues, but become so through a process. This calls our attention to the social constructedness of security. Waever's conceptualization of security as a speech act is useful in understanding the constructed nature of security.[4] "In this usage, security is not of interest as

---

as a process through which an issue comes to be conceived as a security issue. "When a problem is 'securitized', the act tends to lead to specific ways of addressing it: threat, defence, and often state-centered solutions" (ibid., 65).

4. Ibid.

a sign that refers to something more real; the utterance itself is the act."[5] In other words, issues become security issues by virtue of a process of social construction, that is, securitization. Waever suggests that securitization is an instrument that power holders can use to gain control over an issue. While this may be accurate in some cases, it is misleading to limit our understanding of securitization to an instrumental process that is controlled by elites and power holders. Theories of social construction and understandings of language/discourse as a productive practice, which seems to be what Waever is getting at in his security-as-speech-act approach, suggest a more subtle and nuanced manner in which issues becomes socially constructed as particular kinds of issues. This is especially the case when we move away from the more traditional and narrow understandings of security discussed below. It is important that we leave open the possibility that securitization of an issue can come from varied and dispersed locales, for example, from below, so to speak, from the masses. Language is too unwieldy for elites to control it totally or to limit our understanding of its productive power to a one-way instrumental process. While elites and other power holders may be key participants in the social construction of security issues, they are by no means always the only or the most significant actors. Nor is the state the only entity that can label an issue a security problem. Whether it comes from below or from elites, though, securitization is a very political process that has important policy implications. In this section I discuss three modes of securitization and the political implications of each. These modes are summarized in Table 1 below.

The national security mode of securitization is arguably the dominant way security has been understood in international relations. The focus here is on the security of the nation-state as an entity. Security is defined in political/military terms as the protection of the boundaries and integrity of the state and its values against the dangers of a hostile international environment.[6] An issue becomes securitized when it is understood as a threat or potential threat to the stability or survival of the state. This has, of course, been the predominant understanding of security as it has been defined traditionally in the field of security studies. The major recent statement that exemplifies this mode is Walt's,

---

5. Ibid., 55.
6. J. Ann Tickner, "You Just Don't Understand: Troubled Engagements Between Feminists and I. R. Theorists," *International Studies Quarterly* 10, no. 4 (December 1997): 611–32.

which warns against the destruction of the "intellectual coherence" of security studies by broadening the concept of security to include issues such as poverty, the environment, and AIDS.[7] According to Walt, including these kinds of issues in the realm of security studies would make it more difficult to devise solutions to them, though no argument is made as to why this would necessarily be the case. For Walt, the essence of security studies must be "the study of the threat, use, and control of military force."[8] There are numerous things which can

Table 1

THREE MODES OF SECURITIZATION

Mode of securitization	Logic	Type of politics
National security	Classical security logic, self-other inextricably linked to territory	Realpolitik
Societal security	Logics of exclusion and inclusion, self-other linked to territory	Realpolitik, assimilation, identity politics
Human security	Inclusionary	Radical pluralism

have an impact on the use of military force, for example, domestic political regimes, ideas, etc., but the notion of security, for Walt, ultimately refers back to the security of the nation-state. While Walt's agenda for contemporary security studies has been broadly criticized, the criticism that is especially relevant for my purposes has to do with the attempt to harness and indeed the belief that is it possible to harness the meaning of the term security.[9] Walt's essay simultaneously asserts an essential meaning to security and demonstrates the fragility and precarious nature of that essential meaning. Permeating the article is the notion that there is a proper meaning to security that runs the

7. Stephen M. Walt. "The Renaissance of Security Studies," *International Studies Quarterly* 35, no. 2 (June 1991): 211–39.

8. Ibid., 212–13.

9. For an excellent critique of Walt, see Edward A. Kolodziej,. "Renaissance in Security Studies? Caveat Lector!" *International Studies Quarterly* 36, no. 4 (December 1992): 421–38.

risk of being contaminated by the inclusion of those issues that Walt seeks to exclude. The very need to banish these other notions, however, attests to the inherent overdetermination of security itself.[10] By opening up the research agenda to domestic politics, the power of ideas, and the linkages between economic resources and security, Walt opens up a Pandora's box of potentially insecurity-producing items that disrupt the narrow, conventional understanding of security he seeks to preserve. There is an almost infinite number of ways that these things affect security, pointing in directions that those proposing alternative conceptualizations of security might like to explore. Only by vigilantly patrolling the ways that domestic politics, ideas, and economics may be permitted into the imagery of security studies can Walt maintain his narrow state-centric understanding of security.[11] Walt and others who try to harness the meaning of security seem more interested in the coherence and legitimacy of security studies as an academic field than in the real world of human beings whose lives are affected by the issues that Walt wants to exclude from the agenda.

Some of the recent academic calls for a broadening of security concerns, while moving away from Walt's narrow focus on military force, nonetheless fall within a mode of securitization that unproblematically accepts the nation-state as the ultimate site of security. Ullman, for example, argues against a purely military definition of security, suggesting that security be redefined.[12] "A threat to national security is an action or sequence of events that (1) threatens dramatically and over a relatively brief span of time to degrade the quality of life for the inhabitants of a state, or (2) threatens significantly to narrow the range of policy choices available to the government of a state or to private nongovernment entities (persons, groups, corporations) within the state."[13]

10. I use the term overdetermination to suggest that we should be suspicious of attempts to essentialize the concept of security, or any concept for that matter. Gilles Deleuze, *Nietzsche and Philosophy*, trans. Hugh Tomlinson (New York: Columbia University Press, 1983), 4, suggests that "A thing has as many meanings as there are forces capable of seizing it." While this understanding of meaning might not sit well with attempts at parsimony and prediction, it may in fact better capture the workings of the "real" world that social scientists are at least to some degree concerned with.
11. James Der Derian, "The Value of Security: Hobbes, Marx, Nietzsche, and Baudrillard," in Lipschutz, *On Security*, 24–45, notes Walt's attempt at "theoretical damage control," reflecting the insecurity on the part of the theorists who engage in such facile attempts to discredit those critical theorists whose threatening work they generally do not bother to read.
12. Richard H. Ullman, "Redefining Security," *International Security* 8, no. 1 (summer 1983): 129–53.
13. Ibid., 19.

While Ullman's redefinition of security could include many issues beyond the purely military, security remains a concept which is operable
only within the bounds of states.

Myron Weiner's frequently cited article on security and immigration
is another instance of an attempt to broaden the concept of security by
including the issue of immigration.[14] Weiner, however, still locates security and insecurity as terms which a priori depend upon the notion
of clearly defined and bounded nation-states. This can be seen in Weiner's identification of three broad categories of security problems associated with immigration: (1) Forced migration can be an instrument
of government policy used against internal targets such as minorities
and dissidents. (2) Refugees and immigrants can pose threats to sending
(home) countries by working to undermine or overthrow the regime
in their home country by using the host country as a base for arming
themselves and/or engaging in terrorist acts. They can also destabilize
host countries by changing ethnic balances, exacerbating social and
economic problems, and disrupting notions of political and cultural
identity. (3) Interstate conflict may result from the use of armed force
to prevent or stem the flow of migration. I am certainly not suggesting
that these ideas regarding security and immigration are necessarily
wrong, but rather that they remain within a state-centered mode of
analysis that precludes considerations such as those suggested by
Waever which are discussed in greater detail below.

Within policy making and other arenas we find similar understandings of the ways in which immigration poses a threat to security. A
case in point is when Senator Alan Simpson expressed concern over
the national security implications of a porous U.S. border: "You could
take a crack outfit of 100 people, sprinkle them in through the borders...and they could meet at some predetermined point. They could
pick up their equipment on this side of the border....We wouldn't
even know what was going on."[15] The type of politics associated with
this mode of securitization is that of realpolitik. The term "hyper-
realism" is an apt description of the transference of the signs and symbols of realist realpolitik into areas such as immigration which have
not been traditionally associated with national security.[16] Such hyper-

14. Myron Weiner, "Security, Stability, and International Migration," *International
Security* 17, no. 3 (winter 1992/93): 91–126.
15. John Dillin, "Spies, Terrorists and United States' Borders," *Christian Science
Monitor*, 24 March 1986, 1.
16. I borrow the term "hyper-realism" from Timothy W. Luke, "The Discipline of
Security Studies and the Codes of Containment: Learning from Kuwait," *Alternatives*

realism is evident in immigration discourses and policies. Immigration and refugee movements come to be seen as invasions necessitating strategic action along the lines of more traditional threats to national security. The recent overwhelming focus on reinforcing the U.S.-Mexico border is an example of a hyper-realist policy orientation. While most illegal immigration is not due to illegal border crossings, the emphasis in terms of a solution is predominantly concentrated on the border.[17] Other recent examples of hyper-realism include Malaysia's labeling of foreign workers as a national security threat and its plan to raze immigrant squatter settlements, and Europol's declaration that organized illegal immigration is the police organization's greatest concern.[18]

Despite the dominance of the national security mode of securitization, a rethinking of security has recently taken place among a small group of international relations scholars who have suggested that security concerns increasingly center on society rather than on the state. Ole Waever attempts to capture this new phenomenon with the concept of societal security. Societal security refers to the ability of a society to persist in its essential character under changing conditions and possible or actual threats. Societal security is inextricably linked with the notion of identity. Societal security represents a fundamental rethinking of security and is an important shift in the concerns traditionally expressed in the security studies subfield of international relations. It provides an opening, indeed an opportunity, to address issues heretofore ignored. It moves us into the realm of society and all its various aspects that are relevant to the processes whereby identities are constructed and societies come to perceive their identities as being threatened. Importantly this concept has the potential to move us away from a purely statist understanding of security. Waever carefully stresses that earlier understandings of societal security which retained the state as the referent object are untenable. Instead, Waever suggests a fundamental reconceptualization of the security field as one with two organizing centers: a duality of state security and societal security. The

---

16, no. 3 (summer 1991): 315–44. See also Der Derian, "The Value of Security: Hobbes, Marx, Nietzsche, and Baudrillard,"37–41. See Roxanne Lynn Doty, "The Double-Writing of Statecraft: Exploring State Responses to Illegal Immigration," *Alternatives* 21, no. 2 (April–June 1996): 171–89, for a discussion of how this relates to immigration policies.

17. For example, the Clinton administration has increased the number of Border Patrol agents by about 45 percent (Eric Schmitt, "Milestones and Missteps on Immigration," *New York Times*, 26 October 1996), 1, 9.

18. "Malaysian Foreign Workers Are Security Threat," *Migration News* 3, no. 5 (May 1996): 8.

referent for societal security is not the state, but society. While survival for a state is a question of sovereignty, survival for society is a question of identity, and while societal security can be relevant for state security, it is also relevant in its own right.[19] In an important sense societal security is even more fundamental than state security. Whenever state security is invoked in response to various perceived threats, an implicit presumption is made that society is already in place. Sovereignty, which is what is at stake when it comes to questions of state security, implicitly invokes the notion that the state represents an identifiable presence, a political community, a society.[20] As many contemporary events suggest, this presumption is becoming increasingly problematic as it becomes obvious that in many cases it is society itself that is insecure. Herein lies the tremendous value of the concept of societal security. As Waever points out, the logic that has been associated with national security can be operative in areas not traditionally associated with the security of the state. This can take the form of realpolitik as discussed above, but it can also take the form of identity politics. "Society is about identity, the self-conception of communities, and those individuals who identify themselves as members of a particular community."[21] Identity politics involves attempts to reassert the identity of those who belong to a particular society and simultaneously to define those who will be excluded. In this respect, identity politics resembles realpolitik carried on in a different arena. Identity politics, however, can also take the form of a politics of assimilation, which is not solely an exclusionary politics and moves away from realpolitik and the classical security logic. Great Britain's post–Second World War immigration policies, for example, have been both exclusionary and analogous to realpolitik, but also inclusionary in terms of efforts toward assimilation and improved "race relations."[22] I should stress here that using a societal security framework should not be taken as implying that one must assume that a stable, homogeneous, and coherent societal identity always exists in the particular society that feels threatened. During times when there is no perceived threat, homogeneity,

19. Ole Waever. "Societal Security: The Concept," in *Identity, Migration and the New Security Agenda in Europe*, ed. Ole Waever et al. (Copenhagen: Pinter Publishers, 1993), 22–25.
20. Roxanne Lynn Doty, "Sovereignty and the Nation: Constructing the Boundaries of National Identity," in *State Sovereignty as Social Construct*, ed. Thomas J. Biersteker and Cynthia Weber (New York: Cambridge University Press), 122.
21. Waever, "Securitization and Desecuritization," 67.
22. Doty, "Sovereignty and the Nation."

however illusory, is often taken for granted. It is during times of crisis, such as movements of people who are seen as "different" (ethnically, racially, culturally, and so on), that the problematic nature of this taken for granted homogeneity becomes apparent.

While the concept of societal security, in terms of the openings it creates for addressing contemporary issues such as immigration, is a vast improvement over the more conventional understandings of security discussed above, the two understandings share some important features which create significant constraints in both a theoretical and practical sense. This is especially evident in Waever, who is torn between broadening the concept of security and thus the focus of security studies on the one hand, and on the other hand maintaining a legitimate position within the traditional security discourse. It is significant that he suggests the possibility of simultaneously having two centers in the study of security, that of the state and society. This arguably creates openings for even more centers and a move toward a decentering of security studies. Waever, however, seems to fear this and retreats to a security studies agenda that is compatible with the traditional one. This fear is evident in his efforts to distinguish societal security from that of individual security. "Whenever security is defined via individual security there is a high risk that the core of the classical security problematique, which one is allegedly trying to redefine not forget, will be missed."[23] In presenting the concept of societal security, Waever cautions against moving too far away from the core of the classical security problematique. Better to get at the specific dynamics of the classical security field and "show how these old elements operate in new ways and new places."[24] The argument that Waever offers to support his suggestion is that, while security itself has no essential meaning, but rather is socially constructed, it has been socially constructed through speech acts in a particular way and within a particular community, that is, a community that revolves around discussions of security in a classical sense consistent with the national security mode of securitization outlined above. Waever wants to rethink the concept of security "in a way that is true to the classical discussion." The problem with this is that it implicitly assumes that the logic captured by the classical security field regarding state security is the logic that is operative in the realm of societal security and is, indeed, the only logic worth consider-

23. Waever, "Societal Security: The Concept," 24.
24. Waever, "Securitization and Desecuritization," 51.

ing if one is to contribute to existing conversations on security. This precludes consideration of the possibility that important and relevant logics that cannot be placed entirely within the classical security logic may be operative.[25] Like Walt, Waever simultaneously points to the overdetermined nature of security and then attempts to harness it by assigning a foundational logic to it. This results in merely replacing an essentialization of the object of security (that is, the state) with another essentialization (that is, the logic of security). Societal security may be an important reconceptualization of security, but it does not problematize security itself or its underlying logic. Security reconceptualized to include a duality of state and societal security is essentialist not in terms of its object, but in terms of its logic. The result is that it becomes impossible within this framework to imagine a kind of security that does not depend upon a particular understanding of danger, and a particular understanding of self and other, that is, danger stemming from another that is disruptive or at least potentially disruptive of the self's state or the self's society, thus evoking a certain kind of policy that is consistent with the logic of security. Waever sees this logic as deriving from the logic of war and consisting of a sequence of stimuli and responses.[26] This logic of challenge-resistance/defense-escalation-recognition/defeat can be replayed metaphorically and extended to other than military sectors. Framed by this logic, though, it simply becomes impossible to imagine a security logic which departs from the classical security logic. It becomes impossible to imagine a different "structure of the game," or to imagine security in terms of a metaphor other than a game. Things which threaten the presumed fixedness of the inside versus the outside of states and societies are sources of insecurity and this gives rise to the logic of the classical security problematique. The logic is one of exclusion which depends upon an understanding of self and other that is inextricably linked with territory. Solutions/policy prescriptions for addressing security threats will rely upon an exclusionary logic that seeks to determine the criteria for differentiation between self and other.

There are two related problems with remaining wedded to this classical security logic that preclude adequately addressing the issue of im-

25. See Tickner, "You Just Don't Understand," for an excellent discussion of how traditional security studies and international relations more generally preclude feminists and others understandings of security and thus discount or trivialize research that seeks to address these issues.
26. Waever, "Securitization and Desecuritization," 54.

migration and the politics of security that are associated with it. The first problem with remaining wedded to the classical security logic is that societal security, even as conceptualized by Waever, cannot be confined to this kind of logic. I am not suggesting that this logic is totally absent, but rather that it is not the only logic that is operative. Societal insecurity, for example, can take multiple forms. As noted above, efforts to deal with societal insecurity can focus on assimilatory policies, which follow a quite different logic. The whole notion of the United States as a "melting pot" presumes the success of assimilatory policies. Historically, this has been a significant way of preventing societal insecurity. I am not suggesting that assimilation is either a positive or a negative thing or that it has actually been successful. Recent concerns, such as those expressed by Schlesinger, suggesting that the "historic idea of a unifying American identity" which resulted from assimilation is being replaced by fragmentation and separation illustrate the fear that the logic of assimilation is increasingly less operative than in the past.[27] The point is that assimilation is driven by a logic of inclusion, albeit one that is coupled with exclusion in that the "other" is seen as an imperfect version of one's self which needs to be assimilated. Still, this logic is quite different from the classical security logic.

The second problem with remaining within a classical security logic is that one of the issues that can give rise to societal insecurity and arguably even national insecurity, as traditionally understood, in the first place is driven by a logic that cannot be accounted for by classical security or societal security frameworks and which policy responses must deal with. This is the logic of human security which focuses on the security of people as human beings. Their link with national territory is not a defining or necessary feature. Human security attempts to get at some of the same issues as those who suggest that redefinitions of security are in order, for example, the environment, AIDS, drugs. These issues, however, are not of concern primarily because they potentially pose a threat to the security of nation-states. The normative commitment is not to states but to human dignity and welfare.[28] Difference is appreciated but not reduced to a superior-inferior, us-them kind of logic. The "other" is not reduced to a lesser and potentially assimilable self. It is important to stress that human security is not primarily an individual-level concept. While it is certainly relevant to the lives of

27. Arthur M. Schlesinger Jr., *The Disuniting of America* (New York: Norton, 1992).
28. Mahbub ul Haq, *Reflections on Human Development* (London: Oxford University Press, 1995), 115–16.

individuals, it essentially has to do with the well-being of collectives along various dimensions not included in traditional understandings of national security or societal security as discussed above. It most emphatically cannot be reduced to the individual level. Human security has received virtually no consideration in classical security discourses and very little in discussions of societal security. It is, however, increasingly difficult to ignore. Human security is arguably global and indivisible. It cannot be contained within national borders. While the first two modes of securitization require a radical separation of self and other, inside and outside, human security calls for a reconceptualization of self and other. It requires a rethinking of the very notion of identity. Human security allows for a security that would not be guided by the idea of a fully constituted nation-state or society or a fully constituted exemplary self. It implies a type of politics that can be called radical pluralism. By radical pluralism I mean something like that to which Connolly refers as an ethos of critical responsiveness that goes beyond conventional state-centered pluralism. An ethos of critical responsiveness "does not reduce the other to what some 'we' already is." It rather redefines the relationship between self and other and in the process modifies the very identity of self and other. It opens up cultural space through which the other may consolidate itself into something which is unaffected by negative cultural markings.[29] It implies a deterritorialization of identity, security, justice, and human rights. The nation-state and the society that is presumably embodied by it are just two of many possible sites of security and insecurity. Bruce Cronin suggests much the same with the term transnational identities whereby the definition of self transcends state boundaries.[30] The shared identities to which Kahl and Hampton refer also create openings that are consistent with human security.[31]

What implications does the concept of human security have for immigration? Perhaps the most significant implication is that "radical pluralism," with its appreciation of the ambiguity of boundaries and its

29. William E. Connolly, *The Ethos of Pluralization* (Minneapolis: University of Minnesota Press, 1995), xvi–xvii.

30. Bruce Cronin, "From Balance to Community: Transnational Identity and Political Integration," *Security Studies* 8, nos. 2/3 (winter 1998/99–spring 1999): 270–301.

31. Mary N. Hampton, "NATO, Germany, and the United States: Creating Positive Identity in Trans-Atlantia," *Security Studies* 8, nos. 2/3 (winter 1998/99–spring 1999): 235–69; Colin H. Kahl, "Constructing a Separate Peace: Constructivism, Collective Liberal Identity, and Democratic Peace," *Security Studies* 8, nos. 2/3 (winter 1998/99–spring 1999): 94–144.

sensitivity to the violence involved in the production of boundaries and the identities encompassed by them, would politicize the construction of immigration as a security issue defined in terms of either national security or societal security. One's identity would not be threatened by the presence of an unrecognized and inassimilable other. Concerns might focus on the underlying causes of migration such as poverty and human rights abuses without reducing the necessity to address these causes to a concern for one's own security. Ironically, perhaps, Waever's societal security framework itself opens the door for an even broader understanding of security, an understanding that moves toward human security. Once it is admitted that security can involve issues of self-identity and definitions of who does and does not belong to a particular society, it is just a short step to problemetizing the idea of society itself. If we begin to question understandings of society and recognize its social constructedness, then a move can be made to a broader understanding of society itself and with it a different logic that approaches that of human security. In the following section I examine how the three modes of securitization and their respective logics were operative in the case of Haiti.

SECURITY AND THE HAITIAN CRISIS

BACKGROUND

In this section I very briefly chronicle the relevant events from September 1991 when Haitian president Aristide was overthrown in a military coup to September 1994 when 16,000 troops, mostly from the United States moved into Haiti. On the morning of 30 September 1991 the Haitian military, under the control of Lt. General Raoul Cedras, ousted President Jean-Bertrand Aristide from office. Aristide had served as president for nine months after winning over 67 percent of the votes in the election held in December 1990 and was the first democratically elected president in the history of the Republic of Haiti.[32] Aristide was allowed to leave the country. On 7 October the Organisation of American States condemned the coup and imposed a trade embargo. On 11 October the UN General Assembly condemned the coup and announced that it would not recognize the Cedras re-

---

32. James Ridgeway, *The Haiti Files* (Washington, D.C.: Essential Books, 1995), 205–6.

gime. On 5 November U.S. president George Bush signed a commercial embargo against Haiti on all products and commercial traffic except for humanitarian aid. The Organization of American States (OAS) and U.S. embargoes were never strictly implemented though. Trade with Europe and Japan continued, U.S.-owned export assembly plants in Haiti were exempted, and U.S.-based assets were only partly blocked.[33] In November 1991 the United States repatriated the first boatload of Haitian refugees (538 refugees) since the coup. Over the next two years, the United States repatriated over 30,000 Haitian refugees.[34] The security and human rights situation deteriorated over the next two years and, in June 1993, the UN Security Council said that the situation in Haiti threatened international peace and security. Acting under the UN Charter, Chapter VII, it adopted Resolution 841 which imposed an arms and oil embargo on Haiti and froze its government assets in other countries. On 27 June 1993 negotiations between Aristide and Cedras were held on Governor's Island, New York and were overseen by UN and U.S. diplomats. These negotiations culminated in what became known as the Governor's Island Agreement in which steps were outlined to restore democracy and reinstate President Aristide. A ten-point accord called for the naming of a new prime minister by Aristide, a series of parliamentary reforms of the police and army under UN supervision, a blanket amnesty for those involved in the coup, and the voluntary retirement of Cedras prior to Aristide's return, which was set for 30 October 1993. The embargo was suspended on 27 August 1993 after the Haitian parliament ratified Prime Minister Robert Malval and his new cabinet.[35] Violence continued to increase though and on 11 October, when the USS Harlan County arrived in Port-au-Prince carrying Canadian and U.S. military instructors and was prevented from docking, the UN Security Council reimposed sanctions in Resolution 873. The next day the minister of justice appointed by Aristide was assassinated in Port-au-Prince.[36] With continued violence, rapes, assassinations, arbitrary arrests, and illegal detentions, the United Nations tightened sanctions with Resolution 917 on 6 May 1994, which enacted general trade sanctions and a ban on noncommercial air traffic. The United States also embargoed commercial air traffic. As the situation deteriorated, the UN Security Council passed Resolution 940 on 31 July

33. *World Disasters Report, 1995* (http://www.ifre.org.tubs.wdr).
34. Ridgeway, *The Haiti Files*, 210.
35. Ibid., 225.
36. *World Disasters Report, 1995.*

1994, authorizing member states to form a multinational force under unified command to facilitate the departure of the military leadership consistent with the Governor's Island Agreement. In late September 1994, after negotiations between the military leaders and former U.S. president Jimmy Carter, 16,000 troops, most of them from the United States, moved into Haiti. Aristide was restored to power and the coup leaders left the country.

ANALYSIS

An examination of U.S. policy and discourse during the Haitian crisis of circa 1991–94 reveals just how interrelated the various aspects of security are. All three modes of securitization were operative during this crisis. This case reveals that policymakers themselves either explicitly or implicitly made connections among different definitions of security. This would seem to indicate that it is counterproductive for scholars to hold fast to one particular understanding of either security or a foundational security logic. This calls into question the usefulness of Walt's attempts to harness the meaning of security. It also calls into question Waever's idea of a foundational logic to security, however security may be defined. In distinguishing his approach from other proposed alternatives to traditional understandings of security, Waever discusses problems that arise from attempts such as those of Galtung and Oberg to develop an alternative understanding of security that encompasses goals related to human needs.[37] Waever suggests that such an alternative understanding of security lacks any relevant connection to the core of classical security as a field of study and that there is a lack of political effect on security as traditionally understood. The case of Haiti demonstrates that in fact issues related to human needs or human security can have a very real effect on security as traditionally understood. If this alternative understanding of security lacks connection to the academic field of classical security studies, perhaps the problem lies not with the alternative understanding but with the narrowness of focus found in classical security studies. An examination of the Haitian case illustrates how different security logics can be operative simultaneously. In this section I examine the case of Haiti in light of the three modes of securitization discussed above.

37. Waever, "Securitization and Desecuritization," 48.

In order to take the kinds of actions it did and provide justifications for those actions U.S. policymakers had to consider the Haitian situation relevant to and a potential threat to U.S. national interests. Just how it was relevant was not so obvious to everyone. It is useful to begin with a look at some of the reasons suggested. In October 1993 Alexander Watson, assistant secretary for inter-American affairs suggested that

> The United States has vital interests in Haiti." These vital interests included "the protection of the lives of approximately 10,000 American citizens, nearly 9,000 of whom are dual nationals, and 1,000 of whom are U.S. citizens only; to prevent the outflow of thousands of boat people to the United States from Haiti, many of whom would die in the attempt to flee; to reinforce political stability in a country which shares its small island with the Dominican Republic; a country which is itself struggling to preserve democratic practices; to fulfill the Governor's Island Agreement restoring civilian elected government to Haiti; and ending wanton violence which is destroying the fabric of Haitian society; to comply with the mandatory UN Security Council resolutions imposing sanctions on Haiti; to honor the U.S. and hemispheric commitment to democracy and the protection of human rights, and to discourage other violent challenges to civilian governments in the region; and to enhance U.S. influence and credibility internationally by demonstrating U.S. resolve in a region with strong historical, cultural, economic, and political ties to the United States.[38]

The varied interests expressed by Watson were echoed by others. In a speech on 16 September 1994, President Clinton justified a U.S. invasion if General Cedras refused to yield power in order to "protect its interests—to stop the brutal atrocities that threaten tens of thousands of Haitians; to secure our borders and preserve stability in our hemisphere, and to promote democracy and uphold the reliability of our commitment around the world."[39] Perhaps the most widely accepted of these justifications was the need to secure U.S. borders. If the United States failed to act, "the 300,000 Haitians now in hiding will be the next wave of refugees at our door."[40] National Security Adviser Anthony Lake, insisting the United States "has a great deal at stake" in

38. "Briefing before the Committee on Foreign Affairs," House of Representatives, 103rd Cong., 1st Sess., 20 October 1993, 2.
39. Douglas Jehl, "Clinton Addresses Nation On Threat to Invade Haiti; Tells Dictators to Get Out," *New York Times*, 16 September 1994, 1, 5.
40. Ibid.

Haiti, said that an uncontrolled refugee flow from an unstable Haiti could swamp U.S. shores.[41] Within the discourses offering these justifications for action(s) we can find elements of the different modes of securitization discussed above.

Several important aspects of U.S. policy fit within the national security mode of securitization, most significantly the policy of forced repatriation and the confinement of Haitian refugees to camps in locations outside the United States, for example, on Guantanamo Bay. On 24 May 1992 Bush issued Executive Order 12,807, also referred to as the "Kennebunkport Order," under which all Haitian boats would be interdicted by U.S. Coast Guard cutters and their passengers returned directly to Port-au-Prince with no prior screening for asylum seekers. A 1981 bilateral agreement with the Haitian government had launched the interdiction program. The agreement, however, had stipulated that the United States was obligated to screen Haitians for claims of persecution, thereby recognizing the international principle of nonrefoulment.[42] Under the Kennebunkport Order, no such screening was required. The only hearings available to Haitian asylum seekers was through the in-country processing program (ICP) which was set up in Port-au-Prince in February 1992. This aspect of policy followed a classical security logic. The United States was arguably confronted with a test of will of its ability to fend off a challenge. The discourse of policymakers reveals that one of the overwhelming concerns and justifications for action, and the one the American people were most receptive to, was the necessity of securing U.S. borders. If, as Waever suggests, the classical security logic follows the logic of war in which "combatants each try to function at maximum efficiency in relation to a clearly defined aim" and in which "the ability to fend off a challenge is the criterion for forcing the others to acknowledge its sovereignty and identity as a state," the policy of forced repatriation certainly would fit within this logic.[43] Both the Haitian refugees and the U.S. government tried to function at maximum efficiency to attain a clearly defined aim. The aim of the former was to reach U.S. shores safely, the aim of the latter was to prevent this. While the Haitian refugees were not "enemies" in the traditional sense, the threat was certainly constructed as one that was every bit as serious as security threats emanating from other states.

---

41. Catherine Foster, "Black Caucus Aims to Stiffen Trade Embargo of Haiti," *Christian Science Monitor*, 22 March 1994, 3.
42. Ridgeway, *The Haiti Files*, 192.
43. Waever, "Securitization and Desecuritization," 53.

U.S. policy for dealing with this challenge involved the use of force in the curtailment of the flight of refugees. Haitian refugees were regarded as invaders who threatened the stability of the United States, particularly certain regions such as Florida. There was a twist here, however. The enemy in this case was not another state, but rather the Haitian immigrants or potential immigrants. This twist is significant. While we can find support for the national security mode of securitization, the nature of the enemy raises some of the issues that those who seek alternative understandings of security also raise. The state centricity of classical security studies is criticized by Tickner for not taking into consideration the fact that states and their militaries are frequently antithetical to their citizens.[44] Certainly in the case of Haiti this fact underpinned the whole crisis.

Forced repatriation was the official U.S. policy for dealing with potential refugees from Haiti until, under criticism from human rights groups and amid charges of racism, Clinton announced a major shift in policy on 8 May 1994. The policy, which took effect on 16 June, required the Immigration and Naturalization Service (INS) to conduct interviews at sea and admit refugees judged to be fleeing repression.[45] Still, the United States sought to keep the refugees out when during the first month of the new policy over 17,000 refugees fled Haiti. Those promised asylum were to be sent to other countries. The U.S. embassy broadcast continued messages in Creole over Haitian radio warning potential refuges that "one thing is certain. You won't get to the United States."[46] "The Coast Guard that catches you at sea will not take you to the United States. They'll drop you in a refugee camp in another country. You can spend six months, a year in that camp until the crisis finds a solution, before you can come back to Haiti."[47]

If we pursue the question of why it was so important to keep the refugees out of the United States, we move into the realm of societal security, where the threat is not to the sovereignty of the state as would be the case with the national security mode of securitization. Rather, as discussed earlier, when it comes to societal security the cohesion and very identity of society is at stake. These two kinds of threat are not unrelated. The case of Haiti shows that societal insecu-

44. Tickner, "You Just Don't Understand," 625.

45. Kevin Fedarko, "Haiti-Policy at Sea," *Time*, 18 July 1994.

46. Fedarko, "Haiti-Policy at Sea."

47. Arthus R. McGee, "U.S. Policy Exposed," *Haiti Information* 2, no. 24 (27 August 1994): 2.

rity was a significant factor that led the Haitian refugee crisis to be considered relevant to U.S. national interests and indeed a threat to U.S. national security. While it would be difficult to support an argument that U.S. sovereignty was actually in danger, the rhetoric of "securing our borders" insistently pointed toward policies motivated by the same kind of logic that has driven more traditional security concerns over conflict and war. This supports Waever's suggestion that societal security contains the same logic as that of classical security. The policy of forced repatriation as well as the refusal to grant refugee status to the majority of fleeing Haitians followed this logic. It is worth noting that U.S. acceptance rates of Haiti refugees was incredibly low, 1.2 percent for fiscal year 1992.[48] After Clinton reversed Bush's interdiction policy in May 1994, a Republican congressional staff member, fearing that more "boat people" would be accepted as legitimate political refugees, complained that the increased numbers would "devastate Florida." Shortly after Clinton was elected to his first term, it was suggested that Haitian refugees were his greatest political risk. "Allowing large numbers into south Florida could create a political backlash."[49] Public sentiment in Florida against allowing large numbers of Haitian refugees into Florida must be understood within the context of an increasingly anti-immigrant mood in the United States, where fears such as those expressed by Schlesinger of a "disuniting of America" were increasingly expressed in various arenas. This could certainly lend support to an argument that domestic U.S. politics was a significant factor in motivating U.S. policy toward Haiti. I would not disagree with this argument. What is important to note, though, is that domestic politics was intimately connected to the issue of societal security. It is necessary to pose the question as to why Haitians were a big political risk for Clinton. The answer includes issues of identity, that is, who is understood as belonging to the U.S. or Floridian community and who is perceived as not belonging. Pointing to domestic politics, then, is compatible with a societal security framework.

It is important to note that policies designed to address societal insecurity do not necessarily have to follow the logic of classical security. In the case of Haiti there was a mixture of policies and logics. Forced

---

48. This is in contrast to an acceptance rate of 89.7 percent for Cuban refugees, 89.1 percent for refugees from the former Soviet Union, 95.2 percent for Vietnam, and 79.2 percent for South Africa. See Dorris M. Meissner et al., *International Migration—Challenges in a New Era. Report to the Trilateral Commission,* 44 (1993), 33.

49. Lee Hamilton, "What the United States Should Do About Haiti," *Christian Science Monitor,* 22 December 1992, 19.

repatriation was a realpolitik solution to the Haitian crisis, but the logic that drove this kind of policy was not the only logic at work. While economic sanctions can arguably be regarded as a realpolitik type of policy carried out in the economic arena, other strategies such as the Governor's Island Agreement and Jimmy Carter's diplomacy were not driven solely by a realpolitik logic. Another logic was at work, one that came increasingly to the fore after the U.S./UN intervention. This was a logic that moved toward that of human security. This was evident in the discourse on democracy and human rights. While sceptics may rightfully question the sincerity of U.S. rhetoric and while keeping Haitians out of the United States may indeed have been the overriding U.S. concern, the issues of democracy and human rights were nonetheless ones that received quite a bit of attention and became significant considerations to U.S. policymakers. The name of the U.S. occupation operation that landed U.S. forces in Haiti on 19 September 1994, "Operation Uphold Democracy," conveys the importance of a logic other than that of realpolitik. The national security and societal security of the United States became inextricably linked with the human security of the Haitian people. This link was fairly explicitly articulated by Lee Hamilton, the ranking Democrat on the House Foreign Affairs Committee, when he suggested that U.S. interests in Haiti faced two challenges: "The first is to our commitment to democracy. Haiti is one of only two countries in the hemisphere (the other is Cuba) now ruled by an unelected government. Second, a prolonged crisis will cause a steady flow of refugees. These two challenges are linked: The refugee flow cannot be halted without a resolution to the political crisis."[50] One way to promote the security of the Haitian people and thereby stop the refugee flow was to promote democracy and a respect for human rights. As time passed, it became clear that this could not be done solely with policies dictated by a classical security logic. Rather, what we find is a logic that moved toward an appreciation of the concept of human security. Haq suggests that the end goal in human security is human welfare. Understanding security as human security means that "Security will be interpreted as: security of people, not just territory, security of individuals, not just of nations, security through development, not through arms, security of all people everywhere—in their homes, in their jobs, in their streets, in their

---

50. Hamilton, "What the United States Should Do About Haiti."

communities, in their environment."[51] This may sound rather all-encompassing and unattainable, not to mention idealistic, from an academic point of view. It was precisely these things, however, that were missing from Haiti and that the United States increasingly came to believe must be restored, or put into place in the first place, if U.S. borders were to be secured. This created spaces for a broadened understanding of security that moved away from the logics of national security or societal security.

This does not imply, however, that these spaces were fully explored. U.S. concerns were still dominated by the fear of the other, that is, Haitian refugees "flooding" U.S. borders. This desire to keep "them" out retained the logic of identity linked with territory and thus precluded a complete move to a more radical understanding of human security. Nonetheless, the concern with human rights and the restoration of democracy in Haiti and the subsequent acting upon these concerns does demonstrate at least a partial disaggregation of democracy. Connolly uses this term to refer to the possibility of an understanding of democracy and identity that is not imprisoned by state boundaries and that merely requires "common points of reference through which issues can be defined and pressures for action can be organized."[52] In the case of Haiti, we can find evidence of pressures for action that were articulated along other than national territorial boundaries. Congressman Charles Rangle (D-New York), for example, arguing in favor of toughened U.S. sanctions against the Haitian government, said: "We as African Americans have to recognize that we have the responsibility in this country to protect our own, and taking care of Haiti is only part of our responsibility."[53] The concern expressed here is not for the national or societal security of the United States. Rather, it is illustrative of the kind of common point of reference that Connolly suggests. For Rangle and members of the Black Caucus, and others such as Randall Robinson and members of TransAfrica, this common point of reference may have been race, which illustrates a very different understanding of community than that commonly associated with a community that exists solely within a state's geographical boundaries. There were other groups, however, whose common point of reference seems to have been humanity more generally. Several groups were party to a

51. Haq, *Reflections on Human Development*, 115–17.
52. William E. Connolly, "Democracy and Territoriality," *Millennium: Journal of International Studies* 20, no. 3 (winter 1991): 476–79.
53. Catherine Foster, "Black Caucus Aims to Stiffen Trade Embargo of Haiti."

case heard by the U.S. Supreme Court regarding President George Bush's policy of forced repatriation of Haitian refugees: American Baptist Churches in the U.S.A., Catholic Community Services, Center for Immigrants Rights, Inc., the Child Welfare League of America, Florida Rural Legal Services, Global Exchange, the International Ladies Garment Workers Union, and the U.S. Committee for Refugees. These groups and others demonstrated the kind of critical responsiveness discussed earlier that eventually influenced U.S. policymakers.

This case illustrates that not only are there numerous issues that defy the traditional definitions of security that have dominated the field of security studies but that different logics are at work when it comes to securitizing a particular issue. As Waever carefully points out, a concept such as security is a speech act and as such the act of uttering it moves an issue into a specific area which makes certain means of action possible and legitimate.[54] It has also been pointed out, regarding speech-act theory, that language exhibits a readiness to be grafted into new and unforeseeable contexts such that no appeal to performative intent can serve to delimit the range of possible meanings.[55] Securitization cannot be locked into a particular logic anymore than it can be locked into a particular meaning. Several modes of securitization chacterized by different logics may be operative simultaneously. These can have important policy implications. A world that is increasingly characterized by flows, permeable borders and changing understandings of identity affects the nature of the logic that governs security practices. Security, like many other concepts that are important to international relations, is overdetermined and contested. Its meaning is not fixed, but rather is the result of social-political practices in specific circumstances. This is true both in terms of the meaning(s) assigned to it by scholars as well as the meaning(s) assigned to it by policymakers and society more generally. Efforts to fix either the meaning of security or to preserve a foundation in the form of a defining logic to which issues must fit if they are to be considered relevant to security studies seem counterproductive and exclusionary. Walt argues that issues of war and peace are too important to be "diverted into a prolix and self-indulgent discourse that is divorced from the real world."[56] The case of Haiti and the relationship among the complex elements of security that it illustrates offers support to Walt's words. I would argue, though, that the

---

54. Waever, "Securitization and Desecuritization," 55.
55. Christopher Norris, *Derrida* (Cambridge: Harvard University Press, 1987).
56. Walt, "The Renaissance of Security Studies," 223.

self-indulgent discourse that is divorced from the real world is the narrow one that Walt seeks to promote in his effort to silence more critical approaches to security. Haq suggests that "human security is a concept emerging not from the learned writings of scholars but from the daily concerns of people."[57] It was such concerns that motivated Haitian refugees to flee and seek refuge in the United States and that were significant in the U.S. decision to use its military power. The case of Haiti demonstrates that national security, societal security, and human security can be inextricably linked with one another. Hobsbawm suggests that international migration has made a world of national territories, belonging exclusively to the natives who keep strangers in their place, even less of a realistic option for the twenty-first century than it was for the twentieth.[58] Arguably, this phenomenon, as well as others, that have been excluded from traditional security studies, also makes a narrow understanding of security less of a realistic option for those who seek to address the many contemporary issues that affect the security of people globally.

57. Haq, *Reflections on Human Development*, 116.
58. E. J. Hobsbawm, *Nations and Nationalism Since 1780* (Cambridge: Cambridge University Press, 1992), 182.

CONSTRUCTING A SEPARATE PEACE:

CONSTRUCTIVISM, COLLECTIVE LIBERAL IDENTITY, AND DEMOCRATIC PEACE

COLIN H. KAHL

THE PROPOSITION that democracies rarely, if ever, fight one another has assumed axiomatic status for many students of international politics. Increasingly, confidence in the reality of the so-called democratic peace phenomenon has seeped out of the ivory tower of academia and spread to many Western policymakers as well.[1] These claims stem chiefly from voluminous statistical evidence that suggests that liberal democracies have indeed established a separate peace amongst themselves.[2] Despite an enormous amount of intellectual energy spent on the effort, current explanations for this inductively discovered "law" suffer from a number of inadequacies. One type of explanation locates the source of democratic peace in various characteristics of democratic institutions. In isolation, however, this explanation fails to account for important aspects of inter-democratic relations, such as the tendency of democracies to define their national interests in compatible or collective ways and utilize peaceful means of dispute resolution. A second type of explanation focuses on ideational factors and contends that a common commitment to liberal ideas and democratic norms generates peace among liberal democracies. These explanations provide insights into aspects of democratic peace neglected by institutional arguments, but have not been taken far enough. Especially, the

Colin H. Kahl is a Ph.D. candidate in the Department of Political Science at Columbia University.

I would like to thank Tim Crawford, Ted Hopf, Robert Jervis, Aaron Seeskin, Jack Snyder, Jon Western, Leslie Vinjamuri, and the anonymous reviewers of Security Studies for their helpful suggestions and criticisms.

1. See, for example, "Democracies and War: The Politics of Peace," *Economist*, 1 April 1995, 17–18.
2. For discussions of the statistical literature, see Bruce Russett, *Grasping the Democratic Peace: Principles for a Post–Cold War World* (Princeton: Princeton University Press, 1993); David L. Rousseau et al., "Assessing the Dyadic Nature of the Democratic Peace, 1918–1988," *American Political Science Review* 90, no. 3 (September 1996): 512–33; and Zeev Maoz, "The Controversy over the Democratic Peace: Rearguard Action or Cracks in the Wall?" *International Security* 22, no. 1 (summer 1997): 162–98.

conditions under which democracies come to view one another as liberal, morally legitimate, or deserving of the externalization of certain norms and practices are still undertheorized.

Embedding ideational explanations for democratic peace in constructivist theory offers a way of simultaneously addressing the inadequacies of institutional explanations while helping ideational ones reach their full potential. Constructivism argues that the national interests and foreign policy strategies states adopt are, to a significant degree, a function of state identity. Constructivists contend that some identities lead states to identify negatively with one another. When this occurs, states rely on self-help, compete for relative gains, and become constantly wary of the possibility of violent conflict with others. In contrast to neorealists, however, constructivists do not view this type of behavior as an inevitable outgrowth of an anarchic international system. Rather, constructivists contend that certain social identities entail positive identifications with others, leading to a definition of state interests and appropriate state strategies that facilitates coordination and peaceful relations. I argue that a constructivist analysis holds the key to a more complete understanding of the separate peace established between liberal democracies. States that view one another as liberal democracies positively identify with one another. This collective liberal identity reduces uncertainty and anxiety, leads to cooperative relations, generates a tendency for liberal democracies to ally with one another, and contributes to the peaceful resolution of conflicts of interest. Positive collective identification thus allows liberal democracies to opt out of the Hobbesian world described by neorealists in their relations with one another.

The primary goal of this essay is to demonstrate that it is possible to derive interesting, specific, and empirically testable propositions from constructivist theory regarding relations between liberal democracies. I proceed toward this goal by, first, briefly discussing the current explanations for democratic peace and their shortcomings. I then provide an overview of constructivism, before moving on to a discussion of liberal identity, collective liberal identity, and their implications. Ultimately, I hope to demonstrate that institutional arguments leave a number of important features of democratic relations unexplained or underexplained, that ideational arguments help fill this explanatory gap, and that constructivism provides a good theoretical vehicle for advancing our understanding of the role ideation plays in generating democratic peace. In the last section I suggest that a constructivist approach can productively advance the democratic peace research program by opening it up to interpretive approaches to empirical investigation.

EXPLAINING DEMOCRATIC PEACE

SCHOLARS TYPICALLY explain democratic peace by pointing to the institutional or ideational features of democratic states. In this section, I outline these explanations, point to their merits, and discuss their inadequacies.

INSTITUTIONAL EXPLANATIONS

Institutional explanations for democratic peace come in both monadic and dyadic forms. Monadic institutional explanations emphasize those aspects of democratic institutions that affect the foreign policy dispositions of democratic states, regardless of whether the foreign policy is directed toward a fellow democracy or a non-democracy. This type of explanation emphasizes the powerful constraining role played by institutionalized checks and balances. In particular, it is claimed that democratic decisionmakers are held accountable to the preferences of the median voter by frequent and fair elections. Because the public tends to be wary of war, due to its costs in blood and treasure, they tend to punish decisionmakers who engage in reckless foreign policies and military campaigns. Since decisionmakers expect to be punished if they act imprudently in foreign affairs, they tend to be constrained and refrain form entering into long and costly wars.[3]

Dyadic institutional explanations shift the focus to the specific puzzle that preoccupies most of the democratic peace research program: why democracies tend to be particularly pacific in their relations with

3. Rudolf J. Rummel, "Libertarianism and International Violence Between and Within States," *Journal of Conflict Resolution* 27, no. 1 (March 1983): 27–28; T. Clifton Morgan and Sally Howard Campbell, "Domestic Structure, Decisional Constraints, and War: So Why Kant Democracies Fight?" *Journal of Conflict Resolution* 35, no. 2 (June 1991): 190–91; Jack Snyder, *Myths of Empire: Domestic Politics and International Ambition* (Ithaca: Cornell University Press, 1991); Bruce Bueno de Mesquita and David Lalman, *War and Reason: Domestic and International Imperatives* (New Haven: Yale University Press, 1992): 153–55; David A. Lake, "Powerful Pacifists: Democratic States and War," *American Political Science Review* 86, no. 1 (March 1992): 24–37; Randall L. Schweller, "Domestic Structure and Preventive War: Are Democracies More Pacific?" *World Politics* 44, no. 2 (January 1992): 241–45; and Edward D. Mansfield and Jack Snyder, "Democratization as a Cause of War," *International Security* 20, no. 1 (summer 1995): 5–38.

one another. Dyadic explanations contend that two characteristics of democratic institutions, the slowness of mobilization and the transparency of democratic institutions, are especially important. The complexity of the mobilization process in democracies means that the process of going to war is slow. This reduces the fear of other states that the democracy will launch surprise attacks, and generates an expectation that there will be sufficient time to negotiate a peaceful resolution to conflicts before they escalate. Furthermore, since the mobilization and decision-making processes tend to be public in democracies, they are relatively transparent to other states. This reduces the chance that misperceptions and miscalculations of relative power and resolve will lead to conflict.[4]

Institutional explanations, by themselves, provide an incomplete explanation for democratic peace. Monadic variants are problematic because it is not clear that democracies are, in general, more prudent. While there is some statistical evidence suggesting that democracies are more pacific and less likely to initiate disputes, most studies find that democracies are just as war prone as other types of states.[5] Moreover, the extensive record of liberal imperialism suggests that democracies are capable of aggressive foreign policies toward weak nondemocracies.[6] Monadic institutional logic provides no explanation for the apparent failure of strong democracies to take advantage of similar power asymmetries and engage in low-cost wars against weaker democracies.

Dyadic variants also have limitations. Dyadic explanations focusing on mutual institutional constraints speak only to wars of tragedy triggered by spiral dynamics associated with rapid mobilization and reciprocal fear of surprise attack. Many wars, however, arise over pure conflicts of national interests, however defined, not from tragedy.[7] In addi-

---

4. Bueno de Mesquita and Lalman, *War and Reason*, 155–64; Russett, *Grasping the Democratic Peace*, 38–40; James D. Fearon, "Domestic Audiences and the Escalation of International Disputes," *American Political Science Review* 88, no. 3 (September 1994): 577–92; Ken Schultz, "Domestic Political Competition and Bargaining in International Crises" (Ph.D. diss., Stanford University, 1996).

5. For recent reviews of monadic findings, see Rousseau et al., "Assessing the Dyadic Nature of the Democratic Peace, 1918–1988," 515–17; and Miriam Fendius Elman, "Introduction," in *Paths to Peace: Is Democracy the Answer?*, ed. Miriam Fendius Elman (Cambridge: MIT Press, 1997): 14–20.

6. Michael W. Doyle, "Kant, Liberal Legacies, and Foreign Affairs, Part 1," *Philosophy and Public Affairs* 12, no. 3 (summer 1983): 1156–57; and Doyle, "Kant, Liberal Legacies, and Foreign Affairs, Part 2," *Philosophy and Public Affairs* 12, no. 4 (fall 1983): 323–53.

7. See Dan Reiter, "Exploding the Powder Keg Myth: Preemptive Wars Almost Never Happen," *International Security* 20, no. 2 (fall 1995): 5–34.

tion, since the record of democratic foreign policies toward non-democracies suggests that jingoistic public opinion can push democracies into wars of aggression, there is no institutional reason why democracies would view one another as dove-like and prudent in crisis situations. There must be something special about how democracies perceive one another or interact that is not picked up simply be considering institutional constraints.

Dyadic explanations emphasizing the role of transparency also provide an incomplete picture of war avoidance. Transparency, it is argued, facilitates the deescalation of crises because it allows the parties involved to make proper evaluations regarding each other's relative military capabilities, interests, and resolve. Transparency thus generates a clear picture of relative bargaining power during crises, enables the weaker party to back down, and facilitates negotiated settlements short of war.[8] It is, however, still possible for states having accurate assessments of their relative bargaining power in a crisis to engage in war. Some states may end up fighting rather than opting for a less costly solution if the values involved in the crisis are "lumpy" (that is, indivisible), and thus not amenable to a satisfactory negotiated settlement. In some instances, for example, national survival, sovereignty, political autonomy, and core national values may represent such lumpy issues.[9]

Finally, both monadic and dyadic institutional explanations are relatively silent on other aspects of democratic peace, such as the tendency for democracies to get into fewer militarized crises with one another during peacetime and to ally with one another during wartime.[10] Institutional constraints and transparency should only be activated when the risk of war is high. This only implies that militarized crises should be resolved before they escalate, not that crises should occur less frequently. Institutional constraints and transparency also say little about the bias in alliance behavior because there is no reason to expect that allying with non-democracies is on average more costly than allying

8. See Fearon, "Domestic Political Audiences and the Escalation of International Disputes"; and Fearon, "Rationalist Explanations for War," *International Organization* 44, no. 3 (summer 1995): 379–414.

9. Fearon admits to this possibility, though he optimistically argues that these situations arise infrequently. Fearon, "Rationalist Explanations for War," 381–82.

10. On the infrequency of crises, see Zeev Maoz and Nasrin Abdolali, "Regime Types and International Conflict, 1816–1976," *Journal of Conflict Resolution* 33, no. 1 (March 1989): 3–35; and Maoz, "The Controversy Over the Democratic Peace." On the frequency of alliances, see Rudolf M. Siverson and Julian Emmons, "Birds of a Feather," *Journal of Conflict Resolution* 35, no. 2 (June 1991): 285–306.

with fellow democracies or that more accurate perceptions facilitate such alliance formation. Understanding the lower incidence of inter-democratic crises and the bias in alliance behavior requires an explanation for why democracies appear to more frequently have compatible or collective interests with one another than with other types of states. Institutional explanations simply fail to address this issue.

None of this is meant to suggest that institutional explanations are wrong, only that they provide an incomplete understanding of democratic peace. To fully understand democratic peace and its implications we must turn to ideational approaches. These explanations do not compete with institutional claims, but provide insights into critical aspects of democratic relations that institutional accounts leave unexplained or underexplained.

IDEATIONAL EXPLANATIONS

A second general approach to explaining democratic peace focuses on ideational factors. One strand of ideational explanation contends that the substance of liberal ideas generates democratic peace. Doyle, for example, argues that liberal democracies enjoy mutual respect in their relations with one another, and see one another as legitimate and just because they share a common commitment to liberal principles.[11] More recently, Owen has refined this argument by stressing the specific role played by several key tenets of liberalism. According to Owen, liberal principles hold that (1) all individuals and states share a common interest in self-preservation and material well-being; and (2) peace and freedom are required to advance these interests. For freedom to flourish, all people must be enlightened and live under enlightened political institutions that allow the expression of their interests to shape policy. Consequently, liberals view all individuals and states as having a common interest in peace and deem war desirous only when it is required to bring about more peace on balance in the long term. These ideas, embodied in a liberal foreign policy ideology and empowered by democratic institutions, create democratic peace. Liberal ideas also explain the nature of relations between liberal and illiberal states,

---

11. Doyle, "Kant, Liberal Legacies, and Foreign Affairs, Part 1"; and Doyle, "Liberalism and World Politics," *American Political Science Review* 80, no. 4 (December 1986): 1151–69.

because liberal states tend to view non-democracies with suspicion, and consider them constant dangers to international peace.[12]

A second variant of ideational explanation focuses on democratic norms and practices. This explanation contends that democratic decisionmakers expect to resolve internal conflicts through compromise and nonviolence, and tend to respect the rights and continued existence of opponents. Democracies follow these norms of peaceful conflict resolution with other democracies and expect other democracies to do the same. In this way, internal norms and practices are externalized and a "transnational democratic culture" evolves, where other liberal democracies are seen as possessing rights, and states commit themselves to settling their disputes peacefully.[13]

Ideational approaches hold much promise for addressing critical aspects of democratic peace neglected by their institutional cousins, namely the apparent tendency of liberal democracies to define their national interests in compatible or collective ways and resort to peaceful means of dispute resolution. As such, ideational explanations provide a number of essential building blocks for much of the argument presented here. As currently articulated, however, ideational explanations fail to realize their full potential. First, existing ideational explanations fail to discuss the source of liberal ideas and democratic norms, and thus fail to explain why the majority of public and elite opinion within liberal democracies should be expected to adopt them. Second, the source and mechanism for the shared perceptions between liberal democracies is left almost completely unexplained. This is especially problematic given that these shared perceptions and understanding are the most important components in an explanation seeking to demonstrate how ideational factors generate the special quality of democratic relationships. As Owen concedes, "[m]ore research needs to be done on the question of how a state with democratic institutions comes to be regarded by its peers as liberal."[14]

---

12. John M. Owen, "How Liberalism Produces Democratic Peace," *International Security* 19, no. 2 (fall 1994): 93–104. See also, Owen, *Liberal Peace, Liberal War* (Ithaca: Cornell University Press, 1997); and Owen, "Perceptions and the Limits of Liberal Peace: The Mexican-American and Spanish-American Wars," in Elman, *Paths to Peace*, 153–90.

13. Russett, *Grasping the Democratic Peace*, 30–38; William J. Dixon, "Democracy and the Peaceful Settlement of International Conflict," *American Political Science Review* 88, no. 1 (March 1994): 14–32; Thomas Risse-Kappen, "Democratic Peace—Warlike Democracies? A Social Constructivist Interpretation of the Liberal Argument," *European Journal of International Relations* 1, no. 4 (December 1995): 491–517.

14. Owen, "How Liberalism Produces Democratic Peace," n. 32.

CONSTRUCTING A VIABLE EXPLANATION FOR DEMOCRATIC PEACE

Adler has recently argued that "democratic peace is about...the spread over the world of an intersubjective liberal identity." Therefore, "the 'democratic peace' cries for a constructivist explanation."[15] In the remainder of this essay, I take up Adler's challenge and argue that an explanation for democratic peace grounded in constructivism succeeds in filling many of the theoretical and explanatory gaps left by existing institutional and ideational accounts. To date, Risse-Kappen is the only scholar to explain democratic peace within an explicitly constructivist framework. Risse-Kappen persuasively argues that a common liberal identity helps to stabilize expectations and reduce fear in relations between liberal democracies, thereby preventing war by defusing the security dilemma.[16] My analysis seeks to go beyond Risse-Kappen's in three important ways. First, unlike Risse-Kappen, who is primarily interested in how liberal affinity produces peace, I go to considerable lengths to specify the conditions under which constructivist theory would lead us to expect liberal democracies positively to identify with one another in the first place. Second, when explaining pacific relations, I do not focus solely on the ways in which liberal polities defuse the security dilemma in their relations with one another. Rather, I suggest that liberal democracies might enjoy a particularly robust peace not only because the security dilemma is less acute, but also because they tend to have similarly constituted national interests. Finally, I make greater effort to specify ways in which a constructivist explanation for democratic peace can be operationalized.

CONSTRUCTIVISM

CONSTRUCTIVISM IS a branch of international relations theory that draws on phenomenological variants of sociology and social psychology, particularly structuration theory, symbolic interactionism, ethnomethodology, and role-theory.[17] Given that I seek to explain the

15. Emanuel Adler, "Seizing the Middle Ground: Constructivism in World Politics," *European Journal of International Relations* 3, no. 3 (September 1997): 347.
16. Risse-Kappen, "Democratic Peace—Warlike Democracies?"
17. See Robert O. Keohane, "International Institutions: Two Approaches," *International Studies Quarterly* 32, no. 4 (December 1988): 379–96; Alexander E. Wendt, "Anarchy is What States Make of It: The Social Construction of Power Politics," *International Organization* 46, no. 2 (spring 1992): 391–425; Peter J. Katzenstein, ed., *The Culture of National Security: Norms and Identity in World Politics* (New York: Colum-

foreign policy behavior of liberal democracies, I will mainly focus on constructivist theory as it relates to state identity and collective identity formation.

THE CONSTRUCTIVIST NOTION OF STRUCTURE

There are two major elements in the constructivist notion of structure, both drawn from Anthony Giddens's structuration theory. Material resources represent the first element. Resources are the physical properties and capabilities of actors (in this case states). These include such factors as geography, climate, population, natural resource base, industrial strength, wealth, levels of armaments, and technological and organizational capabilities. Rules make up the second element of structure. As Dessler notes, rules are "frameworks of meaning...the media through which [states] communicate with one another and coordinate their actions."[18] These rules can be "regulative," in the sense of prescribing and proscribing behavior in defined circumstances (for example, norms and other guides to legitimate action), or "constitutive," in the sense of creating or defining new types of behavior and making that behavior meaningful (for example, conventions and shared beliefs about the nature of the world). In addition, these rules can be either explicit or implicit.[19] When the meshing of resources and rules evolves into relatively stable sets of intersubjective meanings across time and space, they are referred to as "institutions." Once "institutionalized" these meanings exist as "objective" and "external" facts defining social reality, and it is only then that structure can be said truly to "exist"[20]

---

bia University Press, 1996); and Adler, "Seizing the Middle Ground." For discussions of structuration theory, see Anthony Giddens, *The Constitution of Society: Outline of the Theory of Structuration* (Berkeley: University of California Press, 1984). For excellent surveys of the relevant social psychological approaches, see Sheldon Stryker, "Symbolic Interactionism: Themes and Variations," in *Social Psychology: Sociological Perspectives*, ed. Morris Rosenberg and Ralph H. Turner (New York: Basic Books, 1981), 3–29; John C. Heritage, "Ethnomethodology," in *Social Theory Today*, ed. Anthony Giddens and Jonathan H. Turner (Stanford: Stanford University Press, 1987), 224–72; and Jonathan H. Turner, *A Theory of Social Interaction* (Stanford: Stanford California Press, 1988).

18. David Dessler, "What's at Stake in the Agent-Structure Debate?" *International Organization* 43, 3 (summer 1989): 453–54.

19. See Dessler, "What's at Stake in the Agent-Structure Debate?" 453–54; and Friedrich V. Kratochwil, *Rules, Norms, and Decisions: On the Conditions of Practical and Legal Reasoning in International Relations and Domestic Affairs* (New York: Cambridge University Press, 1989), 54–57.

20. Giddens, *The Constitution of Society*, chaps. 2–4; and Wendt, "Anarchy is What States Make of It," 405. See also Alfred Schutz, *The Phenomenology of the Social World*

Thus, for constructivists, institutions represent intersubjective social structures. This view stands in sharp contrast to the predominantly materialist notions of structure put forth by both neorealism and neoliberal institutionalism. Under constructivism's broad definition of institutions, notable international institutions include such instantiated elements of international politics as diplomatic and consular practices, international organizations, treaties, regimes, and conventions,[21] transnational political communities, the modern sovereign-territorial state,[22] and certain institutionalized practices such as self-help.[23]

For constructivists, structure provides both an essential enabling context for interaction, and a constraint on that interaction. Without institutionalized resources and rules, interaction would be impossible and unintelligible. It helps determine which actors interact with each other and on what terms. Despite this description, however, constructivists do not view structure as a thing; they view it as a process. It is produced, reproduced, and potentially transformed by interaction within the social structural context existing at any given point in time and space. Thus, there is a duality in the constructivist notion of structure; structure is both the medium for and the outcome of interaction. Agent and structure are distinct, but each is to some extent determined by the other.[24]

ACTION, INTERACTION, AND INTERSUBJECTIVE MEANING

Turning to the agency side of the equation, constructivism contends that all state action is dependent upon a named or classified world. The naming and classification of objects, including other states, provides states with the necessary simplicity and clarity to act in an otherwise complex, confusing, and unintelligible international environment.

(1932; Evanston: Northwestern University Press, 1967); Peter L. Berger and Thomas Luckman, *The Social Construction of Reality* (Garden City: Doubleday, 1966); Ronald L. Jepperson, "Institutions, Institutional Effects, and Institutionalism," in *The New Institutionalism in Organizational Analysis*, ed. Walter W. Powell and Paul J. DiMaggio (Chicago: University of Chicago Press, 1991), 143–63; and Lynn G. Zucker, "Institutionalization in Cultural Persistence," in Powell and DiMaggio, *The New Institutionalism in Organizational Analysis*, 63–82.

21. See Hedley Bull, *The Anarchical Society: A Study of World Order in World Politics* (New York: Columbia University Press, 1977).

22. See John Gerald Ruggie, "Territoriality and Beyond: Problematizing Modernity in International Relations," *International Organization* 47, no. 1 (winter 1993): 139–74.

23. See Wendt, "Anarchy is What States Make of It."

24. Alexander E. Wendt, "The Agent-Structure Problem in International Relations Theory," *International Organization* 41, 3 (summer 1987): 360.

These names and classifications thus provide sets of meanings. States, in turn, act toward these objects based on these meanings.[25]

Constructivists contend that these meanings emerge from social interaction within a given structural context and that these meanings are modified and dealt with through an interpretive process used by states when responding to things encountered. In the realm of social psychology, George H. Mead was the first to argue explicitly that interaction represents a "conversation of gestures." Actors signal their respective courses of action by emitting gestures, and at the same time they interpret the gestures of others. Following Mead, Alexander Wendt argues that signaling, interpreting, and responding complete a 'social act,' beginning the process by which states create ("produce") intersubjective meanings.[26] Social acts thus help generate expectations among states about each other's behavior in future interactions, with each subsequent social act potentially reinforcing ("reproducing") or modifying these meanings and expectations. If actions are repeated frequently and consistently enough (that is, if they are "recursive"), their products become institutionalized. This makes them appear to be relatively stable and external elements of objective social reality, and creates a certain degree of path dependence.[27]

THE FORMATION OF SOCIAL IDENTITY

The "social" identities of states represent the names, ideal types, groups, statuses, and social categories that states are socially recognized, by themselves and others, to be members. As such, social identities are among the key constitutive intersubjective meanings that structure international politics. Like other forms of intersubjective meanings, these identities grow out of social interaction. Insights from symbolic interactionism suggest that states interacting in a given social structural context come to recognize one another as occupants of certain identities. When this occurs, the states invoke certain expectations regarding each

25. Wendt, "Anarchy is What States Make of It," 396–97 and 403.
26. Wendt, "Anarchy is What States Make of It," 405. See also George H. Mead, *Mind, Self, and Society* (1934; Chicago: University of Chicago Press, 1974); and Stryker, "Symbolic Interactionism," 15–16.
27. Dessler, "What's at Stake in the Agent-Structure Debate?" 462; and Roy Koslowski and Friedrich V. Kratochwil, "Understanding Change in the International System: The Soviet Empire's Demise and the International System, *International Organization* 49, no. 3 (summer 1994): 227

other's behavior based on these identities.[28] States also give names to themselves. For constructivists, a state's conception of "self" is largely a meaning existing in the activity of viewing itself reflexively. Interaction is thus critical, because it is only interaction, particularly communication, that permits an actor to attribute sets of meaning to itself by taking the perspective of the other. These "reflective appraisals" then create internalized expectations regarding the state's own behavior.[29]

CORPORATE IDENTITY

Not all aspects of a state's identity are social, in the sense of being defined by taking the perspective of other states. Rather, some important aspects of a state's identity stem from its domestic institutional makeup. These elements represent a state's "corporate" identity. As Wendt explains:

> Corporate identity refers to the intrinsic, self-organizing qualities that constitute actor individuality. For human beings, this means the body and experience of consciousness; for organizations [such as the state], it means their constituent individuals, physical resources, and the shared beliefs and institutions in virtue of which individuals function as a "we."[30]

A state's corporate identity is generated by state formation and political development processes that are, to varying degrees, prior to or independent from interaction with other states.[31] Thus, these elements of a state's identity are at least partially exogenous, rather than endogenous, to the process of interaction between states. It is only "partially" exogenous, however, because a state's relations and interactions with others frequently affects the trajectory of its political and domestic in-

28. See Stephen Walker, "Symbolic Interactionism and International Politics: Role Theory's Contribution to International Organization," in *Contending Dramas: A Cognitive Approach to International Organization*, ed. Martha L. Cottam and Chih-yu Shih (New York: Praeger, 1992), 19–38; and Michael Barnett, "Sovereignty, Nationalism, and Regional Order in the Arab States System," *International Organization* 49, no. 3 (summer 1995), 482–92.
29. Alexander E. Wendt, "Collective Identity Formation and the International State," *American Political Science Review* 88, no. 2 (June 1994): 395; Mead, *Mind, Self, and Society*, 136–40; and Stryker, "Symbolic Interactionism," 24–25.
30. Wendt, "Collective Identity Formation and the International State," 385. In a number of ways, the distinction between social and corporate identity mirrors Paul Kowert's distinction between "internal" and "external" identity. See Paul A. Kowert, "National Identity: Inside and Out," *Security Studies* 8, nos. 2/3 (winter 1998/99–spring 1999): 1–34.
31. See Kowert, "National Identity: Inside and Out," 11–14.

stitutional development to some degree. This is the kind of interactive effect typically pointed to by so-called second-image reversed theorists. It should be emphasized, however, that even these interaction effects are not "social" in the sense discussed above because they are not aspects of a state's identity defined by reflecting on the nature of the self by taking the perspective of the other.

It is important to consider a state's corporate identity for several reasons. First, a state's intrinsic capabilities and institutional make-up place constraints on the possible forms that a state's social identity can take (including the prospects for positive collective identification with others), just as biology does for individuals. Second, a state's corporate identity, and changes in it resulting from internal processes, affects the meanings and social identities of other states. Because a state's corporate identity in part determines its behavior, it effects the patterns of international interaction likely to emerge.[32] The final reason to consider a state's corporate identity is unique to the study of international politics. A state is not completely analogous to an individual acting and interacting within a single system. Instead, in international politics there are at least two systems in which interaction occurs, the domestic and international. Consequently, we need to be conscious of processes operating at both levels.

The notion of corporate identity adds much to the dynamism constructivists see in the international system, because changes in corporate identity due to factors exogenous to state interaction can still have implications for that interaction. In the traditional parlance of international relations theory, this is a way of conceptualizing how "unit-level" factors potentially constitute or transform international systemic properties. For our purposes here, the notion of corporate identity provides a useful device for conceptualizing the ways in which democratic institutions may produce, reproduce, or transform liberal and collective liberal identities.

IDENTITY, INTERESTS, AND BEHAVIOR

When discussing the relationship between state identity and behavior, it is important to note the distinction between interests, which are

---

32. Emanuel Adler, "Cognitive Evolution: A Dynamic Approach to the Study of International Relations and Their Progress," in *Progress in Postwar International Relations*, ed. Emanuel Adler and Beverly Crawford (New York: Columbia University Press), 61; and Koslowski and Kratochwil, "Understanding Change in the International System," 216.

preferences over outcomes, and strategies, which are preferences over actions.[33] Constructivism contends that state identities constitute national interests, and enable and constrain state strategies.[34] Constructivism thus posits that the beliefs, values, norms, and practices embodied in, and manifested by, state identities logically and necessarily matter "all the way down."[35] Specifically, constructivists contend that identity generates state interests and strategies in three interrelated ways. First, the national values inherent in a state's identity establish the ends, gratifications, or utilities sought by states. Thus, identity can literally define a state's interests. Second, certain beliefs embedded in the identities of actors help determine how situations in which action takes place to fulfill these interests should be defined and interpreted.[36] This helps shape state preferences regarding particular actions. As a result, identity matters even with regard to those ends of state policy that tend not to vary across states with different identities. The state interest in physical security provides a case in point. This interest is almost certainly universal, regardless of the specifics of a state's identity. Yet, even when this interest is implicated, as when a state is confronted with the military preparations or actions of a neighboring state, the best policy is rarely unambiguous. What security means to that state, what constitutes a threat to that security, and how the state can best ensure its security in a given social context, are all contingent factors, not objective givens.[37] It is here that a state's identity, and the perceived identity of other states, is likely to play a large part in determining the state's behavior. Finally, identities embrace certain norms and practices that specify which strategies are legitimate and preferable in given situations. This may create constraints on, or powerful incen-

33. Robert Powell, "Anarchy in International Relations Theory: The Neorealist-Neoliberal Debate," *International Organization* 48, no. 2 (spring 1994): 318.

34. See, for example, Rodney Bruce Hall's discussion of the ways in which the territorial-sovereign social identities of European belligerents affected the scope, conduct, terms of engagement, and terms of disengagement during the Seven Years War. Hall, "Territorial and National Sovereigns: Sovereign Identity and Consequences for Security Policy," *Security Studies*, 8, nos. 2/3 (winter 1998/99–spring 1999): 145–97.

35. David Halloran Lumsdaine, *Moral Vision in International Politics: The Foreign Aid Regime, 1949–1989* (Princeton: Princeton University Press, 1993), 20–21; and Alexander E. Wendt, "Constructing International Politics," *International Security* 20, no. 1 (summer 1995): 74.

36. See Adler, "Cognitive Evolution," 46, 52, and 60–61.

37. See Robert Jervis, *Perception and Misperception in International Politics* (Princeton: Princeton University Press, 1976).

tives for, particular foreign policy options that differ from what a simple evaluation of the material and strategic context would suggest.[38]

In contrast, rational-materialist theories, such as neorealism and neoliberal institutionalism, typically fail to take seriously the contention that variations in interests and strategies stem from the corporate and social identities of states.[39] The rationalist component of these theories says nothing about the identity or interests of states. Instead, interests are exogenous, unexplained givens in the model, and are argued to be both ordered and stable. Likewise, variations in identity are also exogenous. The rationalist component is a useful "tool box" used to make predictions about the strategies states will select, and the outcomes likely to emerge from strategic interaction, but does not serve as a sufficient stand-alone explanation for actor behavior. Neorealists and neoliberal institutionalists address this problem, either explicitly or implicitly, by introducing a materialist component that provides the identity and interests of actors, which, in turn, are plugged into the rational (often game-theoretic) choice model. A state's identity (the names given to states, such as "great," "middle," and "lesser" powers) is defined in terms of the state's material capabilities relative to others. Other aspects of a state's identity and internal motivations, whether they stem from regime type or variations in national values, are viewed as less important determinants of state behavior. In short, states are "billiard balls."[40] In general, all states are posited to have a constant interest in material security and wealth. More specific interests are claimed to vary based on a state's relative international position. Furthermore, state identity and interests are also treated as largely exogenous to the process of social interaction. Interaction may shape the "pay-offs" to be achieved from any given encounter and, consequently, shape a state's preferences over actions, but the identity and underlying interests of states are never altered by interaction unless the distribution of relative material capabilities changes.

38. For recent discussions of the role norms play in shaping the legitimacy of certain strategies, see Jeffrey W. Legro, "Military Culture and Inadvertent Escalation in World War II," *International Security* 18, no. 4 (spring 1994): 108–42; and Richard Price, "A Geneology of the Chemical Weapons Taboo," *International Organization* 49, no. 1 (winter 1995): 73–104.

39. See Kowert, "National Identity: Inside and Out," 2.

40. Arnold Wolfers, *Discord and Collaboration* (Baltimore: Johns Hopkins University Press, 1962), 82; Kenneth N. Waltz, *Theory of International Politics* (New York: McGraw-Hill, 1979); and Waltz, "Reflections on *Theory of International Politics*: A Response to My Critics," in *Neorealism and its Critics*, ed. Robert O. Keohane (New York: Columbia University Press, 1986), 323–30.

COLLECTIVE LIBERAL IDENTITY AND DEMOCRATIC PEACE

Now THAT THE basic contours of constructivism have been laid out, it is possible to sketch out a constructivist explanation for democratic peace. A number of scholars have rightly criticized constructivism for failing to offer specific, empirically testable propositions. Critics charge that constructivist concepts are rarely operationalized and appear to be impervious to direct empirical refutation.[41] While this is certainly the case for some constructivist claims, it is incorrect to characterize constructivism as anti-empiricist. Constructivism makes a number of ontological claims about the underlying nature of international politics which, in and of themselves, are difficult to refute empirically. Nevertheless, it is possible to make probabilistic and contingent, but also potentially falsifiable, generalizations from constructivism regarding both the process of identity and collective identity formation, and how we would expect states, and individuals within states, with a given identity or collective identity to behave. To generate propositions from constructivism, we must add substance to the intersubjective meanings that constructivism argues shape state behavior. Specifically, all state identities embody and manifest themselves in a particular cluster of beliefs, values, norms, and practices that influence foreign policy behavior and make it meaningful. Consequently, we can provide a constructivist explanation for democratic peace by deriving propositions from the substance of liberal identity and collective liberal identity regarding the prospects for war and peace. Many of these have been noted already by proponents of ideational explanations for democratic peace. Constructivist analysis adds a broader theoretical framework in which to revisit and refine these arguments and a set of propositions specifying the various processes involved in generating robust ideational bonds among liberal democracies.

In the following sections, I outline the ideational substance of liberal identity, and discuss both the formation and implications of collective liberal identification between states. Before proceeding, three points regarding my treatment of liberalism should be made clear. First, while my discussion touches on both political and economic aspects of liberalism, I place most of the emphasis on political liberalism. I do this because it is the form of liberalism most relevant to questions surround-

---

41. See, for example, Judith Goldstein and Robert O. Keohane, "Ideas and Foreign Policy: an Analytical Framework," in *Ideas and Foreign Policy: Beliefs, Institutions, and Political Change*, ed. Goldstein and Keohane (Ithaca: Cornell University Press, 1993), 6.

ing democratic peace. Economic and political aspects of liberalism are often conjoined in modern capitalist democracies, but economic aspects of liberalism, such as free trade and economic interdependence, do not, in and of themselves, provide persuasive explanations for the separate peace between democracies.[42]

Second, my description of liberalism seeks to outline its contours in the broadest and most generalizable terms. While specific aspects of liberalism, such as the degree of mass political participation seen as desirable or views regarding the responsibility of government to intervene to promote "positive" freedoms and societal welfare, undoubtedly vary across historical contexts, I do not believe this variation undermines any of the basic claims made below. Nevertheless, any analyst seeking to operationalize my arguments must be sensitive to the specific nature of liberalism in the particular spatial and temporal setting being studied.

Finally, my discussion of liberalism as an identity should not be confused with liberal theories of international relations. Liberal international relations theories seek to explain behavior by pointing to the rational-materialist calculations of self-interested individuals and groups.[43] Individuals, groups, or states committed to a liberal identity also subscribe to fixed and transhistorical features of social life, some of which emphasize material components, while others focus on moral components. My intent is not to show that liberal international relations theory explains all human behavior, but to suggest that liberal and collective liberal identity contributes to certain patterns of relations among those actors committed to those identities.

LIBERALISM AND WAR

The foundations of liberal thought can be traced to both philosophers and economists, any complete list of which would include Locke, Rousseau, Montesquieu, Kant, Schumpeter, J. S. Mill, Cobden, Adam Smith, Keynes, and Wilson. Despite a great deal of internal variation, it is possible to make generalizations about the ideational features of liberalism. As John Gray notes, "common to all variants of the liberal

42. Joanne Gowa, "Democratic States and International Disputes," *International Organization* 49, no. 3 (summer 1995): 519–22.

43. See Thomas Risse-Kappen, *Cooperation Among Democracies* (Princeton: Princeton University Press, 1995), 24–27; and Andrew Moravcsik, "Taking Preferences Seriously: A Liberal Theory of International Politics," *International Organization* 51, 4 (autumn 1997): 513–54.

tradition is a definite conception, distinctly modern, of man and society...[and] it is this conception...which gives liberalism a definite identity which transcends its vast internal variety and complexity."[44] The liberal conception of the relationship between individuals and society can be described in terms of three key elements. First, liberalism is individualistic, in that liberals assert the moral primacy of the individual against the claims of any social collectivity. Second, liberalism is fundamentally egalitarian, universalistic, and cosmopolitan. Liberalism is egalitarian in the sense that it confers on all individuals the same moral status and denies that differences in moral worth among human beings have any relevance to the legal or political order. It is universalistic and cosmopolitan in its conception of a moral unity among all human beings and its accordance of only secondary importance to specific historical, cultural, ethnic, or national forms. Third, liberalism is meliorist, embracing an optimistic view of human nature that sees individuals as possessing (1) the moral capacity of forming a conception of the good life, and (2) the intellectual capacity of articulating that conception in attempts to reshape social and political institutions.[45]

Beyond these core conceptual elements, liberalism's view of the individual and society is informed by the contention that all individuals share a fundamental interest in self-preservation and material well-being. The advancement of these interests requires the freedom to follow one's own personal preferences as long as they do not detract from the freedom of others to do the same.[46] Liberals believe that the common interest in self-preservation and material well-being sustains society and all human relationships. They also see coercion and violence as unnecessary for, and corrosive to, political order. For liberals, a stable society is a free society, with the corollary being that repressive societies are unstable and reactionary. More specifically, liberals believe freedom requires the equal protection of certain basic civil liberties and rights to private property and a limited government under the rule of law. Freedom also requires the development of enlightened political institutions that allow governments to be responsive to the needs and ideas of their members. There is no consensus among liberals, however, on exactly what institutions make up the ideal representative government. Democratic government is consistent with liberalism, but

44. John Gray, *Liberalism* (Milton Keynes: Open University Press, 1986), x.
45. See D. J. Manning, *Liberalism* (London: J. M. Dent, 1976).
46. This is the key component in Owen's explanation for democratic peace. Owen, "How Liberalism Produces Democratic Peace," 93–94.

unlimited democratic government risks a tyranny of the majority that is feared by liberals just as much as a tyranny of the minority.[47] In sum, then, liberalism calls for the relative noninterference of society and the independence of the individual, on the one hand, and an entitlement to participate in collective decision making, on the other, but not one specific form of government.

It must be recognized, however, that liberals do not envision a complete harmonization of interest or the total absence of conflict within liberal societies. Indeed, liberals contend that the combination of scarcity and differing positive values make some level of social conflict inevitable.[48] Thus, the fact that liberals posit all individuals to hold certain basic interests in common, does not mean a total synchronization of all interests or the lack of significant disagreements among people (and peoples). Rather, liberals believe that a diversity of opinion must be tolerated and encouraged, because it serves the vital social functions of checking tyranny and encouraging social dynamism.[49]

All of liberalism's views regarding war follow directly from these key tenets. Liberals contend that peace is required to advance the basic common interests in self-preservation and material well-being. They see war as a wasteful diversion of resources from welfare to destruction that is both irrational and unnatural. Liberals believe war is legitimate only as an act of self-defense or the defense of one's friends, or when it is required to free others from the oppression and servitude of tyrannical government. Liberals explain the occurrence of war, despite its irrationality and immorality, by pointing to the governmental structure of certain societies. Liberals see war as arising from the whims and parochial interests of monarchs, statesmen, and soldiers who are unaccountable for their actions, and believe these tendencies would be eliminated if the basic interests of individuals were given expression through constitutional government.[50] As Thomas Paine observed, liberals conclude that "Man is not the enemy of man but through the medium of a false system of government....As the barbarism of the present old governments expires, the moral condition of nations with

47. See Gray, *Liberalism*, 45–62 and 74–75.
48. Moravcsik, "Taking Preferences Seriously."
49. Manning, *Liberalism*, 21.
50. See Michael Howard, *War and the Liberal Conscience* (New Brunswick: Rutgers University Press, 1978), chaps. 1 and 2; and Geoffrey Blainey, *The Causes of War* (New York: Free Press, 1988), chap. 2.

respect to each other will be changed. Man will not be brought up with the savage idea of considering his species his enemy."[51]

THE FORMATION OF COLLECTIVE LIBERAL IDENTITY

Constructivism contends that one significant factor affecting a state's conception of its interests and the appropriate strategies for pursuing these interests, especially how it defines and advances its interest in security, is "the extent to which the self is identified cognitively with the other."[52] Because of this claim, and because it holds the key to understanding the robust peace between liberal democracies, it is essential to explore the conditions that promote positive collective identity formation in greater depth. Constructivism posits that state identities, once produced, are not to be treated as timeless givens, constantly and consistently reproduced by interaction. Instead, they are susceptible to change through the myriad interchanges between actors, whose altering definitions can then reshape the very context and content of interaction. As these identities change through interaction, actors may come negatively to identify with one another, as in the Hobbesian world of self-help envisioned by neorealists. Nevertheless, they may also come positively to identify with one another. This section posits several specific conditions and processes involved in positive collective identification between liberal democracies.

Proposition 1: Positive identification between liberal democracies will be made possible to the extent that the preexisting social structure exhibits sufficient "slack" for positive interaction to occur. Social structures exhibit varying degrees of path dependence. This is the case for several reasons. First, highly institutionalized social structures confront actors as objective and external social facts. This generates a kind of cognitive path-dependency; it becomes difficult for actors to even conceive of alternative arrangements. Second, actors seek to maintain relatively stable conceptions of self and other. This desire is rooted in the desire to minimize uncertainty and anxiety, and to avoid the expected costs of breaking prior commitments.[53] Third, existing social structures privilege certain practices and patterns of behavior whereby actors express themselves as actors. As actors engage in these practices, they of-

51. Quoted in Howard, *War and the Liberal Conscience*, 29–30.
52. Wendt, "Anarchy is What States Make of It," 399.
53. Ibid., 411. See also, Erving Goffman, *The Presentation of Self in Everyday Life* (1959; Woodstock: Overlook Press, 1973).

ten unintentionally reproduce the conditions that make these activities possible. "By analogy, when people walk across a field they may unintentionally create a path. Others subsequently follow and in doing so 'reproduce' the path."[54] Finally, existing social structures also constitute certain national and subnational actors with vested interests in intentionally seeking to maintain the existing order.[55]

The recursive nature of social structure begs a number of questions relevant for our discussion. How does a given social structure at time "t" affect the prospects for positive identification at time "t + 1"? Given the self-reproducing tendencies of social structure, how do we account for change? Or, more specifically, if a given social structure privileges identities and patterns of behavior that foster negative identification between states, how does positive identification between liberal democracies become possible? These questions are crucial to considering the possibility of positive collective identification, because a social structure that is anarchic, hypercompetitive, and predatory may force states to defend egoistic identities, engage in self-help practices, and compete for relative gains, as neorealists suggest. Contrary to the claims of neorealists, however, positive identification between liberal democracies may still be possible even within such a social structure. Three factors help determine the transformative potential of any given social structure in international politics: (1) the "slack" within a given social structure; (2) transformative crises; and (3) changes in a state's corporate identity. Here, I will focus on the first factor. The second and third factors will be discussed in later propositions.

Social structures have varying degrees of slack. Slack represents the level of indeterminacy in a given social structure and therefore delimits the possibilities for transformation.[56] Highly institutionalized structures exhibit very little slack in which transformative activities can occur. In less institutionalized structures, however, there may be more room on the agent side of the agent-structure equation to reshape social relations via positive interaction. Constructivists contend that there is considerably more slack within the so-called self-help system than neorealists assume. Constructivists tend to agree with neoliberals that Darwinian selection, the harshest recursive mechanism for egoistic and

54. Barry Buzan, Charles Jones, and Richard Little, *The Logic of Anarchy: Neorealism to Structural Realism* (New York: Columbia University Press, 1993), 108.

55. See James G. March and Johan P. Olsen, *Rediscovering Institutions: The Organizational Basis of Politics* (New York: Free Press, 1989).

56. See Margaret S. Archer, *Culture and Agency* (New York: Cambridge University Press, 1988), 72–96.

competitive identities, is often muted in international politics.[57] Constructivists also claim that the institution of sovereignty tends to soften or mitigate the institution of self-help, creating a Lockean anarchy in which states enjoy some rights and a certain level of basic security rather than a Hobbesian anarchy characterized by a war of all against all.[58] Of course, as I discuss below, the institution of sovereignty also puts constraints on the degree of positive identification possible. Nevertheless, sovereignty may provide states with a level of discretion not appreciated by neorealists.

Other more specific forms of shared understandings and expectations among certain clusters of states may also generate sufficient slack for positive interaction. Common threat complexes, for example, may allow states who perceive they share a common foe to interact in ways that create a sense of common identification that persists even when the common threat evaporates. In the first decade of the twentieth century, for example, a common perception of the German threat encouraged Britain and France to form the entente cordiale of 1904, thereby establishing a bond between two liberal democracies that persists to this day.[59] Similarly, a constructivist rereading of the cold war would suggest that a common fear of the Soviet Union created the political space for Western democracies (and Japan) positively to identify with one another. As the essays by Mary Hampton and Frank Schimmelfennig in this volume demonstrate, this sense of common identity survived the collapse of the Soviet Union, suggesting that there is more to the Western alliance than neorealism would lead us to expect.[60] Shared perceptions regarding the utility of war as a viable instrument of foreign policy may also generate slack. If states share the belief that war is costly, that defensive military technology and doctrines are rela-

57. Lumsdaine, *Moral Vision in International Politics*, 14; and Robert O. Keohane, *After Hegemony* (Princeton: Princeton University Press, 1984), 82.

58. See Bull, *The Anarchical Society*, 19 and 48–50; Robert H. Jackson and Carl G. Rosberg, "Why Africa's Weak States Persist: The Empirical and the Juridical in Statehood," *World Politics* 35, 1 (October 1982): 1–24; and Wendt, "Anarchy is What States Make of It," 412–15.

59. See Stephen R. Rock, *Why Peace Breaks Out* (Chapel Hill: University of North Carolina Press, 1989), chap. 4.

60. Mary N. Hampton, "NATO, Germany, and the United States: Creating Positive Identity in Trans-Atlantia," *Security Studies* 8, nos. 2/3 (winter 1998/99–spring 1999): 235–69; and Frank Schimmelfennig, "NATO Enlargement: A Constructivist Explanation," *Security Studies*, 8, nos. 2/3 (winter 1998/99–spring 1999): 198–234; See also Richard Ned Lebow, "The Long Peace, the End of the Cold War, and the Failure of Realism," *International Organization*, 48, no. 2 (spring 1994): 249–78; and Risse-Kappen, *Cooperation Among Democracies*, chap. 8.

tively more effective than offensive ones, or that the cumulativity of resources from war is low, then even a neorealist social structure may contain significant slack.[61] Consequently, even if the world is socially constructed in ways broadly compatible with the claims made by neorealism, there may still be room for positive interaction to occur.

Proposition 2: Positive identification between liberal democracies will be fostered by the extent to which structural capacities (spatial relations, physical and technological capacities, and institutional practices) enable or privilege patterns of interaction with other liberal democracies, and/or the extent to which structural constraints "commit" states to take on such identities. The meshing together of resources and rules represent social structural contexts that both enable and privilege certain patterns of interaction. Space and how it is organized (that is, geography and notions of territoriality), the physical and technological capacities of states, and the various institutionalized practices they bring to bear, all help determine which states are likely to interact, as well as how often and on what terms they are likely to do so.[62] This helps shape a state's social identity and the formation of collective identities in two interrelated ways. First, because structure enables and privileges certain patterns of interaction, it helps determine which others matter to the self.[63] Consequently, structure puts some constraints on which other states (or, "significant others") have the greatest impact on the development of a state's social identity. Neighboring countries or states whose geopolitical concerns in particular regions of the globe substantially overlap, for example, are more likely to influence each others' social identities than states structurally predisposed to interact infrequently. Second, insights from role-theory, particularly its notion of "commitment," suggest that the degree to which an actor's relationship to specific sets of important others depends on it "taking" on a particular identity and "playing" a certain role will have a large impact on a state's social identity. In conditions of stark structural asymmetry, certain states may feel compelled to take certain identities and play certain roles if they wish to survive or thrive. To participate in international politics in the post–Second

61. This, of course, borrows from the literature on the security dilemma and the offense-defense balance. The classic here is Robert Jervis, "Cooperation Under the Security Dilemma," *World Politics* 30, no. 2 (January 1978): 167–214. For a recent discussion, see Stephen Van Evera, "Offense, Defense, and the Causes of War," *International Security* 22, no. 4 (spring 1998): 5–43.

62. See Buzan, Jones, and Little, *The Logic of Anarchy*, chap. 4.

63. Morris Rosenberg, "The Self-Concept: Social Product and Social Force," in Rosenberg and Turner, *Social Psychology*, 598–99.

World War era, for example, newly independent polities in Asia and Africa had little choice but to "take" the identity of sovereign-territorial nation-state and accept colonial borders. Likewise, many developing and former communist countries are currently strongly compelled to take on the identity of a "capitalist" and "democratizing" state because favorable social relations with Western states and financial institutions depend on assuming such an identity.[64] States that are not as dependent on a specific identity to maintain critical social relations are structurally less constrained, and more capable of "making" rather than taking their social identities.[65]

This discussion has two implications for the formation of a collective liberal identity. It suggests that liberal states will positively identify most strongly with those liberal states with which they are structurally predisposed to interact most. It also suggests that liberal states are most likely to take on such social identities in structural circumstances in which continued relations with significant others depend on adopting this identity.

Proposition 3: Positive identification between liberal democracies will be fostered by the degree to which the "other" is perceived to resemble the "self," in the sense of sharing liberal beliefs, values, norms, and practices. Following Durkheim's lead, J. H. Turner argues that there will be differentiation in any competitive system where there is the possibility of "falling by the wayside."[66] In international politics, differentiation involves the development of distinctive attributes, such as economic and military capabilities or forms of political organization, that occurs as states seek to better their chances of survival.[67] More specifically, Turner argues that this process tends to result in three basic forms of differentiation: (1) subgroups, whose internal structure is dense relative to other subgroups (in international politics, this includes states, but also integrated transnational organizations, such as the European Union); (2) subcultures, whose stocks of knowledge and repertoires of

64. See, for example, Schimmelfennig's discussion of Eastern European incentives to join NATO in this volume, Schimmelfennig, "NATO Enlargement."

65 Walker, "Symbolic Interactionism and International Politics," 28–31.

66. J. H. Turner, "Analytical Theorizing," in Giddens and Turner, *Social Theory Today*, 185–91.

67. This argument is obviously not consistent with Waltzian neorealism. Waltz holds that the relative functional "sameness" of states tends to minimize the international division of labor. It is not clear how this argument is consistent with Waltz's contention that states have different capabilities to perform similar tasks. This indicates that there *is* differentiation, although for Waltz this is based solely on the distribution of capabilities. See Buzan, Jones, and Little, *The Logic of Anarchy*, 37–47.

beliefs, values, norms, and practices differ from other subcultures (liberal democracies arguably fall in this category, as do transnational ethnic and religious affinities); and (3) hierarchies, which vary in terms of the respective share of material, political, and cultural resources states hold (this includes the traditional distinction between great, middle, and lesser powers).[68]

Generally speaking, differentiation leads to negative identification; the obvious corollary being that the prospects for positive collective identification between states is greater when there is less differentiation. These macro-level processes are supported by the microfoundations provided by various theories in social psychology. Symbolic interactionists contend that categorization is a cognitive necessity to make sense of an otherwise unintelligible environment. Naming oneself and others, and determining what groups one belongs to, represent ways in which states categorize objects in the social world to provide meaning and order. One prominent theory for why actors attach themselves to certain reference groups is based on the process of comparison. According to this argument, when deciding whether they fit into a certain group actors ask: "Do others in the group look and act like me?" More specifically, the perceived congruence of others' ideational commitments with the actor's own has been demonstrated to influence the selection of reference groups.[69] Thus, states are likely to identify positively to some extent with other states that share similar ideational commitments, frequently represented in a state's institutional, cultural, linguistic, historical, or political background.

This leads us to expect that liberal states will positively identify with one another owing to shared common beliefs, values, norms, and practices, instantiated most often in the form of democratic institutions.

Proposition 4: The relative inclusiveness of liberal corporate identity will foster positive identification between liberal democracies. The more exclusive corporate identities of many illiberal states, including illiberal democracies, make extensive positive identification with liberal democracies improbable and may foster negative identification. The corporate need for differentiation and maintenance of a core conception of self, often combined with nationalism and the institution of sovereignty, probably mean that positive identification between states can never be com-

---

68. For a general discussion, see Turner, "Analytical Theorizing," 188.

69. See, John C. Turner, *Rediscovering the Social Group* (Oxford: Basil Blackwell, 1987).

plete.[70] Instead, collective identification represents "a continuum from negative to positive—from conceiving the other as anathema to the self, to conceiving it as an extension of the self," with completely negative and completely positive identifications representing its extremes.[71] This caveat notwithstanding, the specific nature of a state's corporate identity often varies with regard to its inclusiveness and exclusiveness. Certain corporate identities are more universal and inclusive than others. In particular, a liberal corporate identity may be especially inclusive because liberalism's universal and cosmopolitan tenets encourage an expansive notion of the national self. Consequently, we would expect the liberal corporate identity of certain democracies to pose less of a constraint on, and potentially even provide an impetus for, a social identity that positively identifies with other liberal states.[72]

Other more exclusive corporate identities, however, may contribute to negative identification or at least make extensive positive identification with other states improbable.[73] Indeed, a number of democracies in Southern and Eastern Europe, the former Soviet Union, Asia, Africa, and Latin America currently embrace more exclusive conceptions of citizenship and political participation that reject, to varying degrees, liberalism's egalitarian, universal, and cosmopolitan tenets.[74] These illiberal democracies are unlikely to form enduring ideational bonds with liberal democracies. There is also the possibility that democratic norms may not be wholly externalized in democratic dyads containing

70. Wendt, "Collective Identity Formation and the International State," 388. See also Barnett, "Sovereignty, Nationalism, and Regional Order in the Arab States System."

71. Wendt, "Collective Identity Formation and the International State," 386.

72. A similar argument is made by Bruce Cronin in this volume. When explaining the integration of Italy, Cronin notes that this process was facilitated by "the development of a transnational identity that [was] grounded in a cosmopolitan rather than a parochial nationalism" (Bruce Cronin, "From Balance to Community: Transnational Identity and Political Integration," *Security Studies* 8, nos. 2/3 [winter 1998/99–spring 1999]: 271).

73. This argument mirrors the civic-ethnic distinction in the literature on nationalism. See Anthony D. Smith, *The Ethnic Origins of Nationalism* (Cambridge, Mass.: Blackwell, 1986); and Liah Greenfeld, *Nationalism: Five Roads to Modernity* (Cambridge: Harvard University Press, 1992).

74. See Thomas Carothers, "The Democracy Nostrum," *World Policy Journal* 11, no. 3 (fall 1994): 47–54; Donald L. Horowitz, "Democracy in Divided Societies," in *Nationalism, Ethnic Conflict and Democracy*, ed. Larry Diamond and Marc F. Plattner (Baltimore: Johns Hopkins University Press, 1994), 35–55; Ghia Nodia, "Nationalism and Democracy," in Diamond and Plattner, *Nationalism, Ethnic Conflict and Democracy*, 3–22; Samuel P. Huntington, *The Clash of Civilizations and the Remaking of World Order* (New York: Simon & Schuster, 1996); and Fareed Zakaria, "The Rise of Illiberal Democracy," *Foreign Affairs* 76, no. 1 (November/December 1997): 22–43.

such illiberal democracies. In democratic societies where politics is largely organized along cultural, ethnic, or religious lines, the democratic process is likely to be less fluid and more zero-sum. For democratic rules to work, political affiliations and alliances must be somewhat fluid; it must be possible for majorities and minorities to be made and unmade and there must be a certain amount of uncertainty of political outcomes. When the organizing principles of political groups are based on immutable characteristics, such as ethnicity, tribe, or religion, political affiliations are also immutable, and democratic politics loses its fluidity.[75] The exclusivity of these societies may socialize both elites and the public to the view that non-citizens, including the peoples of other democracies, are not deserving of the extension of democratic norms.

Therefore, it is essential to consider the specific substance of a state's corporate identity when trying to determine the likelihood of positive or negative identification with others. With regard to a liberal corporate identity, its universal and cosmopolitan nature is likely to facilitate, rather than impede, positive identification with other liberal states. On the other hand, liberalism's claim that illiberal governments are illegitimate is likely to lead to negative identification with illiberal states, possibly including illiberal democracies.

Proposition 5: Positive identification between liberal democracies will be fostered by the degree, density, many-sidedness, and positive nature of interdependence. Over a given period of time we would expect the degree of collective liberal identification to covary with an increase in these factors. Certain types of interaction can also influence the collective identification of states. These include communication and transaction flows between individuals and social groups from different states, and rising international interdependence. Trade, migration, tourism, cultural and educational exchanges, and advancing means of direct communication can create a "thick social environment" and a "dynamic density," that deepens state opinions about one another. Furthermore, the more direct and many-sided (that is, located in multiple settings and taking multiple forms) these interactions are, the more likely they are to impact the social identities of states. Where a proper foundation exists, as it appears to among many contemporary Western democracies, these processes can create or accentuate feelings of similarity and shared stocks of knowledge, thus accelerating the positive identification be-

75. Horowitz, "Democracy in Divided Societies," 46–47.

tween states.[76] Rising interdependence between states also has implications for the utilities (material and non-material) states receive from interacting with one another. The increased vulnerability and sensitivity of states to the moves of one another "reduces the ability to meet corporate needs unilaterally and increases the extent to which actors share a common fate."[77] Where the maintenance of interdependence creates positive utilities, it generates incentives for states to identify with those states with which they share their fate.

The evolution of liberal affinity between Britain and the United States during the nineteenth century demonstrates these processes at work. Absolute levels of multilayered, sustained, and intimate economic interactions were very high throughout the nineteenth century. Moreover, Anglo-American economic interdependence failed to generate high levels of anxiety between the two states because their interactions were broadly complementary. In the commercial realm, for example, Britain relied on trade with the United States for agricultural goods and raw materials while America imported British manufactured goods.[78] Furthermore, the degree and density of Anglo-American interactions across other spheres of life and between all levels of society increased dramatically over the course of the nineteenth century. Increasingly rapid and efficient forms of communication and transportation played an important facilitating role from the middle of the nineteenth century onward. Private correspondence, transatlantic press coverage, tourism, and intermarriage all increased significantly. As interaction and the reciprocal flow of information increased, so did the warmth of relations. This positive interaction, and the ongoing political development of Britain as a liberal democracy, helped the two

76. See Karl W. Deutsch, *Political Community and the North Atlantic Area* (Westport, Conn.: Greenwood, 1957); Michael Taylor, *Community, Anarchy and Liberty* (New York: Cambridge University Press, 1982).

77. Wendt, "Collective Identity Formation and the International State," 389; and David M. Cheshier and Cori E. Dauber, "The Place and Power of Civic Space: Reading Globalization and Social Geography Through the Lens of Civilizational Conflict," *Security Studies* 8, nos. 2/3 (winter 1998/99–spring 1999): 50.

78. The growth of American industry in the late nineteenth century reduced this complmentarity somewhat, but because Britain continued to rely on American imports, commercial retaliation was not seen as a viable option to assuage the occasional resentment resulting from this increased competition. See Rock, *Why Peace Breaks Out*, 42–48.

countries overcome a long history of competition and distrust to forge a strong sense of liberal affinity.[79]

In relations between liberal countries, the traditional separation between state and society probably facilitates these diverse processes by encouraging the proliferation of autonomous transnational relations between the societal actors of different liberal polities.[80] Of course, high levels of communication, transaction flows, and rising interdependence may lead to a sense of vulnerability and accentuate feelings of difference as much as similarity, and thus generate negative identification. The utilities resulting from interaction could also be highly asymmetric or negative. In contrast to the Anglo-American experience, for example, trade flows between Britain and Germany created an enormous sense of mutual vulnerability.[81] Therefore, these systemic processes cannot be viewed as universally likely to foster positive identification. The positive or negative nature of identification is highly contingent on the preexisting foundation of common understandings and shared stocks of knowledge, as well as the utilities produced by interaction.[82] Nevertheless, when transactions, communication, and positive interdependence increase in degree and density, are manysided, and generate positive utilities between liberal states, we would expect these states to increasingly positively identify with one another. Indeed, this outcome may be more likely to foster positive identification between liberal states than is the case with other types of states because the key tenets of liberalism predispose liberal polities to see such material and ideational intercourse as serving the best interests of both states' peoples.

Proposition 6: Positive identification between liberal democracies will be fostered by repeated cooperation between states with liberal identities. Game theorists have long contended that iteration and lengthening the "shadow of the future" can facilitate cooperation among self-interested actors in situations where market failures and collective action prob-

79. See H. C. Allen, *Great Britain and the United States: A History of Anglo-American Relations (1783–1952)* (New York: St. Martin's, 1955), 27, 32, 109–30, 166, and chap. 6.

80. Doyle, "Liberalism and World Politics," 1161; and Risse-Kappen, "Democratic Peace—Warlike Democracies?" 508.

81. Rock, *Why Peace Breaks Out*, 76–84.

82. This argument is also advanced by Cronin, "From Balance to Community: Transnational Identity and Political Integration," 283–84.

lems would otherwise make such cooperation problematic.[83] As with other rationalist accounts, such analyses tend to see the outcome as resulting merely from changes in expectations about behavior, not changes in the identities and interests of the actors involved. Constructivists suggest, however, that repeated consistent interaction (such as cooperation) institutionalizes sets of intersubjective meanings. As the symbolic interactionist notion of reflective appraisals discussed above suggests, actors come to see themselves in part as others see them. Furthermore, each social act generates expectations regarding the behavior of self and other in future interactions. Thus, through repeated cooperative behavior, states may come positively to identify with one another as they come to internalize a "cooperative" identity, and come to see others as sharing that identity. As Wendt argues, "by teaching others and themselves to cooperate…actors are simultaneously learning to identify with each other—to see themselves as a 'we' bound by certain norms."[84] A sense of "we-ness" shapes identity-based behavioral expectations that, in turn, contribute to a self-fulfilling prophecy of further cooperation and positive identification.[85] This leads us to expect that the degree of positive identification between liberal states will be enhanced over time, as cooperative behavior at time "t" begets even more cooperative behavior at time "t+1." We would also expect liberal-democratic norms and practices of peaceful conflict resolution to reinforce this process.

Proposition 7: When negative identification is already institutionalized, militarized crises will tend to reproduce negative identification. When positive identification is not far advanced, or if militarized crises escalate to war, such events will likely contribute to a significant regression of relations between liberal democracies. If a robust foundation for a collective liberal identity exists, however, disputes and crises that fail to escalate are unlikely to erode positive identification and may even strengthen the bonds between liberal democracies. Once institutionalized, certain types of collective identification tend to become quite robust; institutionalized meanings often become taken-for-granted elements that contribute to path dependence. In such contexts, militarized crises between states can potentially play pivotal roles in reproducing or transforming institu-

83. See Kenneth A. Oye, "Explaining Cooperation Under Anarchy: Hypotheses and Strategies," in *Cooperation Under Anarchy*, ed. Kenneth A. Oye (Princeton: Princeton University Press, 1986), 1–24.

84. Wendt, "Collective Identity Formation and the International State," 390.

85. Risse-Kappen, "Democratic Peace—Warlike Democracies?" 504–5.

tionalized social identities. Militarized crises are likely to contribute to negative identification under a number of circumstances. If negative identification is already firmly institutionalized, militarized crises are likely to reproduce this negative identification by confirming expectations about behavior. Moreover, if states are moving along the continuum away from negative identification toward increasingly positive identification, but are still not very far along, it is likely that militarized crises will contribute to a regression. This is especially likely if the states involved have a salient history of negative interaction that shapes their interpretations of behavior during the crisis.[86] Finally, if a militarized crisis escalates to war, even a robust collective liberal identity may disintegrate. As the work of historical and sociological institutionalists in comparative politics demonstrates, large crises (alternatively referred to as "punctuations," "shocks," or "critical junctures") can fundamentally disrupt the path dependence created by existing institutions.[87] Large crises can radically alter existing institutions by causing actors to question the very foundations upon which their current patterns of interaction are organized. A similar point is made by ethnomethodologists when they speak of the severe irreconcilabilities that sometimes arise between behavior and meaning, referred to as a "breach." A breach results in interaction between actors being unintelligible when based on existing sets of meaning. This increases anxiety and obviates trust, causing actors to reinterpret the world around them.[88]

For reasons discussed in propositions 8–10 below, such severe crises and wars are unlikely between states sharing a robust collective liberal identity. Consequently, once such an identity is established, the violent transformative events that normally promote negative identification become less likely. Furthermore, ethnomethodological experiments indicate that actors who share common understandings enter into relations with one another willing to overlook a great deal. They also tend to do a great deal of accommodative work to normalize interactions

86. See Jervis, *Perception and Misperception in International Politics*, chaps. 4 and 6; and Richard Ned Lebow, *Between Peace and War: The Nature of International Crisis* (Baltimore: Johns Hopkins University Press, 1981), 310–17.

87. See Kathleen Thelen and Sven Steimo, "Historical Institutionalism in Comparative Politics," in *Structuring Politics: Historical Institutionalism in Comparative Analysis*, ed. Kathleen Thelen, Sven Steimo, and Frank Longstretch (New York: Cambridge University Press, 1992), 1–32.

88. Turner, *A Theory of Social Interaction*, 49–50; and Heritage, "Ethnomethodology," 232–35.

that appear to be short-circuiting.[89] As a result, inconsistent behavior and uncertainty are resolved in ways favorable to the maintenance of the relationship and the threshold required for a breach is set very high. The implication of this line of reasoning is that disputes and crises that do not escalate between states which share a positive collective identity are unlikely to dissolve the relationship.

In some cases disputes and crises may actually strengthen the collective bond between liberal democracies. Crises may serve as wake-up calls that clarify the importance of maintaining the relationship and the need to take steps to avoid additional crises down the line.[90] The 1898 Venezuelan boundary dispute between the United States and Britain, for example, served to accelerate and solidify positive identification between the two liberal states. Elite and public opinion in the two countries were terrified by how close the US and Britain came to a "fratricidal" war and resolved themselves to avoid any risk of such a conflict arising in the future.[91] The peaceful resolution of serious disputes and crises may also contribute to positive identification among liberal democracies by confirming identity-based expectations about behavior (that is, the expectation that liberal-democracies will externalize norms of peaceful conflict resolution). Indeed, the deescalation of crises may even contribute to positive identification among members of the liberal-democratic community not directly involved via a kind of demonstration effect.

COLLECTIVE LIBERAL IDENTITY AND PEACE

Positive collective identification between liberal democracies should be expected to generate peace for several reasons.

Proposition 8: States sharing a sense of collective liberal identity should define their national security interests in compatible and/or collective ways. This should preclude wars stemming from irresolvable conflicts of national interest. Compatible and/or collective definitions of national security interests should also lead liberal democracies to ally more frequently with one another, be less fearful of relative shifts in the distribution

89. Randall Collins, "On the Microfoundations of Macrosociology," *American Journal of Sociology* 86, no. 5 (March 1981): 995.
90. A similar argument is made by Benedict Anderson when he discusses the effect civil wars have on bolstering nationalism. See Benedict Anderson, *Imagined Communities* (New York: Verso 1991), 199–203.
91. Rock, *Why Peace Breaks Out*, 50–57.

of military capabilities among members of the liberal community, and avoid taking advantage of opportunities to advance their relative position through the use of violent means. The opposites should be more likely in relations with illiberal states. It is often treated as a truism of international relations that, in the absence of a central authority to provide the collective good of security (that is, in a condition of anarchy), disorder is the rule, competition is fierce and zero-sum, and cooperation is difficult. Nevertheless, these outcomes, while frequently the result of particular anarchic environments, do not necessarily follow from the absence of central authority. Social order can be maintained, and cooperation facilitated, under anarchy if actors enjoy a sense of positive collective identification, or "community."[92] Positive collective identification entails a concern for the welfare of others who fall within the community. It does so by leading to a redefinition of the self-concept, potentially to such an extent that others come to be seen as a cognitive extension of the self rather than independent. While positive identification is unlikely to ever be complete in international politics, this does not mean that feelings of community and solidarity cannot go a long way in generating interests that facilitate policy coordination and pacific relations between certain states. It is important to remember that collective identification represents a continuum from negative to positive. As one moves closer to the positive end, cooperation and pacific relations become more likely. The universal and cosmopolitan qualities of a liberal identity make movement toward the positive end of the continuum more likely between liberal states than may be the case with other identities. Consequently, if any states are likely to identify with one another to such an extent that war begins to look like fratricide, liberal states are likely candidates. Therefore, we would expect the institution of self-help to be transformed in situations of positive collective identification between liberal states.

This conclusion is reinforced by the social psychological findings of minimal group experiments and social identity theory. These findings suggest that once actors positively identify with others, and form a group or community, they tend to accentuate both similarities among the members of their group and differences between their group and other groups. The results of minimal group experiments suggest that even in situations of minimal identification, no history of interaction,

---

92. See Taylor, *Community, Anarchy and Liberty*, chap. 1; and Hampton, "NATO, Germany, and the United States," 229–30.

and no competition over scarce resources, actors seek to maximize the differences between their in-group and the perceived out-group. Actors exhibit a tendency toward self-help and a concern for relative gains between groups, but they also demonstrate strong tendencies toward sharing, cooperation, and perceived mutuality of interests among members of the same group. Social identity theory (SIT) posits the reason for this to be a universal desire for self-esteem, which is enhanced by maximizing distinctions between groups that actors positively identify with and those they do not.[93]

Recently, Mercer has argued that these findings provide a social psychological foundation for neorealism's contention that self-help and concerns for relative gains dominate relations between states. Mercer bases this claim on the assumption that states represent groups that we would expect, according to the minimal group experiments and SIT, to exaggerate their differences with other states, engage in self-help, and compete for relative gains. He thus argues that constructivism is overly optimistic about the prospects of positive identification between states. In Mercer's words, "nature trumps process."[94] Mercer's conclusions, however, do not follow from his analysis of minimal group experiments and the arguments of SIT. Participants in the minimal group experiments were divided into groups based on arbitrary factors. The identity and group status of these individuals were givens in these experiments, because the researchers were not interested in what makes individuals choose certain reference groups over others. Instead, the researchers were only interested in how individuals behaved once they perceived themselves to be in a certain group. This begs the question of what leads to the formation of in-groups and out-groups on the first place? It cannot be assumed that individuals across societies will necessarily see themselves to be in completely distinct groups, just as each collection of individuals within societies do not necessarily form distinctive groups.[95] If states are social, they can form groups based on the factors and processes outlined above. Moreover, in the case of liberal

---

93. See Henri Tajfel and John C. Turner, "The Social Identity Theory of Intergroup Behavior," in *Psychology of Intergroup Relations*, second edition, ed. Stephen Worchel and William G. Austin (Chicago: Nelson-Hall, 1986), 7–24. See also Kowert, "National Identity: Inside and Out," 16–17.

94. Jonathan Mercer, "Anarchy and Identity," *International Organization* 49, no. 2 (spring 1995): 236.

95. See Wolfers, *Discord and Collaboration*, 93–94; and Keohane, *After Hegemony*, 124.

democracies, the universal and cosmopolitan nature of liberalism predisposes these states to see themselves as part of the same group.

Mercer's conclusions result from a confusion over the "self" aspect of "self-help." For Mercer, the contrast is between self-help, emphasized by neorealists, and the possibility of "other-help," emphasized by constructivists. Constructivists, however, do not argue that positive identification leads to the abandonment of self-help. Instead, they simply contend that the "boundaries of the self are not inherently limited to corporate identity," and that positive identification leads to an expanded notion of self.[96] It may be the case that certain forms of other-help could arise from specific altruistic identities, but this is not the same as a positive collective identity that simply makes the self a larger unit. Mercer's conclusions also assume that, for constructivists, positive identification depends on states being empathetic with one another, which he contends is difficult and unlikely.[97] Empathy is not the only route to positive identification, however, and is rarely a necessary condition. Mercer is correct that "perspective taking" plays an essential role as the precondition for social interaction in constructivist theory, but it is well established in social psychology that positive identification can also stem from a perceived congruence of beliefs, values, norms, and practices. This depends very little on successfully taking the perspective of the other. Furthermore, to the extent that empathy is required, it is likely to exist between liberal states that share basic underlying assumptions about the nature of the world. Thus, Mercer is right that there are likely to be in-groups and out-groups in international politics, but each may contain a community of states, and one of those communities is likely to be liberal.

These criticisms notwithstanding, Mercer's analysis is invaluable for understanding the relationship among members of the liberal in-group, and between this in-group and the illiberal out-group. It helps us understand why we would expect liberal democracies to define their basic interests in self-preservation and material well-being in compatible or collective ways, ally more frequently, and put less emphasis on self-help and the distribution of relative gains amongst themselves.[98] It also helps us understand why we would expect liberal states to continue to

---

96. Wendt, "Collective Identity Formation and the International State," 387.

97. Mercer, "Anarchy and Identity," 246–49.

98. For further discussion of positive identification as a source of cooperation, see Michael Spirtas, "French Twist: French and British NATO Policies from 1949 to 1966," *Security Studies* 8, no. 2 (winter 1998/99): 302–346.

adopt self-help and relative gains postures vis-à-vis illiberal states. In the late nineteenth century, for example, the economic and industrial potential of the United States was clearly a greater challenge to British hegemony than the one posed by Germany.[99] Nevertheless, both Britain and the United States saw Germany as a more significant threat. To a significant degree, this disjuncture between material power and threat perception stemmed from positive liberal identification between Britain and America and a common Anglo-American distrust of illiberal Germany.[100]

Proposition 9: States sharing a sense of collective liberal identity should engage in accommodative work for each other, resolve uncertainty favorably, and externalize norms of peaceful conflict resolution. This should preclude wars stemming from the security dilemma. In their relations with illiberal states, however, uncertainty should generate more tension and instances of misperception and conflict. We would expect the existence of shared stocks of knowledge and values to lead states sharing a sense of collective liberal identity to resolve situations of uncertainty favorably. This should make their relations more pacific by defusing the mutual fears and misperceptions that drive the security dilemma. Insights from phenomenology and ethnomethodology suggest that the degree to which actors share certain implicit stocks of knowledge and understandings determines the likelihood that interaction will be intelligible and comfortable. This provides actors with a sense that they share a common universe with certain others, making those social relations more stable than those where actors view the world in fundamentally different ways. Actors should also be expected to do a great deal of accommodative work for one another.[101] This should make the relationship between liberal states robust in the face of all but the most irreconcilable behavior.

This general tendency is reinforced by the specific nature of liberal democratic norms and practices. Liberalism contends that conflicts of interest and disagreements of opinion are natural, legitimate, and socially productive. Therefore, we would expect liberal states to have disagreements and occasional crises, just as individuals and social groups within liberal societies do. Under most circumstances, however,

---

99. See Paul Kennedy, *The Rise and Fall of Great Powers* (New York: Vintage Books, 1987), 242–49.

100. Allen, *Great Britain and the United States*, 257.

101. See Turner, *A Theory of Social Interaction*, 73–84 and 95–98. See also Harold Garfinkel, *Studies in Ethnomethodology* (Cambridge, Mass: Polity, 1984).

we would not expect these crises to call a state's liberal identity into question. Moreover, because liberal states view other liberal states as sharing a common commitment to norms of peaceful conflict resolution, they are unlikely to fear that other liberal states will try to dominate or exploit them, and will tend to adopt strategies in their relations with one another that resolve disputes and crises before they escalate. Thus, collective liberal identification not only works to prevent wars stemming from pure and irreconcilable conflicts of interest, but also helps keep the peace by defusing the security dilemma.[102]

In contrast, the lack of common understandings and divergent approaches to the conduct of foreign policy are likely to increase uncertainty and anxiety between liberal and illiberal states. This increases the risk that misunderstandings and misperceptions will lead to conflict. This general tendency is further compounded by the fact that liberalism posits illiberal states to be unstable, reckless, and aggressive. As a result, liberal states are likely to fear and distrust illiberal ones, aggravating the security dilemma. As Ernest May notes, these dynamics were in evidence during the lead up to American intervention in the First World War:

> What Germany and the United States lacked was precisely the underpinning of mutual comprehension and trust that allowed Britain and America to adjust their differences....When Wilson spoke of "lasting peace"...[m]ost of his countrymen, bred in the Liberal consensus...understood what he meant. So did most Englishmen....Despite Kant's famous essay, few Germans shared the Liberal dream of eternal peace...German-American negotiations were always troubled by differences in meaning, intention, and outlook.[103]

Proposition 10: Democratic institutions facilitate and reinforce the processes whereby collective liberal identification produces peace. Thus far little has been said about the role democratic institutions play in promoting peace between liberal democracies. While institutional explanations for democratic peace, by themselves, provide an incomplete understanding of relations between liberal democracies, a constructivist analysis allows us to envision at least three ways in which democratic institutions contribute to the peace established between liberal states. First, demo-

102. On collective liberal identity and the security dilemma, see Risse-Kappen, "Democratic Peace—Warlike Democracies?" 504–5.
103. Ernest May, *The World War and American Isolation* (Cambridge: Harvard University Press, 1966), 434–35.

cratic institutions potentially provide the mechanism through which liberal tenets influence foreign policy.[104] Second, democratic institutions serve as important mechanisms to socialize individuals, thus helping to maintain the corporate elements of a state's liberal identity.[105] In those societies where the foundation for a liberal identity exists, acts such as voting, exercising free speech, and observing legislative debates and the peaceful accommodation evident in the democratic process at all levels of government assist in the reproduction of liberal beliefs, values, norms, and practices. These ideas in turn serve to legitimize these same institutions. Thus, democratic institutions represent important elements of a liberal state's corporate identity and serve as doubly important intervening variables in a constructivist explanation for democratic peace.

Finally, democratic institutions may serve as important signposts or cues whereby states identify and categorize one another, and themselves, as liberal in the social sense. This is especially likely when these institutions conform to a state's own conception of what it means to be liberal at a given point in time.[106] The transparency of democratic institutions likely facilitates this mutual perception of "likeness" by allowing democratic states and their constituent individuals to recognize similar clusters of beliefs, values, norms, and practices in other democratic polities.[107]

None of this means that the existence of democratic institutions automatically transforms a state into a liberal one, or transforms all clusters of democratic states into liberal communities. As noted previously, there can be democratic institutions in polities committed to more exclusive corporate and social identities. These democracies may be fundamentally illiberal, because they fail to embrace liberalism's egalitarian, universal, and cosmopolitan tenets. Therefore, the existence of democratic institutions is not sufficient to lead liberal democracies to define their interests in compatible or collective ways, lessen concerns about relative shifts in military capabilities, engage in fewer crises, ally more frequently, etc. When we speak of the separate peace established between liberal democracies, both the "liberal" and the

104. See Owen, "How Liberalism Produces Democratic Peace," 93 and 99–101.
105. For a general discussion, see Zucker, "The Role of Institutionalization in Cultural Persistence."
106. Owen, "Perceptions and the Limits of Liberal Peace," 155–59.
107. Risse-Kappen, "Democratic Peace—Warlike Democracies?" 508.

"democratic" part are important to understanding the most robust aspects of the phenomenon.

INTERSUBJECTIVE ONTOLOGY AND INTERPRETIVE EPISTEMOLOGY

The causal variable posited by the constructivist explanation for democratic peace is collective liberal identity. Specifically, this social identity is manifested in the ideational features of liberalism and collective liberal identification that make the foreign policy behavior of liberal states, and their constituent individuals and social groups, meaningful. This sense of community helps foster peaceful relations via the general properties of positive identification (that is, by reducing the concern for relative gains, reducing mutual suspicion, resolving uncertainty favorably, etc.), as well as the specific beliefs, values, norms, and practices inherent in a liberal identity. These tenets define the strategic situation and values involved, and determine which strategies should be undertaken. What security is, what represents a threat to that security, and views regarding the legitimacy of force as the final arbiter of disputes are defined in terms of a shared commitment to liberalism and a recognition by both parties of this commitment. Thus, the constructivist explanation has a fundamentally intersubjective ontology. When a proposed causal variable is grounded in how actors see the world, the only viable epistemological approach is one that takes intersubjective meanings seriously.[108] Consequently, adding a constructivist analysis to the democratic peace research program requires scholars to adopt an interpretive epistemology that seeks to explore the meanings, understandings, and interpretations of the relevant actors, the processes involved in generating these intersubjective meanings, and the behavioral patterns that result.

There are numerous interpretive approaches to social science. All forms of interpretivism share some resistance to the notion that explanations and theories are true only insofar as they correspond to directly observable "facts" and behavior. Interpretivists all emphasize the intimate and symbiotic relationship between subjects and objects and

108. Friedrich V. Kratochwil and John G. Ruggie, "International Organization: A State of the Art on an Art of the State," *International Organization* 48, no. 2 (spring 1986): 764–66.

the challenges this poses for social science. Human subjectivity and intersubjectivity raises a unique challenge for studying social actors and explaining their behavior: the problem of meaningful, value-laden social action. To understand human behavior, analysts must understand the perceptions and understandings of the actors involved, as well as the normative and symbolic contexts in which action takes place; they must engage in what Max Weber called *verstehen*. Intersubjectivity also poses problems from the analyst's point of view. The analyst's own perceptions, prior understandings, experiences, and values are argued by interpretivists to complicate the analyst's ability to detach himself/herself from the social world. In its most extreme form, the second part of this critique leads some to reject objectivity as a fantasy and view "modernist" social science and the quest for causal explanation as a dangerous fraud.[109] This last position is too extreme. Acknowledgment of the challenges posed by intersubjectivity calls for modesty in causal claims and self-awareness and intellectual honesty regarding an analyst's own predispositions, but does not necessarily call for the abandonment of modernist social science. It is possible to make contingent and probabilistic generalizations about the causes of human behavior even if we recognize the phenomenological nature of the world.[110] Indeed, rhetoric that rejects notions of causal explanation and generalization notwithstanding, many interpretivists in practice implicitly incorporate some kind of causal analysis into their discussions of human behavior.

This interpretive approach obviously stands in sharp contrast to the approach adopted by proponents of an extreme, or "hard," positivist position. Hard positivist ontology subscribes to a clocklike view of the social world that envisions human behavior to be guided by transhistorical laws akin to those (believed to exist) in the natural world. Hard positivist epistemology contends that observable physical facts represent all the facts there are and draws a sharp distinction between subject and object, both in terms of explaining human behavior and in

---

109. For examples and discussions of the spectrum of interpretive approaches, see Fred R. Dallmayr and Thomas A. McCarthy, eds., *Understanding and Social Inquiry* (Notre Dame: University of Notre Dame Press, 1977); Daniel Little, *Varieties of Social Explanation* (Boulder: Westview, 1991), chaps. 4 and 11; and Harold Kincaid, *Philosophical Foundations of the Social Sciences* (New York: Cambridge University Press, 1996), chap. 6. For a discussion of interpretivist approaches to the study of ideas in international relations, see Albert S. Yee, "The Effects of Ideas on Policies," *International Organization* 50, no. 1 (winter 1996): 94–103.

110. See Adler, "Seizing the Middle Ground," 325–30.

terms of the analyst's ability to make firm, fact-value distinctions. For these scholars, social theories are supported and falsified based only on observable phenomena and behavior.[111] In short, there is no place for intersubjectivity.

Few political scientists, let alone contemporary philosophers of science, embrace such a hard positivist stance. Indeed, the form of interpretivism advocated here is not a radical disconnection from the approach taken by a large number, perhaps a majority, of political scientists whom we might call "soft" positivists. Soft positivists study politics with methodological rigor, and search for regularities, but are more sensitive to history and the inherent plasticity involved in all "laws" relating to human behavior.[112] Thus, the form of interpretivism advocated here, because it provides an internal critique of the key factors in a particular causal explanation rather than an external critique of the modernist project of causal explanation in general, stakes out a position capable of generating genuine and productive dialogue among a wide range of international relations scholars.

OPERATIONALIZING THE CONSTRUCTIVIST EXPLANATION

If the proposition that collective liberal identity generates democratic peace is to be made susceptible to empirical investigation, the key causal variable, collective liberal identity, must be operationalized in a plausible way. The first step is to recognize the obvious: states are not individuals, they are collectivities of individuals. Up to this point, this essay has been guilty of anthropomorphizing the state in a way not unlike other theories that treat the state as a unitary actor. This is done primarily for heuristic purposes; it simplifies and streamlines analysis. It is imperative that we recognize that terms such as "liberal identity" and "collective liberal identity" refer to macrophenomena that themselves are not directly observable. This does not mean they do not "exist"; they can be very real, in the sense of enabling and shaping behavior. Nevertheless, as Michael Spirtas observes elsewhere in this volume, "to give the concept of identity real value we need to find ways

---

111. See Anthony Giddens, *Studies in Social and Political Theory*, chap. 1.

112. See, for example, Jack Snyder, "Richness, Rigor, and Relevance in the Study of Soviet Foreign Policy," *International Security* 9, no. 3 (winter 1984/85): 89–108; Gabriel Almond and Stephen Genco, "Clouds, Clocks, and the Study of Politics," in *A Discipline Divided: Schools and Sects in Political Science*, ed. Gabriel Almond (Newbury Park, Calif.: Sage, 1990), 32–65; and Atul Kohli et al., "The Role of Theory in Comparative Politics: A Symposium," *World Politics* 48, no. 1 (October 1995): 1–49.

to make it more observable and understandable."[113] To avoid reifying an unobservable, and possibly nonexistent, variable, we require what sociologists call "microtranslations." Microtranslations are descriptions of lower-level phenomena, processes, and behavior embodied in higher order phenomena.[114] Thus, to operationalize the constructivist explanation, we must translate the concept of collective liberal identity into microphenomena. This involves locating collective meanings in the perceptions, understandings, and behavior of individuals.

Two types of microtranslations are required. First, we require microtranslations that get at the sense of collective identity between particular states. Analysts cannot interrogate all the individuals of a given polity in an attempt to discover their perceptions and opinions regarding other states. Instead, we require aggregate data where available, and a representative sample of sources from which we can reasonably infer collective meanings. We also require a multidimensional method of interpreting these sources in order to maximize our ability to identify their central meanings. Second, we require behavioral microtranslations that get at the lower-level processes and patterns of behavior through which collective liberal identity leads to peaceful relations between states. This requires deducing the observable behavioral patterns we would expect logically to follow from the unobservable aspects of the explanation. These microtranslations serve as observable links in a causal chain that allow us to use behavioral evidence empirically to evaluate the constructivist explanation for democratic peace.[115]

TRANSLATING COLLECTIVE MEANINGS

State identity, as it is used here, refers to the beliefs, values, norms, and practices that characterize a particular polity and its foreign policy. These ideational phenomena are collective in nature and are transmitted and modified from one generation of individuals to another through various mechanisms of socialization and recursive patterns of

---

113. Spirtas, "French Twist," 346.
114. Collins, "On the Microfoundations of Macrosociology." Microtranslations differ from "microfoundations," which are lower-level theories.
115. A number of constructivists have drawn on insights from scientific realism, which contends that unobservable phenomena are "real" to the extent that they consistently correlate with outcomes which logically flow from them. See, for example, Wendt, "The Agent-Structure Problem in International Relations Theory"; and Dessler, "What's at Stake in the Agent-Structure Debate?" To make the argument more conducive to testing and potential falsification, however, we need microtranslations.

behavior. Collective liberal identity is a social identity that refers to the sense on the part of members of one state that the boundaries of their political community extend, to varying degrees, to members of another state, and that this community is defined in terms of a shared commitment to liberalism. Consequently, analysts should seek to discover how individuals within states define themselves in relation to others, define the nature of national security and threats to that security, and define the legitimacy of force as a policy instrument in their relations with particular states.

To establish whether states view one another as liberal democracies, analysts should interrogate several different types of sources. To measure public attitudes, researchers should analyze public opinion and voting data (where it is available), and the treatment, images, and representations of other states in newspapers, educational texts, and popular culture. To measure elite attitudes, researchers should analyze the prevailing conceptions that shape the policy discourse among decision-makers. Specifically, analysts should focus on the framing and content of policy debates conducted in national cabinets, legislatures, and the editorial pages of major national newspapers.[116] Obviously, both public records (texts of speeches, legislative debates, public interviews, articles, etc.) and private sources (private minutes, diaries, memoirs, etc.) should be used where available.

When interrogating these sources, analysts should adopt a multidimensional interpretive method that searches for a congruence, or lack thereof, of perceptions and understandings regarding other states. As Johnston has persuasively demonstrated, the more and varied the interpretive techniques, the better the chances of "triangulating" on the central meanings involved. Following Johnston's lead, analysts should use three distinct methods of interpretation.[117] The first approach is to analyze explicit statements made in public and private sources for what they do and do not say about the notions of national identity and the degree of affinity between states. Obviously this approach is, by itself, insufficient; not everything that is meant is said and what is said is not always what is meant. Therefore, we need additional interpretive methods as well. A second method involves interrogating the sources for their causal logics. This calls for the analyst to outline, or "map,"

116. This builds on suggestions made by Charles A. Kupchan, *The Vulnerability of Empire* (Ithaca: Cornell University Press, 1994), 29 and 101–2.

117. See Alastair Iain Johnston, *Cultural Realism: Strategic Culture and Grand Strategy in Chinese History* (Princeton: Princeton University Press, 1995), 49–52.

the structure of means-ends relations across the spectrum of representative sources being interpreted. The more closely these causal logics parallel the means-ends relationships inherent in a liberal identity and sense of collective liberal identity, the more reasonable it is to infer that these forms of identification exist.[118]

A third interpretive approach, symbolic analysis, is more complicated and controversial, and thus requires greater elaboration. Symbols can be any kind of object used to represent meanings that are not inherent in, nor discernible from, the object itself.[119] "Every symbol stands for something other than itself, and it also evokes an attitude, a set of impressions, or a pattern of events associated through time, through space, through logic, or through imagination with the symbol."[120] The symbols that concern us here are what Mead called "significant symbols."[121] These are social symbols, not individualistic and particularistic symbols, that index important elements of liberal identity and a sense of collective liberal identity. Symbols are traditionally divided into "referential symbols" and "condensational symbols." Referential symbols are purely denotative; they are economical ways of referring to objects with no meaning beyond the immediate object to which they refer. The more important type of symbols here are condensational ones. These symbols are socially constructed condensations, or summaries, that evoke shared beliefs, emotions, or experiences associated with an object.[122] These symbols can have both emotive and cognitive components. The emotive component refers to how positively or negatively a particular object, such as another state, is viewed. The cognitive component refers to what actors know and associate with a particular object.[123]

Interpreting condensational symbols for their emotive and cognitive meanings is potentially a powerful means of getting at a polity's collective sense of identification with other states. As Elder and Cobb note:

---

118. See the discussion of "cognitive mapping" in Johnston, *Cultural Realism*, 50 and chap. 3.

119. Charles D. Elder and Roger W. Cobb, *The Political Uses of Symbols* (New York: Longman, 1983), 28. I am indebted to Johnston's citations in *Cultural Realism* for putting me on to this text.

120. Murray Edelman, *The Symbolic Uses of Politics* (Chicago: University of Illinois Press, 1985), 6.

121. Mead, *Mind, Self, and Society*, 71–72.

122. See Edelman, *The Symbolic Uses of Politics*, 6–9.

123. See Elder and Cobb, *The Political Uses of Symbols*, 7–55 and 83.

Because they are simultaneously elements of culture and objects of individual meaning, these symbols provide a linkage between the individual and the larger social and political order. They mediate the relationship between the individual and social reality, structuring people's perceptions and allowing them to find meaning in events beyond their own immediate experience.[124]

Consequently, when seeking to determine a polity's collective perceptions and understandings regarding other states, researchers should search sources for condensational symbols that indicate a sense of affinity, or lack thereof. The types of symbols that could be analyzed are in principle quite varied. To simplify matters, however, it is probably sufficient to focus on verbal symbols, given the tendency for nonverbal symbols to "pass through the relay of language, which extracts their meanings...and names their referents."[125] Thus, analysts should focus on the names, labels, imagery, stories, phrases, metaphors, and analogies used to identify the national self and its relation to others.

BEHAVIORAL MICROTRANSLATIONS

By itself, simply showing how actors see the world does not provide for an adequate explanation of behavior. A complete explanation also requires causal accounts linking these meanings to behavior. The various propositions linking collective liberal identification to peaceful relations between states fleshed out these causal accounts at higher levels of generality. To operationalize them, however, we require behavioral microtranslations. This involves deducing the observable patterns of political behavior we would expect to follow from a sense of collective liberal identification between states. Several behavioral microtranslations follow from the hypothesized causal relationship between collective liberal identity and peace. These can be stated in the form of additional propositions.

Proposition 11: When collective liberal identification exists, significant portions of public and elite opinion should be strongly liberal, trusting, and pacific toward other states perceived to be liberal democracies (a corollary being that they should be more distrustful of states perceived to be illiberal or nondemocratic). The extent and intensity of these opinions should co-

124. Ibid., 30.
125. Lowell Ditmer, "Political Culture and Political Symbolism," *World Politics* 29, no. 4 (July 1977): 567.

vary with the degree of positive collective identification.[126] In a state with a liberal identity we would expect the majority of public and elite opinion to embrace the ideational components of liberalism. Most individuals will undoubtedly be incapable of fully articulating a liberal philosophy, but they should have internalized the substance of liberalism to a sufficient degree that it guides political behavior, however unconsciously. Additionally, we would expect the liberal tenets of domestic life to be preferred by the majority of individuals in foreign relations with states perceived to share these ideational qualities.[127] Thus, the majority of individuals and social groups should agitate for close relations and the peaceful resolution of the conflicts of interest with states perceived to be liberal, and be wary and more disdainful of illiberal states.

Proposition 12: The opinions and perceptions regarding other liberal democracies should be held consistently as long as the hypothesized processes of collective-identity formation operate. If perceptions change, these shifts should be traceable to discernible medium or long-term internal or interactive processes, not short-term material or strategic interests. The manifestations of liberalism in public and elite opinion should be relatively autonomous from the material and strategic interests of states as defined by neorealists. The liberal construction of interests should trump the neorealist construction of interests when the two come into conflict. Furthermore, the perception of a common liberal identity, or lack thereof, should be based on a perceived similarity of political ideals and institutions. If these views change, the change should be the consequence of either a change in the ideals or institutions of the target state, or a discernible medium or long-term interactive or internal process, not the short-term material or strategic interests of the states involved.

Some prima facie support for these first two behavioral microtranslations can be found in the results from recent experimental studies on democratic peace conducted by Alex Mintz and Nehemia Geva. These experiments presented three groups of subjects (American undergraduate students, American nonstudent adults, and Israeli students) with one of two hypothetical situations. In both hypotheticals, a foreign state invaded a small neighbor possessing a resource critical to the

126. This is similar to a hypothesis put forth by Owen. See Owen, "How Liberalism Produces Democratic Peace," 103; and Owen, "Perceptions and the Limits of Liberal Peace," 156.
127. Lumsdaine, *Moral Vision in International Politics*, 22–23.

United States (or Israel), and also took American (or Israeli) hostages. In one hypothetical, however, the aggressor was presented as a democracy, while in the other it was presented as a nondemocracy. Despite the aggressive nature of the action and the clear threat to the material and security interests of the subject's country, the researchers found that individuals in all three groups were less likely to approve of the use of force against a democratic state than a nondemocratic state. They also found that the majority considered the use of force against a democratic aggressor to represent a failure of foreign policy.[128]

Building on these initial microtranslations concerning public and elite opinion, we can also generate microtranslations regarding how exactly we would expect pacific relations between liberal states to be maintained.

Proposition 13: The majority of decisionmakers should be liberal and avoid foreign policies that carry a substantial risk of war with other states perceived to be liberal. Since the majority of public and elite opinion should be liberal, we would expect the majority of key decisionmakers to be liberal as well. Indeed, decisionmakers are more likely than any other kind of individual to internalize liberal tenets, because they regularly benefit from adherence to liberal principles and practices, and have more experience with norms of peaceful conflict resolution.[129] In other words, whereas liberalism may be murky and abstract for any given member of the public, its tenets should be much clearer and more concrete for decisionmakers. When this is the case, decisionmakers should avoid policies that run the risk of war with other states perceived to be liberal.

Proposition 14: When illiberal decisionmakers, or decisionmakers who do not share the perception that another state is liberal, guide the foreign policy of a liberal democracy, they should be constrained by liberal public or elite opinion when and if these decisionmakers adopt belligerent policies that run significant risks of war with another liberal state.[130] The previous proposition notwithstanding, not all the key decisionmakers in a lib-

---

128. See Alex Mintz and Nehemia Geva, "Why Don't Democracies Fight Each Other?" *Journal of Conflict Resolution* 37, no. 3 (September 1993): 484–503; and Nehemia Geva, Karl R. DeRouen, and Alex Mintz, "The Political Incentive Explanation of 'Democratic Peace': Evidence from Experimental Research," *International Interactions* 18, no. 3 (1993): 215–29.

129. See Dixon, "Democracy and the Peaceful Settlement of International Conflict," 16–18.

130. This also parallels a hypothesis put forth by Owen in "How Liberalism Produces Democratic Peace," 103–4.

eral democracy will necessarily embrace liberalism, or act in ways consistent with the tenets of liberalism toward other states. This is the case for at least three reasons: (1) not all individuals in a state with a liberal identity are liberal or liberal to the same degree; (2) not all individuals will share identical perceptions regarding the liberal nature of other states; (3) decisionmakers get elected for their positions on numerous policy fronts and, consequently, their beliefs and perceptions regarding certain other states may not be salient in particular elections. As a result, certain decisionmakers in liberal states may get their countries into military crises with other states that the majority of the public and elite view as liberal. When this occurs we would expect democratic institutions to empower public and elite opinion to agitate for the peaceful resolution of any such crisis, and either successfully constrain or politically punish, the decisionmaker.[131]

RECODING CASES AND RETESTING IDEATIONAL EXPLANATIONS

Existing testing procedures have gone a long way toward establishing the existence of a democratic peace, as well as pointing to the viability of various institutional and ideational explanations. Our confidence in these findings, however, hinges to a significant degree on how concepts such as "democracy" and "liberal" are defined, and thus how cases are coded.[132] Current coding procedures allow persuasive tests of institutional hypotheses because democracy is defined in terms of those observable institutional features posited to generate democratic peace. Some of the existing coding schemes also generate highly suggestive "first-cut" analyses of ideational accounts because it is reasonable to assume that democracies embracing liberal corporate identities (that is, democratic institutions, civil rights and civil liberties, free markets, etc.) will be capable of recognizing these traits in one another.[133] Nev-

---

131. This empowerment may occur to different degrees and privilege certain sectors of the public or elite depending on the exact nature of the democratic institutions involved. See Thomas Risse-Kappen, "Public Opinion, Domestic Structure, and Foreign Policy in Liberal Democracies," *World Politics* 43, no. 4 (July 1991): 479–512; and Susan Peterson, *Crisis Bargaining and the State: The Domestic Politics of International Conflict* (Ann Arbor: University of Michigan Press, 1996).

132. See Robert L Merritt and Dina A. Zinnes, "Democracy and War," in *On Measuring Democracy: Its Consequences and Concomitants*, ed. Alex Inkeles (New Brunswick: Transaction, 1991), 225–27; and Ido Oren, "The Subjectivity of the 'Democratic' Peace: Changing U.S. Perceptions of Imperial Germany," *International Security* 20, no. 2 (fall 1995): 147–84.

133. See, for example, Doyle, "Kant, Liberal Legacies, and Foreign Affairs, Part 1"; and Doyle, "Liberalism and World Politics."

ertheless, to gain sufficient confidence in the validity of ideational claims, including the constructivist propositions laid out here, it is essential to reexamine and "recode" cases to account for the contingency inherent in such intersubjective concepts as "liberal" and "democracy." Because we only know a liberal-democratic community exists based on the shared perceptions and understandings of the actors under study, we must move beyond analyses that define these concepts outside of their specific social and historical contexts. Adopting a more interpretive epistemological position provides an effective means of taking these intersubjective concepts seriously. Therefore, while the nonconstructivist methods used to establish the existence of a democratic peace are perfectly acceptable, providing a sufficient explanation for its existence requires a new approach. The recoding procedure advocated here could, in theory, be used in either large-N quantitative work or small-N comparative case studies, but, given the complexity and lengthy period of time required to explore each case in ways consistent with rigorous interpretivism, it may be more practical to begin with a number of small-N studies.[134]

It may turn out, upon recoding, that ideational explanations for democratic peace have little merit or that the assumptions guiding existing statistical studies are untenable. Such a finding would create a paradox of sorts, because the very statistical studies that suggested the significance of ideational explanations in the first place, and thus justified the constructivist endeavor undertaken here, might be shown by a rigorous constructivist analysis to be untenable. Nevertheless, a negative finding would still vindicate the utility of a constructivist approach. By casting doubt on ideational accounts, a constructivist analysis would point to the need for alternative explanations to account for those features of democratic peace left unexplained or underexplained by institutional approaches. It is also possible that a constructivist analysis would reveal that ideational bonds do promote peace between liberal democracies. The few studies that have adopted an epistemological approach somewhat similar to the one advocated here have resulted in divergent findings. Owen, for example, found substantial support for ideational claims, while Oren found that perceptions regarding the liberal-democratic character of other states tended to be

---

134. The larger the number of cases, the less time on average analysts tend to spend on each case, and the more likely there is to be significant measurement error. See James D. Fearon, "Counterfactuals and Hypothesis Testing in Political Science," *World Politics* 43, no. 2 (January 1991): 174–75.

epiphenomenal to strategic interests. These studies are suggestive but are far from conclusive.[135] Our confidence in the existence, or lack thereof, of the factors emphasized by ideational explanations, as well as our understanding of the various processes involved, would be greatly enhanced by a more rigorous and broad-based constructivist analysis.

CONSTRUCTIVISM AND THE EXPANSION OF DEMOCRATIC PEACE

THE FINDINGS of the democratic peace literature are among the most consequential in recent international relations scholarship. These findings have not only led to productive research and heated academic debate, but appear to have significant influence in current foreign policy discussions as well. Unfortunately, current explanations for democratic peace face certain limitations. By themselves, institutional explanations for the phenomenon leave critical aspects of liberal-democratic relations unexplained or underexplained. Ideational explanations help fill the explanatory gap left by institutional arguments, but have not been taken far enough. At present, ideational explanations suggest that liberal affinity and the externalization of democratic norms facilitate peace between liberal democracies, but the various processes whereby states develop a sense of collective liberal identity in the first place, as well as the full implications of this identification, have not been sufficiently explored.

Constructivist theory paves the way for a more comprehensive and productive elaboration of ideational explanations for democratic peace. Incorporating insights from constructivism allows us to derive a number of specific, interesting, and empirically testable propositions about the causes and consequences of collective liberal identification. This essay has not provided definitive support for these propositions, but rather has sought to take the initial steps toward improving the democratic peace research program by including a constructivist analysis. If

135. Owen, "How Liberalism Produces Democratic Peace"; Owen, *Liberal Peace, Liberal War*; and Oren, "The Subjectivity of the 'Democratic' Peace." Oren's conclusions are particularly problematic. Oren illustrates his major claim by considering the shifting perceptions of Imperial Germany held by two prominent late-nineteenth-century political scientists, Woodrow Wilson and John W. Burgess. Oren's conclusions regarding Wilson are historically controversial. For a contrary view, see May 1966. Moreover, Oren does not study broader elite or public opinion nor does he evaluate a large number of cases. It is thus difficult to evaluate the merit of his specific claims in the Imperial German case, let alone the generalizability of his conclusion that liberal-democratic affinity is epiphenomenal.

further research demonstrates that democratic peace stems in part from collective liberal identification, it would significantly increase our confidence in existing ideational accounts while clarifying the various processes and contingencies involved.

In a world in which the United States and other Western countries appear committed to democracy promotion, it is imperative that we understand the processes whereby states come to see themselves as part of a broader community of liberal democracies. A constructivist analysis suggests that Western powers would be naive to believe that they can rapidly or efficiently expand the size of the liberal-democratic community simply by promoting democracy. The community that now exists in the West was fostered by a common conception of liberal democracy and a common Soviet threat during the cold war. The former provided the foundation for community, while the latter served to mute security competition between traditional Western rivals, thereby providing sufficient structural slack for positive identification to occur. A common threat complex also created the political space for Western states to construct an intricate web of economic and security institutions and interdependencies that serve as mechanisms to reinforce their sense of collective identification despite the collapse of the Soviet Union. It is difficult to conceive of a similar array of circumstances conspiring to promote a substantial broadening of the liberal-democratic community in the post–cold war world. Many non-Western democracies reject Western concepts of liberalism or civic democracy, and the dense web of European and trans-Atlantic institutions is not in evidence elsewhere. Moreover, while other post–cold war processes, such as economic globalization and the expansion of American popular culture, could theoretically serve as catalysts for broader collective identification, these processes may also invite an anti-Western backlash.[136] In this context, further investigation of the democratic peace proposition within a constructivist framework may help clarify the limits to which policymakers can reasonable expect emerging democracies, which may not be liberal or come to view one another as such, to join in the separate peace.

---

136. See Huntington, *The Clash of Civilizations and the Remaking of World Order.* For a more optimistic picture, see Cheshier and Dauber, "The Place and Power of Civic Space."

TERRITORIAL AND NATIONAL SOVEREIGNS:
SOVEREIGN IDENTITY AND CONSEQUENCES FOR SECURITY POLICY

RODNEY BRUCE HALL

I WILL ADDRESS two issues of current interest to students of international relations in this article. The first is the extent to which societal collective identity, and especially national collective identity, has causal significance for international interaction and for the strategic behavior of states that are committed to different forms of sovereign identity. The second is the issue of change in the international system. Both of these issues have been consequential to theoretical debates among scholars approaching the analysis of international politics and global order[1] and have been featured in the disparate writings of realists, Marxists, liberals and institutionalists of various stripes for decades. More recently, the notion that societal collective identity is a crucial component of the social construction of social and political order has become an essential claim upon which, in part, more recent reflectivist[2], constructivist[3], and poststructuralist[4] research programs have been founded.

Rodney Bruce Hall is a postdoctoral fellow in international relations at the Thomas J. Watson Jr. Institute for International Studies at Brown University.

An earlier draft of this article was presented at the 92nd Annual Meeting of the American Political Science Association, 29 August–1 September 1996, San Francisco, California. Portions of this article appear in a somewhat different form in Rodney Bruce Hall, *National Collective Identity: Social Constructs and International Systems* (New York: Columbia University Press, 1999). Thanks to Michael Barnett, Glenn Chafetz, Daniel Deudney, Martin Heisler, Friedrich Kratochwil, Yosef Lapid, Hendrik Spruyt for useful comments on earlier versions of these arguments. Thanks to the anonymous referees of *Security Studies* for useful suggestions for structural and stylistic enhancements of this article. Thanks also to the Watson Institute for International Studies for financial support.

1. An important recent example is Barry Buzan, Richard Little and Charles Jones, *The Logic of Anarchy* (New York: Columbia University Press, 1993).
2. See the work of Friedrich Kratochwil, esp. Friedrich V. Kratochwil, *Rules, Norms, and Decisions: On the Conditions of Practical and Legal Reasoning in International Relations and Domestic Affairs* (Cambridge: Cambridge University Press, 1989).
3. In addition to the work of Kratochwil, see the agency-structure debate literature, esp. Alexander Wendt, "The Agent-Structure Problem in International Relations Theory," *International Organization* 41, no. 3 (summer 1987): 335–70; and David Dessler, "What is at Stake in the Agent-Structure Debate?" *International Organization* 43, no. 3

For structural realists and, especially structural neorealists, actor identities and interests are determined by the context of interaction; the "anarchical" structure of the international system. Actor self-identifications are irrelevant for the subsequent patterns of interaction. Epochal change in the international system is unknown, and change is occasioned only by major positional shifts in the distribution of military and economic power resources among the actors. National actors are simply nationalized state actors. Their self-identification as national-states has no consequences for their subsequent interaction.[5] The system is static but for the name of the hegemon. There is no requirement to identify the "generative moment" of the system, which has always been the same.[6]

For reflectivists-constructivists, and especially for postmodernists-poststructuralists, the social institutions which constitute the structure of international relations are generated by the agency of malleable human societies acting upon historically contingent notions of their own identities and interests. Thus social institutions such as the structural-realist notion of international anarchy are, according to Alex Wendt, "what states make of it."[7] The context of international social interaction is provided by the prevailing, historically contingent, structure of identities and interests in the system. Epochal change in the international system is a function of major transformations in this "structure of identities and interests."[8]

(summer 1989):441–74; Also see Nicholas Onuf and Frank Klink, "Anarchy, Authority, Rule," *International Studies Quarterly* 33, no. 2 (June 1989): 149–74; and Onuf, *World of Our Making* (Columbia: University of South Carolina Press, 1989); Hayward R. Alker, *Rediscoveries and Reformulations: Humanistic Methodologies for International Studies* (Cambridge: Cambridge University Press, 1996); and the collection of essays in Thomas J. Biersteker and Cynthia Weber, eds., *State Sovereignty as Social Construct* (Cambridge: Cambridge University Press, 1996).

4. Notable works include R. B. J. Walker, *Inside/Outside: International Relations as Political Theory* (Cambridge: Cambridge University Press, 1993). See esp. chaps. 5 and 6 in this context. See also Jim George, *Discourses of Global Politics: A Critical (Re)Introduction to International Relations* (Boulder: Lynne Rienner, 1994); and Cynthia Weber, *Simulating Sovereignty: Intervention, the State and Symbolic Exchange* (Cambridge: Cambridge University Press, 1995); and Jens Bartleson, *A Genealogy of Sovereignty* (Cambridge: Cambridge University Press, 1995).

5. See Yosef Lapid and Friedrich Kratochwil, "Revisiting the 'National': Toward an Identity Agenda in Neorealism?" in *The Return of Culture and Identity in IR Theory*, ed. Yosef Lapid and Friedrich Kratochwil (Boulder: Lynne Rienner, 1995), 105–26.

6. See Buzan, Jones, and Little, *The Logic of Anarchy.*

7. Alexander Wendt, "Anarchy is What States Make of It," *International Organization* 46, no. 2 (spring 1992): 391–425.

8. Wendt provides a highly useful development of the meaning of this phrase in ibid. Kahl notes the importance of the historical contingency of social "structure" when he notes that in constructivist theory it "is produced, reproduced and potentially

SOCIAL IDENTITIES AND STATE INTERESTS

W E CAN SEE the dichotomous tension between these opposing views. For structural realists and Marxists, the behavior of international actors in the system is all but determined by structural features that so significantly constrain interaction within the system that this behavior is either immutably fixed, or objectively predetermined. Structure governs behavior. Conversely, for poststructuralists and postmodernists, the power of human agency to transform political structure is so potent that structure is an illusion, projected into eyes of the unwitting to ensure the perpetuation of oppressive and asymmetric social power structures which can be dismantled if only we expose their insidious nature.

For social constructivists, whom, I would argue, take a position somewhere between these epistemological poles,[9] human agency has the capacity to transform social systems, but structure is real and indisputably constrains behavior. The interests of international actors, however, are not objectively or structurally determined. Interests, in this view, do not develop independently of social identities. Identities and interests are co-constituted. Actor motivations are embedded in social identities. The structure that is in fact causally significant for behaviors is the structure of co-constituted identities and interests. A problem that even the analyst who accepts these propositions immediately encounters, however, is that of how to account for social identities in order to apprehend this structure of identities and interests. The analyst must designate actors to construct any theory of the international system. Let me spend a moment considering the manner in which structural neorealist theory approaches this problem, and another moment considering the case of classical realism. The works of Kenneth Waltz and Hans Morgenthau will serve this purpose.

---

transformed by interaction within the social and structural context existing at a given point in space and time" (Colin Kahl, "Constructing a Separate Peace: Constructivism, Collective Liberal Identity, and Democratic Peace," *Security Studies* 8, nos. 2/3 [winter 1998/99–spring 1999]: 103).

9. For a particular view of constructivist method as a *via media*, see Emanuel Adler, "Seizing the Middle Ground: Constructivism in World Politics," *European Journal of International Relations* 3, no. 3 (September 1997): 319–63. Note that I would, however, argue in favor of including most postmodernist and poststructuralist scholarship under a very large "constructivist" umbrella.

In constructing his system theory, Waltz underspecifies the relevant actors in the system by specifying only the unitary state-as-actor.[10] I argue that designation of actors requires some specification of their attributes in a social context. These contexts are not, however, static over time. Waltz is mired perpetually in a system of Westphalian territorial-sovereign states precisely because he has designated these not only as the primary actors but as the only actors in his system, whose structure, in his view, perpetually reproduces the system. He can not explain, for example, nationalist phenomena as he can not perceive nations. They are exogenized from his system, as are all other historically observed forms of political association that preceded the Peace of Westphalia.[11] In order convincingly to define political structure, the analyst must take into account the self-designations of the actors of the system. Had Waltz designated a different sort of actor, he might have discovered a different conception of structure, and might have formulated a very different systems theory.

A common assumption of both classical realist and neorealist theories regards the fixity of the "interests" and motivations of state actors in the conduct of interaction. Hans Morgenthau's formulation of the notion of interest obscures the relationship between interests and power by equating these two distinct concepts. He states boldly, early on in his work, that "[w]e assume that statesmen think and act in terms of *interest defined as power.*"[12] Even in acknowledging in a particular case that an ideational factor like nationalism has consequences that must be accounted for, Morgenthau merely asserts that the factor has been appropriated by statesmen and applies the factor as if it had no consequences for his description of state interests in terms of power. His analysis of the behavior of nation-state actors is an analysis of the behavior of nationalized state actors still ruled by the old power lust. The goals of this will-to-power alone have changed. Morgenthau recognizes that, in the nationalist era, actor identities have changed, but insists that their interests remain constant.[13] He perceives a changing structure of identities, but not a changing structure of interests.

10. Kenneth N. Waltz, *Theory of International Politics* (New York: Random House, 1979).

11. See Richard Little, "Rethinking System Continuity and Transformation," in Buzan, Jones, and Little, *The Logic of Anarchy.*

12. Hans J. Morgenthau, *Politics Among Nations: The Struggle for Power and Peace,* 4th ed. (New York: Knopf, 1967), 5.

13. Martin Griffiths, *Realism, Idealism and International Politics: A Reinterpretation* (London: Routledge, 1992).

Theory that is formulated in such a way as to describe the interests of social actors in terms of power, and in unitary terms, is not capable of making an analytic cut into the discovery of the notion of interests which impel nationalist phenomena.[14] This suggests that interests must sometimes be described in a different language, and that their formulation and expression are far from a unitary process. The analysis of the interaction of sovereign states will remain forever static if it provides no means by which to analyze transformations in collective identity and especially transformations in sovereign identity.

It will not do simply to note that the territorial-sovereign states of modern Europe (and by extension non-European states) have become nationalized, suddenly imagining themselves to have become nations, and then proceed to analyze their behavior as though the same norms of sovereignty are applicable to nation-states as had been the case for dynastic and territorial-sovereigns. Statesmen in the nationalist era have not spoken in voice of the same set of prenational interests. They do not merely articulate a different set of ethics which now simply extend the goals of the state, in relation to those articulated in the prenationalist era. They have spoken in an entirely new voice and have articulated a new set of interests—the interests of an entirely new social entity. In the nationalist era, statesmen were no longer speaking with the voice of a prince, a house, an empire or kingdom. Nor did they any longer articulate these interests and goals. The statesmen of nation-states began speaking in the voice of a sovereign people, a collective actor possessed of a collective identity and collective interests and goals. This is a very different social actor than was the dynastic-sovereign or the absolutist territorial-sovereign. I argue, and will shortly seek to illustrate, that actor self-identification is a critical component of this structure of identities and interests.[15]

Societies with different conceptions of the nature of legitimate authority choose to endow different elements of society with this authority. What or whom is regarded as sovereign is strongly conditioned by the self-understandings of members of domestic society with

14. For a more extended critique of structural neorealism and Morgenthau's formulation of interests in terms of the "will-to-power," see the first chapter of Hall, *National Collective Identity.*

15. Kahl similarly appears to recognize the importance of societal self-identification (at the level of the state in his case) in arguing that "For constructivists, a state's conception of 'self' is in large part a meaning existing in the activity of viewing itself reflexively." Later, on the same page, he argues that "identity can literally define a state's interest" (Kahl, "Constructing a Separate Peace," 107).

respect to legitimate authority. That which we call sovereign says a lot about whom we believe ourselves to be as a polity, whether we are a passive polity (regarding ourselves as subjects of authority) or an active polity (regarding ourselves as sources of authority).[16]

The subject of the dynastic-sovereign state gives his or her allegiance to the Prince, who rules domestic society, and to his creed. The subject of the territorial-sovereign state gives his or her allegiance to the sovereign of that state. The citizen of the national-sovereign state give his or her allegiance to the nation, to the imagined community of shared ancestry, culture or history to which he or she believes himself or herself to be a part.[17] Domestic law is given to domestic society by the prevailing sovereign. The sovereign is that person, institution or community in which legitimate social authority is lodged in accordance with the legitimating principles of the social order.

The emergence of national collective identity transformed sovereign identity within the state. The notion that nations—national communities based upon common language, ethnicity, culture or shared history—are the legitimate wielders of the sword of state sovereignty, has altered the norms, rules and principles of international as well as domestic society.[18] The notion that the nation, however defined or segmented, is inherently sovereign and self-determining, transformed the legitimate purposes of state action.

We must delineate the structure of identities and interests of the territorial-sovereign from that of the national-sovereign. The emergence of national collective identity in Europe resulted in the replacement of the territorial-sovereign legitimating principle of raison d'état with the national-sovereign legitimating principle of national self-determination. Eighteenth-century dynastic, mercantilist absolutism and easy recourse

---

16. A sweeping study of changing identities and polities is found in Yale H. Ferguson and Richard W. Mansbach, *Polities: Authority, Identities and Change* (Columbia: University of South Carolina Press, 1996).

17. See, for example, Benedict Anderson, *Imagined Communities: Reflections on the Origins and Spread of Nationalism* (London: Verso, 1983).

18. It is in this context that I concur with Cheshier's and Dauber's assertion that "constructivists and globalists...insist culture and race and nationality can be overcome, as they all arise out of socially constructed realities" (David M. Cheshier and Cori E. Dauber, "The Place and Power of Civic Space: Reading Globalization and Social Geography Through the Lens of Civilizational Conflict," *Security Studies* 8, nos. 2/3 [winter 1998/99–spring 1999]: 47). Note that, consistent with Doty's emphasis on individuals and societies as well as states, I concur that "while survival for the state is a question of sovereignty, survival for society is a question of identity" (Roxanne Lynn Doty, "Immigration and the Politics of Security," *Security Studies* 8, nos. 2/3 [winter 1998/99–spring 1999]: 78).

to war were practices which developed from the norms, rules and principles of a system legitimated by the territorial-sovereign principle of raison d'état. Territorial-sovereign imperialism was a commercial and strategic venture whose social purpose conformed to the zero-sum nature of dynastic, territorial-sovereign status competition.

The emergence of national-sovereign identity and interests, in the nineteenth century, problematized territorial-sovereign legitimating principles and subsequently transformed the structure of state interests, practice and institutions. The emergence of national collective identity created problems of secessionism and irredentism, and thus new sources of interstate conflict. It enhanced the resources mobilizable by statesmen by enfranchising ever lower economic strata of domestic society, inducing their participation in the projects of the state as members of the nation. Conflicting class and national identity commitments created tools for statesmen to "divide and rule" domestic society, but radically reduced the insularity of their decision-making processes as an enfranchised and nationalized "citizenry" took an interest in the affairs of state with which territorial-sovereign statesmen had not been required to contend. As I will illustrate later in the article, national collective identity engendered statesmen such as Bismarck with the tools to forge a German superstate from the many petty kingdoms and mini-states of German Central Europe. It constrained other statesmen, such as Napoleon III, from "balancing" the creation of a threatening German superstate, and from enjoying the flexibility to form alliances with other powers sufficient to meet the threat of this hostile superstate when the Franco-Prussian War commenced in 1870.

TERRITORIAL-SOVEREIGN IDENTITY AND STRATEGIC BEHAVIOR

BEFORE I proceed to illustrate the behavioral consequences of the transition from territorial-sovereign identity to the behavior induced by national sovereign identity, it is important to pause here to delineate territorial sovereignty from the dynastic form which had preceded it. Territorial sovereignty and mercantilist economic policy can be seen to have operated synergistically in the eighteenth century, with significant and logical consequences for strategic behavior. The principles underlying this form of sovereignty, and the practices associated with it need to be explained before we can understand the changes that came with the later notion of the development of national sovereignty.

TERRITORIAL-SOVEREIGN IDENTITY AND MERCANTILIST
THEORY AND PRACTICE

One of the most significant consequences of the Westphalian settlement and the close of the era of the Wars of Religion had been a shift in both the rationales and character of the system of continental alliances that had structured European international relations between the sixteenth and seventeenth centuries. With the delegitimation of religious ideas and affiliations as sources of interstate conflict, and the rise of the principle of raison d'état, the continent fell away from the familiar pattern of conflict between the Austro-Spanish Hapsburg axis and the coalition of Protestant powers aided by a France encircled by Hapsburg territories. Consequently the continental system became much more multipolar, and increasingly characterized by a loose system of very short-term alliances.[19]

The creation of standing armies and their regular employment in the acquisition of new territory, to buttress state or dynastic status, and to compensate for increasing uncertainty in alliance politics due to the delegitimation of religious-military affiliations, created a pressing need for steady flows of revenues for their maintenance. Continental struggles became wars of shifting, short-term coalitions. Financing these struggles was a challenge for an era characterized by the scarcity of coin and the continued flow of funds to armies of professional soldiers, many of whom were mercenaries recruited from foreign lands and distinctly unmotivated by more than the desire to earn money and to survive. Thus finance was of paramount importance for monarchs who wished to sustain a successful campaign.

An artifact of the segmentation of the political world according to the principle of territoriality[20] was an economic closure corresponding to the political closure segmented by territory. As state-building and territorial consolidation crystallized the state as an institutional form, Europe witnessed the emergence of economies whose boundaries roughly coincided with those of the state.[21] As European monarchs

---

19. Paul Kennedy. *The Rise and Fall of the Great Powers: Economic Change and Military Conflict from 1500 to 2000* (New York: Random House, 1987), 73. For an illuminating discussion of alliance politics during this era, see Evan Luard, *The Balance of Power: The System of International Relations, 1648–1815* (New York: St. Martin's, 1992), 256–80.

20. John Gerard Ruggie. "Territoriality and Beyond: Problematizing Modernity in International Relations," *International Organization* 47, no. 1 (winter 1993): 148–52.

21. James Mayall. *Nationalism and International Society* (Cambridge: Cambridge University Press, 1990), 72.

continued to discover the extent to which success in their martial status-contests relied upon their ability to mobilize the "industrial, commercial, financial, military and naval resources"[22] of their territories, they increasingly viewed these resources as interchangeably fungible, globally scarce, and fundamentally limited. The absolutist regarded the wealth of the state as his or her personal war-chest. The scarcity of coin and precious metals, and the rudimentary nature of early eighteenth-century credit vehicles and banking systems had led to bullionism—the view that all wealth resides in the possession of precious metals, that money had to be secured either by plunder or trade.[23] The crown could tax trade and sell monopolies to individual merchants or trading companies. These revenues made up a crucially significant share of the revenues of the crown, which was anxious to see such economic activity expanded.

The establishment of colonies in large measure resulted directly from the desire to increase the flow of limited tradable commodities. Colonies were, unlike continental territory, coveted not from a desire for conquest, honor, or glory but for the products they could supply and the taxable wealth they could generate. This motivation is fundamentally distinct from the imperial impulses that were to impel the territorial segmentation of the globe in the late nineteenth century, during the nationalist era. In the eighteenth century:

> Europeans did not settle in the remote foreign regions out of a desire for conquest, but to secure access to particular commodities which could be profitably traded in Europe....Except in the Americas, permanent settlement was usually not intended, still less the detailed administrations of local populations.[24]

Trade with one's colonies was an enormously important contribution to the balance of trade. Woloch provides data which indicates that France's colonial trade grew from twenty-five million livres in 1716 to 263 million livres in 1789, which constituted growth from 20 percent to 50 percent of France's total foreign trade.[25] Similarly, Luard's data

---

22. Edward Mead Earle, "Adam Smith, Alexander Hamilton, Friedrich List: The Economic Foundation of Military Power," in *Makers of Modern Strategy: Military Thought From Machiavelli to Hitler*, ed. Edward Mead Earle (Princeton: Princeton University Press, 1973), 118.

23. Mayall, *Nationalism and International Society*, 72.

24. Luard, *The Balance of Power*, 226.

25. Isser Woloch, *Eighteenth Century Europe: Tradition and Progress 1715–1789* (New York: Norton, 1982), 128.

suggests that Britain's North American colonial trade alone constituted 20 percent of her total foreign trade in 1750 and 34 percent by 1785.[26]

The territorial-sovereign state had a powerful incentive to establish colonies, particularly in regions were valuable commodities could be extracted or grown which were unavailable in Europe. Colonies were seen not as strategic liabilities but as economic assets, particularly where they were established by trading companies that maintained their own armed forces, which many did.[27]

The major incentive to establish colonies for eighteenth-century mercantilist regimes, however, lay in the extension of the sovereignty of the state (and its monarch) to the remote colony, not for purposes of accruing status to either, but for the capability, unavailable on the continent, to leverage the terms of trade to the advantage of the mother country and to shield it from competition. Colonial trade was "directed," or "managed" trade. It was reserved to the home country alone and as such constituted "a pure monopoly."[28] Moreover, such managed arrangements could be designed to ensure not only a captive market for the manufactures of the mother country, and a supplier of rare and valuable commodities for those manufactures, but a perpetually captive market as well. Residing under the sovereignty of the mother country, colonists could be obstructed from developing manufacturing industries, and generally were, as manufacturing industries at home needed markets and abhorred competition.[29]

Mercantilist theory and practice routinely subordinated private economic interests to the perceived interests of the state, and raison d'état justified and legitimated this view and practice in as much as wealth and power were so closely coupled in the thought of the day. Edward Earle captures the issues succinctly in a rather extreme formulation.

> In modern terminology, we would say that the predominant purpose of mercantilist regulations was to develop the military potential, or war potential. To this end exports and imports were rigidly controlled; stocks of precious metals were built up and conserved; military and naval stores were produced or imported under a system of premiums and bounties; shipping and the fisheries were fos-

---

26. Luard, *The Balance of Power*, 228.

27. Ibid., 227. Also see Darrett B. Rutman. "The Virginia Company and Its Military Regime," in *The Old Dominion: Essays for Thomas Perkins Abernethy*, ed. Darrett B. Rutman (Charlottesville: University Press of Virginia, 1964), 1–20.

28. Luard, *The Balance of Power*, 228–29.

29. Ibid., 229.

tered as a source of naval power; colonies were settled and protected (as well as strictly regulated) as a complement to the wealth
and self-sufficiency of the mother country; population growth was
encouraged for the purpose of increasing military man power.
These and other measure were designed with the major, if not the
single, purpose of adding to the unity and strength of the nation
[sic].[30]

Of course mercantilist assumptions are highly suspect, and the critiques of the classical economists of the Scottish Enlightenment, specifically that of Smith, began to appear later in the decade.[31] These critiques became influential and began to guide even British economic
policy in the nineteenth century, but certainly not in the eighteenth.
What is important to the present study is not whether or not wealth
and military power are fungible, or whether they are mutually interdependent. The last is a question that is still a point of much contention in international relations theory.[32] What is important is that
eighteenth-century governments believed that they were valid, and
predicated their economic policies on their perceived economic, military and strategic needs, acting on assumptions very similar to those of
classical realist and neorealist theories of international relations.

The critical link between extreme nationalist economic nationalism
and mercantilism is the assumptions regarding the political order in
which economic activity is conducted. Mercantilism "envisages 'a
world not of markets but of states'."[33] Colonies were seen as exten-
sions of the state, and as such sources of raw materials for home industries, of strategic materials and naval goods such as hemp, flax, copper,
pitch and tar. They were seen as provenders of precious metals, as
sources of a positive balance of trade, a means of import saving, sources
of cheap slave labor, markets for manufactures of the mother country,
distress goods markets for mitigating the effects of protectionist tariffs
elsewhere, as well as outlets for surplus production and surplus capital

30. Earle, "Adam Smith, Alexander Hamilton, Friedrich List," 118–19.
31. Adam Smith, *An Inquiry into the Nature and Causes of the Wealth of Nations*,
vols. 1 and 2, ed. R. H. Campbell and A. S. Skinner (Indianapolis: Liberty Press, 1981).
See esp. Book 4, "On Systems of Political Economy," 428–688.
32. See, for example, David A. Baldwin, *Economic Statecraft* (Princeton: Princeton
University Press, 1985).
33. Martin Staniland, *What is Political Economy? A Study of Social Theory and Un-
derdevelopment.* (New Haven: Yale University Press, 1985), 106.

for the mother country. They were generally prized for helping to reduce dependency on other states for commodities and markets.[34]

Thus an important element motivating eighteenth-century colonialism was that it was integral to the state-building exercise, but unlike the continental competition for territory, the competition for colonial territory in the periphery was oriented toward building up the wealth, and consequently, it was thought, the power of the continental state. A real distinction between dynastic interests of earlier centuries, and the state interests that developed significantly in the eighteenth century, regarded the desire to render the sovereignty lodged in the monarch and in the state "impermeable" by shielding it in impermeable territory.[35] Dynasts of earlier centuries desired the loyalty or allegiance of their subjects in the lands they ruled. They cared little for direct control, and expended little effort toward creating unified administrations for this purpose. Each territory acquired might continue on its own path with its customs and institutions undisturbed, and might even extract a pledge from its new ruler to speak the language of the acquired territory.[36] The acquisition of the territory had added honor to the name and revenues to the coffers of the dynastic-sovereign's house. It was yet in this house that the dynast's primary self-identification was lodged, rather than in the institutional structure of a state.

The territorial-sovereign, however, "is sovereign because he has the power to constrain his subjects, while not being so constrainable by a superior power. The decisive criterion thus is actual control of one's 'estates' by one's military power."[37] As the legitimacy of the territorial-sovereign's rule was now predicated on his administrative sovereignty, recognized by his peers, over his lands, and not his dynastic rights by feudal custom or residue, he now required an institutional structure to "house" that legitimacy, and to reproduce it for his scion. It is generally accepted that the Westphalian settlement resolved the legitimation crisis that the segmentation of European international politics along confessional lines had created. An unintended consequence of the settlement was the creation of a crisis of dynastic legitimacy by enshrining territorial rule as the legitimating principle of European government. This dynastic legitimation crisis was simultaneously a dynastic

---

34. Luard, *The Balance of Power*, 232–36.

35. John H. Herz, "Rise and Demise of the Territorial State," *World Politics* 9, no. 4 (July 1957): 478–79.

36. Luard, *The Balance of Power*, 174.

37. Herz, "The Rise and Demise of the Territorial State," 479.

"identity crisis," thus in no small measure an impetus to the state-building projects of territorial-sovereigns. This was so precisely because it was the institution of the modern state which replaced the dynastic house as sanctuary for the continued legitimacy of dynastic rule.

This territorial-sovereign was, however, now vulnerable to the strong winds of the caprice of his peers in a way in which his dynastic house never had been. Dynastic claims to territory based upon custom or ancient privilege no longer held the sway they once had. These claims could now be contended, thus territory was desired "to create readily defensible and powerful states" with rounded frontiers "to create more self-sufficient units" of sovereignty.[38] Territorial-sovereigns had thus developed a passion for contiguous, defensible territories and many conflicts were fought in attempt to unite divided dynastic holdings. Thus the principle of territoriality was the only means of social and political closure available to resolve the legitimation crisis created by the Westphalian settlement.

On the continent, any and all means were employed in the acquisition of state-buttressing territory. War, as we have seen, was considered not only a legitimate means, but the most decisive means, and most wars had clear territorial objectives when they were launched. Negotiation was generally only effective when one had territory in hand to bargain with. Purchase was not uncommon (and is, significantly, quite difficult to imagine in the nationalist era). Matrimony still could serve to acquire territory, but now in a manner limited by the balancing concerns of others. The loss of territory was inevitably bitterly resented and could result in prolonged "wars of recovery."[39] As we shall see, Austria's preoccupation with recovering Silesia, lost to Friedrich the Great of Prussia, served to align the Hapsburg monarchy with its ancient nemesis France during the Seven Years' War, with disastrous consequences for both.

Most significantly, the land-grabbing proclivity that accompanied the state-building of the period, and that was even more pronounced in military struggles for territory in the colonial periphery, was in large measure a direct consequence of this dynastic legitimation crisis. The absence of logical frontiers had not been such a significant impetus to international violence when dynastic-feudal claims had held sway. Now these claims were largely defunct, but neither had they yet been

38. Luard, *The Balance of Power*, 175–76.
39. Ibid., 184–95.

replaced by any clear linguistic, ethnic or cultural alignments within contiguous territories ruled by the emerging, centralized administrative apparatus of the absolutist state. As Luard suggests, "one state had as good a reason to claim a particular territory as another."[40] Certainly this was doubly so in the periphery, where commercial quasimilitary enterprises and the settlers that followed on their heels pushed aside, enslaved, and in most conceivable fashions exploited the indigenous peoples they encountered there, as well as the resources of the lands which these peoples had previously regarded as their homes.[41]

I will begin the analytic section of this article with an illustration of the behavioral consequences of territorial-sovereign identity drawn from the pages of diplomatic history. This article will conclude with a comparative illustration of the behavioral consequences of national-sovereign identity in the nineteenth century. I now proceed with an analysis of the consequences of territorial sovereignty for strategic behavior during an eighteenth-century dispute between Britain and France over which of them would be master on the North American continent.

THE EUROPEAN "DIPLOMATIC REVOLUTION" AND UNSETTLED SCORES

France had by 1750 constructed a series of settlements and fortresses, from New Orleans in the south to Quebec in the North which bisected the continent and threatened to foreclose further British westward expansion. By the middle of the decade it became clear to each side that the issue of supremacy in America would be settled by a test of arms. Britain was anxious to constrain the conflict to the North American periphery where its preponderance of sea power would quickly and economically overwhelm France and deliver mastery of America. France's best hope of victory lay in grinding down British resolve and resources in a continental war, diverting British resources from America. Newcastle, and William Pitt (the Elder) had greatly feared a continental theater of the approaching war as most inimical to British interests, and began to cast about for continental allies strong enough to frustrate this ambition and contain the coming conflict to the seas, and to North America.

---

40. Ibid., 198.
41. A particularly thorough account of the impact of colonial wars on indigenous peoples may be found in Francis Jennings, *Empire of Fortune: Crowns, Colonies and Tribes in the Seven Years War in America* (New York: Norton, 1988).

As Europe prepared for the Seven Years' War it was still fully in the hands of European territorial-sovereigns. The Bourbon-Hapsburg rivalry which had dominated European international relations from the Westphalian settlement through the close of the War of Spanish Succession had begun to give way to a more multipolar arrangement. The issues surrounding the realignment about to occur in Europe were led by the Franco-British competition in the periphery, and the Austrian vendetta against Prussia over the loss of Silesia in 1740. This action by Friedrich the Great had roughly doubled the territory of Prussia, created a Great Power to upset Austrian hegemony over the German states, and enraged the Hapsburg dynasty. The Prussian acquisition had also upset Russia's ambitions in central Europe. We should also consider the importance of the personal caprice of territorial-sovereign monarchs in the equation. The Russian Czarina, Elizabeth, clearly despised Friedrich II of Prussia as an individual, which had added venom to the already bitter potion of dynastic ambition and more than soured the relationship between Berlin and St. Petersburg.[42]

As Britain and France squared off over control of territory in the colonial periphery, Britain had begun to caste about the continent in search of allies there, feeling disinclined to stand alone against France. Dutch fear of a powerful French neighbor, which had clearly recovered its strength so many years after the Treaty of Utrecht had formalized the demise of the last French bid for continental hegemony, had placed the previous British arrangements with the Dutch in question. Prussia had been hostile to Britain since 1753 owing to an unresolved maritime dispute. Moreover, the existing British defensive alliance with Russia was due to expire in 1757. Apprehending the isolation to which these problems threatened to consign them as they contemplated war with France, the British monarch and government instituted a frenetically active diplomacy in 1755 in order to correct this isolation.

The Hanoverian succession of 1714 had dealt Britain another misfortune. As war with France for empire in America loomed, the reigning British monarch, George II, was simultaneously Elector of Hanover on the continent. In the event of continental hostilities, little Hanover was vulnerable to being overrun either by France from the west, or by Prussia from the east. So long as George was attached to his electorate, royal pressure for the provision of the defense of Hanover was to be a factor in every decision taken by Newcastle, and later by Pitt, in the

42. See, for example, Woloch, *Eighteenth Century Europe*, 41.

conduct of British foreign policy. Unfortunately for Newcastle and for Pitt, George was very much attached to Hanover, as his sovereignty over it provided him with a great deal of personal income and enhanced his status as a player in the politics of Central Europe and the flagging Holy Roman Empire. Of course, this dual-sovereignty of a monarch over, in this case, both English and German-speaking territories separated by geography, language, culture and history is no longer possible in the national-sovereign era. Yet such an arrangement was quite unremarkable in the eighteenth-century territorial-sovereign system, and, I will argue, had causal significance not only for the conduct of British diplomacy, but for the British conduct of the war. The causal significance of such an institutional fact[43] is beyond the notice of structural realist and neorealist systems' theoretical explanations which would generally emphasize arguments like this one:

> The Seven Years' War—whatever its immediate causes—represents a deeper structural crisis within the global political system, generated by the need to readjust relations among the core states in the system in line with intervening changes in power distributions and, in a more general sense, to resolve prewar ambiguities in the order and status hierarchy of the system itself.[44]

It is never made clear, when structural realists are generating such sweeping assertions, why these immediate causes are of no interest or significance. Neither is it ever really made clear what these system needs are, or at what point they become dire. Schweizer cites, as his inspiration for this analysis, the power-transition theories of Organski and Kugler, and the cycles-of-hegemonic-war thesis of Robert Gilpin, and other theorists of structural social causation, such as George Modelski and Immanuel Wallerstein.[45] It is puzzling to see a historian acquire the structural realist passion for the reification of functional-structural teleology in this context, and to generate an assertion in which the designation of actors is abandoned in place of the agency of a disembodied "system" that is in "crisis." Social systems are trans-

---

43. For a development of the notion of institutional facts and their role in structuring action, see Friedrich Kratochwil, "Regimes, Interpretation and the 'Science' of Politics: A Reappraisal," *Millennium* 17, no. 2 (summer 1988): 263–84. For a new and more general development of the significance of institutional facts in social life, see John R. Searle, *The Construction of Social Reality* (New York: Free Press, 1995), 79–126.

44. Karl Schweizer, "The Seven Years' War: A System Perspective," in *The Origins of War in Early Modern Europe*, ed. Jeremy Black (Edinburgh: John Donald, 1987), 242.

45. Ibid., 255 n. 4.

formed and replaced when they cease to be reproduced by social actors, but they are sometimes intentionally transformed by the agency
of these actors. Similarly, alliance systems do break down, but in response to specific decisions taken by specific social actors.

The passage quoted above is a very strange argument when the prose
is disaggregated in order to clarify what is being said. We must, by contrast, be careful to point out that France and especially Britain, not
"the system," needed to adjust relations among core states. Britain
needed to do so because France was challenging her in the periphery
and threatening to isolate her on the continent. Britain and France
"needed" to fight the Seven Years' War because they were, respectively, eighteenth-century territorial-sovereign mercantilist oligarchies
and autocracies, and they were playing the game that eighteenth-
century territorial-sovereign mercantilist oligarchies and autocracies
had created to play. Elizabeth of Russia, and Maria Theresa of Austria
needed "to resolve prewar ambiguities in the order and status hierarchy" because Friedrich the Great had played the game well at their expense and they consequently despised and resented his grandson. The
system "needed" the legitimate functioning of mercantilist, oligarchic
and autocratic territorial-sovereigns in order to continue to exist in its
eighteenth-century form. It ceased to exist when these did. Failure to
recognize that the functioning of a system is dependent on the variable
"needs," motivations, interests and agency of social actors, which must
be designated in the ontological construction of a system theory, is the
greatest error of structural realist teleologies of this form. Let us return
to the European theater of the war for further illustration. The discussion will deepen my critique of structural realist system theory by
demonstrating that, without correction, it cannot adequately explain
the notion of interest that informs the practice even of territorial-
sovereign alliance formation. I will demonstrate that commitments to
particular territories cannot be explained by structural realist theory
without incorporating a more rigorous analysis of the prevailing, historically contingent, structure of sovereign identities and interests.

THE DEFENSE OF HANOVER AND ISSUES OF TERRITORIAL SOVEREIGNTY

The devastating seventeenth-century English civil war that had toppled
the Stuarts, and created the monarchical vacancy that the Hanoverian
succession was designed to fill, had also resulted in a distrust of a large
standing army that had remained with Britain to the eve of the Seven

Years' War. It was a measure of the value which Britain placed in further westward expansion in North America at the expense of France when Parliament voted £1,000,000 on 22 March 1755 to enhance the army and navy.[46] It was generally felt in Britain that its forces were adequate to deal with the French on the North American continent, and on the seas approaching and surrounding it, as the British had established "a clear working superiority"[47] over the French in naval forces. The relatively diminutive size of Britain's standing army, and the lack of enthusiasm for strongly enhancing it, however, suggested to the British that they would need to fight the French on the continent with the forces of others. This could be accomplished only by alliance diplomacy, or by the payment of subsidies, or with a combination of these strategies.[48]

The territorial-sovereign practice of payment of subsidies implied either subsidizing the armed forces of allies engaged in hostilities for their own casus belli, or payment of cash to the sovereign of troops who would serve under British colors and orders for a period of time specified by treaty. Such an arrangement was essentially a contract for mercenary troops, whatever the arrangement might be called. In significant contrast with the national-sovereign era, there were, during the period of the Seven Years' War, a large number of states that seemed to specialize in these services, and whose sovereigns relied upon the revenues from such contracts to make ends meet.[49]

Eldon's 1938 study of the British policy of subsidies to the continent during the Seven Years' War provides an appendix which details the annual British subsidies to no less than ten such states. According to this data, Britain provided subsidies to, or contracted troops from Mentz, Brunswick-Wolfenbüttel, Bavaria, Saxony, Hesse-Cassel, Hanover, Prussia, Brunswick, and Portugal.[50] Britain also subsidized Russia for a time early in the war. Among these states, Russia and

---

46. Carl William Eldon, "England's Subsidy Policy Towards the Continent During the Seven Years' War" (Ph. D. diss., University of Pennsylvania, 1938), 11.

47. Julian S. Corbett, *England in the Seven Years' War: A Study in Combined Strategy*, vol. 1, (London: Longmans, Green, 1918; reprint, New York: AMS, 1973), 23.

48. Kennedy, *The Rise and Fall of the Great Powers*, 111–13.

49. For all of these reasons Hampton correctly observes that, during this period, the "norms shared by the great powers did not erase the option of implementing force between them" (Mary N. Hampton, "NATO, Germany, and the United States: Creating Positive Identity in Trans-Atlantia," *Security Studies* 8, nos. 2/3 [winter 1998/99–spring 1999]: 229).

50. Eldon, *England's Subsidy Policy*. See the appendix, "Table II—Subsidy Payments," 160.

Prussia, at least, were belligerents in their own right, and should not be seen merely as provenders of mercenaries in order to glean state revenues. Russia, of course, fought on the side of France. Eldon demonstrates that the diplomatic record provides evidence that Saxony and Bavaria, however, were highly dependent upon subsidy money to maintain themselves as states.[51] Both of these states approached Britain for such arrangements. Saxony was initially engaged for the defense of Hanover (to quell the fears of George), with the understanding that Britain would defend Saxony if attacked, presumably by Prussia.[52] Clearly Saxony's armed forces did not exist solely for the purpose of defending Saxon territory, a finding somewhat at odds with the assumptions of the structural realist position. Bavaria was not to be thus engaged by Britain during the war as the Bavarian Elector demurred on renewal of an existing subsidy arrangement with Britain until he could ascertain the sentiments of Austria,[53] whose immanent presence and preponderance of force no doubt weighed heavily on his mind.

Parliamentary debate on the issue of the defense of Hanover had come about indirectly through debate on a measure to provide a subsidy to Hanover to pay and provision 8,000 Hanoverian troops for its defense. That this measure would be advanced by the government—men who were appointed by and beholden to the king—could not have been a surprise for the Whig oligarchy assembled in parliament. Such a measure allowed George II to ensure the defense of his Electorate with troops, paid with British money, and to ensure his own revenues into the bargain. Pitt, then still in opposition, included in his arguments against the measure the fascinating dilemma that the government's emphasis of the defense of Hanover demonstrated that treaties made with other powers for the defense of Hanover had been made in the interests of the Electorate of Hanover, namely George II, not in the interest of Britain. Many felt that the interests of Britain would be best served by surrendering Hanover until the end of the war, and demanding it back as a condition of peace.[54]

Eldon has captured the gist of the debate on the pros and cons of a British subsidy policy on the continent in his study of the pamphlets circulating in Britain in the summer and fall of 1755 that debated the issue. They are worth pausing to discuss, not only as they recount an

51. Ibid., 18.
52. Ibid., 20.
53. Ibid., 14.
54. Ibid., 47.

important debate whose outcome would strongly influence further British conduct of the war, but because they provide a fascinating glimpse of the interests of the eighteenth-century mercantilist oligarchy of Britain.

Those opposed to the subsidies argued that Britain could never gain enough on the continent to compensate for the cost of the subsidies. They argued that the European costs would starve British military forces in America. They asked why Britain should hire German princes to defend their own lands. They argued that France would not, in any case, overrun those countries on the continent with whom Britain was engaged in active trade, and thus saw no benefit to Britain's trade from a continental war. They argued that continental wars had always impoverished Britain in the past, that this was merely to play into French hands and that mercenary troops were, in any case, untrustworthy.[55]

Also gleaned from the pamphlets are the arguments of those favoring the subsidy arrangements. The pro-subsidy forces argue that subsidies were the best and cheapest way of diverting France, and conversely the most expensive for France. They argued that the Russian subsidy would prevent Prussian aggression, by cowing Prussia and thus neutralizing Friedrich. They argued that German subsidies would permit their continental fight to take the offensive, and would allow Britain to focus on the destruction of the French navy and commercial shipping, and thus to defend the colonies. They argued that it was better to pay in British money than in British lives, and that the destruction of French shipping alone could not destroy French trade owing to the inevitable persistence of land routes and neutral carriers. They argued that there could be no markets for re-exports from British colonies if France overran Europe, and that the maintenance of an English army on the continent would be much more expensive than the provision of mercenary troops. They also argued that an English militia would draw men from economic pursuits, that Britain's real wealth lay in the pursuits of industry, trade and commerce, and thus that it would be wasteful to turn productive workers into soldiers.[56]

The fact that these points were debated, and hotly debated, is highly suggestive in itself, in spite of the fact that many of these arguments are highly problematic upon further examination. Lacking the mercantilist

55. Ibid., 51–52.
56. Ibid., 53–54.

blinders of these eighteenth-century oligarchs, we might find, from our national-sovereign perspective, serious flaws with the premises of most of these arguments. What is particularly noteworthy is that nearly all of these arguments, both pro and con, are predicated on the assumptions and notions of state interest that were consistent with the legitimating principles of mercantilist, oligarchic or absolutist, eighteenth-century territorial-sovereign identity. In this *Weltanschauung*, as we have seen, international economic competition is a zero-sum game. What helps you must hurt your opponent. Men, money, commodities, trade, armed force are all fungibly interchangeable.[57] Colonies are valuable as they promote trade and gain wealth. More is better, thus more colonies are war objectives. Continental allies with whom one trades minimally are expendable. British subjects are too valuable for the commodity value of their labor to risk losing to French cannonade.

These people thought like capitalists, not like patriots, let alone nationalists. This is not to suggest that there was no "love of country" in eighteenth-century Britain or France, but that this sentiment did not appear to influence significantly either decisions to go to war, or war objectives, or the conduct of war, or even who would do the fighting. These decisions, at least in the British case, appear to have been more strongly influenced by love of profit than of country. Here is, in many dimensions, the model of the state-as-firm in the competitive market place that inspires nearly all theories of rational choice in the literature on international relations. Debates such as these certainly lend these theories some credence. These theories, however, fail to mention the extent to which the character and issues of such debates change when the notion of state (or now, national) interest changes. Such a transformation in the British notion of state interest was to begin before the end of the eighteenth century, with the humiliating loss of the North American colonies, and the delegitimation of mercantilist thought by the development of liberal economic theory of the later Scottish Enlightenment. The debate was settled when Parliament voted 301 to 105 in December of 1755 to retain the pledge of assistance to Hanover with the lame assertion the British "honor" was at stake in Hanover. George had his way. Russian and Hessian subsidy treaties were also approved that month.[58]

---

57. Kennedy, *The Rise and Fall of the Great Powers*, 113.
58. Eldon, *England's Subsidy Policy*, 55–57.

An active British diplomacy had also turned toward Berlin and Vienna in the hope that if defensive alliances could be arranged with both of these, France would wisely eschew continental hostilities and be forced to confine these to the sea and North America, where Britain had a strong advantage in forces deployed and deployable. Prussia had not been a natural British ally, but Friedrich's seizure of Silesia from Austria in 1740 had transformed Prussia into a considerable continental power, and Friedrich was still anxious merely to maintain and consolidate Prussian control over it by 1755. Neither is it inconceivable that dynastic loyalties played some role in this British-Prussian diplomacy when we realize that George II was Friedrich's uncle.[59] By the end of November 1755 Britain had promised to renew its guarantee of Prussian control of Silesia and to settle Prussia's grievance regarding the ships Britain had seized from Prussia if only Prussia guaranteed Hanover's neutrality in any future conflict. The result of this diplomacy was the Convention of Westminster, signed on 16 January 1756, in which each party pledged peace and friendship.[60] This alliance poisoned British diplomacy with Austria, however, and the Austrian Empress, intent on recovering Silesia from Friedrich, "refused point-blank to subscribe to a treaty in which Prussia was a party."[61]

The Convention of Westminster, concluded in large measure to secure Prussian defense of George's Hanover, triggered the rest of the European realignment that has become known as the "diplomatic revolution." The hasty arrangement of the Convention, and the fact that it was concluded without consultation with other interested parties, namely France, Russia and Austria, strongly irritated these courts and set in motion the diplomacy that led to their own alliance. It was not lost on the court in St. Petersburg that the British subsidy arrangement with Russia that had just been signed in December was starkly contradicted by the Convention as it "provided for Russians coming into Germany [sic], the former for keeping them out."[62] The Austrian vendetta regarding Prussian control of Silesia assured that the Hapsburgs had at last found a common cause with the Bourbons, in their capacities as territorial sovereigns, that their common Catholicism had never been able to foster when, in their capacities as purely dynastic sover-

---

59. Ibid., 58.
60. Ibid., 61.
61. Ibid., 62.
62. Ibid., 71.

eigns, Catholic Hapsburgs had squared off against the Catholic Valois and Bourbon kings of France in centuries past.[63]

This rapprochement was cemented in a Franco-Austrian alliance with the signing of the First Treaty of Versailles on 1 May 1756. Britain declared war against France two weeks later, Russia promised assistance to Austria in the event the latter was attacked by Prussia, and Franco-Russian rapprochement strengthened with an exchange of ministers in May. By June, Friedrich's strategic-political position was quite precarious. Certain of the imminence of hostilities, he decided on a preemptive move to strengthen his strategic-military position and invaded Saxony, against British wishes and advice to the contrary. Russia mobilized in response and promised assistance to France and Austria. Newcastle then suspended British subsidy payments to Russia lest they be used to fight Friedrich.[64]

This series of events suggests that it is less illuminating than it would at first appear to intone that "whatever it's immediate causes...[the war]... represents a deeper structural crisis in the global political system."[65] The British requirement to provide for the defense of Hanover resulted directly from the dual-sovereignty of George II over Britain and Hanover, and from this consideration alone. The Prussian alliance was clearly designed primarily to enssure Prussian defense of Hanover. France was to be belligerent in any case, and neither Russia nor Austria were situated geographically to provide a credible guarantee of Hanover's security, thus they were not approached in this regard. Only Prussia possessed the geographical proximity and military capability either to defend Hanover as a British ally from a powerful and belligerent France, or to seize it as an enemy of Britain. In the absence of the requirement to defend Hanover, and the Prussian alliance that predominantly secured this defense, British diplomacy would have been free to pursue, and much more likely to secure, Austrian and Russian alliances that might well have prevented any French action on the continent.

It is therefore quite reasonable to argue that one of the major immediate causes of the continental theater of the war was the unique character of George II's dual-territorial-sovereignty over Britain and Hano-

---

63. For a discussion of the pattern of French pragmatism on the matter of alignment in accordance with confessional factors, see Mark Greengrass, *The French Reformation* (Oxford: Basil Blackwell, 1987); and Emannuel Le Roy Ladurie, *The Royal French State 1460–1610*, trans. Juliet Vale (London: Blackwell, 1994).

64. Eldon, *England's Subsidy Policy*, 73–78.

65. Schweizer, 'The Seven Years' War: A System Perspective," 242.

ver. It is not at all clear from the diplomatic record that (1) either Britain or France perceived any "structural crisis they needed to resolve" on the European continent, or (2) hostilities initiated in the North American periphery would have migrated to a European theater at all without British anxiety over the status of Hanover.

The European alliance realignment that we now call the diplomatic revolution occurred entirely subsequent to the signing of the Convention of Westminster, and in reaction to it. The realignment was not due to any parsimonious, disembodied, structural determinism latent within the system, but occurred because Austria had an axe to grind with Prussia, and Russia had ambitions in central Europe that could be much more easily achieved subsequent to the demise of Prussia. The European theater of the Seven Years' War was thus engaged largely because the whims and caprice of eighteenth-century territorial-sovereigns led to decisions (George's insistence on the defense of Hanover at all costs, Maria Theresa's insistence on the recovery of Silesia at all costs, Friedrich's anxiety to leave a Prussia augmented by Silesia to his heir, Czarina Elizabeth's loathing of Friedrich) that had unintended consequences. Opposition to the will of the king in Hanoverian England could have cost the average ambitious Whig oligarch dearly in patronage and position,[66] and the whims and words of Maria Theresa, Friedrich and Elizabeth were law in their lands.

In the conduct of the war the defense of Hanover appeared to take precedence over many other objectives as well, including sound military and political strategy. With William Pitt the Elder, the earlier opponent of continental subsidies, in charge of the government in 1758, George II again displayed the division of his loyalties between Britain and Hanover. Friedrich was now receiving British subsidies to the tune of £670,000 sterling per year. Subsequent to the Prussian defeat at the Battle of Kolin in June 1758, and the subsequent Prussian evacuation of Bohemia (in which much of Friedrich's mercenary army had disappeared in mass desertions), Friedrich had gathered his strength and prepared to resume the offensive. Pitt wanted to send Friedrich a strong letter of British support of this intention, but George wanted the forces under Friedrich's command in Hanover excluded from the campaign under the lame pretense that this would be impossible "due to his [George's] obligation to accept an Austrian agreement regarding

---

66. H. T. Dickinson, "Whiggism in the Eighteenth Century," in *The Whig Ascendancy: Colloquies on Hanoverian England*, ed. John Cannon (New York: St. Martin's, 1981), 43.

Hanover's neutrality."[67] After leaving George's presence, Pitt expressed the opinion that a separate peace for Hanover would be an intolerable breach of faith with Friedrich and ordered Newcastle "to give Prussia the strongest assurance of support" counter to George's wishes.[68]

George had evidently moved privately to obtain a separate peace for Hanover in any case, perhaps leery of a direct clash on the matter with the formidable Pitt, whom he needed as Britain grappled with war on two continents. In any event, later in the year, George's son, the Duke of Cumberland, concluded the Convention of Closterseven and a separate peace for Hanover, acting on the full powers of his father. The temerity of George when confronted with this breach of faith was remarkable. As Eldon recounts it: "The king [George] insisted falsely that the convention had been signed contrary to his orders."[69] Not even the equally audacious Pitt had a stomach for questioning the king's veracity, but Pitt, in his capacity as head of the government, insisted upon the abrogation of the treaty in vehement terms, and refused to allow the exchequer to send any more funds to Hanover until the troops there were again in motion against France.[70] Later, in the summer of 1759, George declared that his Hanoverian revenues were only sufficient to pay his 42,000 Hanoverian troops, and that consequently Britain would have to pay all other expenses associated with the defense of Hanover. An angry Pitt refused and instead spoke of terminating all continental operations.[71]

CONQUERING AMERICA IN GERMANY?

In reading such accounts, it is both fascinating and terrible for those of us reared in the era of national-sovereignty to watch an eighteenth-century statesman be required to negotiate with, and to outmaneuver his monarch in order to ensure that the latter conducted foreign policy in a manner consistent with the "interests" and security of the state whose throne he had mounted. A conflict in the "interests" of the sovereign qua king of Britain and the empire, and the interests of the sovereign qua Elector of Hanover, could be acknowledged and debated, as

---

67. Eldon, *England's Subsidy Policy,* 100.
68. Jeremy Black, "Chatham Revisited," *History Today* 41, no. 8 (August 1991): 38.
69. Eldon, *England's Subsidy Policy,* 101.
70. Ibid., 103.
71. Ibid., 118.

Pitt had done while still in opposition. Ultimately, however, precisely because the interests of the king qua dynast and the interests of the king qua territorial sovereign could not be decoupled, the "interests" of George in both capacities had to be accommodated, and reconciled with those of the British empire, as Pitt had done when he left the opposition and agreed to lead George's government. The same William Pitt the Elder who had so vehemently opposed the defense of Hanover and the expense of the system of continental subsidies designed to ensure it, was now called upon to defend the subsidy policy as expenses mounted with the progress of the war. As Schweizer himself suggests, though he does not grasp the extent to which the assertion damages his structural realist explanation of the origins of the war:

> Although Englishmen often resented the union of Hanover and Britain, abandoning Hanover was strategically [sic] and politically [much more to the point] unfeasible...the impossibility of severing the connection insured that Hanover's interests would be considered by British administrations, and, on occasion, would predominate. It also meant that Britain was obliged to make provisions for Hanover's defense and thus for continental war, by subsidies to allies, through a British expeditionary force or both.[72]

It is difficult to argue, in the face of this realization, that British "sovereignty" was so firmly lodged with the people or with the Parliament as Britons then and now might wish to believe. George may have had a Parliament and the wishes and interests of British oligarchs to contend with, but his arrangement of the defense of Hanover throughout the war, in the teeth of voices and evidence that suggested that this policy could not be easily reconciled with the seemingly objective political and strategic interests of the British empire, demonstrates that George II was an eighteenth-century territorial-sovereign in his own right. Even though it would appear he acted to protect personal and dynastic interests, the principle of raison d'état still legitimated his actions to the extent that he successfully extended his sovereignty over, and to, German Hanover on the continent. When it was clear that he insisted upon this extension, the British notion of "state interest" adjusted to incorporate the necessity of the defense of Hanover. As this is the case, and as this example serves to help illustrate, it becomes quite problematic to speak of the "objective interests" of the

---

72. Schweizer, "The Seven Years' War, A System Perspective," 248.

state in a trans-historical or an ahistorical fashion.[73] It is difficult to see how any structural model of rational choice, let alone structural neorealism, can account for this. One suggestion which emerges from this discussion is that the interests of whatever institutional form of collective action which forms the units that populate a given historical system are not static, not "an object of rational determination,"[74] or objectively given even within the time span of a single military conflict, let alone across the time frame in which that "system" is dominant, or across "systems" that I argue are constituted and reconstituted by transformations in the prevailing forms of collective identity.

British conduct, and especially Pitt's conduct to the end of the war, illustrate that certainly British war objectives had expanded from colonial territorial aggrandizement in the periphery at least to encompass extracting Britain from the European theater of the conflict without surrendering or endangering Hanover, and without undue cost in lives or money. Money may have won out over lives near the end, as British finances became strained, and Pitt acceded to the introduction of British troops to the "German war" by May 1760, upon learning how much money Friedrich demanded in exchange for allowing Britain to conclude a separate peace with France.[75] Further, by the close of 1759, in the North American periphery, the strategic points of Niagara, Ticonderoga, Crown Point and Quebec had all fallen to British forces and Pitt had begun to realize, contrary to his earlier opinion, the real benefits that the British free hand in the North American theater, occasioned by the continental subsidy policy, had gained for Britain at the expense of France.

Other British war objectives and interests had remained constant. As Montreal fell in September of 1760, the British conquest of North America was moving to mopping-up operations and Pitt and Newcastle had determined to continue the war only to obtain the most favorable (and lucrative) settlement from France. Pitt was now kept quite busy defending the "German war" before the restless Parliament that was the first to convene with a new king, George III, on the throne. Prussia's price in money for a separate British peace with France remained too high, however, and Russian diplomacy under Elizabeth

73. It is equally problematic, *contra* Marx, to speak of the "objective interests" of a socio-economic class, and for similar reasons, but this is a topic for another article.
74. Raymond Aron, *Peace and War: A Theory of International Relations* (New York: Praeger, 1966), 285.
75. Eldon, *England's Subsidy Policy*, 131–32.

insisted on Russian acquisition of Prussian territory in return for a Russian cessation of hostilities.[76] At this point, Pitt provided the final demonstration of his extreme mercantilist proclivities as head of the British government when Spain, hoping to bolster its own colonial empire, concluded an alliance with France in mid-August of 1761. Spain's miscalculation was grave and its timing bad. Pitt was anxious to use the alliance as a pretext to declare war on Spain in order to allow the British navy to capture Spanish treasure fleets.[77] Spanish gold from America would alleviate severely strained British finances and defray the long-term expenses of the unexpectedly expensive war for Britain. Outvoted on this measure, he resigned on 5 October 1761, and consigned himself to defending, as a private member of Parliament, the continental war "for having diverted the energies of France. 'America', he said, has been conquered in Germany'."[78]

Irrespective of the merits of this claim, Parliament was not consoled by the fact that America had been conquered so long as the war raged on in Europe at a ruinous cost, principally in British money. Fortunately for British coffers, for Prussian territorial integrity, and for Pitt's reputation, the irascible Russian Czarina Elizabeth died in January of the following year, "when Friedrich II's military fortunes were at their lowest point,"[79] to be succeeded by the Pro-Prussian Peter III, who offered Prussia peace on terms so favorable that Austria and France, in recognition that they could now hope for a return to the status quo ante bellum at best, were forced to sue for peace.[80] The 1763 Peace of Paris left Great Britain in control of the North American continent east of the Mississippi River, the Indian subcontinent, and a number of strategic islands.[81]

Thus this eighteenth-century, transcontinental war ended with Britain overwhelmingly the big winner.[82] Had America been conquered in Germany? Pitt has today long been lionized by historians as the strategic visionary who saw that the strategic division of French energies between two continents and an ocean, made possible by the system of

76. Ibid., 137–9.
77. Ibid., 140.
78. Ibid., 143.
79. Karl W. Schweizer and Carol S. Leonard, "Britain, Prussia, Russia and the Galitzin Letter: A Reassessment," *Historical Journal* 26, no. 3 (March 1983): 531.
80. Kennedy, *The Rise and Fall of the Great Powers,* 114.
81. Corbett, *England and the Seven Years' War*, vol. 2, 377–90. Corbett provides the English language text of the treaty in the appendix to his second volume.
82. See, for example, Kennedy, *The Rise and Fall of the Great Powers,* 114.

subsidies to the continent, had left British forces free to ride herd over the Atlantic and Caribbean and the North American continent, in spite of the evidence that he clearly held the opposite opinion while in opposition and vacillated while in office.[83] Pitt may well have been, and probably was, convinced of the efficacy of this policy at some point, most likely in the annus mirabilis of 1759, when French colonies fell to British forces around the globe. More important than the answer to this question, in my view, is the notion of state interest that animated the subsidy policy. To illuminate this, I will conclude this section, appropriately, with a citation from the last paragraph of Eldon's study of the subsidy policy.

> Whether we take the word of the [British] pamphleteer who wrote: "if you take your people from their work, and make soldiers of militia man...you will certainly be the cause of its (money) going abroad, never to return again," or whether we quote the ministerial doctrine that "we must be merchants while we are soldiers,"... we can see operating even in war time the belief that it is better to work for one's country than to die for it.[84]

These sentiments, particularly the notion that it is better to work and produce for your country than to die for it, are quintessential tenants of the notion of interest that animated the eighteenth-century, mercantilist, territorial-sovereign state system. This last sentiment, as we shall see, was to become quintessentially alien to the national-sovereign collective identity that was soon to break upon America and Western Europe, and from there to Central and Eastern Europe and the globe.

In light of the analysis above, what is the reason that, in 1756, George II could rearrange a hitherto stable system of European alliances, to the effective disadvantage of a notion of British interests as calculated within a rational instrumental logic predicated on the assumption of the state as a unitary actor? How could he have induced his ministers and nation to accept a painfully expensive continental war which might have been averted by abandoning Hanover? The explanation lies in the nature of eighteenth-century territorial sovereignty and the self-understandings of the relevant actors. Even in Britain, which had earlier ended a Stuart dynasty with an act of regicide, George was sovereign of both Britain and Hanover, and so long as this

---

83. Ibid., 98.
84. Eldon, *England's Subsidy Policy*, 160.

was the case he was able to extend his sovereignty over each. British national interests could not be neatly decoupled from George's personal interests qua sovereign of Britain and Hanover. Even the enfranchised Whig oligarchy was unable, at the level of policy, to decouple their interests qua British national interests from the personal, dynastic interests of George II. Let me move to analysis of the strategic behavior and the fate of a nineteenth-century emperor who reigned a century after the close of the Seven Years' War, in the national-sovereign era, where matters were quite different.

NATIONAL-SOVEREIGN IDENTITY AND STRATEGIC BEHAVIOR

LOUIS BONAPARTE, a nephew of Napoleon, was elected president of the Second French republic in 1848. He seized power in a military coup four years later and had himself crowned Napoleon III, emperor of the Second French Empire, subsequent to a plebiscite in which the French people had declared themselves weary of republicanism. Louis Napoleon had, as Marx caustically observed, replaced "liberté, egalité, fraternité, with cavalry, infantry, artillery."

Napoleon III's reign was not to be conducted with the carefree, unselfconscious, pseudo-autocratic authority that Friedrich-Wilhelm managed to carry off in Prussia, in spite of the parliamentary window-dressing that the latter had been required to give to his government from 1848. Napoleon III wished to reign as had his grand-uncle, but he found it unexpectedly difficult to carry off the trappings of absolutism. The violent manner in which he had established his empire rankled Great Britain and all republicans. The plebescitory manner in which he had formally acquired his title left serious questions regarding his legitimacy as a monarch in the eyes of his continental peers. In any event his dynasty was distressingly young and quixotically nouveau royale from the perspective of the courts of Vienna, St. Petersburg, Berlin and Madrid. Consequently they had been very hesitant to grant him the full, official recognition that was due to a brother-monarch, and they addressed him in their official correspondence, throughout his reign, and to his considerable irritation as "*notre très cher ami* [our very dear friend] rather than *Sire mon frère* [Majesty my brother]."[85]

---

85. Ibid., 15.

It was not possible to legitimate the Second Empire with recourse to the dynastic, divine right that the other monarchies of mid-nineteenth-century Europe still so resolutely relied upon. Whether by design or by default, Napoleon III inherited the nationalist credentials of his uncle. France had chosen the Second Empire in lieu of the Second Republic in her craving for a return to the national glory of the first Empire.[86] A Bonaparte served this purpose. He professed a belief in the power of the development of "completed nation-states" as a progressive, organizing, and modernizing force of history and was soon to play the champion of the principle of nationality in the conduct of his foreign policy. Kissinger argues that Napoleon "was driven to dependence on public opinion [to maintain his legitimacy], and his policy fluctuated with his assessment of what was needed to sustain his [domestic] popularity."[87] He was only consistently popular when that policy consistently defended the principle of nationality.

NATIONALITY AND LEGITIMACY IN THE SECOND EMPIRE:
CONSEQUENCES FOR ALLIANCE FORMATION

By 1854 Napoleon had entered the Crimean War on the side of England, in part to check Russian expansion into the collapsing Ottoman empire. This move was quite popular at home precisely because it avenged France against Russia's role in the defeat of the first empire of a Napoleon. Later in the decade he was to bring French troops into the fray of a War of Italian liberation against Austria. This conflict posed a conflict of state and "national" interests that became a classical pattern for the hybrid international system of the nineteenth century—a mixed system of the competing territorial-sovereign and national-sovereign entities. The Austrian interest in engaging in the Italian campaign was the maintenance of "social order, political legitimacy and religious faith...[against]....Bonapar- tism, nationalist passions and secularization."[88] Having already made an enemy of Russia, Napoleon's Italian campaigns now earned him the permanent enmity of Hapsburg Austria, at whose expense the Italian unification had come.[89] Significantly,

86. Theo Aronson, *The Fall of the Third Napoleon* (Indianapolis and New York: Bobbs-Merrill, 1970), 15.

87. Ibid.

88. James J. Sheehan, *German History 1770–1866* (Oxford: Clarendon, 1989), 865.

89. Cronin provides an excellent constructivist account of Italian unification in this issue. See Bruce Cronin, "From Balance to Community: Transnational Identity and Political Integration," *Security Studies* 8, nos. 2/3 [winter 1998/99–spring 1999]: 270–

it also earned him the mistrust of Francophobe Great Britain, which was by no means pleased to witness new Napoleonic military activity such a short time after the Battle of Waterloo was supposed to have ended it once and for all. Neither had his Italian campaigns earned Napoleon the good will of the Pope. The advancing unification of Italy presented an obvious threat to the Papal States, and Napoleon had been forced in 1848, when still president of the Second Republic, to send a substantial French garrison to Rome in order to protect Pius IX from Garibaldi and the Roman Republic. Pius had issued his continued defense of his temporal authority in the forms of the encyclical *Quanta cura* and the December 1864 *Syllabus errorum*. Thus, as Prussian aggression and German unification loomed on Napoleon's eastern horizon, he could not yet remove the garrison without inflaming devout French Catholic opinion.[90] Unfortunately for Napoleon, French domestic opinion might have adored the principle of nationality, but not at the expense of the papacy. French identity might have been national, but it was also overwhelmingly Catholic. The papacy might be defied, as it had been during the first Empire, for the sake of the expression of French national identity,[91] but not for the sake of Italian national identity.

Worst of all, his actions in Italy had not even earned him the unequivocal gratitude of Italian patriots, who were upset that Napoleon had not freed all of northern Italy, as he had promised, and were no more pleased that the French garrison in Rome prevented the eternal city from becoming the capital city of the united Italy that the Risorgimento insisted it must become.[92] This was later to cost Napoleon the potential for an alliance with Italy, when he was to cast about in vain for help against the threat of a war with Prussia. In spite of the fact that Napoleon had wed his cousin, Prince Jerome Napoleon (who was known in France, irreverently, as Plon-Plon) to Clotilde, daughter to the Italian King Victor Emanuel II, Italy would not ally with France while French troops still protected the temporal power of the pa-

---

301). While I treat the German case, I share Cronin's use of the puzzle of unification as a "voluntary cession of sovereignty by a group of independent states to create an entirely new political authority" and also emphasize the irrationality of such an act in the structural realist and neoliberal institutionalist frameworks (ibid., 270, 273–74).

90. Eric Eyck, *Bismarck and the German Empire* (New York: Norton, 1968), 102–3.

91. See, for example, Woloch's treatment of the anticlerical nature of French domestic educational policy during the First Republic and much of the First Empire. See Isser Woloch, *The New Regime: Transformations of the French Civic Order, 1789–1820* (New York: Norton, 1994), 173–236.

92. Aronson, *The Fall of the Third Napoleon*, 20–21.

pacy.[93] This was so because the papacy had for long been so effective in sustaining political fragmentation on the Italian peninsula.

It is worthwhile to pause here and observe the extent to which the insularity of decision making for statesmen, which had been complete a century before the reign of Napoleon III, had become so badly eroded by this time that Napoleon could not make the move required to lock up an alliance with an emerging nation that he had helped to create. By the 1860s, Napoleon III, ruling France without the constraints of a constitution (until months before the end of his reign), found himself unable to take a decision to abandon a militarily helpless papacy to Italian nationalists in order to maximize his opportunity to gain a military ally which otherwise had been given every reason to support him. He could not do so precisely because such a decision would so badly inflame domestic opinion that his regime likely would not have survived the domestic aftershocks of such a decision. Napoleon could take no decision on foreign or domestic policy which could not be soundly excoriated in the *corps legeslatif* or in the press. Each major decision that Napoleon III had taken resulted in an unofficial plebiscite in France regarding the question of whether his rule and his dynasty would continue to be tolerated.

Napoleon was soon to further aggravate his strained relations with Russia by playing the champion of the cause of the long-suffering nationalists of partitioned Poland when they revolted against Alexander II in 1863. This policy played well to the appreciative Parisians, but gained the lasting enmity of Alexander. According to Aronson:

> Nor had a recent state visit [by Alexander] to Paris done anything to endear the Russian Emperor to Napoleon III's regime. His [Alexander's] arrival had been greeted by shouts of "Long live Poland!" and, on driving back one day with Napoleon from Longchamps, he had been shot at by a young Polish patriot. Napoleon's tactful observation that as the two of them had been under fire together they were now "brothers-in-arms" was frigidly received by the outraged Tsar. He returned to Russia in a very bad humor.[94]

Neither had Napoleon's ill-advised policy in Mexico endeared him to the court in Madrid. Napoleon had acceded to the encouragement of his Empress of Spanish birth, Eugenie, to install Maximilian, the brother of the Hapsburg Austrian Emperor, as a Catholic puppet em-

93. Ibid., 55.
94. Aronson, *The Fall of the Third Napoleon*, 56.

peror in republican Mexico.[95] This feat, and the subordinate relationship of Maximilian's "Empire" to the French Empire made France appear glorious in the eyes of domestic French nationalists of all political opinions. The glory this move bestowed on France allowed most Frenchmen to ignore the fact that Maximilian had essentially imposed a Catholic Hapsburg imperial government on a national republican Mexico. Similar to his policy of supporting the papacy against Italian nationalists, the installation of a puppet emperor in Mexico was another clear move away from support for the principle of nationality, though it won him rabid approval by domestic French nationalists.

NATIONAL IDENTITY AS A TOOL OF STATESMEN: BISMARCK
ENGINEERS THE DANISH AND AUSTRO-PRUSSIAN WARS

Napoleon's Prussian nemesis Bismarck, conversely, had been able to utilize an emerging sense of national identity among the German-speaking peoples of Central Europe to pursue quite traditional territorial-sovereign objectives for the Prussian crown.[96] From the inception of his administration, Bismarck consistently steered Prussian policy on a unilateral course oriented toward Prussian aggrandizement. Bismarck indeed sought the unification of the German states, but he sought this unification only as he envisioned it; under Prussian rule. He was masterfully to employ popular pan-German nationalist sentiment as a tool toward the attainment of this goal.[97] To that end Prussian policy under Bismarck, from 1863, set out to destroy the "legitimate structure of Europe" that had been codified in the 1815 Vienna treaties.[98] Like Napoleon III, Bismarck's policy was entirely subversive of the legitimating principles, and the agenda of Metternich's Vienna system. The Vienna system had been predicated on the assumption of common Austrian and Prussian interest in the maintenance of conservative institutions as

95. Ibid., 17.

96. Here, as Spirtas argues in a different context, "group identification contributes to intimate international cooperation" (Michael Spirtas, "French Twist: French and British NATO Policies from 1949 to 1966," *Security Studies* 8, nos. 2/3 [winter 1998/99–spring 1999]: 302).

97. As Cronin observes in the similar case of pan-Italian nationalism, "a more broadly conceived nationalism can extend the definition of one's community to include populations from other established states" (Cronin, "From Balance to Community," 280). The significance and "rational utility" of this fact was clearly not lost upon Bismarck.

98. Eyck, *Bismarck and the German Empire*, 71.

a bulwark against the forces of liberalism and democracy in the domestic opposition of each.[99]

Unfortunately for Austria, Bismarck did not feel that he required this bulwark to maintain order and conservative monarchical rule within Prussia. Austria was at this time, as it had always been, much more dynastic than territorial in outlook. Due to its polyglot ethnic and linguistic composition, cemented by a coextensive division of ethnicity with geography, the Austrian state had never been and could never become a national state. In deference to their imperial subjects traditions, the Hapsburgs had of old taken separate coronation oaths for the regions that they ruled. "Hapsburgs swore to defend each province and to respect its traditional customs, laws, privileges, and religion."[100] In doing so, the Austrian Hapsburgs attempted to govern a fairly conventional Empire along the lines of the Roman model of antiquity, subsequent to what Michael Doyle has described as the Augustan revolution of imperial administration.[101] The Austrian Hapsburg Empire was at this time, at the most, what Michael Mann calls a "confederal state" subjected to a dynastic, monarchical, absolutist rule softened only by the mitigating parameters of Hapsburg respect for cultural and linguistic particularism.[102] It became increasingly difficult for confederal Austria simply to maintain what it held in an age when centrifugal nationalism was making its rounds in Europe, and while Russia was frustrating Austria's hopes of expansion into the soft areas of south-eastern Europe created by the quickening Ottoman collapse. The very last thing that Austria wanted to do at this time was to struggle with Prussia for regional hegemony of the German lands of central Europe.[103] Equally unfortunate for Austria, Prussia felt it had to struggle with Austria to gather up these lands. Austrian Hapsburg princes had been continuously elected Holy Roman Emperors by the German Electors from 1438 until the last Holy Roman Emperor had resigned and done away with the office in the first decade of the nineteenth century. While this office was gone, the allegiance to Hapsburg Austria among the many remaining German princes had not receded. This was so particularly in the Catholic south of German central Europe. Bis-

99. Henry Kissinger, *Diplomacy* (New York: Simon and Schuster, 1994), 122.

100. Michael Mann, *The Sources of Social Power*, vol. 2, *The Rise of Classes and Nation-States, 1760–1914* (New York: Cambridge University Press, 1993), 330–31.

101. Michael Doyle, *Empires* (Ithaca: Cornell University Press, 1986), 92–97.

102. Mann, *The Sources of Social Power*, vol. 2, 331.

103. Sheehan, *German History*, 856.

marck was eventually to determine that he must remove the sparkle from the imperial Hapsburg diadem in order to bring the German states under the rule of Prussia. He was soon to provide such a drubbing of Austrian prestige.

Austria, however, was not to be the first victim of Prussian aggression in the developing Bismarckian scheme to employ pan-German national identity to unite the German lands under Prussian rule. That misfortune was to befall a non-German state, specifically Denmark. Significantly, Denmark attracted Bismarck's attention in this regard precisely because it was a non-German power. Even before, and especially after an 1848 insurrection by the German-speaking inhabitants of the Danish-ruled Duchies of Schleswig and Holstein, tangled disputes had emerged regarding to whom the titles to the Duchies would revert upon the death of the Danish King Friedrich VII.[104] Schleswig-Holstein was a region of mixed Danish-German ethnicity. Friedrich had held title to both while he lived. The dispute had been an essentially legal, titular dispute of the sort common in the eighteenth century. It had been an issue of contended dynastic succession, of the sort that was to become very uncommon in the more recent era of national-sovereign identity—which prince would own and rule the territory upon the death of their present sovereign.

Upon the death of the Danish sovereign in 1863, Bismarck quickly reduced the issue to a German national irredentist claim to recover separate ethnic Germans. Of course, Bismarck had never viewed the Schleswig-Holstein affair from the perspective of a German nationalist and was unlikely to have given a fig for whether or not the ethnic Germans had been mistreated by their Danish rulers. Yet claims that such mistreatment had occurred had been advanced and German nationalists throughout the German-speaking states of central Europe expressed enthusiasm for the separation of the Duchies from Danish rule. The Danish king had died without issue, and Bismarck became anxious to take advantage of the controversy regarding the right of succession over these Duchies in the name of the German nationalist cause, not because he had any sympathy for this cause but because "Prussia did not have, either in law or in history, the smallest title to

---

104. In the German case, as in the Italian case, the "permissive cause of integration was the revolutions of 1848" (Cronin, "From Balance to Community: Transnational Identity and Political Integration," (ms. p. 24.). This was a "permissive cause" of the Second French Empire as well.

the Duchies."[105] He has earlier written, to Manteuffel, "I have not the smallest doubt that the whole Danish business can be settled in a way desirable for us only by war. The occasion for such a war can be found at any moment we consider favorable for waging it."[106] The death of the Danish king provided that moment.

Bismarck was able to take advantage of German nationalist sentiment in this context in large measure because Friedrich VII had, somewhat foolishly and autocratically, attempted to "impose a new constitutional order on Schleswig without the promised consultation" back in March 1863.[107] Upon Friedrich's death, rival claims by Prince Christian of Glücksburg (to both Schleswig-Holstein and the Danish crown) and Prince Augustenburg (a progressive candidate supported by most German liberals) were evaluated by the Diet of the German Confederation in late November. The Diet was effectively powerless except as a negotiating forum for delegations of the German princes of the loose Confederation formed at the end of the Napoleonic Wars, but among its delegates were many German liberal nationalists. A consensus in support of Augustenberg's candidacy emerged.[108] This was the combined result of inflamed and nascent German nationalist passion over the alleged mistreatment of the German minority in the Duchies, the attempt by a Danish prince to impose a constitutional order on them without consultation with the estates, and the prospect of the continuation of this alleged state of affairs under a new Danish sovereign.

What is essential to my analysis of the period is the difference in Austrian and Prussian motivation in cooperating in the joint conquest of Schleswig-Holstein, and the insights that analysis of this difference provides in understanding the growing cleavage in the Austrian and Prussian notions of their state interests. This rift was critical in bringing the curtain down on the Vienna system, and ending the prolonged period of peace among conservative dynasts that had characterized the functioning of the Concert of Europe. As Sheehan describes the situation, Bismarck and the Austrian foreign minister, Count Johann Bernhard von Rechberg, were laboring over a very different set of assumptions regarding the significance of their cooperation in operations against Denmark for the future of Austro-Prussian relations. The dif-

105. Eyck, *Bismarck and the German Empire*, 81.
106. Ibid.
107. Sheehan, *German History*, 890.
108. Ibid.

ference is hardly surprising, given Austria's reliance upon the continuation of Metternich's Vienna system to avoid conflict with Prussia while nationalist and secessionist trouble was appearing in its multi-ethnic empire. It is less surprising still when we consider the character of Rechberg, who "called himself a Conservative statesman and a pupil of Metternich."[109]

> Rechberg saw the Schleswig-Holstein problem as the occasion for creating the constellation of forces that he had always wanted: a Confederation dominated by an Austro-Prussian condominium directed against liberal nationalism and in favor of the status quo. His interest in Schleswig-Holstein *per se* was minimal; his principal aim was to lay the basis for a broad and lasting set of agreements with Berlin. This was not Bismarck's intention. Although he did not reveal his goals to anyone for another year, he was attracted to the idea of annexing the Duchies to Prussia. Moreover, his agreement to work with Vienna in support of the treaties of 1852 [with the Confederation, which Denmark had violated] was purely tactical, a way to keep the game going while he waited to see what would develop.[110]

In his dedication to conservative principles of government, the place of the ancient aristocracy in the leadership of domestic society, and to monarchical rule, Bismarck was every bit Rechberg's match. Unlike Rechberg, however, and unlike many of his Prussian peers such as Gerlach, Bismarck did not regard adherence to the Vienna system as in any way essential to the maintenance of dynastic rule in Prussia. This led him to reject the premises, advice and wishes of Prussian conservatives. As Kissinger has recently argued, Bismarck "challenged the conventional wisdom which identified nationalism with liberalism."[111] Thus Bismarck did not see any inherent liberal threat to the Prussian monarchy or social order in a pan-German policy which excluded Hapsburg Austria. Instead, he believed "the illusion of the need for an Austrian alliance served above all to inhibit Prussia from pursuing its ultimate goal of unifying Germany"[112] under the Prussian crown. In rejecting the necessary identification of nationalism with liberalism, however, a linkage that was almost axiomatic to the adherents to Metternich's doctrine when he constructed the Vienna system in 1815,

109. Eyck, *Bismarck and the German Empire*, 64.
110. Sheehan, *German History*, 891.
111. Kissinger, *Diplomacy*, 128.
112. Ibid.

Bismarck also rejected the proposition that liberal institutions were required to achieve the unification of Germany. This was a proposition that had been equally axiomatic among the German liberals who had gathered in Frankfurt after the 1848 revolution to construct an all-German constitution. Bismarck felt that the legitimacy of the Prussian monarchy and the strength of the Prussian state was of an order that rendered it impervious to the threat of this logic. Thus he could flirt with the Prussian left, the liberals, and the Prussian, German nationalists when it suited him, and he could employ what he regarded as their delusional, pan-German, national enthusiasms for his own purposes. As Bismarck had himself written in this context:

> The sense of security that the King remains master in his country even if the whole army is abroad is not shared with Prussia by any other continental state and above all by no other German power. It provides the opportunity to accept a development of public affairs much more in conformity with present requirements....The royal authority in Prussia is so firmly based that the government can without risk encourage a much more lively parliamentary activity and thereby exert pressure on conditions in Germany.[113]

On the basis of Rechberg's delusions regarding his intentions, Bismarck had, in January 1864, engineered the joint invasion of Schleswig by Austrian and Prussian forces. They crossed the frontier on 1 February.[114] With annexation of the Duchies as his aim, Bismarck carefully avoided all overtures for a peaceful settlement throughout the ensuing conflict and Denmark was forced to sue for peace by August, and to cede the Duchies to the joint control of Austria and Prussia. Schleswig-Holstein was to be administered by an Austro-Prussian condominium of the sort Rechberg had favored, in spite of the fact that this arrangement favored Prussia, which was geographically situated to exercise an authority over the area that Austria could not.[115]

Bismarck wished, of course, to annex both Duchies directly to Prussia, but could not employ such a demand as a legitimate basis for war with Austria, a war which he desired in order to humble Austria in the eyes of the Confederation as well as to complete the Prussian conquest of Schleswig-Holstein. Neither his sovereign, the Crown Prince of Prussia, nor the opinion of the smaller German states that he wished to

113. Ibid., 129. Kissinger is citing Bismarck's *Werke* here. The cited passage was written in March 1858.
114. Eyck, *Bismarck and the German Empire*, 90.
115. Ibid., 92–94.

woo under the sovereignty of the Prussian crown, would tolerate such a selfish act of aggression.[116] The Prussian sovereign and his son would not tolerate it, as it would constitute a blatant breach of faith with a brother-monarch, violating his primary aristocratic identity commitment to his social class. The smaller German states would not tolerate it, as it would constitute a blatant breach of faith with a brother-German, violating their emerging pan-German identity commitments. The best that Bismarck could therefore manage to advance his design, for a time, was to engineer the Convention of Gastein which ended the condominium arrangement by dividing the Duchies between them, awarding Schleswig, in the north, to Prussia and Holstein, in the south, to Austria. The convention was completed on 14 August 1865.[117] This division was extremely unpopular throughout the Confederation.

Unfortunately for Austria, however, the Convention of Gastein was signed in the nature of a provisional, not a permanent settlement. This provided Bismarck with the opportunity to manufacture grievances against conduct of the Austrian administration of Holstein, and continuously to badger the Austrian ambassador and court with a series of hostile notes until Austria was provoked into sending a very sharp note to Bismarck in response.[118] This note upset the Prussian king and was now allowed to serve as a pretext for the creation of a rift in Prussian relations with Austria, particularly in light of the growing realization in Berlin that a military conflict with Austria might provide a means of suspending the escalating constitutional crisis between the Prussian parliament and the Prussian crown.

Bismarck had met with Wilhelm on 21 February to consider how to deal with the crisis and had convinced Wilhelm "that only three alternatives were now open to him: a liberal ministry [an idea which repelled Wilhelm], a coup d'état against the constitution [which also repelled him as the document had been drafted by his father], or war."[119] Thus when Wilhelm called a Crown Council on 28 February 1866 to formulate future Prussian policy he was persuaded without difficulty to grant Bismarck permission to begin negotiations with Italy for a military alliance against Austria. This was concluded by 8 April. The following day, Bismarck instructed the Prussian minister in Frankfurt

116. Ibid., 100.
117. Ibid., 106.
118. Ibid., 107–10.
119. Sheehan, *German History,* 900.

to introduce to the Diet of the German Confederation a proposal to convene a German parliament elected on the basis of universal suffrage![120] This was precisely the franchise that the Frankfurt Parliament which had convened in the aftermath of the Revolution of 1848 had sought, and had been denied when the Prussian king had refused to accept the imperial German crown and to vitalize that franchise. The move was carefully and cynically calculated to gain sympathy for the Prussian government as an administration of progressive design which supported liberal, pan-German national unity in comparison with the creaking, dynastic, particularistic Hapsburg court in Vienna. The move served its purpose admirably. It was a singular success for Bismarck when one realizes that the move helped to convince the peoples of the German Confederation that Prussia was demonstrating itself to be not only liberal, but German nationalist in outlook, while at the same time in essence it demolished the German Confederation by concluding an alliance with Italy against another German member of the Confederation. Bismarck admitted as much when he confided to Benedetti, the French foreign minister:

> I have induced a King of Prussia to break off the intimate relations of his House with the House of Hapsburg, to conclude an alliance with revolutionary Italy, possibly to accept arrangements with Imperial France, and to propose in Frankfurt the reform of the Confederation and a popular parliament. That is a success of which I am proud.[121]

Bismarck's reference to "arrangements with Imperial France" refer to the ultimately unsuccessful negotiations that he had been conducting with Napoleon III. Bismarck had hoped to bring Napoleon into the war against Austria, or at the least to ensure Napoleon's benevolent neutrality, by suggesting to Napoleon that if France wished to incorporate all French-speaking regions of Europe (clearly alluding to Belgium) into the Empire, in accordance with the Emperor's devotion to the principal of nationality, that Prussia would take no notice. These overtures to Napoleon III had scandalized Gerlach, Bismarck's mentor and Wilhelm's military adjutant. Gerlach regarded Napoleon as an illegitimate upstart, as had been his great uncle before him, and counseled rapprochement between Vienna and Berlin in order to isolate illegitimate and chronically revolutionary France. In the margin of a letter

120. Eyck, *Bismarck and the German Empire*, 115.
121. Ibid.

from Gerlach, protesting to Bismarck that "Napoleon is our natural enemy," Bismarck had scrawled, "What of it?"[122] For most conservatives, even so late in the nineteenth century, the legitimacy of the principles of the Vienna system was ironclad. Men like Gerlach listened to the mechanized hum of Bismarck's radical, realpolitik move away from Metternich's creation with incomprehension and incredulity. Yet Bismarck appears to have realized that in order for Prussia unambiguously to wrest leadership of German central Europe from Hapsburg Austria, Prussia would have to exploit pan-German national sentiment and was qualified to do so in a fashion that Austria was not. As Kissinger has recently argued:

> Had Prussia sought [earlier] to exploit German nationalism, it could have challenged Austrian pre-eminence in Germany a generation before Bismarck...[but]...refrained from pursuing their advantage because it ran counter to the dominant principle of maintaining the status quo. Austria, seemingly on its death bed after Napoleon's [I] onslaught was given a new lease on life by the Metternich system, which enabled it to survive for another hundred years.[123]

In a similar sense, Bismarck's move to bring a motion for universal suffrage before the Diet of the German Confederation was astonishing. Universal suffrage certainly existed nowhere in the German states at that time. In a masterstroke, Bismarck made the severe, autocratic and parochial Prussian government appear to be both democratic and pan-German nationalist, when it was neither. Bismarck had calculated that his motion to grant universal suffrage for confederal elections would take the wind out of the sails of his domestic parliamentary adversaries, especially the liberal, bourgeois Progressive party, in the upcoming elections. The move made him appear to support German unification as well—in as much as nationalism and liberalism were such cognitively linked concepts in the minds of Prussian and other German liberals, as well as in the minds of their conservative adversaries. Bismarck had no doubts that he would succeed in his aim by these moves; he had seen it accomplished before, in France. As Eyck argues persuasively:

> His [Bismarck's] practical model was Napoleon III, whose government was sustained by the masses and opposed by a portion of the educated upper middle class; Napoleon had introduced universal

122. Kissinger, *Diplomacy*, 124–25. Kissinger's quotations of the exchange between Gerlach and Bismarck are taken from p. 125.
123. Ibid., 85.

suffrage to get rid of the Second Republic [in 1852] and had been successful in that. Bismarck was confident that he would be able to achieve the same success.[124]

Bismarck did achieve the same success, and more. War between Austria and Prussia finally came and Prussia prevailed quickly and spectacularly, in spite of the fact that the Prussian army had been universally thought to be no match for the Austrian forces. The Austrian forces, however, were defeated at Sadowa a mere three weeks after Prussian troops had crossed the Saxon frontier.[125] The armistice was concluded on 26 July 1866 in Nikolsburg.

The terms of the armistice were extraordinarily moderate for Austria. Bismarck had wished to humble the Hapsburgs in order to turn the eyes of the Confederation squarely to Prussia for future leadership of a united German Empire. He had not wished to make of Austria a permanent and implacable enemy. He had been required to argue at great length, and at significant personal cost, with an obsessively triumphant and momentarily vindictive Wilhelm, that no Austrian lands should be annexed to Prussia as part of the settlement. Prussia was not to be so moderate in its terms for the northern German states who had supported Austria in the war. Hanover, Hesse-Cassel, Nassau and the Free City of Frankfurt were annexed to the Prussian crown,[126] their monarchs were deposed, and they ceased to exist as independent actors in the international arena. Saxony, which had also favored Austria, was spared this fate only by vociferous Austrian opposition, yet Saxony was required under the terms of the peace to enter the new confederation that would be formed under the leadership of Prussia.

NATIONAL IDENTITY AS A CONSTRAINT FOR STATESMEN:
THE SECOND EMPIRE'S FAILURE TO BALANCE

Quite contrary to Bismarck's expectations, his subordinate, Goltz, had induced Napoleon III to accept this annexation of vast tracts of northern Germany, along with its three to four million inhabitants, into the Prussian state. The fact that Napoleon did not oppose this annexation, despite the fact that it created a more powerful, and therefore more dangerous German state on his western border, is also quite contrary

124. Eyck, *Bismarck and the German Empire*, 116.
125. Ibid., 128.
126. Ibid., 132–33.

to the expectations of realist balance-of-power theories of international relations, quite irrespective of whether they are of the classical realist, or of the neorealist variant.[127]

The structural neorealist variant argues that a state can balance internally, by arms racing, as easily as externally, by alliance formation. Waltz has argued that "[b]alance-of-power politics prevail wherever two, and only two, requirements are met: that the order be anarchic and that it be populated by units wishing to survive."[128] Waltz constructs this argument in order to argue that bipolar superpower competition in the twentieth century was not inconsistent with the classical realist notion of the balance of power as an explanation of state behavior. Certainly the notion should have therefore been just as applicable in the late nineteenth century, in a clearly multipolar European system which featured, at a minimum, Austria, Britain, France, Prussia and Russia as Great Powers. Any variant of balance-of-power theory would argue that it was explicitly inimical to French state interests to sit idly by and watch large tracts of central Europe and up to four million people, and their goods and wealth, become annexed to an already powerful Prussian neighbor to the east. Yet this is precisely what Napoleon III did, however much hand-wringing might have accompanied his inactivity. How might this behavior be explained?

The major component of the explanation appears to lie in the manner in which Napoleon III's regime had been legitimated. This legitimating principle derived directly from the collective identity of the French nation. Throughout his reign Napoleon had consistently posed as the defender of national self-determination and had attacked the Vienna system coterie of traditionally legitimated, conservative monarchs on this basis.[129] His nationalist rhetoric and campaigns had been inspired in no small measure by a store of personal conviction that the future belonged to national-states and not dynastic states. Kissinger has

---

127. For the balancing expectations of classical realist scholarship, see Hans J. Morgenthau, *Politics Among Nations*, 161–215; Robert Gilpin, *War and Change in World Politics* (Cambridge: Cambridge University Press, 1981), 156–210; Edward Hallett Carr, *The Twenty Years' Crisis, 1919–1939: An Introduction to the Study of International Relations*, 2nd ed. (New York: Harper and Row, 1964), 102–46; A. F. K. Organski and Jacek Kugler, *The War Ledger* (Chicago: University of Chicago Press, 1980), 13–62. Neorealist expectations of balancing activity among states are best described in Waltz, *Theory of International Politics*, 102–28; and the "expected utility" model presented in Bruce Bueno de Mesquita, *The War Trap* (New Haven and London: Yale University Press, 1981).

128. Waltz, *Theory of International Politics*, 121.

129. Kissinger, *Diplomacy*, 107.

argued that Napoleon III in fact "dreaded German unification but was sympathetic to German nationalism and dithered about solving that insoluble dilemma."[130] Moreover, a great deal of his popularity and legitimacy within France derived from his role as a symbol of the progressive future of national-states. Irrespective of its acceptance of a Second Empire, France still regarded itself to be one of these. France may have chosen an imperial form of government with the 1852 plebiscite that resulted in Napoleon's installation as Emperor, but it was a national-imperial state which had enthusiastically supported Napoleon's nationalist campaigns throughout the continental periphery in the intervening years between the proclamation of the Second Empire in 1852 and the Austrian debacle at Sadowa in 1866. A major difficulty for Emperor Napoleon III, was that over the years he had been "driven to dependence on public opinion, and his policy fluctuated with his assessment of what was needed to sustain his [domestic] popularity."[131]

Napoleon's seeming inability to play the balance-of-power game when it would bring his policy into conflict with the principle of nationality—which had served so admirably to legitimate his regime—indicates that his decision-making procedures could not be conducted with the insularity of more traditionally legitimated statesmen. Just as he had been unable to abandon the papacy for fear of inflaming domestic Catholic opinion, neither could he oppose the operation of the principle of nationality in central Europe without inflaming radical domestic nationalist opinion. To oppose the principle of nationality, which had long served to legitimate his foreign policy and his domestic rule, would simultaneously risk exposing himself as a traditional autocrat. A Second Empire which represented and glorified the French nation was popular when successful and at least tolerated when not. A Second Empire which represented the Bonaparte family and dynasty, and nothing else, would be unpopular and domestically illegitimate even when successful and deposed when unsuccessful. The legitimating principles of the Second Empire were the principles of nationality and the belief that the imperial institutional form of collective action was best suited to glorify the French nation and thus manifest the agency of the French nation abroad.

Bismarck was, of course, not immune to the pressure of domestic opinion in the formulation and conduct of his policy, but he had sev-

---

130. Ibid., 114.
131. Ibid., 107.

eral crucial advantages over Napoleon. First, Bismarck served an autocratic Prussian monarch whose legitimacy to rule in that capacity was unquestioned by the broad mass of Prussian society. The only elements of Prussian society which conceivably questioned the legitimacy of Wilhelm's reign were the radical liberals and socialists. Both of these elements were marginalized fringe groups in the context of the prevailing Prussian political discourse of the 1860s. Second, Wilhelm's legitimacy was enhanced by his emergence as a rallying point for pan-German nationalist sentiment. Bismarck's skillful maneuvers in the Diet of the German Confederation had created the illusion of a liberalizing, German-nationalist Prussian monarchy. The illusion was enhanced by a number of institutional facts.[132] One of these had emerged with the failure of the decisions of the Frankfurt Parliament to be implemented by the Prussian crown. Pan-German nationalist sentiment could only realize its ambition to become institutionalized in a German nation by attaching itself to, or becoming adopted by, an existing German prince or state in order to acquire an institutional form. The Hapsburg Austrian state was both unsuitable for this purpose by virtue of its polyglot demography, and disinclined to serve this role by virtue of the dynastic, Hapsburg conception of Austrian state interests. Thus Bismarck could play the nationality card to his domestic audience, and to a broader central European audience, as a German nationalist leader. He could annex the defeated German powers which had sided with Austria in the Austro-Prussian War into a *Norddeutscher Bund*, as part and parcel of a legitimate irredentist claim[133] to gather up the German-speaking lands of central Europe into a greater German Reich.

In order to oppose this move, Napoleon would have been required to repudiate the legitimating principle of his own regime and its foreign policy in its entirety. As Kissinger has recently argued, Napoleon effectively had two options. First, he could adhere to the tried and true strategy of Richelieu and strive to keep central Europe fragmented. Adopting this policy would, however, have cost him his credentials as a nationalist, with all the attendant potential consequences that I have just outlined above. Otherwise, he could strive for the leadership of Europe by placing himself and his Empire at the head of a nationalist

132. Kratochwil, "Regimes, Interpretation and the 'Science' of Politics," 270–72.
133. For a discussion of the problem of irredentism to the stability of international order see Mayall, *Nationalism and International Society*, 57–61.

crusade, as had his uncle before him.[134] Instead, "[u]nfortunately for France, Napoleon pursued both strategies simultaneously."[135]

As the Austro-Prussian War progressed, "Bismarck threw Napoleon the sop of letting him mediate the peace,"[136] though this attempt at intervention also failed and was ultimately exercised only after Austria had been defeated. Napoleon believed that he could not ask for anything for France so long as he was in the process of mediating the Austro-Prussian peace, but when this task was completed he sent Benedetti to Bismarck on 23 July to ascertain Bismarck's attitude to a French proposal for a secret convention between France and Prussia that would award France with its 1814 frontiers, and Luxembourg as well.[137] It would appear, then, that Napoleon was suffering from the illusion—which Bismarck had taken no small pains to encourage—that he had achieved an understanding with Prussia, based on the principle of nationality—a principle that Bismarck was proclaiming falsely. Prussia would be allowed to gather up German states in central Europe, and would in return wink at French annexation of Belgium and Luxembourg. It is a tribute to the growing strength of pan-German national sentiment, in what was soon to become Germany, that Bismarck found it impossible to yield Germanophile Luxembourg to France.[138] Yet we should not delude ourselves that such an annexation was Napoleon's intent before the Austro-Prussian war began. This does not salvage either classical or neorealist understandings of the balance of power. Napoleon did not intend to balance Prussian gains in central Europe with acquisitions of the significant French-speaking territories that lay between France's northeastern frontier and the Rhine. At least, he did not intend to do so before the Austrian defeat at Sadowa.

Napoleon attempted to retrieve the situation by calling for a European congress. While his call was ignored, Bismarck allowed him to mediate the peace in bilateral negotiations between the belligerent parties. Napoleon faintly hoped to intervene sufficiently with his mediation efforts to avoid the "complete reversal of the European balance of power"[139] that was developing as a result of the war. Bismarck, how-

134. Kissinger, *Diplomacy*, 108.
135. Ibid., 109.
136. Ibid., 117.
137. Ibid., 136.
138. Ibid., 156.
139. Eyck, *Bismarck and the German Empire*, 129.

ever, had procrastinated in these diplomatic efforts to terminate hostilities, while simultaneously hinting broadly that Napoleon should make an ultimatum to the Belgian King that Belgian integration into the Second Empire would be essential to offset Prussian political and territorial gains as a result of the Austrian war.[140]

The rapid Austrian military collapse, coupled with Bismarck's hints that France could be compensated for its neutrality in a manner consistent with French devotion to the principle of nationality, especially in Belgium, appears to have secured that neutrality. Upon the attainment of a peace, however, Bismarck lost interest in the question of French irredentist interests in Belgium and Luxembourg. Napoleon pursued this issue in order to obtain compensation subsequent to the Prussian territorial gains and the humiliation of Austria. French balancing was, however, somewhat tardy. It was a forlorn hope, ex post facto of the Prussian fait accompli. The French failure to balance Prussian aggrandizement prior to the Prussian victory had effectively and permanently ended the French hegemony in central and western Europe that France had enjoyed since the reign of Louis XIV.

Certainly, as I have indicated, Louis Napoleon appears to have been badly outmaneuvered by Bismarck. Bismarck's duplicity and superior statecraft, however, cannot in themselves explain Napoleon's failure to balance Prussian aggrandizement. Napoleon had surely not failed to understand where the consequences of the Danish and Austro-Prussian wars were tending, or their implications for French security. It was, in my own view, precisely the hybrid character of the French regime, the fact that it was simultaneously an imperial, or pseudo-monarchical institutional form of collective action, and legitimated by the principle of nationality, and a country rife with popular nationalism, that rendered it so difficult for Napoleon III successfully to balance Prussian aggrandizement in central Europe. Napoleon was an emperor so long as he and his empire served to embody French national aspirations. The Second Empire provided an institutional form of collective action that provided a serviceable vehicle for the expression and agency of French national collective identity so long as Napoleon's goals were at unity with the will of French national aspirations. French national aspirations willed the demise of the Vienna system, which had been constructed to shackle the French people, and all the peoples of Europe, to a legitimate scion of the ancien regime. This system constituted, by

140. Ibid., 130.

design, the uncompromising nullification of the idea of the nation. Napoleon's Second Empire served, for a time, as an institutional form for the collective action of the French nation because its goals were indeed at unity with the will of the nation. His regime provided an institutional form of collective action capable of serving as an instrument for the effective execution of the agency of pre-existing French national collective identity. French national identity sought demolition of the Vienna system that had been created to constrain it.

> Napoleon's ultimate goal was to abrogate the territorial clauses of the Vienna settlement and to alter the state system on which it had been based. He never understood, however, that achieving his goal would also result in a unified Germany, which would forever end French aspirations to dominate Central Europe.[141]

That Napoleon's attainment of his goal of demolishing the Vienna system did entail these consequences meant that the French failure to balance the Prussian creation of the *Norddeutscher Bund* spelled the beginning of the end for the Second Empire. The Prussian aggrandizement resulting from the defeat of Austria not only created an obstacle to the advancement of specifically French national aspirations, but created an aggressive and expansive Prussian power which could muster an army four times the size of that of France.[142] By failing to balance this power, the Second Empire had acceded to the forging of the tool of its own destruction.[143]

---

141. Kissinger, *Diplomacy*, 107.

142. According to Eyck, having cowed the southern German states by his annexation of most of those in the north, Bismarck had been careful to obtain alliances, stipulated in secret treaties, with nearly all of these states to the effect that they would put their forces at the disposal, and under the command of the King of Prussia in the event of a future Prussian war with, particularly, France. See Eyck, *Bismarck and the German Empire*, 136. As a consequence, according to Howard, the Prussian army had at its disposal as many as 1,200,000 men compared to 288,0000 Frenchmen under arms at the end of 1866. See Michael Howard, *The Franco-Prussian War: The German Invasion of France, 1870–1871* (New York: Collier, 1969), 29. Note here also that, as with Cronin's emphasis of the importance of "fighting together as Italians," the experience of having fought together against the common French foe was an important element in solidifying pan-German national identity and the integration of the German states under the Prussian crown. See Cronin, "From Balance to Community: Transnational Identity and Political Integration," (ms. pp. 291ff.).

143. It might be interesting, in a larger study where more space is available, to consider in this context the reasons why Russia and Britain also failed or declined to balance Prussian expansion. Paul Schroeder suggests answers to this question in separate but relevant arguments. First, Schroeder argues that the system of the Concert period was not a "balance of power" system but a hegemonic system dominated by superpowers in Russia and Britain. See Paul W. Schroeder, "Did the Vienna Settlement Rest on a Balance of Power?" *American Historical Review* 97, no. 6 (June 1992): 683–735. One

REPRISE: IDENTITIES, INTERESTS, AND INSTITUTIONS

THE SEVEN YEARS' WAR provides a highly effective illustration of the causal significance of the territorial-sovereign structure of identities and interests for the security conduct of territorial-sovereign states. I have argued that the scope, conduct, terms of engagement, and terms of disengagement of belligerents during the Seven Years' War are inexplicable without recourse to analysis of the manner in which the interests of the belligerents were structured by their territorial-sovereign social identities. Analysis of George's dual territorial-sovereignty over Britain and Hanover is required to explain the scope of the war and the diplomatic revolution which demolished a classical European system of alliances which had stood for centuries as more consistent with the balancing requirements of European actors. The choice of alliance partners and the theaters of conflict are otherwise inexplicable. They are equally inexplicable without analysis of the consequences for alliance formation of the whims and caprices of the territorial-sovereign monarchs who were to become belligerents. No argument predicated on assumptions of rational instrumental decision making on the part of belligerents can explain why a continental European theater of the war should have been opened, unless the interests of actors are properly understood to be structured by historically contingent territorial-sovereign social identities.

Similar analysis is required to apprehend the terms of engagement of the war. On the part of the British, the peripheral war was fought primarily by the British navy and provincial troops over whom the British crown had extended sovereignty, but to whom the crown had not awarded full citizenship. The British oligarchy reasoned like capitalists, not like patriots, evincing evidence of their love of profit rather than love of country in decision making regarding whether or not to conduct the war, for what objectives, and with whom. The state-as-firm model is nearly reified in this portrait of mercantilist, oligarchic, territorial-sovereign decision making. The notion of state interests which emerges from this portrait, however, is a construction of a very

---

might then surmise that Russia and Britain could afford to take an indulgent view of Prussian expansion at the expense of France. In another argument, Schroeder points out the Britain had both instrumental and cultural affinities for Prussia, which "would be a peaceful, satiated, progressive, Protestant power, a useful commercial partner, and a good guarantor of Peace in Europe against a restless France" (Paul Schroeder, "Historical Reality vs. Neo-realist Theory," *International Security* 19, no. 1 [summer 1994]: 108–48). The passage quoted is found on p. 146.

specific structure of social identities, and theories which exogenize this notion of interests by assumption to all actors in quite different systems consequently severely limit their potential explanatory utility.[144] I have argued that similar analysis is required to apprehend the conduct of the war. On the British side, the primacy of the defense of Hanover was continuously elevated over other, more likely genuinely strategic priorities, in decision making regarding the application of strategic resources: namely, troops and subsidy funds for more troops. In the person of one territorial-sovereign individual and his system-legitimated proprietary sovereign interests, we are witnesses to the spectacle of a conflict of interests between the sovereign and the rational, objective, strategic and pecuniary interests of the nation. This dichotomy was to become an impossible contradiction in terms in the national-sovereign system that followed. In the system structured by territorial-sovereign identities and interests, however, the division had to be accommodated and reconciled. The British notion of state interests had to adjust to accommodate the proprietary and territorial interests of the sovereign's second territorial sovereignty. Thus we observe that it is ineffectual to theorize about the objective interests of state or nation in a transhistorical or ahistorical fashion; a fashion in which socially constructed and empirically verifiable notions of state or national interests are disregarded in some accounts in favor of a priori assumptions.

Lastly, I have argued that similar analysis is required to apprehend the terms of disengagement from the war. It is certainly true that France had suffered serious military defeats in the periphery and might well have been financially exhausted in the last year of the war. It is also certainly true that the death of Catherine and the accession of a capriciously pro-Prussian Peter to the Russian throne had left France bereft of continental allies with the resources to assist France effectively in a successful conclusion to the continental theater of the war.

The discussion of the demise of the Second Empire and birth of the Second Reich has analyzed the consequences of the development of national collective identity for the conduct of national-state security policy in the nineteenth century in the context of critical areas of state

---

144. It is in this context that I heartily endorse Schimmelfennig's suggestion that "rationalist and constructivist explanations do not have to exclude one another but can be combined in different ways." See Frank Schimmelfennig, "NATO Enlargement: A Constructivist Explanation," *Security Studies* 8, nos. 2/3 [winter 1998/99–spring 1999]: 230).

conduct, in which realist and neorealist theory predict state security behavior that is at variance with the observed behavior of nation-states.

Both classical realism and structural neorealism predict that states will balance the attempts of powerful neighbors and adversaries to expand their territory. Yet, as has emerged in my analysis, Napoleon III was unable to take action to frustrate Bismarck's projects to unify the German states, in spite of the fact that French ascendancy over continental affairs was seriously endangered by the creation of the *Norddeutscher Bund* at the close of the Austro-Prussian War. Napoleon allowed himself to be goaded by Bismarck, and the French nationalist press, into initiating a war against Prussia for which he clearly believed France to be unprepared. France fought Prussia, in 1870, for no purpose whatever consistent with an instrumentally rational definition of the interests of the French state. I have explored the impact of French domestic nationalist agitation in the origins of the Franco-Prussian War. I have developed the manner in which the legitimacy of Napoleon III's reign was predicated on his policy of upholding the principle of nationality in French policy toward the Italian Peninsula, the German states of central Europe, and the Polish reaction against its partition by Russia and Prussia. I have argued that, by the time Bismarck's policy of unification came to fruition, the policy of the liberal Empire of France was at the service of the popular French conception of the principle of nationality.

The interests of societies, whatever institutional form of collective action they employ to express these interests, is demonstrated to be influenced by the self-perceptions of the society they represent. I argue that interests are not static or exogenously given, but are a function of historically contingent societal collective identity. The structure of state interests of the Second Empire of Napoleon III, and that of Bismarck's Prussia emerge as distinctly different conceptions, derived from distinctly different notions of the nature of sovereign identity. The regime of Napoleon III, legitimated as it was by Napoleon's antidynastic support for the principle of nationality, led him to take decisions that were not formally rational or consistent with the rational-instrumental logic that Bismarck was able to apply as chancellor of a traditionally legitimated Prussia. Significantly Bismarck, though a confirmed monarchist, was able to employ French and pan-German national sentiment as a tool to obtain his rational-instrumental objectives. Thus a major consequence of the development of national collective identity is that it could be employed as a tool or alternately suffered as a constraint for statesmen. Variations in the structure of state identities and interests, predicated on the legitimating principles of a given regime, determined whether or not the principle of nationality (later followed by national self-determination) was a constraint or a tool for statesmen who might like to pursue rational instrumental policies. Domestic nationalist ferment sometimes transforms the structure of state interests, impelling statesmen to pursue formally irrational policies. I argue that this is precisely what occurred to induce Louis Napoleon to launch the Franco-Prussian War, which resulted in the demise of his Second Empire and in the birth of the Second German Reich.

It was precisely the hybrid nature of the liberal Empire—that it neither served as an appropriate institutional form of collective action to manifest monarchical territorial sovereignty nor French popular and national sovereignty—which doomed it to extinction at the first serious transnational difficulty. The symbolism of earlier French national glory, latent within the imperial office and the name of Bonaparte, was cast aside like a tarnished ornament when delegitimated by defeat. Louis Napoleon's legitimation crisis came into being and passed away in a day, at Sedan. The imperial institutional form of collective action could no longer manifest French national collective identity. It suited, however, as a wholly appropriate institutional form to manifest the national collective identity of the newly forged pan-German nation.

NATO ENLARGEMENT:
A CONSTRUCTIVIST EXPLANATION

FRANK SCHIMMELFENNIG

At its Madrid summit in July 1997, NATO invited three central
and eastern European (CEE) countries to accession talks: the
Czech Republic, Hungary, and Poland. In December of the
same year, the accession protocols were signed. In this article, I seek to
explain NATO enlargement. More precisely, I ask (1) why CEE countries
strive to become NATO members;[1] (2) why NATO decided to expand to
the east;[2] and (3) why (only) the Czech Republic, Hungary, and Poland were invited to become NATO members.[3]

I argue that the most prominent rationalist international relations
approaches to the study of alliances and international institutions cannot answer these questions convincingly. In both their neorealist and
their neoliberal variations, they may be able to account for the CEE
countries' bid to join NATO but fail to explain the interest of NATO in
expansion (see "Rationalist Puzzles" below). This puzzle for rationalism is solved by a constructivist approach to the study of international
institutions which analyzes enlargement as a process of international
socialization. In the constructivist perspective, NATO is a specialized
organization—the "military branch"—of the Euro-Atlantic or Western
community of liberal-democratic and multilateralist values and norms.

Frank Schimmelfennig teaches at Darmstadt University of Technology.

In preparing the first version of this article, I benefited from a discussion in the research seminar of the Center for International Relations at the University of Tübingen.
I also gratefully acknowledge the comments made by the reviewers of *Security Studies*
as well as by Kai Alderson, Jeff Checkel, Gunther Hellmann, Hans Peter Schmitz, and
Bernhard Zangl.

1. Only twelve out of nineteen central European countries (I do not count the
Transcaucasian and central Asian OSCE members as part of this group) have formally
applied for NATO membership. Among the NATO Partners, the most notable exceptions are the CIS members (Belarus, Moldova, Russia, and Ukraine).

2. The study ends with the decisions made in 1997; it does not include the ratification process.

3. The general decision to expand and the decision to invite the three central European countries are distinct because they were made independently of each other in
1994 and 1997, respectively.

The international socialization approach gives an answer to all three questions: (1) CEE countries strive for NATO membership inasmuch as they share the community values and norms and seek identification with, and recognition by, the West; (2) NATO decided to expand in order to strengthen liberal democracy and multilateralism and to build, in central and eastern Europe, a stable peace based on these values and norms. When a country has internalized the community values and norms and has changed its domestic and foreign policy practices accordingly, it is admitted as a full member to the organization as a reward for its efforts and because of the community's moral commitment to guarantee the security of countries that share its principled beliefs; (3) the Czech Republic, Hungary, and Poland were invited to join NATO first, because they were more advanced than the other CEE countries in the internalization of the community values and beliefs.

The constructivist explanation of enlargement as international socialization is backed up by an analysis of the enlargement process: In the section "Enlargement Discourse," I show that the discourse of NATO and its members reflects the value-rational motivation for enlargement. Furthermore, the stages of enlargement, above all the PfP Program, fit the image of a process of socialization in which the Western alliance teaches its values and norms to its cooperation partners and evaluates their learning progress. The only facts that constructivism cannot explain (and are better accounted for by rationalism) are the bid to join NATO of rather authoritarian governments (like the Romanian government until 1996 and the Meciar government in Slovakia) and the exclusion of Slovenia from the first round of expansion.

The aim of the study is to give a convincing explanation of NATO enlargement. I do not claim to refute rationalist institutionalism in international relations theory. To begin with, the research design does not allow a thorough test of theories. Moreover, such "paradigmatic" approaches to the study of international institutions (and social phenomena in general) as rationalism or constructivism are impossible to refute empirically. Finally, rationalist and constructivist explanations do not necessarily exclude each other but can be combined.

I seek to demonstrate, however, that a constructivist approach to the study of international institutions provides a superior explanatory framework. The core propositions or "theorems" of the dominant rationalist approaches to the study of alliances—the assumption of rational egoism based on relative gains and balance-of-power concerns (neorealism) or based on absolute gains and welfare maximization con-

cerns (neoliberal institutionalism)—have serious difficulties in accounting for NATO expansion. A constructivist approach—the international
socialization of states to the basic norms of an international community of values—offers a parsimonious explanation of the enlargement
process. Constructivist and rationalist propositions can be combined to
explain NATO enlargement, but the rationalist propositions are only
correct when applied within a larger constructivist framework.

RATIONALIST PUZZLES

RATIONALISM, INTERNATIONAL ORGANIZATION, AND ENLARGEMENT

Rationalist theories of international politics and international institutions have dominated the theoretical debate in international relations
throughout the 1980s.[4] Despite their many differences, neorealism and
neoliberalism share the rationalist premises of individualism, egoism,
and instrumentalism. Rationalist explanations of international interaction start with the actors whose identities, interests, and preferences
they take as exogenously given and stable. Rationalism assumes that
individuals as well as corporate actors act egoistically and instrumentally, that is, they choose the behavioral option which promises to
maximize their utility.[5] Institutions are supposed to influence the options available to the actors and their cost-benefit calculations but not
their identities and interests.

These premises also characterize the rationalist analysis of international organizations and their enlargement. Rationalist theories start
from the assumption that international organizations are instrumental
associations which help their members to maximize their utilities. Decisions on membership in international organizations are made according to criteria of instrumental rationality. They are based on exogenously given and stable preferences of both members and candidates
for membership.

4. For an overview, see David A. Baldwin, ed., *Neorealism and Neoliberalism. The
Contemporary Debate* (New York: Columbia University Press, 1993); and Andreas
Hasenclever, Peter Mayer, and Volker Rittberger, *Theories of International Regimes*
(Cambridge: Cambridge University Press, 1997).
5. To be sure, the assumption of egoism is no assumption of rational-choice theory
as such but a general feature of rationalist institutionalism in international relations.
See, for example, Robert O. Keohane, *After Hegemony. Cooperation and Discord in the
World Political Economy* (Princeton: Princeton University Press, 1984), 66.

The basic rational-choice approach to the issues of membership and size of organizations is club theory. A club is defined as a voluntary group deriving mutual benefit from sharing a good characterized by excludable and partially divisible benefits.[6] This definition is held to suit most international organizations. NATO provides nuclear deterrence and conventional defense. Both goods are excludable, but while deterrence is basically indivisible, the provision of conventional forces and weapons creates divisible benefits.[7] Whereas extended nuclear deterrence protects all alliance members simultaneously, conventional forces used to defend one alliance member cannot be used to defend another ally at the same time. It is easier for individual NATO countries to withhold their conventional forces from an ally than it is to exclude an individual alliance member from the nuclear umbrella.

If an international organization provides divisible goods, membership becomes a problem because additional members are rival consumers. Enlargement can lead to crowding or congestion, that is, members cannot use the good as much or as often as they would like to because of other members using the good as well. International organizations, then, only expand if the costs of increased congestion are matched by equivalent "cost reductions owing to the sharing of provision expense," that is, contributions by the new members.[8] This applies to all members and candidates for membership individually. Thus, for a club-type international organization to expand, each member state must expect positive net benefits in order to approve of expansion, and each state outside the organization must expect to gain positive net benefits in order to join the organization.

Neorealism and neoliberalism differ with regard to the utilities and the cost-benefit assessments that determine the choices of state actors.

---

6. This definition is, in abbreviated form, from Richard Cornes and Todd Sandler, *The Theory of Externalities, Public Goods, and Club Goods* (Cambridge: Cambridge University Press, 1986), 24–25, which also provides an overview of club theory. Clubs are "voluntary in the sense that members would not join (or remain in the club) unless a net gain resulted from membership" (Todd Sandler and John T. Tschirhart, "The Economic Theory of Clubs: An Evaluative Survey," *Journal of Economic Literature* 18, no. 4 [December 1980]: 1491). A good is indivisible "when a *unit* of the good can be consumed by one individual without detracting...from the consumption opportunities still available to others from that *same* unit"; it is excludable if its benefits can be "withheld costlessly by the owner or provider" (Cornes and Sandler, *The Theory of Externalities*, 6). The seminal article is James M. Buchanan, "An Economic Theory of Clubs," *Economica* 32, no. 125 (February 1965): 1–14.
7. Todd Sandler, "Impurity of Defense: An Application to the Economics of Alliances," *Kyklos* 30, no. 3 (1977): 443–60.
8. Cornes and Sandler, *The Theory of Externalities*, 159–60.

The neorealist analysis of international politics starts from the assumption that the international system is an anarchical self-help system in which states must be primarily concerned with their security if they want to survive and protect their autonomy.[9] The most useful instrument to achieve this objective is power, above all military power. Therefore states are sensitive to changes in the distribution of power in the international system. They worry about relative gains of other states and seek to defend and—if possible—to enhance their position in the international power structure. In principle, states prefer not to align because alliances reduce their freedom of action and entail the risk of entrapment. Alliances are only formed out of necessity, that is, if states are unable to maintain their security and defend their position in the international power structure by autonomous efforts.

Snyder gives an apt and concise account of the cost-benefit calculations that enter into alliance choices:[10]

> Security benefits in a mutual defence alliance include chiefly a reduced probability of being attacked (deterrence), greater strength in case of attack (defense) and prevention of the ally's alliance with one's adversary (preclusion). The principal costs are the increased risk of war and reduced freedom of action that are entailed in the commitment to the partner. The size of these benefits and costs for both parties will be determined largely by three general factors in their security situations: (1) their alliance "need," (2) the extent to which the prospective partner meets that need, and (3) the actual terms of the alliance contract. Alliance need is chiefly a function of the ratio of a state's capabilities to those of its most likely antagonist(s), and its degree of conflict with, or perceived threat from, that opponent.

The most important neorealist hypotheses about alliance formation differ mainly with regard to the main determinant of alliance need. Whereas balance-of-power theory emphasizes "capabilities," balance-of-threat theory gives precedence to the "perceived threat."

Balance-of-power theory predicts that states align with the weaker side:

> If states wished to maximize power, they would join the stronger side, and we would see not balances, but a world hegemony forged.

---

9. The basic text is Kenneth N. Waltz, *Theory of International Politics* (New York: Random House, 1979).

10. Glenn H. Snyder, "Alliance Theory: A Neorealist First Cut," *Journal of International Affairs* 44, no. 1 (fall 1990): 110.

This does not happen because balancing, not bandwagoning, is the behavior induced by the system. The first concern of states is not to maximize power but to maintain their positions in the system.[11]

This calculation not only applies to great powers but also to "secondary powers." They "flock to the weaker side; for it is the stronger side that threatens them. On the weaker side, they are both more appreciated and safer."[12] An alliance with the stronger side may provide small countries with security against outside states. At the same time, however, they risk of being dominated or subjugated by their "protector."

In order to come to terms with some of the anomalies which balance-of-power theory encounters in reality—in particular, that balances of power often fail to form—Walt developed a balance-of-threat theory of alliances which is supposed both to refine and subsume balance-of-power theory.[13] According to this theory, states seek allies to balance threats. Whereas the overall capabilities emphasized by balance-of-power theory are an important ingredient of states' threat perceptions, alliance choices are determined by other factors as well: the higher not only a state's aggregate power, but also its geographic proximity, offensive capabilities, and aggressiveness of perceived intentions, the stronger the tendency for a state to align with others to oppose the threat.[14] It is the factor of "perceived intentions" that makes the biggest difference to balance-of-power theory.[15] The core realist proposition concerning enlargement can be summarized in the following conditional expectation: NATO expands if enlargement is a necessary and efficient means for both old and new members in order to balance superior power or perceived threats.

In the neoliberal perspective, the international system is characterized by complex interdependence.[16] Owing to increasing interdependence, military power is losing its effectiveness and fungibility as a

11. Waltz, *Theory of International Politics*, 126.

12. Ibid., 127. See also George Liska, *Nations in Alliance. The Limits of Interdependence* (Baltimore: Johns Hopkins University Press, 1962), 13.

13. Stephen M. Walt, *The Origins of Alliances* (Ithaca: Cornell University Press, 1987).

14. Ibid., 32.

15. Although Walt does not clearly say whether intentions outweigh capabilities in all instances, I will focus on this factor in order to stress the difference between both neorealist theories. In addition, note that, by emphasizing perceptions, Walt departs from the materialist foundations of neorealism.

16. Robert O. Keohane, Joseph S. Nye Jr., *Power and Interdependence. World Politics in Transition* (Boston: Little, Brown, 1977).

means to achieve state objectives in international politics. At the same time, survival ceases to be the primary concern of states. As a consequence, security is not the only and not even the main benefit that states seek by forming and expanding international organizations. Instead of relative losses, states worry most about maximizing their absolute (welfare) gains under conditions of (primarily economic) interdependence in a variety of issue-areas. States create international institutions to manage interdependence and to increase gains from international cooperation. Accordingly, it is the core neoliberal proposition concerning NATO enlargement that NATO expands if both old and new members expect net absolute gains from enlargement.

In the neoliberal analysis, it is inherently difficult to determine the utilities of international actors and their cost-benefit calculations theoretically because there is no clear hierarchy of issues and goals. In the words of Schweller, a "balance of interests" rather than a balance of threat or a balance of power determines alliance choices.[17] While states are expected to balance for security, they may bandwagon for profit. Threat assessments enter into the equation but they are neither the only nor necessarily the decisive variables. That complicates the analysis considerably compared to neorealism. I will, therefore, concentrate on the most important categories of costs and benefits usually itemized in economic analyses of alliances and specifically mentioned in the 1995 "Study on Enlargement." Moreover, the test of the rationalist hypotheses will be limited to an overall qualitative assessment of the cost-benefit calculations for the two main groups of countries involved, that is CEE countries and NATO members. In the order of growing complexity, I begin with balance-of-power theory, move on to balance-of-threat theory, and end with the economic analysis of alliances.

THE CENTRAL AND EASTERN EUROPEAN COUNTRIES AND NATO MEMBERSHIP

Balance-of-power theory fails to explain the interest of CEE countries in NATO membership. Their bid to join NATO is a clear instance of bandwagoning and thus contradicts the theory. The only exception from balancing behavior that Waltz concedes is the case that the weaker coalition does not achieve "enough defensive or deterrent strength to dissuade adversaries from attacking."[18] Russia, however, could have effec-

---

17. Randall L. Schweller, "Bandwagoning for Profit. Bringing the Revisionist State Back In," *International Security* 19, no. 1 (summer 1994): 99.
18. Waltz, *Theory of International Politics*, 127.

tively provided its smaller Western neighbors with the security benefits of deterrence and defense. In spite of all economic and political difficulties, its nuclear second-strike capability has remained intact and
credible.[19] At the same time, Russia's reduced power would have given
the allies more leeway than they had in the Soviet era.

Balance-of-threat theory explains the behavior of the CEE countries.
Although NATO has increased its relative power vis-à-vis Russia and is
closer geographically to the central European countries than the eastern superpower, it is not perceived as aggressive. U.S. military hegemony in western Europe has been benign and has excluded the use of
force against allies. By contrast, the CEE societies have had a long history of Russian and Soviet domination and, even under the current
circumstances, they still are suspicious of Russian intentions. Therefore, it is reasonable for them to balance a potential Russian threat by
joining NATO—just as west European countries flocked to the United
States during the cold war, although the Soviet Union has always been
the weaker superpower.

This result is confirmed by a neoliberal assessment of the costs and
benefits of membership. Most importantly, by joining NATO as full
members, the CEE countries receive a place under the nuclear umbrella
and the right to military assistance by the other members in the case of
an acute threat or an attack. They thus acquire a degree of external security that they could not provide on their own (given their status as
non-nuclear weapon states and their limited financial and personal resources) and that allows them to spend less on the military than if they
had to rely exclusively on their own defense. From the viewpoint of
CEE countries, the costs incurred by the need to modernize and adjust
their armed forces and military facilities to NATO standards in order to
achieve a minimum of compatibility and interoperability are preferable
to the costs expected from autonomous defense provision.[20]

Furthermore, membership confers upon the CEE countries the right
to vote in the NATO Council, to be represented in the military com-

19. Kenneth N. Waltz, "The Emerging Structure of International Politics," in *The Perils of Anarchy. Contemporary Realism and International Security*, ed. Michael E. Brown, Sean M. Lynn-Jones, and Steven E. Miller (Cambridge: MIT Press, 1995), 50.

20. See the Polish study on the costs of NATO enlargement quoted in Institut für Friedensforschung und Sicherheitspolitik an der Universität Hamburg (IFSH), *Sicherheit in einem ungeteilten Europa. Die NATO-Osterweiterung als Chance nutzen*, Hamburger Informationen zur Friedensforschung und Sicherheitspolitik 20/1997 (Hamburg: IFSH, 1997), 10. For Hungary, see the interview with Minister of Foreign Affairs Kovacs, "Budapest will auf die 'Überholspur'," *Süddeutsche Zeitung*, 14 June 1997.

mand structure of NATO, and to participate in the NATO intelligence processes. Membership thus enhances their possibility to influence NATO decisions. At the same time, they are bound by NATO decisions and obliged to assist other NATO members in the case of attack (Article 5 of the Washington Treaty). On balance, the benefits probably outweigh the costs. First, given the highly asymmetrical interdependence in Europe, CEE countries are strongly affected by NATO policies whether they are members or not. Membership at least gives them some say. Second, it is highly unlikely that NATO will be attacked. Moreover, since the only country capable of threatening NATO is Russia, the CEE members' individual interests to protect their territory are hardly distinct from their obligation to protect the borders of NATO; there is virtually no entrapment risk for CEE countries. Finally, participation in out-of-area missions is voluntary.

NATO MEMBER STATES AND EASTWARD ENLARGEMENT

Realism and neoliberal institutionalism share the rationalist belief that, ceteris paribus, alliances with few members are preferable to alliances with many members: "Small is beautiful." Generally, the larger the size of an international organization, the smaller the "marginal policy contribution" of an additional member, the higher the diffusion of gains from cooperation, the higher the likelihood of free riding, and the higher the administrative costs as well as the costs of finding agreement.[21] In a club-theoretical perspective, then, the marginal benefits accruing to the members of the international organization from enlargement have to be considerably higher than the marginal costs of crowding. They also have to balance the increasing costs of organization, decisions, and compliance. It is difficult to see, however, that benefits of enlargement could be large enough to make old NATO members interested in the accession of CEE countries.

Realists expect NATO to disintegrate rather than to expand.[22] Even if NATO survived, it would have no need to enlarge itself. In a balance-of-

---

21. See Michele Fratianni and John Pattison, "The Economics of International Organizations," *Kyklos* 35, no. 2 (1982): 252; Mancur Olson, *The Logic of Collective Action. Public Goods and the Theory of Groups* (Cambridge: Harvard University Press, 1971), 35; and Bruce Russett, "Components of an Operational Theory of Alliance Formation," *Journal of Conflict Resolution* 12, no. 3 (September 1968): 286. For a realist assertion of the virtue of small numbers in alliances, see Liska, *Nations in Alliance*, 27.

22. See Waltz, *Theory of International Politics*, 126; and at a U.S. Senate hearing in 1990 ("NATO is a Disappearing Thing"), quoted by Gunther Hellmann and Reinhard

power perspective, the position of NATO in the international power structure has benefited so greatly from the dissolution of the Warsaw Pact and the Soviet Union that no further action is required.[23] The Russian threat has diminished at least as much as Russian power. If anything, balance-of-threat theory appears to predict an even more rapid and far-reaching disintegration of NATO than balance-of-power theory because the perceptions by NATO of a Soviet or Russian threat were reduced faster and to a greater extent than the actual capabilities of the Eastern superpower.[24]

In the realist perspective, preclusion is the only plausible reason for NATO enlargement. Russia's relative weakness provides a unique opportunity to expand NATO eastwards. If in the future Russia regained strength and returned to its traditional policy toward central and eastern Europe, an enlarged NATO would be able to deny Russia the restoration of the former Soviet hegemonic sphere. Even this explanation, however, is not fully satisfactory. As Walt claims, expansion may cause the disease it pretends to cure.[25] It fuels Russian suspicions, strains the relationship between the West and Russia, and may thus provoke a threat in the future where there is none at present. More importantly, assuming that preclusion is the main objective of enlargement, it is difficult to understand the selection of new members. If the window of opportunity had really been so small that immediate action was required, NATO should either have completed enlargement in a single round or should have focused on Ukraine and the Baltic countries, because these countries border on Russia and are the main objects of Russian revisionism. Instead, the first wave of expansion includes countries that could still have joined NATO after a potential manifestation of Russian expansionism in the former Soviet republics. Timing and scope of enlargement do not fit the preclusion hypothesis well. In any case,

---

Wolf, "Neorealism, Neoliberal Institutionalism, and the Future of NATO," *Security Studies* 3, no. 1 (autumn 1993): 17. Even according to traditional realism, NATO may endure longer than neorealism predicts but will eventually decline in the absence of a common threat. See Randall L. Schweller and David Priess, "A Tale of Two Realisms: Expanding the Institutions Debate," *Mershon International Studies Review* 41, suppl. 1 (May 1997): 21.

23. It may be argued that expansion increases the power of the alliance members. Just as bandwagoning, however, maximizing power is not covered by balance-of-power theory.

24. See the November 1991 "Rome Declaration on Peace and Cooperation," and "Strategic Concept" of NATO. See also Robert B. McCalla, "NATO's Persistence After the Cold War," *International Organization* 50, no. 3 (summer 1996): 451.

25. Stephen M. Walt, "Why Alliances Endure or Collapse," *Survival* 39, no. 1 (spring 1997): 173.

neorealism is indeterminate: the counterfactual event—the refusal of
NATO to enlarge—would not have been interpreted as an anomaly for
neorealism and would have corroborated its balancing hypotheses
more easily than enlargement.

Whereas the realist analysis emphasizes the lack of balancing needs,
the neoliberal analysis stresses the absence of absolute gains for the
NATO members. The current debate on the costs of NATO enlargement
focuses on the monetary contributions that NATO members must make
in the future in order to finance enlargement. Whereas initial U.S. calculations ranged from around $30 billion (RAND Corporation, Depart-
ment of Defense) to about $125 billion (Congressional Budget Office),
depending on the scenario, current NATO estimates are below $2 billion
and are based on the October 1997 decision that, for the most part, the
new members will have to bear the costs of force modernization themselves. Although this figure is contested and may be motivated by an
effort to ease ratification in the member states' parliaments, most observers agree that the costs of NATO enlargement are "moderate and
affordable."[26]

This is not the only cost factor, however. Crowding effects are to be
expected from spatial rivalry and entrapment risks. As far as spatial
rivalry is concerned, the inclusion of the Czech Republic and, above
all, Poland lengthens the "Eastern front" of NATO. Hungary does not
even share a single border with any other NATO country. Entrapment
risks, that is the probability of a higher than average consumption of
the club good, result from expansion into a politically unstable region
and toward Russia, which is not only the most powerful country outside of NATO but also opposed to NATO expansion. Hungary borders
on Croatia and Serbia, Poland on Russia and Belarus.[27] These costs are
not prohibitive, but they act as further disincentives to enlargement.

It is highly unlikely that the organizational and decisional costs of an
enlarged membership, the additional monetary contributions by the
old members and disproportionate crowding effects on the use of col-

---

26. Richard L. Kugler, *Costs of NATO Enlargement. Moderate and Affordable*, Strategic Forum 128 (Washington, D.C.: Institute for National Strategic Studies, 1997). See
also Jonathan Eyal, "NATO's Enlargement: Anatomy of a Decision," *International
Affairs* 73, no. 4 (October 1997): 711–12.

27. It is assumed, of course, that once a country is a member of NATO, solidarity is
quasi-automatic. In theory (even according to the NATO Treaty), it is possible that the
members decide case by case according to their cost-benefit assessments. In practice,
however, the decision not to defend a member would probably spell the breakdown of
NATO.

lective defense will be balanced by higher than average contributions of the new members. This is mainly because they still are in the process of economic transformation, and their GNP per capita is at the low extreme of NATO members. As a consequence, the joint contribution of the Czech Republic, Hungary, and Poland to the military budget of NATO will probably amount to no more than 4.5 percent. Furthermore, their armed forces are in a poor state, according to internal NATO reports.[28]

In compensation, this technological gap between old and new members gives rise to expectations of high private benefits from CEE orders to the defense industries of the United States and western Europe. Substantial profits, however, are unlikely because the post–cold war arms market is a highly competitive buyers' market and because the budgets of the new members will not allow major expenses. If large-scale sales take place at all, they will most probably be accompanied by indirect and direct offsets as well as Western military aid and credits.[29]

In sum, the main rationalist approaches to the analysis of international institutions explain the interest of the CEE countries in joining NATO but do not convincingly account for the decision of NATO to expand to the east. Starting from neorealist or neoliberal premises, international relations scholars must arrive at the conclusion that Partnership for Peace is "preferable to expanding NATO"[30] and constitutes the more "efficient institutional solution."[31]

THE CONSTRUCTIVIST EXPLANATION

ENLARGEMENT AS INTERNATIONAL SOCIALIZATION

Since the beginning of the 1990s, (social) constructivist approaches to the study of international relations have increasingly challenged the

---

28. See, for example, "NATO Concerned About Polish Military," *RFE/RL Newsline*, 20 January 1998, referring to a report from NATO headquarters.

29. Joanna Spear, "Bigger NATO, Bigger Sales," *The World Today* 53, no. 11 (November 1997): 272–74.

30. Walt, "Why Alliances Endure or Collapse," 179 n. 55.

31. Thomas Bernauer, "Full Membership or Full Club? Expansion of NATO and the Future Security Organization of Europe," in *Towards a New Europe. Stops and Starts in Regional Integration*, ed. Gerald Schneider, Patricia A. Weitsman, and Thomas Bernauer (Westport, Conn.: Praeger, 1995), 186–87.

rationalist paradigm.[32] Constructivism rejects the basic metatheoretical and theoretical premises of rationalism. It problematizes the actors' identities, interests and preferences which rationalism takes as given and stable. In the constructivist perspective, actors and their dispositions are socially constituted and subject to social change. Instead of providing the given starting points for the analysis of international interaction, identities and interests must be explained as the products of intersubjective social structures (culture, institutions) and social interaction. Moreover, constructivists reject the assumptions of egoism and instrumentalism. They claim that international actors are committed in their decisions to values and norms and choose the appropriate instead of the efficient behavioral option.[33]

On the basis of these assumptions, constructivists analyze international institutions not merely as regulatory institutions that constrain the behavioral options available to actors and influence their cost-benefit assessments. Constructivism posits that the origins and the constitution as well as the goals and the procedures of international organizations are more strongly determined by the standards of legitimacy and appropriateness of the international community they represent than by the utilitarian demand for efficient problem-solving.[34] In-

32. In International Relations, "constructivism" has established itself as the generic term for various approaches emphasizing the causal preponderance of intersubjective social structures. See the representative outlines of this research program by Emanuel Adler, "Seizing the Middle Ground: Constructivism in World Politics," *European Journal of International Relations* 3, no. 3 (September 1997): 319–63; Martha Finnemore, *National Interests in International Society* (Ithaca: Cornell University Press, 1996); Ronald L. Jepperson, Alexander Wendt, and Peter J. Katzenstein, "Norms, Identity, and Culture in National Security," in *The Culture of National Security. Norms and Identity in World Politics*, ed. Peter J. Katzenstein (New York: Columbia University Press, 1996), 33–75; Alexander Wendt, "Anarchy is What States Make of It. The Social Construction of Power Politics," *International Organization* 46, no. 2 (spring 1992): 391–425; and Wendt, "Collective Identity Formation and the International State," *American Political Science Review* 88, no. 2 (June 1994): 384–96. In particular, I share their view that constructivism provides, above all, an ontological, rather than an epistemological or methodological, alternative to rationalism and materialism.

33. Finnemore emphasizes the "logic of appropriateness" (Finnemore, *National Interests in International Society*, 29–30). This logic was opposed to the rationalist "logic of consequentiality" of James G. March and Johan P. Olsen, *Rediscovering Institutions. The Organizational Basis of Politics* (New York: Free Press, 1989), 160–62. In a similar vein, Max Weber contrasts instrumental rationality (*Zweckrationalität*) with value-rationality (*Wertrationalität*). See Max Weber, *Economy and Society. An Outline of Interpretive Sociology* (New York: Bedminster, 1968), 25.

34. See Peter J. Katzenstein, "United Germany in an Integrating Europe," in *Tamed Power. Germany in Europe*, ed. Peter J. Katzenstein (Ithaca: Cornell University Press, 1997), 12; Christian Reus-Smit, "The Constitutional Structure of International Society and the Nature of Fundamental Institutions," *International Organization* 51, no. 4 (autumn 1997): 569; and Steven Weber, "Origins of the European Bank for Recon-

ternational organizations are the institutional articulation of international communities of values and norms whose "definitions, rules, and principles are encoded in the prescriptions" they elaborate "for nation-state practice."[35] Moreover, constructivists view international organizations as constitutive institutions that contribute to shaping actors' identities, values and interests, and emphasize their "ability…to impose definitions of member characteristics and purposes upon the governments of its member states."[36] In their external relations, international organizations seek to defend the community against competing values and norms and to expand the community by disseminating its principles and precepts.

In the constructivist perspective, the enlargement of an international organization is primarily conceived of as a process of international socialization.[37] In general, "socialization" means the internalization, by a social actor, of the constitutive beliefs and practices of a social community. In this way, the actor acquires the collective identity of the community. Most commonly, "internalization" is used as a psychological concept that, strictly speaking, only applies to individuals. In the case of states, "internalizing" can be defined as the process of embedding the constitutive beliefs and practices of an international community in the domestic decision-making processes.[38] At an institutional level, a successful internalization is indicated by the integration of the fundamental community norms into the state constitution and their translation into (stable) domestic laws; at a cognitive level, it is reflected in consensual affirmative references to these fundamental norms in the domestic discourse. Both at the institutional and at the cognitive level, internalization is a matter of degree. Successful internalization, however, requires that the community beliefs and practices embedded in domestic institutions and discourses effectively determine state behavior.[39] Thus,

---

struction and Development," *International Organization* 48, no. 1 (winter 1994), 4–5 and 32.

35. Connie L. McNeely, *Constructing the Nation-State. International Organization and Prescriptive Action* (Westport, Conn.: Greenwood, 1995), 27.

36. Ibid., 33.

37. For an explication of the concept of socialization and a discussion of its uses in international relations, see Frank Schimmelfennig, "Internationale Sozialisation neuer Staaten. Heuristische Überlegungen zu einem Forschungsdesiderat," *Zeitschrift für Internationale Beziehungen* 1, no. 2 (December 1994): 335–55.

38. Kai Alderson, "Dimensions of Internalization" (unpubl. ms., 1997), 1.

39. Internalization does not presuppose that international values and norms are never challenged domestically. Domestic institutions and actors, however, must be strong enough to resist these challenges and successfully defend the internalized values and norms. (See, for examples from regime analysis, Harald Müller, "The Internaliza-

socialization is more than just an opportunistic and superficial adaptation. In order for an actor to become a member of the community, the community's constitutive beliefs and practices must become an integral part of the actor's identity and must be acted upon independently of external stimuli.

In international socialization, an international community and its organizations "teach" their constitutive norms and values to states and societies,[40] either as active promoters or as passive role models. As international organizations only dispose of a weak coercive and legislative authority compared to states, their influence as agencies of socialization is highly dependent on a combination of cultural diffusion or ideological infusion, on the one hand, and resource manipulation or power, on the other.[41] The relationship of states with the community and its organizations depends on the degree to which they base their identity and their interests on the community values and norms. In order to become members, they have to learn the lessons taught by the community's organizations, that is, to internalize their values, norms, and practices. They also have to pass a probationary period during which the community assesses whether the applicants are internalizing its identity or simply adapting to it superficially. Full membership is granted when socialization has sufficiently progressed and the community regards the applicant state as "one of us."[42]

---

tion of Principles, Norms, and Rules by Governments. The Case of Security Regimes," in *Regime Theory and International Relations*, ed. Volker Rittberger with the assistance of Peter Mayer [Oxford: Clarendon Press, 1993], 361–88.) Likewise, individual internalization does not imply the absence of deviant thoughts but requires the individual's conscience to prevent these thoughts from becoming norm-violating deeds.

40. Finnemore, *National Interests in International Society*, 11–12.

41. See Thomas M. Franck, *The Power of Legitimacy among Nations* (New York: Oxford University Press, 1990), 36–39; and McNeely, *Constructing the Nation State*, 28 and 35–36. The relative importance of ideational and material factors differs among authors (and probably among real world socialization processes). Whereas Franck stresses the "legitimacy" of rules, "hegemony" is presupposed by both realist and Marxist accounts of international socialization (see G. John Ikenberry and Charles Kupchan, "Socialization and Hegemonic Power," *International Organization* 44, no. 3 [summer 1990]: 283–315; and Robert W. Cox, "Gramsci, Hegemony and International Relations: An Essay in Method," in *Gramsci, Historical Materialism and International Relations*, ed. Stephen Gill [Cambridge: Cambridge University Press, 1993], 61–63). Note that, whereas the socialization process can be characterized by reinforcement based on material power or rewards, the socialization outcome requires that external reinforcement or monitoring no longer be necessary in order to ensure compliance.

42. The process of socialization is a special case of the process of positive identification leading to the formation of collective identities analyzed by Colin H. Kahl, "Constructing a Separate Peace: Constructivism, Collective Liberal Identity, and Democratic Peace," *Security Studies* 8, nos. 2/3 (winter 1998/99–spring 1999): 94–144. Socialization is special because it consists of an asymmetrical process between an estab-

In the perspective of socialization analysis, material costs and benefits clearly play a subordinate role both for the international organization and for the countries aspiring to membership. In the case of the organization, the commitment to its constitutive values and norms creates an obligation to diffuse them internationally and to grant membership to all states which share them—even in the case of material losses to the members of the organization. This obligation requires neither self-denial nor immediate membership. It does not extend to costs that are beyond the capabilities of the member states and would threaten the existence of the organization.

For an applicant state and society, accession to an international organization mainly fulfills the needs of identification and legitimation. Being accepted as a member of a group of like-minded countries assures governments and societies of their identity and of the legitimacy of their political and social values. In addition, membership facilitates the assertion of these values against competing values in the domestic as well as in the international arena because it enhances both the material and immaterial resources for their defense. Aspirations to membership vary with a country's perception of the community values and norms. The more the applicant state identifies with the community and perceives its values and norms as legitimate, the greater is its interest in membership and the less costly the requirements for membership appear to this state. The general constructivist hypothesis about the enlargement of international organizations then is: A state is accepted as a member by an international organization if it reliably shares the community values and norms. The faster it internalizes them, the earlier it becomes a member.

NATO AND THE VALUES AND NORMS OF THE EURO-ATLANTIC COMMUNITY

From a constructivist viewpoint, NATO is best understood neither simply as a form of alignment (as in neorealism) nor as a functional international institution (as in neoliberalism) but as an organization of an international community of values and norms. NATO is embedded in the Euro-Atlantic or "Western" community and represents its

---

lished community preserving its collective identity, on the one hand, and outside actors exchanging their former identity for the collective identity of the community, on the other. The community and its organization(s) serve as the "reference other" in the way this concept is used by Bruce Cronin, "From Balance to Community: Transnational Identity and Political Integration," *Security Studies* 8, nos. 2/3 (winter 1998/99–spring 1999): 270–301.

"military branch." This community is most fundamentally based on the liberal values and norms shared by its members. Liberal human rights, i.e. individual freedoms, civil liberties, and political rights are at the center of the community's collective identity. The liberal principles of social order—pluralism, the rule of law, democratic political participation and representation as well as private property and the market economy—are derived from, and justified by, these rights. They are the "constitutive values that define legitimate statehood and rightful state action" in the domestic and the international realm.[43]

The liberal community values define the basic purpose of the alliance, determine its interpretation and strategy of security and peace, and serve to identify the main threats:

(1) In the preamble to the North Atlantic Treaty, the signatory states declare the protection of their values, rather than just the preservation of national autonomy or the balance of power, as the basic purpose of NATO: "They are determined to safeguard the freedom, common heritage and civilisation of their peoples, founded on the principles of democracy, individual liberty, and the rule of law."

(2) Art. 2 of the treaty summarizes the two most important strands of the liberal theory and strategy of peace—republican and commercial liberalism or, in other words, peace through joint democracy and peace through trade (and the intensification of other transnational transactions):[44]

> The Parties will contribute toward the further development of peaceful and friendly international relations by strengthening their free institutions, by bringing about a better understanding of the principles upon which these institutions are founded, and by promoting conditions of stability and well-being. They will seek to eliminate conflict in their international economic policies and will encourage economic collaboration between any or all of them.

(3) On the threat perception of NATO members, Risse-Kappen argues from a constructivist perspective

43. Reus-Smit, "The Constitutional Structure of International Society," 558.

44. See Andrew Moravcsik, "Taking Preferences Seriously: A Liberal Theory of International Politics," *International Organization* 51, no. 4 (autumn 1997): 513–53. For a constructivist interpretation of the liberal theory of peace, cf., Emanuel Adler, "Imagined (Security) Communities: Cognitive Regions in International Relations," *Millennium* 26, no. 2 (summer 1997): 249–77; Kahl, "Constructing a Separate Peace"; and Thomas Risse-Kappen, "Democratic Peace—Warlike Democracies? A Social Constructivist Interpretation of the Liberal Argument," *European Journal of International Relations* 1, no. 4 (December 1995): 491–517.

that the sense of community, by delimiting the boundaries of who belonged to "us," also defined "them," that is those outside the community who were then perceived as a threat to the common values. In other words, the collective identity led to the threat perception, not the other way round.[45]

Furthermore, the common liberal values underlie the alliance norms governing the behavior of alliance members toward each other. Whereas, in a rationalist perspective, a hegemonic U.S. alliance organized as a "series of bilateral deals with each of the subordinates" would have been the expected institutional form and decision-making structure,[46] NATO is based on the norms of multilateralism. Ruggie defines multilateralism as a generic institutional form that

coordinates relations among three or more states on the basis of generalized principles of conduct: that is, principles which specify appropriate conduct for a class of actions, without regard to the particularistic interests of the parties or the strategic exigencies that may exist in any specific occurrence.[47]

These "generalized organizing principles logically entail an indivisibility among the members of a collectivity with respect to the range of behavior in question" and generate "expectations of 'diffuse reciprocity'." According to Weber, these principles govern the praxis of NATO:

Within NATO, security was indivisible. It was based on a general organizing principle, that the external boundaries of alliance territory were completely inviolable and that an attack on any border was an attack on all. Diffuse reciprocity was the norm.[48]

The principles of multilateralism correspond to the basic liberal idea of procedural justice, that is, "the legislative codification of formal, reciprocally binding social rules" among the members of society.[49] In the constructivist perspective, they are an effect of the liberal-democratic identity of the alliance members:

45. Thomas Risse-Kappen, *Cooperation Among Democracies. Norms, Transnational Relations, and the European Impact on U.S. Foreign Policy* (Princeton: Princeton University Press, 1995), 32.
46. Steve Weber, "Shaping the Postwar Balance of Power: Multilateralism in NATO," in *Multilateralism Matters. The Theory and Praxis of an Institutional Form*, ed. John Gerard Ruggie (New York: Columbia University Press, 1993), 235.
47. John Gerard Ruggie, "Multilateralism: The Anatomy of an Institution," in Rugie, *Multilateralism Matters*, 11.
48. Weber, "Shaping the Postwar Balance of Power," 233.
49. Reus-Smit, "The Constitutional Structure of International Society," 577.

Democracies externalize their internal norms when cooperating with each other. Power asymmetries should be mediated by norms of democratic decision making among equals emphasizing persuasion, compromise, and the non-use of force or coercion....Norms of regular consultation, of joint consensus-building, and non-hierarchy should legitimize and enable allied influence.[50]

Regarding NATO enlargement, constructivism then hypothesizes: A state seeks, and is granted, membership in NATO if it reliably shares the liberal values and the multilateralist norms of the Western community. The faster it internalizes these values and norms, the earlier it becomes a member.

THE CONSTRUCTIVIST EXPLANATION OF NATO ENLARGEMENT

How well does the constructivist hypothesis answer the three questions of why CEE countries seek NATO membership, why NATO expands to the east, and why the Czech Republic, Hungary, and Poland were invited to the first round of enlargement? For each question, I will first give the constructivist response and then discuss whether the conditions postulated by constructivism are necessary and sufficient to explain enlargement.

(1) Since the breakdown of the communist domestic and international system, the central and eastern European countries have strived to acquire a new identity and a new "home" in the international system. The "return to Europe," of which NATO membership is an important element, has become their central foreign policy objective.[51] This goal generally enjoys a broad consensus among the major political forces in those CEE countries that have applied for NATO membership and has been pursued no less by postcommunist (for example, in Po-

---

50. Risse-Kappen, *Cooperation Among Democracies*, 33.

51. See Fouzieh Melanie Alamir and August Pradetto, "Identitätssuche als Movens der Sicherheitspolitik. Die NATO-Osterweiterungsdebatten im Lichte der Herausbildung neuer Identitäten im postkommunistischen Ostmitteleuropa und in der Allianz," *Osteuropa* 48, no. 2 (February 1998): 134–47; Adrian G. V. Hyde-Price, "Democratization in Eastern Europe. The External Dimension," in *Democratization in Eastern Europe. Domestic and International Perspectives*, ed. Geoffrey Pridham and Tatu Vanhanen (London: Routledge, 1994), 225 and 235; George Kolankiewicz, "The Other Europe: Different Roads to Modernity in Eastern and Central Europe," in *European Identity and the Search for Legitimacy*, ed. Soledad García (London: Pinter, 1993), 108; George Kolankiewicz, "Consensus and Competition in the Eastern Enlargement of the European Union," *International Affairs* 70, no. 3 (July 1994): 481–82; and Iver B. Neumann, "Russia as Central Europe's Constituting Other," *East European Politics and Societies* 7, no. 2 (spring 1993): 349–69.

land, Hungary or Lithuania) than by other governments. From a constructivist point of view, the "return to Europe" results from a strong identification with Western values and norms as well as with the Western international community from which these countries were cut off under communist rule. The Western international community constitutes the model of the "good" domestic and international order which inspired the Eastern European revolutions of 1989 and 1990 and which the CEE countries try to emulate in their transformation processes. For the CEE countries, membership in NATO is a symbol for having successfully transformed themselves into modern European countries and for being recognized as "one of us" by their Western role models. At the same time, it indicates that they have broken links with their Soviet Communist past and have cast off their "Eastern" identity.

Furthermore, the prospect of membership in Western organizations serves as an important additional source of legitimacy for the proponents of liberal democratic reform in central and eastern Europe. Changes in domestic and foreign policy as well as the hardships of transformation are easier to justify and implement if they are demanded by Western organizations as a condition of closer cooperation and accession (or can be legitimized this way). The eventual accession to Western organizations confers political prestige upon the CEE governments, strengthens the self-esteem of CEE societies and makes authoritarian reversals more difficult.

Identification with the values and norms of the Western international community is a sufficient but not a necessary condition for the CEE countries' desire to join NATO. It is a sufficient condition because all CEE countries that strongly identify with the West and make a great effort to institutionalize Western norms have applied for NATO membership. On the other hand, as shown above, membership in NATO is attractive for instrumental reasons alone, that is, in order to balance a potential Russian threat, to provide for national security more efficiently, and to gain more influence on NATO decision making. A strong identification with Western values and norms is not necessary for countries to seek membership: Romania and Slovakia have done so under governments with authoritarian tendencies.

(2) According to the constructivist hypothesis, NATO decided to enlarge to the east in order to promote and strengthen liberal values,

(liberal democratic) peace and multilateralism in this area.[52] The prospect of NATO membership serves to give CEE countries an incentive to further pursue democratic reform and consolidate the transformation of their domestic systems as well as to manage international conflicts in this area peacefully, multilaterally, and on the basis of international law. Countries which share the liberal values of the Western community, have made sufficient progress in the internalization of its constitutive norms, and have behaved accordingly for a certain period of time are recognized as "Western." This recognition entails the commitment to grant full membership to this country in the Western organizations and to come to its assistance in the case of a military threat or attack.

The constructivist hypothesis establishes a necessary as well as sufficient condition for enlargement because rationalist theories have severe difficulties in explaining NATO behavior. In the absence of the desire to diffuse and stabilize Western values and norms in central and eastern Europe, and without the moral obligation to admit successfully socialized countries, enlargement would not have occurred given the net material losses involved for NATO members. This makes the value-rational commitment of NATO a necessary condition. It is also a sufficient condition because no other conditions have to be present in order for enlargement to occur.

(3) NATO chose the Czech Republic, Hungary, and Poland as its first new members because these three countries are more advanced than other CEE countries in their internalization of Western values and norms. They are closest to western Europe not only in terms of geography but also in terms of common history and political culture. More than other CEE countries, they can rightly claim to be a part of the "common heritage and civilisation" of NATO countries. More importantly, they are the forerunners and paragons of liberalization and democratization in the region. Already under Soviet domination, popular movements in Hungary (in 1956), Czechoslovakia (1968), and Poland (1956, 1970, 1980) revolted against the Communist system. In 1989, they led the way in the democratic transformation of the region—with Poland inventing the "round table" of peaceful transition and Hungary opening the "iron curtain" for GDR refugees. Meanwhile, the consolidation of the democratic system is well advanced in these countries. In

---

52. See Patrick M. Morgan, "Security Prospects in Europe," in Ruggie, *Multilateralism Matters*, 345–46, for the importance of the Western post-war multilateralist experience as a guide to dealing with present developments in eastern Europe.

Hungary and Poland, even the postcommunist parties which came into power through regular elections have not deviated from the path of transformation and integration into the Western organizations. Moreover, none of the three central European countries has been engaged in major territorial and ethnic conflict with its neighbors or in major domestic ethnic conflict. All of them have shown the willingness and capability to manage such conflicts as there were by peaceful means. Poland granted minority rights to its German-speaking population and made no claims to Lithuanian, Belarusian, and Ukrainian territory that had belonged to its prewar area. The Czech Republic used no force or pressure against Slovak separatism but agreed to a peaceful dissolution of Czechoslovakia. The Hungarian government has stayed away from irredentism despite sizable Hungarian minorities abroad. In the face of considerable domestic opposition and repressive policies against the Hungarian minority in Slovakia and Romania, it has actively and successfully pursued the conclusion of basic treaties with both neighboring countries.

The speed of, and progress in, the internalization of community values and norms is a necessary but not a sufficient condition for the selection of new members in the first round of NATO enlargement. It is obvious that no country is invited without having made such progress and proven its adherence to the community values and norms in word and deed over a certain period of time. Moreover, the Czech Republic, Hungary, and Poland were more advanced in the socialization process than the other CEE countries. In Bulgaria and Romania, liberal-democratic transformation has stagnated under postcommunist governments until the elections in late 1996 and early 1997. The Baltic countries have advanced very far on the way of economic liberalization and democratic consolidation but still have to contend with difficulties in the integration of the Russian minorities (and with Western criticism about their minority policies). Slovakia had ranked as high on the list of potential NATO members as the Czech Republic until President Meciar and his party embarked upon a course of authoritarian governance and minority discrimination. Only Slovenia matches the liberalization and democratization record of the Czech Republic, Hungary, and Poland, and after the initial short period of war has successfully insulated itself from the Balkan conflicts. It lags behind these three states, however, with regard to the duration of its participation in the socialization process. Thus, if only three countries were to be invited, constructivism would have predicted the actual choice.

Yet, nothing in the constructivist hypothesis predicts that NATO should limit its initial round of enlargement to three countries in the first place. Whereas one could make a plausible argument for why most aspiring states are not ready for full membership, at least the exclusion of Slovenia cannot be justified on the basis of insufficient socialization. Therefore, the constructivist explanation does not sufficiently account for the choice of new members. Rather, the discussions on the eve of the Madrid summit suggest that the number of new members was restricted mainly because of the United States' resolute opposition against the initiative of France and other European member states to include Slovenia and Romania in the first round of enlargement. The most important reasons given for this limitation were that the admission of further countries would become too costly for NATO, endanger its cohesion, and call into question ratification by the U.S. Senate. Furthermore, it was said that Slovenia's population and armed forces were too small and too weak to make much of a military contribution to collective defense.[53]

To sum up, the first round of NATO enlargement to the east corroborates the constructivist hypothesis about the enlargement of international organizations to a very large extent. The international socialization approach to enlargement stands out most obviously with regard to the central explanandum of this article which, at the same time, constitutes a puzzle for mainstream rationalist approaches to the study of international organizations: the readiness of NATO to admit CEE countries as full members. The constructivist hypothesis provides both a more elegant and a more determinate explanation of enlargement than the main rationalist hypotheses. First, whereas a possible rationalist explanation must be based on the rather marginal preclusion hypothesis and on uncertain future expectations (of a Russian neoimperialism), the constructivist explanation starts from the core hypothesis of international socialization and from factual conditions (the state of liberal transformation in central and eastern Europe). Second, whereas the rationalist explanation would have explained the absence of enlargement as well (and probably more convincingly than its presence), the constructivist hypothesis would have failed if NATO had denied

---

53. See "Albright on Potential New NATO Members," *RFE/RL Newsline*, 30 May 1997; Michael Mihalka, "Why Only Three Countries Will Likely Be Included in First Wave of NATO Enlargement," *RFE/RL Newsline*, 7 July 1997; "Kohl und Clinton auf einer Linie," *Süddeutsche Zeitung*, 7 June 1997; and "Clinton für drei neue NATO-Länder," *Süddeutsche Zeitung*, 13 June 1997.

membership to the most consolidated CEE democracies. The constructivist hypothesis, however, cannot explain why governments that are not willing to adopt the constitutive values and norms of the Western community nevertheless apply for membership, and why Slovenia was not invited to join the organization together with the Czech Republic, Hungary, and Poland. These facts are better accounted for by instrumental calculations. Moreover, rationalist theories of international organization give a convincing alternative explanation for the CEE countries' interest in becoming NATO members.

The claim that constructivism provides a better explanation for NATO enlargement than rationalism is mainly based on its ability to explain the interest of NATO in, and its criteria for, admitting CEE countries as full members. So far the constructivist explanation rests on a correlational and conditional account. In other words, I have tried to show that the general constructivist hypothesis about the enlargement of international organizations covers, and establishes a necessary and sufficient condition for, NATO enlargement to the east. The case for constructivism would be even more convincing if it could further be shown that not only the results but also the process of NATO enlargement was congruent with the international socialization perspective. The method of "process-tracing"[54] goes beyond the analysis of correlations and conditions by seeking to establish whether the independent variable(s) postulated by a theory really are at work as causal factors in the production of the fact or event to be explained. In order to provide additional evidence for the constructivist explanation, I shall argue (1) that the presumed cause of NATO enlargement, the community of values and norms, is reflected in the enlargement discourse, that is, in the basic statements and documents supporting enlargement, and (2) that the stages of enlargement resemble, and are regarded as, a process of teaching and learning community values and norms.

54. On this method, see Alexander L. George, "Case Studies and Theory Development: The Method of Structured, Focused Comparison," in *Diplomacy: New Approaches in History, Theory and Policy*, ed. Paul Gordon Lauren (New York: Free Press, 1979), 46; and Alexander L. George and Timothy J. McKeown, "Case Studies and Theories of Organizational Decision Making," in *Advances in Information Processing in Organizations*, vol. 2, ed. L. S. Sproull and P. D. Larkey (Greenwich, Conn.: JAI Press, 1985), 21–58.

ENLARGEMENT DISCOURSE

The enlargement discourse is composed of the oral and written public statements in favor of and against NATO enlargement in both the member and the aspiring countries as well as in transnational and international fora. In order to confirm the constructivist explanation of NATO enlargement, it is not necessary to demonstrate that arguments based on power and threats or, more generally, on costs and benefits, were absent in the enlargement discourse. We should expect, however, that such arguments were mainly put forward by the opponents of enlargement. By contrast, the advocates of enlargement ought consistently to justify their viewpoint by value-based considerations. Value-rational actors would not simply deny that NATO enlargement was against the egoistic security and material interests of its members (in which case they would appear as irrational or, at best, subjectively rational utility-maximizers). Rather, they would argue that the interest of NATO must be interpreted in terms of commitments to its values and norms and that material losses from enlargement must be accepted (as long as they are manageable) in order to honor these commitments. The most important "pieces of evidence" are the basic texts produced by NATO during the enlargement process, that is the 1994 Partnership for Peace (PfP) Framework Document and the 1995 Study on Enlargement. These documents reflect the shared understandings of NATO members and serve as consensual and official guidelines for enlargement. No less important are statements by the representatives of the most important NATO member states. Given the paramount position of the United States in the alliance, it is justifiable to focus on U.S. documents and the U.S. debate.

The opponents of enlargement have voiced their skepticism mainly in specialized journals and on the op-ed pages of the leading newspapers. The antienlargement campaign in the United States has reached its apex in two letters sent to President Clinton in late June 1997, one by more than twenty senators, the other by more than forty former senior officials and government experts representing the opposition among the foreign policy establishment.[55] The opponents based their contra-arguments consistently (but usually implicitly) on rationalist assumptions. First, they argued that Russia, for the foreseeable future,

---

55. See Sonia Winter, "NATO: Expansion Critics Write To Clinton," *RFE/RL Newsline*, 27 June 1997. The following references are examples from the op-ed pages of the *International Herald Tribune*.

would be too weak to pose a threat to the other CEE countries.[56] Instead, the security of the CEE countries that do not become members would be reduced.[57] Second, they expected that NATO expansion would harden Russian resistance to further nuclear disarmament that would serve U.S. and NATO security better than the new allies in central and eastern Europe.[58] Third, the opponents put forward the view that enlargement would weaken NATO by creating more costs than security benefits and by causing internal divisions about the states to be invited and about the distribution of enlargement costs.[59] Finally, Fred Iklé criticized that NATO enlargement was regarded as a "nursery for the young democracies" of east and central Europe instead of asking whether new members were security producers or consumers.[60]

NATO documents and statements by leading U.S. government officials confirm Iklé's perception. They corroborate the constructivist view of the basic motivation for enlargement—the most fundamental contribution to the security of the North Atlantic area is the spread of liberal democracies and multilateralist cooperation—and of the basic preconditions for states to be admitted: adherence to liberal values, to the liberal strategy of security and peace, and to the alliance norms of multilateralist and consensual decision making. Already the PfP Framework Document (§2) establishes the values to be served by the program:

> Protection and promotion of fundamental freedoms and human rights, and safeguarding of freedom, justice, and peace through democracy are shared values fundamental to the Partnership. In joining the Partnership, the member States of the North Atlantic Alliance and the other States subscribing to this Document recall that they are committed to the preservation of democratic societies,

56. See George F. Kennan, "NATO Expansion Would Be a Fateful Blunder," *International Herald Tribune*, 6 February 1997, 8; and William Pfaff, "European Security Isn't Broken, So Why Try to Fix it Now?" *International Herald Tribune*, 18 February 1997, 8.

57. Francois Heisbourg, "At This Point, Only Washington Can Slow the Reckless Pace," *International Herald Tribune*, 28 November 1996, 8.

58. Thomas L. Friedman, "Forgetting that Russia's Nuclear Weapons Are the Problem," *International Herald Tribune*, 3 June 1997, 6.

59. Frederick Bonnard, "NATO: Slow Down and Be Sure the Alliance Remains Strong," *International Herald Tribune*, 4 July 1997, 8; and Philip H. Gordon, "Will Anyone Really Pay to Enlarge NATO—and If So, Who?" *International Herald Tribune*, 30 April 1997, 8.

60. Statement at a NATO Roundtable organized by the Konrad Adenauer Foundation, cited according to Josef Joffe, "Kinderhort für die jungen Demokratien," *Süddeutsche Zeitung*, 3 June 1995, 9.

their freedom from coercion and intimidation, and the maintenance of the principles of international law.

In chapter 1 (§2) of the Study on NATO Enlargement, entitled "Purposes and Principles of Enlargement," NATO describes security and democracy as inextricably linked:

> The benefits of common defence and...integration are important to protecting the further democratic development of new members. By integrating more countries into the existing community of values and institutions...NATO enlargement will safeguard the freedom and security of all its members.

NATO secretary-general Solana emphasizes the identity- and legitimacy-building functions of NATO enlargement as "a means of reinforcing the new democracies with a confidence in their destiny and giving them a sense of belonging." Although he also sees "many practical benefits," he stresses the "moral obligation for us to help them fulfil their legitimate aspirations."[61] Strobe Talbott, U.S. deputy secretary of state, regards it as a part of the post–cold war mission of NATO

> to open its door to the new democracies that have regained their sovereignty. They aspire and deserve to be part of the trans-Atlantic community. All of Europe will be safer and more prosperous if these postcommunist lands continue to evolve toward civil society, market economies and harmonious relations with their neighbors.[62]

Finally, Ronald Asmus, then an analyst at the RAND Corporation and now deputy secretary of state, named as "the goal" of NATO enlargement "to do for Eastern Europe what was done for Western Europe—create a security framework under which these countries can safely complete their transition to Western democratic societies."[63]

The representatives of the invited central European countries have also emphasized the community of values and the moral obligations of NATO in order to promote the cause of enlargement against the skeptics in the NATO member countries. Vaclav Havel, the Czech president, probably enjoys the highest authority with the Western public:

61. Javier Solana, "Preparing for the Madrid Summit," *NATO Review* 45, no. 2 (March-April 1997), 3.
62. Strobe Talbott, "Why the Transformed NATO Deserves to Survive and Enlarge," *International Herald Tribune*, 19 February 1997, 8.
63. Ronald D. Asmus, "Stop Fussing About NATO Enlargement and Get On With It," *International Herald Tribune*, 9 December 1996, 8.

The alliance should urgently remind itself that it is first and foremost an instrument of democracy to defend mutually held and created political and spiritual values. It must see itself not as a pact of nations against a more or less obvious enemy, but as a guarantor of European-American civilization....The opportunity to make decisions about common defense should not be denied a priori to countries that have embraced and advanced Euro-American political and cultural values.[64]

NATO documents and statements by members of the U.S. administration strongly suggest that political conditions pertaining to shared values and alliance norms are the primary and indispensable prerequisites for membership. U.S. president Clinton plainly summarized which countries do not qualify:

> Countries with repressive political systems, countries with designs on their neighbors, countries with militaries unchecked by civilian control, or with closed economic systems need not apply.[65]

Also, Secretary of State Albright made clear that liberal values and norms are a sufficient condition of membership, since "no European democracy will be excluded because of where it sits on the map."[66]

By contrast, the factors emphasized by rationalist approaches to the study of alliances (balances of power or threat, the costs and benefits of sharing defense, or organizational costs) play only a secondary role in the Western alliance's catalogue of enlargement conditions. They are cast in rather vague terms. In the Study on NATO Enlargement, no military threat is named. Instead, NATO prefers to speak of "risks" which are "hard to predict and assess" (§10). True, "the ability of prospective members to contribute militarily to collective defence and to the Alliance's new missions will be a factor in deciding whether to invite them to join the Alliance" (§75). Yet, NATO only demands minimum standards of interoperability and a general ability to contribute to its tasks; it does neither require a certain quality or quantity of contributions nor that the new members' contributions equal their prospective utilization of the alliance goods and compensate the old members for the disproportionate organizational costs they cause. Rather, NATO demands "a contribution level based, in a general way, on

---

64. Vaclav Havel, "The Euro-American Alliance Needs to Deepen as it Expands," *International Herald Tribune*, 15 May 1997, 8.
65. Cited in http://www.nato.int/usa/info/info2.htm.
66. Speech at the North Atlantic Council Ministerial Meeting in Sintra, 29 May 1997, cited in http://www.nato.int/usa/specials/970529-a.htm.

'ability to pay'" (§ 65)—which will be fairly limited in the case of CEE members.

A PROCESS OF TEACHING AND LEARNING

In preparing the candidate states for membership, NATO emphasizes the importance of active participation in Partnership for Peace. Whereas the rationalist analysis regards PfP as the equilibrium solution to the asymmetrical interests of NATO members and CEE countries, constructivism suggests interpreting PfP as an intermediary and probationary stage in the socialization of potential new members. During this stage, NATO teaches the values, norms, and practices of the Western international community to the aspiring states and tests whether they meet the learning objectives.[67] The Study on NATO Enlargement, in paras. 38 and 39, confirms this interpretation:

> Through PfP planning, joint exercises and other PfP activities, including seminars, workshops and day-to-day representation in Brussels and Mons, possible new members will increasingly become acquainted with the functioning of the Alliance....Possible new members' commitment to the shared principles and values of the Alliance will be indicated by their international behaviour and adherence to relevant OSCE commitments; however, their participation in PfP will provide a further important means to demonstrate such commitment as well as their ability to contribute to common defence. For possible new members, PfP will contribute to their preparation both politically and militarily, to familiarise them with Alliance structures and procedures and to deepen their understanding of the obligations and rights that membership will entail.

Since enlargement could put a strain on the principle of consensual decision making, NATO further stresses that "it will be important that prospective new members become familiar with the Alliance decision-making process, and the modalities and traditions of consensus and compromise, before joining." Finally, the "varying degree of participation is a key element of the self-differentiation process" (§46). NATO explicitly states that countries which take part in the Planning and Review Process (PARP) and are ready to reinforce and deepen their Individual Partnership Programmes, thus distinguishing themselves by

---

67. See Risse-Kappen, *Cooperation Among Democracies*, 224.

"demonstrating their capabilities and their commitment," enhance their prospects of (early) NATO membership (§40–41). During the probationary period starting with Partnership for Peace, the aspiring countries have regulary received "grades" for their progress on the way to membership. Former U.S. secretary of defense Perry, for example, toured central and eastern Europe in September 1995, confirming that the Czech Republic met all prerequisites for NATO membership whereas Slovakia would have to intensify the democratization process.[68] According to the proponents of NATO enlargement, this socialization process has been a success. At the NATO Ministerial Meeting in Sintra on 29 May 1997, Albright said that

> we want to give the nations of Central and Eastern Europe an incentive to make the right choices about their future. We want to encourage them to resolve old disputes, to consolidate democracy, and to respect human rights and international norms. So far, that is exactly what the prospect of enlargement has done.

Asmus concurs with the view that the

> prospect of NATO enlargement has already contributed enormously to reform and reconciliation in Eastern Europe. From the Baltic to the Black Sea, foreign and defense policies are being reconstructed in order to bring these countries into line with alliance norms. Rarely has a Western policy had such an impact in eliciting such positive change.[69]

The many bilateral basic treaties between CEE countries concluded to settle territorial disputes and ethnic minority conflicts are the most important foreign policy changes attributed to the conditions of membership explicitly stated by NATO. Among the domestic changes, the introduction of civilian control of the military can most clearly be linked to the prospect of NATO membership—above all in Poland where it was long contested and had to be secured by the dismissal of the Polish chairman of the joint chiefs of staff in the spring of 1997.

In April 1997 NATO discussed and adopted individual reports on the 12 candidates for NATO membership in order to give a precise picture of the political and military situation of each aspiring state as well as of

68. Interestingly, Perry praised Slovenia as a role model for the rest of Central Europe and as a strong candidate for membership in NATO (see "Perry: Slowenien ist Vorbild für Mitteleuropa"; "Perry ruft Slowaken zu mehr Demokratie auf"; and "Perry: Prag erfüllt Bedingung für NATO-Beitritt," *Süddeutsche Zeitung* 19, 20, and 21 September 1995).
69. Asmus, "Stop Fussing About NATO Enlargement," 8.

the consequences of its accession, on which the political representatives of the member states could then base their decision about the countries to be invited to become members.[70] The decision to choose only the Czech Republic, Hungary, and Poland for the first round of enlargement was justified by their progress in the internalization of alliance values. The chairman of the U.S. Joint Chiefs of Staff, General Shalikashvili, said that these three countries had

> come far toward political democratization and an opening of their economies...had large and competent military forces and had made important strides politically and economically. All had contributed importantly to the peacekeeping operation in Bosnia.[71]

As to Slovenia and Romania, whose membership was supported by a majority of the European NATO members, Defense Secretary Cohen praised their "efforts to qualify for NATO membership, but said the reform process undertaken by those governments had not had sufficient time to become firmly rooted."[72] NATO encouraged these countries, though, to proceed further on the path of liberal reform and peaceful conflict management in order to qualify for later rounds. In its Madrid Declaration, it specifically recognized the progress achieved in Romania, Slovenia, and the Baltic countries. Finally, at their joint press conference at the Madrid summit, the heads of state or government of the Czech Republic, Hungary, and Poland confirmed the view of membership as a consequence of successful socialization and as a boost to their identity and legitimacy:

> We see the invitation extended to us in Madrid as recognition of the tremendous efforts undertaken by our societies following the changes in 1989/1990. We are indeed very proud that the transformation of our political systems and economies have made us eligible to be considered as an integral part of the Alliance.[73]

---

70. "Reformvorschläge des NATO-Militärausschusses," *Neue Zürcher Zeitung*, 24 April 1997, 2.

71. Brian Knowlton, "Top General Defends U.S. Choices for NATO," *International Herald Tribune*, 17 June 1997, 2.

72. William Drozdiak, "Europeans Protest Clinton's Limit on Widening NATO," *International Herald Tribune*, 13 June 1997, 1 and 11.

73. Cited in http://www.nato.int/docu/speech/1997/s970708h.htm.

PUTTING THE CONSTRUCTIVIST EXPLANATION IN PERSPECTIVE

IN THIS ARTICLE I have attempted to show that a constructivist approach to the study of international organizations based on the notion of international socialization provides an elegant explanation for NATO enlargement to central Europe, whereas the most prominent rationalist approaches, namely neorealism and neoliberal institutionalism, have difficulties in accounting for the decision of NATO to accept the Czech Republic, Hungary, and Poland as full members. In this final section, I will add some qualifications to the refutation of rationalist approaches and suggest some avenues for further research necessary to substantiate the constructivist explanation.

(1) I do not claim that there are no rationalist explanations for the interest of NATO in enlargement. My argument is limited to the core propositions of the mainstream rationalist approaches which have, to a very large extent, framed the academic debate about international institutions and international cooperation in the last two decades. In principle, it is possible to find some rationalist (as well as, probably, constructivist) explanation for any social event if the necessary modifications or qualifications to the original propositions are introduced. Neorealist propositions on alliance-building and international integration, in particular, have been modified considerably in order to account for anomalous empirical phenomena.[74] Moreover, it may be possible to find explanations for NATO enlargement that do not fit in with the neorealist or neoliberal frameworks but are based on the assumption of egoistic instrumental action nevertheless. For instance, a "critical" or "radical" explanation of NATO expansion as a means to protect the assets and interests of Western multinationals appears to have some plausibility given the fact that the three CEE countries selected for full membership have attracted by far the largest share of

---

74. For modifications to Waltz's balance-of-power theory, see Walt, *The Origins of Alliances*; and Schweller, "Bandwagoning for Profit." For the study of European integration, see Joseph M. Grieco, "State Interests and Institutional Rule Trajectories: a Neorealist Interpretation of the Maastricht Treaty and European Economic and Monetary Union," *Realism: Restatements and Renewal*, ed. Benjamin Frankel (London: Frank Cass, 1996), 261–306. See John A. Vasquez, "The Realist Paradigm and Degenerative vs. Progressive Research Programs: An Appraisal of Neotraditionalist Research on Waltz's Balancing Proposition," *American Political Science Review*, 91, no. 4 (December 1997): 899–912, for a critical review of these efforts (as well as the realist rejoinders in the same issue).

Western direct investments in the region.[75] The international socialization approach is preferable, though, because it provides the more parsimonious and determinate explanation of NATO enlargement and it is, at the same time, more in tune with the core propositions of its research program than any of the rationalist approaches.

(2) Rationalist and constructivist explanations do not have to exclude one another but can be combined in different ways:

(a) It may be the case that one group of state actors, the CEE governments, are motivated by egoistic interests, whereas the other, the NATO governments, act value-rationally. This would be compatible with the finding that rationalist approaches are able to explain the behavior of CEE countries and with the observation that governments leaning toward authoritarianism have not refrained from applying for NATO membership.

(b) There is some evidence that, even though the general decision to expand NATO is best explained as a value-rational action, the concrete terms and steps of enlargement are also motivated by instrumental considerations. The fact that the first round of enlargement was limited to three countries (and did not include Slovenia) is best explained by U.S. concerns about ratification and the costs of enlargement. The (temporary) exclusion of the Baltic states cannot be attributed only to the unsolved minority question in Estonia and Latvia, but, perhaps more convincingly, to the Western desire not to antagonize Russia completely. Finally, instrumental cost-benefit calculations explain best why NATO continually presses for the candidates to raise their defense expenditures and why its members decided to make the CEE countries bear the costs of modernizing their armed forces.

(c) If one starts from the assumption that NATO represents the military branch of the Western community of liberal values whose members share not only the purpose of protecting and disseminating their beliefs, but also the perception that undemocratic governments are a threat to their preferred world order, and the belief that peace depends on joint democracy, then the democratic socialization of countries bordering on the Western community becomes an instrumentally rational strategy for advancing the security of NATO members.[76] It is obvious, however, that in all these combinations of rationalist and con-

---

75. I thank one of the anonymous reviewers of *Security Studies* for alerting me to such alternative explanations.

76. I thank Bernhard Zangl and one of the reviewers for pointing out this combination of constructivist and rationalist explanations to me.

structivist explanations, the constructivist element is more fundamental: The liberal democratic identity of NATO members determines the ideas and purposes on which NATO enlargement is based and toward which instrumental action is oriented.

(3) Further research is required in order to substantiate the constructivist explanation. In this article, I have focused on a single organization, a single region, a single round of enlargement, on NATO as a collective, and on the enlargement outcomes. For this reason, the analysis of enlargement should be extended in five ways.

(a) In order to test the constructivist explanation offered here, the integration of central and eastern Europe into NATO should be compared to the eastward enlargement processes of other Western international organizations. As I have tried to show elsewhere, the eastern enlargement of the European Union resembles NATO expansion: It is driven by the same commitment to liberal values and norms, especially since the costs of enlargement exceed the benefits for the current members even more clearly than in the case of NATO.[77]

(b) Furthermore, the eastward enlargement must be compared to enlargement processes in other regions of Europe. As Mary Hampton shows, the integration of West Germany into NATO can be regarded as the prototype case of a successful socialization of a former enemy by the Western international community.[78] Another salient case is southern Europe. Here, the explanation of enlargement as the international socialization of formerly authoritarian countries to the values and norms of the Western international community appears to hold as well—most obviously for the accession of Greece, Portugal, and Spain to the Council of Europe (in the 1970s) and to the European Community (in the 1980s). The picture is less clear for NATO: Whereas Spain joined the alliance after the democratization of the country, Greece, Portugal, and Turkey became or remained NATO members in spite of periods of authoritarian rule. Moreover, the international socialization approach appears to be less suitable prima facie in the cases of "northern enlargement." If Austria, Finland, or Sweden were to join NATO, this could certainly not be explained by the diffusion of liberal

---

77. Frank Schimmelfennig, "Liberal Norms and the Eastern Enlargement of the European Union: A Case for Sociological Institutionalism," *Österreichische Zeitschrift für Politikwissenschaft* 27, no. 4 (December 1998).

78. See Mary N. Hampton, "NATO at the Creation," *Security Studies* 4, no. 3 (spring 1995): 610–56; and Mary N. Hampton, "NATO, Germany, and the United States: Creating Positive Identity in Trans-Atlantia," *Security Studies* 8, nos. 2/3 (winter 1998/99–spring 1999): 235–69.

democratic values which these countries have shared with NATO since its foundation. If constructivism was to provide a convincing explanation for these possible enlargements, it would have to demonstrate that the internalization of the community norm of multilateral and common defense as opposed to the previously dominant norm of neutrality was the decisive factor.

(c) The future development of NATO expansion is a crucial test for the constructivist explanation of enlargement as international socialization. Further rounds of enlargement in which the countries with the best record of liberal democratic transformation and multilateralist foreign policies accede to NATO would support this explanation. If NATO enlargement, however, stopped with the first round or did not include the Baltic countries in spite of further progress in the peaceful and democratic management of their minority problems, or if Slovakia and Croatia became NATO members without a thorough democratization of their political systems, the constructivist account would run into severe difficulties.

(d) To treat NATO as a collective and the United States as its representative member, as I have done in this article, is a highly simplifying assumption. This summary analysis should therefore be complemented by an analysis of the enlargement preferences and policies of the (main) individual member countries. As a consequence, the constructivist explanation may have to be refined. As it stands, constructivism would lead us to expect a uniform position of all member countries on the desirability of enlargement and the choice of individual new members. In reality, however, the enlargement preferences varied—less so with regard to the decision to enlarge NATO at all and to the choice of the Czech Republic, Hungary, and Poland, but very much so with regard to the speed of enlargement and the accession of further CEE countries.[79]

(e) The focus of this article is on the enlargement decisions and outcomes. The analysis of process has been largely limited to showing that the motivation of the actors implied in the constructivist explanation of enlargement as international socialization is consistent with their basic texts and statements and the stages of the enlargement. One im-

---

79. Even Chancellor Kohl pleaded for postponing enlargement and criticized the U.S. administration for forcing the pace in February 1996, although the German government had declared itself in favor of enlargement early on. The division on the number of CEE countries to be invited in the first round of enlargement lasted until the final decision was reached at the Madrid Summit on 8 July 1997.

portant question relating to process is not treated and answered: How did the value-based preference for enlargement form and assert itself? The present explanation seems to suggest that NATO has had the preference to enlarge to the democratic CEE countries ever since the east European revolutions and has pursued enlargement as its new "grand strategy" since the end of the cold war and after containment had become an obsolete doctrine. This was clearly not the the case. Whereas the central European countries began to raise the question of NATO membership almost immediately after the dissolution of the Warsaw Pact and the Soviet Union, the United States and then NATO did not firmly commit themselves to enlargement before 1994. The enlargement process of NATO was not the implementation of a "grand strategy" but was characterized by "halting diplomatic discussions and haphazard, last-minute decision making, [and] of symbolic gestures made through 'photo opportunities'."[80]

There are competing suppositions as to why enlargement occurred nevertheless, which reach from the courting of the voters of central and eastern European origin by the Clinton administration to the successful lobbying by CEE governments (and perhaps the German government). In order to be consistent with constructivism, process-tracing would have to show that persuasive appeals to the shared values and to the moral obligation of NATO members to act in solidarity with the democratic CEE countries produced this outcome. It is conceivable that the constant reference by NATO and its members to liberal values, the democratic international community, and its solidarity with the (former) "captive nations" of central and eastern Europe created an argumentative self-commitment that NATO members could not ignore—or only at the expense of their own credibility.[81] There are strong indications, indeed, that such a process was at work: In his analysis of U.S. decision making, Goldgeier indicates that President Clinton was persuaded of NATO expansion after he had met with the

---

80. Jonathan Eyal, "NATO's enlargement," 695.
81. Cf., Elster's discussion of the "civilizing force of hypocrisy" and the problems of opportunistic argumentation in Jon Elster, *Arguing and Bargaining in Two Constituent Assemblies*, Storrs Lecture (New Haven: Yale Law School, 1991); and Jon Elster, "Arguing and Bargaining in the Federal Convention and the Assemblée Constituante," in *Rationality and Institutions. Essays in Honour of Knut Midgaard*, ed. Raino Malnes and Arild Underdal (Oslo: Universitetsforlaget, 1992), 13–50. Thus, the analysis of process provides further opportunities for combining constructivist and rationalist factors.

presidents of the Czech Republic and Poland, Havel and Walesa, at the opening of the Holocaust Museum in Washington in April 1993:

> These two, having struggled so long to throw off the Soviet yoke, carried a moral authority matched by few others around the world. Each leader delivered the same message to Clinton: Their top priority was NATO membership. After the meeting, Clinton told [national security adviser] Lake how impressed he had been with the vehemence with which these leaders spoke, and Lake says Clinton was inclined to think positively toward expansion from that moment.[82]

Finally, the process of socialization and internalization needs to be unpacked. How does NATO socialize the CEE states and societies? Who exactly does the "teaching" of constitutive beliefs and practices, and by what means? How are community values and norms internalized in the CEE countries? Which learning processes occur at what level? A full account of international socialization has to address the agency dynamics not only within the the organization and its member countries but also within the candidate societies.[83]

---

82. James M. Goldgeier, "NATO Expansion: The Anatomy of a Decision," *Washington Quarterly* 21, no. 1 (winter 1998): 86–87. See, however, his more cautious assessment of the causes of the U.S. decision (ibid., 100–101).

83. Thanks to Jeff Checkel for insisting on this point. See also his review of some of the constructivist literature (Jeffrey T. Checkel, "The Constructivist Turn in International Relations Theory," *World Politics* 50, no. 2 [January 1998]: 324–48).

NATO, GERMANY, AND THE UNITED STATES:
CREATING POSITIVE IDENTITY IN TRANS-ATLANTIA

MARY N. HAMPTON

A S NATO begins its second life and expands eastward, analysts and policymakers alike are occupied with defining the alliance. To many, NATO always represented something more than a balancing mechanism in a bipolar system. Aside from its obvious mission of countering the Soviet threat, its creators intended it to be the flagship institution for building a trans-Atlantic security community of likeminded democracies. Inherent to the NATO enterprise was the promotion of transnational democratic integration, as stated in the Preamble and Articles 1 and 2 of the North Atlantic Treaty. The mission of constructing a Western community of democracies was to avoid the slide into war among potential antagonists by achieving positive identification among NATO members. Foremost to American policymakers was that its success depended not only on incorporating and democratizing Germany, but in forging a common identity between West Germany and the West.[1]

The task of this paper is twofold. First, I examine the theoretical claim that positive identification occurs among democratic states. Sec-

Mary N. Hampton is associate professor of political science at the University of Utah.

I have many people to thank for their help and comments on this paper. First, I thank NATO. Because of my receiving a NATO Research Fellowship for 1997/98, I was able to complete much of the research for the paper in Germany. I also want to thank the Hessische Stiftung für Frieden und Konflikt Forschung (HSFK) in Frankfurt, Germany. Thanks to the director, Harald Mueller, I had an office at the institute and was able to use the excellent library there. I thank Drs. Bruno Schoch, Matthias Dembinski, Kinka Gerke, Berthold Meyer, and Joachim Spanger for their helpful comments. In Bonn, I thank especially Drs. Peter Weilemann and Karl-Heinz Kamp for their assistance in allowing me to have an office at the Konrad Adenauer Stiftung, and for their help in establishing research connections and for providing access to research materials for me. They and Dr. Martin Hoch also gave me insightful comments on my work. I also thank Drs. Holger Mey and Michael Ruehle for their excellent comments. In the United States, I thank Drs. Ronald Rogowski and Mary Reddick for their comments. I am also particularly grateful to Joseph Roberts and Jennifer Mann for their computer assistance. Finally, I thank the anonymous reviewers of *Security Studies*, and am especially grateful to the editor, Benjamin Frankel, for his guidance.

1. Mary Hampton, "NATO at the Creation," *Security Studies* 4, no. 3 (spring 1995): 610–56.

ond, I focus empirically on the U.S.-German security relationship that developed in the NATO context and argue that a positive security identity has emerged. The paper therefore shows, concurring with other contributions in this volume, that the phenomenon of positive identity between states can be identified, and that it is significant for our understanding of state behavior.

The German-American case is critical since many analysts argue that the seismic changes of 1989 and after will alter German behavior and preferences. Debate abounds as to whether united Germany will continue the practices of preunification West Germany or set out on a new course as the country's capitol moves from Bonn to Berlin. Structural realists assume that the change in German material capabilities and placement in the hierarchy of states will necessarily lead to a change in German interests, and therefore in its behavior.[2] Structural realism posits the rationalistic behavior of states, where interests are exogenous to state interaction. John Mearsheimer and those who seek explanation for state behavior in the realm of material capabilities and distribution of power often argue that united Germany will behave differently from the former Federal Republic; that it will behave more independently and aggressively; that it will outgrow the institutions that bound the slighter Bonn. Peter Katzenstein states: "For Mearsheimer German unification in 1990 is the opening chapter of the third edition of the German catastrophe."[3] In contrast, I argue that the presence and influence of positive identity formation confirm the contrary: that interaction between states is endogenous to the formation of state interests, and in fact directly influences the formulation of state interests.[4]

Studies that focus on various historical and cultural domestic explanations for German behavior similarly predict the demise of Western cohesion in the wake of German unification, although for different

2. See John J. Mearsheimer, "Back to the Future: Instability in Europe After the Cold War," in *The Cold War and After: Prospects for Peace*, ed. Sean Lynn Jones (Cambridge: MIT Press, 1992), 141–92.

3. Peter Katzenstein, "Taming of Power: German Unification, 1989–1990," in *Past as Prelude: History in the Making of a New World Order*, ed. Meredith Woo-Cumings and Michael Loriaux (Boulder: Westview, 1993), 61.

4. Alexander Wendt, "Collective Identity Formation and the International State," *American Political Science Review* 88, no. 2 (June 1994): 384–96. See also Colin H. Kahl, "Constructing a Separate Peace: Constructivism, Collective Liberal Identity, and Democratic Peace," *Security Studies* 8, nos. 2/3 (winter 1998/99–spring 1999): 94–144.

reasons.[5] An extreme example is represented by Conor Cruise O'Brien, who argues that German unification was the turning point for European integration and Germany's place therein. Drawing on past German behavior, he posits that since unification, which freed Germany from the Western institutional constraints of the cold war, "German nationalism is on the rise, and it seems likely that Germans, in the near future, will interpret their own past in an increasingly nationalist way, placing strains on relations within the Community."[6] Some U.S.-German policy analysts like Werner Weidenfeld also fear the worsening of the trans-Atlantic relationship in the post–cold war era, as the United States and Germany adjust to their redefined interests.[7]

By analyzing German-American relations in the NATO context, I choose one of the most important cases for testing the existence of transnational positive identity formation. Because NATO is the most developed transnational institution binding the United States and Germany, and because security identity goes to the heart of national identity, the emergence of positive identification in this context is significant. In arguing that positive security identification has evolved between Germany and the United States, I examine two issues that are directly linked to an understanding of German security identity and its perception of others. First, I analyze the role of historical memory as it pertains to German-American relations. I argue that one aspect of the NATO mission was to forge a positive identity among member states by helping to create a shared sense of history and destiny. This socialization process was intended to change the way West German elites and the public perceived the West, and especially the United States. To change West German perceptions meant reconstituting the subjective meanings West Germans attached to themselves, to the West, and to the United States.[8] I discuss the impact that the reconstruction of shared history has had in creating a sense of "solidarity, community,

---

5. For a good discussion of these competing approaches, see Andrei S. Markovits and Simon Reich, "Should Europe Fear the Germans?" in *From Bundesrepublik to Deutschland*, ed. Michael G. Huelshoff, Andrei Markovits, and Simon Reich (Ann Arbor: University of Michigan Press, 1994), 271–90.

6. Conor Cruise O'Brien, "Pursuing a Chimera," in *The Question of Europe*, ed. Peter Gowan and Perry Anderson (New York: Verso, 1997), 77–84; quote from p. 83.

7. See, among others, Werner Weidenfeld, *Kulturbruch mit Amerika? Das Ende transatlantischer Selbstverstaendlichkeit* (Guetersloh: Verlag Bertelsmann Stiftung, 1996).

8. See Ido Oren, "The Subjectivity of the Democratic Peace: Changing U.S. Perceptions of Imperial Germany," in *Debating the Democratic Peace*, ed. Michael E. Brown, Sean M. Lynn-Jones, and Steven E. Miller (Cambridge: MIT Press, 1996), 263–300.

and loyalty" between Germany and its trans-Atlantic ally, and how much of a role German membership in NATO has had in influencing that process.[9]

Second, I focus on the current German debate about military security. Any change in German security identity would be reflected in Bonn-Washington relations. While there was a brief flirtation in post-unification Germany with reassessing its security interests in light of changed domestic and international opportunities, that moment has passed. The fact that German policymakers have quickly retreated from revisionist scenarios and recentered German security interests within the U.S.-led NATO framework is significant. The German predilection to maintain the bonds of positive identity with the United States forged through NATO therefore remains strong.[10] It is a phenomenon that runs counter to realist expectations concerning trans-Atlantic relations in the post–cold war period. The tendency toward either balancing against, or reassessing the German security relationship with, the United States in light of changed circumstances has not emerged. Both tendencies could be expected according to analyses based on interest calculations, especially when applied to an increasingly multipolar world, or according to certain cultural/historical explanations.

I argue that the German rerallying around the NATO relationship is best explained through my focus on positive identity formation. The German identity complex forged with the United States through membership in NATO has been internalized to the point that Germans link their security identity to the United States through the alliance. The positive security identity that evolved has created a set of habits and expectations in German security policy, and has likewise directly influenced the German self-image, or the "sets of meaning" Germans ascribe to themselves and their role in the world.[11]

Theoretically, I combine the approaches of democratic theory literature and political psychology regarding group identity formation to explain the emergence of positive identity in German-American relations. Many proponents of democratic theory have recently depicted

9. Wendt, "Collective Identity Formation and the International State," 386.

10. For a realist analysis that predicts potential balancing against the U.S. among its cold war allies, see Christopher Lane, "The Unipolar Illusion: Why Great Powers Will Rise," in *The Perils of Anarchy: Contemporary Realism and International Security*, ed. Michael E. Brown, Sean Lynn-Jones, and Steven E. Miller (Cambridge: MIT Press, 1995), 130–76.

11. Kohl, "Constructing a Separate Peace."

the trans-Atlantic area as a security community of democracies. While it is usually implicit in arguments concerning the emergence of community among democratic states, the concept of positive identification developing between democratic states is understudied, often confined to the term "special relationship." While many analysts, for example, claim that a community of democracies has developed within the trans-Atlantic area, few explain precisely if and why NATO members achieve something more than cooperation with each other. If in fact positive identity forms between member states, it would mean that transnational relationships have developed such that states see each other "as a cognitive extension of the self, rather than independent."[12] In so doing, the member states come to share a positive identity that transcends relationships built on particular interest calculations, which could include cooperative behavior, and enters the realm of nonrational, positive affective relations.

According to findings from political psychology, such a phenomenon reveals the emergence of group identity. Margaret Hermann and Charles Kegley summarize this literature in the following way: "In building their own identity, people are more acceptant of those who are familiar and similar and distance themselves from those who are dissimilar and less familiar."[13] This formulation of interactive relations means that one group of people comes to view its own destiny as tied to that of another group, and that between them arises group loyalty and empathy that is affective, rather than only rational, in nature. The evolution of this type of interaction defines positive identity, and stands in contrast to the negative identity between states assumed by neorealism, where states construct their interests according to relative gains calculations.[14]

For international relations theory, such a development is profound, for it means nothing short of dislodging the primacy of the security dilemma in Western interstate relations. Under the security dilemma, interstate relations necessarily tend toward the negative end of the identity continuum. To discuss seriously the possibility that something like positive identity can develop and be maintained over time between

12. Wendt, "Collective Identity Formation and the International State," 386.
13. Margaret G. Hermann and Charles W. Kegley Jr., "Rethinking Democracy and Democratic Peace: Perspectives from Political Psychology," *International Studies Quarterly* 39, no. 4 (December 1995): 511–34, quote is from p. 517.
14. Wendt, "Collective Identity Formation and the International State," 386. See also the discussion by Kahl on negative-positive identity among states: "Constructing a Separate Peace."

states, one must assume that international relations is more complicated than core structural realist assumptions that leave states existing
in a condition of anarchy as self-interested, security-seeking actors who
measure their success and each other in relative power terms. The
claim supports Rodney Bruce Hall's argument that "the interests of
international actors are not objectively or structurally determined....Identities and interests are co-constituted."[15]

Structural realism in fact has a difficult time accounting for what
looks like a solid tendency toward bandwagoning rather then balancing behavior among Western members of NATO even as their positions
in the international system change.[16] The emergence of positive security identity between the United States and Germany therefore leaves
unfounded predictions of a negative downturn in trans-Atlantic security relations based on the redistribution of power among them and
the subsequent rearticulation of interests within each in the post–cold
war era.[17]

COOPERATION AND POSITIVE IDENTIFICATION AMONG DEMOCRACIES

IT IS NOW common practice among liberal international relations analysts to argue that the trans-Atlantic area is some form of community. The definition of community most often used is the one first offered by Karl Deutsch, where security communities exist when there
"is a group of people which has become integrated," and wherein
members of the security community (amalgamated or pluralistic) attain
"a 'sense of community' and of institutions and practices strong
enough and widespread enough to assure, for a long time, dependable
expectations of 'peaceful change' among its population."[18] This definition of community implies that more than cooperative behavior has
emerged between member states. Implicit or explicit in such arguments

15. Rodney Bruce Hall, "Territorial and National Sovereigns: Sovereign Identity
and Consequences for Security Policy," *Security Studies* 8, nos. 2/3 (winter 1998/99–
spring 1999): 145–97.

16. See discussion by Stephen Walt, *The Origins of Alliances* (Ithaca: Cornell University Press, 1987); see also Frank Schimmelfennig's discussion of why realism and neorealism falter in their explanations of NATO enlargement, in his "NATO Enlargement: A
Constructivist Explanation," *Security Studies* 8, nos. 2/3 (winter 1998/99–spring 1999):
198–234.

17. See Lane, "The Unipolar Illusion."

18. Karl Deutsch et al., *Political Community and the North Atlantic Area* (Princeton:
Princeton University Press, 1957), 5.

is the claim that, because of their shared values, democracies achieve a sense of positive identification with each other. Otherwise, discussing a "sense of community" between them would be meaningless.

To claim, however, that states identify with each other through shared values and maintain collectively held norms does not take us very far in determining the nature or level of identity that emerges among them. Michael Doyle, for example, argues that eighteenth and nineteenth century European great powers shared "a relative homogeneity of domestic structures." He posits that the great powers of Europe held positive values and norms concerning civilization and legitimacy, and because of these shared views the survival of each was held up as an accepted principle.[19] Yet as he surveys the landscape of eighteenth century great power behavior, he finds that the norm condemning the unprovoked dismemberment of legitimate states was broken a number of times, and that although the great powers prevented hegemonic challenges from within their ranks, and maintained a consistent number of states in the club, peace was not kept between them. In fact, Doyle observes that there was more warfare between the great powers at this time than before or since.[20] Clearly, the norms shared by the great powers did not erase the option of implementing force between them, nor did they develop the affective bonds of positive identity.

What makes positive identity formation among democracies possible and critical according to the liberal position in international relations is that the norms shared between like democracies include the delegitimization of violence between them, and hence the opportunity is created of developing positive identity that is preserved through a culture of consultation and persuasion, as is the case in democratic domestic politics. G. John Ikenberry observes: "Democracies do not just sign agreements; they create political processes that reduce uncertainty and build confidence in mutual commitments."[21] Therefore, unlike the identity complex that may form between nondemocratic states, the role of violence and force is erased as a plausible foreign policy option for democratic states. Mobilizing against another in-group democratic state is

---

19. Michael Doyle, "Balancing Power Classically: An Alternative to Collective Security?" in *Collective Security Beyond the Cold War*, ed. George Downs (Ann Arbor: University of Michigan Press), 133–65; esp. 142–44.
20. Ibid., 160–61.
21. G. John Ikenberry, "The Myth of Post-Cold War Chaos," *Foreign Affairs* 75, no. 3 (May/June 1996): 79–91, quote from p. 87.

simply not an option. Instead, the door is left open to construct among members a collective identity that includes solidaristic loyalties.[22]

Bruce Russett concurs with the above view by arguing that the norms in democracies, backed up by practice, "permit compromise and peaceful resolution of conflicts without the threat of violence," and are transferable to the international system and other democracies.[23] From this process a democratic political culture based on positive affective relations can emerge wherein positive identification with each other forms. In his book, *Grasping the Democratic Peace*, for example, Russett argues that Deutsch's notion of security community characterizes the relationship between democracies and that the community between them emerges from mutual expectations based on shared norms concerning conflict resolution. He states that while the term community is difficult to "observe reliably," one can measure the existence of community, since democracies refrain from fighting each other and mostly refrain from even threatening to fight each other. He posits that it is this characteristic of democracies that forges the community between them, and implies that positive identification has emerged.[24]

I go further than most analysts in the field in suggesting that democracies therefore create the space for developing positive affective relations between themselves. In terms of its affective requirements, the relationship between democracies is akin to the contested "special relationship" construct that has been used to denote particularly close, thick culture-bound relations between liberal democracies, as in the cases of the American-British or American-Israeli friendships. Peace between democracies is maintained by the affective and institutional bonds that are forged between them as well as by the domestic values that they share.[25]

Michael Doyle takes a different tack at explaining the emergence of community between democratic states, or what he calls instead the "zone of peace" that exists between liberal democratic states. Following Immanuel Kant, Doyle argues that the democratic peace is a process through which republican states eventually establish a culture of caution between them. The shared norms, values, and institutions of do-

---

22. Wendt, "Collective Identity Formation and the International State," 387.
23. Bruce Russett, *Grasping the Democratic Peace: Principles for a Post–Cold War World* (Princeton: Princeton University Press, 1993), 31.
24. Ibid., esp. 30–42, quote from p. 42.
25. See discussion by Andrew Moravcsik, "Federalism and Peace: A Structural Liberal Perspective," *Zeitschrift für Internationale Beziehungen* 3, no. 1 (1996): 123–32.

mestic liberal orders help establish the culture of caution and keep the peace between independent democratic states.[26] For Doyle, however, the identity that emerges between the member states lies somewhere in between on the negative-positive continuum. A zone of peace in the international order is best guaranteed when "one liberal state" stands "preeminent among the rest, prepared and able to take measures...to sustain economically and politically the foundations of liberal society beyond its borders."[27] According to Doyle, competing interests between liberal democracies can otherwise lead to the breakdown of domestic liberal orders, or to a situation in which differences between states escalate into hostility. In the end, then, Russett's transnational democratic community appears more stable than Doyle's zone of peace because Russett implies the emergence of strong positive identification among democracies that transcends potential clashes of egoistic interest while Doyle does not. In Doyle's analysis, competing interests still exist between democracies and need to be mitigated or controlled by external agencies. In his community of democracies, group identity, or positive identity, is limited.

There is obviously little agreement on the scope and definition of positive identity in a transnational democratic community. To establish the extreme ends of the continuum, I turn to Robert Bellah's differentiation of enclaves and communities. I represent his concepts as ideal types. An enclave is a collectivity forged by members who share specified and short-term interests. The example he uses to illustrate the concept is the lifestyle enclave, where people are bound to one another through features they hold in common, but where the bond is easily and quickly broken once the underlying condition of their agreement is broken. Thus, for example, in a so-called singles community, the factor that binds members together is their marital status, which creates only limited group identity between them by narrowly defining the self-other distinction. Once someone from the group marries, however, there is nothing more to bind that member to the group.[28] In this social construct, the term positive identity has limited value, since the relationship is based on narrowly conceived shared interests and a limited notion of shared experience. Extending the analogy to the tran-

---

26. Michael Doyle, "Kant, Liberal Legacies, and Foreign Affairs," in *Debating the Democratic Peace*, ed. Michael E. Brown, Sean M. Lynn-Jones, and Steven E. Miller (Cambridge: MIT Press, 1996), 3–57.

27. Ibid., 28.

28. Robert Bellah et al., *Habits of the Heart* (Harper and Row, 1985), 71–75. I thank Peter Diamond for his helpful comments on these points.

snational context, the traditional interest-driven alliance and the eighteenth century great power consensus are similar to the enclave.

At the other end of the continuum, Bellah defines community by revisiting what he deems to be the best of American republicanism. For him, a community is "an inclusive whole, celebrating the interdependence of public and private life and of the different callings of all."[29] Robert Booth Fowler observes that in this ideal type, community members must embrace "shared virtues and shared history."[30] For Fowler, the above model of community shares features with other models; they imply an "affective or emotional dimension," wherein "a shared life, self-consciously accepted, is required."[31] In this definition of community, positive identity emerges in a subjective way that validates the solidaristic loyalty between members.

Michael Spirtas observes that "group formation is an inherently social process."[32] So especially is positive identity formation, and in order for it to emerge between states, socialization patterns between them must emphasize not only shared democratic values, but the creation of a sense of shared history and common destiny. As David M. Cheshier and Cori E. Dauber argue, individuals in different states come to identify with one another more when they share experiences and "lived traditions."[33] I argue that the creation of a shared history and destiny was promoted through the NATO relationship, where "ongoing socialization and collective patterns of persuasion" have had significant value in creating positive identity in the German-American relationship.[34]

GERMANY, THE UNITED STATES, AND POSITIVE SECURITY IDENTITY

I FOCUS ON Germany because it is crucial to the survival of the NATO relationship and because so many questions have been raised about the motives and nature of the united Germany. It is a country that has

29. Ibid., 72.
30. Robert Booth Fowler, *The Dance With Community: The Contemporary Debate in American Political Thought* (Lawrence: University of Kansas Press, 1991), 40.
31. Ibid., 4.
32. Michael Spirtas, "French Twist: French and British NATO Policies from 1949–1966," *Security Studies* 8, nos. 2/3 (winter 1998/99–spring 1999): 302–46.
33. David M. Cheshier and Cori E. Dauber, "The Place and Power of Civic Space: Reading Globalization and Social Geography Through the Lens of Civilizational Conflict," *Security Studies* 8, nos. 2/3 (winter 1998/99–spring 1999): 35–70.
34. Ibid.

experienced much discontinuity in its past and its western half was a stable democracy for less than fifty years. Critical to understanding contemporary Germany is the knowledge that it was politically and socially transformed after 1945. Its institutions were altered from the bottom up, its education system was modified, its economy was changed, and, of course, its political system was completely over-hauled.[35] Also important, however, is the fact that the transnational norms guiding interstate conduct were altered within the Western context. Congruence between the German domestic political culture and Western institutions was achieved through German integration in NATO and the European Union. Tony Smith observes that Woodrow Wilson's view of building a strong community in Europe necessarily meant that "to change Germany internally was to change Europe, and to change Europe was to change the world."[36] American foreign policymakers located the source of past German aggression not so much in its power capabilities, but in its undemocratic political system. To encourage the habits of democracy, Germany's domestic political system was radically altered and the Federal Republic was brought in as a member state with equality of status to a host of Western institutions, including NATO.

One of the chief objectives of early postwar American policymakers, such as Dean Acheson, and then especially John Foster Dulles, was therefore to democratize Germany as it was being integrated into Western institutions. The NATO relationship was seen as the central institution through which West Germany could be successfully socialized into the West. Frank Schimmelfennig observes that the international socialization process "means the internalization of the constitutive beliefs and practices of a social community by a social actor."[37] The logic in the NATO mission was to establish and validate the values and norms of democracy domestically as West Germany became integrated internationally. It was envisioned that West Germany would come to identify its own democracy with those of the West through the institutions it joined. To forge positive identity between Germany and its Western allies, or to create a "common positive experience of

35. See discussion by Peter Katzenstein, "Taming of Power," 59–81.
36. Tony Smith, *America's Mission* (Princeton: Princeton University Press, 1995), 331.
37. Schimmelfennig, "NATO's Enlargement: A Constructivist Argument."

high intensity,"[38] the negative historical memories of two world wars had to be replaced with a reconstructed sense of shared history and destiny with its Western allies, or with its former adversaries.

West Germany's first postwar leader, Chancellor Konrad Adenauer, was more than aware of the necessity of changing German identity by integrating the country into the Western democracies. He observed of the German people after the war that they "must be given a new ideology."[39] His friend, U.S. secretary of state John Foster Dulles, became assured of West Germany's place at the Western table of democracies largely because Adenauer "came to represent for Dulles the incarnation of German democracy."[40]

Over time these changes were accepted by West German elites and the public and heavily imprinted the German identity. It is therefore of utmost importance to explain how and why the affective "habits of the heart" that bind Germany to the United States through the alliance are strong enough to survive current systemic change at the international level and German unification's transformation of the domestic context.[41]

CREATING A SHARED HISTORY THROUGH NATO

Has Germany, through historical learning and NATO membership, been able to overcome its own negative collective past and the negative collective memories of others and develop positive identification with democracy and its trans-Atlantic ally? If so, the phenomenon provides evidence that a stable positive security identity can develop between democracies and that in the U.S.-German case it can endure current domestic and systemic changes.

The continued salience of historical lessons, collective memory, and the beliefs they spawn regarding domestic and foreign policy making is perhaps clearer for Germany than is true with any other Western democracy. I accept Andrei Markovits's definition of collective memory,

38. Bruce Cronin, "From Balance to Community: Transnational Identity and Political Integration," *Security Studies* 8, nos. 2/3 (winter 1998/99–spring 1999): 270–301.

39. Konrad Adenauer, quoted in Hans-Peter Schwarz, *Konrad Adenauer: Volume One: From the German Empire to the Federal Republic, 1876–1952* (Providence: Berghahn, 1995), 612.

40. Alfred Grosser, *Germany in Our Time* (New York: Praeger, 1971), 308.

41. "Habits of the heart" was a term used by de Tocqueville in his famous analysis of American democracy, *Democracy in America*. It has been recycled by Bellah et al. in their updated study of American mores in *Habits of the Heart*.

that it is "a contemporary experiencing and constant reinterpretation of the historic past....It is in constant flux, subject to mood swings and relatively sudden changes."[42] This definition of collective memory is similar to Robert Bellah's use of the term "community memory": in order not to forget the past, "a community is involved in retelling its story," and the stories it retells "are an important part of the tradition that is central to a community of memory."[43] Both collective memory and community of memory point toward the future, but are also about the past and present.[44] For each case, the construction of memory is social and helps define a people's identity.

Because of their past, German elites and the public have been forced through the collective memories of others and their own to prove that they have achieved strong democratic beliefs and institutional safeguards against backsliding.[45] The so-called German question emerges not just from history, but from the mists of compelling collective memories concerning the German past and doubts about a stable German identity. Negative collective memories about Germany occasionally reach critical mass and can affect governmental policies between Germany and other states.

To overcome the negative collective memories, an essential part of the NATO mission has been to rewrite the history that exists between the West and Germany. The NATO relationship intentionally helped create a positive shared history in the trans-Atlantic area, thereby seeking to establish a sense of empathy and common destiny between its members. Obviously, the construction of group loyalty was greatly helped during the cold war by the clearly defined out group. The Soviet threat, linked ideologically to nondemocratic societies, helped create a shared sense of values, trust, and destiny between the newly evolving West German society and the West. Because the United States was the ultimate security guarantor in the relationship, the potential for forging a community of shared values between the West Germans and America was great. As I argue below, the dominant military role of the United States also created a protector-protectee relationship in matters of military security.

42. Andrei S. Markovits, "The Contemporary Power of Memory: The Dilemmas for German Foreign Policy" (paper presented at the 1995 American Political Science Association, Chicago, Ill, September 1995.)

43. Bellah et al., *Habits of the Heart*, 153.

44. Markovits, "The Contemporary Power of Memory."

45. For an interesting discussion of the various "memory maps" that influence German policymakers and elites, see Markovits, "The Contemporary Power of Memory:"

Aside from mobilizing against the Soviet threat, a component of the American mission was to have Germany internalize as part of its national identity its identification with the United States. Controversy still surrounds the role of the United States and Great Britain in rehabilitating Germany immediately after the war. Despite the earnestness of the de-Nazification program, there is evidence that U.S. policymakers decided not to push punitive policies to the extreme in order to begin a positive rehabilitative process of the fledgling and vulnerable West German democracy. American policymakers pursued a balancing act of seeking punishment of Nazi war criminals and beginning the rehabilitation process of the West German public and political elites. The widespread unpopularity in the defeated Germany of Allied policy targeting German war criminals, especially regarding high-ranking generals and the *Bundeswehr*, gave leverage to West German policymakers like Konrad Adenauer, in arguing that the process was undermining the democratic experiment being launched in Bonn.[46] Such punitive policies also stood in the way of creating a positive identification between West Germans and the United States. Norbert Frei observes of High Commissioner John McCloy's dilemma:

> McCloy knew that a significant step was required to ensure that the war criminal issue did not become a major disturbance in the German-American relationship. Exactly how big a step was needed, in order to not frustrate the Germans on one hand, while not shocking the Americans on the other hand: that was what he sought to explore at the end of 1949 and into 1950.[47]

Once the Korean War broke out in 1950, the balance of U.S. policy tipped toward more rapid rehabilitation of the West Germans and their enlistment in the common goal of containing the communist threat.

Therefore, a U.S. objective was to begin, immediately after the Second World War, the process of reconstructing German identity vis-à-vis its former adversaries away from one of hostility and to one of friendship, or to move the relationship away from the negative end of the identity continuum toward the positive. Walther Leisler Kiep, a former leading Christian Democrat (CDU) politician, said of the American-German alliance: "In effect, it provides a second constitution for

---

46. See the study by Norbert Frei, *Vergangenheitspolitik: Die Anfaenge der Bundesrepublik und die NS-Vergangenheit* (Munich: C. H. Beck, 1996).

47. Frei, *Vergangenheitspolitik*, 192. My translation.

our country."[48] In the elite socialization of the German military, for example, the values and norms of democracy and trans-Atlanticism were emphasized and remain the cornerstone of German military elite identity and of the German military training program. As one German general put it, "NATO has become a part of our ego."[49] It is clear from recent polls that top German military elites, especially generals and admirals, are consistently more supportive of NATO than are other elites and German military personnel from the lower ranks. Military elites are also most supportive of the continued American role in Europe. This has to do with their socialization into NATO, and their association of the American presence with German democracy and identity.[50]

NATO has maintained extremely high levels of support among other German elites as well. A recent RAND-Friedrich Naumann Foundation interview series shows a support level of 92 percent for NATO among German elite groups, including representatives from politics, law, military, economy, media, academia, churches, and the unions.[51] In a similar vein, 73 percent of these elites want to maintain American troops in Germany, with no further reductions. Those who support the maintenance of American troops reaches a high of 94 percent among military elites.[52] While such poll results do not directly measure levels of identification, they do reveal a tendency among German elites to eschew any break in the trans-Atlantic security relationship in the post–cold war era based on revised German interest calculations in a transformed international system. As I discuss below, there was a brief flirtation among some elites and the public with questioning the necessity of NATO for German security interests in the heady days directly following German unification, but these ruminations have largely subsided.

Symbolic political-security acts have also been key to forging positive identity with America among the German public. Events such as

48. Walther Leisler Kiep, quoted in Ikenberry, "The Myth of Post–Cold War Chaos," 89.

49. Background interview, Germany, April 1997.

50. Dietmar Schloessler, Reiner Albert, Frank Kostelnik, *Deutschland, die NATO und Europa: Die sicherheitspolitische Lage im Spiegel von Elite-Gruppen-Meinungen* (Muenster: Lit Verlag, 1995). These findings were further verified in a series of background interviews I conducted with current and former top military officers in Bonn, 1997.

51. "Das Meinungsbild der Elite in Deutschland zur Aussen- und Sicherheitspolitik," (Berlin: Infratest Burke in affiliation with RAND and the Friedrich Naumann Foundation, 1996), 21.

52. Ibid., 23.

the Berlin airlift of 1948, memorialized as a monument in Berlin, and the addresses delivered to the German public by American presidents at the Berlin Wall, helped tie the German identity to the United States. The stationing of hundreds of thousands of American troops on German soil acted as a conduit through which closer German popular cultural affinity to the United States was created. Although an understudied phenomenon, it is clear that the actual presence of these American troops in Germany influenced the German popular culture and forged a direct link between German security identity and the United States.[53] It is therefore no surprise that currently many Germans worry about the negative effect the removal of American troops may have on German-American cultural affinity.[54]

High levels of public support for U.S.-German relations mirror those of the elites and are registered in public opinion polls during and since the end of the cold war. In one public opinion poll, 75 percent of German respondents in 1994 continued to view NATO as vital to their security.[55] In EMNID polls taken between 1966 and 1989, German public support for an unchanged NATO actually increased in the 1980s. In 1966, 63 percent of West German respondents supported an unchanged NATO. In 1989, as unification became certain, 72 percent of German respondents backed an unchanged NATO.[56] A poll taken by EMNID in 1996 that attempts to measure German public sympathy with various other states reveals that the United States is the country with whom most German respondents sought better relations: 92 percent chose the United States, followed by 90 percent for the French and British.[57] While the distance separating the United States and the two West European allies of Germany does not appear very statistically significant, it is an important finding in that it reveals the continued high identification of Germans with the United States, despite the waning of the cold war and the claims being made regarding an emerging European positive identity through the European Union.

53. In "Immigration and the Politics of Security," *Security Studies* 8, nos. 2/3 (winter 1998/99–spring 1999): 71–93, Roxanne Lynn Doty examines the importance of societal security and how it relates to the identity formation of a society.

54. See, for example, Leo Wieland, "Das Deutschland Bild in Amerika," *Frankfurter Allgemeine Zeitung* 13 February 1997, 1.

55. Ronald Asmus, quoted in Tom Heneghan, "Germans More Willing to Lead Than Their Leaders," *Reuters Community Report* 7 (March 1995).

56. Michael Wolffs, Stefan Beil, *Documentation: Deutsche Einheit, Nationalbewusstsein und Westbindung: in Meinungsklima der Bevoelkerung* (Sankt Augustin: Konrad Adenauer Stiftung, 1991), 71.

57. *EMNID Umfrage & Analyse*, Heft 3/4, 1996, 29.

Further, the Bush administration's unequivocal backing of German unification in 1989 and 1990 reinforced German positive identity with the United States among both German elites and the public. U.S. support was based on the American principle of self-determination and on the alliance's obligation to support German unification "in peace and in freedom" which was forged upon West Germany's entry into NATO in 1955. By meeting its allied obligation to Germany, the American position reinforced the trust that Germans placed in the security relationship and the empathy felt for the United States. It also laid to rest the cynicism shared by many analysts and policymakers regarding American sincerity on the unification issue.[58] Washington's official line was mirrored by high levels of support for German self-determination among the American public. According to several polls, the American public registered a higher level of sympathy for German unification during 1990 than did publics throughout Europe.[59]

That German elites and the German public appreciated the U.S. posture was reflected in political statements, press releases, and public opinion polls. In reminiscing about German unification, Chancellor Kohl stated: "I am filled with a feeling of gratitude. Many contributed to German unity. Who doesn't think of George Bush as well as Michael Gorbachev in that regard?"[60] Likewise, in an editorial that appeared in 1990 in the most important German daily paper, the *Frankfurter Allgemeine Zeitung* (FAZ), Guenther Gillessen praised the Bush administration's support for German unification, and noted that the American position was unique among international actors. He ends by saying that: "The Germans have reason to thank President Bush for his handling of the German question."[61] In another article from the FAZ, in July 1990, Dieter Buhl goes even further:

> Nowhere outside of the German borders could the joy over the German-German development be more sincere than in Amer-

---

58. David Schoenbaum and Elizabeth Pond, *The German Question and Other Questions* (New York: Oxford University Press, 1997).

59. Wolffs and Beil, *Documentation*, 14. According to a number of polls, for example, American public support for German unification ranged between 61 and 76 percent during 1989–90, while in France, the country reflecting the next highest level of support, the public backed unification within a range of 60–63 percent during the same period.

60. Helmut Kohl, *Ich Wollte Deutschlands Einheit*, written with Kai Diekmann and Rolf Reuth (Berlin: Propylaen, 1996), 10 (my translation).

61. Guenther Gillessen, "Mit amerikanischem Beistand," *Frankfurter Allgemeine Zeitung*, 3 May 1990 (my translation). See also Leo Wieland, "Der ueberzeugendste Verbuendete," *Frankfurter Allgemeine Zeitung*, 16 May 1990.

ica....The demonstrations in Leipzig and the fall of the wall corre-
sponded to their [Americans'] respect for freedom. The manner and
means with which the Germans are managing the unification process complies with their fondness for decisiveness and dynamism....Perhaps most representative for many Germans was the
way that the telephone operator from the Foreign Office responded
on the night of the wall's opening as she connected Hans-Dietrich
Genscher with his colleague: "Thank you, Mr. Minister," she
shouted to James Baker, "God save America."[62]

When asked in a public opinion poll how they perceived the political relationship between the United States and Germany, German respondents answering "good" (as opposed to "bad" or "no answer") registered a high of 92 percent in 1990, compared to 74 percent in 1984,
80 percent in 1988, and 89 percent in 1989.[63]

The positive American response was particularly illuminating when
compared with the negative reception German unity received in other
Western capitals, such as in London and Paris. The Nicholas Ridley
affair in Britain, which occurred during German reunification, revealed
the continued residue of negative sentiment about Germany among
important segments of British society and elites.[64] That Ridley lost his
job in Prime Minister Thatcher's government for his publicly stated
analogy of contemporary Germany and the Third Reich does not erase
the fact that he tapped into existing strong currents of negative emotions and beliefs concerning the nature of German intentions.
Thatcher herself held some of the negative views regarding German
aggressive tendencies, which were reinforced during the Chequers
seminar in 1990, when she had various German experts assess the
German character. Her negative opinion of that character led her to
criticize French president François Mitterrand for not joining her in
resisting rapid German unification.[65] Mitterrand did in fact reveal his
own reservations regarding German unification in a number of foreign
policy gestures, such as announcing without consulting the Germans

---

62. Dieter Buhl, "Vom Paten zum Partner Bonns," *Die Zeit*, 20 July 1990 (my translation).

63. EMNID poll series, cited in Wolffs and Beil, *Documentation*, 83.

64. See Katzenstein's discussion of this incident in "Taming Power," 65–67. While I
agree with him that such thinking as expressed by Ridley and others regarding German
"character" is "dubious," it nonetheless is symbolically important to considerations of
collective memory.

65. Margaret Thatcher, *Downing Street Years* (New York: Harper Collins, 1993).

that all French troops would be removed from German soil in the immediate post-unification period.[66]

Finally, the success of tying German security identity to NATO and the United States has been reflected by the near absence of backlash to be seen among members of the German elite class regarding West German dependence on the NATO relationship. While what Jacob Heilbrunn calls the new right in Germany has developed revisionist feelings concerning Germany's rights as a sovereign state with unique interests, and German identity is still subject to a "war of memories,"[67] the German political class and public clearly maintain their allegiance to NATO and the United States. Without entering the polemics spawned by Heilbrunn's article regarding the importance or influence of the new right, we should note how small an impact the group has had on German politics and among the German public.

What the new right in fact reflects is a domestic posture one might expect of a newly empowered Germany that subsequently revises its security interests and identity in light of changed international realities. Heilbrunn, for example, says of the new right that they view the Bonn Republic as a historical detour for Germany "that substituted self-flagellation for an assertion of German national interests and honor."[68] He observes that another member of what he terms the new right, Klaus Rainer Roehl, "portrays the Bonn political class as quislings who sold out to the United States."[69] The new right, still only a latent political force in German politics, has so far found few takers in Germany, and Josef Joffe observes of Rainer Zittelmann, one of the self-appointed voices of the new right, that he has lost his position of influence in journalistic circles.[70]

The success of fostering positive identification between Germany and the United States at the elite and public levels through the alliance has not been complete, however. A few examples will suffice. First,

66. See discussion of English and French policy regarding German unification in Schoenbaum and Pond, *The German Question and Other Questions*, 178–79.

67. Jacob Heilbrunn, "Germany's New Right," *Foreign Affairs* 75, no. 6 (November/December 1996): 80–98. For a study of the politics of historical memory, see Peter Reichel, *Politik mit der Erinnerung: Gedaechtnisorte im Streit um die national-sozialistische Vergangenheit* (Munich: Carl Hanser, 1995).

68. Ibid., 82–83.

69. Ibid., 94.

70. Josef Joffe, "Mr. Heilbrunn's Planet," *Foreign Affairs* 76, no. 2 (March/April 1997): 157. On the latent potential of the new right, see William Drozdiak, "Germany's Far Right Just Can't Find Votes," *International Herald Tribune*, 14 June 1997, 2.

alongside the symbolic and real events that were meant to create a shared history and positive identity between the United States and Germany, instances like the Vietnam War and the American civil rights conflicts of the 1960s affected German public and elite beliefs about the United States in a negative way. Thus, for example, many of the so-called '68ers, or the Germans who came of age in the late 1960s, pursued a distancing from the United States both in their own identity and in their willingness to identify German interests and values with those of the United States Today, the effects of that process are still observable. A significant minority of the Social Democrats (SPD) and a majority of the Greens' rank and file members, the two parties most influenced by the '68ers, continue to promote security and foreign policies for Germany that demand distancing from the United States. Further, the posture is reflected in public opinion polls; while Germans regard the United States as generally sympathetic and often as the most significant security ally, Germans also find America a bad model regarding values of social justice and equality.[71] That said, however, in an unprecedented move, the German Green Party revised their security platform for the first time in 1998 to accept continued German membership in NATO. Until that point, the party, dominated by its "fundi" (fundamentalist) rank and file members, advocated the dissolution of NATO as part of its program. I will return to this event below.

Second, the residue of negative sentiment in the United States regarding German history is still in evidence. The ironic twist of the Bitburg debacle in 1985, for example, showed the still powerful force of negative collective historical memory in and outside of Germany. The poorly conceived plan to have President Reagan and Chancellor Helmut Kohl visit the cemetery of those fallen in the Second World War was a gesture meant to reflect German reconciliation with its important NATO partner and to reflect the shared history and positive identity forged between them for thirty years. The event turned into a political fiasco upon the discovery of Waffen SS graves at the site.[72] Collective memories were stirred in the United States about the Holocaust, and were reflected in American public opinion polls. A *Wall Street Journal* poll taken in April 1995, commemorating the fiftieth

71. Ronald D. Asmus, *Germany's Political Maturation: Public Opinion and Security Policy in 1994* (Santa Monica: RAND, 1995), 38–39.

72. For a recent discussion of Bitburg, see David B. Morris, "Bitburg Revisited: Germany's Search for Normalcy," *German Politics and Society* 13, no. 4 (winter 1995): 92–109, esp. 101.

anniversary of the fall of the Third Reich, revealed that 44 percent of Americans believed another Nazi-like regime in Germany would be possible. Another 47 percent of American respondents thought that Germany had not assumed enough responsibility for the Second World War.

The incident evoked negative memories in Germany concerning perceived German victimization since the end of the war.[73] The new right and other revisionist groups made their entry in contemporary German politics through such events by deploring what they perceive as continued German servitude to the legacy of the Holocaust and to the United States, and thereby failing to develop a "normal" and independent national identity.[74] To this way of thinking, the identity that links Germans to the United States is alien and keeps Germany subordinate. As I discuss below, because the positive identity forged between Germany and the United States was a limited protector-protectee relationship, the demand by revisionists on the right and the left for Germans to break with their dependent past occasionally finds echoes among the political class and in the public. While predictions are difficult to make regarding when affective relations change, the basis of the German positive identity with the United States could tend more toward the negative end of the spectrum should such revisionist sentiment gain a stronger foothold. The recent electoral victory of the SPD/Green coalition government will prove a test case of German positive identity with the United States, since much of the German challenge to positive identity with the United States has emanated from the ranks of these two parties.

The reservations concerning the extent of positive identification between allies notwithstanding, it is clear that learning occurred in the postwar West German context because the initial changes made in internal and external policies were institutionalized and, by the end of the 1950s, finally won legitimacy among the political class and the public with regard to the value of democracy and Western integration.[75] The success of the half-century-long democratization and integration

---

73. For a discussion of the victim sentiments aroused in West Germany during Bitburg, see Moishe Postone, "Germany's Future and Its Unmastered Past," in *From Bundesrepublik to Deutschland: German Politics after Unification*, ed. Michael Huelshoff, Andrei S. Markovits, and Simon Reich (Ann Arbor: University of Michigan Press), 291–99.

74. Heilbrunn, "Germany's New Right."

75. See polls cited in Peter Merkl, "A New German Identity," in *Developments in German Politics*, ed. Gordon Smith et al. (Durham: Duke University Press, 1992).

processes, including a dominant U.S. presence inside West Germany, has forged strong beliefs among the German elite and public as to the necessity of maintaining a strong German security identity with the United States through NATO, a security identity that helped rehabilitate and unify Germany, and bring it legitimacy among nations.

The example of German-American establishment of positive security identity through NATO stands in contrast to the experience of the Soviet-East German security relationship. For a half century, East German and Soviet political elites attempted to forge a group identity through a sense of shared socialist history and destiny between the German Democratic Republic and the Soviet Union. During the cold war, the goal of constructing the socialist group identity was to be assisted through ideological antagonism with the West. Mirroring the case of West Germany, the elite and public of the German Democratic Republic were therefore summoned to construct a shared history and destiny with the Soviet protector.

Decades of ideological programming and political incentives failed to create in the East German society a common identity with the Soviet sponsor state. The programmatic construction of socialist brotherhood was therefore enforced through political control at all social and political levels in the GDR, or from the cradle to the grave. Yet, by the 1970s, and especially in the 1980s, East Germans increasingly linked their identity to the West, via media exposure and through growing webs of interpersonal contacts between West and East Germans. At the official public and mass level, "real socialism" was maintained through government-sponsored or condoned institutions and programs, but at the individual level the basis of East German identity and loyalty was already being defined elsewhere. Given their first real chance in 1989, East Germans began dismantling the system that had never won their loyalty and never constructed a group identity. In the end, it was apparent that the core of the GDR-Soviet relationship was one of East German elite dependency on the Soviet leadership.[76]

The effects of German positive identity with the United States is strongly reflected by the recent and current German debate about military security policy in the post–cold war era.

---

76. For in-depth analysis of East German politics and society, see the four-volume study by the Enquete-Commission, *Getrennte Vergangenheit, gemeinsame Zukunft*, (Munich: DTV, 1997).

MILITARY SECURITY POLICY AND GERMAN POSITIVE IDENTIFICATION
WITH NATO

Important to understanding the construction of the U.S.-West German security identity complex was that it was a limited protector-protectee relationship. In terms of military capabilities, the United States played and continues to play the dominant role. The nature of the relationship, however, is also social and political, and maintained bilaterally as well as through the multiple socialization and consultation mechanisms built into the NATO relationship. In the realm of social and political interaction, the U.S.-German NATO relationship is less hierarchical. Numerous examples from the 1950s onward reveal that German egoistic security interests were projected onto the NATO and U.S. foreign policy agendas without threatening or challenging the solidaristic loyalty of the relationship, while the dominant military role of the United States has helped shape and cement the German national self-image as a democratic and non-militaristic state.

In 1955, for example, West Germany entered NATO on the understanding that it renounce the production of nuclear weapons, although it improved its situation from the 1952 European Defense Community (EDC) talks by not being required to renounce the right to acquire the nuclear weapons of others, or to produce nuclear power for nonmilitary use.[77] In exchange for renuncing nuclear weapons production, Bonn demanded to enter NATO on the terms of equality of status and nondiscrimination, and that the alliance assume responsibility for supporting the eventual reunification of Germany.

All three elements of the 1955 agreement were important in cementing German positive identification with the United States First, the absence of an active nuclear role in German politics has come to form a significant basis of the German self-image: one of a democratic and nonaggressive state. The current enhanced relative and absolute power capabilities of unified Germany have not undermined this element of the national self-image, and therefore the role of the United States as the ultimate nuclear and military guarantor remains intact.

An example that reflects the ability of Germany to pursue its own interests within the political framework of the alliance as a member with equal status occurred during the period of East-West détente that began in the 1960s. In 1969, after adoption of the Harmel Report in

77. Matthias Kuentzel, *Bonn and the Bomb: German Politics and the Nuclear Option* (Boulder: Pluto, 1995), esp. 2–5.

NATO that declared détente to be the second component of the allied security mission, the West Germans were able to construct their own version of détente through Ostpolitik.[78] Despite misgivings in Washington and other Western capitals concerning the pace and motives of Ostpolitik, Washington never openly questioned the West German right to pursue the policy. In fact, by the 1980s, when the Reagan administration refocused U.S.-Soviet relations on strategic competition, the West German governments of Helmut Schmidt and Helmut Kohl maintained the West German right to keep the political and economic aspects of the allied Harmel understanding alive.

The greatest single example of Germany projecting its interests onto the NATO agenda while not threatening solidaristic loyalty with the United States came with unification in 1989–90. Kohl could and did openly speak of the 1954 allied pledge to accept as a NATO obligation the unification of German. As I argued above, the unquestioning support of the United States through that process reconfirmed to the Germans both the reliability of its trans-Atlantic ally and the two-way basis of the security relationship.

For a short time after German unification, however, the trans-Atlantic security relationship began to be seriously reassessed in Germany in light of changed circumstances. Germany was now fully sovereign for the first time since 1945, was clearly emerging as the major European power, and therefore could redefine its security relationships that were established during the cold war.

REASSESSING GERMAN INTERESTS IN 1990–94

Immediately after German unification, there were indications among the German elite class and in public opinion polls that NATO's role as the cornerstone of German security in Europe was at least open to debate. Through 1990–94, freed from the political constraints of the cold war and fully sovereign for the first time since 1945, debate among German political elites and intellectuals flourished about whether a European or German security alternative to NATO was possible. On the right and the left, alternative security frameworks to NATO, and thereby the centrality of the trans-Atlantic security relationship, were openly contemplated.

78. See Hampton, "NATO at the Creation."

For many on the left, the Organization for Security and Cooperation in Europe (OSCE) was envisioned as an alternative security model to NATO. For years, central figures in the SPD had been promoting a Europe-wide security structure that would include the Soviet Union, the United States, and the Europe in between. For many, 1989–90 represented a watershed. With the cold war over and a united Germany situated in the heart of Europe, the time was perceived as ripe for constructing a post–cold war security structure that rejected both Soviet and American dominance in Europe, and that would instead promote the development of a collective security system wherein the military power of both superpowers played diminished roles. The former members of the Eastern and the Western blocs would start anew in creating an inclusive Europe-wide security structure. The 1990 Paris summit, where the OSCE was granted new powers as a crisis management organization, was seen as the first major step in realizing that goal. Throughout 1990–91, many in the SPD and Green parties concentrated on promoting the pan-European security framework that could bind Germany in Europe and balance against U.S. military dominance on the continent.[79]

Among many in the center-right and right, new emphasis was given to Franco-German security cooperation and the rapid development of European security structures like the WEU. A paper published by Karl Lamers and Wolfgang Schaeuble, two leading members of the CDU, called for the immediate invigoration of a strong European security identity to be forged through the EU, with France and Germany serving as the nexus.[80] Upon publication, the paper caused a storm in the German, Italian, French and British presses, with much criticism focusing on what was perceived by some as potentially imperial inclinations on the part of the German policymakers. The paper was seen by many as demanding that France take its place next to Germany as the engine of European unity, while basically warning Great Britain of the consequences of missing the integration train that was ready to depart, and leaving other EU members like Italy in a subordinate position.

There was even discussion in German intellectual and academic circles of pursuing a more independent German foreign policy course,

79. See discussion in Andrew Denison, "The European Dilemmas of the German Left: The Social Democratic Party and West European Security Cooperation" (Ph.D. diss., Johns Hopkins University, 1996) (Ann Arbor: UMI Dissertation Services, 1996), esp. chaps. 3–5.
80. Karl Lamers and Wolfgang Schaeuble, "Überlegungen zur europaischen Politik," CDU/CSU Fraktion des Deutschen Bundestages, 1 September 1994.

one less dependent on the Western transnational institutions that embedded West Germany during the cold war.[81] Hans-Peter Schwarz, for
example, argued: "The time is past when a German government could
present the results of policy negotiations within NATO or the European
Community (EC) as identical with German interests, and this now applies to security questions as well."[82] Official German criticism of U.S.-
NATO policy was also on the menu, as revealed in 1994 by a leaked
government memorandum from Hermann von Richthofen, the German ambassador to NATO. Criticizing what he perceived as U.S. unilateralism on the issues of Bosnia intervention and NATO enlargement,
Richthofen warned of "cracks appearing in the alliance."[83]

The ambivalence among the political class was reflected in important
ways in public opinion polls taken during 1990–91. In the first year
after unity, for example, one public opinion poll registered only 53
percent of German respondents who supported the continuation of
NATO and the American presence in Germany. Despite the high levels
of continued support for NATO and the United States, an Infas poll
from 1990 showed that a full 79 percent of German respondents
thought it was equally important to maintain good relations with both
the United States and the Soviet Union, while only 2 percent felt it
was more important to maintain above all good relations with the
United States[84] Further, a series of polls from this period also found
that for the first time since the 1960s, a majority of German respondents felt that German security could be guaranteed without the presence of American troops. In 1970, 20 percent of West Germans believed that German security could be guaranteed without American
troops in Germany; in 1990, 54 percent thought this was the case.[85]

By 1995, much of the debate among German elites concerning future security options faded into a renewed consensus centered on rein-
vigorating NATO. The main focus of debate among the political class in
Germany shifted to enlarging the alliance and negotiating German
military intervention in Bosnia through NATO under the Dayton Accords. As with the elites, so too did public opinion appear to recenter
around the NATO consensus. By the end of 1994, 75 percent of German

81. Heilbrunn, "Germany's New Right."
82. Hans-Peter Schwarz, "Germany's National and European Interests," *Daedalus*
123, no. 2 (spring 1994): 81–105, quote from p. 89.
83. "Bonn's NATO-Botschafter warnt vor Spaltung der Allianz und erhebt schwere
Vorwuerfe gegen die Politik der USA," *Sueddeutsche Zeitung*, 1 December 1994.
84. Wolffs and Beil, *Documentation*, 86.
85. Ibid., 77.

respondents saw NATO as vital to German security, with a large in-crease in support for NATO coming from former East Germans.[86] The margin of Germans' sympathy for the United States versus Russia likewise widened considerably in favor of the United States. This reral-lying around NATO, and therewith the German security identity with the United States, can be explained at a number of levels.

Germans have reinvigorated their loyalty to NATO according to what can be interpreted as egoistic calculations. First, because of reductions in defense budgets across Europe, a phenomenon that is especially ap-parent in Germany, it has become increasingly evident that a viable European security identity is still a vision of the future rather than a concrete current policy option. Because of the high costs associated with the German unification process, and the strained monetary and economic situation created in Germany based on the drive to create the Euro, German defense spending will be constrained into the near future.

Second, Franco-German cooperation, the envisioned axis of a Euro-pean security identity, still falters on the shoals of the French prefer-ence for sovereignty regarding matters of national security. Despite progress in a number of areas of Franco-German cooperation, includ-ing developing a European nuclear deterrent, the willingness of France to transcend its independent posture regarding matters of national de-fense remains suspect.

Third, the reality of the wars in the former Yugoslavia, ending at the negotiating table in Dayton, Ohio, reinforced the importance of the American presence and leadership role in European security matters. Not only did a common European position and subsequent policy never materialize on the crisis in former Yugoslavia, negative collective memories were stirred that reflected continued differences in national interests and beliefs. The German policy of recognizing Croatia, which was endorsed by the EU, spawned extremely negative historical analo-gies in the French and British presses regarding German historical ties to Croatia during the Third Reich.

Fourth, the flexibility of NATO, as is being reflected through its eastward expansion and internal reform policies, allows Germany to project its own security interests onto an organization that is already in place and that has achieved a high degree of legitimacy and credibility. Thus, for example, the "NATOization" of the WEU was begun at the

---

86. Asmus, *Germany's Political Maturation*, 13–26.

1996 NATO meeting in Berlin, when it was argued that the WEU could depend on NATO assets in future military missions. This act gives NATO, and thereby the United States, a role in WEU operations, but saves Germany and the other European participants money by placing much of the financial burden on NATO.[87]

Fifth, and finally, the potential renationalization of European security policy that the demise of NATO could spawn stands as a nightmare to German policymakers, who have achieved through NATO membership a first in German history: the abolition of the German historical fear of being isolated in Europe. The current NATO policy of enlargement multiplies that benefit by assuring that Germany will be surrounded only by allies.

These are all explanations for the continued German support of NATO that lend themselves to interest-calculation arguments and need no reference to the existence or absence of positive identity in the NATO relationship. The problem is that one can produce a number of counter-scenarios that could also serve German interests. As members of the minimal German new right and some on the German left maintain, for example, the newly united Germany could view continued dependence on the United States and NATO as counterproductive to emerging German interests as a post–cold war European power. The development of a credible European security identity and framework would increase the influence of Germany as a member, and reduce the risks of producing a dissatisfied Russia. Maintenance of the NATO relationship indeed keeps Germany and Europe dependent on the United States, and recent estimates of the military technology gap between the United States and Europe show that dependence to be projected well into the future. Likewise, continued German dependence on the United States through NATO deflates potential domestic arguments that would summon more defense spending to enhance German security interests and capabilities.

I would argue that a more plausible explanation for German behavior regarding NATO is in fact related to the argument concerning positive identity, and is one that can subsume the above explanations as well. As Michael Spirtas argues in this issue regarding group identity

87. I learned much on this topic from briefings attended during the German-American Research Group (DAA) conference held in Frankfurt, Strasbourg, and Bonn in June 1996. I especially thank Wolfgang-Uwe Friedrich for the invitation to participate in the conference. I thank Karl-Heinz Kamp of the Adenauer Stiftung for his helpful discussion of the "NATOization" of the WEU.

among states: "Those that are deeply devoted to a group identity are unlikely to be swayed by late-breaking events or newly discovered facts."[88] The Germans are devoted to the self-identity that has evolved out of and is dependent on their relationship with the United States through NATO. The Germans have placed their trust in the trans-Atlantic security relationship, and have now found persuasive reasons not to remove that trust. The Greens have endorsed the NATO relationship for the first time. Among leading members of the SPD, the lessons of 1989 and 1990 affirmed the virtues of the Western alliance as newly democratizing states in the former east bloc sought entry into NATO as well as the EU. SPD foreign policy expert, Karsten Voigt, for example, criticized those in the SPD who still pursue the OSCE or other frameworks as alternatives security structures for the new Europe. In response to a Green Party spokesman's criticism of the NATO enlargement policy and his plea for the construction of an alternative all-European security framework, Voigt admonished: "This position shows that you, at least those of you who hold this opinion, have never understood in reality the meaning of the democratic revolutions and the people's movement." He goes on to repeat a comment made by the Dane Hans Haekkerup: "The Germans and the Danes have had hundreds [sic] of years of problems with each other. I want to say openly that since we've been in NATO, we enjoy the best relationship we've ever had."[89] The rush to join the trans-Atlantic alliance by the new democracies in east and central Europe thus reaffirms the basis of German-U.S. positive identity. All of the developments listed above therefore preserve NATO, keep the United States in Europe, and maintain the German self-image.

It is no surprise that most resistant to alternative security scenarios have consistently been members of the German military elite, many of whom tend to view the potential retreat of the United States from NATO not just as a security threat to Europe, but as a threat to European democracy. Because NATO membership has led to a culture in Europe where military security is largely denationalized, the removal of NATO is seen as representing the potential renationalization of European security identity. In this way, the notion of German security interests becomes enmeshed with the concept of German security iden-

---

88. Michael Spirtas, "French Twist: French and British NATO Policies from 1949–66," *Security Studies* 8, nos. 2/3 (winter 1998/99–spring 1999): 302–46.

89. Karsten Voigt, speech delivered in German Bundestag, 25 June 1997. His comment was a response to Green member Ludger Volmer.

tity with NATO and the United States. Further, it is significant that there is still little momentum in Germany for enhancing its defense posture or changing its nuclear status to match its power position. Those close to or involved in the German defense industry warn of an increasing tendency inside Germany toward reducing the national military capability to a point of danger. By the end of 1997, an estimated 100,000 jobs had been lost in the German defense sector.[90]

This domestic resistance to developing a high German military profile is reflected in the absence of a nuclear debate as well. Based on his strict structural realist reading of European security, John Mearsheimer has predicted and prescribed the conditions for the emergence of a nuclear Germany.[91] The lack of German appetite for a nuclear role in the postwar period has been constant save for occasional raised voices from the right. During the 1940s and 1950s the disposition against nuclear weapons and armaments generally was a direct result of lessons learned from the Second World War experience, but was reinforced and compensated for through German membership in NATO. German influence on NATO nuclear policy has been in effect since the 1960s through the Nuclear Planning Group, which compensates for its lack of nuclear status without raising the specter of a nuclear Germany.[92]

The contemplation of a reconfigured German nuclear role even inside the European context rings alarms inside Germany. In an unanticipated move, for example, the French government invited the Kohl government in 1995 to begin serious discussion of Europeanizing the French nuclear deterrent to cover Germany and include it in nuclear decision making. German defense minister Volker Ruehe responded to the French offer by saying that "[o]ur most important defense shield is NATO"; he stated further that there would be no substitute for the American nuclear umbrella, including not "in the future."[93] *Der Spiegel's* editor, Rudolf Augstein, further illuminates the German position by explaining how Adenauer only accepted a nonnuclear role for Germany upon achieving German admittance to NATO. "Since then, it's become clear that the problematik from that period has been over-

---

90. I thank Holger Mey for his observations in this regard.
91. Mearsheimer, "Back to the Future."
92. See discussion by Karl Heinz Kamp, "Déjà Vu: The Never Ending Story of a European Nuclear Deterrence," Institute Français des Relations Internationales (IFRI), 1997.
93. Volker Ruehe, quoted in "Voellig von der Rolle," *Der Spiegel*, 11 September 1995, 22–23, quotation from p. 23 (my translation).

come...NATO, always including the United States, is our umbrella and shield."[94]

Following an agreement signed between Kohl and French president Chirac in December 1996 to continue the bilateral dialogue on nuclear weapons and deterrence, German resistance to disrupting the rockbed of America's nuclear guarantee through NATO remained unmoved. Ruehe caused an uproar in France, for example, after the 1996 German-French "security and defense concept" agreement was made public. He referred to the event as reflecting the "NATOization" of France, where France actually signed on to the proposition that: "The highest security guarantee of the allies will be maintained through the nuclear forces of the alliance, and especially the United States"[95] The contribution of the German government in edging bilateral European relations closer to the NATO framework was viewed as positive by much of German press coverage.[96]

Most illuminating in explaining the continued lack of German interest in building up its defense industry and acquiring nuclear weapons are therefore the factors of the reconstituted German self-image and positive identity that developed with the United States through NATO, wherein American military and nuclear power have sufficed for German security requirements. That relationship helped construct postwar German identity and continues to diminish the attractiveness of a high defense posture or a pronuclear position in Germany today. The German self-image, shared by the elites and the public, is that of a democratic and nonaggressive state, and depends on a continued low military profile in its national security identity and in its pursuit of egoistic national interests. German identity and self-image are therefore constituted by the established relationship in NATO with the United States, and in this sense the identity construction constrains German elite and public attitudes toward issues like nuclear weapons.[97]

94. Rudolf Augstein, "Der vertrackte Freund," *Der Spiegel*, 11 September 1995, 24 (my translation).

95. "Gemeinsames deutsch-franzoisisches Sicherheits- und Verteidigungskonzept," in *Bulletin*, 5 February 1997. The quotation was reproduced as signaling a positive development in "Bonn's militärische Koordination mit Paris," *Neue Zuercher Zeitung*, 30 January 1997.

96. On Ruehe's statement, see Jan Bielicki and Franz Josef Hutsch, "Weltmacht Europa?" *Die Woche*, 7 February 1997. For German press coverage, see "Bonn's militärische Koordination mit Paris," *Neue Zuercher Zeitung*, 30 January 1997.

97. See the discussion of identity and interests in Colin H. Kahl, "Constructing a Separate Peace: Constructivism, Collective Liberal Identity, and Democratic Peace," this volume. He states, "state identities constitute national interests, and enable and constrain state strategies."

In the political culture of contemporary Germany, therefore, the constitutive norms admonishing against the use of German military force and the acquisition of the means of coercion are powerful and have worked as clear guideposts on military security issues. They have also conformed to a positive identity with the United States through the allied relationship, which has in turn contributed to the German national self-image of being a democratic and nonagressive state. The German security identity and self-image therefore evolved in a unique way, based on a particular set of relationships. How Germany has defined its security has been path dependent and influenced by its identification with another state, which, as Roxanne Lynn Doty observes, "calls our attention to the social constructedness of security."[98]

While recent and current changes in German military policy and identity have incrementally signaled a slight change in the German attitude toward military intervention, such as the German decision to intervene militarily in Bosnia alongside its NATO allies, the changes have been carefully implemented within the context of the NATO relationship and according to the history and destiny shared by Germany and other NATO members. Thus, while the norm of military nonintervention was strong in postwar West Germany, a lesson learned after the disastrous Second World War experience, another lesson that was learned in the context of West Germany's rebirth as a NATO democracy has guided unified Germany's way toward accepting military intervention under certain conditions: since democracies vanquished Nazism, Germany must be willing to intervene in the name of democracy with its democratic allies.[99] German politicians and generals therefore speak of Germany's obligation to act in "solidarity" with its democratic allies.

In sum, an important effect of German membership and participation in the Western security alliance has been the stabilizing of German democracy and the evolution of a positive German security identity with NATO and the United States. Significant has been the diminution of the security dilemma as a dynamic force in German domestic security-thinking concerning the West, an increase in the trust that Germany places in its trans-Atlantic relationship, and the effective lack of political will in openly to challenge the U.S. military leadership role,

98. Roxanne Lynn Doty, "Immigration and the Politics of Security," *Security Studies* 8, nos. 2/3 (winter 1998/99–spring 1999): 71–93.

99. I thank Matthias Dembinski for his helpful comments on the subject of historical lessons.

despite changes in potential and real German material and political power capabilities. This phenomenon has not diminished with the end of the cold war, although German officials continue to criticize what they see as American inclinations toward unilateralism. The resilience of German positive identification with the United States will be further tested by the new Schroeder government, which, as noted above, contains the seeds of possible revisionism.

CONCLUSION: ASSESSING THE POWER OF POSITIVE IDENTITY

MEASURED BY the goals set by its founders, NATO has had a powerful effect in creating positive security identification between the United States and Germany. Because Germans have come to identify NATO and the U.S. role therein with their own democracy, initial sentiments in post unification Germany for setting upon a potentially different security policy course have withered, although not disappeared. To challenge the U.S.-German security connection would mean no less than reopening the national debate about Germany's security identity in the international system, the role of the military in a sovereign Germany, and the relationship of German democracy to German power. In essence, the trans-Atlantic security relationship between the United States and Germany has secured a positive identity that has moved beyond explanations that focus on rationalistic behavior, and is one that Germans have not been willing to forfeit because the relationship is a cornerstone of the German self-image.

The powerful evidence for the existence of positive identification between Germany and its trans-Atlantic partner since the 1950s does reveal two areas of weakness, where the relationship registers on the negative end of the identity continuum. The continued salience of negative historical memories concerning the German past, and German misgivings about American social values, temper the evidence that forty years of positive shared history in NATO has led to positive identification between Germany and its American partner. The caveats, however, do not overshadow the greater body of evidence that supports the existence of the positive security identity that Germany has developed with the United States through NATO. Even the fact that the positive identity was based on a military protector-protectee basis has not undermined the stability of the relationship in light of the material and political changes following German unification.

The question that has not been answered, but which is essential to the overall identity complex between the U.S. and Germany, concerns the viability of this positive identity in light of aspects of the U.S.-German relationship that fall outside the NATO security dimension. While I have shown, for example, that the German security identity with the U.S. is intimately connected with the German self-definition of democracy, such a connection does not necessarily exist in other vital components of the trans-Atlantic relationship, such as in trade and monetary relations, and is not necessarily transferable to them. Despite optimism about the "liberal manifesto," or the liberal world order that is meant to have created an overarching democratic community in the trans-Atlantic area, U.S.-German economic relations tend to be under-institutionalized, and they are adversarial more frequently in the post–cold war period than was the case previously.[100] The clash of interests and disputes concerning sovereignty issues tend to be pronounced in trans-Atlantic economic relations, despite shared values regarding liberal trade practices and positive assumptions about the necessary processes of consultation and mediation. Placing the economic relationship along the identity continuum, it is somewhere in between the two extremes.

While shared norms regarding economic and monetary relations exist, a shared history and sense of destiny were never forged in this issue area in the way that they were in the U.S.-German security relationship. A critical factor in German national identity as a democracy, and one that also evokes the lessons of history, is economic well-being. Yet, socialization of German elites in the economic arena has occurred mostly in the European Union framework, not in an institutionalized trans-Atlantic framework. Therefore, in the area of economic relations, Germany has been much more willing to challenge not only U.S. leadership and policy, but American economic and monetary models. German elites often couch the push for greater European economic integration in terms of competition with the U.S. Public opinion polls reflect this ambivalence as well. Between 1991 and 1994, for example, polls show that while between 88–90 percent of Germans sought an "expanded partnership among equals with USA" in European economic affairs, between 59–63 percent of those same respondents viewed the

---

100. Among others, see Ikenberry, "The Myth of Post Cold War Chaos."

European economic relationship as creating "greater independence and a counterweight to USA."[101]

In sum, while Germans have been resilient in their continued security identification with the United States through NATO, the lack of positive identity in the vital arena of national economic identity has led to a bifurcation of the trans-Atlantic relationship. A tension therefore exists in the U.S.-German relationship, where balancing and egoistic behavior could potentially dominate in the economic relationship, while a positive identity has arisen in the security relationship. Whereas security matters dominated in the cold war era, economic issues have tended to top foreign policy agendas since 1989. The importance of the positive security identity will, therefore, be increasingly tested. It is possible that the diffuse but efficacious German cultural affinity with the United States that emerged through the evolution of shared history in the security relationship could at least mute the problems emerging in other aspects of the trans-Atlantic relationship. That being said, predicting the outcome of the process wherein these contradictory impulses are played out is well beyond the scope of this paper, but is fertile ground for further research.

101. Asmus, *Germany's Political Maturation*, 33.

FROM BALANCE TO COMMUNITY:

TRANSNATIONAL IDENTITY AND POLITICAL INTEGRATION

BRUCE CRONIN

H OW DO STATES distinguish friends from enemies, partners from competitors, and communities from outsiders? Why does this change over time? Why are interests defined in parochial terms at some points and in more cosmopolitan terms at others? Traditionally, the international relations literature has examined these questions through the study of alliances and institutions, that is, forms of cooperation through which states attempt to achieve specific, well-defined, but limited goals. While neorealists focus primarily on alliances and neoliberals on institutions, both approaches are based on a model of strategic interaction by autonomous, self-interested states. They necessarily hold constant the state as an analytical unit. That is, the state itself is presented as an unproblematic given, endowed with a set of fixed attributes and a fixed identity. As a result, there is little room for the examination of complex relationships that go beyond expediency and calculation.

This article will attempt to demonstrate the deficiencies of purely structural models in explaining the nature of interstate relationships by examining an anomaly that cannot be easily explained either by neorealist or neoliberal theories of cooperation: the voluntary cession of sovereignty by a group of independent states to create an entirely new political authority. Specifically, I examine why the Italian peninsula transformed from a competitive balance-of-power system of independent states to an amalgamated security community in the mid-nineteenth century. In doing so, I explore the conditions under which a disparate group of states will redefine themselves in transnational terms so as to form a new political community.

Bruce Cronin is assistant professor at the Department of Political Science, University of Wisconsin, Madison.

An earlier version of this article was presented at the 92nd annual meeting of the American Political Science Association, 29 August–1 September 1996. I wish to thank Michael Barnett, Glenn Chafetz, Benjamin Frankel, Rodney Bruce Hall, Joseph Lepgold, Alexander Wendt, and the anonymous reviewers of *Security Studies* for their helpful comments.

In the following pages, I will develop a set of theoretical principles drawn from social identity theory and symbolic interaction sociology and argue that political integration requires two conditions: the development of a transnational identity that is grounded in a cosmopolitan rather than a parochial nationalism, and a "reference other" which embodies this identity and around which the independent units can coalesce. Under these conditions, juridical borders are no longer viewed as a protection of autonomy, but as impediments toward unity. This occurs when a group of states sharing a common experience of high intensity and long duration, a common relationship to the region's other states, and a positive interdependence, develops a political consciousness that identifies them as a unique and exclusive community.

In shifting the focus from strategic interaction to the construction of cohesive transnational relationships, I conceptualize political integration as a process through which states create an amalgamated security community (ASC). An ASC is a cohesive security arrangement characterized by the formal merger of at least two states' administrative, security and political institutions. It is based on a concept of a common good and a shared sense of self, giving its members a positive stake in building and maintaining internal relationships.[1] By examining integration as a type of cohesive security arrangement, I highlight the political rather than economic variables.

POLITICAL UNIFICATION AS A THEORETICAL ANOMALY

TWO OF THE most fundamental assumptions in the study of international relations are, first, that states wish to survive as sovereign entities and, second, that they will not voluntarily allow themselves to become entangled in relationships that significantly compromise control over their own affairs. These are not controversial propositions. Most scholars and practitioners accept the eighteenth-century doctrine of raison d'état, which holds that the motive and rule of political action in international relations is to advance the political, security and economic interests of the state.[2] Our notion of security is therefore

1. The concept of amalgamated security community was first suggested by Karl Deutsch and his associates in *Political Community and the North Atlantic Area* (Princeton: Princeton University Press, 1957). This definition, however, is mine.
2. See Derek McKay and H. M. Scott, *The Rise of the Great Powers, 1648–1815* (New York: Longman, 1983), 210–11.

usually understood in terms of the survival and expansion of state power.

The breakup of a unified state into smaller units is more easily explained than the amalgamation of independent states into a cosmopolitan community. From an elite perspective, leaders of self-defined political communities could profit by breaking away from the central state and forming a new base of power under their leadership. From the vantage point of the population, political divorce would allow for greater control of their political, cultural, social and economic destinies.[3] While secession results in the creation of multiple centers of authority, however—providing material rewards to those advocating it—political integration requires existing authorities to subordinate themselves to a larger collective. Unlike the creation of an empire, where independent units are conquered and absorbed into the center, integration is a synthesis of the component units and the creation of an entirely new political community. Thus, while there may be incentives for political actors to secede, only a conqueror gains materially from amalgamation. As a result, the question of political, as opposed to economic, integration has been generally absent from the literature over the past few decades.[4]

If political integration is a theoretical anomaly, the integration of Italy is also a historical one. Ever since the emergence of independent states and principalities during the fifteenth century, the Italian peninsula was governed by a classic balance-of-power system. Following the Peace of Lodi in 1454, five states of relatively equal power emerged— Milan, Venice, Florence, Rome and Naples. A century later Piedmont was created by the House of Savoy. Not only did the principalities regularly fight among themselves, they often allied themselves with

---

3. For two studies of secession, see Alan Buchanan, *Secession: the Morality of Political Divorce From Fort Sumter to Lithuania and Quebec* (Boulder: Westview, 1991); and Lee Buchheit, *Secession: The Legitimacy of Self-Determination* (New Haven: Yale University Press, 1978).

4. The early neofunctionalists tried to explain political integration through an economic functionalist model, arguing that the requirements of an integrated economy across borders set in motion a self-reinforcing process of political institution-building. Economic integration produces spill-over effects requiring ever deepening levels of political cooperation, regulation, standardization and ultimately integration. Besides the empirical difficulties, the key problem with these theories is that the variables which integrationists use to explain economic integration cannot necessarily account for political integration. See, inter alia, Ernst Haas, *The Uniting of Europe: Political, Social and Economic Forces, 1950–57* (Stanford: Stanford University Press, 1958); and Leon Lindberg and Stuart Scheingold, *Europe's Would-Be Polity: Patterns of Change in the European Community* (Englewood Cliffs: Prentice-Hall, 1970).

European great powers against one another, a classic balancing practice.

The reorganization of the peninsular by Napoleon did not significantly change this situation. While he consolidated some states and
absorbed others into his empire, after his defeat the Congress of Vienna recreated the original prewar borders and restored the traditional
royal families to their thrones. With the restoration of the old political
boundaries came the old rivalries. As Austrian foreign minister Clemens von Metternich correctly observed at the time, "If disorder broke
out in Florence, the inhabitants of Pisa or Pistoria would take sides
with the opposition because he hates Florence. And so it happens that
Naples is resentful of Rome, Rome of Bolgna, Leghorn of Ancona and
Milan of Venice."[5]

Moreover, contrary to the myths promoted by the early romantic
historians, Italian history did not even leave a legacy that could account for a national or ethnic consciousness to develop in the nineteenth century. The peninsula and islands that we now know as Italy
were originally the territories of the Hellenic, Carthaginian, Etruscan,
and Roman peoples. For a time they were united—along with much of
Europe and the Middle East—under the Roman empire. Ancient
Rome, however, was the capital of a Mediterranean empire, not an Italian state, and its legacy was not Italy, but the Papacy.[6]

When "Italy" reappeared during the Renaissance, it was not as a single political unit but rather a peninsula of city-states. The Teutonic
peoples predominated in the north, and Greek peoples in the Basilicata
and Puglie regions. Arab, Norman and Spanish stock had left their
marks in Sicily, while the old Italic and Etruscan peoples remained in
Tuscany.[7] In fact, there was not even a common language to tie them
together. Regional dialects were the dominant form of communication;
beyond that, Latin was the most common language in Rome, French
in Turin, and Spanish in Naples, Sicily and Sardinia.[8] The integration
of Italy is thus a hard case for integration theories since so many factors were working against transnational cohesion.

5. Clemens Von Metternich, *Memoirs of Prince Metternich*, ed. Prince Richard Metternich, vol. 2 (New York: Scribner's, 1882), 188.

6. Derek Beales, *The Risorgimento and the Unification of Italy* (New York: Barnes
and Noble, 1971), 30.

7. Bolton King, *A History of Italian Unity: A Political History of Italy From 1814–
1871*, vol. 1 (1899; New York: Russell and Russell, 1924).

8. Denis Mack Smith, ed., *The Making of Italy, 1796–1870* (New York: Walker,
1968).

Neorealist or neoliberal institutionalist approaches cannot easily account for these puzzles primarily because both present the state as an ontological given without making analytical distinctions between the different forms it could take. For the purpose of analysis, a state is a state and interaction occurs among predefined units. The nature of these units, and thus their identities, are not considered to be relevant for understanding behavior.

From a neorealist perspective, all states are analytically the same, differing only in size and capabilities. Kenneth Waltz argues that the ends to which states aspire are similar, and that only their capabilities vary.[9] He holds that in an anarchical environment, states are compelled to act alike—that is self-interested in the pursuit of power and wealth—lest they "fall by the wayside." Thus, a single set of primary attributes, roles and behaviors are wrapped up in this political unit. In addition, for both neorealists and neoliberals, sovereignty is equated with social autonomy from other states. That is, state development is purely internal and its relationships with other states affect only strategy and calculation, not its social or political construction. The tie between the population (or at least the elites) and the state is considered to be primary, and in an anarchic environment it is by necessity also exclusive.[10]

In this model, there is little room for political actors to develop transnational attachments that could lead to the formation of new communities. Rather, neorealist alliance theory suggests that cooperation is achieved through the expediency of power balancing brought about through changes in the distribution of power.[11] Friends are distinguished from enemies through strategic calculation based on the demands of realpolitik and the necessities of the balance of power. Since neorealism is concerned only with capabilities and not intentions, neorealists speak in terms of allies rather than partners or friends. As Waltz argues, the state's interest provides the spring of action; the necessities of policy arise from the unregulated competition of states; calculation based on these necessities can discover the policies that will

9. See Kenneth N. Waltz, *Theory of International Politics* (New York: Random House, 1979), 96.

10. Hans J. Morganthau, *Politics Among Nations: The Struggle for Power and Peace*, 6th ed. (New York: Knopf), chap. 1.

11. See, for example, Waltz, *Theory of International Politics*, chap. 6; Barry R. Posen, *The Sources of Military Doctrine: France, Britain and Germany Between the World Wars* (Ithaca: Cornell University Press, 1984); and John J. Mearsheimer, "A Realist Reply," *International Security* 20, no. 1 (summer 1995): 82.

best serve a state's interests; and success is defined as preserving and strengthening the state.[12]

Why, then, would states, in particular the Italian principalities, cede their sovereignty to create an entirely new political entity? A realist may suggest that the cession of sovereignty was undertaken in the 1850s to ensure survival against outside powers, specifically Austria and France. The war against Austria in 1859 demonstrated the vulnerability of small states to occupation and coercion by great powers. Thus, integration would be explained by political necessity in an anarchic world. This, however, brings us back to the question of how states distinguish friends from enemies in the first place.

The Italian peninsula had been under domination by the Spanish, the Bourbons and the Hapsburgs for three centuries. Far from making a common cause against the European great powers, however, the principalities regularly supported and sometimes instigated invasion by these powers to help them against neighboring Italian states.[13] At the time, they were considered to be no more foreign than the other principalities. Moreover, during the early nineteenth century, the feared power was not Austria or France but Piedmont, the state with whom the principalities would eventually merge. This was reinforced by the fact that many of the northern and central principalities were ruled by monarchs with dynastic ties to the Austrian Hapsburgs.

It was not until the political actors in the principalities reconceptualized themselves as Italians that Austria was seen as the foreign enemy. As long as the principalities continued to define themselves in dynastic terms, an alliance with Austria reflected the interests of the political elites in the northern principalities. Under these conditions, integration was never a possibility, since the accumulation of power in the hands of rulers over several generations inevitably produced dynastic interests that were at variance with any concept of nation. Austrian control of Lombardy and Venetia was not seen as a problem for the rest of the peninsula, since there was no perceived tie between those regions and the sovereign states of Italy. In fact, during this period, many of the elites saw Austria as an ally in helping them to maintain their rule domestically and in balancing the power of the other principalities.

12. See Waltz, *Theory of International Politics*, 117.
13. Smith, *The Making of Italy*, 2.

At the same time, realists could argue that political integration was the result of changes in the balance of power in southern Europe. Among the major changes that occurred in the mid-nineteenth century was in the relative capabilities of the great powers. France became stronger, and with the rise of Louis Napoleon more aggressive, while Austria was weakened by domestic revolts in Vienna, Prague, Budapest and Bohemia. This provided the Italian states with an external ally against a distracted hegemon. While this could account for the ability of the Italian states to attempt integration without external interference, it does not explain why the states would wish to do so in the first place. In fact, given the long history of rivalry and conflict on the peninsula, it is counterintuitive.

Finally, a realist could argue that integration was facilitated by an increase in Piedmont's relative capabilities and the rise of a new breed of modern politicians willing to manipulate both the international situation and nationalist aspirations to their own advantage.[14] In this case, integration can be explained by the ascension of Camillo Benso, Count of Cavour, and his attempt to extend Piedmontese hegemony over the peninsula.[15] Yet as the case below will show, integration was not Piedmont's preferred outcome until the late 1850s. In fact, in some cases, annexation of the other principalities was thrust upon the Piedmontese by the leaders of the principalities themselves. Moreover, if Piedmont had attempted to impose its will on the other states, one should expect the principalities to have formed a balancing coalition in an attempt to thwart Piedmont's supposed power grab. This never occurred. Thus, while balance-of-power theory can explain why the northern and central Italian states would ally against Austria during the war of 1859, it cannot account for their subsequent integration.

In sum, traditional structural approaches toward security cannot adequately account for either the theoretical puzzle of integration or the historical anomaly of Italian unification.

14. See the discussion of these approaches in Lucy Riall, *The Italian Risorgimento: State, Society and National Unification* (New York: Routledge, 1994), 63–66.
15. See, for example, John Breuilly, *Nationalism and the State* (Chicago: University of Chicago Press, 1994), 96–114.

TRANSNATIONAL IDENTITY FORMATION AS AN EXPLANATORY VARIABLE

TO UNDERSTAND how a balance-of-power system could evolve into a political community, I suggest that we shift our focus from structural variables to intersubjective ones, specifically the formation of transnational identities and cohesive security communities. There is a growing literature that holds that the dynamics of international politics is neither natural nor given, but rather is "socially constructed" by political actors through their actions and relationships. On one level, constructivist social theory focuses on how political actors define their situations and relationships vis-à-vis other actors, by examining the connection between what actors do and what they are.[16] On another level, it focuses on how patterned interactions can shape state identity and state interests. The model proposed in this article is in the spirit of this research program. Specifically, I use social identity theory (SIT) and symbolic interactionist sociology (SIS) to explain how political elites can reconceptualize their loyalties and identities and in the process construct new transnational relationships.

Social identity theory argues, in part, that individuals are socially constructed by the conceptual groups to which they belong.[17] It holds that actors develop conceptual ties to one another through the creation of social identities, defined as those parts of one's self-concept that are derived from the social categories to which one is associated (for example, democratic state, Arab, and great power). These identities can lead to group solidarity and collective action. SIT models place the social group in the center of investigation by emphasizing the social forces and psychological pressures that help members of social groups to differentiate themselves from other groups, for example, classes, ethnici-

16. For an overview of various constructivist approaches, see John Searle, *The Construction of Social Reality* (Berkeley: University of California Press, 1995); Alexander Wendt, "Anarchy is What States Make of It: The Social Construction of Power Politics," *International Organization* 46, no. 2 (spring 1992): 391–425. Nicholas Onuf, *World of Our Making* (Columbia: University of South Carolina Press, 1989); Friedriech Kratochwil, *Rules, Norms, Decisions* (Cambridge: Cambridge University Press, 1989); and Peter Katzenstein, ed., *The Culture of National Security: Norms and Identity in World Politics* (New York: Columbia University Press, 1996).

17. For a sample of this literature, see Henri Tajfel, ed., *Social Identity and Intergroup Relations* (Cambridge: Cambridge University Press, 1982); John Turner, *Rediscovering the Social Group* (New York: Basil Blackwell, 1987); Michael Hogg and Dominic Abrams, *Social Identifications: A Social Psychology of Intergroup Relations and Group Process* (New York: Routledge, 1988); and Dominic Abrams and Michael A. Hogg, *Social Identity Theory: Constructive and Critical Advances* (New York: Springer-Verlag, 1990).

ties, and political communities. SIT research thus seeks to explain intragroup solidarity and intergroup conflict by showing the ways in which individuals identify themselves and their interests with the group.

Symbolic interaction theories hold that the "self" (in this case, the sovereign state) is always in the process of being (reproducing) and becoming (changing). The main premise of SIS is that human beings do not typically respond directly to stimuli, but rather assign meanings to the stimuli and act on the basis of these meanings. SIS thus focuses primarily on the way actors create, interpret, and define (or redefine) social situations through the use of symbols, framing and role-making.[18] These situations are defined and interpreted by the participants, who act toward each other on the basis of their intersubjective definitions. Thus, actors assign meaning to acts, objects and individuals in terms of their joint relationship to the situation.[19] Identities and the social roles that are derived from them influence the way meaning is assigned and therefore influence behavior. Action, then, is influenced by social interaction and definitions of the present situation.[20] I argue that one's identity helps to structure the roles and meanings that guide perception and behavior.

It is my position that one cannot understand the political dynamics that lead to transnational integration without taking into account the role of social identity. Identities provide a frame of reference from which political leaders can initiate, maintain and structure their relationships with other states. These relationships can range from symbiosis to hostility, but embedded within them are a set of expectations concerning the nature of the actors. Structures, rules and norms can motivate, constrain, guide and generate behavior, but ultimately political leaders evaluate the intentions, capabilities and behaviors of other

---

18. Symbolic interactionism grew from the work of George Herbert Mead, although it also has roots in German idealism, Scottish moralism, and American pragmatism. It was further developed by Herbert Blumer, particularly in his *Symbolic Interactionism: Perspective and Method* (Englewood Cliffs: Prentice Hall, 1969). See also Erving Goffman, *The Presentation of Self in Everyday Life* (Garden City: Doubleday Anchor, 1959); Tamotsu Shibutani, "Reference Groups as Perspectives," *American Journal of Sociology* 60, no. 6 (May 1955): 562–69; Sheldon Stryker, *Symbolic Interaction: A Social-Structural Version* (Menlo Park, Calif.: Benjamin/Cummings, 1980); and Joel M. Charon, *Symbolic Interactionism: An Introduction, An Interpretation, An Integration Method* (Englewood Cliffs: Prentice Hall, 1979).

19. John Hewitt, *Self and Society: A Symbolic Interactionist Social Psychology* (Boston: Allyn and Bacon, 1976), 115.

20. Charon, *Symbolic Interactionism*, 24.

states, not abstract structures.[21] All human relationships involve inter-action between oneself and an other or among groups of selves and others. Thus, the way in which one defines self and other greatly influences the nature of the relationship.

To understand the relationship between identity and integration, let us first consider why states would wish to remain independent. Although this is assumed in most of the international relations literature, it is not immediately obvious from a security or economic perspective why states should not combine to produce a stronger more prosperous society. Anarchy explains why states may be wary of trusting the intentions of other states, but it does not explain why the boundaries that define a state cannot be expanded to include other political communities. Obviously the state as an integrated set of institutions has a material incentive to survive; however, the state as a trustee for its society must be concerned with the security and prosperity of that society. In fact when Morganthau argues that states are morally compelled to act with extreme prejudice in promoting their self-interest, he uses a states-as-trustee model rather than an institutional survival approach.[22]

If one was to adopt this perspective, then the identity of the political community over which the state rules is important in determining state interests and social attachments. The primary factor that allows for each state to develop its own identity is its distinction from other states. That is, the construction of state identity is achieved through the creation of conceptual boundaries that separate the domestic (the self) from the foreign (the other). Thus even at its most basic level, the sovereign state develops its identity as a state through its associations within the nation-state system. Its unique consciousness is formed by differentiation from other states. The identity of being French, for example, provides a rationale for developing a particularly "French interest," rather than a European or Catholic one, but only because the political actors distinguish themselves from non-French states. Through its interaction and communication with other states, it categorizes, compares itself to, and occasionally tries to emulate them. Its agents became self-conscious, and this affects both the meaning and future development of its institutions.

Thus, the way in which political actors draw conceptual boundaries greatly influences the way in which the state and its population distin-

21. David Dessler, "What's at Stake in the Agent-Structure Debate?" *International Organization* 43, no. 3 (summer 1989): 441–73.
22. Morganthau, *Politics Among Nations*, chap. 1.

guishes itself and its interests in international society. To the extent that the juridical, geographic and social boundaries that divide one society from another arise from a variety of historical rather than natural factors, they can change over time.

A narrowly conceived nationalism, for example, places a clear boundary between one's ethnic or civic community and all others.[23] Broader attachments are considered less important or even detrimental, and interests tend to be defined in highly parochial terms. Yet a more broadly conceived nationalism can extend the definition of one's community to include populations from other established states, for example, pan-Arabism, pan-Slavism or pan-Italianism. It depends upon how the relevant political actors define "the nation." At the same time, a broadly conceived cosmopolitanism, for example Europeanism, extends the definition of self to include a far broader conceptual category of people and societies than does nationalism. While political actors and populations having such identities retain attachments to their more parochial communities, they also identify themselves and their interests with those of a broader group that crosses political borders. In this sense, the primary issue in determining these attachments is not state power but state identity.

The concept of patriotism as loyalty to one's own country presupposes a conceptual tie between the population, or at least the political elites, and the state. This tie is presumed to be greater than other bonds, such as religion, ethnicity, and regionalism. The institution of sovereignty provides the material foundation for this bond; however, this is by no mean static or unalterable. Since national identities, like other types of group consciousness, are constructed they are capable of being reconstructed or transformed. T. A. Elliot demonstrates, for example, how racial identities in Africa became reclassified as national when they became attached to a particular territory.[24] In fact, in many of these states, political stability and independence depends more on

23. There is a large literature examining how these boundaries are constructed. For a sample of the various approaches, see Walker Connor, *Ethnonationalism: The Quest for Understanding* (Princeton: Princeton University Press, 1994); Anthony D. Smith, *The Ethnic Origin of Nations* (Oxford: Oxford University Press, 1986); Ernest Gellner, *Nations and Nationalism* (Ithaca: Cornell University Press, 1983); and Benedict Anderson, *Imagined Communities: Reflections on the Origins and Spread of Nationalism* (London: Verso, 1983).

24. T. A. Elliot, *Us and Them: A Study in Group Consciousness* (Aberdean, Australia: Aberdean University Press, 1986). Robert Jackson demonstrates, however, that this process has often been unsuccessful. See his *Quasi-States: Sovereignty, International Relations and the Third World* (Cambridge: Cambridge University Press, 1990).

securing loyalty to national over transnational or tribal identities than it does on increasing state power vis-à-vis their neighbors.[25] To the extent that transnational identities are dominant, as in the case of the Hutus and Tutis in Rwanda and Burundi, the state is not the most important focus of loyalty and security is not necessarily equated with the state.

Identities are social locations relative to the various individuals and social categories with whom actors come into contact.[26] They are neither autonomously developed nor are they externally imposed, although both domestic and systemic factors play an important role. Rather, they evolve through interaction among societies and through a process of differentiation. Identities are a synthesis between a self and an other. As sociologist George Herbert Mead argues, identities arise in the process of social experience and activity. They develop as a result of one's relations to the process as a whole and to other individuals within that process.[27] It is through our interaction with others that we become conscious of our similarities and differences, and this consciousness forms the basis for an identity.

Thus, states as institutional actors (represented by their agents) achieve an understanding of "self" identity through the process of social comparison and categorization. One cannot deduce these identities apart from the historical context through which this interaction occurs. As with the case of individuals, a particular characteristic of a society can either be rendered significant or irrelevant depending upon the context. Dynastic lineage, for example, was the most salient character in defining self and interest within the states of central Europe for much of the seventeenth and eighteenth centuries. The dynastic system encouraged monarchs to develop transnational loyalties and political attachments through marriage and family compact. Rulers were conscious of their position as part of a transnational family and of their responsibilities to it.[28] With the rise of nationalism, however, dynastic identities were downplayed in favor of cultural or ethnic attributes in defining the state and previous attachments were rendered irrelevant.

---

25. Jackson discusses this type of problem in *Quasi-States*.
26. Hewitt, *Self and Society*, 101.
27. George Herbert Mead, *Mind, Self and Society from the Standpoint of a Social Behaviorist*, ed. Charles W. Morris (Chicago: University of Chicago Press, 1934), 135.
28. Jeremy Black, *The Rise of the European Powers* (New York: Routledge, Chapman and Hall, 1990), 150.

Identities can affect definitions of friend and enemy by providing a standard of comparison and expectation, but also by influencing ones choice of reference groups and the degree to which these groups are viewed positively or negatively. As actors develop relationships with others, they develop a cumulative sense of the others who are important to them, either positively or negatively. Sociologists refer to these as "reference others" or if they comprise conceptual categories, "reference groups."[29] Reference others help individuals to form judgments about themselves by serving as points of comparison or standards of judgment, thus facilitating the process of self definition and identity formation. Individual and institutional actors continually compare themselves to others, positively and negatively, in part to better define who they are and, equally importantly, who they are not. The stronger the identification with one's reference group, the stronger one identifies oneself with or against that group's interests. Integration represents a strong positive identification in the form of symbiosis.

Hogg and Abrams argue that there is a continuum of self-conception ranging from exclusively social to exclusively personal identity and that when social identities become more salient than personal identities, the resulting behavior is qualitatively different.[30] Thus, one can be both a German and a European and behave differently in circumstances where one is more salient than the other. Moreover, actors have many "selves" with each related to the interactions with which he or she is involved.[31] Thus, each actor is a unique combination of various characteristics and social locations. As we interact with others we become aware of ourselves as objects (as well as subjects) and come to see, assess, judge and create identities. This interaction among our various selves constitutes a parochial identity.

The significance of one's identity for understanding behavior often depends upon the particular social situation. Actors often know what to expect of each other in particular situations because they know that various types of people behave in typical ways under particular circumstances.[32] In its relations with non-Arab states, for example, leaders

---

29. See Shibutani, "Reference Groups as Perspectives," 562–69.
30. Hogg and Abrams, *Social Identifications*, 25.
31. Mead, *Mind, Self and Society*; Hewitt, *Self and Society*, 77–82.
32. John Hewitt refers to this as "typification." See his *Self and Society*, 122–24. See, also, Alfred Schultz, *On Phenomenology and Social Relations* (Chicago: University of Chicago Press, 1970), 11–122.

of Egypt and Saudi Arabia are often pressured by their domestic populations and their neighbors to "act like an Arab," even though they may have more national interests to promote. In this sense, identities are "situated" within specific contexts. Mead thus argues that the self is complex and differentiated. Once the self arises, it continues to be defined and redefined through interaction.

States represent a variety of societal institutions and practices that gain social meaning when they are contrasted with other types of institutions and practices. States, however, not only represent societies defined by their intrinsic qualities—culture, history, geography, political institutions—but also by their association with broader conceptual social groups that transcend juridical borders.[33] These groups together furnish states with a repertoire of discrete category memberships (social identities) that help to define them in their relations with other states. The mutual recognition by particular states that these social categories are part of their self-concepts, as well as their knowledge that they belong to certain social groups, forms the basis for transnational identities.

Transnational identities—social identities that transcend juridical borders—express a change in the level of abstraction of self-categorization, that is, a shift from a definition of self as unique and distinct to one that perceives the self as part of a conceptual social category or group that transcends state boundaries. Put another way, it expresses a change in the way states make "self-other" distinctions. Political integration is facilitated when definitions of the self are extended to include what were previously considered to be foreign societies. Social identity theory holds that a transformation of identities can occur when actors develop conceptual attachments to selective others through the processes of recategorization, recomparison and reidentification.[34] When a group of states recognize that they share a common set of social characteristics and experiences that define them as a unique group in distinction from other conceptual groups, they have created a transnational identity.

---

33. A social group is defined as two or more actors who share a common identification and perceive themselves to be members of the same social category. See John Turner, "Towards a Cognitive Redefinition of the Social Group," in *Social Identity and Intergroup Relations*, ed., Henri Tajfel (Cambridge: Cambridge University Press, 1982), 15.

34. Henri Tajfel and John Turner, "An Integrative Theory of Intergroup Conflict," in *The Social Psychology of Intergroup Relations*, ed. W. G. Austin and S. Worchel (Monterey, Calif.: Brooks/Cole, 1979), 33–47.

Transnational identities can alter the social environment through which a group of states relate to each other by creating what Mead would call a community of attitudes or "generalized other." These communities develop particular frameworks that inform the members of the appropriate ways of responding to a situation.[35] Thus, the generalized other provides the criteria for self-assessment, reflection, signaling, and interpreting the signals of others. In Meadian terms, states sharing a transnational identity often assume the organized social attitudes of their group (or community) toward the social problems that confront them at any given time. When a community of attitudes develops such that definitions of self eliminate the juridical and geographic borders that separate sovereign states, the foundation for political integration has been laid. The units then come to perceive themselves as the interchangeable exemplars of a social category, rather than only as unique actors. In the extreme, the result is pan-nationalism, a political program that places one's transnational identity above or at least on par with one's parochial identity. This requires all of the following necessary conditions:

First, the units must share a common positive experience of high intensity. Such experiences, such as a war of liberation, tend to create close bonds among the units. The more positive the experience and the higher the intensity and duration, the closer the bonds. Second, the units must share a common relationship to the other units in the system. The more unique and exclusive the relationship, the greater the perception of commonality that distinguishes them as a social group. This means that the units must not only perceive themselves to share this unique relationship, but also be treated this way by the other units in the system. Under these conditions, juridical and political boundaries are broken down.

Third, there must be a high level of positive interdependence between the units such that the political elites perceive their fortunes as linked. Interdependence lowers the conceptual boundaries that are created by juridical borders, and this can help to lead to a broader definition of "self" that moves beyond territorial distinctions. The interdependence must be positive—that is, mutually rewarding—otherwise it could lead to resentment. When a group of actors depend upon each other to satisfy at least one of their primary political needs and achieve

35. Mead, *Mind, Self and Society,* 155–58.

satisfaction from their association, they develop feelings of mutual attraction that strengthens the group.[36]

Fourth, there must be some "reference other" that can provide a political center around which the units can coalesce. This center must embody the transnational identity that forms the basis for a new political community.

While these factors do not guarantee that integration will occur in a given situation, they furnish the permissive conditions, or motivation, that can lead political actors to seek such an outcome. Chance, opportunity and ideational factors also come into play. Without a concept of nationalism, for example, there could be no foundation upon which to build a national state. For this reason, historical analysis is needed to understand how and why the four factors discussed above converge during a particular period. This can be understood when examining the integration of Italy in the nineteenth century.

COMPETING IDENTITIES AND THE ORGANIZATION OF THE PENINSULA

FOR THE FIRST few decades following the conclusion of the Napoleonic wars, few political actors either wanted or expected the creation of a unified state on the Italian peninsula. Under the Vienna system (the European order created at the Congress of Vienna in 1815), the peninsula was populated by independent monarchic states, some of which were tied to the other European powers through dynastic lineage. Lombardy-Venetia was a kingdom within the Austrian empire; the Kingdom of the Two Sicilies was ruled by Bourbon monarchs with ties to France; Modena and Tuscany were ruled by archdukes with dynastic ties to the Hapsburgs. Only the Papal States, which were ruled by the Pope, and Piedmont, which was ruled by the House of Savoy, were governed by monarchs without ties to a European family. From this hodgepodge of competing political units, there was no obvious model for how the peninsula would be organized even if the great powers were to renounce their interest in its future.

To the extent that nationalist feeling existed, it was of a provincial rather than of a cosmopolitan type. This is captured well by Genovese delegate Pareto, who wrote a letter to Lord Castlereagh during the

---

36. Jonathan Turner, Michael Hogg, Oakes S. Reichter, and M. Wetherell, *Rediscovering the Social Group: A Self-Categorization Theory* (New York: Blackwell, 1987).

Congress of Vienna opposing a proposal to merge Piedmont with Genoa:

> [National spirit] certainly could not exist in the amalgamation of two peoples, Genoese and Piedmontese, divided by their character, their habits, and by an invincible antipathy...vain would be the attempt to make them one nation.[37]

This reflected a typical feeling throughout the post-Napoleonic era: few Italians wished to form a unified state.[38] In fact, following his return to Piedmont, King Victor Emmanuel—whose son would later lead a war of independence against Austria—set out to destroy every trace of "Italian" institutions, seeking in essence to de-Italianize his state.[39]

THE 1848 REVOLUTIONS AND THE REDEFINITION OF STATEHOOD

The explanations for the transformation of the peninsula can be found in the social changes that swept Europe during the mid-nineteenth century and the process through which integration occurred. That is, integration developed from an amalgamated security community rather than as a result of economic interdependence, a nationalist uprising, or a cultural revolution. Leading up to the rapid series of events that changed the political map of southern Europe, a transnationalist Italian identity evolved from the following factors: the Congress of Vienna, which had created a shared relationship among the Italian principalities to the rest of Europe; a positive interdependence among democratic leaders in the various states; a common experience during the wars between Lombardy and Austria in 1849 and 1859; and the emulation of Piedmont by the other principalities as their "referent society" embodying pan-Italian ideal.

The permissive cause of integration was the revolutions of 1848. Until that time, there was little resistance to Austrian domination of the northeastern and central peninsula, apart from small conspiracies among the *Carbonari* and other secret societies.[40] 1848, however, saw a

---

37. T. C. Hansard, *The Parliamentary Debates From 1813 to the Present Time*, vol. 29 (London, 1815), 398.

38. David Ward, *1848: The Fall of Metternich and the Year of Revolution* (New York: Weybright and Talley, 1970), 84.

39. Hannah Alice Straus, *The Attitude of the Congress of Vienna Toward Nationalism in Germany, Italy and Poland* (New York: Columbia University Press, 1949), 92.

40. The exception to this was the failed revolutions in 1820, which were directed less against Austria and more in opposition to the monarchies in Naples and Piedmont.

systemic shock that reached every part of Europe, including the peninsula. Beginning in Paris and spreading throughout the continent, there was a widespread series of revolutions and uprisings against the very authorities that provided the foundation for restoration Europe. The European revolutions of 1848 were the culmination of a series of economic, social and political crises. They were diverse and multifaceted, and caused by a number of different factors unique to the period. As a European phenomenon, however, they were not only domestic revolts against kings, princes and emperors; they represented a transnational uprising against the political order established by the Vienna treaties in 1815.[41]

Revolutions occurred in every Italian state except Piedmont, undermining both the institution of monarchy and the dynastic foundations of sovereign authority. The principle aim of most of the revolutionary movements was not integration but to acquire a constitution for each state and to see that it was respected.[42] Dynastic rulers were driven out of the northern Italian states, the Bourbons expelled from the Kingdom of Two Sicilies, and the Pope and his government expelled from the Papal states. A Roman republic was declared. While the revolutions were later defeated by Austrian and French troops, the legitimacy of the Italian princes was badly undermined and their dynastic rights were no longer respected. This provided the permissive condition for integration: the breakdown of traditional forms of sovereign authority, which allowed for a redefinition of the state.

The 1848 revolutions in Lombardy and Venetia were directed mostly against Austrian rule and this ultimately brought the Italian nation into conflict with the Hapsburg state for the first time. Taking advantage of domestic unrest in Austria, revolutionaries overthrew the local administration and temporarily drove Austrian security forces out of Milan. The revolution transformed Lombardy from a dynastic state with ties to the Hapsburgs to a liberal state with ties to other newly formed liberal states on the peninsula. This encouraged the new elites to reevaluate their state's relationships to the other principalities and to the great powers of Europe. As a result, after much debate, the provisional government voted for union with Piedmont, a significant move given their traditional animosity. This can be explained in part by their desire to strengthen their ties to other constitutional regimes.

41. See Ward, *1848*.
42. Delio Cantimori, "Italy in 1848," *in The Opening of an Era, 1848: An Historical Symposium*, ed. Francois Fejto (1948; New York: Howard Fertig, 1966), 119.

Piedmont's constitution was the most progressive on the peninsular, indeed in most of Europe. For the first time, Piedmont was viewed by democrats as the liberal hope of the peninsula. This set the stage for the events of 1849, which I will examine below.

A COMMON RELATIONSHIP TO EUROPE

One of the factors that helped to facilitate the development of a common transnational consciousness on the peninsula was the states' external treatment by the Great Powers of Europe. For almost three-quarters of a century prior to 1848, the Italian principalities shared a unique common relationship to the rest of Europe. Although none of the Great Powers wished to create a unified Italian state, they (and Napoleon before them) treated the Italian principalities collectively as a single administrative unit in building the new order. This was done primarily for the sake of convenience, as it would help to secure a European equilibrium in the south. Rather than approaching each state as an autonomous sovereign unit—as was done with the other secondary states of Europe such as Spain or Belgium—both the French empire and the Great Powers considered the individual states to be part of a broader "Italian question."[43] These perceptions were projected onto the Italian states, making the concept of "Italy" as a political idea both thinkable and a topic for discussion by the European community.[44]

Moreover, Europe's hegemonic states inadvertently contributed to the breakdown of political divisions among the principalities by keeping them internally weak. Had Napoleon and the Great Powers supported the establishment of strong independent Italian monarchies, the political basis for a unified Italian nation would have likely been missing.[45] By keeping the Italian states under Great Power tutelage, the big powers helped to prevent the development of strong state institutions and loyalties among the rulers, elites and population.[46] Thus, when dynastic authority ultimately collapsed in the early 1850s, the new

43. Paul Schroeder, *The Transformation of European Politics, 1763–1848* (Oxford: Clarendon Press, 1994).

44. References to the Italian problem are common in both the primary and secondary literature of this period.

45. This is consistent with Theda Skocpol's thesis that social revolutions are more likely in countries where the state structures are weak. See her *States and Social Revolution* (Cambridge: Cambridge University Press, 1979).

46. Compare this situation to that of the Arab states as discussed by Michael Barnett in "Sovereignty, Nationalism and Regional Order in the Arab State System," *International Organization* 49, no. 3 (summer 1995): 479–510.

authorities could not simply assume the machinery of the state, as had been the case in much of Europe. The state was the monarchy and without the latter the former did not have a strong independent existence. This limited the extent to which political elites could develop strong loyalties to the state.

Consequently, in an ironic twist, the Vienna system itself helped contribute toward the eventual development of a transnational identity among the Italian states. In designating Austria as the sole Great Power responsible for maintaining security and overseeing Italy's economic development, the Great Powers isolated the peninsula both politically and geographically from the rest of Europe. In short, it made the peninsula politically, economically and militarily impenetrable. Thus, a unique relationship developed among the Italian states, that of object rather than participant in the European order. While the other secondary powers, such as Spain, Holland and Portugal were treated as important parts of the Vienna system, the Italian states became objects for securing a European equilibrium. The "self-other" distinction that is often the basis for nationalist identification was in part created by the Congress.

The geographic isolation also helped to facilitate an exclusive form of cooperation among the elites of the principalities. From 1839 through 1847, for example, scientific congresses were held annually in Pisa, Turin, Florence, Padua, Lucca, Milan, Naples, Genoa and Venice. These gatherings brought together scientists and naturalists from every principality. While they were largely scientific in nature, in the words of historian Bolton King, it became "impossible for Italians of different states to come together without giving something of a national complexion to their meetings."[47] That is, since only people from the peninsula attended, the congresses were defined partly by their particularism. Beginning in 1844, the congresses began to elect committees of members representing various states to study such common problems as elementary education, the search for coal deposits, the silk industry, the reintroduction of a uniform metric system, steam power, and deficiency diseases.[48] Besides facilitating cooperative relationships among the principalities on educational, economic and scientific matters, the

47. King, *A History of Italian Unity*, 150.
48. Smith, *The Making of Italy*, 93.

congresses forged a new cultural unity in the peninsula, testifying to the economic and intellectual interdependence of its states.[49]

The 1848 revolutions also helped to create a positive interdependence among republicans and liberals throughout the peninsula. Drawing on each other for support within their own states, the various networks of democratic activists helped to create a transnational community among the educated and elite classes. These networks played an important role in deemphasizing the juridical divisions among the Italian states in favor of ideological solidarity. In the struggle against monarchy, one's democratic credentials were more important than in which state one happened to reside. Ideological solidarity replaced provincial patriotism as their focus of loyalty. As one historian argues, the activists created among themselves a special sense of group solidarity that was built upon a shared intellectual heritage and a common ideology.[50] Democratic movements had existed in every major city within the peninsula since the early 1830s, although until the mid-1940s they tended to remain secretive and isolated from each other. Most of these movements had the dual goal of expelling the Austrians from their states and establishing constitutional systems within them. Many also sought to curb the Church's spiritual and ideological power, a move that was necessary for the creation of a single state on the peninsula.

During the period surrounding the 1848 revolutions, activists within local and regional movements began to make more formal contacts with similar activists in other regions and states.[51] The flow of volunteers from throughout the peninsula to help Piedmont in its war against Austria in 1849 (see below) further developed this network and deemphasized the juridical divisions. All of this culminated in widespread participation in the Lombard Campaign (against Austria), the Five Days in Milan (the Venetian revolution), and the proclamation of the Roman Republic following an insurrection in the Papal states. While these revolutions were eventually defeated, the experiments helped to strengthen the movements for independence and democracy. This would have lasting effects. Spencer Di Scala estimates that as many as 50,000 exiles from these movements migrated to Piedmont.[52]

49. Denis Mack Smith, *Victor Emmanuel, Cavour and the Risorgimento* (London: Oxford University Press, 1971), 3.

50. Clara Lovett, *The Democratic Movement in Italy, 1830–1876* (Cambridge: Harvard University Press, 1982), 9.

51. See Lovett, *The Democratic Movement in Italy*, chap. 5.

52. Spencer Di Scala, *Italy: From Revolution to Republic* (Boulder: Westview, 1995), 98.

Once there, many decided to place independence and unity above republicanism as their immediate goals and helped to influence Piedmontese policy (particularly that of Prime Minister Cavour) concerning
Italy. In sum, as the democratic activists began to act together as Italians, their outlooks became more cosmopolitan. Changing practices
created new identities. This had an important impact on the future political elites in the northern and central regions who would ultimately
win political power.

A COMMON EXPERIENCE: FIGHTING TOGETHER AS ITALIANS

The 1848 revolution in Lombardy necessarily brought that state into
conflict with Austria. By overthrowing the Hapsburg monarch, the
Lombards posed a direct challenge to Austrian rule. Thus, when Austria sent in troops to crush the rebellion, they were acting within their
centuries-old traditional role as protectors of the Lombard monarchy.
The difference this time was not in Austrian behavior but in the reaction by Piedmont, a traditional Austrian ally. If history was any guide,
Piedmont should have been expected to aid Austria in its war against
Milan (the provincial capital of Lombardy). This which would have
helped Piedmont to maintain its hegemony in the region. When the
Lombards appealed to Piedmont for support in the name of Italian
solidarity, however, King Charles Albert was forced to choose between
his conflicting roles as head of the House of Savoy and as the leader of
an Italian state. The King's decision to take up the Lombard's cause
was the first indication that Piedmont would shift its loyalty from dy-
nasticism to nationalism by defending a fellow Italian state. This required a reconception of Piedmontese identity and interest.

Piedmont's behavior was an indication that it would not use strictly
balance-of-power calculations in determining its alliances. Austria's
actions were not a threat either to Piedmont or to its position on the
peninsula. Venetia was legally part of the Austrian empire, an arrangement that had continued for more than three decades. The Austrian campaign against Lombardy was in the spirit of this arrangement.
At the same time, one can not ascribe expansive motives to Piedmont.
Its political elites was ambivalent at best about whether they wished to
challenge Austria's traditional position on the peninsula. In fact, although Lombardy had requested annexation to Piedmont—a move
that would certainly have increased Piedmont's authority in the northern peninsula—the Piedmontese leadership was divided on whether

they should accept it. Charles Albert had seen Piedmont as a state of its own, not to be submerged in a union of other Italian states.[53] Adding Lombardy's territory and population to Piedmont would have meant bringing in an economically backward "foreign" people into its fold, without increasing either its military or political power.

Thus, while the 1848 revolution in Vienna may have provided the means for Piedmont to have challenged Austrian authority it did not provide the motivation. Rather, the revolutions throughout Italy had a significant effect on Piedmont's understanding of itself vis-à-vis the other Italian states. This understanding was reflected in future Prime Minister Cavour's statement to Charles Albert prior to Piedmont's entrance into the war:

> The nation is at war with Austria already. The whole nation is rushing to the succor of the Lombards, the volunteers have crossed the frontiers, our fellow citizens are openly making munitions and sending them to the Milanese.[54]

Charles Albert's response is also illustrative of his changing understandings:

> We, out of love for our common race, understanding as we do what is now happening, and supported by public opinion, hasten to associate ourselves with the unanimous admiration which Italy bestows upon you. Peoples of Lombardy and Venetia...we are now coming to offer you in the latter phases of your fight the help which a brother expects from a brother.[55]

One explanation for this change can be traced to the new role that Piedmont had assumed in the region. As argued above, roles are formed within social settings, always in relation to others.[56] This concept of roles is key to the explanation of Piedmont's behavior in the integration process. As a dynastic state representing the House of Savoy, Piedmont traditionally viewed Austria as an ally against other Italian principalities. After his accession in 1831, Charles Albert argued that Austria was Piedmont's best partner in the legitimist cause against the threat of liberalism.[57] The Piedmontese army had been trained to

53. J. A. S. Grenville, *Europe Reshaped: 1848–1878* (Sussex, England: Harvester, 1976), 47.

54. Smith, *The Making of Italy*, 146.

55. Ibid., 148.

56. Mead, *Mind, Self and Society*, section 18.

57. The legitimist principle stated that dynastic lineage was the only legitimate foundation for sovereign authority on the continent.

fight for the dynasty and the Holy Alliance side-by-side with Austria and had no sympathy for Italy. They loathed the Tricolor (the symbol of Italy).[58] Acting as an Italian state rather than as a dynastic one, however, brought it into conflict with Austria, which was trying to maintain dynastic rule over the northern part of the peninsula.

Several points are illustrative in understanding how Piedmont's identification with "Italy" influenced its choice of allies. First, they were woefully unprepared for war, suggesting that the decision to enter was not preplanned.[59] Militarily is was not a wise decision. Piedmont's interests, however, did not appear to be either dynastic expansion or territorial aggrandizement. Rather, in the words of Cavour, "The moral effect of an opening of hostilities and the relief of Milan would be of more use to the Italian cause than the defeat of a body of five hundred men would injure it."[60]

Second, at a crucial point, instead of concentrating on fighting the war, Charles Albert insisted on holding plebiscites in both Lombardy and Venicia on whether they wished to merge with Piedmont. This move was criticized as a major military blunder by contemporaries and historians alike.[61] While this made little sense from a military point of view, it was crucial if Piedmont was serious about building an amalgamated security community based on national sovereignty. A national state requires the legitimization of the population, something only a plebiscite could confirm.

Third, even after the Italian coalition was defeated in late 1848, Charles Albert resumed the war against Austria in 1849—after the Emperor suppressed the Austrian revolution and rebuilt Austrian power—largely because he was committed to winning Italy's independence and building a unified Italian kingdom. His resumption of the war was on behalf of Italy, not Piedmont.[62] From a purely Piedmontese perspective, resuming the war in support of Lombardy made little sense. From an Italian perspective, however, it was a war of national liberation. To be an Italian meant one had to act like an Italian.

After the peace agreement, Austria had offered to give Piedmont the principality of Parma and a waiver of indemnity if it would modify its

---

58. Cantimori, "Italy in 1848," 119.
59. Edgar Holt, *Risorgimento: The Making of Italy, 1815–1870* (London: Macmillan, 1970).
60. Smith, *The Making of Italy*, 147.
61. Ibid., 149.
62. Holt, *Risorgimento*, 160.

constitution and rejoin the legitimist alliance. King Victor Emmanuel, Charles Albert's son, who assumed the throne upon his father's abdication, refused, saying, "I will hold the tricolor high and firm."[63] He remained loyal to this position even in the face of revolution against a neighboring monarch. Although cabinet minister Gioberti proposed that Piedmont send troops into Tuscany to restore order after the republicans took power in 1849, both the King and cabinet refused, arguing that they could not send Italians to fight Italians. This was a radical departure from the diplomatic history of the Italian states.

The wars of 1848 and 1849 demonstrate several other points about the development of a transnational identity among the sovereign states of Italy. First, prior to the revolutions and war, Piedmont did not see itself as an Italian state. It was only through its participation in the war of independence on behalf of another state—a common experience—that it developed the notion that the war was an Italian one. This presents a good example of how process and interaction can help to create new identities. Second, and somewhat related to the first point, the war against Austria was not aimed at building a united Italian nation. It was purely anti-Austrian, focused on achieving independence for the two northern states. Once the war took on a national character, however, it changed the understandings of the participants. They became Italians by acting as Italians. Mead's "community of attitudes" had been formed, providing a framework from which the political leaders could evaluate the appropriate ways to respond to the situation.

Victor Emmanuel's strong support for the other principalities in his negotiations with Austria highlighted the special relationship that existed among the Italian states and confirmed the House of Savoy as the acknowledged leader of Italy.[64] The final result of the war was to increase the prestige of Piedmont as the leader of all Italy, a phenomenon that would have been unthinkable in almost any previous period in the history of the peninsula. In the years prior to 1848–49, Piedmont had been regarded as a dangerous rival. In fact, previous attempts by other Italian states to involve Austria in a defensive league derived largely from anxiety about Piedmont.[65] The change in Piedmont's perception can be explained by the fact that the other Italian states had begun to

63. King, A History of Italian Unity, vol. 1, 356.

64. Arthur James Whyte, The Evolution of Modern Italy (Oxford: Basil Blackwell, 1944), 85; and Holt, Risorgimento, 163.

65. Stuart Woolf, A History of Modern Italy, 1700–1860: The Social Constraints of Political Change (London and New York: Methuen, 1979), 416.

think of themselves as Italians, with Piedmont thus no longer a dangerous adversary but a leader of a pan-Italian community.

In sociological terms, Piedmont became a positive reference group which embodied the transnational Italian identity. This view was articulated by Tuscan leader Bettino Ricasoli who said, "I want to make Tuscany a province of Piedmont, for that is the only way for her to become a province of Italy.[66] In Milan, where animosity and suspicion toward Piedmont had traditionally been strong, the members of the government peace commission wrote: "Despite our losses, the foundations of free and independent Italy still stand firm in Piedmont, that when conditions of Europe permit us to claim the rights of our common nationality, all Italy may turn to her, as the natural champion of this cause...."[67]

The identification of Piedmont with Italy was particularly appealing to the liberals and republicans who would later assume power in the central principalities. Piedmont was the only state on the peninsula to emerge from the 1848 revolutions and the Austrian war with its constitution intact.[68] Its steadfast defense of the constitution against Austria's wishes lifted Piedmont to first claim on liberal Italy's hope and gratitude.[69] For the liberals, Piedmont was a model state to emulate.

THE CREATION OF AN ITALIAN SECURITY COMMUNITY

The integration of Italy ultimately required all of the sovereign states to cede much of their sovereignty to an abstract concept, Italy. In practical terms, this meant merger with Piedmont. The creation of Italy occurred in four stages, beginning with the construction of an amalgamated security community among the northern and central Italian states. This was a direct outgrowth of fighting together as a single unit against Austria in 1859.

During the summer of that year, Piedmont conspired with France to provoke a war with Austria, hoping to expel the latter from the peninsula. According to the secret agreement, France would support the merger of Lombardy and Venetia with Piedmont into a Kingdom of North Italy, as originally proposed during the 1849 war, and in return Piedmont would cede Nice and Savoy to France. With the support of

---

66. King, *A History of Italian Unity*, vol. 1, 60.
67. Ibid., 360.
68. See Riall, *The Italian Risorgimento*, 14.
69. Whyte, *The Evolution of Modern Italy*, 85; and Holt, *Risorgimento*, 163.

France secured, the Piedmontese leaders reached out to their historical rivals in the name of pan-Italianism. Speaking in terms of a transnational Italian community, Victor Emmanuel made his famous "cry of anguish" speech to parliament, calling for all Italians to fight as one against Austria. Thousands of volunteers from each of the northern and central principalities responded by joining Piedmont's efforts on behalf of Italy.

The war was short and inconclusive, ending with an armistice between France and Austria that did not include leaders from Piedmont. France sold out Piedmont by agreeing to leave Venetia within the Austrian sphere. Echoing a time-honored tradition, the two Great Powers sought to settle the "Italian question" between themselves. This time, however, the situation was different. The participation of volunteers from throughout the peninsula under the command of Piedmont blurred the conceptual boundaries that had previously divided the states and created a new type of security arrangement. The disparate states were not only military allies but also symbiotic partners. Therefore the agreement would be impossible to enforce without the force of arms directed against the entire peninsula.[70]

This became clear when revolutionaries overthrew the ruling monarchs in Tuscany, Parma and Modena. The revolutions were not initially nationalist; they were aimed at toppling discredited dynasties kept in power by Austria.[71] Immediately following the insurrections, however, the political leaders of these states each announced their interest in joining the Piedmont-Lombardy union, much to the disapproval of France.[72] The French-Austrian agreement had called for restoring the dispossessed princes in the central duchies; however, Parma and Tuscany refused to go along with this agreement and announced their union with Piedmont. Their interest in creating this amalgamated security community was in part a recognition that they shared a unique common relationship to the Great Powers and thus their fortunes would rise and fall together.

The rulers of these former duchies then set out to "Piedmontize" their states by unifying their currencies, customs and postal arrangements.[73] The leaders pledged their loyalty to Victor Emmanuel, in effect ceding their sovereignty to a foreign king. Even at this point,

---

70. See Di Scala, *Italy*, 106–10.
71. Smith, *Victor Emmanuel, Cavour, and the Risorgimento*, 203–4.
72. Di Scala, *Italy*, 108–10.
73. Beales, *The Risorgimento and the Unification of Italy*, 128.

Piedmont was unsure whether it wanted to merge with the states of central Italy, as this would have meant the end of the House of Savoy as a political entity. For the monarchy, questions of identity were as important than those of territory. Prior to the war, Cavour had not intended to annex Tuscany; he preferred a united but independent central Italy as an ally against Austria.[74] Thus, Piedmont at first hesitated to accept annexation of the central duchies. As Cavour continued to modernize Piedmont and identify it more closely with Italian aspirations, however, broad support grew for the creation of an Italian state.[75]

Despite grave misgivings, Piedmont could not deny an Italian state entry into its newly formed security community. This was particularly so given the level of sacrifice the central states were willing to make. As pro-unionist Tabarrini argued, "either the Florentines do not know what they are doing or if they do, they are giving the greatest possible proof of self-sacrifice for Italy...the Florentines are committing political suicide."[76]

As a result, Tuscany decided in favor of transnational solidarity over autonomy. Tuscany's decision was followed by annexation movements throughout the central duchies. Much of political foundation for this movement was laid by the National Society, which at the time did not foresee a united Italy.[77] Over time, however, the leaders of the National Society moved from regionalism to pan-Italianism. The nature of their association influenced their understanding of self and interest. The new Italian parliament responded by voting to approve annexation by means of plebiscite of any Italian territory that wished to be part of Italy. The link between the House of Savoy and Piedmont had ended.

Italian integration was not without its opponents. The resistance by traditional regional authorities to integration, and in particular to Piedmont's attempt to build a strong national government, demonstrates how entrenched traditional institutions and regional loyalties were within the peninsula. The strongest opposition came from a competing transnational authority, the Church, which challenged integration both from within and outside the Papal states. Not surpris-

74. J. M. Thompson, *Louis Napoleon and the Second Empire* (New York: Columbia University Press, 1983), 132.
75. Beales, *The Risorgimento and the Unification of Italy*, 128.
76. M. Tabarrini, "Dario 1859–1860," in Smith, *The Making of Italy*, 302.
77. Ibid., 128.

ingly, the Papacy was strongly opposed to the construction of a secular, national state on the peninsula. It not only threatened the loyalty
of Italians toward the Church as a political authority, but also challenged the very existence of the Papacy as a temporal power. One of
the failed alternatives to national integration, promoted by the Neo-
Guelph movement, called for the construction of a transnational
Catholic community centered within the Italian peninsular. To this
end, they proposed uniting Italy into a federation of Catholic states
under the rule of the Pope. While Pope Pio IX had both the moral and
institutional power to enforce its instructions, his refusal to support
the war against Austria at the crucial moment in 1849 forever discredited him and the Papacy as a force for national leadership.[78]

There was also strong opposition from the dynastic rulers who
stood to lose everything from integration. Their loyalties were toward
their transnational families and local monarchic institutions. A national state would not only threaten their local authority, but would
undermine the very legitimacy of dynastic ties as a justification for
rule. They became so discredited after the revolutions of 1848, however, that they held little influence over the political elites. Ultimately,
they succumbed to revolution and by the late 1850s only the Bourbon
rulers in Sicily remained in power.

Finally, there was local and regional resistance to the centralization
of authority, particularly Cavour's attempt to Piedmontize the political and administrative institutions of the former sovereign states. This
move was unpopular in many segments of the educated population and
later served to emphasize rather than undermine regional rivalries and
local resistance. This opposition, however, was strongest after integration, since the new elites who came to power during the crises of 1849–
1859 were generally committed to building a national state.[79]

COOPERATION AND THE LIMITS OF ANARCHY

THE INTEGRATION of Italy demonstrates that under certain conditions, the conceptual boundaries that divide societies can be rede-

---

78. The Pope argued, logically from a Catholic perspective, that he could not sanc-
tion a war of one Catholic country against another.

79. For an excellent account of this resistance, see Lucy Riall, "Elite Resistance to
State Formation: the Case of Italy," in *National Histories and European History*, ed.
Mary Fulbrook (Boulder: Westview, 1993).

fined so that transnational attachments outweigh parochial loyalties. In these circumstances, state power is less important than state identity in distinguishing between friends and enemies. The competitive balance-of-power system that governed the peninsula for almost four centuries was transformed into an amalgamated security community within a relatively short period of time. The principle factor facilitating this transformation was not a change in the distribution of capabilities within the European system, but a change in the identities of the units. As dynastic states changed into liberal ones, legitimate authority became rooted in the population rather than in the royal family. This provided the permissive condition for reevaluating the juridical borders that had separated the various populations.

This suggests several implications for the study of interstate relationships in general and alliances in particular. First, the creation of an amalgamated security community out of a balance-of-power system suggests that there is not a single enduring logic of anarchy that, in the words of Waltz, obtains whether the system is comprised of tribes, nations or even street gangs.[80] Contrary to much of the traditional security literature, states can and have built cohesive security relationships with other states that go beyond expediency and strategic calculation. The study of alliances has been traditionally concerned with the politics of necessity arising out of the balance of power. As a result, interstate security cooperation is largely seen as limited to the creation of institutions whose primary purpose is to enhance state capabilities through combination with others in the face of a defined threat. As Joseph Grieco argues, in an anarchic world where states are forced to emphasize relative gains, states must avoid becoming entangled in complex relationships that could inhibit their ability to pursue state interests.[81]

While this characterization of international politics is useful for understanding the behavior of states in the face of a defined threat, it unnecessarily assumes a set of fixed interests common to all states. Sometimes this assumption is a valid one for evaluating the intentions of state leaders. When state structures are stable and regional or global rivalries are institutionalized, the distinctions between friend and en-

---

80. See Kenneth N. Waltz, "Realist Thought and Neorealist Theory," *Journal of International Affairs* 44, no. 1 (summer 1990): 21–37.

81. Joseph Grieco, "Anarchy and the Limits of Cooperation: A Realist Critique of the Newest Liberal Institutionalism," *International Organization* 42, no. 3 (summer 1988): 485–507.

emy or between partner and competitor can be made on the basis of necessity and political expediency. When the identity of the state changes, however, its interests can no longer be assumed. The transformation of the Italian peninsula from a region of dynastic states to one of liberal states altered the social environment through which the units interacted. The new elites perceived that they shared a common relationship and a positive interdependence and this helped to lead to a consciousness that they constituted an exclusive community. They became Italians.

Second, the study suggests that participation in alliances can not only change state interests, as predicted by liberal institutionalist theory, but also state identity. Piedmont's political elites did not view their country as a primarily Italian nation, nor did they wish to form an integrated Italian state until after they began to fight alongside the other states on the peninsula against what became a foreign enemy. The self-other distinction which is the basis of identity was created during this process. This suggests that NATO may have played a more important role in creating a European identity than has been previously acknowledged.

Third, the article suggests that as important as the balance of power is in helping to determine alliance patterns, it is not a universal factor. Piedmont's behavior during and after the wars of 1849 and 1859 cannot be explained by balance-of-power theories of alliances. Rather, its decision to support its historic rivals against its traditional ally was made on the basis of transnational solidarity with the pan-Italian nation. Similarly, the interests of the principalities were largely framed by the type of states they wished to form, indicating that the identity of the units are indeed relevant in determining the type of security arrangement that develops within a region. Once Piedmont was seen as the embodiment of Italy's aspirations, it changed from a dangerous rival to a trusted ally. Rivalries and distrust were overcome only when the principalities reconceptualized themselves as Italians rather than as Tuscans, Parmans, or Piedmontese. Until this occurred, the political elites did not consider integration to be in their interest.

Finally, the preceding pages suggest that while the concept of anarchy can be useful for explaining some of the barriers to cooperation and systemic cohesion in international affairs, as a theoretical assumption it is too broad for understanding the features and dynamics of an international or regional order. Definitions of self and other can influence and sometimes change the social environment through which states interact without a corresponding change in structure. This supports the constructivist claim that there can be different types of anarchy. Once anarchy becomes a variable rather than a constant condition, we are freed from the assumption that rational egoism is necessarily the starting point of analysis. Thus, there is a greater range of possible security arrangements, and other factors come into play in determining which is ultimately constructed during a particular period. Power is an important factor in understanding behavior, yet it does not provide grounds for purposive or meaningful action, only the means to take action. In some circumstances, states may use power forcibly to attain specific ends at the expense of other states. In other situations, states may use their power to facilitate more cohesive relations with selected states. As a result, power is also indeterminate.

FRENCH TWIST:

FRENCH AND BRITISH NATO POLICIES FROM 1949 TO 1966

MICHAEL SPIRTAS

G ROUP IDENTIFICATION contributes to intimate international cooperation; lack of group identification makes such cooperation
less likely. I apply this social-psychological principle to explain
British and French policies toward the North Atlantic Treaty Organization (NATO). When leaders and their publics perceive their state to be
part of a group of states, they are more likely to favor cooperation
within this group. My argument explains why two relatively similar
countries have followed different policies toward military cooperation,
in particular, why Britain supported cooperation in NATO from 1949 to
1966 (and beyond), and why the French cooperated with NATO in 1949
but withdrew from its coordinated military command in 1966.

Since conflict and cooperation is a widely studied and highly complex subject, I narrow my focus to potential intimate cooperative
agreements. The requirements for intimate international cooperation
differ from other cooperative agreements in their intensity and intru-
siveness upon the states involved. Intimate cooperation involves a high
level of policy coordination in important issue areas that have wide-
ranging effects on the health of the states involved. Alliance cooperation in NATO during the cold war qualifies as intimate because the
states involved pledged to deter and defend one another against attack
in a systemic war. After the growth of nuclear arsenals and missile
technology, this cooperation became even more intimate because the
alliance pledge raised the possibility that deterrence efforts could lead

Michael Spirtas is a fellow at the Center for National Policy and research fellow at U.S.
CREST.

For their assistance, I thank Christopher L. Ball, Frédéric Bozo, Richard K. Betts,
Glenn Chafetz, Charles Cogan, Sheena Singh Danziger, Pierre Façon, Barbara Farn-
ham, Allyson Ford, Philip H. Gordon, Robert Jervis, Helen V. Milner, Dominique
Moïsi, Galia Press, Glenn H. Snyder, Georges-Henri Soutou, Maurice Vaïsse, Geoffrey
Warner, and the anonymous reviewers of *Security Studies*. I also thank the interviewees
listed at the end of the article.

to the devastation of the countries included.[1] States are wary of entering cooperative arrangements which may diminish their freedom of action in the future.

Social psychologists have established that individuals who believe themselves to belong to a common group are more likely to engage in cooperative behavior with other group members than individuals who lack such beliefs.[2] The perception of common group membership enhances the possibility of cooperation. A group is "two or more individuals who share a common social identification of themselves or...perceive themselves to be members of the same social category."[3] Although there are limits to the use of social-psychological insights to understand international relations,[4] there are enough similarities to merit cross-fertilization. State decisionmakers, like the subjects of psychological experiments, think of themselves and their states as belonging to groups.

International group identification is often a relatively long-term process that shapes basic perceptions of other states with respect to their suitability as partners in cooperative agreements. Identity does not switch on and off. Instead, identity shifts are gradual processes that can orient people toward or away from allegiance with a group of states. Some identities can be held stable over decades. Nevertheless, it is important not to take too static a view of identity. Large numbers of people can and do experience identity shifts in short periods of time.[5]

1. An example of nonintimate international cooperation is the creation of free trade zones. Lowering tariffs does have an effect on a state's economy, but the effect is felt primarily through microeconomic mechanisms such as product price levels. In contrast, currency cooperation, which does qualify as intimate cooperation, requires that states renounce powerful macroeconomic policy tools that affect the entire economy at once, and leave the state's economy more vulnerable to circumstances in other states than is the case with tariff cooperation.

2. Harvey A. Hornstein, "Promotive Tension: The Basis of Prosocial Behavior from a Lewinian Perspective," *Journal of Social Issues* 28, no. 3 (1972): 191–218; Harvey A. Hornstein, *Cruelty and Kindness: A New Look at Aggression and Altruism* (Englewood Cliffs: Prentice-Hall, 1976), esp. chap. 7; John C. Turner "Towards a Cognitive Redefinition of the Social Group," in *Social Identity and Intergroup Relations*, ed. Henri Tajfel (Cambridge: Cambridge University Press, 1982); John C. Turner, "Social Categorization and Social Discrimination in the Minimal Group Paradigm," in *Differentiation between Social Groups*, ed. Henri Tajfel (London: Academic Press, 1978).

3. Turner, "Towards a Cognitive Redefinition of the Social Group," 15.

4. See Siegfried Streufert and Susan C. Streufert, "The Development of Internation Conflict," in *Psychology of Intergroup Relations*, ed. Stephen Worchel and William G. Austin (Chicago: Nelson-Hall Publishers, 1986).

5. Deutsch, Karl W. Deutsch et al., *Political Community in the North Atlantic Area: International Organization in the Light of Historical Experience* (New York: Greenwood, 1957), 12.

Group identification affects behavior significantly enough to be considered an important variable, and it can change enough to explain policy changes. Such changes do not occur every day, but they do occur and have important effects on our behavior. Group identities are likely to change more often when current group loyalties are relatively weak. The faint-hearted are the most likely to change their minds. Those that are deeply devoted to a group identity are unlikely to be swayed by late-breaking events or newly discovered facts.

To adapt the concept of group identity formation to international relations, I devise a method to measure the relationship between the perceived similarities within a potential group and within other potential groups.[6] Since group formation is an inherently social process, this paper examines the context in which a potential group member finds herself. Group identities only become salient when they are accessible to potential group members and when they fit the potential group members.[7]

Accessibility is a necessary condition for the creation of group identity. If an identity is not available in the perceiver's environment, the perceiver will be unable to adopt that identity. One cannot be what one is not familiar with. It makes no sense to be a devotee of Beethoven if one has never heard his work; or to be a Muslim if one has never seen a mosque. Proximity can make an identity accessible by decreasing the distance between the perceiver and the identity.[8] Technological advances in travel and communications have affected how people perceive distance, so perceptions of proximity have changed over time.[9] I measure proximity with travel and telecommunications data. High

---

6. John C. Turner refers to this as the metacontrast principle: "any collection of individuals in a given setting is more likely to categorize themselves as a group (become a psychological group) to the degree that the subjectively perceived differences between them are less than the differences perceived between them and other people (psychologically) present in the setting (i.e. as the ratio of intergroup to intragroup differences increases)" (John C. Turner, *Rediscovering the Social Group: A Self-Categorization Theory* [Oxford: Basil Blackwell, 1987], 51–52)

7. Penelope Oakes, "The Salience of Social Categories," in Turner, *Rediscovering the Social Group*, 126–32.

8. See Turner, "Towards a Cognitive Redefinition of the Social Group," 25; and Hornstein, "Promotive Tension," 202–3.

9. Daniel Bell, *The Cultural Contradictions of Capitalism* (New York: Basic Books, 1976), 100–101; and Deutsch et al., *Political Community and the North Atlantic Area:*, 51–54. Also see Karl W. Deutsch, *Nationalism and Social Communication: An Inquiry into the Foundations of Nationality* (New York: Technology Press of the Massachusetts Institute of Technology and John Wiley & Sons, 1953), 16; and Bruce M. Russett, *Power and Community in World Politics* (San Francisco: W. H. Freeman, 1974), 331.

volumes of traffic and telecommunications data show a high level of interaction between states.

Accessibility alone is not enough for a group identity to develop, however. Familiarity often breeds contempt. In addition to being accessible, an identity must fit its owner to be adopted. There must be some match between the perceiver and the group. Three factors can contribute to the fit of a particular identity. First, perception of a common affinity can bind people together.[10] I measure this factor with public opinion polls. Favorable responses to poll questions about another state indicate a sense of common affinity. Second, the existence of a common threat can also bind people together. If two or more countries perceive a common threat, they are likely to perceive themselves as a group with a shared interest in fending off the danger.[11] I measure common threat by surveying statements by state decisionmakers about perceived threats to their state. When state elites agree about the tangibility of a menacing state or group of states, a common threat exists. Third, idea convergence contributes to fit a group identity to a perceiver.[12] People like people who share their opinions. I measure idea convergence by examining policy debates. Decisionmakers demonstrate idea convergence when they agree about the end goal of a particular policy and the proper means to achieve this end.

In addition to considering group identity, I examine another variable: external pressure. External pressure can contribute to cooperation by highlighting the contribution that other states may be able to provide to an embattled state. High levels of external pressure can make cooperation less likely if the threatened state adopts an isolationist stance, and eschews help from others. If state elites feel that there are no acceptable potential partners, they may choose isolation, even in

10. See, Alexander Wendt, "Collective Identity Formation and the International State," *American Political Science Review* 88, no. 2 (June 1994): 389–90; Wendt cites Barry Buzan, "From International System to International Society: The English School Meets the American Theories," *International Organization* 47, no. 3 (summer 1993): 327–52; and John G. Ruggie, "Continuity and Transformation in the World Polity: Toward a Neorealist Synthesis," in *Neorealism and Its Critics*, ed. Robert O. Keohane (New York: Columbia University Press, 1986), 131–57. For a social-psychological perspective on common affinity and group formation, see Jacob M. Rabbie and Murray Horwitz, "Arousal of Ingroup-Outgroup Bias by a Chance Win or Loss," *Journal of Personality and Social Psychology* 13, no. 3 (November 1969): 269–77.

11. Arnold Wolfers, *Discord and Collaboration: Essays on International Politics* (Baltimore: Johns Hopkins University Press, 1962), 27–29.

12. Wendt, "Collective Identity Formation," 389; Virginia Hensley and Shelley Duval, "Some Perceptual Determinants of Perceived Similarity, Liking, and Correctness," *Journal of Personality and Social Psychology* 34, no. 2 (August 1976): 159–68; and Deutsch et al., *Political Community and the North Atlantic Area*, 46–50.

dire times. When external threats are high, cooperation is still not a given. When external pressure is low, states are less constrained and have more leeway to pursue secondary interests. Cooperation decisions will not be constrained in one way or another.

To measure external pressure, I examine means that could potentially harm a state. In military issues arms buildups, troop deployments and belligerent policy statements and actions from foreign governments constitute external pressure upon a state. The careful reader will note that external pressure is similar to the level of common threat, which affects the accessibility of a group identity. Common threat refers to how previous and current threats contribute to the group identity process, while external pressure refers only to currently perceived threats. Previous and current levels of external pressure may contribute to group identity by enhancing perceptions of common threat, while current external pressure may or may not contribute to cooperation. A gradually increasing perception of threat can contribute to cooperation both by (1) increasing the accessibility of a particular group identity, which raises the salience of the identity; and (2) raising the necessity for cooperation. The first instance refers to common threat, the second to level of external pressure.

HYPOTHESES

WE CAN DRAW several specific hypotheses to show how group identity and external pressure interact to determine whether or not a state will choose to cooperate with others.

If group identity is high and external pressure is low, a state will engage in voice negotiation. A state engages in voice negotiation when it would like to cooperate, but vehemently insists that the cooperative agreement be shaped according to its preferences. The state will adjust its policies, which is consistent with our definition of cooperation, but will insist that the cooperative agreement corresponds closely to its preferences. Since external pressure is low, the state is not compelled to cooperate to counter a threat. In addition, high group identity makes it likely that decisionmakers will take the view that state interests are best served by cooperating within the group. Although some tension between the desire to cooperate and the desire to maximize state interests may exist, it will probably be resolved by remaining in the group. The state will still have to adjust its policies as part of the cooperative agreement, which will lead some groups within the state to argue that the cooperative agreement constitutes an unacceptable loss of policy autonomy. Policymakers will defend their decision to cooperate by arguing that state interests are best served by staying within the group, and that the state will enjoy more autonomy by working with the group rather than leaving it and facing the international environment alone.

If both group identity and external pressure are high, states will be highly constrained to cooperate with others. Policymakers will be likely to see cooperation as imperative to state interests, and will agree to cooperate even when the terms of cooperation are less than ideal for the state. They will argue that the importance of countering the external pressure outweighs the need for an ideal agreement. This is an example of submissive cooperation.[13] State leaders will go along with other group members even if the agreement is not the best possible one for their state, and will practice diffuse reciprocity in negotiations with their partners.[14]

If group identity and external pressure are low, a state will only choose to enter a cooperative agreement with others if the agreement is highly compatible with the state's interests. State leaders will pursue a unilateral policy just as much as they will seek to cooperate with other states. Policymakers will hold out for concessions during international negotiations and, if these concessions are not forthcoming, they will not cooperate. I call this type of behavior acquisitive negotiation. Instead of going along with the agreement if it is diffusely reciprocal, these state leaders will insist on specific reciprocity and will guard their interests closely. Because group identity is low, other states do not appear to be attractive partners. Owing to low external pressure, acquisitive states will not be constrained to cooperate. Even if they cooperate, they will be more likely to use the agreement to advance their particular interests than for the good of the group as a whole. Concessions to the other cooperators will be minimal.

If group identity is low and external pressure is high, a state will be unlikely to cooperate with others. Policymakers will likely see cooperative agreements as hindrances to coping with the pressure rather than an

---

13. Arthur Stein argues that when states face common aversions, they are playing a coordination game. See his "Coordination and Collaboration: Regimes in an Anarchic World," *International Organization* 36, no. 2 (spring 1982): 299–324.

14. On the concept of diffuse reciprocity see Robert O. Keohane, "Reciprocity in International Relations," *International Organization* 40, no. 1 (winter 1986): 1–27.

effective way of countering it. States in this sector will *exit* rather than cooperate. Policymakers will argue that the state is better off on its own than in a group. The high level of external pressure makes the state's interests clear, and the low level of group identity enhances the differences between the state's interests and those of the would-be group.

Table 1

NEGOTIATION, COOPERATION, AND NONCOOPERATION

		External Pressure	
		Low	High
Group identity	Low	Acquisitive negotiation	Exit noncooperation
	High	Voice negotiation	Submissive cooperation

Current efforts to explain international cooperation require assistance. Neorealist explanations often contain unspecified theories of the domestic sources of cooperation.[15] Explanations that focus on the role of domestic institutions and ideas cannot show why a state might cooperate at one time and not another.[16] We need an explanation that can illuminate the process of preference formation, that can show how preferences can change over time, and that can be applied to more than one case.

15. Helen V. Milner, "International Theories of Cooperation Among Nations: Strengths and Weaknesses," *World Politics* 44, no. 3 (April 1992): 466–96; Alexander Wendt, "The Agent-Structure Problem in International Relations Theory," *International Organization* 46, no. 2 (spring 1992): 335–70. For an example of a realist explanation of European monetary integration, see Joseph M. Grieco, "State Interests and Institutional Rule Trajectories: A Neorealist Interpretation of the Maastricht Treaty and European Economic and Monetary Union," *Security Studies* 5, no. 3 (spring 1996): 261–306. For a modified neorealist interpretation of alliance formation, see Stephen M. Walt, *The Origins of Alliances* (Ithaca: Cornell University Press, 1987).

16. For an explanation of NATO that focuses on common ideals, see Thomas Risse-Kappen, "Collective Identity in a Democratic Community: The Case of NATO," in *The Culture of National Security: Norms and Identity in World Politics*, ed. Peter Katzenstein (New York: Columbia University Press, 1996).

Constructivists argue that the formation of group identities affects the likelihood of cooperation. They urge us to examine the strategies and positions of the players, as well as the intersubjective understandings that influence players' calculation of their interests.[17] It is not enough, however, for political scientists to suggest that group identity formation influences cooperation. I show how group identities form and how that process affects cooperation decisions.

THE PUZZLES: FRANCE, GREAT BRITAIN
AND THE NORTH ATLANTIC TREATY ORGANIZATION

E VEN HERCULES would have balked at the labors facing French leaders in the aftermath of the Second World War. The French sought not only to rebuild a country utterly devastated by war and occupation, but to rebuild French international influence. French goals of economic reconstruction and global resurgence were probably contradictory.[18] Economic recovery would be difficult enough, requiring enormous political will to inspire a war-weary populace to rebuild a broken land. The reestablishment of French political leadership on the world stage, however, would require the use of scarce resources. Nevertheless, the French were determined to pursue both tasks. Even General Charles de Gaulle realized from his wartime experiences that strength of personality could only achieve limited results. De Gaulle was outraged at not being invited to the Yalta conference, and refused to meet Franklin D. Roosevelt during the American president's return trip from the meeting.[19] French suspicions of their marginalization were confirmed by their exclusion from Potsdam and Dumbarton Oaks as well.

The French faced other contradictions in the postwar world. France would have to build a different relationship with a divided and ruined

17. For studies of cooperation based on game theory, see Kenneth A. Oye, ed., *Cooperation Under Anarchy* (Princeton: Princeton University Press, 1986). For constructivist modifications, see Wendt, "Collective Identity Formation and the International State," 390–91; and Jonathan Mercer, "Anarchy and Identity," *International Organization* 49, no. 2 (spring 1995): 229–52. Wendt uses the word "collective" the way I use the word "group." I prefer the latter because it emphasizes the contribution of the social psychologists and because it avoids jargon.

18. Wolfram Hanrieder and Graeme P. Auton, *The Foreign Policies of West Germany, France, and Britain* (Englewood Cliffs: Prentice-Hall, 1980), 292.

19. Rene Girault, "The French Decision-Makers and their Perception of French Power in 1948," in *Power in Europe?* ed. Josef Becker and Franz Knipping (Berlin: W. de Gruyter, 1986), 47.

Germany. In addition, the French discovered threats to their newly found independence. Despite a clear inclination not to reinforce the division of the world into two camps led by the United States and the Soviet Union, the French would choose to join the United States and the United Kingdom in a Western anticommunist coalition. The Soviet threat entailed the possibility of reoccupation, but the French also perceived the United States to be a threat to their independence. At the same time, French opposition to colonial independence movements in North Africa and East Asia would inevitably draw resources away from efforts to increase French independence. The French faced these obstacles with weak Fourth Republic governments that did not often outlast the political challenges of the day. Beset by difficulties on all sides, the French rose to meet the challenges of the postwar world.

French postwar security policy presents a puzzle in need of a solution. The French were able to bolster their security by engaging the United States in NATO, and by influencing NATO policy to embrace the doctrine of forward deployment of troops. How the French were able to influence the establishment of such a favorable alliance despite their weakened position following the Second World War constitutes one puzzle. Other puzzles arise from French behavior within the alliance. Despite receiving this security assistance, in addition to generous economic aid, the French were somewhat wary of their benefactors. After proposing the European Defense Community (EDC), a collaborative approach to ensuring West European security, the French destroyed their own creation, refusing to ratify the EDC treaty. Why did the French propose the EDC only to reject it? French travails continued throughout the 1950s, and so do the puzzles that arise from their policies. Despite French and British partnership during the Suez debacle, for example, the French drew considerably different lessons from the misadventure than the British did. The British resolved to increase their influence by working quietly with the United States, while French dissatisfaction with their influence within the alliance led to formal proposals for alliance reform. When the French were not satisfied with the reaction to these proposals, they began a gradual withdrawal from key alliance structures, denying that doing so could potentially jeopardize French security. Despite oft-repeated and well-justified fears of Soviet invasion, fueled by memories of other invasions of French territory, the French placed their position within NATO in jeopardy by withdrawing from its integrated military command. The twists and turns of French alliance policy from 1949 to 1966 present a number of interesting cases to which I can apply my hypotheses. I will attempt to explain four different cases: (1) the creation of NATO; (2) the EDC debacle; (3) Suez, Sputnik, and de Gaulle's tripartite memorandum; and (4) de Gaulle's decision to withdraw from NATO's integrated military command.

Like France, Great Britain attempted to restore its international power position after the Second World War while recovering from the war. When the British realized that the United States and the Soviet Union would be the only two superpowers, they adopted another goal: to become the closest ally of the United States, and to maintain this position. If the United Kingdom could no longer shape international politics unilaterally, it could still attempt to exert power indirectly by influencing U.S. policies. This would require that U.S. policymakers think of the British as their closest partners, ahead of other states. Implementing this strategy required that Britain prevent other states from coming between it and the United States, and the British were willing to take such steps, especially with respect to the French.

The British maintained the view that they would be best off by remaining close to the United States. This view arose from a strong sense of belonging to a North Atlantic group of states, particularly by identifying with the United States, the leader of this particular group. Many have written about the importance of the "special relationship" between the United Kingdom and the United States.[20] It is not surprising that the United Kingdom sought close partnership with the United States. The two states had shown the ability and willingness to cooperate with one another in the past, and close cooperation allowed the two states to play key roles in winning the Second World War. The post–Second World War relationship continued the past trend.

Despite this continuity, however, it was far from given that the United Kingdom would seek intimate cooperation with the United States in the post–Second World War era. Prior to the war the United Kingdom ranked among the greatest of world powers, and even after the war some placed the British alongside the United States and the Soviet Union.[21] Nevertheless, soon after the war it became apparent that the British would have to adjust to a lesser international role than

20. For just a few examples, see John Baylis, *Anglo-American Defense Relations 1939–1984: The Special Relationship* (New York: St. Martin's, 1984), esp. xiv–xv; and William Roger Louis and Hedley Bull, eds., *The 'Special Relationship'* (Oxford: Clarendon, 1986).

21. William T. R. Fox, *The Superpowers: The United States, Britain and the Soviet Union and Their Responsibility for Peace* (New York: Harcourt and Brace, 1954).

they had previously enjoyed. Earlier episodes of U.S.-U.K. cooperation generally featured the British in a superior or at least equal position with respect to the United States, but post–Second World War relations between the two countries assumed a different dynamic, with the United States in the dominant role. Decline cannot be easy to accept. It was far from obvious that the British would choose to work under their former colony rather than seek an alternative.

Notwithstanding this difficulty, the British sought intimate cooperation with the United States, initiating talks leading to the North Atlantic Pact and remaining a vital NATO member to this day. This is not to imply that Anglo-American relations were always good during this era, however. The Suez crisis and the Skybolt controversy caused friction (see later in this article). To understand British policy toward the North Atlantic community, we should unearth the underlying supports of British group identification, and examine how it interacted with external pressure to influence British foreign policy.

GROUP IDENTIFICATION

ACCESSIBILITY

Despite considerable gaps in half-century-old data, enough travel data exist to support some analysis of accessibility. French travel to selected North Atlantic area countries increased substantially from 388,695 in 1948 to 998,937 in 1949.[22] Along with the number of Allied troops that had been stationed in France at the end of the war, the North Atlantic identity was accessible to the French. As the French recovered from the devastation of the war, they also increased their proximity to North Atlantic area countries, with French travel to these countries increasing to 5,518,966 in 1966. The French withdrawal from NATO's integrated military command did not result from lack of contact between the French and their allies. If we separate French travel to North America from French travel to West Europe, we can see that

---

22. Travel data come from various editions of the *UN Statistical Yearbook* (New York: United Nations Statistical Office). The numbers refer to trips taken. I use raw numbers, even when comparing British and French travel, because the populations of both countries are almost equal during this period. For example, the populations of Britain and France, respectively, in 1966 were 54,643,000 and 49,184,000. If I were to make comparisons using travel data (and other data that is sensitive to the number of people in a state) between states with different populations, it would be necessary to present travel as a percentage of the total population.

the French were less proximate to North America than they were to Europe. French travel to North America did increase from 35,016 in 1949 to 75,804 in 1966, but as a percentage of total French population the travel might not have had a large effect on the country as a whole. The level of accessibility of the North Atlantic identity to France becomes clearer in comparison to British accessibility to the identity. From 1948 to 1949 British travel to selected North Atlantic countries almost doubled, increasing to 1,175,678 from 631,582. British travel to these countries increased to 2,659,702 in 1966. While the British had not yet reached the level where they would out-travel the French in Europe, British proximity to the North Atlantic during this period was quite good. It is interesting to note that the British report almost three times as much travel to North America as the French did in 1949 (92,584 compared to 35,016). As a proportion of the population, even British travel to North America is not a large figure, but this disparity between the British and the French proximity to North America, especially to the United States, the most important NATO member, had implications on their identifications with the North Atlantic group.

Accessibility is a necessary condition for group identification, and its importance in the cases should not be denied. Without accessibility, the identities would not be available for adoption. Despite the comparatively low level of French travel to North America in 1949–66, there was enough contact between the French and the North Atlantic identity to allow the necessary conditions for group identification.

FIT: COMMON AFFINITY

Polls conducted in 1949–66 allow a rough measurement of French and British common affinity with the North Atlantic group in this period. Public opinion data show that the French displayed positive attitudes toward the United States in 1949. The French were grateful for U.S. financial assistance, and supported the presence of American troops in France. This indicates a fairly high level of common affinity, which aided NATO's formation.[23] In the 1950s, however, French perceptions of common affinity faded as the French began to chafe at U.S. influence

23. *Sondages, Revue Française de l'Opinion Publique* 15, no. 2 (1953): 7. These results are from a 1950 poll, after the French signed the North Atlantic Pact, so French entrance into the pact could have inflated these figures. Other French opinion data at this time are indicative of French opinion before 1949, but this poll gives an accurate indication of French regard for the Americans and British prior to the establishment of the North Atlantic Pact.

FIGURE 1
BRITISH TRAVEL BY DESTINATION

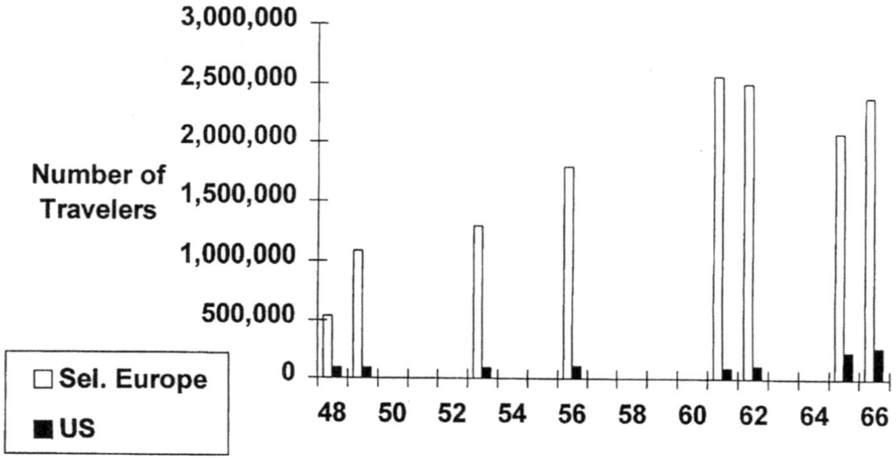

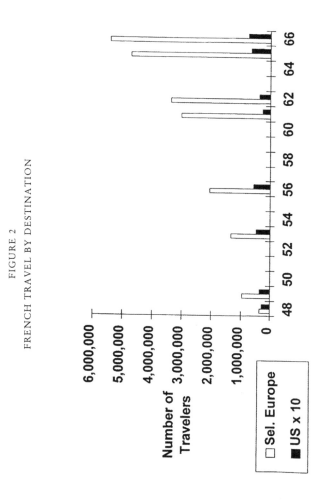

FIGURE 2

FRENCH TRAVEL BY DESTINATION

over French policy.[24] The French saw the United States as inexperienced in foreign policy and obsessed with communism. While support for U.S. troops in France remained high, the perception of common affinity declined to a moderate level in the mid-1950s.[25] As time passed, the perception of common affinity dropped further. In 1963 a majority of French respondents expressed the desire that their country work with Europe independently of the United States.[26] The drop in French perceptions of sharing a common affinity with the North Atlantic community corresponds well with increasing French intransigence toward intimate cooperation within that group.

One might argue that this trend in the public opinion data reflects Gaullist policy choices instead of influencing them. There is probably some truth to this. The French public, for example, initially disapproved of de Gaulle's withdrawal from the integrated military command, but they eventually approved of the move.[27] Still, this consideration does not weaken my account of the influence of group identification on state policy for two reasons. First, even though leaders of democratic states may follow policies that are not immediately supported by their publics, such policies often are rooted in more fundamental sources consistent with public opinion not always captured by opinion polls. Decisionmakers may make unpopular choices, but without some undergirding of support, which is present in the French NATO case, such leaders will not remain in office for long. Second, just as group identification affects state policy, reciprocal effects are likely as well. This makes analysis difficult, but reality is often complicated. The question becomes whether the reciprocal interaction between policy and group identification prohibits the use of group identification to explain policy. I contend that this is not the case. Knowing that policy can affect group identification, which in turn may eventually affect future policies, indicates that the considerations of group identification in this book are policy relevant and should be taken into account by astute decisionmakers.

---

24. Michel Winock, "Les Attitudes des Français face à la Présence Américaine (1951–1967)," in *La France et l'OTAN 1949–1996*, ed. Maurice Vaïsse, Pierre Mélandri and Frédéric Bozo (Armées: Éditions Complexe, 1996), 323–30.

25. *Sondages*, respectively, 24, 28, 39, and 9; also see *Sondages* 18, no. 3, (1956): 35; and *Sondages* 20, no. 1 (1958): 46.

26. *Sondages*, no. 1 (1963): 94.

27. Jean-Paul Brunet, "Le Retrait de la France de l'OTAN: La Scène Intérieure," in Vaïsse et al., *La France et l'OTAN 1949–1996*, 394.

In contrast to the French experience, the British reported relatively high levels of common affinity from 1949 to 1966. The close U.S.-U.K. relationship during the Second World War undoubtedly contributed to sentiments that the two countries would continue to be bound together in the new era. Polling data from the 1950s is consistent with this view.[28] The high perception of common affinity continued into the cold war, even during the midst of the Suez crisis, when 77 percent of British citizens polled noted that Britain's basic interests were either very much or fairly well in agreement with the basic interests of the United States.[29] This figure dropped slightly, to 74 percent, in 1962, but continued to demonstrate a high level of common affinity. High common affinity continued into the mid-1960s, illustrated nicely by the 56 percent of British respondents who picked the United States as Britain's "best friend."[30] Constantly high common affinity helps explain constant British identification with the North Atlantic group during this period, and the mostly supportive stance of British NATO policy from 1949 to 1966.

FIT: COMMON THREAT

In the aftermath of the Second World War, the French continued to view Germany as a threat. The Soviet Union, however, began to emerge as an unambiguous menace as Stalin's expansionist intentions became clear. Soviet obdurateness over the future status of Germany in general and the Saar in particular convinced the French that it would not be possible to play a role independent of the United States and the West, which pushed the French toward the North Atlantic group.[31] Signs of Soviet belligerence such as the Prague coup and the Berlin blockade firmly established the Soviets as a common threat to the North Atlantic community.[32] The French soon joined the British in urging the United States to take a more active role in European secu-

28. Compare British views of the U.S. to British views of the Soviet Union and China in Richard L. Merritt and Donald J. Puchala, *Western European Perspectives on International Affairs: Public Opinion Studies and Evaluations* (New York: Praeger, 1968), 244, 246, 248.
29. Ibid., 254–55.
30. George H. Gallup, ed., *The Gallup International Public Opinion Polls: Great Britain*, vol. 2, *1965–1975* (New York: Random House, 1976), 789.
31. For Bidault's impressions, see letter from Bidault to Auriol from Moscow, 10 Avril 1947, Archives Auriol, 552 AP, Carton 63, Archive Nationale (hereafter AN).
32. Grosser, *The Western Alliance*, 85; Grosser, *La IVe République*, 224.

rity.[33] Despite Bidault's and other French officials' perception of the Soviets as a threat, other French policymakers, such as Auriol, held a more benign view of the Soviets and urged that France assume a neutral role.[34] Because of this split within French foreign policy circles, I code French perception of the Soviets as a common threat as moderate during the formation of the alliance.

The French continued to see the Soviets as a moderate threat to the North Atlantic group during the early 1950s. The Korean War and insurrection in Indochina occurred in the East, yet both events fueled fears of Soviet adventurism to the West as well. The expanding reach of Soviet atomic power contributed to French concerns. Over the decade the French continued to perceive the Soviets as a threat.[35] The Soviet repression of Hungary and the second Berlin crisis did little to hinder this view. The turning point in French perception of common threat came after the Cuban missile crisis, an episode where the French demonstrated firm support for U.S. policy.[36] Despite this show of alliance solidarity, after the crisis the French perception of the Soviet threat declined significantly. Like many others, the French viewed the crisis as a defining moment, a point in time where the Soviets had shown that they were not willing to risk open war to advance their aims. Though the French did not view the Soviets as a benign international force after Cuba, they no longer viewed the Soviet Union as a common threat that menaced the North Atlantic community during the 1960s. This decline in the French perception of the Soviets as a common threat contributed to a decrease in French identification with the North Atlantic group, fueling their eventual decision to withdraw from the integrated military command.

Some might argue that my measurement of French perception of common threat is colored by French justification of their policies, that the French downplayed the Soviet threat and questioned the credibility of the U.S. commitment to justify their intransigence within NATO and their eventual withdrawal from the integrated military command. This may be true to an extent. Public opinion data and archival sources,

33. Georges Bidault, *Resistance: The Political Autobiography of Georges Bidault*, trans. Marianne Sinclair (London: Weidenfeld & Nicolson, 1967), 155–56.
34. Letter from Auriol to Georges Bidault, 4 Mars 1947, Archives Auriol, 552 AP, Carton 63, AN.
35. *Sondages* 20, no. 1 and 2 (1958): 53.
36. Maurice Väisse, "Une hirondelle ne fait pas la printemps. La France et la crise de Çuba," in *L'Europe et la Crise de Cuba*, ed. Maurice Väisse (Paris: Armon Colin Éditeur, 1993), 89–107.

however, provide two different sources that are untainted by the need to justify French policy, as memoirs and public elite statements often are. My views on threat perception are based on all four types of sources, and should be consistent with other scholarly views on the subject.

The British perception of the Soviets as a common threat contrasts with the French view. While the Chiefs of Staff of the military services were less than obsessed with the Soviet threat in the years immediately after the Second World War, the Foreign Office grew increasingly wary of the Soviet Union as postwar conferences became increasingly confrontational.[37] Even Bevin, who had hoped to work with the Soviets, became disillusioned with the former ally and led the drive, both within the British government and in international circles, that resulted in the formation of NATO.[38] After the creation of the alliance, the British continued to perceive long-term Soviet goals as hostile to the North Atlantic group, even if there was little likelihood of imminent attack. This perception continued throughout the 1950s, as Stalin's death and Khrushchev's denunciation of Stalin yielded little change in Soviet international behavior, and into the early 1960s, as Macmillan argued that the Soviets were in the midst of a political offensive.[39]

While the British perceived more of a Soviet threat during the 1950s than the French did, the divergence between British and French views becomes most evident after the Cuban missile crisis. As I noted above, the French viewed the crisis as a cold war benchmark beyond which the Soviets no longer appeared to be the menace that they had been earlier. The British did perceive less of a Soviet threat after the Cuban crisis than before, but not to the same extent as the French. Unlike the French, the British never seriously entertained the idea that they could forge a new relationship with the Soviets. For the British, the Soviets continued to embody a common threat, albeit to a lesser degree, during the first half of the 1960s.

---

37. John Baylis, *The Diplomacy of Pragmatism: Britain and the Formation of NATO, 1942–1949* (Kent, Ohio: Kent State University Press, 1993). For a Foreign Office view of the Soviets as a common threat to the North Atlantic community, see C. F. A. Warner, Report, "The Soviet Campaign Against this Country and our Response to It," Public Records Office (hereafter PRO), FO 371/56832 Soviet Union 1946.

38. For an indication of Bevin's thinking, see Memorandum by the Secretary of State for Foreign Affairs, 5 January 1948, "Review of Soviet Policy," PRO, CAB 129 23, CP (48) 7.

39. Harold Macmillan, *At the End of the Day 1961–1963* (London: Macmillan, 1973), 142.

FIT: IDEA CONVERGENCE

In the years following the Second World War a softening of the French position toward Germany created additional convergence between the French and their British and American counterparts. Nevertheless, the EDC controversy illustrates how French diverged from those of their allies. The French sought British membership in the EDC, but when the British refrained from complete membership in the organization, the French began to fear that establishing a European Army would lead to American and British detachment from continental Europe, a fear which fueled the eventual French refusal to ratify the EDC Treaty.[40] French idea divergence from their allies increased both during and after the Suez crisis. The French decision to plan the military raid angered the Eisenhower administration, and after American pressure forced the French to withdraw from Egypt the French increasingly questioned NATO. The United States and France subsequently differed over the French nuclear force and U.S. intervention in the Middle East and Far East.

Debates over alliance nuclear strategy during the early 1960s deepened French differences with their allies. Instead of viewing the flexible response strategy as a realistic step in the evolution of a credible nuclear deterrent, the French viewed McNamara's proposal as tacit acknowledgment of American unwillingness to place its own population at risk.[41] The gulf between U.S. and French nuclear strategy had practical implications. Just as the United States embraced counterforce targeting of Soviet military capability, allowing for a variety of responses to Soviet aggression, the French were advocating countervalue targeting of Soviet population centers. Some French advocated using their nascent nuclear force to trigger the U.S. force should the Americans

40. Letter from Massigli to Parodi, 18 Mars 1949, Ministére des Affairs Étrangères (hereafter MAE), PA-AP 217, Papiers Massigli, vol 100, 101, 102 (microfilm).
41. As early as 1953 Pierre Gallois met with de Gaulle to lecture him on the unreliability of the U.S. deterrent and the need for an independent French nuclear capability (Gallois, interview with author, Paris, February 1966). There was a spirited debate in France over flexible response. For the standard argument against flexible response, see Pierre Gallois, *The Balance of Terror: Strategy for the Nuclear Age* (Cambridge: Houghton Mifflin, 1961); for a critique of Gallois and a defense of flexible response, see Raymond Aron, *The Great Debate: Theories of Nuclear Strategy*, trans. Ernst Pawel (Garden City: Doubleday, 1965), chap. 3. For a more detailed discussion of French opposition to flexible response than the one in this paragraph, see Jane E. Stromseth, *The Origins of Flexible Response* (London: Macmillan 1988), chap. 6.

prove reluctant to enter into a future conflict.[42] American officials were not pleased with the prospect of having their hands tied by the French, and the French were not content with the idea that they might have to force their ally into action. The French were also concerned that American policies threatened the independence of the French nuclear force. French decisionmakers referred to the value of an independent nuclear force when they rejected Kennedy's offer of Polaris missiles tied to an alliance nuclear force. Similar concerns drove the French to oppose proposals for the Multilateral Force (MLF). The widening gulf between French and American nuclear strategy contributed significantly to the decline in French identification with the North Atlantic group which culminated in the French withdrawal from the military integrated command of NATO in 1966.

Unlike the French, the British displayed a moderate to high degree of idea convergence with the United States during the period under consideration. In the period prior to the formation of NATO, the British differed with the United States over the Middle East and the lack of American assistance for the British nuclear program, but fundamentally agreed over Germany and European security.[43] This moderate level of idea convergence continued into the 1950s, when, despite differences over the Korean war, the British and Americans both began to increase their emphasis on nuclear weapons instead of conventional means to ensure West European security.[44] Interestingly, British overestimation of the level of idea convergence between the United Kingdom and the United States contributed to the British decision to intervene in Egypt during the Suez crisis. Some evidence suggests that British decisionmakers believed that the United States would support the Franco-British intervention, but was restrained from joining its allies

---

42. Alfred Grosser, *French Foreign Policy Under De Gaulle*, trans. Lois Ames Pattison (Boston: Little, Brown, 1967), 102–3; André Beaufre, *Deterrence and Strategy*, trans. R. H. Barry (New York: Praeger, 1965), 80–86.

43. Note from Frank Roberts reporting on a conversation between the secretary of state and Hamilton Fish Armstrong, 1 June 1948, PRO, FO 800/843, Private Papers of Ernest Bevin, North Atlantic Pact 1948–1950; and Frank Roberts, *Dealing with Dictators: The Destruction and Revival of Europe: 1930–1970* (London: Weidenfeld & Nicolson, 1991), chap. 16.

44. On differences between the United States and the United Kingdom over the Korean War, see Stuart Croft, *The End of Superpower: British Foreign Office Conceptions of a Changing World, 1945–51* (Aldershot: London, 1994), 150; For British views on nuclear weapons, see Margaret Gowing, *Independence and Deterrence: Britain and Atomic Energy, 1945–1952*, vol. 1, *Policy Making* (New York: St. Martin's, 1974), 440–43; and Baylis, *Anglo-American Defense*, 52.

by domestic public opinion.[45] After the Suez debacle the British resolved to maintain close relations with the United States, and to seek
to influence U.S. views from a position of collaboration rather than
confrontation.[46] Despite specific differences over the Berlin crisis and
the independence of the British nuclear program, the relevant British
policymakers of the time essentially agreed with American views of the
world during the early 1960s.[47] This level of agreement was evident in
British accord with the United States over the concept of flexible response. Even when the British disagreed with U.S. policy, they countered in a nonconfrontational manner. For instance, the British subtly
undercut the American-proposed MLF by proposing an alternative, the
Atlantic Nuclear Force (ANF) and then quietly failed to follow through
on their proposal.[48] By working in this manner, the British were able
to maintain close agreement between their views and American views,
perhaps even persuading U.S. officials to change their policies so that
they would be closer in line to policies favored by the British. Owing
to the level of agreement detailed in the case study, high British idea
convergence with the United States fueled a high degree of British
group identification with the North Atlantic community, which made
possible close British cooperation within this community.

EXTERNAL PRESSURE

The French experienced moderate to low external pressure during the
formation of NATO. Soviet aggressiveness during the Prague coup and
Berlin blockade pressured the French, but neither event directly im-
pinged on French security or made French policymakers fear imminent invasion.[49] Tension increased during the Korean War, but
dropped off after Stalin's death and the signing of an armistice in Korea

45. Note from Eden to Churchill, undated, PRO, PREM 11/1690.
46. Sir Harold Caccia, "Annual Review of U.S. for 1956," 1 January 1957, PRO, FO
371 126666; and "The Present State of Anglo-United States Relations," Note from Sir
Harold Caccia to Selwyn Lloyd, 1 January 1957, PREM 11 2189.
47. Annual Review for 1961, 1 January 1962, 10, PRO, FO 371 162578; and Annual
Review for 1962, 1 January 1963, 8, PRO, FO 371/168405.
48. The British Defence Minister, Peter Thorneycroft, argued that the MLF could
lead to West German possession of nuclear weapons. "Brief for the Secretary of State,"
E. J. W. Barnes, 29 May 1963, PRO, FO 371 173440. For more detail on the British
attitude toward MLF and their ANF proposal, see Stromseth, *The Origins of Flexible
Response*, chap. 6.
49. Michael M. Harrison, *The Reluctant Ally: France and Atlantic Security*
(Baltimore: Johns Hopkins University Press 1981), 9; and Hervé Alphand,
L'étonnement d'être: Journal 1939–1973 (Paris, Fayard, 1977), 207.

in 1953. The relative lack of external pressure allowed the French the opportunity to refrain from ratifying the EDC. External pressure remained relatively low until the Suez crisis, when both superpowers, the United States and the Soviet Union, urged the French to withdraw their forces. After the subsequent withdrawal, external pressure returned to its previously low level. When de Gaulle returned to office, he capitalized upon the low level of external pressure to further French independence from the North Atlantic group, particularly the United States.[50] France's withdrawal from Algeria and the growth of the French nuclear arsenal under his administration contributed to French perceptions of low external pressure, and made conceivable France's eventual withdrawal from close cooperation in the integrated military command of NATO. Tension increased during the 1961 Berlin crisis, but soon decreased after the construction of the Wall. The Cuban missile crisis increased external pressure, but the location of the crisis in the Western Hemisphere eased the burden considerably. After the crisis, external pressure resumed a low level for the French for the rest of the period under consideration.[51]

Similar to the French, the British experienced moderate to low levels of external pressure prior to the creation of NATO. Soviet intransigence contributed to the birth of the cold war, but the British did not believe another world war was impending.[52] The successful development of British atomic capability increased British status and lowered stress. The British were concerned that the Korean War could escalate, but once the conflict subsided external pressure assumed a low level. Tension remained low for the British until the Suez crisis, when it increased considerably and helped shift British policy toward a more conscious effort to work with the United States and within the alliance to forward British goals. Like the French, the British were concerned during the Berlin and Cuban crises, but after the resolution of the latter crisis external pressure upon the British returned to a low level. The consistently low level of external pressure during this period corresponds with the constant British NATO policy of voice negotiation.

50. Charles de Gaulle, *Memoirs of Hope: Renewal and Endeavor*, trans. Terence Kilmartin (New York: Simon and Schuster, 1970), 200–201.

51. Maurice Couve de Murville, *Une Politique Étrangère*, 189. Couve de Murville's private remarks match his published recollections. MAE, *Secrétariat Général*, Entretiens et Messages, Carton 114, Conversation tête-à-tête, Couve-Schroeder, 2 November 1965.

52. See, for example, Bevin's remarks in Memorandum by the Secretary of State for Foreign Affairs, "Review of Soviet Policy," 5 January 1948, 2, PRO, CAB 129 23, CP (48) 7.

THE DEPENDENT VARIABLE: FRENCH AND BRITISH NATO POLICY

FRANCE: FROM VOICE TO ACQUISITIVE NEGOTIATION

My hypotheses predict that under moderate to high group identification and moderate to low external pressure, a state will conduct a policy of voice negotiation. French behavior in 1949 confirms this hypothesis. The initiative for the talks came from Bidault and Ernest Bevin, his British counterpart, and not from the United States.[53] In addition, the French were able to secure a pledge from the United States to defend continental Europe from Soviet attack. As treaty negotiations progressed, many U.S. officials favored a peripheral strategy that would allow the United States to refrain from immediate intervention in the heart of the European continent. Instead, the United States would form a defense line at the English Channel and the Pyrenees. The French objected to this plan and successfully encouraged alliance military planners to extend the line of defense eastward into Germany.[54] In addition, the passage of the Military Assistance Act by the U.S. Congress later in 1949 supplemented the North Atlantic treaty and constituted another success for the French as they became the primary recipient for U.S. military aid to Europe.[55]

The French were ambivalent about accepting economic and security assistance from the United States. While they desperately needed economic aid to rebuild their economy, and while they knew that the continental European states would be unable to counter a Soviet attack without American help, the French were also concerned about undue U.S. influence over European and French policies.[56] France faced the unenviable task of recovering from the war. This task was complicated by French insistence on spending money and troops in an attempt to maintain order in their Asian and North African colonies. At the same time the French were ever vigilant against American infringement

---

53. Georges Bidault, *Resistance: The Political Autobiography of Georges Bidault*, 155–56.

54. Guillen, "Les Militaires Français," 83–84.

55. Irwin M. Wall, "France and the North Atlantic Alliance," in *NATO: The Founding of the Atlantic Alliance and the Integration of Europe*, ed. Francis H. Heller and John R. Gillingham (New York: St. Martin's, 1992), 46.

56. For an argument on the French need for American assistance, see, "Note pour le President," from the Secretaire General, 16 juin 1948, Archives Auriol, 552 AP, Carton 71, AN; for a more ambivalent discussion after the signing of the North Atlantic Pact, see "Pròces Verbal du Comite de Défense Nationale," 29 aôut 1949, Archives Auriol, 552 AP Carton 44, AN.

upon French independence. The French were grateful for the Marshall aid, but were wary of strings attached to it that would limit future policies. The Quai d'Orsay even favored a proposal, which was discussed with the United States, to link the Organization for European Economic Cooperation to NATO in order to increase European influence in the latter organization.[57] At a higher level, Schuman proposed secret tripartite U.S.-U.K.-French cooperation, especially on Middle Eastern issues.[58] Just prior to signing the North Atlantic Treaty, the French insisted on the creation of the Standing Group, which consisted of tripartite U.S.-U.K.-French membership, in an attempt to institutionalize French influence into alliance decision making.[59] The Standing Group was incorporated into the newly born NATO, but never possessed the policy clout that the French had envisioned. Despite the failure of the Standing Group to achieve real influence, this and the other aspects of the French negotiating stance discussed above show that the French engaged in voice negotiation during the talks that led to the signing of the North Atlantic Treaty.

Likewise, low external pressure and relatively high identification with the North Atlantic group led to French voice negotiation during the EDC saga. Several elements of the case point to this conclusion. First, the French proposed the idea of the EDC. They also insisted upon British participation in it. As this goal was thwarted by British reluctance to involve itself directly in continental defence, the French could no longer support the EDC and were unable to ratify the treaty. In the aftermath of the EDC collapse, the French "voice negotiated" once again when they successfully linked West German rearmament to the WEU. The French were also given assurances preventing West Germany from procuring heavy armaments.

Even though the French were able to obtain some concessions by linking West German rearmament to the WEU, the failure of the EDC dealt a serious blow to NATO. The French were sufficiently disturbed by alliance friction that they considered an idea that had been shelved

57. "Note Pour le Président," from Direction Générale des Affaires Economiques & Financiéres, Service de Coopération Economique, O. Wormser, 15 décembre 1951, MAE, Series DE-CE 1945–1960, #467; A 30 3, OTAN April 1949–Octobre 1952.

58. Conferences Internationales 1949–1951, Box 53, Folder V, "Réunion des Ministres des Affaires Étrangères de France, de Grande Bretagne et des Etats-Unis Tenue a Washington en Septembre 1951," 1ere Seance, 12 septembre 1951, document pp. 8–13, MAE, Secretariat general.

59. Guillen, "Les Militaires Français," 81; and Pierre Gerbet, "La Rôle de la France dans la Négociation de l'Alliance Atlantique," in Vaïsse, Mélandri, and Bozo, *La France et l'OTAN 1949–1996*, 100.

following the 1947 Moscow conference: constituting a third force, independent of the U.S.-U.K. and Soviet blocs and able to reconcile the differences between the two. During the final months of the EDC crisis, one influential official in the Quai d'Orsay wrote a series of memos that considered returning to such a strategy. Jean Saubargnargues, who would eventually become the French ambassador to Germany, suggested two solutions to the problem of German rearmament.[60] The first category was that of an enlarged Europe, which involved creating a confederal European superpower, independent of the United States. The other solution, which he termed as Atlantic, would allow German entrance into NATO. The problem with the Atlantic solution, he noted, was that there would be no way to limit German rearmament, which could result in high troop levels and dangerous arms under German control. Saubargnargues favored the enlarged European solution in order to avoid an unbridled, rearmed Germany. In another memo, Saubargnargues urged that German rearmament be handled in such a manner that it would not provoke the Soviet Union. He even considered a possible Franco-Soviet entente.[61] These notes show that, during times of alliance strife, the French could still consider a "third path" between the United States and the Soviet Union. French yearnings for independence, evident in Saubargnargues' work, would continue to influence French alliance policy.

De Gaulle's return to power in 1958 brought the French desire for independence to the fore. French policy switched from voice to acquisitive negotiation. The French exhibited moderate perceptions of sharing common affinity and common threat with the North Atlantic community in that year. In addition, French and U.S. ideas about security policy diverged. Though the North Atlantic identity was accessible to the French, it did not fit them well at all. As external pressure was low in 1958, the French followed a policy of acquisitive negotiation, seeking to redefine the terms of the Western alliance. French identification with the North Atlantic group dropped between 1954 and 1958. The French probably exhibited a moderate level of identification with the group in November 1956, when they followed a submissive policy of cooperation by heeding the wishes of the United States and withdrawing their troops from Egypt. The remnants of

60. Note No. 3, "Remarques au sujet des solutions de rechange," 26 juin 1954, MAE, Secretariat Général, CED V, Carton 16.
61. Note No. 6, "Sécurité et coexistence," 2 juillet 1954, MAE, Secrétariat Général, CED V, Carton 16.

higher levels of the North Atlantic group identity, along with the high level of external pressure experienced by the French during the crisis contributed to this result. The forced retreat led the French to question the U.S. commitment to support French policies, however. The French owed a great deal to the United States, which had freed France from occupation, and provided them with massive economic and military aid. Yet the French now witnessed firsthand how dependence on their ally placed real limits on French policies. The Foreign ministry report on the conclusions of Suez stressed the need to convince the United States to support French aims, but realistically noted that, if this was not possible, the French would be forced to follow U.S. policies.[62] Suez also highlighted the perils of integrating French troops with those from other states, and this lesson fueled the hesitation later French governments later displayed when asked to place their troops under NATO command. The French policy of submissive cooperation during the retreat from Suez is consistent with my hypotheses.

French policy in 1958 also confirms the hypothesis as external pressure and French identification with the North American community both receded. Most notably, the French engaged in acquisitive negotiation when de Gaulle proposed the creation of a tripartite U.S.-U.K.-French directorate within NATO and the expansion of the geographical scope of the alliance in his September 1958 memorandum to Eisenhower and British prime minister Harold Macmillan. De Gaulle also sought increased French control over any nuclear weapons placed in France and institutionalized consultation over any U.S. use of nuclear weapons outside of use for U.S. national defense, on the grounds that such use would affect the credibility of the U.S. strategic deterrent. The memorandum remains the focus of controversy among scholars, who argue over whether it was a serious proposal, or if de Gaulle meant to use it as a pretext for later French intransigence.[63] British and Ameri-

---

62. *Documents Diplomatiques Français*, vol. 3, "Note de la Direction Générale Politique (redigee a l'intention du Secrétaire générale)," by Etienne de Crouy-Chanel, 10 novembre 1956, 271–72.

63. De Gaulle claims in his memoirs that the memo was a pretext. See de Gaulle, *Memoirs of Hope: Renewal and Endeavor*, 203. For an argument that the memo was not a pretext, see Frédéric Bozo, *Deux Stratégies pour l'Euope: De Gaulle, les Etats-Unis, et l'Alliance Atlantique 1958–1969* (Paris: Plon; Fondation Charles de Gaulle, 1996) 39; and Harrison, *The Reluctant Ally*, 100–101; For an argument that the memo was a pretext see Wilfrid Kohl, *French Nuclear Diplomacy* (Princeton: Princeton University Press, 1971), 74–80. For consideration of how the 1958 memo compares to Fourth Republic Foreign Policy, see Maurice Vaïsse "Aux origines du mémorandum de septembre 1958," *Relations Internationales* 58 (summer 1989): 253–68.

can politicians believed that accepting the memorandum would have given the French greater ability to veto proposed alliance policies. The British and American governments did not give the memorandum an entirely negative hearing, and Eisenhower even suggested setting up a subcabinet tripartite group and joint planning on policy toward Africa, but these revisions only angered de Gaulle.[64] De Gaulle's proposals were presented in a "take it or leave it" manner and not as a serious proposal forwarding give-and-take negotiations over alliance reform. When the proposals were not accepted de Gaulle did not respond immediately; instead he formulated a gradual response that would take seven years. The rejection of the memorandum set the French on a path that would continually diverge from their alliance partners and would eventually lead the French to withdrawal from the integrated military command of NATO.

The period following de Gaulle's memorandum contains some notable examples of acquisitive negotiation. I discuss two here. One instance is the French reaction to the U.S. offer of Polaris missiles that followed. The United States had offered the missiles to the British at their meeting at Nassau to compensate for the U.S. decision to cancel the Skybolt program. Kennedy feared that offering Polaris to the British would fuel French concerns of inferior treatment, so the president extended his offer to them as well, on the same terms as those negotiated with the British at Nassau.

After considering the offer, de Gaulle refused on the grounds that the French had neither the submarines nor the warheads necessary to deploy Polaris. This reasoning was plausible, although it is more likely that the French refused the Polaris offer because they did not want to depend on U.S. technology for their nuclear force.[65] Relying on the United States could place limits on how the French could deploy the missiles. The French considered that British acceptance of Polaris compromised British independence, a compromise that the French would not accept.[66] In addition to the Polaris offer, the French began to protest against another U.S. proposal involving nuclear cooperation: the multilateral nuclear force (MLF) that would consist of a fleet of surface ships, equipped with nuclear weapons and manned by multina-

64. David Schoenbrun, *The Three Lives of Charles de Gaulle* (New York: Atheneum, 1966), 303.

65. Raymond Aron, *The Great Debate: Theories of Nuclear Strategy*, trans. Ernst Pawel (Garden City: Doubleday, 1965), 95.

66. Bozo, *Deux Stratégies pour l'Europe*, 56.

tional crews. De Gaulle did not accept the idea of integrating nuclear forces, and insisted that French nuclear weapons, the first of which were then under development, must remain solely under French control.[67] The French were not alone in their opposition to the MLF, but they did display the most vehement objection to it. The French openly attacked the idea while the British worked quietly against it.[68] In a conversation with Couve de Murville, Kennedy argued that, by offering the French Polaris and the MLF, the United States was treating the French in the same manner as the British. Couve de Murville responded that the French refused because the offer would have jeopardized the independence of the French national force. When forced to choose between equality with Britain and independence, the French chose the latter.[69] British acceptance of Polaris also confirmed French suspicions that when forced to choose between Europe and the United States, the British opted for the latter.[70]

Another notable example of the French policy of acquisitive negotiation was their gradual withdrawal from military integration within NATO. Fearful of having French ships placed under a British admiral, the French withdrew their officers and ships from the Mediterranean fleet of NATO in March 1959. From April to May of that year the French asked that American nuclear bombers based in France be redeployed, as de Gaulle argued that the material risk of having the bombers on French soil outweighed strategic advantages. In September 1960, after months of arguing over the establishment of an integrated Western air defense, the French worked out an agreement that would keep French forces under national command, an agreement that made more political than military sense.[71] Franco-American relations deteriorated further after Kennedy's assassination. De Gaulle recognized communist China and announced his disapproval of U.S. Vietnam policy in January 1963. The French also refused to support U.S. efforts to promote nuclear nonproliferation. In addition, the French refused to participate in the "Fallex" exercise in 1965, a simulated conventional de-

---

67. Entretiens et Messages, 1963, Carton 69, "Audience Accordee par le General de Gaulle à Monsieur Charles Bohlen," 4 Janvier 1963, MAE, Secrétariat Général.
68. Colette Barbier, "La France et la Force Multilaterale (MLF)," in Vaïsse, Mélandri, and Bozo, *La France et l'OTAN 1949-1996*, 285-306.
69. Entretiens et Messages, 1963, Carton 69, "Entretien entre le Président des Etats-Unis et le Ministre des Affaires Étrangères," 25 mai 1963, MAE, Secrétariat Général.
70. In addition to the document cited in the previous note, see Geoffrey Warner, "The United States and the Western Alliance, 1958-1963," *International Affairs* 71, no. 4 (1995): 818.
71. Bozo, *Deux Stratégies pour l'Europe*, 60-61.

fense against Soviet attack that followed the dictates of flexible response. Finally, in March 1966, in a letter to U.S. president Johnson, de Gaulle declared that he would withdraw French forces placed under NATO command, end French staff participation in NATO command structures, and ask that all NATO bases and offices, including the offices of the Central European command and the supreme allied commander in Europe, be removed from French territory. The move was consistent with low French group identification with the North Atlantic community and low external pressure.

GREAT BRITAIN: PREDOMINANCE OF VOICE NEGOTIATION

When state decisionmakers encounter high levels of group identification and low levels of external pressure I expect them to engage in voice negotiation. British policy during the negotiations which created NATO qualify as a good example of voice negotiation. First, the British, acting primarily through Bevin, were the main instigators of the talks. Prior to signing the Brussels Pact, Bevin decided that a direct U.S. role in European security would be essential, and doggedly set out to secure U.S. commitment to play such a role. It was Bevin who promoted the idea of an airlift to counter the Soviet blockade of Berlin. The United States initially took a less strong stance and went along only after Bevin had already committed the British to the project.[72]

Perhaps the most interesting single document that can illuminate British policy during this period is a committee brief by the Permanent Undersecretary's Committee, entitled "A Third World Power or Western Consolidation?" The paper was completed in May 1949, after the signing of the North Atlantic pact, but the paper was drafted during the negotiations of the pact and can be viewed as a representation of elite British foreign-policy opinion in this period. The Committee considered several alternatives for British security: consolidating the Commonwealth; building a united Europe independent of both the United States and the Soviet Union; and allying with the United States. After careful consideration, the paper argued that there was little likelihood that the British could unite the Commonwealth and convert it into a world power. The Committee questioned the likelihood of Britain developing West Europe into a political force independent of the

---

72. Frank Roberts, *Dealing with Dictators*, chap. 17; Elisabeth Barker, *The British Between the Superpowers, 1945–50* (London: Macmillan, 1983), chap. 5.

superpowers, saying that continental Europe's economic and military weaknesses precluded British efforts to unite West Europe without U.S.

Table 2

FRENCH NATO POLICY

	1949	1954	1958	1966
Group id.	high	high/mod.	low/mod.	low
Ext. press	mod./low	mod./low	low	low
Policy	voice negotiation	voice negotiation	acquisitive negotiation	acquisitive negotiation
Hypothesis	confirmed	confirmed	confirmed	confirmed

help. Moreover, the Committee noted that uniting Europe raised the difficult issue of whether and how to incorporate Germany into global politics in the postwar era. The brief, which Bevin later presented to the Cabinet, concluded that the best course for British policy would be to work closely with the United States to further British goals. It considered the problem of potential U.S. domination, but argued that U.S. dominance predated the signature of the Atlantic Pact, and would likely occur regardless of efforts to thwart it. The paper argued that due to commonality of goals between the United States and the United Kingdom, there was little possibility that the United Kingdom would be entrapped into supporting policies with which it did not agree, and noted that the "kinship of ideas" between the United States and the United Kingdom was greater than that between the United Kingdom and other European states, notably Germany. The policy brief shows that, even when weighing the possibility of following an independent route, the British preferred to work with the United States in the aftermath of the war.[73]

Once they decided on the need for U.S. involvement in European security, the British successfully cajoled the Americans into hosting the talks that led to the creation of NATO. The British worked hard to overcome the objections of U.S. policymakers such as Charles Bohlen

73. Permanent Under-Secretary's Committee Brief, Chaired by William Strang, "A Third World Power or Western Consolidation?" 9 May 1949, PRO, FO 371/76384. The paper is also reprinted in DBPO, 54–63.

and George Kennan, who were skeptical of the need for NATO. By securing direct American participation in an alliance, the British successfully exercised voice.

Low external pressure and high group identification led the British to adopt a policy of voice negotiation during the EDC episode as well. The British did not want to take an active role in the EDC, and did not do so, despite constant pressure from the French and a belated U.S. effort to increase their role. British reluctance stemmed from the European character of the EDC proposal. Since the British were keen to maintain American participation in European security, were skeptical of the ability of the Europeans to unite effectively without American assistance, and were wary of developments that could jeopardize their position as the U.S. closest ally, they opposed more than token U.K. participation in the EDC. The strength of British identification with the North American group drove these considerations and precluded British close cooperation with the European group. British identification with the North Atlantic group drove their policy and was stronger than their identification with the West European group. If the relative strength of the two identities were reversed, it is likely that the British would have been amenable to direct participation in the EDC.

After the French refused to ratify the EDC the British played a key role in crafting the compromise that allowed for limited West German rearmament.[74] The British also committed troops to continental Europe for the first time following the failure of the EDC. The British feared that by joining the EDC they would have diluted their standing in the alliance by becoming just another West European state. Thus, their adamant refusal to commit troops to the proposed European army was consistent with the over-arching goal of maintaining their position as the second most important state in NATO. It is not surprising that the British were willing to send troops to the continent as long as those troops were not placed under the command of a European subdivision of Western defense.

The British mostly agreed with the U.S. over the matter of the EDC. Like the Americans, the British were keen to harness West German military resources in support of the efforts of NATO in Europe. When the French proposed the EDC, the British were initially skeptical, but came to see the European army as a tool that would allow West German rearmament while paying heed to French sensitivities. As we have

74. Roberts, *Dealing with Dictators*, 158–59.

seen, the British saw no reason to take an active role in the EDC. This was not a problem for the United States until it became apparent that British abstention from direct EDC involvement detracted from the likelihood of French ratification. Subsequent U.S. pressure on the British to become more involved in the EDC did lead to friction between the two states, but not of the same magnitude as between the United States and France. The British exercised voice by refusing to take part in an institutional entity that could have changed British stature within NATO. This outcome is consistent with my hypotheses.

Following the EDC episode, the Suez crisis of 1956 again tested intra-NATO relations. After the Franco-British action at Suez, external pressure on the British increased significantly. Both superpowers acted against the British. Diplomatic condemnation at the UN embarrassed the British and economic sanctions drove them perilously close to bankruptcy. Thus, the level of external pressure rose greatly after the Franco-British invasion of Egypt.

Consistent with my hypotheses, the shift in pressure corresponds to a shift in policies. Prior to the Franco-British action, low pressure and high identification led the British to follow a policy of voice negotiation. In a way, British Egyptian policy in 1956 echoed their earlier attempt in 1951 to establish a Middle East Defence Organization. Unable to obtain American participation, the British worked with the French to weaken Nasser and force him to reverse his nationalization of the canal. After the invasion, which incurred unexpected American condemnation (and an increase in external pressure), the British shifted to a policy of submissive cooperation. Interestingly, the initial British reaction to the forced withdrawal was one of defiance. Eden considered abandoning the strategy of working closely with the United States, a strategy that was formed during the early days of the cold war. Instead, He considered working more closely with Western Europe.[75] Eden would soon step down as prime minister, however, as the British sought to reestablish close ties with the United States and heal the rift in the U.S.-U.K. relationship.[76] This effort found success as the two states agreed to the deployment of American IRBMs in Britain, and as the amendment of the McMahon act allowed closer cooperation between

---

75. Note, "Prime Minister's Thoughts following Suez," 30 December 1956, PRO, PREM 11 1138.

76. "Annual Review of U.S. for 1956," Sir Harold Caccia, 1 January 1957, PRO, FO 371 126666; and "The Present State of Anglo-United States Relations," Note from Sir Harold Caccia to Selwyn Lloyd, 1 January 1957, PREM 11 2189.

the two countries on atomic weapons.[77] The Suez crisis had a considerably different effect on the British than it did on the French. The French saw the crisis as proof that the United States had too much influence over French foreign policy. Accordingly, the French worked to increase their independence from U.S. influence. In contrast, the British viewed the crisis as proof that they would have to accept constraints on their policy choices if they were to benefit from collaboration with the United States.

When external pressure is low and group identification is high, I expect a state to engage in voice negotiation, and this expectation is fulfilled by the British in December 1962. The Macmillan government and others saw the Polaris agreement as a success for the British. They U.S. State Department had objected to giving the British Polaris on the grounds that doing so could harm British entrance into Europe.[78] Macmillan thought that Kennedy's open-mindedness led the president to give in at Nassau.[79] Ormsby-Gore argued that only the United Kingdom could have achieved the Nassau compromise.[80] The authoritative U.S.-authored account of the Nassau negotiations notes that Kennedy gave more than he desired to give.[81] The British stance during the Skybolt affair is a good example of voice negotiation, influenced by the level of external pressure and group identification.

British voice negotiation continued through 1966, the end point of my inquiry. High group identity led the British to believe that they were best off cooperating with the North Atlantic community, and low external pressure encouraged them to assert their views. Regarding the MLF, the British worked within alliance channels to promote the Atlantic Nuclear Force as an alternative to the American proposal. When the alternative was accepted, and quietly faded away, the British succeeded in defeating the MLF without openly opposing it or causing intraalliance tension over the disagreement.

77. Baylis, *Anglo-American Defense Relations*, 89–90.

78. De Gaulle did point to Polaris as an example of U.K. dependence on the United States and as a pretext for vetoing British entrance into the EC. Nevertheless, there is considerable evidence that instead of having their entrance vetoed, the British were unwilling to enter the EC in 1962. See Alan Milward, text of his LSE speech, summer 1996.

79. Prime Minister's Personal Minute No. M. 340/63, Note from the Prime Minister to the Foreign Minister, 21 September 1963, PRO, FO 371 173440.

80. Annual Review for 1962, 8, PRO, FO 371/168405.

81. Richard E. Neustadt, *Alliance Politics* (New York: Columbia University Press, 1970), 54.

Table 3

BRITISH NATO POLICY

	1949	1954	1956	1962	1966
Group Id.	high	high	high	high	high
Ext. Press.	mod./low	low	low →high	mod./low	low
Policy	voice negotiation	voice negotiation	voice→co-ordination	voice negotiation	voice negotiation
Hypothesis	confirmed	confirmed	confirmed	confirmed	confirmed

Yet another example of the British policy of voice negotiation was the instrumental role they played in the Nuclear Planning Group (NPG), a regular meeting of NATO defense ministers that made and reviewed alliance policies regarding nuclear strategy. Where the MLF failed to bring the European members of NATO into discussions concerning nuclear strategy, the NPG created a forum where such states could voice their concerns, obtain additional information concerning U.S. nuclear policies, and thus avoid intra-alliance tensions.[82] Within the NPG, Healey helped create a plan for the use of tactical nuclear weapons based in Europe.[83] Again, we see the British working constructively, from the inside of the alliance, to promote alliance policies that correspond with their preferences. The British role in the NPG, along with the manner in which they dealt with the MLF/ANF episode, shows that British NATO policy qualifies as an example of voice negotiation. When the French withdrew from the integrated military command of NATO, the British admitted to themselves that they were not always pleased with American policies, but consistently maintained that it would be best to influence U.S. policies from the inside, by working as closely as possible with the United States, instead of following the strategy of dissent and withdrawal favored by the French.[84]

82. David N. Schwartz, *NATO's Nuclear Dilemma* (Washington, D.C.: Brookings, 1983), 190–91; Stromseth, *The Origins of Flexible Response*, 182–86.
83. Stromseth, *The Origins of Flexible Response*, 167.
84. See the argument made by Foreign Secretary Michael Stewart to the Cabinet, 23 September 1965, 364, PRO, CAB 128/39, CC (65) 49th Conclusions.

FRANCE

In addition to my approach, other explanations make contributions toward explaining French NATO policy from 1949 to 1966. Stephen Walt's balance-of-threat theory should be applicable to French alliance policy. To explain the French stance toward the formation of the Atlantic alliance, the balance-of-threat approach expects the rise of the Soviet threat to spur North Atlantic states to band together to guarantee their mutual security. The French did in fact perceive a common Soviet threat to the North Atlantic leading up to the formation of NATO. While the Soviet threat existed for the French, they did not see the threat as imminent, however, which implies a slight difficulty for the balance-of-threat approach in this case. Without an imminent threat, it is less clear from this perspective why the French would join NATO or why they would work so diligently to enlist U.S. membership in the alliance. Advocates of the balance-of-threat approach might counter that for the French, the German threat spurred their eagerness to join NATO. This argument takes into account French sensitivity over Germany, but ignores the fact that NATO was created with the Soviet threat in mind. Nevertheless, this is not a serious weakness in the balance-of-threat perspective. As I have shown, the French did perceive the Soviets to be a common threat to the North Atlantic group, even if the threat was not imminent. My approach, which differentiates between the existence of a threat (common threat) and the level of threat (external pressure) indicates one modification that could strengthen the balance-of-threat approach.

For the failure of the EDC, the balance-of-threat approach could point to the end of the Korean war and Stalin's death as decreases in Soviet threat that lessened French ardor for a European army. This explanation is quite plausible. The decline in French support for the EDC paralleled perceived declines in Soviet threat, and an explanation that links the two has some plausibility. As for de Gaulle's 1958 memorandum, the balance-of-threat approach could be used to show that declining French perceptions of threat led them to place less of a stake in the alliance, inducing them to seek more advantageous terms in interalliance bargains. The neorealist argument that states seek to maximize relative gains could be applied in support of neorealist balance-of-threat theory to show that the French sought to increase their ability to influence alliance policy.[85] With the Soviet threat subsiding, the French needed NATO less and pressed for policies more to their liking. Similarly, the balance-of-threat approach could generate a plausible explanation of the gradual French retreat from alliance structures that culminated in their withdrawal from the integrated military command in 1966. The waning of the Soviet threat, especially after the Cuban missile crisis, helps to explain increasing French belligerence toward their allies. As the Soviet threat declined, so did French willingness to follow U.S. leadership within NATO. Despite its slight difficulty with French support for the formation of NATO, balance-of-threat theory could be used to elucidate the causes of French NATO policy up to 1966.

The balance-of-threat approach does a decent job of explaining early French policy toward NATO, and has more success in the later cases. In contrast, Thomas Risse-Kappen's common ideals approach best explains early French policy, but is increasingly unable to explain later developments. Since the approach focuses on the manner in which common ideals contribute to a sense of community, it is understandable that a group of Western capitalist democracies would perceive common interests in forming an alliance. Risse-Kappen's approach argues that the Soviet threat enhanced the cause of the alliance, but did not create the community from which the alliance emerged.[86] An approach premised upon commonalities among states is likely to perform well when international cooperation occurs. When there is discord among partners, however, or when cooperation breaks down, such an approach will falter unless there is a corresponding divergence in common ideals.

The ideals that Risse-Kappen focuses on are too broad, however, to explain short-term divergences in French NATO policy. Despite the internal strife of the Fourth Republic and the Algerian crisis, France remained a capitalist, democratic state. French refusal to support the EDC had little to do with changing French ideals. Additionally, the tough bargaining that took place between the allies is not expected by this approach, which expects interalliance bargaining to follow consulta-

---

85. Kenneth N. Waltz, *Theory of International Politics* (New York: McGraw-Hill, 1979), 105; Joseph M. Grieco, *Cooperation among Nations* (Ithaca: Cornell University Press, 1990), 44–45.

86. Thomas Risse-Kappen, *Cooperation Among Democracies: The European Influence on U.S. Foreign Policy* (Princeton: Princeton University Press, 1995), 32; and Risse-Kappen, "Collective Identity in a Democratic Community," 19.

tion norms.[87] Similarly, de Gaulle's 1958 memorandum did not arise out of a fundamental change in French society, nor did the 1966 French withdrawal from the integrated military command. Instead of searching for deep changes in ideals within French society, changes that are not yet evident, Risse-Kappen would do better to examine the relationship between French ideas about security policy with those of other members of the North Atlantic community, which did change over time. To his credit, Risse-Kappen honestly admits that his approach insufficiently explains Franco-American differences and needs to be supplemented with institutionalist arguments.[88] I would suggest that Risse-Kappen's common ideals approach be supplemented with other components that affect group identification, as well as an emphasis on the role of external pressure.

BRITAIN

One might argue that my approach relies heavily upon the concept of external threat to explain state alliance policy. After all, past and present levels of threat influence group identification, and the current level of threat determines the level of external pressure placed upon a state at a given time. Perhaps it would be better to adopt Walt's balance-of-threat approach, which focuses solely on threat, and do away with the troublesome concept of group identity. The balance-of-threat approach would have some success in explaining British NATO policy. The British did not perceive a high level of threat during the formative period of the alliance, but Soviet belligerence undoubtedly played a role in convincing Bevin to work toward the establishment of NATO.

Relying on threat alone to explain British NATO policy from 1949 to 1966 is problematic. It is difficult to explain U.K. policy toward the EDC by referring to British threat perception. It is unclear why the British would perceive a level of threat high enough to justify the formation of NATO a few years prior to the discussions over EDC, while not perceiving enough of a threat to play more than an observer's role in the European army. In addition, the balance-of-threat approach provides

---

87. Risse-Kappen, *Cooperation among Democracies*, 36–37; and Risse-Kappen, "Collective Identity in a Democratic Community," in Peter J. Katzenstein, ed. *The Culture of National Security. Norms and Identity in World Politics* (New York: Columbia University Press, 1996), 357–99. Risse-Kappen does note that allied states may engage in hard bargaining with one another "in conflictual situations," but offers no guide as to when these situations are likely to arise.

88. Risse-Kappen, *Cooperation among Democracies*, 103–4, 213–15.

little ground from which to explain British policy during and after the Suez crisis. If the British perceived enough of a threat to play an important role in NATO, why did they fail to consult the United States, their principal ally within the organization, over the plan to intervene in Egypt? Additionally, why did the British seek to return to a close relationship with the United States so soon after being abandoned by their ally during the crisis? Since the Soviet launch of Sputnik in October 1957 preceded the U.S.-U.K. rapprochement, the level of threat alone is unlikely to explain this event. Considering the Skybolt affair, standard realist thought would not be surprised at British efforts to maintain their independent deterrent and their willingness to press the United States to provide them with Polaris. Nevertheless, the British negotiating position was not directly related to their perception of Soviet threat. Rather, the British perception of Soviet threat acted as a background factor necessitating maintenance of a nuclear deterrent. The existence of the threat says little about the specific negotiating stance adopted by the United Kingdom in this case.

Even more troublesome to the balance-of-threat approach is the last case examined in this paper, British policy toward NATO from 1963–66. The British perceived a lessening of the Soviet threat after the Cuban missile crisis, yet the decline in threat had little perceivable effect on British NATO policy. The British did seek to direct alliance policies to correspond with British interests, but they did not engage in the same sort of hard-line tactics, such as demands for structural reform of the alliance and unilateral withdrawal of troops from alliance commands, which preceded the French decision to withdraw from the alliance's integrated military command in 1966. Instead, the British continued to support the alliance, and worked within it in a consensual manner. It should be clear from these examples that in addition to the level of threat, other factors should be considered to explain British NATO policy from 1949 to 1966.

Mention of consensual bargaining tactics brings to mind another approach that can help understand British NATO policy. Risse-Kappen focuses on the role of common values in intra-alliance relations, and focuses specifically on NATO during the period examined above. On the formation of the alliance, Risse-Kappen could point out that all NATO members' status as liberal democracies is a factor consistent with his expectation that states sharing common domestic political orders would be able to institutionalize their security community. It is less clear what Risse-Kappen's interpretation of the British stance toward the EDC would be, however. The commonalities that allowed the British to join an alliance with other like-minded states was not enough to entice the British into taking an active role in the EDC. It is unclear why this would be the case. In addition, Risse-Kappen's approach cannot point to the sources of British policy toward Suez.

With respect to Suez, Risse-Kappen argues that sometimes norms are violated, and that the violation of a norm does not falsify his approach.[89] He argues that the British believed that the United States would accept and support the Franco-British action after it took place, due to the strength of the community of allies. He explains the decision not to consult with the United States as a tactic taken to free the United States from responsibility for the action, as it could plausibly deny being involved, and because acting against a U.S. veto of the plan would be more damaging than acting without prior consultation.[90] These considerations are plausible, yet they do not work well with the main thrust of Risse-Kappen's approach, which expects allies to consult with one another. Risse-Kappen notes that sometimes norms are violated, but does not indicate the circumstances under which we should expect norm violations to occur. Risse-Kappen's approach would benefit from some sort of consideration of when norms will affect state behavior and when they are likely to be disregarded.

Despite this drawback, however, the approach does help explain British NATO policy during most of the period examined above. The general nature of Risse-Kappen's approach, which makes it difficult for it to explain the variation in French NATO policy, is consistent with the continuity in British NATO policy from 1949 to 1966. The willingness to work with the United States after Suez is just one example. In addition, Risse-Kappen's approach helps an understanding of the British reliance on consensual bargaining before and after the Nassau conference. After the U.S.-U.K. agreement to supply Polaris to the United Kingdom, a successful test of Skybolt threatened to reopen the dispute between the two allies, but such an outcome was avoided by Macmillan's restrained reaction.[91] The common norms approach also helps explain British willingness to work within alliance channels to defeat the MLF and the consensual nature of candid discussion within the Nu-

---

89. Risse-Kappen, *Cooperation Among Democracies*, 83.

90. Ibid., 90.

91. Alistair Horne, "The Macmillan Years and Afterwards," in *The Special Relationship: Anglo-American Relations Since 1945*, ed. William Roger Louis and Hedley Bull (Oxford: Clarendon, 1986), 87–102.

clear Planning Group. Risse-Kappen's approach helps explain the sub-
dued nature of the British approach to NATO politics which prevailed,
despite a few exceptions, throughout the period examined here.

COMPARING BRITISH AND FRENCH POLICY

Both the balance-of-threat and common ideals approaches run into difficulty when called on to differentiate between British and French
NATO policies. Walt's balance-of-threat approach is unable to explain
variation between French and British alliance behavior during the cold
war. Britain and France occupied similar international positions as fad-
ing great powers during the cold war, yet they did not behave similarly. Both states joined NATO when it was founded in 1949, but in
1966 France dropped out of the organization's military command,
while Britain remained at the center of the alliance. From the formation of NATO to the moment of withdrawal, French policymakers
sought to change the alliance better to serve French needs, while the
British were content to work on behalf of the alliance as a whole, arguing that what was good for the alliance was good for Britain.

Walt's modified structural neorealist explanation of alliance formation expects states to ally when they perceive a common threat to their
security. He would have to argue that French perceptions of the Soviet
threat to French security decreased before or during 1966, but that
British perceptions of the Soviet threat to British security remained
constant, to explain the divergence in French and British policy toward NATO. This is puzzling because France, situated in continental
Europe, had been invaded numerous times, while the United Kingdom, protected by the English Channel, was not as vulnerable to conventional attack. In material terms, the French faced a greater threat
than the British, yet the British remained in the integrated military
command of NATO while the French conducted their partial withdrawal. Like other neorealist approaches to international relations,
Walt's balance-of-threat approach is unable to explain why states in
similar international positions would follow different policies.

The other approach I have considered is Thomas Risse-Kappen's
common ideals approach. There is little reason to quarrel with the notion that ideals matter in the policymaking process. Commonalities
among the Western democracies certainly contributed to a sense of
community among them that made the formation of NATO possible.
Risse-Kappen, however, overemphasizes the role of ideals in the NATO

case, which hinders his ability to explain several important aspects of the case. First, in his attempt to find fault with realism, he denies that the common fear of the Soviet Union played a role in the creation of a collective identity among the Western democracies. It is impossible to create an "us" without simultaneously creating a "them." There can be no insiders if there are no outsiders. Even if the Soviets presented little or no threat to the West following the war, the creation of a security alliance among the Western powers implies a difference between the members of that alliance and outsiders.

Second, Risse-Kappen's description of how ideas influence policy is too blunt to be helpful. He speaks in the broadest terms about "liberal republicanism," "liberal democracies," and "republican liberalism," and defines the general concepts that he associates with these terms; but he does not explain why cooperation is more likely to occur in one issue area than another. Liberal democracies do not cooperate on every foreign policy issue. What is special about democracies that makes them amenable to cooperate with one another in alliance policy, but not in sharing nuclear weapons technology, for example? Common domestic orders may provide some base level of trust that is amenable to group identification and cooperation, but this similarity is not sufficient to explain particular instances of cooperation. We need recourse to variables that can explain how states with similar domestic orders could choose different policies in a given area.

Third, and related to the above point, Risse-Kappen overemphasizes the role of ideas at the expense of the role of material factors.[92] He argues, for example, that democracies do not use their material power resources to affect intra-alliance bargaining, denying that democratic states use material power resources to coerce better bargains out of their partners, and declaring that the community of values has no relation to the economic orders within these countries, but is solely based on the states' political orders.[93]

State power resources play a vital role not just in deciding who will ally with whom, but in almost all intra-alliance politics. States that need the alliance necessarily cede control over alliance policy to less dependent states. This dynamic includes democracies and other types

---

92. This was discussed above in general, but not specifically with regard to the NATO case.

93. For the latter point, see Risse-Kappen, *Cooperation among Democracies*, 30.

of states.[94] Material power resources play an important role in bargaining, even if these resources are not consciously used by the participants. Risse-Kappen implies that coercion is too crude a tool for democracies to use when they bargain with one another.[95] Nonetheless, coercion is an inescapable element of any bargaining process that leads to cooperation. We noted above that in the vast middle ground between the poles of complete harmony and complete hostility parties have room to bargain with one another to settle on a cooperative solution. There is often a range of possible cooperative solutions, but the parties agree to only one.[96] During the bargaining process, any move by one party to attempt to shape the agreement more to its liking involves coercive power. Coercion requires that one party gets another party to do what they would otherwise not do by manipulating their incentives, while brute force involves the actual use of violence to accomplish a goal.[97] In NATO, the fact that the United States had nuclear weapons and an economy that had almost completely avoided direct attack during the Second World War made the Americans the undisputed leaders of the alliance. Both the British and the French took this into account when deciding to join the alliance. The case studies show that much of the tension within the alliance was based on member states' concern with their relative influence on alliance policy. We must turn to both material and ideal factors to account for this tension and the resulting differences in French and British policy.

Risse-Kappen's approach prevents him from explaining one of the most interesting events in the history of the alliance: the French withdrawal from the integrated military command. In his attack against realism he argues that even sophisticated realists cannot account for the interaction patterns in alliances. The French withdrawal was a major event in the alliance and, as an interaction pattern, member withdrawal should lie under Risse-Kappen's purview. Risse-Kappen's focus on ideas and collective identity could explain the change in French policy by pointing to a change in French identity; but before, during, and after their withdrawal from the alliance the French state was and continues to be a liberal democracy. Their ideas about democracy have not

94. For an excellent treatment of this subject, see Glenn H. Snyder, "The Alliance Security Dilemma."

95. Risse-Kappen, "Collective Identity in a Democratic Community," 12.

96. See Stephen Krasner, "Global Communications and National Power: Life on the Pareto Frontier," *World Politics* 43, no. 3 (April 1991): 336–66.

97. Thomas C. Schelling, *Arms and Influence* (New Haven: Yale University Press, 1966), 4.

differed greatly from those held by the British, yet the two states have not behaved similarly with regard to NATO. If French values allowed them to share in the collective identity of the original members of the alliance, did French values change significantly in the years prior to 1966? The values that Risse-Kappen focuses on did not change for France during this period. Risse-Kappen would be unable to explain discrepancies in cooperation policies of states with similar domestic orders such as France and Britain.

Examining the role of perception of threat or common values in isolation allows us to weigh the relative importance of each factor, but neither approach is sufficient to explain the variance in state policies over time. Both alternative approaches focus on one aspect of a complex causal scheme. I have borrowed from both alternatives in building my approach. I examine, for example, perceptions of common threat as one of the factors that influences the fit of a particular group identity. In addition, I examine the role of common ideas as another factor that may contribute to group identification. By combining these factors along with others, and by showing how these factors interact to influence state policy, I hope to offer a plausible, generalizable, and applicable approach that can be used to explain state policies toward intimate cooperation.

One might consider another approach that could be capable of contrasting the two states' policies. An approach that focused on the make-up of internal institutions might be used to point to the impact of institutional differences between the two states.[98] Since the shift in French policy occurred at about the same time that de Gaulle established the Fifth Republic, such an approach seems auspicious. Nevertheless, in my view there does not seem to be sufficient evidence that internal institutional changes brought about by the institution of the Fifth Republic led to the shift in French policy. As I have shown, the roots of French yearning for independence from U.S. influence were evident during the Fourth Republic.

Yet another approach that might be used to account for the difference between British and French policies would be to point to the importance of individuals such as Charles de Gaulle. De Gaulle's reemergence in French politics and his well-known emphasis for, or some might say obsession with, French independence would seem to explain

---

98. For an example of domestic institutionalism applied to economic policy, see Peter Hall, *Governing the Economy: The Politics of State Intervention in Britain and France* (New York: Oxford University Press, 1986).

why the French would withdraw from the integrated military command of NATO while the British, without their own de Gaulle, would
choose differently. I will not attempt to enter fully into the debate
over the relative weight of individuals versus broader social forces in
history. In addition, I do not dispute de Gaulle's place as one of the
great figures of our century. He played an important role in French
military policy, and his growing exasperation with U.S. leadership of
the North Atlantic community certainly limited French involvement
with NATO during his tenure. Nevertheless, de Gaulle's influence over
French military policy was not the case of an idiosyncratic individual
who happened to hold power at a certain moment and shaped policy
to his wishes. De Gaulle was an individual, but there were forces at
play in addition to his own iron will. He could not have led France's
gradual withdrawal from the military command of NATO if the public
and his fellow policymakers were irrevocably opposed to such a policy. Despite his reputation for being a nonconformist, de Gaulle could
never have obtained and maintained his position as French president
had he been unable to represent important sectors of French opinion.
These sectors, as well as individuals such as de Gaulle, are influenced
by the group identity variables that I discuss.

IDENTIFYING PRIMARY SOURCES

POLICYMAKERS OFTEN argue that they make decisions based upon
careful analysis of available options. They seek out relevant information and attempt to design the best possible course of action for
their state. Some argue that during crises, such decision making is constrained. Time pressures limit available information, lack of sleep
clouds otherwise clear heads, and stress limits logic. Even during less
immediately pressing times, I argue, factors other than those that have
a direct effect on the utility of a given policy play a role in policy
choice. I have focused on one of these factors—group identification—
and have shown how it played a role in French and British decision
making concerning intimate cooperation in both military and economic cooperation. If we are to make real progress explaining the evolution of preferences for various policies, we must continue to focus on
factors such as group identification and the role that these factors play
in specific policies. At the same time, we must also refrain from vague
generalities that might plague such a project and doom it to faddish-

ness. I have attempted to define the group identification process in real terms, and to measure the variables that contribute to it using discernible variables and indicators of these variables that are vulnerable to independent scrutiny. Some might question my recourse to indicators such as trade dependency and tourist travel to discern the particular group identification prevalent in a state at a particular time. Those who will question this project will have reason to do so. Nevertheless, criticism of this project will be more productive if it suggests better ways to conceptualize and measure various group identities that impact upon policy choice instead of casting aspersion upon a preliminary effort to understand complex yet important phenomena. To give the concept of identity real value we need to find ways to make it more observable and understandable. This is bound to be difficult, as identities are internal processes that are not readily available for external observation. Nevertheless, there is room for real progress.

INTERVIEWS

London

Lord Field Marshal Michael Carver
Sir Frank Cooper
Rt. Hon. Denis Healey
Sir Arthur Hockaday
Sir Frank Roberts

Paris

Prime Minister Maurice Couve de
  Murville
General Pierre Gallois
Ambassador François de Rose
Ambassador Etienne Burin des
  Rosiers
Gilles Andréani

ABANDONING IRAQ:
JORDAN'S ALLIANCES AND THE POLITICS OF STATE IDENTITY

MARC LYNCH

"Won't [the peace treaty with Israel] lead Jordan to settling with the enemy and enmity with our friends, a turn of 180 degrees on yesterday's alliances?"

Bahjat Abu Ghurbiya, *al-Majd*, 17 October 1994.

ETWEEN 1990 and 1995 Jordan shifted its position from Iraq's strongest Arab supporter to one of the most outspoken critics of the Iraqi regime. Jordan's refusal to join the American coalition against Iraq in the Gulf war startled most observers, who expected Jordan to side with its traditional friends in the West and the majority of the Arab League against a threatening neighbor. Jordan's turn against Iraq just five years later represents an equally important and unexplained policy choice. Neither rationalist nor constructivist theories can adequately account for Jordanian behavior toward Iraq in the 1990s. The changes and continuities in Jordanian behavior can best be explained in terms of the public contestation of state identity. The political struggles over Jordanian policy toward Iraq invoked competing definitions of state identity and interests in multiple public spheres. Each decision set in motion identity debates which significantly affected the success or failure of the policy at home and abroad. The domestic consensus in support of the Gulf war policy and the international hostility to the Jordanian position, as opposed to the domestic hostility to the reversal and its enthusiastic international embrace, al-

Marc Lynch is assistant professor of political science at Williams College.

I would like to thank Shibley Telhami, Michael Barnett, Peter Katzenstein, and anonymous *Security Studies* reviewers for helpful comments on earlier versions. Financial support for the research in this paper came from the Social Science Research Council International Predissertation Fellowship Program, the USIA Dissertation Research Fellowship Program, administered by the American Center for Oriental Research in Jordan, and the MacArthur Foundation Postdoctoral Research Fellowship administered by the Institute for International Studies, University of California, Berkeley. I also gratefully acknowledge Mustafa Hamarneh and the Center for Strategic Studies, University of Jordan, for research support.

lows a useful comparison of the interaction between domestic and international public sphere debate on state identity.

Jordanian policy toward Iraq highlights the extent to which rationalist and constructivist approaches underdetermine state behavior. While plausible explanations for each policy choice can be constructed from rationalist premises based on power, threat, or political economy, equally plausible explanations for the opposite behavior could be deduced as logically. Constructivist concepts of communicative action and social structure are necessary to explain the definition of threat and the specification of interests which underlie strategic interaction. Jordanian policy toward Iraq involved a deeply contested reorientation of Jordanian identity, intimately tied up with the struggles over the peace process and the nature of regional order and institutions. Jordanian behavior was both strategic and a contested attempt to assert and institutionalize a new set of identities and interests. Only by incorporating both the strategic and the communicative dimensions of international behavior can a full explanation be developed. This paper should therefore be read as an attempt at synthesis, in which the contestation of identity interacts dynamically with strategic considerations.

This paper seeks to demonstrate the theoretical and empirical potential of a public sphere approach by engaging with rival hypotheses and by a detailed reconstruction of the process by which public sphere produced—or failed to produce—consensus on state identity and interests. First, I sketch the contours of the public sphere approach (Section 1). I then consider several possible explanations for Jordanian behavior either found in the literature or deduced from important rationalist approaches, including balance of threat and political economy.[1] I argue that each of these approaches underdetermines Jordanian behavior. In each case, public sphere interaction provides the crucial linkage between the strategic setting, the definition of interests, and state behavior. Because consensus formation followed very different paths, comparing the cases allows some evaluation of the extent to which communicative action matters for state behavior. The Gulf war case reveals the process of the formation of a powerful domestic consensus emerg-

1. The evidence for behavior and discourse is based upon a collection of commentaries in the Jordanian press, including the semiofficial daily press and the independent weekly press, between 1990 and 1997; international and Arab press reports; collections of policy statements by Jordanian, Israeli, American and other actors; and interviews and discussions conducted in Jordan between June 1994 and June 1995. For more details, see Marc Lynch, *State Interests and Public Spheres: The International Politics of Jordan's Identity* (New York: Columbia University Press, forthcoming).

ing from public debate inside a newly potent domestic public sphere (Section 2). The demands of this public consensus and state interests in securing international economic and political support increasingly clashed in following years (Section 3). Finally, the turn against Iraq demonstrates regime success in achieving international consensus in support of Jordanian policy but its failure to produce a domestic consensus, and the ensuing instability in both domestic politics and in foreign policy (Section 4). I conclude with some observations on the contributions of the two approaches and the possibilities of synthesis between a public sphere approach to identity politics and rationalist models of strategic behavior.

IDENTITY AND THE PUBLIC SPHERE

IN THIS ARTICLE, I use identity to refer to collective definitions of self: publicly asserted conceptions of the nature and purpose of a collectivity.[2] The focus is upon intersubjective, collective identities rather than upon privately held, subjective identities. State identity refers not only to the conceptions held by leaders, but by the set of beliefs about the nature and purpose of the state expressed in public articulations of state actions and ideals. The identity and social purpose of the state can often be seen most clearly in the justifications and explanations of foreign policy offered by leaders and contested by publics. In other words, Jordan's state identity is more than the personal convictions of King Husayn, despite his clear centrality to foreign policy formation in the Hashemite Kingdom. Jordan's identity incorporates the institutions, norms, and public discourse by which the citizens of the state participate in and invoke a collective purpose. The identity of a collectivity is established, reinforced, and changed by exchanging of public claims, assertions, and arguments as well as by the public observance of ritual and celebration of shared myths. Institutions reflect a consensus on collective identity which was achieved through public discourse.[3]

---

2. Peter J. Katzenstein, *The Culture of National Security: Norms and Identity in World Politics* (New York: Columbia University Press, 1996). Compare to the definition of identity offered by Glenn Chafetz, Michael Spirtas, and Benjamin Frankel in their "Tracing the Influence of Identity on Foreign Policy," *Security Studies* 8, nos. 2/3 (winter 1998/99–spring 1999): vii–xxii.

3. On the relationship between contested identity and national institutions, see Peter J. Katzenstein, *Cultural Norms and National Security: Police and Military in Postwar Japan* (Ithaca: Cornell University Press 1996).

This definition of identity, rooted in public discourse and institutional structures, offers useful and observable indicators for empirical research.

Identity politics directly affect behavior, as groups with competing conceptions of state identity and state interests struggle for influence. While state officials attempt to justify policy on the basis of the identity and social purpose of the state, by articulating a specific definition of the national interest, the existence of a public sphere provides the opportunity for political actors to contest the official definition of state interests and to offer competing conceptions. When these political struggles take the form of public communicative action, state identity and interests at least potentially can change in the political process. At the heart of the rationalist-constructivist debate is the question of preference stability.[4] Rationalists have generally argued for holding preferences constant, explaining change in terms of shifts in strategies, while constructivists have focused upon the origin of preferences and the possibility of their change through interaction. The public sphere approach argues that state interests remain stable most of the time, but that during periods of crisis, in which interests become explicitly contested in an effective public sphere, they can potentially change. Identity is not always at stake, but at certain moments the public consensus on state identity becomes open to critical discussion within the public sphere. During periods of "normal" politics, identity is unproblematic, and rationalist models which hold identity and interests constant might fare well.[5] When identity becomes the subject of explicit, public contestation, however, the institutionalized conceptions of collective identity and attendant conceptions of interest can no longer be taken for granted. Political behavior will differ significantly in such moments of thematized identity. The goal for theory building, therefore, should be to identify those points at which change becomes likely.

The existence of a public sphere suggests that certain kinds of political structures will produce political action oriented toward the ex-

4. Alexander Wendt, "Collective Identity Formation and the International State," *American Political Science Review* 88, no. 2 (June 1994): 384–96. For discussion, see Jeffrey T. Checkel, "The Constructivist Turn in International Relations Theory," *World Politics* 50, no. 2 (January 1998): 324–48; Ted Hopf, "The Promise of Constructivism in International Relations Theory," *International Security* 23, no.1 (summer 1998): 171–200; and Emmanuel Adler, "Seizing the Middle Ground: Constructivism in World Politics," *European Journal of International Relations* 3, no. 3 (September 1997): 319–63.
5. This approach to identity differs significantly from those postmodernist approaches which consider identity to be always in flux.

change of argumentation oriented toward consensus.[6] The "will to consensus" is not assumed, but rather represents an important variable. For public debate to lead to change in identity or interests, there must exist a shared concern for achieving consensus, such that a less preferred outcome within a consensus is preferable to a higher payoff without consensus. This consensus refers not to outcomes, but to procedure: a concern for the continuation of the dialogue and the maintenance of shared institutions and relationships, rather than a consensus on the distribution of goods within them.[7] Jordan's preference for a political position within an Arab consensus over an "objectively better" position outside such a consensus has powerfully influenced its behavior over the decades. Where the will to consensus exists, actors at least potentially engage in *communicative action*.[8] Unlike *strategic action*, in which actors manipulate opportunity and power in pursuit of predefined goals, or *normative action*, in which actors demonstrate ritual adherence to predefined values, communicative action is the attempt to arrive at consensus through the exchange of arguments. Communicative action implies the potential negotiation of new conceptions of identity and interests. Such deliberation does not automatically imply change: public discourse might in the end reinforce dominant understandings of identity and interests.

Communicative action occurs within identifiable structures which define the boundaries and the content of the identity at stake. I define the public sphere as a contested participatory site in which actors rou-

6. See the following works by Jürgen Habermas: *Theory of Communicative Action*, vol. 1, *Reason and the Rationalization of Society* (Boston: Beacon Press 1984); *Theory of Communicative Action*, vol. 2, *Lifeworld and System* (Boston: Beacon Press 1987); and *Between Facts and Norms: Contributions to a Discourse Theory of Law and Democracy* (Cambridge: MIT Press, 1996). As noted by the contributors to Craig Calhoun, ed., *Habermas and the Public Sphere* (Cambridge: MIT Press, 1992), Habermas neglects the potential for change in conceptions of identity in the process of public sphere interaction.

7. James Bohman, *Public Deliberation* (Cambridge: MIT Press, 1996), argues for defining consensus in terms of procedure and the will to continue discussion; also see Simone Chambers, *Reasonable Democracy: Jürgen Habermas and the Politics of Discourse* (Ithaca: Cornell University Press, 1996). The relationship between strategic interaction and "deliberative democracy" models of communicative action is discussed in Jon Elster, ed., *Deliberative Democracy* (New York: Cambridge University Press, 1998); and James Bohman and William Rehg, eds., *Deliberative Democracy* (Cambridge: MIT Press, 1997).

8. Habermas, *Theory of Communicative Action*, develops these distinctions among action types. Elster argues that bargaining within market structures differs qualitatively from argument in a public forum, with important implications for explaining political interaction; see "The Market and the Forum," in Bohman and Rehg, *Deliberative Democracy*, 3–34.

tinely reach understandings about norms, identities and interests through the public exchange of argument.[9] Public spheres are not necessarily coterminous with the borders of the state.[10] Multiple public spheres, within or across state borders, compete with national public spheres as the primary site of contestation. The relationship between these multiple public spheres as sites of contestation is an important structural variable for explaining the process of norm and interest formation in international relations. In Arab politics, the existence of a hotly contested transnational public sphere primarily concerned with collective Arab interests in the 1950-60s, and its transformation in the 1970-80s into a more state-centric structure, produce fundamentally different patterns of state behavior in the two periods.[11]

There are no guarantees that consensus can be achieved through public deliberation. The process of struggling for consensus is a political one, a point which is often concealed by Habermas's ideal of rational argumentation. There are important differences, however, between bargaining, in which actors pursue predefined interests, and communicative action, in which persuasion plays a more central role. I make no assumptions about the willingness or ability of actors to set aside their interests or their power in order to evaluate competing positions by the force of the better argument. What is important for the purposes of identifying moments of potential change is the empirical introduction into the public sphere of open discourse on identity.

The concept of strategic framing developed in recent social movement literature offers a bridge between public sphere structure and political outcomes. Argumentation involves overlapping struggles to es-

---

9. This definition is adapted from Margaret Somers, "Citizenship and the Place of the Public Sphere: Law, Community, and Political Culture in the Transition to Democracy," *American Sociological Review* 58, no. 4 (October 1993): 587–620; Calhoun, *Habermas and the Public Sphere*; Jürgen Habermas, *Structural Transformation of the Public Sphere* (Cambridge: MIT Press, 1989); and Habermas, *Between Facts and Norms*.

10. This argument that the public sphere is not necessarily identical with the state is not one which Habermas himself has made. See Habermas, "Citizenship and National Identity: Some Reflections on the Future of Europe," *Praxis International* 12, no. 1 (April 1992): 1–19, for his skepticism about the growth of an international public sphere in Europe. Bruce Cronin, "From Balance to Community: Transnational Identity and Political Integration," *Security Studies* 8, nos. 2/3 (winter 1998/99–spring 1999): 270–301, discusses the implications of a transnational public sphere in the case of Italian unification.

11. Michael N. Barnett, "Institutions, Roles and Disorder: the Case of the Arab States System," *International Studies Quarterly* 37, no. 3 (September 1993): 271–96; and Barnett, "Sovereignty, Nationalism and Regional Order in the Arab States System," *International Organization* 49, no. 4 (summer 1995): 479–510.

tablish interpretive frames.[12] Each frame claims to best interpret reality by providing an overarching conception of the identity, interests, and position of the collectivity. A frame provides a structure for interpreting and understanding the behavior of one's state and of others. In strategic framing, the actions and justifications of each state provide the public with opportunities to evaluate the relative explanatory power of each frame. Communicative action calls dominant frames into question by forcing the articulation and justification of positions and interests. Material power, while important, does not alone determine the outcome of these struggles. Argumentation, the ability to mobilize public support, and the success of prediction and explanation of the behavior of others matters. When the Jordanian government resorted to the application of repressive force against the opposition, the public took this as evidence that the government had lost the debate. These framing processes drive outcomes in a wide range of international issues, as evidenced by the essays in this volume. The competition to frame NATO expansion as "allowing new democracies into the West" vs. "expanding the containment of Russia," for example, has important implications for the mobilization of support for the policy.[13]

Such periods of thematized identity produce different kinds of behavior than would be expected under "normal" circumstances of stable identities and interests. A number of hypotheses can be proposed based on the presence or absence of a public sphere. When an effective public sphere exists, states will make alignment decisions which more closely fit state identity. Where important alignments cannot be justified in such terms, governments will either attempt to change state identity through public contestation or will attempt to repress the expression of public opposition. If identity change through contestation is chosen, actors will tend to most conform most to publicly expressed positions, as they attempt to establish the credibility of their frame. Even self-interested actors might choose to sacrifice short-term interest in the interests of living up to their public rhetoric and thereby establishing a

12. Doug McAdam, John D. McCarthy, and Mayer N. Zald, eds., *Comparative Perspectives on Social Movements: Political Opportunities, Mobilizing Structures, and Cultural Framings* (New York: Cambridge University Press, 1996); Sidney Tarrow, *Power in Movement: Social Movements, Collective Action and Politics* (New York: Cambridge University Press 1994); Bert Klandermans, Hanspeter Kriesi and Sidney Tarrow, *From Structure to Action: Comparing Social Movement Research Across Cultures* (Greenwich, Conn: JAI Press, 1988).

13. Franz Schimmelfennig, "NATO's Enlargement: A Constructivist Explanation," *Security Studies* 8, nos. 2/3 (winter 1998/99–spring 1999): 198–234.

reputation for credibility. If consensus is achieved, the new conceptions of identity and interest can become institutionalized and actors are likely to resume strategic behavior based on stable interests and preferences. In the absence of a workable consensus, however, escalating state-society tensions are likely to plague the state and force a reconsideration of the foreign policy, even if the objective interests at stake have not changed.

Jordan has experienced three interrelated identity crises in the past decade, each of which has entered into the public sphere in different forms. First, the severing of ties with the West Bank in 1988 introduced a crisis in the Jordanian-Palestinian dimension of Jordanian identity. Public deliberation eventually produced a powerful consensus on a new Jordanian identity centered on the East Bank. Second, the Gulf crisis brought on a crisis in Jordan's Arab identity, which is the primary focus of this paper. Third, the peace treaty with Israel challenged the foundations of Jordan's state identity, a crisis which remains unresolved and which has been met with more repression than engagement.

THE GULF CRISIS, 1990–91

R ELATIONS BETWEEN Jordan and Iraq in the decade prior to the Gulf crisis had developed to the point of a close alignment, after a long period of suspicion and hostility beginning with the Iraqi revolution of 1958 and the overthrow of King Husayn's Hashemite kinsmen. In the late 1970s, Jordan turned toward Iraq as the state most likely to provide both strategic depth and economic benefits.[14] The 1980 war between Iran and Iraq facilitated the consolidation of Jordanian-Iraqi relations. In light of Jordanian public support of Iraq in 1990, it is interesting to note that the public reaction to the embrace of Iraq in 1980 was far from positive. As one political activist remembers, "most Jordanian politicians were against the war, many going to the point of hoping the Iraqis would fail militarily...the popular sentiments were similarly against Iraq...all despite the official position of the King."[15] Pro-Syrian Arabists, most Palestinian factions, and pro-Iranian Isla-

14. Laurie A. Brand, *Jordan's Inter-Arab Alliances: The Political Economy of Alliance Making* (New York: Columbia University Press, 1994); Brand, "Economics and Shifting Alliances: Jordan's Relations with Syria and Iraq, 1975–81," *International Journal of Middle East Studies* 26 (summer 1994): 393–413.

15. Jamal Sha'ir, *A Politician Remembers* (in Arabic) (London: Riyad al-Ris, 1987), 270–72.

mists all initially opposed the official tilt to Iraq. The closed and underdeveloped Jordanian public sphere, restricted to privately circulated letters to the King, had little impact on state policy. Opinion changed in Iraqi favor in the early 1980s, with official media encouragement, growing economic interaction, and popular anger inflamed by Syria's threatening behavior. By the late 1980s, official relations had grown unusually close, culminating in the formation of the Arab Cooperation Council as an important axis in inter-Arab politics. The development of Jordanian-Iraqi relations involved growing positive identification and a sense among Jordanians of a common destiny and shared interests which went beyond a temporary convergence of interests.[16] While public identification with Iraq grew close over time, the negative public response, only a decade before the Gulf crisis, belies assertions of organic, essential or eternal pro-Iraqi public opinion. Identification with Iraq developed during a decade of close interaction and active construction of such a consensus.

During the Gulf crisis, Jordan's refusal to join the American coalition surprised many observers, who considered Jordan among the closest and most reliable American allies in the region.[17] Jordanian behavior in this period is often misunderstood, both by its supporters and its critics. Popular perceptions of a Jordan enthusiastically supporting Iraqi aggression against Kuwait are as misleading as are revisionist ar-

16. The development of positive identification with Iraq parallels the emergence of positive identification among states discussed by Colin Kahl, "Constructing a Separate Peace: Constructivism, Collective Liberal Identity, and Democratic Peace," *Security Studies* 8, nos. 2/3 (winter 1998/99-spring 1999): 94–144; also see Wendt, "Collective identity formation." Amatzia Baram, "Baathi Iraq and Hashemite Jordan: from hostility to alignment," *Middle East Journal* 45, no. 1 (winter 1991): 51–70, provides important evidence of the depth of positive identification between the two polities.

17. For overviews of the Gulf crisis, including Jordanian policy, see Dilip Hiro, *Desert Shield to Desert Storm* (New York: Routledge 1992); Lawrence Freedman and Efraim Karsh, *The Gulf Conflict 1990–1991: Diplomacy and War in the New World Order* (Princeton: Princeton University Press, 1993); Majid Khadduri and Edmund Ghareeb, *War in the Gulf, 1990–91: The Iraq-Kuwait Conflict and Its Implications* (New York: Oxford University Press 1997); Mohamed Hasanayn Haykal's *The Gulf Crisis* (in Arabic) (Cairo: al-Ahram, 1992). *The White Book*, published by the Jordanian Ministry of Information in 1991, is invaluable as a reflection of the ideas held by Jordanian policymakers and how they wanted their position understood. On Jordanian policy, see Laurie A. Brand, "Liberalization and Changing Political Coalitions: The Bases of Jordan's 1990–1991 Gulf Crisis Policy," *Jerusalem Journal of International Relations* 13, no. 4 (1991): 1–46; Joseph Nevo, "Jordan's Relations with Iraq: Ally or Victim?" in *Iraq's Road to War*, ed. Amatzia Baram and Barry Rubin (New York: St. Martin's, 1993), 135–47. For Jordanian analyses, see Abdullah Naqrash, "The Official Jordanian Political Position in the Arab Gulf Crisis" (in Arabic), *Dirasat* 21a, no. 4 (1994): 319–49; Ghazi Saleh Nahar, *Jordanian Foreign Policy Decisions Towards the Gulf Crisis* (in Arabic) (Amman: Dar al-Majdlawi, 1993).

guments that Jordanian policymakers reluctantly sided with Iraq only because of irresistible popular or economic pressure. From the outset of the crisis, King Husayn condemned the Iraqi invasion of Kuwait. Shuttling among world and Arab capitals, Husayn sought to find an acceptable solution within an Arab framework. After the failure of initial diplomatic efforts, the U.S.-led coalition intervened in force. Jordan campaigned consistently for a peaceful solution through dialogue within the Arab framework. The American deployment shifted the nature of the crisis from a controversial aggression by one Arab state against another to a face-off between an Arab power and the United States. From this shift emerged a common position: against the Iraqi invasion, but even more against the Western intervention.[18] Jordan adhered to the letter of UN resolutions, even as it came under punitive inspection regimes and accusations of sanctions-busting, and consistently maintained its neutrality in international fora.

Several rationalist explanations for this behavior have either been advanced in the literature or can be reasonably extrapolated from existing theoretical positions. While each offers a useful cut at Jordanian decisions, each underdetermines Jordanian behavior. After discussing each hypothesis, I argue that Jordan's behavior in the Gulf crisis is best explained in terms of the perceived failure of the Arabist order and the construction of an identity frame in the Jordanian public sphere powerfully linking Jordanian interests to Iraqi survival.

THREAT BALANCING

Rationalist explanations of Jordanian behavior in the Gulf crisis share the assumption of a rational unitary state actor pursuing objective, predefined interests, though they differ in the dimension of interest accorded analytical primacy. Stephen Walt's influential account of alliance behavior argued that states tend to balance against threat, rather than directly against power.[19] Walt's state-centric conception of threat was modified by analysts focusing on the developing world, who noted that state decisionmakers often responded more to internal threats to

18. Yezid Sayigh, "The Gulf Crisis: Why the Arab Regional Order Failed," *International Affairs* 67, no. 3 (July 1991): 487–507; George Joffe, "Middle Eastern Views of the Gulf Conflict and Its Aftermath," *Review of International Studies* 19 (April 1993): 177–99; Barbara Ebert, "The Gulf War and Its Aftermath: An Assessment of Evolving Arab Responses," *Middle East Policy* 1, no. 4 (1992): 77–95.

19. Stephen M. Walt, *The Origin of Alliances* (Ithaca: Cornell University Press, 1987).

regime stability than to external military threats.[20] The wide range of threats from which Jordanians had to choose during the Gulf crisis renders even the more nuanced threat-based explanations problematic, however.[21] Israel, Iraq and domestic turbulence each posed a serious threat to Jordanian security and/or regime survival. Why did Jordan balance with one and bandwagon with the other? Which threat motivated Jordanian behavior? While Walt points to objective indicators of threat, such as proximity, offensive capabilities, or perceptions of aggressive intent, such indicators fail to capture the process by which threats were transformed into policy prescriptions.[22] Because of uncertainty and the perception of multiple threats emanating from every direction, interpretation necessarily played a major role in the specification of threat.

A number of threat-based interpretations of Jordanian policy seem plausible and could have easily been invoked to explain almost any Jordanian policy during the crisis. First, Jordan could be seen as balancing an Israeli threat by allying with Iraq. Even prior to the crisis, Jordanians publicly feared Israeli intentions to launch a war in order to facilitate the expulsion of West Bank Palestinians into Jordan and create a Palestinian state on the East Bank.[23] Israeli press discussions of Jordan's diminishing value for Israeli interests and militant declarations that Jordan was Palestine fed these fears.[24] These arguments contained

20. Steven R. David, "Explaining Third World Alignment," *World Politics* 43, no. 2 (January 1991): 233–57; Mohammed Ayoob, "The Security Problematic in the Third World," *World Politics* 43, no. 3 (January 1991): 257–83.

21. Richard Harknett and Jeffrey VanDenBerg, "Alignment Theory and Interrelated Threats: Jordan and the Persian Gulf Crisis," *Security Studies* 6, no. 3 (spring 1997): 112–53, apply threat-balancing theories to Jordanian policy in the Gulf crisis.

22. Michael N. Barnett discusses Walt's threat-balancing theory in the Middle East context in "Identity and Alliances in the Middle East," in Katzenstein, *The Culture of National Security*, 400–50; David Campbell, *Writing Security: United States Foreign Policy and the Politics of Identity* (Minneapolis: University of Minnesota Press, 1991), emphasizes the discursive and social construction of external threats, suggesting that threat might be better understood as a dependent than as an independent variable. Michael Spirtas, "French Twist: French and British NATO Policies from 1949 to 1966," *Security Studies* 8, nos. 2/3 (winter 1998/99–spring 1999): 302–46, argues for the role of identity in producing threat perception between states.

23. Shibley Telhami, "Arab Public Opinion and the Gulf War," *Political Science Quarterly* 108, no. 3 (fall 1993): 437–52. For the Jordanian perspective, see Taher al-Masri, "Speech to the Arab Professionals Conference" (in Arabic), *al-Dustur* (Amman) 14 May 1990; and the roundtable discussions in *The Gulf Crisis in Jordanian Political Thought* (in Arabic) (Amman: Dar al-Sha'ab, 1991).

24. Randa Sharara, "Israel in the Gulf Crisis: The Position on Jordan" (in Arabic), *Majellah al-Dirasat al-Filastiniyya* 4 (fall 1990): 72–83; Colin Shindler, *Israel, Likud and the Zionist Dream: Power, Politics, and Ideology from Begin to Netanyahu* (London: I. B. Tauris, 1995); Yehuda Lukacs, *Israel, Jordan and the Peace Process* (Albany: State Uni-

a direct, public threat: acting on pro-Iraqi public opinion would be grounds for an Israeli intervention.[25]

While Israel posed a threat, there are strong reasons to think such threats were less cause than justification for Jordanian behavior. Since the American war effort promised to achieve Israel's strategic interests without Israeli involvement, there was little rational reason for Israeli military action. Indeed, the Americans publicly lobbied Israel to stay out of the hostilities in order to keep the coalition together and to prevent linkage between the Kuwait occupation and the Israeli occupation of Palestine. On the other hand, Israeli strategic policy had been massive retaliation for any attack, so even such strong disincentives could not be taken as a guarantee. Can leaders rely on the "rationality" of other leaders in such tense moments?[26]

More relevant, then, were Jordanian-Israeli communications and signaling during the crisis.[27] Israeli prime minister Shamir reportedly promised King Husayn that Israel would intervene if and only if Iraqi troops entered Jordan and "Israel's eastern border became hostile," while Husayn promised not to allow such an Iraqi movement. Foreign Minister David Levy publicly reassured Jordan during the crisis that Israel had no hostile intentions against Jordan, and that it considered Jordanian stability to be a fundamental Israeli strategic interest, but that "any threat coming from Jordan against Israel...or movement of troops from outside Jordan into Jordan will be a warning signal to Israel."[28] Levy claims to have sent Husayn such reassurances through an intermediary and to have received a satisfactory response.[29] Prime Minister Mudar Badran alluded to these reassurances publicly, declaring that Iraqi troops would not enter Jordan except in response to an Is-

versity of New York Press, 1997); Ian S. Lustick, *Unsettled States, Disputed Lands: Britain and Ireland, France and Algeria, Israel and the West Bank-Gaza* (Ithaca: Cornell University Press, 1994), discuss the various stances on Jordan in Israeli politics.

25. Prime Minister Shamir warned against an Iraqi deployment in Jordan in the Knesset session broadcast on Israeli Radio, 15 October 1990, in FBIS-NES-90-200.

26. R. Ned Lebow, *Between Peace and War: The Nature of International Crisis* (Baltimore: Johns Hopkins University Press 1981).

27. James A. Baker, *The Politics of Diplomacy* (New York: Random House 1995), 386; Leslie Susser, "Secret Route to Public Dialogue," *Jerusalem Report*, 11 August 1994, 21.

28. David Levy on Israeli TV, 20 August 1990, in *Israeli Foreign Relations* vol. 12, Document 153, 372–73.

29. Foreign Minister David Levy on Israeli TV, 18 October 1990, in FBIS-NES-90-204, 22 October 1990, 21–25, quote at 24.

raeli incursion.[30] Such a precise specification of the meaning of signals facilitated the efficient exchange of information.[31] These communications at the highest levels must have alleviated official Jordanian concern with this threat. While Jordanian officials continued to refer to the Israeli threat, this served more as a public justification and demonstration of valor than as an indication of their motivations.

Second, Jordan could be seen as bandwagoning with Iraq in order to protect itself against an Iraqi threat. Perhaps the real strategic concern was that Iraq, surrounded on all sides, would decide to break out by invading Jordan en route to Israel in order to spark a general Arab-Israeli war and break up the coalition. Were the border to be closed and Iraq to be fully isolated, it would have little to lose by expanding the war into now-hostile Jordanian territory. The recent Iraqi aggression against a small neighboring state provided an important signal about its possible offensive intentions. By maintaining friendly relations with Iraq, Jordan could presumably forestall such an Iraqi threat. Realism would suggest that Jordan would incline toward balancing Iraqi power rather than bandwagoning, however. Aligning with the U.S. coalition in order to secure a credible balance against an Iraqi threat would be a plausible response to a perceived Iraqi threat. While Arabist norms in the past would have prohibited such an alliance choice, the participation of Egypt, Syria and Saudi Arabia in the coalition certainly provided sufficient cover.[32] Israel exercised deterrence on Jordan's behalf independently of Jordanian policy by making the presence of Iraqi troops in Jordan a red line. Aligning with Iraq in order to forestall an Iraqi attack would have been superfluous. Finally, no evidence exists that Iraq conveyed any threat, explicit or implicit, to Jordan that it would attack if Jordan did not take its side; even in King Husayn's revisionist speeches on the crisis since 1995, in which he has sharply criticized Saddam Husayn's policies, he has not accused Iraq of threatening Jordan with invasion.

30. Prime Minister Mudar Badran quoted in *Jordan Times*, 12 January 1991, 1, in FBIS-NES-91-009, 13 January 1991, 76–77.
31. James D. Fearon, "Signaling Foreign Policy Interests: Tying Hands versus Sinking Costs," *Journal of Conflict Resolution* 41, no. 1 (February 1997): 68–90, discusses the complexities of signals and the difficulties of making signals credible.
32. The importance of Arabist norms in eliminating Israel as a viable choice of alliance partner is itself an important point whose significance rationalists fail to appreciate. Nothing in the power or threat standards upon which their theories ostensibly rely explains the consistent rejection of relations with Israel by all Arab states. Even Jordan, which enjoyed a working relationship and many common interests with Israel, refused to make this alignment public.

Third, King Husayn could be seen less as bandwagoning with Iraq than as bandwagoning with domestic pro-Iraqi political actors in order to protect his regime from domestic upheaval. Perhaps the most popular explanation of Husayn's decision has been his fear that his regime could not stand before a mobilized, united public opinion.[33] As Brand argues, "the clear and vociferous anti-American/pro-Iraqi message of a largely united Jordanian people during a period of transition from authoritarianism meant that a Gulf policy even remotely pro-coalition might well have led to severe instability, if not the end of the monarchy."[34] The threat to regime survival tends to be assumed rather than specified, however. While many observers have reported the charged atmosphere of late 1990 and the heady mobilization of the population, none has produced evidence that the army, the security services, or even major political groupings would have acted to overthrow the king had he sided with the American coalition. Jordanian diplomatic history is a recitation of instances of Husayn's decisions taken against the express desires of the majority of the Jordanian political public, none of which has prompted serious rebellion. Furthermore, the regime's ability to sign a peace treaty with Israel without any serious threat of revolution suggests its relative stability in the face of popular displeasure. The causal argument for domestic threat rests on a counterfactual that seems highly implausible based both on historical experience and contemporary evidence. This does not mean that the democratic opening of 1989 was unimportant: the opening of the public sphere was crucial for determining Jordanian behavior, but not by way of posing a threat to regime survival.

The plausibility of such different causal paths suggests that "threat" is not sufficient to explain Jordanian behavior. Some other process seems to be at work which made some behavior seem more threatening than others. In the context of profound uncertainty, the construction of threat through a communicative process, rather than a response to an objectively existing threat, most characterizes foreign policy. The threat motivating Jordanian behavior emerged from the process of public sphere debate, which quickly moved to identify the dimensions and scope of the threat. In the process of framing, a consensus quickly

33. Harknett and VanDenBerg , "Alignment Theory and Interrelated Threats," place great emphasis on the potentially revolutionary situation in Jordan during the crisis (135–39). Their primary evidence, however, consists of post facto interviews with government officials, who have a clear incentive to overstate these fears in order to justify their behavior.

34. Brand, "Liberalization and Changing Political Coalitions," 2–3.

emerged that "the threat to Iraq is a threat to Jordan," uniting interests and identity into a simple and compelling formula. The King's formulation of this position therefore rested firmly on a consensus which emerged, uncoerced, from the Jordanian public sphere.

POLITICAL ECONOMY

Economic interests are another widely cited explanation for Jordanian behavior: "Behind [King Husayn's] positions lies a Jordanian-Iraqi interdependence that has grown deep in recent years. Jordan has grown so dependent on Iraq as a market for its exports and as a source of cheap oil that destruction of the Iraqi economy threatens to destroy Jordan's economy as well."[35] A direct, unmediated relationship between material interests and political positions is assumed. Like threat-based explanations, the political economy argument underdetermines outcomes. For all Jordan's trade dependence on Iraq, it also received vital budget subsidies from Kuwait and Saudi Arabia. Brand's "budget security" explanation of Jordanian foreign policy demonstrates the importance of direct subsidies for the maintenance of the rentier state, which suggests that state actors should give higher priority in their articulation of interests to sources of budget subsidies than to markets.[36] Besides direct budget support, the remittances of Jordanians and Palestinians employed in the Gulf to Jordanian banks represented an essential pillar of Jordan's political economy. Finally, Jordan relied heavily upon international aid, both from the United States and from international lending agencies. Support for Iraq in the crisis clearly and unambiguously threatened all of these. Why were trade relations with Iraq valued more highly than the massive budget supports from these states ranged on the other side of the confrontation? Brand's argument that Jordanian officials had grown weary of the unreliability of Gulf subsidies offers no answer; the definite promises of financial aid made by the United States and its allies would have responded to precisely this concern.

The necessary link between economy and political position might be provided by a closer look at the form of Jordanian-Iraqi economic rela-

---

35. Stanley Reed, "Jordan and the Gulf Crisis," *Foreign Affairs* 69, no. 5 (winter 1990/91): 21–35.

36. Brand, *Jordan's Inter-Arab Relations*, chap. 2, and 284–95. In "Liberalization and Changing Political Coalitions," Brand reviews these competing economic interests and admits that the conflicting interests prevent a causal political economy explanation.

tions and the development of trade networks and positive identification. Rather than being limited to direct budget subsidies, Iraqi support took the form of investment in an infrastructure to support trade relations. The port of Aqaba, in particular, received Iraqi investment attention; in addition, Iraq invested in joint ventures and paid special attention to the transport sector.[37] The trade networks, tying together individuals, corporations, and governments, penetrated far more deeply than did the direct budget subsidies from Gulf states, producing a more direct articulation of common identity and interests. As Iraq became the single largest Jordanian trade partner, a "strong pro-Iraqi business lobby" emerged.[38] In other words, where budget subsidies might create an institutionalized expectation of cooperation at the state level, trade relations create networks of interest at the level of society.

In economic terms, Jordan clearly made the wrong decision. This decision cannot be explained by a lack of information or by a failure to consider the probable outcomes. Decisionmakers and the public were painfully aware of the likely impact of the crisis on the Jordanian economy. The press published frank evaluations of the probable loss of Gulf aid, of the blockade of the Port of Aqaba, of the mass return of Jordanians and Palestinians from jobs in the Gulf. At the same time, Jordanians knew of the American inducements to its Arab coalition partners: "Jordan is fully aware of the size of the bribe it would have received had it agreed [to join the coalition]. We know that our foreign debts would have been canceled with a stroke of a pen, that the siege [of Aqaba] would have been lifted...and that aid and money would have poured into Jordan from all directions, as they pour into the U.S. Arab 'allies'...in the largest sale of consciences in history."[39] Nothing in public discourse suggested any expectation that support for Iraq would prove financially rewarding in the short or medium term: "All Jordanians know that this position will cost Jordan dearly financially...but Jordan is governed by considerations deeper than money."[40]

37. Baram, "Baathi Iraq and Hashemite Jordan," 56, notes that, in 1980, Jordan received $189.2 million in loans and $58.3 million in grants, "much of which went to expand the facilities at Aqaba and improve the highway from Aqaba to the Iraqi border."

38. Baram, "Baathi Iraq and Hashemite Jordan," 58.

39. "The Arab Individual that Washington Does Not Know," (in Arabic), al-Dustur, 1 February 1991, 1, 15, in FBIS-NES-91-023, 68–69.

40. Jamil Nimri, "Husayn and the Diplomacy of the Arabist Position" (in Arabic), al-Ahali, 5 September 1990, 3.

This last assertion introduces the important point that economic ties to Iraq were interpreted within the Jordanian public sphere as holding normative value deeper than their economic value. Ties to Iraq took on an heroic quality as an expression of Arab solidarity. Economic relations were interpreted, and became politically relevant, through the lens of identity. The nature of the Jordanian-Iraqi economic relationship supports this argument. Jordan's economy was tied to the Iraqi market in more than volume of trade. Trade with Iraq involved the development of infrastructure, supply networks, regularized patterns of exchange, and product specialization which could not simply be redirected in the way that direct budget subsidies theoretically could be. While a Japanese budget subsidy could frictionlessly replace a Saudi subsidy, the Iraqi market and the capital, transportation and information investments underlying it could not be replaced with similar ease. Furthermore, no comparable markets existed in the area to replace the Iraqi market. As a Jordanian political scientist explains, "Iraq was the only Arab state that could solve Jordan's long-term economic problems."[41] The argument that trade relations between Jordanians and Iraqis had built networks of community of identity and interests—a constructivist argument—is thus more satisfying than a straightforward equation of economic interdependence and political interests, and better explains why Jordanian society placed higher value on Iraqi rather than Gulf economic relations.

PUBLIC OPINION

Explanations of Jordanian behavior in the crisis regularly import public opinion into ostensibly state-centric accounts to overcome the underdetermination of such explanations.[42] Brand, for example, modifies the budget-security argument in the Gulf war case by proposing that "[above all] King Husayn was responding to...popular opinion in the Jordanian street."[43] Virtually every account of Jordanian policy stresses the importance of public opinion, without allowing this admission to

41. Naqrash, "The official Jordanian Position in the Gulf Crisis," 330–32.

42. Shibley Telhami, "Arab Public Opinion in the Gulf War"; and "Power and Legitimacy in Arab Alliances" (paper presented at the American Political Science Association annual meeting, Washington, D.C., August 1994), examines the influence of public opinion on the foreign policies of Arab states. Also see David Pollock, *The 'Arab Street'? Public Opinion in the Arab World*, Paper no. 32 (Washington, D.C.: Washington Institute for Near East Studies Policy, 1992).

43. Brand, *Jordan's Inter-Arab Relations*, 288.

infiltrate the general reliance on variables such as power, economics, or threat. After admitting that the preferred theory underdetermines Jordanian behavior, each analyst introduces a stylized reading of public opinion on an ad hoc basis to fill in the gap. A public sphere theory can better specify the scope conditions for the role of public opinion and provide a theoretical grounding for its incorporation into a coherent account of state behavior.

The public sphere processes emphasized here should not be reduced to public opinion.[44] Rather than the process of interest and identity formation through public debate, public opinion is generally conceptualized as objectively existing, static, and exogenous. The rationalist use of public opinion posits a sharp distinction between state interests and public opinion, each an independent and objectively specified category. Public opinion at most represents a constraint upon the rational action of states. It does not contribute to the formation of state interests, which are conceptualized as external to the process of political struggle. Therefore, in the explanation of the Gulf crisis, the Jordanian "street" emerged as a powerful constraint, preventing the government from effectively pursuing Jordan's "real" interests. A unified, mobilized Jordanian political society put irresistible pressure on a beleaguered king who knew better but could not stand against it. Support for Iraq welled up from the deep Arabist convictions of the people, who were emotionally swept away by the appearance of a "new Saladin" bidding to unite the Arab world and confront the West. Because of the liberalization of 1989, the public now had the means through which to declare and act upon its convictions. Since the democratization had become essential for regime legitimacy, the regime could not afford repression and could not oppose the will of the aroused public.

This familiar account misrepresents the nature of Jordanian public opinion formation. It assumes a prior and constant degree of support for Iraq among all sectors of political society which was then revealed by liberalization and the Gulf crisis rather than formed in the political process. It reads political behavior directly from essentialized, ascribed identities: Jordanians supported Saddam because of their nature as "Islamic fundamentalists" and "Palestinians," without explaining why these identities, rather than other possible political identities, became the most important for purposes of the understanding of interests. Given the existence of multiple identity choices, the interesting ques-

---

44. Habermas, *Between Facts and Norms*, 361–63.

tion should be why identity came to be framed in such a way that "Arab" or "Islamist" identities trumped others.

A public sphere account, in contrast, views public opinion as constructed in the process of dialogue and as constitutive of interests. Rather than conceptualizing the public as solely a constraint on state behavior, it considers the public sphere structures in which state policymakers are embedded to be formative of their conceptions of the state's interests. In other words, Jordan's interests are defined by the consensus achieved in the public sphere, and should not be viewed as external to these public conceptions. The liberalization process in Jordan did more than allow the "street" to operate as a more effective constraint. During this period of perceived internal and external crisis, the Jordanian public sphere emerged as the primary site for defining Jordanian identity and interests. Interaction in this public sphere during the Gulf crisis produced an effective consensus in support of Iraq which had a powerful effect on state behavior. Active debate in the Jordanian public sphere produced convincing interpretations of Jordanian interests, based in a powerful identity claim rooted in Jordan's Arab character, which state actors accepted and upon which they acted.

I argue that the Jordanian commitment to Iraq emerged through the process of public debate, which established a consensus around an Arabist collective identity frame. A Jordanian identity defined by shared sacrifice and valorous support of an Arabist cause emerged in the heady days of late 1990. Where "Palestinians" or "Islamists" rallied to Iraq, it was because of the successful articulation of a collective identity claim and an attendant specification of interests, threats, and prescriptions for behavior. For the emergent Jordanian consensus, "the unjust war did not only target Iraq but also all who stand beside Iraq and its Arabist message."[45] This consensus, in which Jordan's identity was directly tied to Iraq, was both the outcome of public sphere debate and an important causal variable for subsequent Jordanian behavior.

Participants and analysts disagree about the precise relationship between opinion leaders and public opinion in forming this consensus. The editor of a major daily contends that "during the Gulf war, the press was primarily responsible for the mass mobilization on the side of Iraq...the press crystallized and focused popular sentiment."[46] Opin-

---

45. Hamada Fara'na, "Jordanians and Palestinians in One Trench" (in Arabic), *al-Dustur*, 12 March 1991, 25.
46. Nabil Sharif, editor of *al-Dustur*, interview by author, Amman, 16 March 1995.

ion leaders played an important role in interpreting the crisis and influencing the direction of public mobilization.[47] Not all participants accept the proposition that the press created or even led public opinion, however. In the midst of the crisis, the respected opposition journalist Fahd Rimawi located the real force of the consensus in the public: "Most of the time I feel that the writer follows public opinion and does not create it...he represents the dictatorship of mass frenzy and does not oppose it."[48] This interpretation removes all agency from the explanation, portraying an authoritative consensus which emerged on its own. While this captures the sense of helplessness felt by many Jordanians in the face of the relentless slide to war, it unnecessarily slights the importance of public sphere actors in shaping the political consensus. Political entrepreneurs deployed the Arabist frame, which proved extremely successful in mobilizing people. Once established, this frame quickly achieved near-hegemonic status, and virtually all public discussion accepted its terms of reference. The press established the interpretive frame by which the public understood the crisis, while the subsequent political process of public argumentation produced a powerful, binding consensus.

The argument that the public sphere process produced the consensus begins from the important but overlooked fact that the initial reaction was far from unanimous. In the first few days after the invasion, a wide array of reactions appeared in the press and public discourse. No single interpretation appeared among all Jordanians, or among all opinion leaders, and no "official" discourse dictated by the Palace controlled the field. Many who later led public support for Iraq initially condemned the invasion as an impermissible Arab-Arab bloodletting. Commentators weighed, with varying results, the norms of sovereignty and peaceful resolution of inter-Arab conflicts against the merit of Iraqi claims against Kuwait and Kuwaiti intransigence. Most writers were impressed by Iraqi arguments but profoundly uneasy about the precedent of the military annexation of one Arab country by another. The initial reaction, hesitant and frightened of the implications for regional security, belies the post facto reconstruction of Jordanian opinion as fervently pro-Iraqi from the beginning.

This intense public-sphere contestation did not last long, however. Near-unanimity of opinion followed closely upon the shifting of the

---

47. Marwan Barakat, *The Gulf War in the Jordanian Press* (in Arabic) (Amman: Mu'assisat Rum, 1992).

48. Fahd al-Rimawi, quoted in Barakat, *The Gulf War in the Jordanian Press*, 129.

terms of debate from "Iraq vs. Kuwait" to "Iraq vs. United States" in the first weeks of the crisis. The rise of this interpretation of the conflict to a hegemonic, consensus interpretation is essential to understanding the process of consensus formation in the Jordanian public sphere. Once the conflict left the inter-Arab framework, many of the ambiguities of the interpretive process disappeared: "We don't incline towards Iraq or towards Kuwait...we incline to ourselves and to all Arabs."[49] Rather than weighing the violation of Kuwaiti sovereignty against the manifest injustice of the distribution of Arab wealth, observers now saw an intervention by the imperial powers against an Arab challenger. In such an interpretive frame, Arab identity and Arab interests demanded resistance to foreign power and support for Iraq. In the absence of this frame, it is not clear that the Jordanian public would have settled upon consensus support of Iraq. After all, defense of state sovereignty, a rejection of imposed Arab unity, and the impermissibility of acquiring land by force had been consistent Jordanian norms for decades and could easily have shaped a frame against the Iraqi occupation. The importance of communicative action in translating identity into behavior in this case serves as a warning against overly structural constructivist arguments. The equation of Arab identity and the Iraqi position emerged from the public negotiation of a consensus interpretation, rather than from preexisting or objective factors. Once this consensus interpretation of the crisis crystallized, it translated quickly into an articulation of Jordanian interests and prescriptions for behavior. The consensus proved extremely effective at uniting opinion, guiding behavior, and framing the interpretation of subsequent events.

This consensus forged in the Jordanian public sphere reflected the process of communicative interaction in the Arabist arena. The transition to an "Arab vs. American" frame took place across the Arab world, with Jordan's open public sphere offering one of the few outlets for its expression. Consensus formation at the official Arab level did not follow Arab norms, and the Cairo Summit Resolution was denounced as not representing an authentic Arabist consensus. Numerous reports of the proceedings of the closed summit discussions have emphasized the tight Egyptian control over debate and voting, and the refusal to allow the Arab League to play a genuine role in mediating the conflict and preventing an American intervention.[50] Jordanian of-

---

49. Fahd al-Fanik, quoted in Barakat, *The Gulf War in the Jordanian Press*, 25.

50. Ghareeb and Khadduri, *War in the Gulf*, elaborate this version of events, drawing heavily on the analysis of Mohammed Hassanayn Haykal.

ficials accused Egypt of changing its position under American pressure, a charge which Egypt angrily denied; such a charge essentially denies the Arab authenticity of the Egyptian stance and the Cairo Resolution. In the face of the rejection of the Cairo Summit, and the opposition to the American coalition and support for Iraq in every Arab country which allowed public freedoms, support for Iraq was articulated as the position associated with Arab identity. Jordan's Arab identity, as well as its security, were identified with support for an Arab solution and a refusal to participate in the war coalition despite American and Arab pressure.

As should be clear, I am not arguing that the public commitment to Arabism forced Jordan to act against its state interests. On the contrary, my argument is that the interpretations of Arabism in the Jordanian public sphere led Jordanians to understand state interests as best served by not joining the anti-Iraq coalition. Husayn's surprising policies were widely interpreted as a rare convergence in the public and the official conceptions of Jordanian interests. Once consensus had been achieved, few voices questioned the assertion of a Jordanian interest in supporting Arab Iraq; the suffocating force of this consensus reflects the concerns expressed by some liberal theorists about the pressures for conformity in Habermas's ideal.[51] The consensus on the interpretation of the crisis in Arabist terms largely determined the formulation of interests and then behavior. The rejection of Jordanian argumentation in the Arabist and international public spheres only increased the power of the Jordanian public sphere, enhancing the feelings of solidarity and unity underlying the policy consensus.

MENDING FENCES, 1991–94

AFTER THE Gulf War, the Jordanian public sphere enjoyed efficacy, primacy, and a relative freedom unique in its history. The democratic opening had become a major element in the regime's legitimacy, with high normative value accorded to responsible dissent and open debate. The Arabist public sphere, fragmented by the Gulf war, had yet to be reformulated. The international public sphere remained hostile to Jordan because of Jordanian behavior in the Gulf war. Since the

---

51. Nicholas Rescher, *Pluralism: Against the Demand For Consensus* (New York: Oxford University Press, 1993); Seyla Benhabib, ed., *Democracy and Difference: Contesting the Boundaries of the Political* (Princeton: Princteon University Press 1996).

1988 disengagement with the West Bank, the Jordanian public sphere even enjoyed relative autonomy from the Palestinian public sphere, a separation reinforced by the 1993 Oslo accords.[52] Finally, the Jordanian public sphere was widely credited with having influenced state behavior during the Gulf crisis, which built the confidence of public sphere participants in the efficacy of their participation. Between 1991 and 1994, the Jordanian public sphere was dominated by openly contested domestic issues: the repeal of martial law, the press and publications law, the political parties law, corruption, the role of the Islamists in democracy, and Jordanian-Palestinian relations. Spirited public debate of national issues within a broad consensus on Jordanian international identity and interests characterized this period. Even the peace process did not cause great public sphere confrontation in this period.

The structural changes in the public sphere opened up access to the print media to an unprecedented range of voices and issues, as the government lost some degree of control over the public agenda. Beginning in 1990, independent weeklies which relentlessly pushed the boundaries of acceptable discourse appeared. By 1993, a dense network of weekly newspapers and magazines oriented toward public political debate existed. For the first time, diverse sectors of political society had a consistent voice in the Jordanian public arena, to which the government felt compelled to respond. Achieving public consensus now involved far more print debate, not least because of the continued tight government control of the electronic media. Serious political discussion moved out of the closed, elitist salons and into the open, transforming the nature of political opinion formation. This network of newspapers formed a real, unified public sphere. It could reasonably be assumed that policymakers and public sphere participants read all the major columns which appeared in the two main dailies and in the major weeklies; according to a 1996 opinion poll, 52 percent of Jordanians read the daily press and 39 percent read the weeklies, a readership which certainly includes and transcends the entire political elite.[53] The

52. The Jordanian public sphere could never be truly isolated from the Palestinian public sphere, but after the 1988 severing of ties a conscious effort was made to create a distinctly Jordanian public sphere in which only Jordanian identity and interests served as a legitimate reference point. For details, see Lynch, "Rightsizing Jordan: Moving Borders and the Politics of Identity" (paper presented to the annual meeting of the International Studies Association, Minneapolis, MN, 19–22 February 1998).

53. Center for Strategic Studies, University of Jordan, "Democracy in Jordan 1996"; and "Democracy in Jordan 1997." It is significant that in 1997, after significant government repression of the press, the numbers dropped to 34 percent reading the daily press and 17 percent reading the weekly press, demonstrating that people were aware

government took these debates seriously enough to monitor them closely and to intervene when challenged; the 1997 revision of the Press and Publications Law became the most hotly contested issue of public freedoms.

Government and opposition alike recognized the heavy economic and political price Jordan had paid for its Gulf war position, but they disagreed over the appropriate response. The tension between the desire of state policymakers to restore Jordan's position with its traditional Western and Gulf allies and the strong normative commitment to Iraq became more important as Jordan participated in the Arab-Israeli peace process and moved to reestablish a place in the pro-American camp. The contradiction manifested itself in the diametrically opposed public stances demanded by the Jordanian and the international public sphere. On the one hand, the United States and the Gulf demanded compliance with the sanctions regime and a full Jordanian apology, a confession that its support of Iraq had been politically and even morally wrong. On the other hand, the regime's newfound legitimacy rested in no small part upon its Gulf war policies. The crisis had unified the population around a shared identity, no small achievement for Jordan's traditionally fragmented political society. The regime made much of the sacrifices and hardships Jordan had suffered for its principles, and sought to justify all other policies from within this consensus. Jordanian policy rested upon a normative focal point which could not be lightly reversed: Jordan, unlike most other Arab states, had done the right thing during the Gulf crisis. The newly secured Jordanian identity rested upon this defining moment of unity and shared sacrifice.

Between 1991 and 1995, the Jordanian government tried to reconcile this normative consensus with Western and Gulf demands. Jordanian policy adhered to a set of consistently articulated principles: maintaining the unity and integrity of the Iraqi state; nonintervention in Iraqi affairs; and humanitarian concern for the Iraqi people. Until the 1995 reversal, these norms set the boundaries for Jordanian maneuver in the state's efforts to win back Western and Gulf support. The regime made a number of attempts to distance itself from the Iraqi regime and find a place within the international consensus without departing from these norms. In November 1992, King Husayn distanced himself from Sad-

---

of and responded to changes in the ability of the press to address important and sensitive topics. See, "Jordan: Clamping Down on Critics," *Human Rights Watch* 9, no. 12 (E) (October 1997): 1–34, for details of the government repression of the press.

dam Husayn by suggesting that the time had come for Iraqis to achieve democracy.[54] In early 1993, he suggested that Saddam Husayn's "relentless grip on power" had become a burden on the Iraqi people and hinted that he personally would step down if he ever became such a burden. These moves foundered upon the reticence of the Gulf states, which did not respond to Jordanian overtures, and the unwillingness of the Jordanian public to "grovel" before the Saudis and Kuwaitis. Shortly after the November 1992 speech, Husayn lashed out in frustration at the Kuwaitis and Saudis, to unexpectedly strong public applause which only reinforced the limited public sphere interest in Gulf reconciliation compared to concern with Iraqi suffering.[55] As long as Jordanian policy remained within the bounds of its domestic consensus, it could not satisfy its Arab and international critics.

The consensus norms institutionalized in the Jordanian public sphere directly conflicted with government efforts to repair relations with the Gulf states. State policymakers placed far more emphasis on the need for Gulf financial support and American approval than did most of the public. Intensely proud of Jordan's stance in the Gulf crisis, most of Jordanian political society fiercely opposed any concession to the Gulf demands for a Jordanian apology: "the benefits which might come to Jordan from Saudi Arabia and Kuwait simply do not justify desecrating our country's policies in the war."[56] At stake was not material interest but a normative stance. The "magic words" of apology would have likely brought a direct, significant monetary reward. For the Jordanian public sphere, however, such an apology meant a repudiation of the normative consensus which had bound and constituted the new democratic system and shared identity.

The divergence between this public consensus and the pragmatic orientations of state policymakers became sharper in 1994, as Jordan moved to formalize a peace treaty with Israel. Policymakers, keenly interested in reclaiming Gulf budget subsidies and American political and economic support, resented the efficacy of public opinion in binding their options on Iraq as much as they were infuriated by popular resistance to moves toward peace with Israel. At this point, the concep-

54. See Yousif Ibrahim, "Jordan's King Urges Iraqis to Put an End to the Hussein Era," *New York Times*, 8 November 1992, A1, A20; and Ibrahim, "Jordan Finds Saudis Are Unwilling to Forgive," *New York Times*, 31 December 1992, A11.

55. Mariam Shahin, "The King Lashes Out," *Middle East International*, 4 December 1992, 3–4.

56. Tareq Masarweh, "Relations with the Gulf and Arab Interests" (in Arabic), *al-Ufuq* 119, 14 September 1994, 3–4.

tion of the public sphere as constraint, rather than as a source of state interests, begins to more accurately describe the situation, as the government moved to increase its autonomy from public opinion and to crack down on opposition. This official anger manifested itself in escalating complaints about the abuse of "responsible" press freedoms. Prime Minister Majali "blamed the Jordanian media for continued strains in relations between the Kingdom and the Gulf states."[57] After the Jordan-Israel peace treaty, this criticism escalated into repression, with editors charged with the crime of "harming relations with a friendly states" for publishing attacks on the Gulf monarchies. Officials suggested that the writers and the papers producing such articles were tied to foreign interests working against Jordan. In September 1995, the Arabic daily al-Hayat cited documents alleging massive Iraqi penetration of the media establishment, which was being mobilized to "create a trend opposed to official Jordanian policy."[58] The campaign against "Iraqi influence" represented a major escalation in the regime efforts to deny Jordanian identity to those who opposed official foreign policy. Even more, it attempted to discredit the Jordanian public sphere by denying its autonomy, its loyalty and its authenticity as an expression of Jordanian identity and interests.

The conflict over the meaning of Jordanian-Iraqi relations extended to a reinterpretation of the value of Jordanian-Iraqi economic relations. Businessmen, who amassed considerable profits from trade with Iraq even under sanctions, had a rather different perspective than state policymakers, who expressed increasing doubts about the merits of the Iraqi market. As early as the mid-1980s, trade with Iraq depended on Jordan's provision of export credits, on which Iraq had amassed a billion dollar debt.[59] While businesses prospered, the state was losing money, actively subsidizing the private-sector profits. While this provides a material basis for the state-society differences over Jordanian interests, this should not be taken too far. The state also profited from the Iraqi connection through discounted Iraqi oil, bartered at prices less than half of the world market price. Therefore, a direct inference

57. Prime Minister Abd al-Salam al-Majali, quoted in Jordan Times, 11 January 1994; in FBIS-NES-94-007, 38–39.

58. Salam'ah Nima't, "Jordanian Fears of Iraqi Penetration" (in Arabic), al-Hayat, 20 September 1995, 1; and Nima't interview in al-Hadath, 27 September 1995; in FBIS-NES-95-188, 28 September 1995, 53.

59. Brand, Jordan's Inter-Arab Relations, describes the economic impact of the Export Credits Scandal of the mid-1980s and the Jordanian subsidy of trade with Iraq, 223–25 and 237.

that Jordanian economic interests as interpreted by the state drove the abandonment of Iraq is difficult to sustain.

THE REVERSAL, 1995-97

R EALISM OFFERS a straightforward explanation of the Jordanian reversal: Jordan bandwagoned with the ascendant Israeli-American pole. Jordan was not balancing against an Iraqi threat or Iraqi power· by moving closer to Israel; incremental shifts in Iraqi power were only marginally relevant for Jordanian policy. The growing conviction that the blockade on Iraq would never be lifted as long as Saddam Husayn remained in power perhaps facilitated the decision. More importantly, as the peace process developed, the payoffs of aligning with the Israeli-American coalition seemed to outweigh the dangers of the policy change. The strategic decision to align with Israel, which for realism represents a rational calculation of Jordanian interests in a changing regional and international environment, came first. Abandoning Iraq stood as the price of admission to an alignment with Israel and the United States. The goals of Jordanian policy were widely understood, both in Jordan and abroad, as a move to cement Jordan's position with Israel and the United States and to secure a reconciliation with the Gulf states.

This rationalist argument seems correct in its broad contours, in that the single most important factor in Jordan's turn against Iraq was its peace treaty with Israel. Jordan's behavior, however, was not justified in these terms. On the contrary, Jordanian officials explained their new policy in terms of concern for the Iraqi people and a conviction that Saddam Husayn's regime no longer served their interests; and in terms of the need to reconstruct regional order along new lines. Jordanian behavior toward Iraq is explained not only by its interest in cementing ties with the United States and Israel, but also in its interest in creating new regional and domestic political structures. The regime came to view economic and political ties to Iraq as a threat and a constraint rather than as a benefit. Security, in the new strategic vision, would be secured through the United States and Israel, against threats posed by Iraq and Syria. Securing Jordan's role in a new regional structure involved a reformulation of state identity as much as it involved the pursuit of any compelling economic or security interests. Ties to the Iraqi economy, however lucrative, stood in sharp tension with visions of a Middle East market in which Jordan mediated between Israel and the Arab states and developed a Jordan-Palestine-Israel development zone. Much of the Jordanian public sphere rejected this articulation of threat and opportunity, arguing that Jordan's interests were best served by continued ties with Iraq and an Arab, not Middle Eastern, regional order. The conflict over Jordan's economy and security arrangements reflected the political struggle over Jordanian identity.

After Jordan moved toward peace with Israel, King Husayn embarked on a comprehensive redefinition of Jordan's identity as the standard-bearer of the "Peace Camp." This new identity claim incorporated relations with Israel and the West, a focus on economic cooperation and regional institutions, and replacing Arab/Israeli opposition with Peace Camp/enemies of peace opposition. The turn against Iraq formed a major part of this bid to redefine Jordan in the international public sphere. While some effort was made to explain and justify the Peace Camp identity inside of Jordan, this discourse was clearly oriented toward the norms of the international public sphere. In dozens of speeches, King Husayn and Prince Hassan argued for a new regional order based on the peace process and economic development. The success of these efforts in the West can be seen in the appreciative analysis of the *New Republic*: "The King has well atoned for his sin [of supporting Saddam]."[60] Clinton administration officials argued before Congress that "King Hussein is demonstrating great courage as he takes a stalwart stand against the regime of Saddam Husayn...[he has] initiated a series of actions...that have decisively distanced Jordan from the Iraqi dictator."[61] Based on Jordan's peace treaty with Israel and its turn against Iraq, Congress approved long-withheld arms sales (including F-16 fighter planes), and military and intelligence cooperation escalated dramatically.[62] The reversal of Iraq policy should be understood as the result of peacemaking with Israel, not only as a similar adjustment to power realities but as part of a coherent identity project. This assertion of a new Jordanian identity remained fundamentally contested at the level of the Jordanian public. The opposition rejected the new identity

60. "Jordan and the Peace," *New Republic*, 16 October 1995, 9.

61. Bruce Riedel, deputy assistant secretary of defense for near east and south Asia, testimony during Hearing and Business Meeting of the Committee on International Relations, House of Representatives, 104th Congress, 2nd Session, 13 March 1996, 4.

62. Robert Pelletrau, assistant secretary of state for near eastern affairs, Statement before the House Appropriations Committee, Washington, D.C., 6 March 1996, justifies the American decision to sell F-16s in terms of Jordan's commitment to peace with Israel and the increased threat posed by Iraq in the wake of the reversal.

frame, which denied the integrity of the Arabist order, set Jordan against Iraq, and accepted the Israeli label of its opponents as terrorists. The assertion of this new identity claim extended to a struggle over the public sphere to which claims should be addressed. The regime oriented its argumentation toward the Western public sphere. Unable to convince the Jordanian public of these claims through argumentation, and unable to establish a workable consensus on state identity or interests, the regime moved drastically to curtail the Jordanian public sphere. The years after the peace treaty witnessed a sharp decrease of state tolerance of public criticism.[63] Jordanians, who had developed expectations of the right to free expression in the last four years, resisted the incursions on the public sphere as an active site for Jordanian norm, identity and interest-formation. The more that international society celebrated Jordanian behavior, the more alienated the Jordanian public became. Husayn complained bitterly about this disjuncture in a heated address to the nation in November 1995, fuming that "every newspaper in the world has lauded [the Amman Economic Summit]...every foreign official has hailed Jordan and its achievements....In the internal arena, however...we have only found a few echoes of all this."[64] He questioned the value of a public sphere in which critical voices "undermine national unity and blow up everything of value, tarnishing every achievement of this country." Of the critical voices, he said: "I do not feel that there are any media in this country that identify with this country." The divorce between public sphere consensus and the new Jordanian foreign policy, and the contrast to 1990, could hardly be more clear. The reversal of position on Iraq thus brought on a major confrontation with a Jordanian public sphere already mobilized around the Israeli peace treaty and the repression of public freedoms. The closure of the public sphere undermined the stability of the state itself. An uprising which swept the south of Jordan in August 1996 was blamed by the government on Iraqi provocateurs, although few believed this. Violent uprisings in February 1998 explicitly concerned the right to hold pro-Iraq rallies during a tense American-Iraqi showdown.

State-society polarization over the peace process and the increasing state repression was deepened by the break with Iraq. By 1994 a semi-

63. For details, see "Jordan: Clamping Down on Critics."

64. King Husayn speech delivered 9 November 1995; published (in Arabic) in *al-Dustur*, 10 November 1995, 1; in FBIS-NES-95-218, 13 November 1995, 52–55, quote at 52.

permanent coalition of Arab nationalists, leftists, Islamists, and "old guard" Jordanian nationalists had formed in opposition to the reorientation of Jordanian foreign policy. While these parties disagreed on their positive program, they shared a basic consensus on Jordan's identity and interests and a belief that the new foreign policy harmed both. Where the Gulf crisis forged a powerful state-society consensus, the peace process and the turn against Iraq generated a unified public opinion in opposition to the government. As one senior political figure remarked, "since independence I don't remember a time when there was such complete divergence between regime policies and popular opinion."[65] From 1990–94, then, the regime and the opposition worked within the bounds of the Gulf war consensus. After 1994, the consensus broke down, replaced by a generalized opposition between societal and state interpretations of Jordanian interests.

The reversal of Jordanian policy crystallized around the acceptance of two high-level Iraqi defectors on 11 August 1995. After allowing the longtime head of Iraqi military development, Husayn Kamil, to hold a dramatic press conference from the royal palace denouncing Saddam Husayn, King Husayn moved aggressively to reposition Jordan in the Western camp. Speaking to the Israeli press, Husayn declared that "the time is now for change in Iraq," a claim he would repeat often in the next few months. On 23 August Husayn delivered a manifesto of a new Jordanian policy hostile to the Iraqi regime, reframing the Gulf war and emphasizing the harm inflicted on Jordan by Iraqi behavior.[66] The Jordanian press interpreted the speech as "rewriting the history of Jordanian-Iraqi relations... [and] banishing all the norms of Jordanian discourse."[67] A senior Jordanian official was quoted the next day as confirming that, with this speech, "the break with Baghdad is now sealed, totally and brutally."[68] The speech was followed by an effusion of cables of support for Husayn and his policies published in the daily press, a Jordanian political tradition reserved for major and unpopular policy decisions. After the reversal, the King regularly attacked Iraqi

---

65. Mohammed al-Qadah, "When Cohesion. When Opposition?" *al-Majd* (in Arabic), 7 November 1994, 7.

66. King Husayn speech delivered 23 August 1995; published in *al-Dustur*, 24 August 1995, 1, 4; in FBIS-NES-95-164, 24 August 1995, 43–47.

67. 'Arib Rentawi, "The Second White Book on the Position Towards Iraq and the Gulf" (in Arabic), *al-Dustur*, 27 August 1995, 1, 28; Mohammed Subayhi, "Reading Husayn's Speech" (in Arabic), *al-Dustur*, 26 August 1995, 1, 43.

68. Quoted by Randa Habib, Paris AFP in English, in FBIS-NES-95-164, 24 August 1995, 47.

behavior during and after the Gulf war as deliberately harmful to Jordanian interests, in a concerted effort to disassociate Jordanian and Iraqi shared identity and interests and to undercut the positive identification between the two states. While always emphasizing his deep concern for the suffering of the Iraqi people, Husayn argued that the interests of the Iraqi nation were no longer served by its leadership.

The United States ostentatiously guaranteed Jordanian security against Iraqi retaliation for this new policy. This display of American power bore little relation to the actual behavior of Iraq, which publicly and privately assured Jordan that it had no offensive intentions.[69] Jordanian dailies quoted Tariq Aziz, the senior Iraqi diplomat, as insisting that "the claims of Iraqi threats to Jordan are an American invention."[70] It suited the United States and King Husayn to pretend that such an Iraqi threat existed, in order to justify closer security cooperation. The Jordanian public expressed extreme skepticism, asserting forcefully that they felt no threat from Iraq and would not accept efforts at constructing such a threat.[71] In fact, the threat perceived and expressed by many Jordanians was that Jordan would get sucked in to an American plot to destabilize Iraq. In other words, the Jordanian public sphere showed more concern that Jordan might threaten Iraq than that Iraq threatened Jordan!

Seeking to capitalize on Jordan's newly prominent position in the Western coalition within the Arabist arena, King Husayn tried to rally Arab leaders in support of an activist policy toward change, in sharp contrast to Jordan's longstanding advocacy of moderation and nonintervention. The Jordanian government took numerous steps to back up its rhetoric. Border controls with Iraq were tightened, along with stricter enforcement of residence visa regulations for the tens of thousands of Iraqis who had sought refuge in Amman. Jordanian customs agents seized and turned over to UN inspectors several shipments of parts allegedly intended for missiles and chemical weapons. Trade with Iraq was slashed in half, to the consternation of Jordanian business sec-

69. On Iraqi reassurances to Jordan, see "Iraq Emphasizes Its Close Relations to Jordan," *al-Hayat*, 29 August 1995, 1; and "Iraqi Letter to Prince Hassan: We Want to Preserve Our Strong Relations with Jordan" (in Arabic), *al-Hayat*, 9 September 1995, 1.

70. "Tariq Aziz: The Claims of an Iraqi Threat Are an American Invention" (in Arabic), *al-Dustur*, 12 August 1995, 1.

71. *Al-Hayat*, 20 August 1995, 4 (in Arabic), notes that Jordanian writers "are not hiding their anger at how the U.S. was exploiting the defection." For expressions of this anger, see Taher al-Udwan, "Iraqi Threat?" (in Arabic), *al-Dustur*, 13 August 1995, 25; Mohammed Ka'oush, "Us and Iraq and America" (in Arabic), *al-Dustur*, 18 August 1995, 25.

tors. Measures were taken to reduce Iraqi influence, including the expulsion of embassy staff and a campaign against pro-Iraq journalists.

In late November 1995, Husayn met with Iraqi opposition leaders in London, and offered Jordan as a base for political (but not military) activities. A number of prominent Iraqi defectors took up residence in Amman, establishing opposition political and information offices.[72] The Iraqi National Accord [al-Wifaq] set up a radio station broadcasting violent denunciations of Saddam Husayn into Iraq. While the government insisted that no armed activities would be permitted, and that therefore Jordan had not violated international norms of nonintervention, most observers felt that a line had been crossed and that Jordan was now actively involved in the effort to topple Saddam Husayn.[73] Press reports even indicated Jordanian involvement in a failed CIA-sponsored coup attempt based in the Kurdish autonomous zones. Speculation about Jordanian ambitions in Iraq, whether through a Hashemite restoration or through a territorial partition of Iraq, circulated widely despite regular Jordanian denials. King Husayn stepped up his attacks on Saddam after Kamil's return to Baghdad and brutal murder in February 1996. Jordan continued to hedge its bets, however, abstaining from direct involvement in overthrow attempts and maintaining economic ties. Jordan focused its attacks on the Iraqi regime, justifying its new opposition to Saddam Husayn on the basis of its deep concern for the Iraqi people, and publicly opposing any outside intervention or partition of Iraq.

The new policy caused an important split within the ruling elite, much of which had built personal, political and business ties to Iraq during the long years of close alliance. Numerous prominent figures publicly objected to the break with Iraq, which helped lead to the formation of Abd al-Karim Kabariti's "White Revolution" government in February 1996.[74] Husayn's appointment of Kabariti seems to have

---

72. Minister of Information Marwan Mu'asher told al-Sharq al-Awsat (6 May 1996, 1), that Jordan had received twenty-three requests from Iraqi opposition groups to open offices in Jordan. On the development of Jordan's relations with the Iraqi opposition, see "Rapid Jordanian Movement to an 'Understanding' with the Iraqi Opposition" (in Arabic), al-Sharq al-Awsat, 30 November 1995, 4; and Huda al-Husayni, "Iraqi Opposition Looks to Jordanian Desire for Confederation" (in Arabic), al-Sharq al-Awsat, 7 December 1995, 8.

73. Prime Minister Kabariti quoted in "Kabariti: Jordan Will Not Be Used As a Base for Striking Iraq" (in Arabic), al-Hayat, 28 March 1996, 4.

74. See Samih al-Mayateh, "Report on Kabariti's First 90 Days" (in Arabic), al-Sabil, 9 April 1996, 24; Saleh al-Qullab, "Tensions Grow in the White Revolution" (in Arabic), al-Sharq al-Awsat, 13 July 1996, 4.

been a pointed step toward the removal of the "old guard," now viewed as too closely tied to Iraq and too closed-minded with regard to relations with Israel. Kabariti, the architect of the Iraq reversal as foreign minister, was seen as hostile to the Iraqi regime and thus able to execute Husayn's vision of Jordanian interests. Kabariti's appointment was widely interpreted as a major departure in Jordanian politics, intimately bound to the new foreign policy orientation and the resistance of Jordanian society. The spokesman of the Islamic Action Front made identity his primary concern when discussing the government change: "We want a government that understands the identity of the umma [nation] and preserves this identity."[75] Kabariti's appointment, by contrast, involved a concerted struggle for a changed conception of Jordan's identity and interests. Public debate of Kabariti's policies crystallized around foreign policy, especially the peace treaty with Israel and Iraq policy, and generated a focused debate on Jordan's Arab identity.[76]

The extent of elite dissatisfaction with these changes shows the degree to which the reinterpretation of Jordanian interests came from the very top levels alone and the regime's failure to construct convincing justifications. Jordanian policymakers, increasingly oriented to the international public sphere and hostile to the dominant trends expressed in the Jordanian public sphere, derived conceptions of Jordanian interests from the international sphere. The desire to forge closer and deeper ties with the United States and Israel took priority over the interest in nurturing a Jordanian consensus. The Jordanian public sphere continued to serve as a primary source of norms, identity and interests for most Jordanians, however, who resisted the new conception of Jordanian interests and the implicit dismissal of the Jordanian public sphere.

From the political economy perspective, the domestic conflict might be interpreted in terms of a contradiction between the trade interests of Jordanian businessmen in Iraq against the budget subsidy-seeking state.[77] The behavior of the state could plausibly be interpreted as rent-seeking behavior, with state actors preferring Gulf and American subsidies to the Iraqi market. Economic sectors with interests in the Iraqi market naturally cared more for maintaining the Iraqi market than

75. Hamza Mansour, "The Government We Want" (in Arabic), *al-Sabil*, 5 February 1996, 15; also see Kamron Daghi, "The Meaning of the Change" (in Arabic), *al-Hayat*, 11 February 1996, 13.

76. Fahd al-Fanik, "Kabariti's Government" (in Arabic), *al-Ra'i* (internet edition: http://www.accessme.com/Al-Ra'i), 26 October 1996.

77. Brand, *Jordan's Inter-Arab Relations*.

about the Gulf. There is substantial evidence that such a conflicting understanding of economic interests existed. Many Jordanian businessmen feared that the anti-Iraq policy would cost them the privileged position in a reopened Iraqi market for which they had so patiently waited. As noted above, however, the Jordanian state also had considerable direct economic interests in relations with Iraq, notably access to Iraqi oil. The state budget could not easily live without the oil that Iraq provided at half the world market price. While some Jordanian officials claimed that Jordan had many alternatives to Iraqi oil and would make decisions on that basis, and both Kuwait and Saudi Arabia floated proposals to replace the Iraqi supply, none materialized and Jordan maintained its oil deal with Iraq.[78]

Rationalist ascription of economic interests should be supplemented with an appreciation of the constructivist dynamic, as discussed above. The Jordanian-Iraqi trade relationship was both an expression of and a force in creating the shared identity and norms of the two states: "the organic ties have formed this class into Iraqi allies who oppose any move to reorient the Jordanian economy" away from Iraq, regardless of potential profits elsewhere.[79] Writers heaped scorn on the idea that "our brotherly relations with Iraq are based on trade or oil deals and that they will end if the trade or oil stops."[80] For these Jordanians, a common identity bound Iraq and Jordan together, rather than self-interest.[81] In other words, economic interests took on political meaning through the process of interpretation within a master frame of shared identity.

The political economy perspective, then, can be used to supplement the constructivist argument developed here. Jordanian policymakers

---

78. As reported in *al-Hayat* (in Arabic): "Jordan: We Have Many Alternatives to Iraqi Oil," 17 August 1995, 1; "Kuwait Offers to Compensate Jordan for Iraqi Oil," 23 August 1995, 1; "Washington Announces Continuation of International Blockade of Iraq; Expects Deterioration of Jordanian-Iraqi Relations," 1 September 1995, 1; "Iraq Offers Jordan Oil at Concessionary Prices," 3 September 1995, 1; and "United States Reservations about Jordan-Iraq Oil Deal," 18 September 1995, 1.

79. Salim Nassar, "Kabariti's Cabinet Establishes Change in the Style of Government" (in Arabic), *al-Hayat*, 10 February 1996, 12.

80. Mohammed Ka'oush, "Us and Iraq and America" (in Arabic), *al-Dustur*, 15 August 1995, 25.

81. Baram, "Baathi Iraq and Hashemite Jordan," goes so far as to argue that an unofficial Jordanian-Iraqi federation had come into being, based on the extent of these shared identities and interests. This interpretation overstates the case; at no point has there been any serious expression of interest in political unity, and the ideas floated in the Western and Arab press about the possibility of a Hashemite restoration in Iraq received a negative response in Jordan.

faced a strategic choice about the future of the Jordanian political economy, crudely summarized as a choice between facing east or facing west. The tight Jordanian-Iraqi interconnections bound the Jordanian economy to certain kinds of production and left it dependent on a single market. With the peace treaty, Jordanian planners—notably Prince Hassan—envisioned a Jordan at the center of a rapidly developing Middle Eastern regional market. "[For these] ambitions of becoming a center of regional economic activities...Jordanian relations with Saddam Husayn are a major obstacle."[82] It is highly suggestive that Jordan's break with Iraq came two months before the Amman Economic Summit, heralded in Jordanian official discourse as the foundation of the Middle East market. In other words, the break with Iraq had an economic dimension, but as mediated through identity. The decision to seek a Middle East identity based on acceptance of Israel, of which the economic signature was the Amman Economic Summit, defined the break with Iraq.

As societal resistance to the foreign policy change mounted, King Husayn became personally involved with the policies of peace with Israel and distancing from Iraq to an unprecedented degree. As the King became increasingly active in the public sphere debate, his carefully crafted aura of neutrality frayed and the norm of refraining from direct criticism diminished. In June 1996, a prominent lawyer told a press conference that there were more than 200 lawsuits currently being tried on the charge of *Italat al-Lissan* (slandering the King).[83] Such unprecedented numbers offer an intriguing indicator of the extent to which the King had lost his invulnerability to direct criticism in the Jordanian public sphere.

Within the Arab arena, Jordan's new policy also foundered. Kuwait proved intransigent in its refusal to normalize relations with Jordan, sparking fierce resentment among Jordanians who saw the sacrifice of ties with Iraq going in vain. As early as September, "fresh Kuwaiti criticism of Jordan...soured moves to end their rift."[84] The Jordanian press regularly lambasted Kabariti for his futile efforts to win over the

---

82. Sami Shoursh, "Change in Policy and Practice in the Middle East" (in Arabic), *al-Hayat*, 9 September 1995, 19; Hazim Saghiya, "Jordan and the 'Struggle for Iraq'" (in Arabic), *al-Hayat*, 10 September 1995, 13.

83. "Two Hundred Suits before the Courts on the Charge of Slandering the King" (in Arabic), *Al-Sharq al-Awsat* (internet edition: http://www.asharqalawsat.com), 19 June 1996.

84. For example, see "To the Prime Minister" (in Arabic), *Shihan*, 30 June 1996, 3.

Kuwaitis.[85] Prominent commentators challenged the very idea that the direct budget subsidies to be found in the Gulf were more valuable to Jordanian national interests than the trade relations and strategic depth offered by Iraq.

In addition to the difficulties in capitalizing on the Iraq reversal with Gulf states, Jordan's policy on Iraq worried Syria and Egypt. Harsh media campaigns followed, notably a long denunciation of King Husayn by the editor of an official Egyptian daily and furious responses by Jordanian writers.[86] An Arab consensus emerged, welcoming Jordan's denunciation of the Iraqi regime but rejecting any active involvement in efforts to bring down Saddam Husayn. In September this consensus was articulated in the statement of a Syrian-Egyptian minisummit in Cairo. Egypt seemed most worried that Jordan's increasingly prominent role in American and Israeli strategy could come at the expense of its influence, while Syria worried about the progress of the peace process, which seemed to be bypassing it.

Jordan found itself frustrated by its inability to impose an authoritative interpretation of its own actions. The turn against Iraq generated Arabist debate which Jordan could neither ignore nor carry. This is ironic, because in many ways the Jordanian reversal put it in line with rather than against the Arab consensus. Syrian and Egyptian anger was over Jordan's adoption of their own policy. Jordan was forced to defend itself in the Arab public sphere, and ultimately adjusted its positions and its behavior in order to fit into the Arab consensus. Because of its interest in rehabilitation in the Arabist public sphere in order to restore relations with the Gulf, and because of its consistently expressed normative desire to restore the Arabist dialogue, Jordan could not ignore the demands of Arabist argumentation. As a site of interpretive framing and interest formation, however, the Arabist public sphere was less relevant than the international public sphere. The primary source of the redefinition of Jordanian identity and interests was the international arena, in which the identity claims of a "peace camp" took shape.

85. For the brief Jordanian-Kuwaiti thaw, see "All Jordanian Prisoners in Kuwait Freed!" (in Arabic), *al-Dustur*, 17 February 1996, 1; "Jordan and Kuwait Decide on Normalization" (in Arabic), *al-Hayat*, 15 February 1996, 1.
86. *Al-Hayat*, 19 September 1995, 1, reports talks between Kabariti and Egyptian foreign minister Amru Musa. For examples of the Egyptian-Jordanian exchange, see Abdullah al-Qaq, "In Whose Interest Opening Old Wounds?" (in Arabic), *al-Dustur*, 30 August 1995, 1; and Ahmad al-Hasban, "Our Diplomatic Discourse Will Remain Level" (in Arabic), *al-Dustur*, 31 August 1995, 1.

While the reversal was welcomed by the international public sphere and challenged in the Arabist public sphere, the Jordanian public sphere expressed fundamental reservations about the new policy. As one commentator noted, "this is a retreat from all declared Jordanian political norms...to the extent that even discussing these norms is seen as provocative!"[87] The opposition worked to bring their objections into the public sphere and to force the government to articulate and defend its new policies: "The Jordanian public must raise their voices and repeat what they say in their private conversations....The government knows that as long as the opposition continues to whisper, then the field is open for it alone to make the necessary changes by reversing the nation's constant principles, beliefs, and cultural identity."[88] Objections were cast in terms of generalizable Jordanian interests within the opposition's interpretive frame. By framing the reversal as the inevitable consequence of the peace treaty, the opposition successfully linked the two issues in the political arena. In its regular declarations, the opposition coalition called for an end to the sanctions on Iraq and denounced policies hostile to Iraq almost as frequently as it denounced normalization with Israel. In this opposition frame, Iraq stood as the leading symbol of the Arab identity abandoned by the regime in its pursuit of cooperation with Israel.

Opposition to the reversal grounded its discourse in both interests and identity. First, commentators asked what Jordanian interest was served by fomenting instability in Iraq: "The United States and Israel may have an interest in fragmenting Iraq...but where is Jordan's interest?"[89] With this critique demanding the public articulation of Jordanian interests, the opposition both imposed its frame of state/society conflict and made unimpeachable claims toward public sphere dialogue and national interests. Second, the opposition cast the reversal in terms of a challenge to Jordan's Arab identity, claiming that the new policy replaced Iraq with Israel and foolishly severed Jordan from its true Arab nature: "Every day something happens further revealing the official policy to do all it can to formulate a new identity for Jordan and Jordanians. This identity has nothing to do with Arab and Islamic

---

87. Hilmi al-Asmar, "Norms" (in Arabic), *al-Sabil*, 29 August 1995, 24.

88. Layth Shubaylat, "Open Letter" (in Arabic), in *al-Ahali*, 7 September 1995; in FBIS-NES-95-175, 11 September 1995, 57–58.

89. Fahd Rimawi, "Who Benefits from Dividing Iraq?" (in Arabic), *al-Majd*, 4 December 1995, 12; in FBIS-NES-95-234, 31.

principles."[90] Finally, the opposition pointed to potential economic losses from any fallout with Iraq.

Civil society institutions played an important role in forming and expressing public opinion against the new Iraq policy. Professional associations, cultural associations, women's organizations and political parties were outspoken in their condemnation of state policy. Even the normally apolitical Chamber of Commerce joined in the criticism. A coalition of opposition parties released regular statements countering official foreign policy, allowing no action to go unchallenged; calls to support Iraq were almost as frequent as the calls to resist normalization with Israel. In June 1996 a "Popular Jordanian Delegation" toured Iraq to express Jordanian solidarity. Including more than seventy leading political figures, the delegation declared that it "represented most sectors of society and expressed the position of the majority of the Jordanian people."[91] Explicitly claiming that official Jordanian positions were not those of the Jordanian people, the delegation offered a competing frame of state interests.

Parliament, while unable to check government decisions due to a progovernment majority, did provide a platform for heated debate which forced the government clearly to articulate and defend its policies. In August 1995, Prime Minister Zaid bin Shakir held a contentious meeting with Parliament to explain the new policy. Iraq policy similarly dominated debate during Kabariti's confidence vote in February 1996. After winning confidence, Kabariti claimed that his Iraq policy had been vindicated.[92] Still, a number of influential deputies challenged the new prime minister on the subject. Taher al-Masri, a liberal former prime minister who had led Jordan into the peace process, warned passionately about cutting Jordan off from its Arab roots. According to Masri, adhering to Jordanian norms of nonintervention and support for Iraqi unity "serves Jordanian security and stability and investments."[93] Furthermore, "any call to change Jordan's strategic and

90. Shubaylat, "Open Letter."

91. "Jordanian Delegation to Baghdad to Express Support for Its Position" (in Arabic), al-Sharq al-Awsat, internet edition, 13 June 1996; "The Jordanian Delegation Expresses Its Solidarity with Iraq," al-Sharq al-Awsat, internet edition, 16 June 1996. Also see Taher al-Udwan, "The Jordanian Solidarity Delegation" (in Arabic), al-Dustur, 14 June 1996, 26.

92. "Kabariti Attacks Baghdad Regime" (in Arabic), Al-Hayat, 5 March 1996, 4.

93. Taher al-Masri speech reported in "Taher al-Masri Calls to Not Build 'Blockade Policies' towards Iraq" (in Arabic), al-Hayat, 3 March 1996, 5; the subsequent debate, and demands for clarification of Jordanian policy by a Parliament, is recounted in detail in "Upheaval on Kabariti Led by Members of the Senate!" (in Arabic), al-Sabil, 26

economic ties from Arab to Middle Eastern threatens to isolate Jordan from its Arab identity and community." Islamist Bisam al-Amoush responded forcefully that "we stand against this...and we represent the pulse of the Jordanian street, which rejects these developments toward Iraq." Such exchanges forced the government to articulate and defend its conceptions before a highly skeptical public.

In August 1996, Jordan's south erupted in riots reminiscent of 1989, sparked by the government's decision to remove bread subsidies in line with IMF guidelines. While the army occupied the principal southern cities and the capital, controlling the riots and restoring stability, the events struck deep into the political and social system. King Husayn blamed Iraqi agents for igniting the conflict, to the extreme skepticism of virtually all observers and participants.[94] Others classified the riots as a typical reaction to IMF demands. A more convincing explanation lay in the combination of escalating economic hardship, exacerbated by the closing of the Iraqi market, and the increasing repression of the public sphere. The level of political frustration and alienation over the peace treaty with Israel, the turn against Iraq, and the government's clashes with an impotent Parliament and harassed press and civil society, was evident to all. Faced with decreasing opportunities for economic survival and political expression, Jordanians took to the streets.

The relationship between the Jordanian government's commitment to new regional structures and its policies toward Iraq is demonstrated by the impact of the deterioration of the peace process on Jordan's Iraq policy. As the international consensus on the sanctions regime frayed, and the United States and Iraq engaged in a series of tense military showdowns, Jordan began to renew its calls for an end to the sanctions and for an American-Iraqi dialogue. Relations between Jordan and Iraq remained tense, despite Jordan's diplomatic efforts in this regard, as Jordanian officials sought to prevent a resurgence of positive identification between the two states. In December 1997, an Iraqi decision to execute four Jordanian students accused of smuggling aroused considerable furor in Jordan. The government gleefully exploited the crisis, attempting to whip up popular hostility to Iraq to muster popular support for its policy. Despite the claim by an Iraqi defector that the executions were in fact in retaliation for Jordanian involvement in a

---

March 1996, 1; and "Kabariti: Jordan Will Not Be Used as a Base for Striking Iraq" (in Arabic), *al-Hayat*, 28 March 1996, 4

94. Husayn speech accusing "foreign elements" for the violence published in *al-Rai* (in Arabic), 17 August 1996, 1.

foiled coup attempt, public anger did indeed mount. Several weeks later, an Iraqi diplomat and three others were murdered in spectacular fashion, in what many observers interpreted as a sign that "internal Iraqi battles are being waged on the streets of Amman."[95] In January 1998, the Iraqi government directly appealed to the Jordanian public by releasing all Jordanian prisoners in Iraqi prisons by way of an apology "because of its deep respect for the Jordanian people." Rather than release the prisoners to a representative of the Jordanian government, the Iraqi government chose Layth Shubaylat, an outspoken critic of Jordanian foreign policy. While the official media could not ignore the release of prisoners, it downplayed Shubaylat's role and tried to minimize the significance of the Iraqi action.[96]

The difficulties of abandoning Iraq, and the ongoing importance of public sphere argumentation, can be seen in Jordanian policy during the U.S.-Iraqi crisis of February 1998. During this crisis, Jordan again tried to play a mediating role, warning against the use of military force and calling for a diplomatic solution. As in 1990, Jordan feared the consequences of a military confrontation, sealing the border to prevent refugee flows and working for a diplomatic solution. Unlike 1990, where the government allowed free expression to public opinion, however, in 1998 the government tightly controlled popular mobilization. On 11 February the government announced that all rallies, under any slogan and for any purpose, would be banned. Security forces broke up a massive pro-Iraq rally at the Husayni Mosque in Amman on 14 February. Deputy Prime Minister Abdullah al-Nasour blamed Iraq for growing unrest in Jordan, explaining that "we do not fear the opinion leaders and party chairmen and association officials, because they are principled, but we fear the agitators and the agents and the fifth columnists, who must be resisted at all costs."[97] This restrictive policy on public rallies denied the right of opposition groups to rally public opinion in support of Iraq as they had in 1990. In response, major riots broke out in the cities of the south which were put down with

---

95. Patrick Cockburn, "Jordan at Risk of Becoming Cockpit for Proxy Wars," *Independent* (internet edition: http://www.independent.co.uk/), 24 January 1998, 12.

96. Layth Shubaylat, interviewed in *Shihan* (in Arabic), 26 January 1998 (internet edition: http://www.alarab-alyawm.com.jo/shihan/).

97. Nasour's remarks reported in *al-Rai* (internet edition in Arabic: http://www.accessme. com/Al-Ra'i/), 12 February 1998, 1. For the opposition's insistence on the right to hold public rallies, see *al-Sabil* (internet edition, in Arabic: http://www.assabeel.com/), 11 February 1998, esp. comments by Sulayman Arar, president of the National Committee to Support Iraq.

military force. Security forces placed several cities under curfew for an extended period, arrested dozens of political activists, and imprisoned Layth Shubaylat for incitement to riot.

The February 1998 crisis showed the sharp divergence between popular and official positions toward Iraq, but it also suggested that "abandoning Iraq" might be beyond the capabilities of Jordanian policy. In November 1997, the inability of the United States to prevent linkage between its tense confrontation with Iraq and the collapsing Arab-Israeli peace process demonstrated the need to reformulate policies on both fronts. Jordan's turn against Iraq depended on the peace process and the construction of new regional economic and security structures; the collapse of those efforts undermined Jordan's Iraq policy. King Husayn publicly lobbied the United States to rethink its policies toward Iraq, including an appeal for a direct American-Iraqi dialogue, and to take a more active role in the peace process. Given the failure to bring about a change in Iraq's regime, and the ongoing importance of Iraq to the Jordanian economy, Jordan moderated its overt hostility. The near collapse in the Palestinian-Israeli peace process, after Israeli settlement construction in Jerusalem in March 1997, the failed Israeli assassination attempt of a Hamas leader in Amman, and King Husayn's publicly avowed loss of trust in Benjamin Netanyahu combined to push Jordan back to an Arabist policy and to surrender hope of a transformation of regional institutions. As the peace process collapsed, so did the main justification for the new policy toward Iraq.

ALLIANCES AND IDENTITY

THE rationalist perspective can explain the broad contours of Jordan's strategic realignment, but it neglects important dimensions of the Iraqi-Jordanian relationship and its role in Jordanian politics. This relationship should not be understood as an alliance based on interest between autonomous, unified state actors. Positions toward Iraq and Israel extended deep into the political identity of Jordanians and into the norms and structures of the Jordanian polity. Enmity to Israel and affinity with Iraq exceeded calculation of interests, power, or threat, constituting Jordanian identities, worldviews, and interpretation of interests. These norms and identities underlay the economy, political system, and civil society. The peace treaty and the turn against Iraq failed to generate and institutionalize a new consensus.

This failure stands in stark contrast to the Gulf crisis, in which a powerful consensus was achieved on a frame linking Iraq and Jordan. Relations with Iraq came to stand for an Arabist identity threatened by the move to peace with Israel and the calls for a Middle Eastern identity. The Gulf crisis transformed the alliance with Iraq into not only an indicator, but the central indicator of Arab identity. Jordan's decision to stand by Iraq galvanized and consolidated the Jordanian public. Enjoying virtual consensus and universally interpreted as the expression of the popular will, the policy bound the public together as an extremely powerful normative locus of identity. Rallies of solidarity with the Iraqi people and calls to lift the sanctions could unite a public deeply divided over many issues. Support for Iraq in the war served as a foundation myth for Jordanian democracy, a moment of unity which overpowered cleavages such as Jordanian-Palestinian, urban-tribal, or state-society. The Jordanian people were revealed as an integral unified whole by the consensus decision to stand by Arabist identity and principles. The shared economic and political suffering of the next few years only confirmed this identity-securing myth. The impact of Jordan's turn against Iraq on Jordanian politics must be understood in light of the centrality of this norm to the new Jordanian identity and the legitimacy of the regime's foreign policy.

The mid-1990s shift away from Iraq and toward Israel represented a bid to alter the foundations of Jordanian identity. Without winning the battle for public consensus over these new identity claims, the government could not guarantee domestic stability or consistency in its foreign policy. The story of Jordanian politics in the mid-1990s is the struggle to find a workable public-sphere consensus on Jordanian identity and interests which could legitimate the international alliances King Husayn chose in response to American hegemony. The fundamental question for the Jordanian polity is whether such a consensus could be reached through public-sphere debate, or whether the state would exert power to shut any debate down. The conflict with a mobilized public opinion was not a byproduct or an unwanted constraint: it was an intended and essential component of the shift. The failure of this project of transformation, and the failure to achieve the desired international results, prevented enmity to Iraq from being institutionalized. The Jordanian government has pushed for negative identification with the Iraqi government since 1995, but the Jordanian public has largely maintained its positive identification.

BIBLIOGRAPHY

Abrams, Dominic, and Michael A. Hogg. *Social Identity Theory: Constructive and Critical Advances* (New York: Springer-Verlag, 1990).

Adler, Emanuel. "Seizing the Middle Ground: Constructivism in World Politics." *European Journal of International Relations* 3, no. 3 (September 1997): 319–63.

Adler, Emanuel. "Imagined (Security) Communities: Cognitive Regions in International Relations." *Millennium* 26, no. 2 (summer 1997): 249–77.

Adorno, Theodor W., et al. *The Authoritarian Personality* (New York: Harper, 1950).

Agnew, Joh. *Place and Politics: The Geographical Mediation of State and Society* (Boston: Allen & Unwin, 1987).

Alderson, Kai. "Dimensions of Internalization" (unpubl. ms., 1997).

Anderson, Benedict. *Imagined Communities: Reflections on the Origin and Spread of Nationalism* (London: Verso, 1983).

Ang, Ien. *Watching Dallas: Soap Opera and the Melodramatic Imagination* (London: Methuen, 1985).

Antony, Louise M., and Charlotte Witt. *A Mind of One's Own: Feminist Essays on Reason and Objectivity* (Boulder: Westview, 1993).

Ashley, Richard, and R. B. J. Walker. "Reading Dissidence/Writing the Discipline: Crisis and the Question of Sovereignty in International Studies." *International Studies Quarterly* 34, no. 3 (September 1990): 367–416.

Asmus, Ronald D. *Germany's Political Maturation: Public Opinion and Security Policy in 1994* (Santa Monica: RAND, 1995).

Asmus, Ronald D. "Stop Fussing About NATO Enlargement and Get On With It." *International Herald Tribune*, 9 December 1996, 8.

Augstein, Rudolf. "Der vertrackte Freund." *Der Spiegel*, 11 September 1995, 24.

Ayoob, Mohammed. "The Security Problematic in the Third World." *World Politics* 43, no. 3 (January 1991): 257–83.

Baker, James A. *The Politics of Diplomacy* (New York: Random House 1995).

Baldwin, David A., ed. *Neorealism and Neoliberalism. The Contemporary Debate* (New York: Columbia University Press, 1993).

Baram, Amatzia, and Barry Rubin, eds. *Iraq's Road to War* (New York: St. Martin's, 1993).

Baram, Amatzia. "Baathi Iraq and Hashemite Jordan: From Hostility to Alignment." *Middle East Journal* 45, no. 1 (winter 1991): 51–70.

Barash, David P., and Judith Eve Lipton. *The Caveman and the Bomb* (New York: McGraw-Hill, 1985).

Barber, Benjamin R. *Jihad vs. McWorld: How Globalism and Tribalism are Reshaping the World* (New York: Ballantine, 1995).

Bargh, John A., and Kimberly Barndollar. "Automaticity in Action: The Unconscious as Repository of Chronic Goals and Motives." In *The Psychology of Action: Linking Cognition and Motivation to Behavior*, ed. Peter M. Gollwitzer and John A. Bargh (New York: Guilford, 1996).

Bargh, John A. "The Automaticity of Everyday Life." In *Advances in Social Cognition*, ed. R. S. Wyer Jr. (Mahwah, N.J: Erlbaum, 1996).

Barnett, Michael. "Sovereignty, Nationalism and Regional Order in the Arab State System." *International Organization* 49, no. 3 (summer 1995): 479–510.

Barnett, Michael. "Institutions, Roles, and Disorder: The Case of the Arab States System." *International Studies Quarterly* 37, no. 3 (autumn 1993): 271–96.

Bartleson, Jens. *A Geneaology of Sovereignty* (Cambridge: Cambridge University Press, 1995).

Bauman, Zygmunt. *Legislators and Interpreters: Modernity, Post-Modernity and Intellectuals* (Ithaca: Cornell University Press, 1987).

Beales, Derek. *The Risorgimento and the Unification of Italy* (New York: Barnes and Noble, 1971).

Beer, Francis, and Robert Hariman, eds. *Post-Realism: The Rhetorical Turn in International Relations* (East Lansing: Michigan State University Press, 1996).

Bellah, Robert, et al. *Habits of the Heart* (Harper and Row, 1985).

Benhabib, Seyla, ed. *Democracy and Difference: Contesting the Boundaries of the Political* (Princeton: Princteon University Press 1996).

Bickford, Susan. *The Dissonance of Democracy: Listening, Conflict, and Citizenship* (Ithaca: Cornell University Press, 1996).

Billig, Michael, and Henry Tajfel. "Social Categorization and Similarity in Intergroup Behavior." *European Journal of Social Psychology* 3, no. 1 (1973): 27–52.

Black, Jeremy. *The Rise of the European Powers* (New York: Routledge, Chapman and Hall, 1990).

Blanton, Shannon Lindsey. "Images in Conflict: The Case of Ronald Reagan and El Salvador." *International Studies Quarterly* 40, no. 1 (March 1996): 23–44.

Bloom, William. *Personal Identity, National Identity, and International Relations* (Cambridge: Cambridge University Press, 1990).

Blumer, Herbert. *Symbolic Interactionism: Perspective and Method* (Englewood Cliffs, N.J.: Prentice-Hall, 1969).

Bogert, Carroll. "Mullah Melee." *New Republic*, 19 January 1998, 12–15.

Bohman, James, and William Rehg, eds. *Deliberative Democracy* (Cambridge: MIT Press, 1997).

Bohman, James. *Public Deliberation* (Cambridge: MIT Press, 1996).

Bonnard, Frederick. "NATO: Slow Down and Be Sure the Alliance Remains Strong." *International Herald Tribune*, 4 July 1997, 8.

Bradley, Robert N. *Racial Origins of English Character* (1926; London: Kenni-kat Press, 1971).

Brand, Laurie A. "Economics and Shifting Alliances: Jordan's Relations with Syria and Iraq, 1975-81." *International Journal of Middle East Studies* 26 (summer 1994): 393-413.

Brand, Laurie A. "Liberalization and Changing Political Coalitions: The Bases of Jordan's 1990-1991 Gulf Crisis Policy." *Jerusalem Journal of International Relations* 13, no. 4 (1991): 1-46.

Brand, Laurie A. *Jordan's Inter-Arab Alliances: The Political Economy of Alliance Making* (New York: Columbia University Press, 1994).

Braudel, Fernand. *The Identity of France: History and Environment*, vol. 1, trans. Sean Reynolds (New York: Harper & Row, 1986).

Breuilly, John. *Nationalism and the State* (Chicago: University of Chicago Press, 1994).

Brewer, Marilyn. "The Social Self: On Being the Same and Different at the Same Time." *Personality and Social Psychology Bulletin* 17, no. 5 (October 1991): 475-82.

Bronfenbrenner, Urie. "The Mirror-Image in Soviet-American Relations: A Social Psychologist's Report." *Journal of Social Issues* 17, no. 3 (1961): 45-56.

Brown, Michael E., Owen R. Cote Jr., Sean M. Lynn-Jones, and Steven E. Miller, eds. *Nationalism and Ethnic Conflict* (Cambridge: Massachusetts, 1997).

Brown, Michael E., Sean M. Lynn-Jones, and Steven E. Miller eds. *The Perils of Anarchy. Contemporary Realism and International Security* (Cambridge: MIT Press, 1995).

Brown, Michael E., ed. *The International Dimensions of Internal Conflict* (Cambridge: MIT Press, 1996).

Brzezinski, Zbigniew. *Out of Control: Global Turmoil on the Eve of the Twenty-First Century* (New York: Scribner's, 1993).

Buchanan, Alan. *Secession: the Morality of Political Divorce From Fort Sumter to Lithuania and Quebec* (Boulder: Westview, 1991).

Buchanan, James M. "An Economic Theory of Clubs." *Economica* 32, no. 125 (February 1965): 1-14.

Buchheit, Lee. *Secession: The Legitimacy of Self-Determination* (New Haven: Yale University Press, 1978).

Bull, Hedley. *The Anarchical Society*, (Oxford: Oxford University Press, 1977).

Buzan, Barry. "From International System to International Society: The English School Meets the American Theories." *International Organization* 47, no. 3 (summer 1993): 327-52.

Calhoun, Craig, ed. *Habermas and the Public Sphere* (Cambridge: MIT Press, 1992).

Campbell, David. *Writing Security: United States Foreign Policy and the Politics of Identity* (Minneapolis: University of Minnesota Press, 1992).

Chafetz, Glenn, Michael Spirtas, and Benjamin Frankel. "Tracing the Influence of Identity on Foreign Policy." *Security Studies* 8, nos. 2/3 (winter 1998/99–spring 1999).

Chafetz, Glenn, Hillel Abramson, and Suzette Grillot. "Role Theory and Foreign Policy: Belarussian and Ukrainian Compliance with the Nuclear Nonproliferation Regime." *Political Psychology* 17, no. 4 (December 1996): 727–58.

Chafetz, Glenn. "The Political Psychology of the Nuclear Nonproliferation Regime." *Journal of Politics* 57, no. 3 (August 1995): 743–75.

Chafetz, Glenn. "The Struggle for a National Identity in Post-Soviet Russia." *Political Science Quarterly* 111, no. 4 (winter 1996): 661–94.

Chambers, Lain, and Lidia Curti, eds. *The Post-Colonial Question: Common Skies, Divided Horizons* (New York: Routledge, 1996).

Chambers, Simone. *Reasonable Democracy: Jurgen Habermas and the Politics of Discourse* (Ithaca: Cornell University Press, 1996).

Charon, Joel M. *Symbolic Interactionism: An Introduction, An Interpretation, An Integration* (Method (Englewood Cliffs, N.J.: Prentice-Hall, 1979).

Chatterjee, Partha. *Nationalist Thought and the Colonial World: A Derivative Discourse?* (London: Zed, 1986).

Checkel, Jeffrey T. "The Constructivist Turn in International Relations Theory." *World Politics* 50, no. 2 (January 1998): 324–48.

Cheshier, David M., and Cori E. Dauber. "The Place and Power of Civic Space: Reading Globalization and Social Geography Through the Lens of Civilizational Conflict." *Security Studies* 8, nos. 2/3 (winter 1998/99–spring 1999): 35–70.

Clark, John. "Ethno-Regionalism in Zaire: Roots, Manifestations and Meaning." *Journal of African Policy Studies* 1, no. 2 (1995): 23–45.

Prestowitz, Clyde, et al. "The Fight over Competitiveness: A Zero-Sum Debate?" *Foreign Affairs* 73, no. 4 (July/August 1994): 186–97.

Cockburn, Patrick. "Jordan at Risk of Becoming CockPit for Proxy Wars." *The Independent* (Internet Edition: http://www.independent.co.uk/), 24 January 1998, 12.

Connolly, William E. *The Ethos of Pluralization* (Minneapolis: University of Minnesota Press, 1995): xvi–xvii.

Connolly, William E. "Democracy and Territoriality." *Millennium: Journal of International Studies* 20, no. 3 (1991): 476–79.

Connor, Walker. "A Nation is a Nation, is a State, is an Ethnic Group." *Ethnic and Racial Studies* 1, no. 4 (October 1978): 378–400.

Connor, Walker. *Ethnonationalism: the Quest for Understanding* (Princeton: Princeton University Press, 1994).

Connor, Walker. "Nation-Building or Nation-Destroying?" *World Politics* 24, no. 3 (April 1972): 319–55.

Cornes, Richard, and Todd Sandler. *The Theory of Externalities, Public Goods, and Club Goods* (Cambridge: Cambridge University Press, 1986).

Cottam, Martha. "The Carter Administration's Policy Toward Nicaragua: Images, Goals and Tactics." *Political Science Quarterly* 107, no. 1 (spring 1992):123–46.

Cottam, Richard. *Foreign Policy Motivation: A General Theory and a Case Study* (Pittsburgh: University of Pittsburgh Press, 1977).

Cowhey, Peter F. "Domestic Institutions and International Commitments." *International Organization* 47, no. 2 (spring 1993): 299–326.

Cox, Robert W. "Gramsci, Hegemony and International Relations: An Essay in Method." In *Gramsci, Historical Materialism and International Relations* (Cambridge: Cambridge University Press, 1993).

Crawford, Neta C. "A Security Regime Among Democracies: Cooperation Among Iroquois Nations." *International Organization* 48, no. 3 (summer 1994): 345–85.

Cronin, Bruce. "From Balance of Power to Political Community: Transnational Identity Formation and the Integration of Italy." *Security Studies* 8, nos. 2/3 (winter 1998/99–spring 1999): 270–301.

Crosswhite, James. *The Rhetoric of Reason: Writing and the Attractions of Argument* (Madison: University of Wisconsin Press, 1996).

Dahl, Robert. *Polyarchy: Participation and Opposition* (New Haven: Yale University Press, 1971).

"Das Meinungsbild der Elite in Deutschland zur Aussen- und Sicherheitspolitik" (Berlin: Infratest Burke in affiliation with RAND and the Friedrich Naumann Foundation, 1996).

Dauber, Cori E. *Cold War Analytical Structures and the Post Post-War World: A Critique of Deterrence Theory* (Westport, Conn.: Praeger, 1993).

David, Steven R. "Explaining Third World Alignment." *World Politics* 43, no. 2 (January 1991): 233–56.

Denison, Andrew. "The European Dilemmas of the German Left: The Social Democratic Party and West European Security Cooperation" (Ann Arbor: UMI Dissertation Services, 1996).

Der Derian, James. "The Value of Security: Hobbes, Marx, Nietzsche, and Baudrillard." In *On Security*, ed. Ronnie D. Lipschutz (New York: Columbia University Press, 1995), 24–45.

Dessler, David. "What"s at Stake in the Agent-Structure Debate." *International Organization* 43, no. 3 (summer 1989): 441–74

Deutsch, Karl, et al. *Political Community and the North Atlantic Area* (Princeton: Princeton University Press, 1957).

Deutsch, Karl. *Nationalism and Social Communication: An Inquiry into the Foundations of Nationality* (Cambridge: MIT Press, 1966).

Di Scala, Spencer. *Italy: From Revolution to Republic* (Boulder: Westview, 1995).

Diamond, Larry, ed. *Political Culture and Democracy in Developing Countries* (Boulder: Lynne Rienner, 1994).

Dittmer, Lowell. and Samuel S. Kim, eds. *China's Quest for National Identity* (Ithaca: Cornell University Press, 1993).

Doty, Roxanne Lynn. "Immigration and the Politics of Security." *Security Studies* 8, nos. 2/3 (winter 1998/99–spring 1999): 71–93.

Doty, Roxanne Lynn. "Sovereignty and the Nation: Constructing the Boundaries of National Identity." In *State Sovereignty as Social Construct*, ed. Thomas J. Biersteker and Cynthia Weber (New York: Cambridge University Press).

Doty, Roxanne Lynn. "The Double-Writing of Statecraft: Exploring State Responses to Illegal Immigration." *Alternatives* 21 (1996): 171–89.

Douglas, Mary. *How Institutions Think* (Syracuse: Syracuse University Press, 1996).

Downs, George, ed. *Collective Security Beyond the Cold War* (Ann Arbor: University of Michigan Press).

Doyle, Michael. "Kant, Liberal Legacies, and Foreign Affairs, Part 1." *Philosophy and Public Affairs* 12, no. 3 (summer 1983): 205–35.

Druckman, Daniel. "Nationalism, Patriotism, and Group Loyalty: A Social Psychological Perspective." *Mershon International Studies Review* 38, no. 1 (April 1994): 43–68.

Duara, Prasenjit. *Rescuing History from the Nation: Questioning Narratives of Modern China* (Chicago: University of Chicago Press, 1995).

Ebert, Barbera. "The Gulf War and Its Aftermath: An Assessment of Evolving Arab Responses." *Middle East Policy* 1, no. 4 (1992): 77–95.

Eisenstadt, Abraham, ed. *Reconsidering Tocqueville's Democracy in America*, (New Brunswick: Rutgers University Press, 1988).

Eley, Geoff, and Ronald Grigor Suny, eds. *Becoming National* (Oxford: Oxford University Press, 1998).

Elliot, T. A. *Us and Them: A Study in Group Consciousness* (Aberdean, Australia: Aberdean University Press, 1986).

Elster, Jon Elster. *Rational Choice* (New York: New York University Press, 1986).

Elster, Jon. *Arguing and Bargaining in Two Constituent Assemblies* (New Haven: Storrs Lecture, Yale Law School, 1991).

Elster, Jon, ed. *Deliberative Democracy* (New York: Cambridge University Press, 1998).

Erikson, Erik. *Childhood and Society* (New York: Norton, 1950).

Eyal, Jonathan. "NATO's Enlargement: Anatomy of a Decision." *International Affairs* 73, no. 4 (October 1997): 711–12.

Farell, Thomas B. *Norms of Rhetorical Culture* (New Haven: Yale University Press, 1993).

Fearon, James D. "Signaling Foreign Policy Interests: Tying Hands versus Sinking Costs." *Journal of Conflict Resolution* 41, no.1 (February 1997): 68–90.

Fejto, Francois, ed. *The Opening of an Era, 1848: An Historical Symposium* (1948; New York: Howard Fertig, 1966).

Festinger, Leon. *A Theory of Cognitive Dissonance* (Stanford: Stanford University Press, 1966).

Finnemore, Martha. *National Interests in International Society* (Ithaca: Cornell University Press, 1996).

Finnemore, Martha. *National Interests in International Society* (Ithaca: Cornell University Press, 1996).

Fishkin, James S. *Democracy and Deliberation: New Directions for Democratic Reform* (New Haven: Yale University Press, 1991).

Fiske, Susan T., and Shelley E. Taylor. *Social Cognition.* 2nd ed. (New York: McGraw-Hill, 1991).

Flinn, Michael W., and T. Christopher Smout. *Essays in Social History* (Oxford: Clarendon Press, 1974).

Forbes, H. D. *Commerce, Culture, and the Contact Hypothesis* (New Haven: Yale University Press, 1997).

Fouzieh, Melanie Alamir, and August Pradetto. "Identitssuche als Movens der Sicherheitspolitik. Die NATO-Osterweiterungsdebatten im Lichte der Herausbildung neuer Identitten im postkommunistischen Ostmitteleuropa und in der Allianz." *Osteuropa* 48, no. 2 (February 1998): 134–47.

Fowler, Robert Booth. *The Dance With Community: The Contemporary Debate in American Political Thought* (Lawrence: University of Kansas Press, 1991).

Franck, Thomas M. *The Power of Legitimacy among Nations* (New York: Oxford University Press, 1990).

Frankel, Benjamin, ed. *Realism: Restatements and Renewal* (London: Frank Cass, 1996).

Fratianni, Michele, and John Pattison. "The Economics of International Organizations." *Kyklos* 35, no 2 (1982).

Freedman, Lawrence, and Efraim Karsh. *The Gulf Conflict 1990–1991: Diplomacy and War in the New World Order* (Princeton: Princeton University Press, 1993).

Frei, Norbert. *Vergangenheitspolitik: Die Anfaenge der Bundesrepublik und die NS-Vergangenheit* (Munich: C. H. Beck, 1996).

Friedman, Thomas L. "Forgetting that Russia's Nuclear Weapons Are the Problem." *International Herald Tribune*, 3 June 1997, 6.

Fromm, Erich. *Escape from Freedom* (New York: Farrar & Rhinehart, 1941).

Gaertner, Samuel, et al. "The Common Ingroup Identity Model." In Wolfgang Stroebe and Miles Hewstone, eds. *European Review of Social Psychology* 4 (New York: John Wiley and Sons, 1993): 1–26.

Garcia, Soledad, ed. *European Identity and the Search for Legitimacy* (London: Pinter, 1993).

Geertz, Clifford. *The Interpretation of Cultures: Selected Essays* (New York: Basic Books, 1973).

Geertz, Clifford, ed. *Old Societies and New States* (Glencoe, Ill.: Free Press, 1963).

Gellner, Ernest. *Nations and Nationalism* (Ithaca: Cornell University Press, 1983).

Giddens, Anthony. *Modernity and Self-Identity: Self and Society in the Late Modern Age* (Oxford: Polity Press, 1991).

Gillessen, Guenther. "Mit amerikanischem Beistand." *Frankfurter Allgemeine Zeitung, 3 May 1990.*

Gilpin, Robert. *U.S. Power and the Multinational Corporation: The Political Economy of Foreign Direct Investment* (New York: Basic, 1975).

"Global Security Beyond 2000, Executive Summary" (Pittsburgh: Pittsburgh: University of Pittsburgh, Center for West European Studies, November 1995).

Goffman, Erving. *The Presentation of Self in Everyday Life* (Garden City: Doubleday, 1959).

Goldgeier, James M. "NATO Expansion: The Anatomy of a Decision." *Washington Quarterly* 21, no. 1 (winter 1998): 86–87.

Gordon, Philip H. "Will Anyone Really Pay to Enlarge NATO—and If So, Who?" *International Herald Tribune,* 30 April 1997, 8.

Gorer, Geoffrey. *Exploring English Character* (London: Criterion Books, 1955).

Gorer, Geoffrey. *The People of Great Russia: A Psychological Study* (New York: Chanticleer Press, 1950).

Gorer, Geoffrey. *The American People: A Study in National Character* (New York: Norton, 1948).

Gowan, Peter, and Perry Anderson. *The Question of Europe* (New York: Verso, 1997).

Grenville, J. A. S. *Europe Reshaped: 1848–1878* (Sussex, England: Harvester, 1976).

Grieco, Joseph M. "State Interests and Institutional Rule Trajectories: A Neorealist Interpretation of the Maastricht Treaty and European Economic and Monetary Union." *Security Studies* 5, no. 3 (spring 1996): 261–306.

Grieco, Joseph M. "Anarchy and the Limits of Cooperation: A Realist Critique of the Newest Liberal Institutionalism." *International Organization* 42, no. 3 (summer 1988): 485–507.

Grosser, Alfred. *Germany in Our Time* (New York: Praeger, 1971).

Grund, Francis J. *The Americans in Their Moral, Social, and Political Relations* (London: Longman, Rees, Orme, Brown, Green, 1837).

Gurr, Ted Robert, and Barbara Harff. *Ethnic Conflict in World Politics* (Boulder: Westview, 1994).

Guttman, Amy, and Dennis Thompson. *Democracy and Disagreement: Why Moral Conflict Cannot be Avoided in Politics, and What Should Be Done About It* (Cambridge: Harvard University Press, 1996).

Haas, Ernst. *Beyond the Nation State: Functionalism and Inter-National Organization* (Stanford: Stanford University Press, 1964).

Haas, Ernst. *The Uniting of Europe: Political, Social, and Economic Forces* (Stanford: Stanford University Press, 1958).

Habermas, Jürgen. *Between Facts and Norms: Contributions to a Discourse Theory of Law and Democracy* (Cambridge: MIT Press, 1996).

Habermas, Jürgen. "Citizenship and National Identity: Some Reflections on the Future of Europe." *Praxis International* 12, no.1 (April 1992): 1–19

Habermas, Jürgen. *Structural Transformation of the Public Sphere* (Cambridge: MIT Press, 1989).

Habermas, Jürgen. *Theory of Communicative Action*, vol. 2, *Lifeworld and System* (Boston: Beacon Press 1987).

Habermas, Jürgen. *Theory of Communicative Action*, vol. 1, *Reason and the Rationalization of Society* (Boston: Beacon Press 1984).

Hall, Rodney Bruce. "Territorial and National Sovereigns: Sovereign Identity and Consequences for Security Policy." *Security Studies* 8, nos. 2/3 (winter 1998/99–spring 1999): 145–97.

Hampton, Mary N. "NATO, Germany, and the United States: Creating Positive Identity in Trans-Atlantia." *Security Studies* 8, nos. 2/3 (winter 1998/99–spring 1999): 235–69.

Hansard, T. C. *The Parliamentary Debates From 1813 to the Present Time*, vol. 29 (London: 1815).

Haq, Mahbub ul. *Reflections on Human Development* (London: Oxford University Press, 1995).

Hardin, Russell. *One For All: The Logic of Group Conflict* (Princeton: Princeton University Press, 1995).

Harding, Sandra. *The Science Question in Feminism* (Ithaca: Cornell University Press, 1986).

Harkavy, Robert E. "Defeat, National Humiliation, and the Revenge Motif in International Politics." Paper presented at the Annual Scientific Meeting of the International Society of Political Psychology, Vancouver, British Columbia 1996.

Harknett, Richard, and Jeffrey VanDenBerg. "Alignment Theory and Interrelated Threats: Jordan and the Persian Gulf Crisis." *Security Studies* 6, no.3 (spring 1997): 112–53.

Hartshorne, Thomas L. *The Distorted Image: Changing Conceptions of the American Character Since Turner* (Cleveland: Case Western Reserve University Press, 1968).

Harvey, David. *The Condition of Postmodernity: An Enquiry into the Origins of Cultural Change* (Cambridge: Basil Blackwell, 1989).

Hasenclever, Andreas, Peter Mayer, and Volker Rittberger. *Theories of International Regimes* (Cambridge: Cambridge University Press, 1997).

Havel, Vaclav. "The Euro-American Alliance Needs to Deepen as it Expands." *International Herald Tribune*, 15 May 1997, 8.

Haykel, Mohamed Hasanayn. *The Gulf Crisis* (in Arabic) (Cairo: al-Ahram, 1992).

Hedley, R. Alan. "Identity: Sense of Self and Nation." *Canadian Review of Sociology and Anthropology* 31, no. 2 (May 1994): 200–14.

Heider, Fritz. *The Psychology of Interpersonal Relations* (New York: Wiley, 1958).

Heilbrun, Jacob. "Germany's New Right." *Foreign Affairs* 75, vol. 6 (November/December 1996): 80–98.

Heisbourg, Francois. "At This Point, Only Washington Can Slow the Reckless Pace." *International Herald Tribune*, 28 November 1996, 8.

Hellmann, Gunther, and Reinhard Wolf. "Neorealism, Neoliberal Institutionalism, and the Future of NATO." *Security Studies* 3, no. 1 (autumn 1993).

Hensley, Virginia, and Shelley Duval. "Some Perceptual Determinants of Perceived Similarity, Liking, and Correctness." *Journal of Personality and Social Psychology* 34, no. 2 (August 1976): 159–68.

Hermann, Charles F., Charles Kegley, and James Rosenau, eds. *New Directions in the Study of Foreign Policy* (Boston: Unwin Hyman, 1987).

Hermann, Charles F., et al. *CREON: A Foreign Events Data Set* (Beverly Hills : Sage Professional Papers Series, 1973).

Hermann, Margaret G., and Charles W. Kegley Jr. "Rethinking Democracy and Democratic Peace: Perspectives from Political Psychology." *International Studies Quarterly* 39 (December 1995): 511–34.

Hermann, Richard K., James F. Voss, Tonya Y. E. Schooler, and Joseph Ciarrochi. "Images in International Relations: An Experimental Test of Cognitive Schemata." *International Studies Quarterly* 41, no. 3 (September 1997): 403–33.

Herrmann, Richard, and Michael P. Fischerkeller. "Beyond the Enemy Image and Spiral Model: Cognitive-Strategic Research After the Cold War." *International Organization* 49, no. 3 (summer 1995): 415–50.

Herrrmann, Richard K. *Perceptions and Behavior in Soviet Foreign Policy* (Pittsburgh, University of Pittsburgh Press, 1985).

Herrrmann, Richard K. "The Power of Perceptions in Foreign-Policy Decision Making: Do Views of the Soviet Union Determine the Policy Choices of American Leaders?" *American Journal of Political Science* 30, no. 4 (November 1986): 841–75.

Hewitt, John. *Self and Society: A Symbolic Interactionist Social Psychology* (Boston: Allyn and Bacon, 1976).

Hiro, Dilip. *Desert Shield to Desert Storm* (New York: Routledge 1992).

Hobsbawm, E. J. *Nations and Nationalism Since 1780* (Cambridge: Cambridge University Press, 1992).

Hogg, Michael A., Deborah J. Terry, and Katherine M. White."A Tale of Two Theories: A Critical Comparison of Identity Theory with Social Identity Theory." *Social Psychology Quarterly* 58 (December 1995): 259–62.

Hogg, Michael, and Dominic Abrams, eds. *Group Motivation: Social Psychological Perspectives*, (London: Harvester Wheatsheaf, 1993).

Hogg, Michael, and Dominic Abrams. *Social Identifications: A Social Psychology of Intergroup Relations and Group Process* (New York: Routledge, 1988).

Holsti, K. J. *Why Nations Realign* (London: Allen & Unwin, 1982).

Holsti, K. J. "National Role Conceptions in the Study of Foreign Policy." *International Studies Quarterly* 14, no. 3 (September 1970): 233–309.

Holt, Edgar. *Risorgimento: The Making of Italy, 1815–1870* (London: Macmillan and Company, 1970).

Hopf, Ted. "The Promise of Constructivism in International Relations Theory." *International Security* 23, no.1 (summer 1998): 171–200.

Hornstein, Harvey A. *Cruelty and Kindness: A New Look at Aggression and Altruism* (Englewood Cliffs, N.J.: Prentice-Hall, 1976).

Hornstein, Harvey A. "Promotive Tension: The Basis of Prosocial Behavior from a Lewinian Perspective." *Journal of Social Issues* 28, no. 3 (1972): 191–218.

Horowitz, Donald L. *Ethnic Groups in Conflict* (Berkeley: University of California Press, 1985).

Hroch, Miroslav. *Social Preconditions of National Revival in Europe: A Comparative Analysis of the Social Composition of Patriotic Groups among the Smaller European Nations* (Cambridge: Cambridge University Press, 1985).

Huelshoff, Michael G., Andrei Markovits, and Simon Reich, eds. *From Bundesrepublik to Deutschland* (Ann Arbor: University of Michigan Press, 1994).

Huntingon, Samuel P. *The Clash of Civilizations and the Remaking of World Order* (New York: Simon and Schuster, 1996).

Huntington, Samuel P. "The Clash of Civilizations?" *Foreign Affairs* 72, no. 3 (summer 1997): 197–216

Hurwitz, Jon, and Mark Peffley. "How Are Foreign Policy Attitudes Structured? A Hierarchical Model." *American Political Science Review* 81, no. 4 (December 1987): 1100–20.

Hurwitz, Jon, and Mark Peffley. "Public Images of the Soviet Union: The Impact on Foreign Policy Attitudes." *Journal of Politics* 52, no. 1 (February 1990): 3–28.

Hurwitz, Jon, Mark Peffley, and Mitchell Seligson. "Foreign Policy Belief Systems in Comparative Perspective: The United States and Costa Rica." *International Studies Quarterly* 37, no. 3 (September 1993): 245–70.

Ikenberry, G. John, and Charles Kupchan. "Socialization and Hegemonic Power." *International Organization* 44, no. 3 (summer 1990): 283–315.

Ikenberry, G. John. "The Myth of Post–Cold War Chaos." *Foreign Affairs* 75, no. 3 (May/June 1996): 79–91.

Inkeles, Alex, ed. *On Measuring Democracy: Its Consequences and Concomitants* (New Brunswick: Transaction Books, 1991).

Inoguchi, Takashi. Inoguchi. *Sekai Hendo no Mikata* (The standpoint of global change) (Tokyo: Chikuma Shobo, 1994).

Jackson, Robert. *Quasi-States: Sovereignty, International Relations and the Third World* (Cambridge: Cambridge University Press, 1990).

Jackson, Sally, ed. *Argumentation and Values: Proceedings of the Ninth, SCA/AFA Conference on Argumentation* (Annandale, Va.: Speech Communication Assoc., 1995).

Janis, Irving L., and Leon Mann. *Decision Making: A Psychological Analysis of Conflict, Choice, and Commitment* (New York: Free Press, 1977).

Jervis, Robert, and Jack Snyder, ed. *Dominoes and Bandwagons: Strategic Beliefs and Great Power Competition in the Eurasian Rimland* (New York: Oxford University Press, 1991).

Joffe, George. "Middle Eastern Views of the Gulf Conflict and Its Aftermath." *Review of International Studies* 19 (April 1993): 177–99.

Joffe, Josef. "Mr. Heilbrunn's Planet." Foreign Affairs 76, no. 2 (March/April 1996).

Johnson, Gary R. "The Evolutionary Roots of Patriotism." in *Patriotism In the Lives of Individuals and Nations*, ed. Daniel Bar-Tal and Ervin Staub (city: publisher) 1996.

Lynn-Jones, Sean M., et al., eds. *The Cold War and After: Prospects for Peace* (Cambridge: MIT Press, 1992).

Kahl, Colin. "Constructing a Separate Peace: Constructivism, Collective Liberal Identity, and Democratic Peace." *Security Studies* 8, nos. 2/3 (winter 1998/99–spring 1999): 94–144.

Kamp, Karl Heinz. "Deja Vu: The Never Ending Story of a European Nuclear Deterrence." Institute Francais des Relations Internationales (IFRI), 1997.

Kaplan, Robert. *The Ends of the Earth: A Journey to the Frontiers of Anarchy* (New York: Vintage, 1996).

Kariel, Henry S. *The Desperate Politics of Postmodernism* (Amherst: University of Massachusetts Press, 1989).

Karklins, Rasma. 1994. *Ethnopolitics and Transition to Democracy: The Collapse of the USSR and Latvia* (Baltimore: Johns Hopkins University Press, 1994).

Katzenstein, Peter J. *Cultural Norms and National Security: Police and Military in Postwar Japan* (Ithaca: Cornell University Press 1996).

Katzenstein, Peter J., ed. *Tamed Power. Germany in Europe*, (Ithaca: Cornell University Press, 1997).

Katzenstein, Peter J., ed. *The Culture of National Security. Norms and Identity in World Politics* (New York: Columbia University Press, 1996).

Keddie, Nikki, and Mark Gasiorowski. *Neither East Nor West* (New Haven: Yale University Press, 1990).

Keith, Michael, and Steven Pile, eds. *Place and the Politics of Identity* (New York: Routledge, 1993).

Kenichi Ohmae. "Global Consumers Want Sony, Not Soil." *New Perspectives Quarterly* (fall 1991).

Keohane, Robert O. "Reciprocity in International Relations." *International Organization* 40, no. 1 (winter 1986): 1–27.

Keohane, Robert O. *After Hegemony. Cooperation and Discord in the World Political Economy* (Princeton: Princeton University Press, 1984).

Keohane, Robert O., and Joseph S. Nye Jr. *Power and Interdependence. World Politics in Transition* (Boston: Little, Brown, 1977).

Khadduri, Majid, and Edmund Ghareeb. *War in the Gulf, 1990–91: The Iraq-Kuwait Conflict and Its Implications* (New York: Oxford University Press 1997).

Khong, Yuen F. *Analogies at war: Korea, Munich, Dien Bien Phu, and the Vietnam Decisions of 1965* (Princeton: Princeton University Press, 1992).

Kindleberger, Charles P. *The World in Depression, 1929–1939* (Berkeley: University of California Press, 1973).

King, Bolton. *A History of Italian Unity: A Political History of Italy From 1814–1871*, vol. 1 (1899; New York: Russell and Russell, 1924).

Klandermans, Bert, Hanspeter Kriesi, and Sidney Tarrow. *From Structure to Action: Comparing Social Movement Research Across Cultures* (Greenwich, Conn: JAI Press, 1988).

Klare, Michael. *Rogue States and Nuclear Outlaws: America"s Search for a New Foreign Policy* (New York: Hill and Wang, 1995).

Klotz, Audie. *Norms in International Politics: The Struggle against Apartheid* (Ithaca: Cornell University Press, 1995).

Kohl, Helmut, with Kai Diekmann and Rolf Reuth *Ich Wollte Deutschlands Einheit* (Berlin: Propylaen, 1996).

Kolankiewicz, George. "Consensus and Competition in the Eastern Enlargement of the European Union." *International Affairs* 70, no. 3 (July 1994): 481–82.

Kolodziej, Edward A. "Renaissance in Security Studies? Caveat Lector!" *International Studies Quarterly* 36, no. 4 (December 1992): 421–38.

Kowert. Paul A. "National Identity: Inside and Out." *Security Studies* 8, nos. 2/3 (winter 1998/99–spring 1999): 1–34.

Krasner, Stephen D. "State Power and the Structure of International Trade." *World Politics* 28, no. 3 (April 1976): 317–47.

Kratochwil, Friedrich. *Rules, Norms, Decisions* (Cambridge: Cambridge University Press, 1989).

Krause, Keith, and Michael C. Williams, eds. *Critical Security Studies: Concepts and Cases* (Minneapolis: University of Minnesota Press, 1997).

Krugman, Paul. "Competitiveness: A Dangerous Obsession." *Foreign Affairs* 73, no. 2 (March/April 1994).

Kubalkova, Vendulka, Nicholas G. Onuf, and Paul Kowert, eds. *International Relations in a Constructed World* (Armonk: M. E. Sharpe, 1998).

Kuentzel, Matthias. *Bonn and the Bomb: German Politics and the Nuclear Option* (Boulder: Pluto Press, 1995).

Kugler, Richard L. *Costs of NATO Enlargement. Moderate and Affordable* (Strategic Forum 128, Washington: Institute for National Strategic Studies, 1997).

Laitin, David. *Hegemony and Culture: Politics and Religious Change among the Yoruba* (Chicago: University of Chicago Press, 1986).

Laitin, David. *Identity in Formation* (Ithaca: Cornell University Press, 1998).

Lake, Anthony. "Confronting Backlash States." *Foreign Affairs* 73, no. 2 (March/April 1994): 45–55.

Lake, David. "Beneath the Commerce of Nations: A Theory of International Economic Structures." *International Studies Quarterly* 28, no. 2 (June 1984): 143–70.

Lamers, Karl, and Wolfgang Schaeuble. "Ueberlegungen zur europaischen Politik." *CDU/CSU Fraktion des Deutschen Bundestages*, 1 September 1994.

Lapid, Yosef, and Friedrich Kratochwil, eds. *The Return of Culture and Identity in IR Theory* (Boulder: Lynne Rienner, 1996).

Larson, Deborah Welch. "The Role of Belief Systems and Schemas in Foreign Policy Decision-Making." *Political Psychology* 15, no. 1 (March 1994): 17–33.

Lasch, Christopher. *The Culture of Narcissism: American Life in an Age of Diminishing Expectations* (New York: Norton, 1979).

Lasswell, Harold. *Psychopathology and Politics* (Chicago: University of Chicago Press, 1930).

Lasswell, Harold. *World Politics and Personal Insecurity* (New York: McGraw-Hill, 1935).

Lauren, Paul Gordon, ed. *Diplomacy: New Approaches in History, Theory and Policy* (New York: Free Press, 1979).

Lawrence Grossberg. *Dancing in Spite of Myself: Essays on Popular Culture* (Durham: Duke University Press, 1997).

Lebow, Richard Ned. *Between Peace and War: The Nature of International Crisis* (Baltimore: Johns Hopkins University Press 1981).

Legro, Jeffrey W. "Culture and Preferences in the International Cooperation Two-Step." *American Political Science Review* 90, no. 1 (March 1996): 118–37.

Lemarchand, Rene. *Rwanda and Burundi* (New York: Praeger Publishers, 1970).

Lewis, Martin, and Karen Wigen. *The Myth of Continents: A Critique of Meta-geography* (Berkeley: Univerisyt of California Press, 1997).

Lindberg, Leon, and Stuart Scheingold. *Europe's Would-Be Polity: Patterns of Change in the European Community* (Englewood Cliffs, N.J.: Prentice-Hall, 1970).

Linville, Patricia W. "Self-Complexity and Affective Extremity: Don't Put All Your Eggs in One Cognitive Basket." *Social Cognition* 3 (spring 1985): 94–120.

Linville, Patricia. "Self-Complexity as a Cognitive Buffer Against Related Depression and Illness." *Journal of Personality and Social Psychology* 52 (April 1987): 663–76.

Liska, George. *Nations in Alliance. The Limits of Interdependence* (Baltimore: Johns Hopkins University Press, 1962).

Lovett, Clara. *The Democratic Movement in Italy, 1830–1876* (Cambridge, Mass: Harvard University Press, 1982).

Lovibond, Sabina. "Feminism and the Crisis of Rationality." *New Left Review* no. 207 (September/October 1994): 72–86.

Lukacs, Yehuda. *Israel, Jordan and the Peace Process* (Albany: State University of New York Press 1997).

Luke, Timothy W. "The Discipline of Security Studies and the Codes of Containment: Learning from Kuwait." *Alternatives* 16, no. 3 (date 1991): 315–44.

Lustick, Ian S. *Unsettled States, Disputed Lands: Britain and Ireland, France and Algeria, Israel and the West Bank-Gaza* (Ithaca: Cornell University Press, 1994).

Lynch, Marc. "Abandoning Iraq: Jordan's Alliances and the Politics of State Identity." *Security Studies* 8, nos. 2/3 (winter 1998/99–spring 1999): 347–89.

Lynch, Marc. "Rightsizing Jordan: Moving Borders and the Politics of Identity" (paper presented to the annual meeting of the International Studies Association, Minneapolis, MN, 19–22 February 1998).

Lynch, Marc. *State Interests and Public Spheres: The International Politics of Jordan's Identity* (New York: Columbia University Press, forthcoming).

Majstorovic, Steven. "Ancient Hatreds or Elite Manipulation: Memory and Politics in the Former Yugoslavia." *World Affairs* 15, no. 4 (spring 1997).

Malnes, Raino, and Arild Underdal, eds. *Rationality and Institutions. Essays in Honour of Knut Midgaard* (Oslo: Universitetsforlaget, 1992).

March, James G., and Johan P. Olsen. *Rediscovering Institutions. The Organizational Basis of Politics* (New York: Free Press, 1989).

McAdam, Doug, John D. McCarthy, and Mayer N. Zald, eds. *Comparative Perspectives on Social Movements: Political Opportunities, Mobilizing Structures, and Cultural Framings* (New York: Cambridge University Press, 1996).

McCalla, Robert B. "NATO's Persistence After the Cold War." *International Organization* 50, no. 3 (summer 1996).

McGee, Arthur R. "U.S. Policy Exposed." *Haiti Information* 2, no. 24 (27 August 1994).

McKay, Derek, and H. M. Scott. *The Rise of the Great Powers, 1648-1815* (New York: Longman, 1983).

McNeely, Connie L. *Constructing the Nation-State. International Organization and Prescriptive Action* (Westport, Conn.: Greenwood Press, 1995).

Mead, Margaret. *And Keep Your Powder Dry: An Anthropologist Looks at America* (New York: Morrow, 1942).

Mearsheimer, John. "A Realist Reply." *International Security* 20, no. 1 (summer 1995): 82.

Meissner, Dorris M., et al. "International Migration: Challenges in a New Era." *Report to the Trilateral Commission* 44 (1993).

Mercer, Jonathan. "Anarchy and Identity." *International Organization* 49, no. 2 (spring 1995): 229-52.

Miles, Robert. "Recent Marxist Theories of Nationalism and the Issue of Racism." *British Journal of Sociology* 38, no. 1 (March 1987): 24-43.

Milner, Helen V. "International Theories of Cooperation Among Nations: Strengths and Weaknesses." *World Politics* 44, no. 3 (April 1992): 466-96.

Mitrany, David. *A Working Peace System: An Argument for the Functional Development of International Organizations* (London: Royal Institute of International Affairs, 1944).

Bukovansky, Mlada. "American identity and neutral rights from independence to the War of 1812." *International Organization* 51, no. 2 (spring 1997).

Modelski, George, et al. "Special Issue: Evolutionary Paradigms in the Social Sciences." *International Studies Quarterly* 40, no. 3 (September 1996).

Monroe, Kristen Renwick. "Psychology and Rational Actor Theory." *Political Psychology* 16 (March 1995): 1-21.

Moore-Gilbert, Bart. *Postcolonial Theory: Contexts, Practices, Politics* (New York: Verso, 1997).

Moravcsik, Andrew. "Federalism and Peace: A Structural Liberal Perspective." *Zeitschrift fuer Internationale Beziehungen* 3, no. 1 (1996): 123-32.

Moravcsik, Andrew. "Taking Preferences Seriously: A Liberal Theory of International Politics." *International Organization* 51, no. 4 (autumn 1997): 513-53.

Morganthau, Hans. *Politics Among Nations: The Struggle for Power and Peace*, 6th ed. (New York: Knopf).

Morris, Charles W., ed. *Mead, Mind, Self and Society from the Standpoint of a Social Behaviorist*, (Chicago: University of Chicago Press, 1934).

Morris, David B. "Bitburg Revisited: Germany's Search for Normalcy." *German Politics and Society* 13 (winter 1995): 92-109.

Moynihan, Daniel Patrick. *Pandaemonium: Ethnicity in International Politics* (Oxford: Oxford Univ. Press, 1993).

Nahar, Ghazi Saleh. *Jordanian Foreign Policy Decisions Towards the Gulf Crisis* (in Arabic) (Amman: Dar al-Majdlawi, 1993).

Nairn, Tom. *The Break-Up of Britain: Crisis and Neo-Nationalism* (London: Verso, 1977).

Naqrash, Abdullah. "The Official Jordanian Political Position in the Arab Gulf Crisis" (in Arabic), *Dirasat* 21a, no. 4 (1994): 319–49.

Nash, Roderick. *Wilderness and the American Mind* (New Haven: Yale University Press, 1982).

Neack, Laura, Jeanne A. K. Hey, and Patrick Haney, eds. *Foreign Policy Analysis: Continuity and Change in Its Second Generation* (Englewood Cliffs, N.J.: Prentice-Hall, 1995).

Nelson, John, Allan Megill, and Donald McCloskey, eds. *The Rhetoric of the Human Sciences: Language and Argument in Scholarship and Public Affairs* (Madison: University of Wisconsin Press, 1987).

Neumann, Iver B. "Identity and Security." *Journal of Peace Research* 29, no. 2 (May 1992): 221–26.

Neumann, Iver B. "Russia as Central Europe's Constituting Other." *East European Politics and Societies* 7, no. 2 (spring 1993): 349–69.

Neumann, Johanna. *Lights, Camera, War: Is Media Technology Driving International Politics?* (New York: St. Martin's, 1996).

Newbury, Catharine. *The Cohesion of Oppression: Clientship and Ethnicity in Rwanda, 1860–1960* (New York: Columbia University Press, 1988).

Nisbett, Richard E., and Lee Ross. *Social Inference: Strategies and Shortcomings of Social Judgment* (Englewood Cliffs, N.J.: Prentice-Hall, 1980).

Norris, Christopher. *Derrida* (Cambridge: Harvard University Press, 1987).

O'Boyle, Leonard. "The Problem of an Excess of Educated Men in Western Europe, 1800–1850." *Journal of Modern History* 42, no. 4 (December 1970): 471–95

O'Tuathail, Gearoid. *Critical Geopolitics, Borderlines*, vol. 6 (Minneapolis: University of Minnesota Press, 1996).

Oakes, Penelope. "The Salience of Social Categories." In *Rediscovering the Social Group: A Self-Categorization Theory*, ed. John C. Turner, et al. (New York: Basil Blackwell).

Okin, Susan M. *Women in Western Political Thought* (Princeton: Princeton University Press, 1979).

Olson, Mancur. *The Logic of Collective Action. Public Goods and the Theory of Groups* (Cambridge: Harvard University Press, 1971).

Onuf, Nicholas. *World of Our Making: Rules and Rule in Social Theory and International Relations* (Columbia: University of South Carolina Press, 1989).

Perry, Ralph Barton. *Characteristically American* (Ann Arbor: University of Michigan, 1949).

Pfaff, William. "European Security Isn't Broken, So Why Try to Fix it Now?" *International Herald Tribune*, 18 February 1997, 8.

Pollock, David. *The 'Arab Street'? Public Opinion in the Arab World*, Paper no. 32 (Washington, D.C.: Washington Institute for Near East Studies Policy, 1992).

Posen, Barry. *The Sources of Military Doctrine: France, Britain and Germany Between the World Wars* (Ithaca: Cornell University Press, 1984)

Pridham, Geoffrey. and Tatu Vanhanen, eds. *Eastern Europe. Domestic and International Perspectives* (London: Routledge, 1994).

Putnam, Robert D., with Robert Leonardi and Raffaella Y. Nanetti. *Making Democracy Work: Civic Traditions in Modern Italy*, (Princeton: Princeton University Press, 1993).

Rabbie, Jacob M., and Murray Horwitz. "Arousal of Ingroup-Outgroup Bias by a Chance Win or Loss." *Journal of Personality and Social Psychology* 13, no. 3 (November 1969): 269–77.

Reed, Stanley. "Jordan and the Gulf Crisis." *Foreign Affairs* 69, no. 3 (winter 1990/91): 21–35.

"Reformvorschlage des NATO-Militarausschusses." *Neue Zurcher Zeitung*, 24 April 1997, 2.

Reichel, Peter. *Politik mit der Erinnerung: Gedaechtnisorte im Streit um die nationalsozialistische Vergangenheit* (Munich: Carl Hanser, 1995).

Renan, Ernest. "Qu'est-ce Qu'une nation?" *Oeuvres Compltes*, vol. 1 (Paris: 1947–61), 887–907.

Rescher, Nicholas. *Pluralism: Against the Demand For Consensus* (New York: Oxford University Press, 1993).

Reus-Smit, Christian. "The Constitutional Structure of International Society and the Nature of Fundamental Institutions." *International Organization* 51, no. 4 (autumn 1997).

Riall, Lucy. "Elite Resistance to State Formation: the Case of Italy." In *National Histories and European History*, ed. Mary Fulbrook (Boulder: Westview, 1993).

Riall, Lucy. *The Italian Risorgimento: State, Society and National Unification* (New York: Routledge, 1994).

Richmond, Anthony. "Ethnic Nationalism and Postindustrialism." *Ethnic and Racial Studies* 7, no. 1 (January 1984): 4–18

Richter, James G. "Perpetuating the Cold War." *Political Science Quarterly* 107, no. 2 (summer 1992): 271–301.

Ridgeway, James. *The Haiti Files* (Washington, D.C.: Essential Books, 1995).

Riesman, David, Reuel Denney, and Nathan Glazer. *The Lonely Crowd: A Study of the Changing American Character* (New Haven: Yale University Press, 1950).

Risse-Kappen, Thomas. *Cooperation Among Democracies. Norms, Transnational Relations, and the European Impact on U.S. Foreign Policy* (Princeton: Princeton University Press, 1995).

Risse-Kappen, Thomas. "Democratic Peace—Warlike Democracies? A Social Constructivist Interpretation of the Liberal Argument." *European Journal of International Relations* 1, no. 4 (December 1995): 491–517.

Rittberger, Volker, ed., with the assistance of Peter Mayer. *Regime Theory and International Relations* (Oxford: Clarendon Press, 1993).

Rooney, Phyllis. "Recent Work in Feminist Discussions of Reason." *American Philosophical Quarterly* 31, no. 1 (January 1994): 1–21.

Rosecrance, Richard. *The Rise of the Trading State: Commerce and Conquest in the Modern World* (New York: Basic Books, 1986).

Rosenau, James. *Along the Domestic-Foreign Frontier: Exploring Governance in a Turbulent World* (New York: Cambridge University Press, 1997).

Rosenau, James, ed. *Comparing Foreign Policies: Theories, Findings, and Methods* (New York: Wiley, 1974).

Rosenau, Pauline Marie. *Post-Modernism and the Social Sciences: Insights, Inroads, and Intrusions* (Princeton: Princeton University Press, 1992).

Rothschild, Joseph. *Ethnopolitics: A Conceptual Framework* (New York: Columbia University Press, 1981).

Ruggie, John G. "Continuity and Transformation in the World Polity: Toward a Neorealist Synthesis." *World Politics* 35, no. 2 (January 1983): 261–85.

Ruggie, John Gerard, ed. *Multilateralism Matters. The Theory and Praxis of an Institutional Form* (New York: Columbia University Press, 1993).

Russett, Bruce. "Components of an Operational Theory of Alliance Formation." *Journal of Conflict Resolution* 12, no. 3 (September 1968).

Russett, Bruce. *Grasping the Democratic Peace: Principles for a Post–Cold War World* (Princeton: Princeton University Press, 1993).

Said, Edward W. *Culture and Imperialism* (New York: Knopf, 1993).

Said, Edward W. *Orientalism* (New York: Vintage, 1979).

Sandler, Todd, and John T. Tschirhart. "The Economic Theory of Clubs: An Evaluative Survey." *Journal of Economic Literature* 18, no. 4 (December 1980).

Sandler, Todd. "Impurity of Defense: An Application to the Economics of Alliances." *Kyklos* 30, no. 3 (1977): 443–60.

Sargent, S. Stansfeld, and Marian W. Smith. *Culture and Personality*, (New York: Wenner-Gren Foundation, 1949).

Sayigh, Yezid. "The Gulf Crisis: Why the Arab Regional Order Failed." *International Affairs* 67, no. 3 (July 1991): 487–507.

Schiappa, Edward, ed. *Warranting Assent: Case Studies in Argument Evaluation* (Albany: SUNY Press, 1995).

Schiller, Herbert I. *Communication and Cultural Domination* (New York: International Arts and Sciences Press, 1976).

Schiller, Herbert I. *Mass Communication and American Empire* (New York: A. M. Kelley).

Schimmelfennig, Frank. "NATO Enlargement: A Constructivist Explanation." *Security Studies* 8, nos. 2/3 (winter 1998/99–spring 1999): 198–234.

Schimmelfennig, Frank. "Internationale Sozialisation neuer Staaten. Heuristische ‹berlegungen zu einem Forschungsdesiderat." *Zeitschrift fur Internationale Beziehungen* 1, no. 2 (December 1994): 335–55.

Schlesinger, Arthur M., Jr. *The Disuniting of America* (New York: Norton, 1992).

Schloessler, Dietmar, Reiner Albert, Frank Kostelnik. *Deutschland, die NATO und Europa: Die sicherheitspolitische Lage im Spiegel von Elite-Gruppen-Meinungen* (Muenster: Lit Verlag, 1995).

Schneider, Gerald, Patricia A. Weitsman, and Thomas Bernauer, eds. *Towards a New Europe. Stops and Starts in Regional Integration* (Westport, Conn.: Praeger, 1995).

Schoenbaum, David, and Elizabeth Pond. *The German Question and Other Questions* (New York: Oxford University Press, 1997).

Schroeder, Paul. *The Transformation of European Politics, 1763–1848* (Oxford: Clarendon Press, 1994).

Schultz, Alfred. *On Phenomenology and Social Relations* (Chicago: University of Chicago Press, 1970).

Schulze, Hagen. *States, Nations and Nationalism: From the Middle Ages to the Present*, trans. William E. Yuill (Oxford: Blackwell, 1996).

Schwarz, Hans-Peter. *Konrad Adenauer: Volume One: From the German Empire to the Federal Republic, 1876–1952* (Providence: Berghahn, 1995).

Schweller, Randall L., and David Priess. "A Tale of Two Realisms: Expanding the Institutions Debate." *Mershon International Studies Review* 41, suppl. 1 (May 1997).

Schweller, Randall L. "Bandwagoning for Profit: Bringing the Revisionist State Back In." *International Security* 19, no. 1 (summer 1994).

Searle, John. *The Construction of Social Reality* (Berkeley: University of California Press, 1995).

Seton-Watson, Hugh. *Nations and States: An Enquiry into the Origins of Nations and the Politics of Nationalism* (Boulder: Westview, 1977).

Sha'ir, Jamal. *A Politician Remembers* (in Arabic) (London: Riyad al-Ris 1987).

Shapiro, Michael, and Hayward Alker, eds. *Challenging Boundaries: Global Flows, Territorial Identities, Borderlines*, vol. 2, (Minneapolis: University of Minnesota Press, 1996)

Sharara, Randa. "Israel in the Gulf Crisis: The Position on Jordan" (in Arabic). *Majellah al-Dirasat al-Filastiniyya* 4 (fall 1990): 72–83.

Shaw, R. Paul, and Yuwa Wong. *The Genetic Seeds of Warfare: Evolution, Nationalism, and Patriotism* (Boston: Unwin Hyman, 1989).

Sherif, Muzafer Sherif, et al. *Intergroup Conflict and Cooperation: The Robbers Cave Experiment* (Norman: University of Oklahoma Book Exchange, 1961).

Sherif, Muzafer Sherif. *Group Conflict and Cooperation: Their Social Psychology* (London: Routledge and Kegan Paul, 1966).

Sherif, Muzafer. *In Common Predicament: Social Psychology of Intergroup Conflict and Cooperation* (Boston: Houghton Mifflin, 1966).

Shibutani, Tamotsu. "Reference Groups as Perspectives." *American Journal of Sociology* 60, no. 6 (May 1955): 562–69

Shimko, Keith L. "Reagan on the Soviet Union and the Nature of International Conflict." *Political Psychology* 13, no. 3 (September 1992): 353–77.

Shimko, Keith L. *Images and Arms Control: Perceptions of the Soviet Union in the Reagan Administration* (Ann Arbor: University of Michigan Press, 1991).

Shindler, Colin. *Israel, Likud and the Zionist Dream: Power, Politics, and Ideology from Begin to Netanyahu* (London: I. B. Tauris, 1995).

Silverstein, Brett. "Enemy Images: The Psychology of U. S. Attitudes and Cognitions Regarding the Soviet Union." *American Psychologist* 44, no. 6 (June 1989): 903–13.

Skocpol, Theda. *States and Social Revolution* (Cambridge: Cambridge University Press, 1979).

Smith, Anthony D. "National Identity and the Idea of European Unity." *International Affairs* 68 (1992): 55–76.

Smith, Anthony D. *National Identity* (Reno: University of Nevada Press, 1991).

Smith, Anthony D. *The Ethnic Origin of Nations* (Oxford: Oxford University Press, 1986).

Smith, Dennis Mack. *Victor Emmanuel, Cavour and the Risorgimento* (London: Oxford University Press, 1971).

Smith, Denis Mack, ed. *The Making of Italy, 1796–1870* (New York: Walker, 1968).

Smith, Gordon, et al., eds. *Developments in German Politics* (Durham: Duke University Press, 1992).

Smith, Steve, Ken Booth, and Marysia Zalewski, eds. *International Theory: Positivism and Beyond* (Cambridge: Cambridge Univ. Press, 1996).

Smith, Tony. *America's Mission* (Princeton: Princeton University Press, 1995).

Snyder, Glenn H. "Alliance Theory: A Neorealist First Cut." *Journal of International Affairs* 44, no. 1 (fall 1990).

Soja, Edward. *Postmodern Geographies: The Reassertion of Space in Critical Social Theory* (New York: Verso, 1990).

Solana, Javier. "Preparing for the Madrid Summit." *NATO Review* 45, no. 2 (March–April 1997): 3.

Somers, Margaret. "Citizenship and the Place of the Public Sphere: Law, Community, and Political Culture in the Transition to Democracy." *American Sociological Review* 58, no.4 (October 1993): 587–620.

Spear, Joanna. "Bigger NATO, Bigger Sales." *The World Today* 53, no. 11 (November 1997): 272–74.

Spirtas, Michael. "French Twist: French and British NATO Policies from 1949 to 1966." *Security Studies* 8, nos. 2/3 (winter 1998/99–spring 1999): 302–46.

Sproull, L. S., and P. D. Larkey, eds. *Advances in Information Processing in Organizations*, vol. 2 (Greenwich, Conn.: JAI Press, 1985).

Stack, John F., ed. *The Primordial Challenge: Ethnicity in the Contemporary World* (New York: Greenwood, 1986).

Stein, Arthur. "Coordination and Collaboration: Regimes in an Anarchic World." *International Organization* 36, no. 2 (spring 1982): 299–324.

Stein, Maurice R., Arthur J. Vidich, and David M. White. *Identity and Anxiety* (Glencoe, IL: Free Press, 1960).

Stokes, Gail. "Cognition, Consciousness, and Nationalism." *Ethnic Groups* 10, no. 1–3 (August 1993): 27–42.

Strauss, Hannah Alice. *The Attitude of the Congress of Vienna Toward Nationalism in Germany, Italy and Poland* (New York: Columbia University Press, 1949).

Stuart, Douglas, and William Tow. *The Limits of Alliance: NATO Out-of-Area Problems since 1949* (Baltimore: The Johns Hopkins University Press, 1990).

Susan Strange. *The Retreat of the State: The Diffusion of Power in the World Economy* (Cambridge: Cambridge University Press, 1996).

Susser, Leslie. "Secret Route to Public Dialogue." *Jerusalem Report*, 11 August 1994, 21.

Tajfel, Henry. *Human Groups and Social Categories: Studies in Social Psychology* (Cambridge: Cambridge University Press, 1981).

Tajfel, Henry, and John Turner. "An Integrative Theory of Intergroup Conflict." in *The Social Psychology of Intergroup Relations*, ed. in W. G. Austin and S. Worchel (Monterey, Calif.: Brooks/Cole, 1979), 33–47.

Tajfel, Henry, ed. *Social Identity and Intergroup Relations* (Cambridge: Cambridge University Press, 1982).

Tajfel, Henry, ed. *Differentiation Between Social Groups: Studies in the Social Psychology of Intergroup Relations* (London: Academic Press, 1978).

Tajfel, Henry, et al. "Social Categorization and Intergroup Behavior." *European Journal of Social Psychology* 1, no. 2 (1971): 149–78.

Talbott, Strobe. "Why the Transformed NATO Deserves to Survive and Enlarge." *International Herald Tribune*, 19 February 1997, 8.

Tarrow, Sidney. *Power in Movement: Social Movements, Collective Action and Politics* (New York: Cambridge University Press 1994).

Telhami, Shibley. "Arab Public Opinion and the Gulf War." *Political Science Quarterly* 108, no. 3 (fall 1993): 437–52.

Telhami, Shibley. "Power and Legitimacy in Arab Alliances." Paper presented at the American Political Science Association annual meeting, Washington, D.C., August 1994.

Thatcher, Margaret. *Downing Street Years* (New York: HarperCollins, 1993).

The Gulf Crisis in Jordanian Political Thought (in Arabic) (Amman: Dar al-Sha'ab 1991).

The White Book (Amman: Jordanian Ministry of Information, 1991).

Thompson, J. M. *Louis Napoleon and the Second Empire* (New York: Columbia University Press, 1983).

Tickner, J. Ann. "You Just Don't Understand: Troubled Engagements Between Feminists and I. R. Theorists." *International Studies Quarterly* 10, no.4 (December 1997): 611–32.

Tilly, Charles, ed. *The Formation of National States in Western Europe* (Princeton: Princeton University Press, 1975).

Turner, Frederick Jackson. *The Frontier in American History* (New York: Holt, 1920).

Turner, John C. *Rediscovering the Social Group* (New York: Basil Blackwell, 1987).

Turner, John C. "Social Categorization and the Self-Concept: A Social Cognitive Theory of Group Behavior." in *Advances in Group Processes,* vol. 2, ed. Edward J. Lawler (Greenwich, Conn.: JAI Press, 1985).

Turner, John C. "Towards a Cognitive Redefinition of the Social Group." In *Social Identity and Intergroup Relations,* ed. Henry Tajfel (Cambridge: Cambridge University Press, 1982).

Turner, John C., Michael Hogg, Oakes, S. Reichter, and M. Wetherell. *Rediscovering the Social Group: A Self-Categorization Theory* (New York: Blackwell, 1987).

U.S. House Committee on Foreign Affairs, Subcommittee on International Security, International Organizations, and Human Rights. "U. S. Security Policy toward Rogue Regimes." 103rd Congress, First Session, 28 July and 14 September 1993.

Ullman, Richard H."Redefining Security." *International Security* 8, no. 1 (summer 1983): 129–53.

Vasquez, John A. "The Realist Paradigm and Degenerative vs. Progressive Research Programs: An Appraisal of Neotraditionalist Research on Waltz's Balancing Proposition." *American Political Science Review* 91, no. 4 (December 1997): 899–912 .

Vertzberger, Yaacov Y. I. *The World In Their Minds: Information Processing, Cognition, and Perception in Foreign Policy Decisionmaking* (Stanford, CA: Stanford University Press, 1990).

Verweij, Marco. "Cultural Theory and the Study of International Relations." *Millennium: Journal of International Studies* 24, no. 1 (spring 1995): 87–111.

"Voellig von der Rolle." *Der Spiegel,* 11 September 1995: 22–23

Von Metternich, Clemens. *Memoirs of Prince Metternich*, vol. 2, Prince Richard Metternich, ed. (New York: Scribner's, 1882).

Waever, Ole. "Securitization and Desecuritization." In *On Security*, ed. Ronnie Lipschutz (New York: Columbia University Press, 1995), 54–58.

Waever, Ole. "Societal Security: The Concept." In *Identity, Migration and the New Security Agenda in Europe* (Copenhagen: Pinter Publishers, 1993).

Waldron, Arthur N. "Theories of Nationalism and Historical Explanation." *World Politics* 37, no. 3 (April 1985): 416–33.

Walker, R. B. J. *Inside/Outside: International Relations and Political Theory* (Cambridge: Cambridge University Press, 1993).

Walker, Stephen, ed. *Role Theory and Foreign Policy Analysis* (Durham: Duke University Press, 1987).

Walt, Stephen M. "Why Alliances Endure or Collapse." *Survival* 39, no. 1 (spring 1997).

Walt, Stephen M. "The Renaissance of Security Studies." *International Studies Quarterly* 35, no. 2 (June 1991): 211–39.

Walt, Stephen M. *The Origin of Alliances* (Ithaca: Cornell University Press, 1987).

Waltz, Kenneth N. *Theory of International Politics* (New York: Addison Wesley, 1979).

Waltz, Kenneth N. "Realist Thought and Neorealist Theory." *Journal of International Affairs* 44, no. 1 (summer 1990): 21–37.

Ward, David. *1848: The Fall of Metternich and the Year of Revolution* (New York: Weybright and Talley, 1970).

Weber, Eugen. *Peasants into Frenchmen: The Modernization of Rural France, 1870–1914* (Stanford: Stanford University Press, 1976).

Weber, Max. *Economy and Society. An Outline of Interpretive Sociology* (New York: Bedminster Press, 1968).

Weber, Renee. and Jennifer Crocker. "Cognitive Processes in the Revision of Stereotypic Beliefs." *Journal of Personality and Social Psychology* 45, no. 5 (November 1983): 961–67.

Weber, Steven. "Origins of the European Bank for Reconstruction and Development." *International Organization* 48, no. 1 (winter 1994).

Weidenfeld, Werner. *Kulturbruch mit Amerika? Das Ende transatlantischer Selbstverstaendlichkeit* (Guetersloh: Verlag Bertelsmann Stiftung, 1996).

Weiner, Myron. "Security, Stability, and International Migration." *International Security* 17, no. 3 (winter 1992/93): 91–126.

Weintraub, Jeff. and Krishan Kumar, eds. *Public and Private in Thought and Practice: Perspectives on a Grand Dichotomy* (Chicago: Universityof Chicago Press, 1997).

Welch, David A. "'The Clash of Civilizations' Thesis as an Argument and as a Phenomenon." *Security Studies* 6, no. 4 (summer 1997): 197–216.

Welch, Stephen. *The Concept of Political Culture* (New York: St. Martin's, 1993).

Wendt, Alexander. "Collective Identity Formation and the International State." *American Political Science Review* 88, no. 2 (June 1994): 384–96.

Wendt, Alexander. "Anarchy is What States Make of It. The Social Construction of Power Politics." *International Organization* 46, no. 2 (spring 1992): 391–425.

Wendt, Alexander. "The Agent-Structure Problem in International Relations Theory." *International Organization* 41, no. 3 (summer 1987): 335–70.

White, Ralph K. *Fearful Warriors: A Psychological Profile of U.S.-Soviet Relations* (New York: Free Press, 1984).

Whyte, Arthur James. *The Evolution of Modern Italy* (Oxford: Basil Blackwell, 1944).

Wieland, Leo. "Das Deutschland Bild in Amerika." *Frankfurter Allgemeine Zeitung* 13 February 1997, 1.

Wilkinson, Rupert, ed. *American Social Character: Modern Interpretations* (New York: Icon, 1992).

Wilkinson, Rupert. *The Pursuit of American Character* (New York: Harper and Row, 1988).

Willard, Charles Arthur. *Liberalism and the Problem of Knowledge: A New Rhetoric for Modern Democracy* (Chicago: University of Chicago Press, 1996).

Winter, Sonia. "NATO: Expansion Critics Write To Clinton." *RFE/RL Newsline*, 27 June 1997.

Wolffs, Michael, and Stefan Beil. *Documentation: Deutsche Einheit, National-bewusstsein und Westbindung: in Meinungsklima der Bevoelkerung* (Sankt Augustin: Konrad Adenauer Stiftung, 1991).

Woo-Cumings, Meredith and Michael Loriaux, eds. *Past as Prelude: History in the Making of a New World Order* (Boulder: Westview, 1993).

Woolf, Stuart. *A History of Modern Italy, 1700–1860: The Social Constraints of Political Change* (London and New York: Methuen, 1979).

Wosrschel, Stephen, and William G. Austin, eds. *Psychology of Intergroup Relations* (Chicago: Nelson-Hall, 1986).

Yee, Albert S. "Thick Rationality and the Missing Brute Fact: The Limits of Rationalist Incorporations of Norms and Ideas." *Journal of Politics* 59, no. 4 (fall 1997): 1001–39.

Yuval-Davis, Nira, and Floya Anthias. *Women-Nation-State* (London: Macmillan, 1989).

Fareed Zakaria, "The Rise of Illiberal Democracy." *Foreign Affairs* 76, no. 1 (November/December 1997): 22–43

Zakaria, Fareed. "Culture Is Destiny: A Conversation with Lee Kuan Yew." *Foreign Affairs* 73, no. 2 (March/April 1994).

INDEX

Titles of Related Interest

Illegal Immigration and Commercial Sex
The New Slave Trade
Phil Williams, *Ridgway Center, University of Pittsburgh*, (Ed)

242 pages 1999
0 7146 4832 9 cloth
0 7146 4384 X paper
A special issue of the journal Transnational Organized Crime

Stability and Security in the Baltic Sea Region
Russian, Nordic and European Aspects
Olav F Knudsen, *Norwegian Institute of International Affairs* (Ed)

304 pages 1999
0 7146 4932 5 cloth
0 7146 4492 7 paper

Culture and Security
Multilateralism, Arms Control and Security Building
Keith R Krause, *Graduate Institute of International Studies, Geneva* (Ed)

264 pages 1999
0 7146 4885 X cloth
0 7146 4437 4 paper
A special Issue of the journal Contemporary Security Policy

Turkey: Anglo-American Security Interests, 1945–1952
The First Enlargement of NATO
Ekavi Athanassopoulou, *The Hebrew University of Jerusalem*

224 pages illus, maps 1999
0 7146 4855 8 cloth

FRANK CASS PUBLISHERS
Newbury House, 900 Eastern Avenue, Ilford, Essex, IG2 7HH
Tel: +44 (0)181 599 8866 Fax: +44 (0)181 599 0984 E-mail: info@frankcass.com
NORTH AMERICA
5804 NE Hassalo Street, Portland, OR 97213 3644, USA
Tel: 800 944 6190 Fax: 503 280 8832 E-mail: cass@isbs.com
Website: www.frankcass.com

Realism: Restatements and Renewal

Benjamin Frankel (Ed)

472 pages 1996
0 7146 4608 3 cloth
0 7146 4146 4 paper
A special issue of the journal Security Studies
Cass Series on Security Studies No.2

Roots of Realism

Benjamin Frankel (Ed)

440 pages 1996
0 7146 4669 5 cloth
0 7146 4203 7 paper
A special issue of the journal Security Studies
Cass Series on Security Studies No.1

If War Comes Tomorrow?

*The Contours of Future
Armed Conflict*

M A Gareev
Edited by Jacob W. Kipp and translated by Yakov Fomenko

192 pages illus 1998
0 7146 4801 9 cloth
0 7146 4368 8 paper
Soviet (Russian) Military Theory and Practice No. 7

The Territorial Management of Ethnic Conflict

John Coakley, *University College, Dublin* (Ed)

256 pages 1999 (Second Edition)
0 7146 4988 0 cloth
0 7146 8051 6 paper

FRANK CASS PUBLISHERS
Newbury House, 900 Eastern Avenue, Ilford, Essex, IG2 7HH
Tel: +44 (0)181 599 8866 Fax: +44 (0)181 599 0984 E-mail: info@frankcass.com
NORTH AMERICA
5804 NE Hassalo Street, Portland, OR 97213 3644, USA
Tel: 800 944 6190 Fax: 503 280 8832 E-mail: cass@isbs.com
Website: www.frankcass.com

Toward Responsibility in the New World Disorder
Challenges and Lessons of Peace Operations
Max Manwaring and John Fishel (Eds)

224 pages 1998
0 7146 4901 5 cloth
0 7146 4456 0 paper
A special issue of the journal

Arms Control
New Approaches to Theory and Policy
Nancy W Gallagher, Wesleyan University (Ed)

184 pages 1998
0 7146 4813 2 cloth
0 7146 4363 7 paper
A special issue of the journal Contemporary Security Policy

Pulling Back From The Nuclear Brink
Reducing and Countering Nuclear Threats
Barry R Schneider and William Dowdy both at the US Air War College (Eds)

328 pages 1998
0 7146 4856 6 cloth
0 7146 4412 9 paper

Contemporary Security Policy
Critical Reflections on Twenty Years of Change
Stuart Croft and Terry Terriff, both at University of Birmingham (Eds)

272 pages 2000
0 7146 4993 7 cloth
0 7146 8061 3 paper
A special issue of the journal Contemporary Security Policy

FRANK CASS PUBLISHERS
Newbury House, 900 Eastern Avenue, Ilford, Essex, IG2 7HH
Tel: +44 (0)181 599 8866 Fax: +44 (0)181 599 0984 E-mail: info@frankcass.com
NORTH AMERICA
5804 NE Hassalo Street, Portland, OR 97213 3644, USA
Tel: 800 944 6190 Fax: 503 280 8832 E-mail: cass@isbs.com
Website: www.frankcass.com

DATE DUE

The

VEGAN
SLOW
COOKER

Revised and Expanded

The
VEGAN
SLOW
COOKER

Revised and Expanded

INCLUDES NEW PHOTOS AND RECIPES

Simply Set It and Go with 160 Recipes for Intensely Flavorful,
Fuss-Free Fare Fresh from the Slow Cooker or Instant Pot®

KATHY HESTER

FAIR WINDS

Brimming with creative inspiration, how-to projects, and useful information to enrich your everyday life, Quarto Knows is a favorite destination for those pursuing their interests and passions. Visit our site and dig deeper with our books into your area of interest: Quarto Creates, Quarto Cooks, Quarto Homes, Quarto Lives, Quarto Drives, Quarto Explores, Quarto Gifts, or Quarto Kids.

First Published in 2018 by Fair Winds Press, an imprint of The Quarto Group,
100 Cummings Center, Suite 265-D, Beverly, MA 01915, USA.
T (978) 282-9590 F (978) 283-2742 QuartoKnows.com

Fair Winds Press titles are also available at discount for retail, wholesale, promotional, and bulk purchase. For details, contact the Special Sales Manager by email at specialsales@quarto.com or by mail at The Quarto Group, Attn: Special Sales Manager, 401 Second Avenue North, Suite 310, Minneapolis, MN 55401, USA.

22 21 20 19 18   1 2 3 4 5

ISBN: 978-1-59233-842-9

Digital edition published in 2018

Library of Congress Cataloging-in-Publication Data available

Design: Laura Klynstra
Photography: Kate Lewis of Art Noodles Studio LLC

Printed in China

I dedicate this book to

all the people who took a chance on a new

author so many years ago. I can't thank

my loyal readers enough. You all made my

first book a success and allowed me to keep

creating new vegan recipes for you. You

have my undying gratitude.

Contents

RECIPES BY CHAPTER

Slow Cooker Love

THE MAGIC LIVES ON

This revised edition of *The Vegan Slow Cooker* comes almost ten years after the first one. I always get asked if I still love my slow cookers, and I answer with a resounding *YES*.

A versatile appliance, the slow cooker goes way beyond preconceived limitations. It can even stand in for a rice cooker or an oven in a pinch. It's a great way to extend your kitchen during the holidays, and it can double as a buffet server, too.

I fell in love with slow cookers when I was a busy and poor grad student. I moved from North Carolina to Missouri with what I could pack in my car. Of course, that included my Mom's old slow cooker and, lucky for me, a huge box of beans and grains from the co-op I worked in.

While I was in grad school, I could throw things together in the morning and come home to a ready-to-eat dinner. Cooking beans from scratch is so much cheaper than buying canned. Eating at home every night saved a ton of money, too.

It's true that I've added even more appliances to my kitchen arsenal since then. I also love my air fryer for crispy food and my Instant Pot for quick and easy meals. (If you'll be slow cooking in an Instant Pot, be sure to read the section about them on page 18.)

I always say that slow cookers and Instant Pots make daily cooking fit into your life better. Deciding what works best for you often comes down to personality or the way you schedule your day. Maybe you prefer chopping up a few things the night before and throwing everything in your slow cooker before you leave for work. Or maybe you have zero time in the morning and still have a little energy when you come home. For most of us, a slow cooker and a pressure cooker are not an either/or choice—it's one you make day by day. That's how I am, and I value the Instant Pot and the

slow cooker for making it so much easier to eat at home on a regular basis without spending a fortune!

The slow cooker is a perfect tool for a vegan kitchen. Instead of buying cans of beans, you can cook yours without all the salt while you're at work or asleep. Soups and stews really meld well together after cooking all day, and you can even make pasta and rice dishes in it. You may just find yourself as enamored with your slow cooker as I am with mine. But try not to accumulate as many slow cookers as I have. People will start to talk!

Going beyond the kitchen, slow cookers come in handy in other places, too. They are great on camping trips (assuming you have a power hookup). It's so much fun to go out on a hike and come back to lunch or dinner ready to go. Slow cookers can also increase your cooking power on big holidays such as Christmas. For great, no-oven holiday dishes try Holiday Tempeh and Sage Loaf on page 96, the Whole-Wheat Rosemary Rolls on page 176, or the Butternut Squash Pie on page 217.

All in all, a slow cooker can make a vegan's life easier—and keep it tasty too!

CHAPTER 1

Vegan Slow Cooker Basics

GETTING STARTED

Some people think a slow cooker is only really useful for cooking meat, and that is just not true. A slow cooker is the perfect tool in a vegan arsenal. I wouldn't be able to eat as many homemade meals without it.

Dry beans cook up like a dream in your slow cooker. It's great for making soups and stews in the winter, and it also has its place in a summer kitchen. Most of us still eat hot foods in the summertime, and a slow cooker is a great way to keep your house from heating up. You can even make a pizza in it!

The slow cooker also buys us time to focus on other things in our lives. If you work during the day, imagine dinner waiting when you walk in the door. If you are a stay-at-home parent or a college student, you can still have nice, nutritious meals without having to keep an eye on the stove or the oven. While it's true that delicate vegetables need to be added about thirty minutes before serving, that's still less effort than cooking everything from scratch on the stove. Plus, there are solutions or vegetable substitutions that you can use to make the recipes fit into your schedule.

Most of the recipes in this book cook from 7 to 9 hours on low. They might be ready before 9 hours, but most of the time the dish will hold for 9 hours. That flexibility provides enough time to drive home from work, etc. without worrying about dinner. If you're cooking on the weekend or work from home, you can check to see when the recipes are ready to eat. In most cases, the dish will be all set. One important exception to this is recipes that include dry beans. You can also speed up cooking by using high when low is called for. It cuts the cooking time in half.

Other recipes will cook faster, usually between 1½ to 3 hours. Pasta or grain dishes just cook faster, and they won't hold for 8 hours without becoming mushy. These recipes may not fit into your workday routine, but they are great for days off or evenings when you want to eat later. There are some grains, such as wheat berries, oat groats, and spelt, that can take all day cook. Try using those when faster cooking grains just won't work for you.

I like to make some of the 2-hour dishes after work, then go for a walk or do a few chores around the house. The best part is I don't have to be in the kitchen while it's cooking.

Most of the recipes in this book can comfortably be made in a 3½ to 5-quart slow cooker. When baking, I prefer to use a 6-quart because cakes and breads that are cooked directly in the crock cook more evenly when they are spread thinner, and they can also fit a loaf pan.

If you don't want to own multiple slow cookers, Hamilton Beach has a model called Right Size. It has one crock with a visible line inside to show you if you are filling it up to the 2, 4, or 6-quart line. So, you can cook all the recipes in it!

RULES YOU REALLY SHOULD FOLLOW

I'm not big on rules and tend to break most of them. However, the ones I talk about here really do have to be followed, and most of them are common sense.

I've cooked in dozens of different slow cookers, and I'm not afraid to use any of them. Experimenting with them has given me a depth of knowledge that can help you on your own slow cooker journey. One thing I can tell you for sure is each one cooks a little differently. You have to *learn* your slow cooker to ensure your recipes come out just the way you want them to.

Rule #1: Stay at Home the First Time You Use Your Slow Cooker

You need to check and make sure the slow cooker is functioning properly before using it without being in the house. As you would with any appliance that heats up, you'll also want to see whether your slow cooker runs on the hotter side, so you can adjust recipes with no mishaps.

Even brand-new appliances can have issues. Though it's rare, I firmly believe that it's better to be safe than sorry.

If you are getting a second-hand slow cooker from a friend or family member, or from my favorite—thrift stores—always make sure none of the cording is frayed. Also check that there are no teeny tiny cracks in the crock that would allow leaks into the metal cooking part.

Rule #2: Fill Your Slow Cooker to the Manufacturer's Recommended Amount

This is the rule I expect will get the most resistance. No one likes to read manuals. And honestly they seem to get less and less helpful. But, in this case, you do need to find out how full your slow cooker model needs to be to cook optimally.

You're probably asking yourself, shouldn't it all be the same? I'm here to tell you that it's not.

In general, your slow cooker should be half to three-fourths full to cook at its proper temperature. This can vary from model to model as well as make to make. Be sure to check your user guide to see what's recommended for your model.

You may find that thicker foods, such as stews and casseroles, burn if this rule is not followed, because the food will cook much hotter than it should. This often happens if you use a larger slow cooker than the recipe calls for, or if you aren't filling the slow cooker up enough. If you have a 6- to 7-quart (5.7 to 6.6 L) slow cooker, you can double many of the recipes to fill your slow cooker up enough. *Note: We will use this to our advantage in some of the baking recipes, by not filling the slow cooker up to the recommended fill line.*

One of the main complaints about newer slow cookers is that they burn everything. But just looking in your manual can help you manage your cooker better. Already threw the manual out or didn't get one when you inherited your slow cooker? Search online for your make and model. Most manufacturers have their manuals online, and you can easily download them.

Rule #3: Use Common Sense

Always make sure the area around the sides of the slow cooker is clear. I also put mine on a large trivet as extra protection for my countertop.

I leave my slow cooker on while I'm away at work or doing errands. In fact, it's made to leave on while you are away from the house.

Remember that the outside parts do get hot. You do not want it near anything that could melt or overheat: think bread wrappers, papers, and the like. I find it easy to just give my slow cooker a clear 6-inch (15 cm) radius all around it.

If you have young children, make sure the slow cooker is where little toddler hands can't grab the hot parts or pull on the cord. If you have pets, be sure to keep the cooker where your cat won't knock it off the counter.

Keep an eye on the plug and cord to make sure they're always in good shape. If you get any signals that the slow cooker may not be working properly, it's time to get a new one.

Rule #4: Check the Settings on Your Slow Cooker

Almost all slow cookers have a low and high setting, and many have a warming setting as well.

Some of the fancier slow cookers have programmable settings. Note that you can't program when the slow cooker starts, but you can program how long it will cook at your chosen setting (low or high). After the allotted time, the slow cooker will switch to warm to keep your food ready to eat until you get home.

One thing to be aware of is an auto setting that is found on some slow cookers. From one of my amazing recipe testers, I found out that, at least in Canada, there is an auto temperature instead of low on some slow cookers. This is not the timing mechanism that controls switching the setting to warm after the programmed time. It is on the dial in place of the low. This auto setting cooks the first 2 hours on high and then automatically switches the cooker to low. You need to treat this like a very hot slow cooker and reduce total times and add extra liquid in most dishes. The 2 hours on high are like 4 on low.

Rule #5: Know Your Slow Cooker—Older vs. Newer Slow Cookers

Older slow cookers cook at lower temperatures than newer models do. Due to food safety concerns over the past few years, slow cooker manufacturers have raised the cooking temperature of their appliances. The new low is almost as hot as the old high!

Please note: You may need to adjust the recipes to suit your slow cooker. If your slow cooker runs on the hotter side, you will have more evaporation. That means you will need to add extra liquid to make up for it. This is especially true of newer models; they tend to cook quicker and hotter than the older ones do. Once you've adjusted recipes to your cooker's needs a few times, it will become second nature.

An older model has the opposite issue. They cook at a lower temperature, so you may need less liquid and/or longer cooking times. Older slow cookers can take extra time to cook, and you may need to decrease the amount of liquids.

Once you cook a few dishes, you'll have a good idea what temperature your slow cooker cooks at. Until then, use caution and add more liquid rather than less. You can always cook something longer. If it burns, it's not always as easy to fix it.

Rule #6: Taste and Re-season Before Serving

Due to the long cooking times, you should always taste the dish before you serve it, re-seasoning as needed. This is especially important with stews and soups. Really, if you get in the habit of doing this, you'll find out it helps make dishes prepared using any cooking method taste better.

Add or readjust fresh herbs right before serving. For example, if you are using fresh ginger in a dish and you cook it all day, you may need to add a little more ginger about thirty minutes before serving.

Do not skip this step! It can be the difference between a meh meal and a great one.

WHAT SLOW COOKER SHOULD I BUY?

There's a lot to consider when buying a slow cooker, and there is no one answer that fits everyone. It depends on your family size, and how simple or complex you like your gadgets to be.

Read on and I'll tell you a little about the differences. Hint: your budget should help make your decision easy.

Question #1: What's Your Budget?

You can get slow cookers anywhere from $10 to more than $400! I know that seems impossible, but it's true. And I'm here to tell you that some fancy name brands don't do any extra for the money, except fit in with your super fancy kitchen. I'm not telling you that you can't spend the money if it's burning a hole in your pocket, but they all accomplish the same task.

If you're on a tight budget, first ask around to see if any of your friends or family have a slow cooker that they no longer use. Free is best on your budget, after all. The second place to look is thrift stores. I've seen brand-new models in pristine condition for under $10.

If you get a programmable slow cooker, it will be a little more expensive than one that just has high, low, and warm. If you have an unpredictable leave-time at work or a long drive, it is nice knowing that it will switch to warm after the cooking time is done. Some of these have a simmer function: It's like the old low setting. That's really nice to have, but it's not a deal breaker.

Get home about the same time every day? Then you can skip the programmable function and get the cheapest 4-quart on the shelf.

Want to cook in all the different sizes but you just don't have room to store them all? I'd recom-mend an all-in-one solution such as the Hamilton Beach Right Size or the Crock-Pot® Choose-A-Crock Programmable Slow Cooker. The Right Size has one crock with lines for 2-, 4-, or 6-quart cooking sizes. The Choose-A-Crock has three nesting crocks for storage, but you cook with only one of them at a time. It has a split 2.5-, 4-, and 6-quart crocks.

Question #2: What Size is Best for You and Your Family?

If you got a slow cooker as a wedding present, it seems like people think the bigger the better. But do you really want 7 or 8 quarts of chili? For me, the answer is no.

The ideal size really depends on how many people you cook for and how many leftovers you like to have. Most of the recipes in this book work great in a 4-quart (3.8 L) slow cooker, and they tend to serve four to six. Recipes that don't follow this pattern will have another size clearly note. You can easily double, or even triple, most of the recipes in this book to fit properly in a larger slow cooker.

An inexpensive 4-quart (3.8 L) with manual controls will work just as well as a more expensive model with a programmable timer. A 4-quart (3.8 L) size can work for two people with leftovers or make a single meal for a family of four or five. A 6- or 7-quart (5.7 or 6.6 L) will feed eight to twelve people, depending on the dish.

This may be the most important question you need to think of before you get a new slow cooker. If you have a small family or it's just you, a 5 or 6-quart slow cooker would keep you in chili or soup long after you've grown tired of it. One benefit of large slow cookers is that you can cook a few pounds of dry beans at a time to store in the freezer. It's really a question of your preferences.

Here are my rules of thumb:

- 1½- to 2½-quart slow cookers are great for couples or singles who don't want to eat the same thing every day.

- 4-quart or 5-quart will feed two with leftovers for lunch the next day or will feed four.

- 6-quart is good for a family of more than four.

- Unless you have a huge family or cook meals ahead and freeze them, you would not need anything more than a 6-quart.

- Note: a 1-quart slow cooker, sometimes know as a Little Dipper, is mainly for keeping dips warm and it is not good for cooking.

I like having a small slow cooker for making breakfast, and a large 6-quart for cooking pumpkins and giant batches of dry beans that I freeze in 1½ cup portions (weight will vary). You'll find that you can adjust recipes to use in other size slow cookers, but keep to your manual's rule of how full the cooker needs to be to cook properly.

Question #3: Do You Need Programmable Settings?

I mentioned these under budget, but just in case you're skipping around I thought I'd address it here, too. If you have unpredictable work times, it might be worth the extra money to get a programmable slow cooker. It doesn't let you put off cooking until a certain time, but it does switch to warm after the time in the allotted time has elapsed. This can save your dinner if you come home a few hours later than planned.

Some of the 3-in-1s and fancier slow cookers are programmable, and the only real reason to say no would be if it's over your budget.

Question #4: Do You Want to Sauté in It?

Every year, something new gets added to the slow cooker list that you have to decide if you want or not.

Most slow cooker brands have at least one model that has a metal crock. The are mostly made of nonstick materials. Check the manufacturer's website for more details. The great thing about a metal crock is that it can be used on your stovetop to sauté things like onions, and then can be put back in the slow cooker to finish up your recipe. That means you are only dirtying up one pan.

Some models, such as the Ninja, actually have a sauté setting so you can do it right in the slow cooker, too. Newer Ninjas have a bake setting, too.

Question #5: Are the Crock Materials Important to You?

Most of the ceramic crocks have a glaze. You can check on their websites or call customer service to verify what they use. Most of the websites will state that they do not use lead in their glazes.

Most of the pans that you can sauté in are nonstick, and some people avoid that. There is a brand that is stainless, 360 Cookware Gourmet Slow Cooker and Stainless Steel Stock Pot with Cover. Just know the price is a premium one.

Another natural option is a VitaClay slow cooker. The crock is made with unglazed red clay. It has a double-lid design and uses something called micro pressure cooking, which results in 60 percent more cooking efficiency. That's the good. The bad is that it cooks much faster than normal slow cookers. You will have to read the manual carefully and adjust all of your slow cooker times in recipes you use that aren't from VitaClay—including the ones in this book.

SLOW COOKING IN YOUR INSTANT POT

Lots of people have jumped on the Instant Pot bandwagon, and I am certainly one of them. I even wrote *The Ultimate Vegan Cookbook for Your Instant Pot*. In that book I mostly use the pressure cooking functions, but I wanted to address some of the Instant Pot's slow cooker possibilities here.

I do use a pot lid instead of the top that came with it. You can buy them online or maybe one of your existing pot lids will be a good fit. You can use the original lid, but make sure it's turned to vented.

You need to know that Instant Pots come in 3 sizes: 3-, 6-, and 8-quart. So, you can make most of this book's recipes in them comfortably—especially soup and stews.

DO NOT use the baking recipes in your Instant Pot on the slow cooker setting. They will fail. A 6-quart slow cooker that I recommend has a large bottom baking area that none of the Instant Pots have. At this writing, Instant Pot does have a Ninja slow cooker competitor. It is a slow cooker first and it can be baked in, but it does not have a pressure cooker setting.

The other issue I've run across with Instant Pot slow cooking is the timing of cooking dry beans. On normal, it can even take unsoaked black-eyed peas more than 8 hours to cook. But on high you can cook unsoaked pinto beans in the 4 hours you'd expect. Of course, beans are a variable in themselves because many beans will be a little old when you buy them in the store. The older the bean the longer it needs to cook. To avoid this timing issue, I recommend that you don't cook the recipes that use dry beans in the Instant Pot, or substitute cooked beans and reduce the water amount in those recipes.

INGREDIENTS TO KNOW

You may be familiar with a lot of vegan ingredients, but still encounter a few new spices or seasoning. If you're new to vegan food, here are some of our secret ingredients—the ones that help make vegan food taste great and provide interesting textures.

Cashew Cream

This a homemade substitute for sour cream that you can use in cooking or as a topping. I love it on the Borscht on page 42.

Liquid Smoke

Where I live in the South, we are huge fan of smoky flavors. Traditionally those smoky flavors come from nonvegan sources, but it's easy to veganize them with this ingredient.

Liquid smoke is one of my go-tos. Some people are afraid of it because they think it's made of chemicals, but they actually burn wood and catch the condensation. I've only found one brand with questionable ingredients, and you can avoid getting that by reading the ingredient labels.

You can also use smoked paprika to make food smoky if that's easier for you to find.

Nondairy Milk

There are so many varieties of nondairy milk now. Be sure to read the labels carefully if you have allergies.

On the occasions that I call specifically for soymilk, it's usually to make a vegan buttermilk because soymilk will curdle once you add vinegar (which is what you want). If you are allergic to soy, you can always substitute a nondairy milk that you can have.

I find that soy and cashew are pretty thick while rice and almond can be thinner. But there are milks made of things such as oat, hemp, hazelnut, pea protein, and so many more.

Be sure to note if the recipe calls for unsweetened (no sugar) vs. plain (has sugar) when you are making recipes.

Nondairy Yogurt
Usually these are made of soy or almond, but more types pop up all the time. Make sure to look for unsweetened when using on savory foods.

Nutritional Yeast
This is a staple in vegan food, and it can add a cheesy or almost a chickeny flavor. It's used in soups, stews, casseroles, vegan cheese, sauces, and more. I buy it a pound at a time from the bulk bin at Whole Foods or my local co-op.

Seitan
Seitan is sometimes called wheat meat. It's made with vital wheat gluten flour and has a meaty texture. If you eat gluten-free, this is not for you and should be avoided.

If you are making one of my seitan recipes, be sure to buy vital wheat gluten flour and NOT hi gluten wheat flour. There's a huge difference, and the recipes will only work with vital wheat gluten flour. You can order it at Amazon if you can't find it in a store near you.

Don't want to be bothered making it? You can buy it premade in stores such as Whole Foods and co-ops.

Spices
I use a lot of spices. Don't be intimidated by some of the Indian recipes. The ingredient lists may be a little long, but most of that is spices and will come together quickly.

Buying spices in containers at regular grocery stores is more expensive than buying them in bulk. Sometimes the markup is 1,000%! If you're trying a spice for the first time, go where you can get bulk spices and get just what you need. You can always get more.

Indian, Asian, and Hispanic markets all have specialty herbs, spices, and vegetables that are much less expensive than a supermarket or Whole Foods.

Of course, you can always get any unusual ingredients online no matter where you live.

Soy
There are a ton of myths around soy and, ultimately, it's between you and your doctor if you eat it or not. My doctor is all for it, and we eat soy products a few times a week in my household.

Myth: All soy is GMO.

Any soy or soy product marked organic or non-GMO is GMO-free. That includes soymilk, tofu, tempeh, and soy curls.

Soy Curls
Soy curls are a brand of non-GMO soybeans that have been smashed and dried. They resemble TVP, but I think they are less processed and taste better. These can be found in some grocery stores or ordered online.

Why aren't all the recipes just dump-and-go?
That's kind of like asking why we boil spaghetti and bake lasagna. Different recipes will need a different level of cooking commitment. For those of you who are extra busy, I have gathered a whole chapter of super easy recipes, starting on page 23. They are quick, and you'll get a good flavorful meal from them, too.

Soy curls can be reconstituted quickly in water or broth. Note that in most of the recipes in this book, I add extra liquid so that they can reconstitute right in the slow cooker!

Tofu

Tofu is made of soy, though you can also buy a soy-free version called hemp tofu. It's not exactly the same, but if you are allergic to soy it's a great substitution.

Tofu is an ancient food that provides texture and protein, and it is filling.

Tempeh

Tempeh is an Indonesian soy food. The beans are split in half and stuck together in a culture. The culture may create white or black areas on the tempeh as it ferments (but it's still fine). Think of it like vegan blue cheese if that helps.

Tempeh is great cubed, but you can also crumble it and use it as a ground beef substitute in some of your old favorite recipes.

Tempeh can have a bitter taste to it, but it mellows out if you cube and steam for about ten minutes.

Time-saving Ingredients

While there is a whole chapter on making your own staples, there's no reason why you can't substitute store-bought version to save time.

I always have vegan bouillon cubes and cans of beans and tomatoes in my pantry, in addition to homemade in the freezer. Use whatever works for you.

Also remember that you can use onion and garlic powder in place of fresh to save time, too.

SPECIAL DIETS

We live in a time where allergies and special diets are prevalent. I try to give substitutions for as many special diets as I can on most recipes. Here are a few ideas that can help with the recipes in this book and recipes of your own as you veganize them.

No matter what your special diet or allergy is, be sure to ALWAYS read the labels on products. Manufacturers can change ingredients as time goes on, so make sure it's safe for you.

Gluten-free

Make sure that grains such as oats are in containers that are clearly labeled gluten-free, especially if you have celiac disease.

There are many gluten-free substitutions available today, even gluten-free soy sauce. Just remember that the original versions do contain gluten, and you have to read the labels carefully.

I recommend subbing Julie's Original gluten-free white cake mix for the Not-from-a-Box Cake Mix recipe (page 224) that contains gluten. You can buy it online. In my other baking recipes, I suggest using your favorite gluten-free baking mixes in place of wheat flour. I know that most gluten-free people already have their favorites and know how to tweak the recipe for it.

Soy-free

There are more soy-free options available today. For tofu, you can substitute hemp tofu. Tempeh can be replaced with seitan, and you have an array of soy-free nondairy milks to choose from.

For soy sauce, you can use coconut aminos. There is also miso made from chickpeas instead of soy beans. When recipes call for edamame, try subbing cooked chickpeas or another large firm cooked beans.

No Oil Added

I know many people follow one of the many oil-free vegan diets, and I want to be here to support you in your health journey.

I label things *no oil added* which means no refined oil is used in the dish or there are instructions for you to use to make oil-free. There may be coconut milk, nuts, or other ingredients that are not fat-free. You can still modify most of the recipes to suit your diet.

One thing to keep in mind is while you can substitute aquafaba, applesauce, or pumpkin purée for oil in baked goods, the result will not have the same texture. They will be a little mushy and not have a defined crumb.

Low or No Salt

Throughout this book I say salt to taste to make it easier for people to salt their food in a way that's right for them. You can always use less or no salt in any of the recipes—except for baking.

TROUBLESHOOTING RECIPES

If you change slow cookers, you will notice various issues you didn't have before. Remember that all slow cookers cook a bit differently. Be sure to read the **Rules You Really Should Follow** section on page 14.

Too Much Liquid at the End of Cooking

If this happens consistently, you have a slow cooker that cooks at a lower setting. This will most likely be an older model from the pre-2000s.

You don't have to get a new slow cooker, but you will need to reduce the amount of liquid that's called for in a recipe.

Some slow cookers have a gasket around the lid, and they seal tightly to secure the cooker for traveling. This makes the slow cooker act like older models—the liquid cannot easily evaporate. Be sure to adjust liquids down, and read about the older models (page 15) because the advice will apply to your cooker, too.

In the meantime, if you're cooking a casserole you can put the crock in the oven and cook the extra liquid off and still save dinner!

Why do you ask me to sauté onions?

Some recipes may require you to sauté onions ahead of time. I'm not just being difficult—it really does elevate your dish. That said, there are a few things that you can do to avoid it: Make a big batch of cooked onions (page 223) and freeze them to use later. It's hands off, and cooks right in your slow cooker.

You can always substitute onion powder in recipes. I use 1 to 2 teaspoons onion powder to take the place of 1 cup (128 g) minced or chopped onion. You can also do the reverse and use sautéed onions where onion powder is called for if you prefer it.

There's no shame in using garlic or onion powder. Remember that it's 100% natural. It's just chopped onion or garlic that has been dried and then ground into a powder.

If you don't like the idea of dirtying up two pans, pick out a slow cooker on page 16 and pay careful attention to the slow cookers that you can sauté in. They don't have ceramic inserts, but are usually nonstick.

Not Enough Liquid or Cooked Too Fast

If your dish didn't have enough liquid or if it cooked too quickly, you probably have a newer slow cooker and one that cooks on the hot side, too. This will be even more noticeable to you if you recently upgraded from an old model.

You don't have to get a new slow cooker, but you will need to add more liquid than the recipe calls for. I usually start with ½ cup (120 ml) in most recipes, and I cook the recipe while I'm at home so that I can monitor the cooking and figure out the right adjustment. This way you'll have a rule of thumb for your slow cooker going forward.

Another reason for a recipe cooking too fast can be a lid that doesn't really seat well into the crock. It's their fault, not yours! You can make a quick fix by covering the crock with a piece of foil, place the lid on top of that and use the extra foil to plug the holes.

Ready Before 7 to 9 hours

A recipe with a 7 to 9 hour cook time means that's how long the recipe will hold in the slow cooker. Some recipes will be edible much earlier, so if you are at home and hungry give it a taste. If it's ready, continue with next steps for the recipe.

Not Cooked after Longest Listed Cook Time

There are usually two reasons for ending up with an undercooked dish at the end of the longest listed cook time. Instant Pots tend to have this issue when you are cooking dry beans on the middle setting. If that's the case, be sure to read the section on Instant Pots on page 18.

It could also be because your slow cooker doesn't cook hot enough (even on high). You might need to replace your slow cooker if this is happening with many recipes.

CHAPTER 2

No-Time-to-Prep Recipes

Sometimes you need to be able to just throw together some-thing quick before you leave the house for work. This is the chapter for all those busy mornings!

These recipes typically use canned or jarred ingredients, pre-prepped veggies, or already homemade staples. Even if you like to use everything homemade, I still suggest that you keep some canned beans in your pantry for times like these.

ASIAN TOFU SOUP

This is a light brothy soup to serve as an appetizer for a DIY Chinese takeout party. You can easily double this recipe if you want.

 GLUTEN-FREE OPTION*   SOY-FREE OPTION**   NO OIL ADDED

1-inch (2.5-cm) piece peeled ginger, cut into large slices, divided

2 cloves garlic, minced

7 to 9 shiitake mushrooms, stems removed and caps sliced

2 carrots cut into coins

1 block (15 ounces, or 420 g) tofu, drained and cut into cubes (**use hemp tofu or cauliflower florets)

2 tablespoons (12 g) vegan chicken-flavored bouillon or 4 tablespoons (24 g) DIY Golden Bouillon (page 237)

1 to 2 teaspoons soy sauce (*use a gluten-free brand or **use coconut aminos)

7 cups (1645 ml) water

SERVING INGREDIENTS

Sliced scallions or garlic chives, for serving

☾ **THE NIGHT BEFORE:** Store the cut-up ginger, garlic, mushrooms, and tofu in an airtight container in the fridge.

☀ **IN THE MORNING:** Combine half of the ginger, the garlic, mushrooms, carrot, tofu, bouillon, soy sauce, and water in the slow cooker. Cook on low for 7 to 9 hours.

20 MINUTES BEFORE SERVING: Add the remaining half of the ginger and cook for 30 more minutes. Taste and adjust the seasonings. Add a little more fresh grated ginger if you need more punch. Top bowls of soup with the scallion.

YIELD: 4 servings
EQUIPMENT: 4-quart slow cooker
COOKING TIME: 7 to 9 hours on low

SPLIT PEA APPLE SOUP

I like the sweet and slightly tart taste of apples combined with the rich mouthfeel of split peas. It makes me feel like my split pea soup has really grown up. Indulge in this soup for your health or for a little cold-weather comfort food. It freezes well, and leftovers are perfect for lunches.

 GLUTEN-FREE SOY-FREE NO OIL ADDED

2 stalks celery, chopped

2 medium-size carrots, chopped

1 medium-size apple, peeled if not organic, cored, chopped, and tossed with lemon juice

1 clove garlic, minced

6 cups (1410 ml) water

2 tablespoons (12 g) vegan chicken-flavored bouillon or 4 tablespoons (24 g) DIY Golden Bouillon (page 237)

2 cups (450 g) split peas

1 bay leaf

1 teaspoon dried thyme or 1 sprig of fresh

1 teaspoon coriander

½ teaspoon nutmeg (grate it fresh, if possible)

Salt, to taste

BEFORE SERVING INGREDIENTS

1 tablespoon (15 ml) balsamic vinegar, plus extra for drizzling

☾ **THE NIGHT BEFORE:** Store the cut-up celery, carrots, apple, and garlic in an airtight container in the fridge.

☀ **IN THE MORNING:** Combine the celery, carrots, apple, garlic, water, bouillon, split peas, bay leaf, thyme, coriander, nutmeg, and salt in the slow cooker. Cook on low for 7 to 9 hours.

Remove and discard the bay leaf and sprig of thyme. Add the balsamic vinegar and stir to combine.

BEFORE SERVING: Purée the soup with an immersion blender or in batches in a countertop blender, being careful of splatters of hot soup, until smooth. Taste and adjust the seasonings, if needed. Drizzle a few drops of extra balsamic on each serving.

YIELD: 4 servings
EQUIPMENT: 4-quart slow cooker
COOKING TIME: 7 to 9 hours on low

SPLIT PEA LENTIL SOUP

When I first became a vegetarian, I had a soup that married split peas and lentils with spinach. It was my favorite, but the recipe became lost over the years. This is my redo of the wonderful memory of that warm, nutritious soup.

 GLUTEN-FREE SOY-FREE NO OIL ADDED OPTION*

2 tablespoons (30 ml) olive oil (water sauté)

1 small onion, minced

1 cup (200 g) lentils

1 cup (200 g) split peas

6 cups (1.4 L) water

2 tablespoons (12 g) vegan chicken-flavored bouillon or 4 tablespoons (24 g) DIY Golden Bouillon (page 237)

2 bay leaves

1 teaspoon dried tarragon

1 teaspoon dried marjoram

¼ teaspoon ground rosemary or 1 teaspoon dried rosemary leaves

Salt and pepper, to taste

BEFORE SERVING INGREDIENTS

6 ounces (170 g) fresh baby spinach, washed

☾ **THE NIGHT BEFORE:** Heat the oil in a skillet over medium heat and sauté the onion until translucent, 3 to 5 minutes. Add the garlic and sauté for 1 minute longer. Store in an airtight container in the fridge.

☀ **IN THE MORNING:** Combine the sautéed onion, lentils, peas, water, bouillon, bay leaves, tarragon, marjoram, rosemary, and salt and pepper in the slow cooker. Cook on low for 7 to 9 hours.

30 MINUTES BEFORE SERVING: add the spinach. Taste and adjust the seasonings. Remove and discard the bay leaves before serving.

YIELD: 6 servings
EQUIPMENT: 4-quart slow cooker
COOKING TIME: 7 to 9 hours on low

What's in the Freezer?
VEGGIE SOUP

This is the easiest recipe you will ever make. Some mornings I only have 5 minutes to start some dinner in the slow cooker before I rush off to start working. You can make this no matter what veggies you have on hand. I always keep a few bags of organic frozen veggies in the freezer for this soup, which you can serve chunky or puréed. Add parsnips, potato, or cauliflower if you want to make it look like a cream soup with none of the fat or calories!

 GLUTEN-FREE  SOY-FREE NO OIL ADDED

6 cups mixed veggies (weight will vary depending on the veggies)

2 cloves garlic, minced

5 cups (1175 ml) water

2 tablespoons (12 g) vegan chicken-flavored bouillon or 4 tablespoons (24 g) DIY Golden Bouillon (page 237)

BEFORE SERVING INGREDIENTS

Your favorite combination of herbs and spices

Salt and pepper, to taste

2 to 4 cups (300 to 600 g) precooked grain or pasta (*use your favorite gluten-free grain or pasta to make this gluten-free)

❉ IN THE MORNING: Put any slow-cooking veggies, garlic, water, bouillon, herbs, spices, and salt and pepper in the slow cooker. Cook on low for 7 to 9 hours.

30 MINUTES BEFORE SERVING: Add green peas, fresh herbs, or any other quick-cooking veggies, such as greens. This is also the time to add any precooked grain or pasta you may want to throw in to make it a little heartier. Taste and adjust the seasonings before serving.

YIELD: 6 servings
EQUIPMENT: 4-quart slow cooker
COOKING TIME: 7 to 9 hours on low

CITRUS BLACK BEAN SOUP

This soup recipe was created at one of my infamous Gothic Dinner Parties. I always throw some things I have on hand into my slow cooker, and it's always the best soup I make all year! This one uses precooked black beans, and it gets its specialness from the spices and citrus juice. Be sure to serve with lime wedges!

 GLUTEN-FREE   SOY-FREE   NO OIL ADDED

2 cloves garlic

4 cans (14½ ounces, or 406 g each) black beans, drained and rinsed, or 6 cups (1.1 kg) homemade (page 230)

1 can (14½ ounces, or 406 g) diced tomatoes or 1½ cups (340 g) Preserve-the-Harvest Diced Tomatoes (page 241)

1 teaspoon cumin

½ teaspoon ground ginger

½ teaspoon onion powder

½ teaspoon garlic powder

½ teaspoon smoked paprika

¼ teaspoon allspice

¼ teaspoon cinnamon

⅛ teaspoon nutmeg

Juice of 1 lime

Juice of 1 orange

SERVING INGREDIENTS

Lime and orange wedges to squeeze into soup

Dollop of cashew cream (optional)

☾ THE NIGHT BEFORE: Mince the garlic and store in an airtight container in the fridge.

☀ IN THE MORNING: Add all the ingredients to your slow cooker. Cook on low for about 8 hours. It will look like a stew now, but later you'll purée it into a thick soup. If your slow cooker runs hot or there's not much liquid in your tomatoes, go ahead and add a cup (235 ml) of water, too.

If desired, purée the soup with an immersion blender or in batches in a countertop blender, being careful of splatters of hot soup, until smooth, or leave the soup chunky. Taste and adjust the seasonings.

YIELD: 6 *servings*
EQUIPMENT: 4-*quart slow cooker*
COOKING TIME: 7 *to* 9 *hours on low*

WHITE BEAN *and* KALE STEW

I like my beans New Orleans-style: thick and creamy. I've found the easiest vegan way to do this is to let some of the beans break down and form their own gravy.

 GLUTEN-FREE SOY-FREE ◯ NO OIL ADDED OPTION*

1 teaspoon olive oil (*water sauté)

1 onion, chopped

2 cloves garlic, minced

Salt and pepper, to taste

1 tablespoon (15 ml) balsamic vinegar

1 tablespoon (4 g) chopped fresh oregano or 1 teaspoon dried

5 cups (1.1 L) water

2 cans (14½ ounces, or 406 g each) white beans, drained and rinsed, or 3 cups (520 g) homemade (page 230)

BEFORE SERVING INGREDIENTS

4 cups (270 g) washed and chopped kale

☾ THE NIGHT BEFORE: Heat the oil in a skillet over medium heat and sauté the onion until translucent, 3 to 5 minutes. Add the garlic and a little salt and pepper and sauté for 1 to 2 minutes longer. Add the balsamic vinegar and stir to combine. Store the sautéed onion and the cut-up kale in separate airtight containers in the fridge.

☀ IN THE MORNING: Combine the sautéed onion, oregano, water, and beans in the slow cooker. Cook on low for 7 to 9 hours.

30 MINUTES BEFORE SERVING: Add the kale. Cook for 30 minutes longer, then taste and adjust the seasonings before serving.

YIELD: 6 servings
EQUIPMENT: 4-quart slow cooker
COOKING TIME: 7 to 9 hours on low

CHEATER CHILI *for* IMPOSSIBLE DAYS

If you need to throw together a quick dinner before you dash out the door, this is the recipe for you. It's simple, and you can raid your pantry for cans or look in the freezer for ingredients you've put up yourself.

 GLUTEN-FREE SOY-FREE  NO OIL ADDED

1 can (14½ ounces, or 406 g) black beans, drained and rinsed, or 1½ cups (340 g) homemade (page 230)

1 can (14½ ounces, or 406 g) pinto beans, drained and rinsed, or 1½ cups (340 g) homemade (page 230)

1 can (14½ ounces, or 406 g) kidney beans, drained and rinsed, or 1½ cups (340 g) homemade (page 230)

1 can (14½ ounces, or 406 g) corn, drained and rinsed, or 1½ cups (195 g) frozen

1 can (28 ounces, or 784 g) diced tomatoes or 3 cups (680 g) Preserve-the-Harvest Diced Tomatoes (page 241)

3 cloves garlic, minced, or ½ teaspoon garlic powder

1 tablespoon (7 g) chili powder

A few dashes liquid smoke

A few dashes Tabasco sauce (to taste)

Salt and pepper, to taste

Combine all the ingredients in the slow cooker. Cook on low for 7 to 9 hours. Taste and adjust the seasonings before serving.

YIELD: 6 servings
EQUIPMENT: 4-quart slow cooker
COOKING TIME: 7 to 9 hours on low

TEFF, MILLET, *and* BEAN CHILI

This chili is full of flavor, and it gets its stick to your ribs feeling from the teff and millet which actually mimics ground meat. Freeze the extras for last-minute meals on nights when you can't cook from scratch.

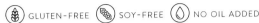 GLUTEN-FREE · SOY-FREE · NO OIL ADDED

4½ cups water

1 can (15 oz/ 425 g) kidney beans, drained and rinsed

1 can (15 oz/ 425 g) pinto beans, drained and rinsed

1 can (15 oz/ 425 g) cannellini beans, drained and rinsed

1½ cups (370 g) pumpkin purée

½ cup (125 g) teff, such as Maskal Teff™ brown teff grain

½ cup (100 g) millet

1 cup (85 g) sautéed onion

2½ teaspoons (6 g) chili powder (salt-free blend)

1½ teaspoon smoked paprika

1 teaspoon dried oregano

1 teaspoon minced garlic

½ teaspoon ground cumin

¼ to 1 teaspoon ground cayenne

BEFORE SERVING INGREDIENTS

2 tablespoons (6 g) nutritional yeast

3 tablespoons (48 g) tomato paste

1 teaspoon dried oregano (in addition to the amount added at the beginning of cooking)

½ teaspoon jalapeño powder (or more if you like it hot)

Salt, to taste

☀ IN THE MORNING: Add the kidney beans, pinto beans, cannellini beans, pumpkin purée, teff, millet, onion, chili powder, smoked paprika, oregano, garlic, cumin, and cayenne to the crock of your 4-quart slow cooker.

Cook on low 7 to 8 hours. Note: If you might be home late, add another ½ cup (120 ml) water to give you some leeway.

BEFORE SERVING: stir in the nutritional yeast, tomato paste and oregano. Stir well, then add salt to taste. Put out your favorite toppings (if using; see below).

You can serve as is in a bowl with a side of tortillas, in tacos, or even in a chili mac!

YIELD: 6 servings
EQUIPMENT: 4-quart slow cooker
COOKING TIME: 7 to 9 hours on low

Serving Suggestion
Top chili with chashew cream, chopped cilantro, and—if you like it spicy—pickled jalepeños.

THAI GINGER PEANUT SAUCE *with* VEGGIE *or* PROTEIN *of Your Choice*

This is my take on my favorite Thai restaurant peanut sauce dish. In my version we cheat a little and use shredded veggies. Make your own broccoli slaw by looking for broccoli with big stems. Peel and grate the stems, and mix with grated carrots.

 GLUTEN-FREE OPTION*   SOY-FREE OPTION**   NO OIL ADDED

SAUCE INGREDIENTS

2 cups (470 ml) water (if you are not using soy curls, leave this out)

1 can (14 ounces, or 392 g) light coconut milk

1 cup (260 g) peanut butter

3 tablespoons (45 ml) soy sauce (*use gluten-free, **use coconut aminos)

1½ tablespoons (12 g) grated ginger

1 tablespoon (15 ml) rice vinegar

2 teaspoons (6 g) minced garlic

½ teaspoon crushed red pepper flakes (or to taste)

2 cups (111 g) dry soy curls* or 1 package (8 ounces, or 225 g) tempeh* or tofu*) or (1 can chickpeas**)

2 cups (170 g) broccoli slaw (or shredded broccoli stems)

2 cups (220 g) shredded carrots

2 cups (140 g) shredded cabbage

SERVING INGREDIENTS

Lime wedges

Chopped cilantro

Chopped peanuts

Steamed rice

☾ THE NIGHT BEFORE: Make the sauce: Blend all the sauce ingredients in a blender or food processor.

Shred the veggies. Store the veggies and sauce in an airtight container in the fridge.

☀ IN THE MORNING: Oil the crock of your slow cooker. Add the soy curls and sauce, and cook on low for 7 to 9 hours.

Serve over rice, squeeze a lime wedge over, and top with the cilantro and peanuts.

YIELD: 4 servings
EQUIPMENT: 4-quart slow cooker
COOKING TIME: 7 to 9 hours on low

Recipe Ideas & Variations
Take this up a notch by adding 2 cups (142 g) broccoli florets and 2 cups (200 g) green beans and turn up the slow cooker to high 40 minutes before serving. Add more water, if needed. It's ready when the veggies are perfectly cooked.

TOFU *or* CAULIFLOWER MASALA

This creamy mild curry will become a family favorite in no time. It's easy to make, and it satisfies your Indian food cravings for less than it costs to eat out. If the spices are new to you, go to a co-op where you can get small amounts to try out—but the real savings kick in when you get them at your local Indian market.

 GLUTEN-FREE   SOY-FREE OPTION*   NO OIL ADDED

SAUCE INGREDIENTS

1 can (14½ ounces, or 406 g) diced tomatoes

1 cup (85 g) sautéed minced onions (or ½ teaspoon onion powder)

1 tablespoon (8 g) garam masala

1½ teaspoons ground cumin

1½ teaspoon ground coriander

1 teaspoon turmeric

½ teaspoon cinnamon

SLOW COOKER INGREDIENTS

1 (16 ounces, or 454 g) package extra-firm tofu or firm tofu that's been pressed (*or 4 cups [528 g] cauliflower florets)

½ cup (120 ml) water

BEFORE SERVING INGREDIENTS

½ cup (120 ml) full-fat coconut milk (or use low-fat or unsweetened nondairy milk)

Salt, to taste

☾ THE NIGHT BEFORE: Make the sauce by combining the diced tomatoes, onions, garam masala, cumin, coriander, turmeric, and cinnamon in your blender. Blend until smooth, then pour into your slow cooker crock. Use a spatula so you don't lose any in the process. Store the sauce in the fridge overnight.

☀ IN THE MORNING: Add in the tofu and water, and cook on low 7 to 9 hours.

BEFORE SERVING: Mix in the coconut milk, and add salt to taste. Serve over steamed brown basmati rice or with an Indian bread, such as naan or roti.

YIELD: 4–6 servings
EQUIPMENT: 4-quart slow cooker
COOKING TIME: 7 to 9 hours on low

SWEET POTATO *and* CHARD DAL

No Indian meal is complete without a lentil dish. This dal, or split pea soup, gets a nutritional boost from the sweet potato and chard. Serve over steamed basmati rice.

 GLUTEN-FREE SOY-FREE NO OIL ADDED OPTION*

1 tablespoon (15 ml) olive oil (*water sauté)

1 small onion, minced

1 teaspoon garam masala

¼ teaspoon turmeric

¼ teaspoon cumin

Pinch of chili powder

Salt, to taste

1 large sweet potato, diced

1½ cups (338 g) yellow split peas

4 cups (940 ml) water

BEFORE SERVING INGREDIENTS

1 bunch Swiss chard, washed, chopped, and spun dry

☾ THE NIGHT BEFORE: Heat the oil in a skillet over medium heat and sauté the onion with the garam masala, turmeric, cumin, chili powder, and salt until translucent, 3 to 5 minutes. Store in an airtight container in the refrigerator. Combine the cut-up vegetables in a separate airtight container and store in the refrigerator.

✳ IN THE MORNING: Combine the sautéed onion, sweet potato, split peas, and water in the slow cooker. Cook on low for 7 to 9 hours.

20 MINUTES BEFORE SERVING: Add the chard and cook until tender, about 20 minutes. Taste and adjust the seasonings.

YIELD: 6 servings
EQUIPMENT: 4-quart slow cooker
COOKING TIME: 7 to 9 hours on low

MASHED POTATO EDAMAME
BURRITO FILLING

From the first time I had a potato burrito, I was hooked! It's mashed potatoes with salsa in a moist tortilla. I've healthied it up a bit with a few veggies and some edamame so there's no need to feel guilty when you eat this amazingly easy comfort food.

 GLUTEN-FREE OPTION*  SOY-FREE OPTION** NO OIL ADDED

4 large Russet Potatoes, chunks

1 cup (235 ml) water

1½ cup (375 ml) mild salsa

1 pound (454g) mix of corn, chopped
red pepper, and edamame (I use
a frozen mix from Trader Joe's) or
**make soy-free by using your blend
of corn, red pepper, and black beans

Salt to taste

SERVING INGREDIENTS

Tortillas (*use gluten-free)

☾ THE NIGHT BEFORE: Peel the potatoes and cut into medium-size chunks. Store in the fridge overnight.

☀ IN THE MORNING: Add the potatoes, water, and salsa into an oiled slow cooker and cook for 6 to 8 hours on low.

1 HOUR BEFORE SERVING: Mash the potato with a potato masher or an immersion blender. Add the mixed vegetables and cook until they cooked through. Taste and add more salt or salsa before serving if needed.

YIELD: 6–8 servings
EQUIPMENT: 4-quart slow cooker
COOKING TIME: 7 to 9 hours on low

Serving Suggestion

If you get low-fat tortillas it helps to steam them before rolling the filling in them. Just put them on top of the filling while it's in the slow cooker for a minute. That should soften them up enough to roll without breaking.

GREEN CHILES REFRIED BLACK BEANS

In my opinion refried beans can be a food group all on their own. If I have some ready in the slow cooker when I get home, I can throw them in a tortilla, serve over rice with avocado, or even just eat a bowl as is. These freeze great, too!

 GLUTEN-FREE   SOY-FREE   NO OIL ADDED

4½ cups (1060 ml) water

1 pound (454 g) dry black beans (about 2 cups)

1 can (4 ounces, or 113 g) diced fire-roasted green chiles

2 teaspoons (6 g) minced garlic

1 teaspoon cumin powder

1 teaspoon chili powder, or add more if you prefer your beans spicy

1 teaspoon liquid smoke (optional)

½ teaspoon jalapeño powder or chipotle powder (optional)

Salt, to taste

IN THE MORNING: Add the water, black beans, garlic, cumin, and chili powder to your slow cooker crock. Cook on low for 7 to 9 hours.

BEFORE SERVING: Remove and reserve any extra liquid. You may need it to thin the beans later. Use your immersion blender and blend until smooth. Alternatively, you can use your blender or mash them with a potato masher depending on the texture you prefer.

YIELD: 6 servings
EQUIPMENT: 4-quart slow cooker
COOKING TIME: 7 to 9 hours on low

Serving Suggestion
I like to freeze leftovers in one-meal-sized freezer bags or stuffed into tortillas for a grab-and-go freezer lunch!

Recipe Ideas and Variations
No black beans? Try using pintos, cranberry beans, lila beans—really any bean except for kidney beans. (See how to cook kidneys on page 230.)

JACKFRUIT CARNITAS

This recipe transforms jackfruit into a flavorful meat substitute that's great for tacos, burritos, or even on its own. If you want a chewier texture, you can bake the mixture after it cooks in your slow cooker—but it's great as is, too!

 GLUTEN-FREE   SOY-FREE   NO OIL ADDED

½ cup (64 g) diced raw onion (use sautéed for a milder flavor)

2 teaspoons (6 g) minced garlic

1 can (1 pound 4 ounces, or 567 g) jackfruit in brine, drained and shredded (Do not get the kind that's in syrup!!)

SAUCE INGREDIENTS

1 tablespoon (15 g) brown or coconut sugar

1 teaspoon dried oregano

1 teaspoon salt, or add last to taste

¾ teaspoon ground cumin

½ teaspoon chili powder (use guajillo chili powder if possible)

½ teaspoon jalapeño powder (optional)

½ teaspoon smoked paprika

¼ teaspoon black pepper

1 cup (235 ml) water

⅓ cup (80 ml) orange juice

❋ IN THE MORNING: Layer the onion, garlic, and shredded jackfruit in your slow cooker crock. Mix all the sauce ingredients together, and pour it over the layers.

Cook on low for 7 to 9 hours.

BEFORE SERVING: Use a spatula to press on the jackfruit chunks and they will begin to shred. Continue until all of it is shredded, and mix well.

Add any additional seasoning that you feel was cooked out, such as a little extra oregano or smoked paprika.

If you'd like this to look meatier, you can spread on a baking sheet and cook at 350°F (180°C or gas mark 4) until it looks drier.

YIELD: 6 servings
EQUIPMENT: 4-quart slow cooker
COOKING TIME: 7 to 9 hours on low

CHAPTER 3

Soups

Soups are one of the easiest and most delicious things to make in a slow cooker. To make it even better most of these soups can cook even longer than their stated times, so if you end up coming home really late from work, your dinner won't be ruined. Still, be sure to add a little extra liquid if your slow cooker runs hot or you know you will be more than an hour or two late just to be on the safe side.

In many of the recipes I do ask that you sauté onions and sometimes garlic before you add them to your soups and stews. You can easily do this the night before when you are cleaning up from that night's dinner or you can make the big pot of onions on page 233 and grab sautéed onions right from your freezer.

If you are in a hurry, or forget to cook them the night before, go ahead and add them raw if you are going to cook it for at least 8 hours. You can also substitute onion powder.

Another thing to note is that you will need to taste the soup and add extra salt, pepper, herbs, or spices before serving. One person will like more seasoning than another, and the long cooking process can dull the flavor of some herbs and spices.

GOLDEN BORSCHT

I don't understand the beets-taste-like-dirt people, and I even live with one. Earthy and dirt just aren't the same thing to me. A good way to sneak them in is to use yellow beets. If the beets aren't red, most people don't notice them and tend to be more open-minded. In this soup, the beets and potatoes are almost the same color after cooking.

 GLUTEN-FREE   SOY-FREE   NO OIL ADDED

3 large yellow beets (about 1½ pounds, or 680 g), peeled and chopped

2 medium-size carrots, cut into half-moons

2 cups (180 g) chopped cabbage

2 cloves garlic, minced

2 fist-size potatoes, peeled if not organic and diced

6 cups (1410 ml) water

2 tablespoons (12 g) vegan chicken-flavored bouillon or 4 tablespoons (24 g) DIY Golden Bouillon (page 237)

4 teaspoons (21 g) tomato paste

1 bay leaf

1 sprig fresh thyme or 1 teaspoon dried

BEFORE SERVING INGREDIENTS

1 teaspoon dried dill

1 teaspoon agave nectar or maple syrup

1 to 2 tablespoons (15 to 30 ml) apple cider vinegar or lemon juice

1 teaspoon pepper (or to taste)

½ teaspoon salt (or to taste)

SERVING INGREDIENTS

Vegan sour cream or Cashew Sour Cream (page 53),

Fresh dill, for serving (optional)

☾ **THE NIGHT BEFORE:** Store the cut-up vegetables in an airtight container in the fridge.

☀ **IN THE MORNING:** Combine the cut-up vegetables, water, bouillon, tomato paste, bay leaf, and thyme to the slow cooker. Cook on low for 7 to 9 hours.

BEFORE SERVING: Remove and discard the thyme sprig. Add the dill, agave, and apple cider vinegar, and adjust the seasonings to make the sweet-sour ratio to your liking. Add the salt and pepper to taste.

Top the bowls of hot soup with a dollop of sour cream and a sprig of fresh dill.

YIELD: 6 servings
EQUIPMENT: 4-quart slow cooker
COOKING TIME: 7 to 9 hours on low

HERBED CARROT *and* BABY TURNIP SOUP

Turnips may not be your favorite veggie, but if you've never had baby turnips you should definitely give them another try. Their flavor is delicate and mild, and they are great steamed on their own, too.

 GLUTEN-FREE   SOY-FREE  NO OIL ADDED

2 pounds (908 g) carrots, tops removed, cut into large chunks

6 baby turnips, tops removed, cut into quarters

6 cups (1410 ml) water

2 tablespoons (12 g) vegan chicken-flavored bouillon or 4 tablespoons (24 g) DIY Golden Bouillon (page 237)

2 sprigs fresh rosemary

5 sprigs fresh thyme, plus extra for garnish

Salt and pepper, to taste

☾ THE NIGHT BEFORE: Store the cut-up vegetables in an airtight container in the fridge.

✷ IN THE MORNING: Combine all the ingredients in the slow cooker. Cook on low for 7 to 9 hours.

BEFORE SERVING: Remove and discard the rosemary sprig. Purée in batches in a food processor or blender, being careful of splatters from the hot soup, adjust the seasonings, and serve. Chop the extra thyme for garnish and sprinkle on top.

YIELD: 6 servings
EQUIPMENT: 4-quart slow cooker
COOKING TIME: 7 to 9 hours on low

CREAMY CORN CHOWDER

Corn chowder is a great summer soup because of the abundant fresh corn and basil. But it works in winter, too, if you keep some frozen corn and basil on hand. Once some of the soup is puréed and the nondairy milk is added, it creates a creamy base studded with veggies and herbs.

 GLUTEN-FREE SOY-FREE  NO OIL ADDED

1 pound (454 g) potatoes, peeled if not organic and chopped

1 bell pepper, chopped

4 cloves garlic, minced

1 pound (454 g) fresh or frozen corn kernels

4 cups (940 ml) water

3 tablespoons (18 g) vegan chicken-flavored bouillon or 6 tablespoons (36 g) DIY Golden Bouillon (page 237)

4 sprigs fresh thyme or 2 teaspoons dried

BEFORE SERVING INGREDIENTS

2 tablespoons chopped fresh basil, plus extra for garnish

2 cups (470 ml) nondairy milk

Salt and pepper, to taste

SERVING INGREDIENTS

Shredded vegan cheddar cheese, for serving, optional

Vegan sour cream or Cashew Sour Cream (page 53), for serving

☾ THE NIGHT BEFORE: Store the cut-up vegetables in an airtight container in the fridge.

✷ IN THE MORNING: Combine the potatoes, pepper, garlic, corn, water, bouillon, and thyme in the slow cooker. Cook on low for 7 to 9 hours.

30 MINUTES BEFORE SERVING: Remove and discard the thyme sprigs and carefully transfer 2 cups (470 ml) of the hot soup to a blender or food processor and purée. Return purée to the slow cooker to thicken the soup. Add the basil and nondairy milk. Turn the slow cooker up to high. Cook for about 30 minutes, until the soup is very hot. Add salt and pepper to taste.

Top bowls of hot soup with the cheese, sour cream, and extra fresh basil.

YIELD: 6 servings
EQUIPMENT: 4-quart slow cooker
COOKING TIME: 7 to 9 hours on low

SUMMER SQUASH BISQUE

This is a light, creamy soup with a hint of lemon from the lemon basil. It's perfect for summer when squash and basil are cheap and plentiful. You can use nondairy milk instead of the creamer if you want to cut down on the fat content.

 GLUTEN-FREE SOY-FREE  NO OIL ADDED

4 cups (480 g) chopped assorted summer squash

2 cloves garlic, minced

3 cups (705 ml) water

2 tablespoons (12 g) vegan chicken-flavored bouillon or 4 tablespoons (24 g) DIY Golden Bouillon (page 237)

1 teaspoon salt

Pepper, to taste

BEFORE SERVING INGREDIENTS

¼ cup (60 ml) unsweetened nondairy creamer or canned coconut milk

10 leaves fresh lemon basil or other variety basil plus juice of ½ lemon

☾ THE NIGHT BEFORE: Store the cut-up squash and garlic in an airtight container in the fridge.

☀ IN THE MORNING: Combine the squash, garlic, water, bouillon, salt, and pepper in the slow cooker. Cook on low for 7 to 9 hours

BEFORE SERVING: Add the creamer and whole basil leaves and stir to combine. Purée the soup with an immersion blender or in batches in a countertop blender, being careful of splatters of hot soup, until smooth. Adjust the seasonings to taste.

YIELD: 6 servings
EQUIPMENT: 4-quart slow cooker
COOKING TIME: 7 to 9 hours on low

ASPARAGUS TARRAGON SOUP

Asparagus is the first veggie of the year to burst out of the dirt. And it tastes brilliant in almost everything, too! This is a delicious, soothing soup. It's the perfect way to celebrate the asparagus harvest.

 GLUTEN-FREE SOY-FREE NO OIL ADDED

2 bunches (about 2 pounds, or 908 g) asparagus

2 cups (470 ml) water

2 tablespoons (12 g) vegan chicken-flavored bouillon or 4 tablespoons (24 g) DIY Golden Bouillon (page 237)

1 tablespoon (4 g) fresh tarragon or 1 teaspoon dried

1 tablespoon (4 g) fresh marjoram or 1 teaspoon dried

BEFORE SERVING INGREDIENTS

½ to 1 cup (120 to 235 ml) nondairy creamer or milk (unsweetened, if possible)

Salt and pepper, to taste

☾ THE NIGHT BEFORE: Wash the asparagus and snap off the woody end of each stalk and discard. Snap the stalks into 1-inch (2.5 cm) pieces. Store in an airtight container in the refrigerator.

☀ IN THE MORNING: Combine the asparagus, water, bouillon, tarragon, and marjoram in the slow cooker. Cook on high for 1½ to 2 hours, until the asparagus is completely cooked.

BEFORE SERVING: Add the creamer and stir to combine. Purée the soup with an immersion blender or in batches in a countertop blender, being careful of splatters of hot soup, until smooth. Add salt and pepper to taste.

YIELD: 4 servings
4- to 6-quart slow cooker
COOKING TIME: 1½ to 2½ hours on high

SPRING MINESTRONE *with* PESTO PARMESAN

Minestrone is great anytime of the year. Serve with focaccia and a big green salad.

 GLUTEN-FREE* SOY-FREE** NO OIL ADDED OPTION***

PESTO PARMESAN INGREDIENTS

15 leaves fresh basil

2 sprigs fresh oregano

¼ cup (36 g) almonds

1 tablespoon (15 ml) olive oil (***optional)

Salt, to taste

MINESTRONE INGREDIENTS

1 tablespoon (15 ml) olive oil (***water sauté)

½ large onion, chopped

2 cloves garlic, minced

1-inch (2.5 cm) piece lemon peel

1 large carrot, chopped

1 yellow squash, cut into half-moons

1 bunch Swiss chard or beet greens, torn into small pieces

5 cups (1175 ml) water

2 tablespoons (12 g) vegan chicken-flavored bouillon or 4 tablespoons (24 g) DIY Golden Bouillon (page 237)

1 can (14½ ounces, or 406 g) white beans or chickpeas, drained and rinsed

1 can (14½ ounces, or 406 g) diced tomatoes

2 vegan Italian sausages, chopped (*omit to make gluten- and **soy-free)

2-inch (5-cm) sprig fresh rosemary

Croutons, for serving

☾ THE NIGHT BEFORE: To make the Pesto Parmesan: Put all the ingredients into a food processor and pulse until it begins to form a grainy paste, but is not smooth. You want the texture to be granular like the grated Parmesan that you buy in a shaker. Store in an airtight container in the fridge.

TO MAKE THE MINESTRONE: Heat the oil in a skillet over medium heat and sauté the onion until translucent, 3 to 5 minutes. Add the garlic and sauté for 1 minute longer. Combine the sautéed onion, lemon peel, and cut-up vegetables in a large airtight container and store in the refrigerator.

☀ IN THE MORNING: Combine all the minestrone ingredients in the slow cooker. Cook on low for 7 to 9 hours. Remove and discard the rosemary sprig. Top bowls of hot soup with the Pesto Parmesan and croutons.

YIELD: 6 servings
EQUIPMENT: 4-quart slow cooker
COOKING TIME: 7 to 9 hours on low

SWEET POTATO WHITE BEAN SOUP

This soup packs tons of nutrients in a tasty package. It's a nice start to a larger meal, or serve it with a salad for a light dinner. The sweetness of the sweet potato hides the slight bitterness of the greens, so it's a great way to get your family to eat more greens.

 GLUTEN-FREE SOY-FREE  NO OIL ADDED

1 medium-size sweet potato, chopped

2 cloves garlic, minced

2 stalks celery, chopped, or 2 sprigs lovage, minced

1 can (14½ ounces, or 406 g) diced tomatoes or 1½ cups (340 g) Preserve-the-Harvest Diced Tomatoes (page 241)

1 can (14½ ounces, or 406 g) white beans, drained and rinsed, or 1½ cups (340 g) homemade (page 230)

5 cups (1175 ml) water

2 tablespoons (12 g) vegan chicken-flavored bouillon or 4 tablespoons (24 g) DIY Golden Bouillon (page 237)

BEFORE SERVING INGREDIENTS

2 cups (134 g) chopped Swiss chard

1 tablespoon (2.4 g) minced fresh thyme

2 sprigs parsley, minced

Salt and pepper, to taste

☾ **THE NIGHT BEFORE:** Store the cut-up vegetables in separate airtight containers in the fridge.

☀ **IN THE MORNING:** Combine the sweet potato, garlic, celery, diced tomatoes, beans, water, and bouillon in the slow cooker. Cook on low for 7 to 9 hours.

20 MINUTES BEFORE SERVING: Add the Swiss chard, thyme, and parsley. Cook until the Swiss chard is tender. Add salt and pepper to taste.

YIELD: 4 servings
4- to 6-quart slow cooker
COOKING TIME: 1½ to 2½ hours on high

CAULIFLOWER *and* CELERY ROOT BISQUE

This recipe was inspired by the Cauliflower Bisque from Anna Thomas's book Love Soup. *Her earlier books opened my mind to exactly how much I could accomplish in my very own kitchen. This soup is tangy from the lemon juice and super creamy and thick from the puréed celery root and cauliflower. It's one of my favorite soups and is great topped with a few croutons.*

 GLUTEN-FREE   SOY-FREE NO OIL ADDED

1 thick slice lemon zest about 1 inch (2.5 cm) long

1 medium-size celery root, peeled and chopped

1 medium-size parsnip, peeled and chopped

4 cloves garlic, minced

30 ounces (840 g) fresh or frozen cauliflower, cut into florets

4 cups (940 ml) water

2 tablespoons (12 g) vegan chicken-flavored bouillon or 4 tablespoons (24 g) DIY Golden Bouillon (page 237)

Juice of ½ lemon

1 tablespoon (7 g) herbes de Provence

Salt and pepper, to taste

☾ THE NIGHT BEFORE: Store the cut-up vegetables in an airtight container in the fridge. If you are using frozen cauliflower, you do not need to defrost it.

✻ IN THE MORNING: Combine all the ingredients in the slow cooker. Cook on low for 7 to 9 hours.

BEFORE SERVING: Fish out the strip of lemon peel, then purée the soup with an immersion blender or in small batches in a countertop blender, being careful of splatters of hot soup, until smooth. Adjust the seasonings to taste.

YIELD: 6 servings
EQUIPMENT: 4-quart slow cooker
COOKING TIME: 7 to 9 hours on low

THAI COCONUT PUMPKIN SOUP

*This tasty recipe has lots of nutrition packaged into a rich, creamy, slightly spicy soup.
It goes great with a big kale salad or the yellow Thai curry on page 120.*

 GLUTEN-FREE SOY-FREE  NO OIL ADDED

1 small pie pumpkin, peeled, seeded,
   and chopped (about 2½ pounds, or
   1135 g)

2 cloves garlic, minced

1½ tablespoons (12 g) peeled and grated
   ginger

1 stalk lemongrass, cut in half and
   bruised with a knife

2 cups (470 ml) water

2 tablespoons (12 g) vegan chicken-
   flavored bouillon or 4 tablespoons
   (24 g) DIY Golden Bouillon
   (page 237)

1 tablespoon (15 ml) agave nectar or
   maple syrup

½ teaspoon turmeric

½ teaspoon cumin

½ teaspoon coriander

½ teaspoon salt

¼ teaspoon chili powder

BEFORE SERVING INGREDIENTS

1 can (14 ounces, or 392 g) light
   coconut milk

Zest of ½ lime

☾ THE NIGHT BEFORE: Store the cut-up vegetables in an airtight container in the fridge.

☀ IN THE MORNING: Combine the pumpkin, garlic, ginger, lemongrass, water, bouillon, agave, turmeric, cumin, coriander, salt, and chili powder in the slow cooker. Cook on low for 7 to 9 hours.

20 MINUTES BEFORE SERVING: Stir the coconut milk and lime zest into the soup. Taste and adjust the seasonings.

You can leave it chunky or purée with an immersion blender or in batches in a countertop blender, being careful of splatters of hot soup, depending on your preference.

YIELD: 8 servings
EQUIPMENT: 4-quart slow cooker
COOKING TIME: 7 to 9 hours on low

HUNGARIAN MUSHROOM SOUP

There is a special place in my heart for Mollie Katzen. I taught myself how to cook from her Moosewood Cookbook. This is one of her recipes that I have veganized and adapted to the slow cooker. It is a thick, super-creamy, earthy treat on a cold winter's night. It's also one of my most requested soups.

 GLUTEN-FREE   SOY-FREE    NO OIL ADDED OPTION*

CASHEW SOUR CREAM INGREDIENTS

¾ cup (100 g) raw cashews

½ cup (120 ml) water

Juice of ½ lemon

SOUP INGREDIENTS

2 tablespoons (30 ml) olive oil (* water sauté)

1 medium-size onion, minced

2 packages (10 ounces, or 280 g each) mushrooms, chopped

2 cups (470 ml) water

½ tablespoon (3 g) vegan chicken-flavored bouillon or 1 tablespoon (6 g) DIY Golden Bouillon (page 237)

Juice of ½ lemon

Salt and pepper, to taste

1 to 2 tablespoons (4 g) minced dill (to taste), plus extra for garnish

2 tablespoons (14 g) paprika

☾ THE NIGHT BEFORE: To make the sour cream: Combine the cashews, water, and lemon juice in a blender or food processor and purée until fairly smooth. Store in an airtight container in the fridge.

TO MAKE THE SOUP: Heat the oil in a skillet over medium heat. Add the onion and sauté until translucent, 3 to 5 minutes. Add the mushrooms and cook until they begin to brown and give off their liquid, 8 to 10 minutes. Store in a separate airtight container in the fridge.

☀ IN THE MORNING: Combine the sautéed vegetables, water, bouillon, lemon juice, salt and pepper, dill, and paprika in the slow cooker. Cook on low for 7 to 9 hours.

BEFORE SERVING: Add the sour cream and stir to combine. Adjust the seasonings to taste.

Garnish bowls of hot soup with extra dill.

YIELD: 4 servings
EQUIPMENT: 4-quart slow cooker
COOKING TIME: 7 to 9 hours on low

TORTILLA SOUP

I just love tortilla soup, and it's hard to find a good vegan version when you're out. Making a batch of this is a perfect excuse to stay in and save some money. You can make it as spicy as you want. After all, it's your kitchen.

 GLUTEN-FREE OPTION*   SOY-FREE ⬦ NO OIL ADDED OPTION**

1 tablespoon (15 ml) olive oil (**water sauté)

1 medium-size onion, minced

2 cloves garlic, minced

1 can (28 ounces, or 784 g) diced or crushed tomatoes or 3 cups (680 g) Preserve-the-Harvest Diced Tomatoes (page 241)

3 tablespoons (48 g) tomato paste

4 cups (940 ml) water

Juice of ½ lime

1 tablespoon (1 g) chopped fresh cilantro, plus extra for garnish

1 teaspoon cumin

½ teaspoon chili powder

¼ cup (120 ml) tequila (optional)

1 teaspoon agave nectar or maple syrup

1 to 2 cups (225 to 450 g) cubed chicken-flavored seitan, store-bought or homemade (page 238, optional, for a heartier soup)

Use reconstituted soy curls or chickpeas to make gluten free

Salt and pepper, to taste

½ avocado, chopped and tossed with some lime juice and chili powder

SERVING INGREDIENTS

Tortilla chips (*use gluten-free), slightly crushed, for serving

🌙 **THE NIGHT BEFORE:** Heat the oil in a skillet over medium heat and sauté the onion until translucent, 3 to 5 minutes. Add the garlic and sauté for 1 minute longer. Store in an airtight container in the fridge.

☀ **IN THE MORNING:** Combine the sautéed onion, tomatoes, tomato paste, water, lime juice, cilantro, cumin, chili powder, tequila, agave, salt, and pepper in the slow cooker. Cook on low for 7 to 9 hours.

Purée the soup with an immersion blender or in batches in a countertop blender, being careful of splatters of hot soup, or leave the soup chunky. Taste and adjust the seasoning. Add optional seitan. Turn slow cooker to high, and cook until soup is warmed thoroughly.

Top bowls of hot soup with the avocado, crushed tortilla chips, and fresh cilantro.

YIELD: 8 servings
EQUIPMENT: 4-quart slow cooker
COOKING TIME: 7 to 9 hours on low

HOT *and* SOUR SOUP

It's hard to find vegan soups at Chinese takeout places in most areas. This is the perfect cold and flu season soup. It clears those sinuses right up! You can adjust the amount of spice until it's just right for you.

 GLUTEN-FREE OPTION*   SOY-FREE OPTION**   NO OIL ADDED

1 package (10 ounces, or 280 g) sliced mushrooms

8 fresh shiitake mushrooms, stems removed and caps sliced

1 can (8 ounces, or 225 g) bamboo shoots, drained and julienned

4 cloves garlic, minced

1 package (15 ounces, or 420 g) firm or silken tofu, cubed (**substitute hemp tofu or add in beans of your choice)

2 tablespoons (16 g) grated fresh ginger, divided

4 cups (940 ml) water

2 tablespoons (12 g) vegan chicken-flavored bouillon or 4 tablespoons (24 g) DIY Golden Bouillon (page 237)

2 tablespoons (30 ml) soy sauce (* use gluten-free or **coconut aminos)

BEFORE SERVING INGREDIENTS

1 teaspoon sesame oil, plus extra for drizzling

1 teaspoon chili paste

2 tablespoons (30 ml) rice wine vinegar or apple cider vinegar

1½ cups (225 g) fresh or frozen peas

☾ **THE NIGHT BEFORE:** Store the cut-up mushrooms, bamboo shoots, garlic, and tofu in an airtight container in the fridge. Store the prepared ginger in another airtight container in the fridge.

☀ **IN THE MORNING:** Combine the mushrooms, bamboo shoots, garlic, tofu, 1 tablespoon (8 g) of the ginger, water, bouillon, soy sauce, sesame oil, chili paste, and vinegar in the slow cooker. Cook on low for 8 hours.

A FEW MINUTES BEFORE SERVING: Add the peas and the remaining 1 tablespoon (8 g) ginger and stir to combine. Taste the broth and add more vinegar or chili if needed. Drizzle a few drops of sesame oil on top of each serving. If you like it milder and your friends like it hot, serve the chili paste on the side.

YIELD: 8 servings
EQUIPMENT: 4-quart slow cooker
COOKING TIME: 7 to 9 hours on low

DELICATA *and* PEAR SOUP

All winter squashes pair well with something a little sweet. I like mixing them with fresh pears and apples in the winter to liven up a soup or casserole. It's unexpected, and a nice change of pace during the colder months.

 GLUTEN-FREE SOY-FREE NO OIL ADDED

1 medium-size delicata or other winter squash

2 medium-size pears or apples

1 small onion, chopped

1 clove garlic, chopped

4 cups (940 ml) water

2 tablespoons (12 g) vegan chicken-flavored bouillon or 4 tablespoons (24 g) DIY Golden Bouillon (page 237)

1 tablespoon (15 ml) port or red wine

1 sprig fresh thyme

1 sprig fresh rosemary

Salt and pepper, to taste

SERVING INGREDIENTS

Finely chopped pistachios, for serving

Minced fresh thyme, for serving

☾ THE NIGHT BEFORE: Cut the delicata squash in half, scrape the seeds out, and then use a vegetable peeler to remove the skin. Chop the flesh into cubes. Peel the pears, core, and chop. Toss with lemon juice to prevent browning. Store the cut-up squash and pears in an airtight container in the fridge.

☀ IN THE MORNING: Combine all the ingredients in the slow cooker. Cook on low for 7 to 9 hours.

BEFORE SERVING: Remove the thyme and rosemary sprigs. Purée the soup with an immersion blender or in batches in a countertop blender, being careful of splatters of hot soup, until smooth. Adjust the seasonings to taste, and add more water or broth if needed. Top with pistachios and minced fresh thyme.

YIELD: 6 servings
EQUIPMENT: 4-quart slow cooker
COOKING TIME: 7 to 9 hours on low

TURBODOG ROOT VEGGIE SOUP

Turbodog is a dark beer brewed by Abita Brewery just outside of New Orleans, Louisiana. All of the beers they brew are vegan and very tasty. The beer adds an almost caramel flavor to the broth. Feel free to mix and match the root veggies that are in season in your area. If turnips aren't your favorite, use a small one, and add extra of one of the other veggies. Or you can simply leave it out—it's your, soup after all!

Note: You want close to an equal amount of each veggie. The sizes will vary depending on the time of year, so just make sure you are selecting by the sizes that are available when shopping.

  GLUTEN-FREE OPTION*   SOY-FREE   NO OIL ADDED

1 medium-size rutabaga

1 medium-size turnip

1 large golden beet

1 small celery root

1 medium-size parsnip

1 large carrot

2 cloves garlic, minced

2 cups (470 ml) water

1 bottle (12 ounces, or 355 ml) Abita Turbodog beer or your favorite vegan dark beer (*buy a gluten-free beer to make this gluten-free)

1 tablespoon (6 g) vegan chicken-flavored bouillon or 2 tablespoons (12 g) DIY Golden Bouillon (page 237)

2 sprigs fresh thyme

1 sprig fresh rosemary

1 bay leaf

Salt and pepper, to taste

☾ THE NIGHT BEFORE: Peel, trim the ends, and dice the rutabaga, turnip, beet, celery root, parsnip, and carrot. Store the cut-up vegetables in an airtight container in the fridge.

☀ IN THE MORNING: Combine all the ingredients in the slow cooker. Cook on low for 7 to 9 hours. Remove and discard the thyme and rosemary sprigs and bay leaf. Taste and adjust the seasonings before serving.

YIELD: 4–6 servings
EQUIPMENT: 4-quart slow cooker
Cooks 7 to 9 hours, 4-quart slow cooker

SMOKED TOFU *and* STARS

This is my favorite soup when I'm sick. It's warm and filling, and evokes memories of childhood soups with fun-shaped pasta.

 GLUTEN-FREE OPTION*   SOY-FREE OPTION **   NO OIL ADDED OPTION***

2 tablespoons (30 ml) olive oil (***water sauté)

1 medium-size onion, minced

4 cloves garlic, minced

2 carrots

2 stalks celery

1 package (8 ounces, or 225 g) smoked tofu (** substitute cooked chickpeas)

2 tablespoons (12 g) vegan chicken-flavored bouillon or 4 tablespoons (24 g) DIY Golden Bouillon (page 237)

8 cups (1880 ml) water

3 sprigs fresh thyme or 1 teaspoon dried

Salt and pepper, to taste

½ teaspoon Cajun seasoning (optional)

BEFORE SERVING INGREDIENTS

1 cup (100 g) small pasta stars or other tiny pasta (*use your favorite gluten-free pasta)

☾ THE NIGHT BEFORE: Heat the oil in a skillet over medium heat and sauté the onion until translucent, 3 to 5 minutes. Add the garlic and sauté for 1 minute longer. Dice the carrots, celery, and tofu. Store everything together in an airtight container in the fridge.

☀ IN THE MORNING: Combine the sautéed vegetables, carrots, celery, tofu, bouillon, water, thyme, salt and pepper, and Cajun seasoning in the slow cooker. Cook on low for 7 to 9 hours. Taste and adjust the seasonings.

You have two choices for adding the pasta. If you plan on eating all of it that night, then add the pasta 20 minutes before serving. Cook until the pasta is al dente. If you will be eating it throughout the week or freezing it, cook the pasta separately on the stove top and add it just before serving. The pasta will get mushy if it stays in the soup too long.

YIELD: 6 servings
EQUIPMENT: 4-quart slow cooker
COOKING TIME: 7 to 9 hours on low

Ann's STUFFED ARTICHOKE SOUP

Ann, from AnUnrefinedVegan.com, re-created this soup to embody the flavors of the stuffed artichokes she grew up on. Ann says: Although the ingredient list is long, it's mostly herbs and spices, and this is a simple soup. One that cooks itself while you're at work or snuggled fast asleep in bed. The "sausage" crumbles and the "cheese" drizzle come together very quickly.

 GLUTEN-FREE SOY-FREE NO OIL ADDED

SOUP INGREDIENTS

1 onion, chopped

1 medium-size carrot, chopped

2 stalks celery, chopped

4 cloves garlic, minced

½ teaspoon fennel seeds

½ teaspoon dried rosemary

½ teaspoon dried oregano

½ teaspoon dried thyme

½ teaspoon garlic powder

Dash red pepper flakes

Dash salt and black pepper

4 cans (14 ounces, or 392 g each) quartered artichoke hearts, drained and roughly chopped

5½ cups (1320 ml) low-sodium vegetable broth, divided

"SAUSAGE" INGREDIENTS

½ cup (28 g) soy curls, soaked in hot water for ~15 minutes

1 clove garlic, roughly chopped

1 teaspoon garlic powder

1 teaspoon rubbed sage

½ teaspoon sweet paprika

⁕ IN THE MORNING: Make the soup: Heat a small skillet over medium-high heat, and add a splash of water or vegetable broth. Sauté the onion, carrot, and celery for about 5 minutes. Add the garlic, herbs, and spices. Cook for an additional 1 to 2 minutes. Remove from the heat and scrape into a 4-quart slow cooker. Add the artichoke hearts and 5 cups (1175 ml) of the vegetable broth.

Turn the slow cooker onto low and cook for about 8 hours.

BEFORE SERVING: Using a stick blender or working in batches in a blender, blend the soup—not so that it's uniform and smooth, unless you prefer it that way—but so that there are still some large pieces of artichoke.

MAKE THE "SAUSAGE": Drain the soy curls well and add them to the bowl of a food processor. Add the herbs and spices, and pulse 5 to 6 times to crumble the soy curls. Heat a skillet over medium-high heat, lightly spritz the pan with olive oil cooking spray (or, to go oil-free, add a splash of water or vegetable broth) and scrape in the soy curl mixture. Cook until very fragrant and beginning to brown. If you're using the no-oil method, add small amounts of water or broth as the soy curls begin to stick to the pan.

Once the "sausage" has browned, deglaze the pan with the red wine. Stir it into the soup just before serving.

½ teaspoon dried oregano

½ teaspoon fennel seeds

¼ teaspoon black pepper

Pinch sea salt

1 to 2 tablespoons (15 to 30 ml) dry red wine or liquid aminos

"CHEESE" INGREDIENTS

½ cup (73 g) raw cashew pieces soaked in ½ cup (120 ml) low-sodium vegetable broth

½ tablespoon (3 g) nutritional yeast

Juice of ½ lemon

½ teaspoon garlic powder

MAKE THE "CHEESE": Put the cashews and the broth they've soaked in into a high-speed blender. Add the nutritional yeast, lemon juice, and garlic powder. Process until very smooth, adding more broth or water so that the consistency is thick but pourable. Set aside until ready to serve the soup.

YIELD: 6 servings
EQUIPMENT: 4-quart slow cooker
COOKING TIME: 7 to 9 hours on low

CREAMY POTATO SOUP

This is another one of my favorite comfort foods. It's great for when you don't feel good, or if it's just chilly outside. It also makes an excellent base for other creamy soups, so add in some broccoli, spinach, or even carrots for a creamy un-cream soup.

  GLUTEN-FREE   SOY-FREE   NO OIL ADDED

4 medium-size russet potatoes, peeled and cut into medium-size cubes

1 clove garlic, minced

4 cups (940 ml) water

2 tablespoons (12 g) vegan chicken-flavored bouillon or 4 tablespoons (24 g) DIY Golden Bouillon (page 237)

1 sprig fresh rosemary or ½ teaspoon dried ground rosemary

Salt and pepper, to taste

BEFORE SERVING INGREDIENTS

1 cup (235 ml) unsweetened nondairy milk

☾ THE NIGHT BEFORE: Store the cut-up potatoes and garlic in an airtight container in the fridge.

☀ IN THE MORNING: Combine the potatoes, garlic, water, bouillon, rosemary, and salt and pepper in the slow cooker. Cook on low for 7 to 9 hours.

BEFORE SERVING: Add the nondairy milk. Remove and discard the rosemary, and mash the potatoes using a potato masher or large spoon.

Taste and adjust the seasonings.

YIELD: 4 servings
EQUIPMENT: 4-quart slow cooker
COOKING TIME: 7 to 9 hours on low

RAINBOW VEGETABLE SOUP

This soup is for those days when you know you need to load up on veggies. You can vary the colors to suit your mood or taste, but remember that some of the purple veggies will turn the broth purple. Is that a bad thing? I don't think so, but it's not the best surprise if you didn't know.

 GLUTEN-FREE SOY-FREE NO OIL ADDED

7 cups (1.7 L) water

3 cups (270 g) chopped green cabbage

2 cups (140 g) chopped mushrooms

1 can (15 ounce, or 420 g) diced tomatoes

2 cups (300 g) quartered baby potatoes (red skin or yellow finn)

1 cup (130 g) carrot half-moons (orange, yellow, or purple)

1 cup (110 g) chopped sweet potato (orange or purple)

1 teaspoon onion powder

1 teaspoon dried marjoram

½ teaspoon dried thyme

½ teaspoon garlic powder

BEFORE SERVING INGREDIENTS

2 cups (220 g) green beans cut into ½-inch pieces

1 cup (67 g) minced kale or collard greens

Salt and pepper, to taste

☾ THE NIGHT BEFORE: Prepare all the soup ingredient vegetables and store in the fridge overnight.

☀ IN THE MORNING: Add the water, green cabbage, mushrooms, tomatoes, baby potatoes, carrot, sweet potato, onion powder, marjoram, thyme, and garlic powder to you slow cooker. Cook on low for 7 to 9 hours.

30 MINUTES BEFORE SERVING: Add the green beans and greens. Season with salt and pepper to taste. Cook 30 minutes, or until the beans are tender.

YIELD: 6 servings
EQUIPMENT: 5- to 6-quart slow cooker
COOKING TIME: 7 to 9 hours on low

COCONUT SOUP *with* MUSHROOMS *and* JACKFRUIT

This is my vegan version of a Thai chicken soup called Tom Kha Gai. I made mine mild, but you can add a little chili oil to spice yours up a bit. There are a few specialty ingredients in this soup, so you will need to find an Asian market where they will be inexpensive. Tamarind concentrate adds a tang, and the kaffir lime leaves, lemongrass, and galangal root are the heart of this aromatic soup. Trust me, it's worth a trip to the market, and it comes together fast once you have the ingredients.

 GLUTEN-FREE OPTION*   SOY-FREE OPTION**   NO OIL ADDED

1 can (10 ounces, or 280 g) jackfruit, drained and shredded by hand

2 cups (140 g) chopped shiitake or button mushrooms

3 (3-inch, or 7.5-cm) pieces of fresh lemongrass

1 (2-inch, or 5-cm) piece galangal root, cut into slices

6 kaffir lime leaves

3 cups (705 ml) water

1 teaspoon tamarind concentrate (*use gluten-free soy sauce or **coconut aminos)

1 teaspoon brown or coconut sugar

1 teaspoon soy sauce

BEFORE SERVING INGREDIENTS

1 cup (235 ml) full-fat coconut milk (you can use light, but it won't be as rich)

¼ cup (24 g) nutritional yeast

1 to 2 tablespoons (15 to 30 ml) lime juice, to taste

Salt, to taste

☾ THE NIGHT BEFORE: Shred the jackfruit. Cut the mushrooms, lemongrass, and galangal. Store in the fridge overnight.

☀ IN THE MORNING: Add the shredded jackfruit, mushrooms, lemongrass, galangal, kaffir lime leaves, water, tamarind, sugar, and soy sauce to your slow cooker. Cook on low 7 to 9 hours.

20 MINUTES BEFORE SERVING: Stir in the coconut milk and nutritional yeast. Add lime and salt to taste, and add garnishes (if using; see below).

YIELD: 4 servings
EQUIPMENT: 4-quart slow cooker
COOKING TIME: 7 to 9 hours on low

Serving Suggestion
Garnish with any of the following: chili oil, lime wedges, chopped cilantro, and shredded carrot.

CHAPTER 4

Stews

Stews and curries are incredibly versatile and make great one-pot meals. Their flavors meld together with long cooking time:s and are perfect for cooking all day while you are at work. The curries are also wonderful served over rice, and all make for leftovers to look forward to!

If your slow cooker runs hot, you will need to add 1 to 2 cups (235 to 470 ml) of extra liquid. You'll also need to taste and adjust the seasonings before serving, because depending on the age of your herbs and how long you cook your stew, their flavors may fade and need a boost.

These recipes are perfect for doing most of the prep work at night before you go to bed. Then when you wake up in the morning it takes very little time to get your dish in the slow cooker. Once you get used to coming home to a ready-made hot dinner, it's hard to remember why you weren't doing this before. Less going out means eating healthier and less expensive food.

ASIAN-STYLE WINTER STEW

This is a hearty stew that can be made with staples and veggies in your pantry. It's perfect for a snowy day, when you can't (or just don't want to) go to the store. It's a warming root stew flavored with miso, then topped with sesame oil.

 GLUTEN-FREE   SOY-FREE OPTION*   NO OIL ADDED OPTION**

2 tablespoons (30 ml) olive oil (**water sauté)

1 medium-size onion, cut in half and sliced

2 cloves garlic, minced

1 tablespoon (8 g) grated ginger

1 small turnip, chopped

3-inch (7.5 cm) piece daikon, chopped

8 baby or fingerling potatoes, cut in half if large

8 ounces (225 g) baby carrots, cut in half if large

4 ounces (113 g) mushrooms (I use a packaged blend of baby bella, shiitake, and oyster), cut into large chunks

2 tablespoons (12 g) vegan chicken-flavored bouillon or 4 tablespoons (24 g) DIY Golden Bouillon (page 237)

2 tablespoons (32 g) miso (*use a soy-free miso)

1 cup (235 ml) water

Salt and pepper, to taste

SERVING INGREDIENTS

Sesame oil, for serving (**omit to make oil-free)

☾ **THE NIGHT BEFORE:** Heat the oil in a skillet over medium heat and sauté the onion until translucent, 3 to 5 minutes. Add the garlic and sauté for 3 minutes longer. Combine the sautéed onion, grated ginger, and cut-up vegetables in a large airtight container and store in the refrigerator.

☀ **IN THE MORNING:** Combine all the ingredients in the slow cooker. Cook on low for 7 to 9 hours.

BEFORE SERVING: Remove and discard the bay leaves. Taste and adjust the seasonings. Serve drizzled with sesame oil if using.

YIELD: *4 servings*
EQUIPMENT: *4-quart slow cooker*
COOKING TIME: *7 to 9 hours on low*

VEGGIE GUMBO *with* CHEATER ROUX

In New Orleans, everyone has his or her own variation on gumbo. It started as a way to use leftovers and make a full meal out of a not-so-full pantry. This recipe is unique because it replaces a slow-cooked traditional roux with a simple thickener that takes less time than the slow browning method, but still retains a smoky flavor.

 GLUTEN-FREE OPTION* SOY-FREE OPTION **  NO OIL ADDED OPTION***

GUMBO INGREDIENTS

2 tablespoons (30 ml) olive oil (**water sauté)

1 small onion, minced

2 cloves garlic, minced

2 stalks celery, minced

2 medium-size bell peppers, chopped

1½ cups (165 g) chopped vegan Italian sausage, tempeh, or tofu **or seitan

12 ounces (340 g) okra

1 can (14½ ounces, or 406 g) diced tomatoes or 1½ cups (340 g) Preserve-the-Harvest Diced Tomatoes (page 241)

4 cups (940 ml) water

3 tablespoons (18 g) vegan chicken-flavored bouillon or 6 tablespoons (36 g) DIY Golden Bouillon (page 237)

1 teaspoon Cajun seasoning

CHEATER ROUX INGREDIENTS

6 roasted or smoked almonds

1 cup (225 g) white beans, drained and rinsed

¼ teaspoon liquid smoke

1 to 3 teaspoons water

SERVING INGREDIENTS

Cooked rice

☾ THE NIGHT BEFORE: To make the gumbo: Heat the oil in a skillet over medium heat and sauté the onion until translucent, 3 to 5 minutes. Add the garlic and celery and sauté for 3 minutes longer. Store the sautéed vegetables and the cut-up bell peppers and sausage together in an airtight container in the fridge.

To make the roux: Place the almonds in a food processor and process until coarse. Add the white beans and liquid smoke and process again. Add the water, 1 teaspoon at a time, until the mixture comes together and blends thoroughly. Store the roux in a separate airtight container in the fridge.

❋ IN THE MORNING: Slice the okra. Combine the okra, sautéed vegetables, bell peppers, sausage, tomatoes, water, bouillon, and Cajun seasoning in the slow cooker. Cook on low for 7 to 9 hours.

ABOUT 20 MINUTES BEFORE SERVING: Stir the roux into the gumbo. Heat through, then taste and adjust the seasonings.

Ladle the gumbo into bowls, then add a scoop of rice to each one, like an island in the middle of the bowl, and serve.

YIELD: 6 servings
EQUIPMENT: 4-quart slow cooker
COOKING TIME: 7 to 9 hours on low

MOJITO PINTO BEANS

Lime, rum, and mint come together to create a bold flavor in these beans. As the rum cooks down with the beans, it creates a rich sauce. The lime juice and mint really brighten up the dish. If you haven't used mint in savory dishes before, add a small amount at first. Serve over rice with a side of steamed veggies for a complete meal.

 GLUTEN-FREE SOY-FREE  NO OIL ADDED

1 small onion

2 cans (15 ounces, or 420 g each) pinto beans, drained and rinsed, or 3 cups (520 g) homemade (page 230)

½ cup (120 ml) water

½ cup (120 ml) rum (dark is best)

½ teaspoon cumin

½ tablespoon (3 g) vegan chicken-flavored bouillon or 1 tablespoon (6 g) DIY Golden Bouillon (page 237)

1 tablespoon (16 g) tomato paste

Juice of 1 lime

Salt and pepper, to taste

BEFORE SERVING INGREDIENTS

Chopped fresh mint, for serving

☾ THE NIGHT BEFORE: Dice the onion and store in an airtight container in the fridge.

☀ IN THE MORNING: Combine all the ingredients in the slow cooker. Cook on low for 7 to 9 hours.

BEFORE SERVING: Taste and adjust the seasonings, then top with the chopped mint.

YIELD: 4 servings
EQUIPMENT: 4-quart slow cooker
COOKING TIME: 7 to 9 hours on low

TOFU BOUILLABAISSE

This is a fragrant, tomato-based stew cooked with saffron and fresh fennel. The potatoes and tofu make it a hearty meal that will even please your nonvegan friends.

 GLUTEN-FREE　NO OIL ADDED

2 tablespoons (30 ml) olive oil (*water sauté)

1 medium-size onion, cut in half and sliced

3 cloves garlic, minced

½ medium-size fennel bulb, chopped

3 stalks celery, chopped

2 carrots, cut into half-moons

3 medium-size potatoes, cut into chunks

1 package (15 ounces, or 420 g) extra-firm tofu, cubed

1 can (28 ounces, or 784 g) diced tomatoes or 3 cups (540 g) chopped fresh

1½ cups (353 ml) water

2 bay leaves

½ teaspoon saffron

Salt and pepper, to taste

Zest and juice of ½ lime

☾ THE NIGHT BEFORE: Heat the oil in a skillet over medium heat and sauté the onion until translucent, 3 to 5 minutes. Add the garlic and sauté for 3 minutes longer. Store the sautéed onion and the cut-up fennel, celery, carrots, potatoes, and tofu in an airtight container in the fridge.

☀ IN THE MORNING: Combine all the ingredients in the slow cooker. Cook on low for 7 to 9 hours. Taste and adjust the seasonings. Remove the bay leaves before serving.

YIELD: 6 servings
EQUIPMENT: 4-quart slow cooker
COOKING TIME: 7 to 9 hours on low

CHINESE-STYLE EGGPLANT
in GARLIC SAUCE

This is a variation on my favorite Chinese takeout dish. You can make it with any kind of eggplant, but it looks amazing using the tiny Fairy Tale variety. Just remove the tops and cook them whole. Be sure to use large chunks or whole small eggplants and note the shorter cooking time.

 GLUTEN-FREE OPTION*   NO OIL ADDED OPTION**

1½ pounds (681 g) eggplant (Italian, Japanese, Indian, Fairy Tale, or other variety)

For the sauce:

4 cloves garlic, minced

2 tablespoons (16 g) fresh grated ginger

½ to 1 cup (120 to 235 ml) water (use the larger amount if your slow cooker runs hot)

1½ tablespoons (9 g) vegan chicken-flavored bouillon or 3 tablespoons (18 g) DIY Golden Bouillon (page 237)

2 tablespoons (30 ml) soy sauce (*use gluten-free)

2 tablespoons (30 ml) hoisin sauce (*use gluten-free)

2 to 3 tablespoons (30 to 45 ml) agave nectar or maple syrup (to taste)

½ to 1 teaspoon sriracha chili sauce (optional)

SERVING INGREDIENTS

Sesame oil (**leave out or use tahini)

☾ THE NIGHT BEFORE: Depending on the variety and size of your eggplants, you can leave them whole (Indian or Fairy Tale variety) or cut into large chunks.

TO MAKE THE SAUCE: Combine all the sauce ingredients in a small bowl and mix thoroughly. Combine the sauce and the eggplant in a large airtight container and store in the refrigerator.

☀ IN THE MORNING: Oil the crock of your slow cooker and add the eggplant and sauce. Cook on low for 5 to 6 hours, longer if you have an older slow cooker. Taste and add more soy sauce or sweetener if needed. Serve topped with a drizzle of sesame oil.

YIELD: 4 servings
EQUIPMENT: 4-quart slow cooker
COOKING TIME: 5 to 6 hours on low

HARD CIDER *and* CABBAGE STEW

This is a sausage and veggie stew that tastes like fall itself. The hard cider mellows out while cooking and makes for a perfect, savory broth.

 NO OIL ADDED OPTION*

2 tablespoons (30 ml) olive oil (*water sauté)

1 small onion, chopped

3 cloves garlic, minced

2 medium-size carrots, sliced into coins

1 small head cabbage (about 14½ ounces, or 406 g), cored and chopped

1 small apple, peeled, cored, and diced

1 package (12 ounces, or 340 g) vegan sausage links (I used Wheat Roast brand smoked apple sage), sliced

2 cups (470 ml) hard cider

2 tablespoons (12 g) vegan chicken-flavored bouillon or 4 tablespoons (24 g) DIY Golden Bouillon (page 237)

2 bay leaves

1 sprig rosemary

2 sprigs thyme

Salt and pepper, to taste

☾ THE NIGHT BEFORE: Heat the oil in a skillet over medium heat and sauté the onion until translucent, 3 to 5 minutes. Add the garlic and sauté for 3 minutes longer. Combine the sautéed onion and cut-up vegetables, apple, and sausage in a large airtight container and store in the refrigerator.

☀ IN THE MORNING: Combine all the ingredients in the slow cooker. Cook on low for 7 to 9 hours. Remove and discard the bay leaves, rosemary sprig, and thyme sprigs. Taste and adjust the seasonings.

YIELD: 6 servings
EQUIPMENT: 4-quart slow cooker
COOKING TIME: 7 to 9 hours on low

RUSTIC SOY CURL STEW

This is down-home stew goodness. It's thick with filling potatoes, sweet carrots, and lots of spices. This is a great fall or winter dish. Serve it with a large piece of whole-grain bread and a kale or spinach salad.

 GLUTEN-FREE  SOY-FREE OPTION* NO OIL ADDED OPTION**

1 cup (128 g) chopped onion, sautéed or the recipe on page 233 (or use 2 teaspoons onion powder)

2 teaspoons (6 g) minced garlic

3 cups (705 ml) water

3 cups (675 g) diced potatoes

2 cups (111 g) dry soy curls or 1½ cups (360g) cooked chickpeas

1 package (12 ounces, or 340 g) baby carrots (rainbow colors if you can find them)

¼ cup (24 g) nutritional yeast

2 teaspoons (2 g) dried marjoram

1 teaspoon dried thyme

¾ teaspoon salt

½ teaspoon paprika

¼ teaspoon pepper

SERVING INGREDIENTS

Sesame oil (**leave out or use tahini)

(optional)

Bread

☾ THE NIGHT BEFORE: Sauté the onions, and store in the fridge along with the garlic and potatoes.

☀ IN THE MORNING: Add the onion, garlic, water, potatoes, dry soy curls, baby carrots, nutritional yeast, marjoram, thyme, salt, paprika, and pepper to your slow cooker. Mix well and make sure the soy curls are pressed under the liquid.

Cook on low 7 to 9 hours. Taste and add extra seasonings and nutritional yeast as needed. I like to serve this stew with a piece of crusty bread.

YIELD: 4 servings
EQUIPMENT: 4-quart slow cooker
COOKING TIME: 7 to 9 hours on low

Did You Know?

What are soy curls? They are a minimally processed non-GMO soy product, that comes out of Oregon. I get mine online at Amazon. The are soy beans that are squeezed and dried, making them look like chick'n tenders.

CARIBBEAN MANGO BLACK BEANS

Sometimes you need something easy to make that's good enough for company. These beans have a hint of sweetness from the mango with a layer of spiciness underneath. You can halve this recipe if you aren't serving a crowd, or you can freeze the leftovers for another night. Serve over rice, in a burrito, or by themselves as a side.

 GLUTEN-FREE SOY-FREE  NO OIL ADDED

3 cloves garlic

2 mangoes

4 cans (15 ounces, or 420 g each) black beans, drained and rinsed, or 6 cups (1040 g) homemade (page 230)

1 cup (235 ml) water

2 tablespoons (12 g) vegan chicken-flavored bouillon or 4 tablespoons (24 g) DIY Golden Bouillon (page 237)

3 tablespoons (24 g) grated fresh ginger

1½ teaspoons paprika

2 teaspoons thyme

¼ teaspoon nutmeg

⅛ teaspoon ground cloves

⅛ teaspoon allspice

⅛ to ½ teaspoon ground hot pepper (to taste)

Salt and pepper, to taste

☾ THE NIGHT BEFORE: Mince the garlic. Cut along both sides of the mango pit to remove 2 cheeks. Using your knife, cut lengthwise into the mango just to the skin. Do the same across widthwise, so that you have a checkerboard. Take the piece in hand and open the crisscross section so it bows out. Now take your knife and run it under the flesh. The fruit will easily fall off into chunks. Repeat with the remaining mango cheek. Store in an airtight container in the fridge.

✳ IN THE MORNING: Oil the crock of your slow cooker and add all the ingredients. Cook on low for 7 to 9 hours. Taste and adjust the seasonings.

YIELD: 8 servings
EQUIPMENT: 4-quart slow cooker
COOKING TIME: 7 to 9 hours on low

CHANA SAAG *(Indian Greens with Chickpeas)*

You can use any combinations of greens here, such as spinach, Swiss chard, turnip greens, and collards, or anything that's plentiful where you live.

 GLUTEN-FREE   SOY-FREE   NO OIL ADDED OPTION*

2 tablespoons (30 ml) olive oil (*water sauté)

1 small onion, minced

2 cloves garlic, minced

1 tablespoon (8 g) grated fresh ginger

1 pound (454 g) assorted greens, washed, torn into bite-size pieces, and spun dry (you can also buy a prewashed mix in a bag)

Zest of ½ lime

1 teaspoon cumin powder

½ teaspoon turmeric

½ teaspoon ground coriander

½ teaspoon garam masala (or to taste)

1½ cups (353 ml) water

2 tablespoons (12 g) vegan chicken-flavored bouillon or 4 tablespoons (24 g) DIY Golden Bouillon (page 237)

BEFORE SERVING INGREDIENTS

1 can (15 ounces, or 420 g) chickpeas, drained and rinsed, or 1½ cups (340 g) homemade (page 230)

½ to 1 cup (120 to 235 ml) plain nondairy creamer or nondairy milk

Salt, to taste

SERVING INGREDIENTS

Rice

☾ THE NIGHT BEFORE: Heat the oil in a skillet over medium heat and sauté the onion until translucent, 3 to 5 minutes. Add the garlic and sauté for 2 minutes longer. Store the sautéed onion, grated ginger, and prepared greens in an airtight container in the refrigerator. Store the lime zest separately in the fridge.

☀ IN THE MORNING: Oil the crock of your slow cooker. Combine the sautéed onion, ginger, greens, spices, water, and bouillon in the slow cooker. Cook on low for 7 to 9 hours.

ABOUT 30 MINUTES BEFORE SERVING: Purée the soup with an immersion blender or in batches in a countertop blender, being careful of splatters of hot soup, until smooth. Add the chickpeas, nondairy creamer, lime zest, and salt to the slow cooker. Cook on high for 30 more minutes, until the beans are heated through. Taste and adjust the seasonings. Serve over rice.

YIELD: 6 servings
EQUIPMENT: 4-quart slow cooker
COOKING TIME: 7 to 9 hours on low

BAIGAN BHARTA *(Eggplant Curry)*

When eggplant cooks down, it gets an almost creamy consistency. Add extra chipotle chile powder to make it spicier, or use a different type of chili to omit the smokiness.

 GLUTEN-FREE   SOY-FREE   NO OIL ADDED OPTION*

2 tablespoons (30 ml) olive oil (*water sauté)

1 small onion, minced

2 cloves garlic, minced

2 teaspoons grated ginger

4½ cups (about 1 pound, or 454 g) chopped eggplant

1 cup (235 ml) water

Salt, to taste

½ teaspoon garam masala

1 teaspoon cumin

½ teaspoon turmeric

Pinch of chipotle chile powder

☾ THE NIGHT BEFORE: Heat the oil in a skillet over medium heat and sauté the onion until translucent, 3 to 5 minutes. Add the garlic and sauté for 2 minutes longer. Combine the sautéed onion, grated ginger, and cut-up eggplant in an airtight container and store in the fridge.

☀ IN THE MORNING: Combine all the ingredients in the slow cooker. Cook on low for 7 to 9 hours. Taste and adjust the seasonings.

YIELD: 6 servings
EQUIPMENT: 4-quart slow cooker
COOKING TIME: 7 to 9 hours on low

ANU'S BLACK-EYED PEA CURRY

My friend Anu is also a recipe developer at SimmertoSlimmer.com and an amazing Indian cook. I talked her into sharing one of her amazing recipes with us. I love the little bit of sweet-and-sour in with the subtly spiced black-eyed peas. I made a few minor changes to make the recipe work better in the slow cooker, but Anu is the genius behind all the wonderful flavors!

 GLUTEN-FREE SOY-FREE  NO OIL ADDED

1ST COOK INGREDIENTS

3 cups (705 ml) water

½ cup (64 g) minced onion

1½ cups (375 g) dry black-eyed peas

2 teaspoons (6 g) minced garlic

1½ teaspoons ground coriander

1½ teaspoons ground cumin

1 teaspoon grated ginger

¼ to 1 teaspoon chili powder such as cayenne, add more to make it spicier

BEFORE SERVING INGREDIENTS

¾ cup (150 g) crushed tomatoes

1 tablespoon grated jaggery, brown, or coconut sugar (weight will vary)

½ tablespoon (8 ml) lime juice

Salt, to taste

SERVING INGREDIENTS

Steamed rice or roti

¼ tablespoon dried methi leaves (optional)

¼ cup (4 g) chopped cilantro leaves

☾ THE NIGHT BEFORE: Cut the onion and store in the fridge. You can also go ahead and measure out the spices if you want.

☀ IN THE MORNING: Add the onion, black-eyed peas, garlic, coriander, cumin, ginger, and chili powder. Cook on low 7 to 9 hours.

30 MINUTES BEFORE SERVING: Stir in the crushed tomatoes, sugar, and lime juice. Add salt to taste. Cook on high for about 30 minutes or until the tomato sauce is hot.

Serve over steamed rice or with roti, and garnish with methi leaves (if using) and cilantro.

YIELD: 4 servings
EQUIPMENT: 4-quart slow cooker
COOKING TIME: 7 to 9 hours on low

EASY VEGGIE CHICKPEA BIRYANI

This is made differently than a traditional biryani. Here we cook the veggies in a stew, then sandwich the stew between layers of cooked rice, instead of cooking the stew between the rice layers in the oven. It has all of the flavor, and if you have a rice cooker you won't heat up the kitchen at all.

GLUTEN-FREE SOY-FREE NO OIL ADDED

2 tablespoons (30 ml) olive oil (*water sauté)

1 small onion, minced

1 bell pepper, diced

2 teaspoons grated ginger

½ teaspoon minced garlic

1 small sweet potato, diced

8 ounces (225 g) fresh or frozen cauliflower, broken into small florets

2 teaspoons (5 g) garam masala

1 teaspoon ground cumin

1 teaspoon ground turmeric

½ teaspoon ground cinnamon

½ teaspoon ground coriander

½ teaspoon ground cardamom

2 cups (470 ml) water

2 tablespoons (12 g) vegan chicken-flavored bouillon or 4 tablespoons (24 g) DIY Golden Bouillon (page 237)

1 can (15 ounces, or 420 g) chickpeas, drained and rinsed, or 1½ cups (340 g) homemade (page 230)

Salt, to taste

4 to 6 cups (660 to 990 g) cooked rice (cook with a pinch of saffron if you have some on hand)

☾ **THE NIGHT BEFORE:** Heat the oil in a skillet over medium heat and sauté the onion until translucent, 3 to 5 minutes.

Add the bell pepper and cook for 2 minutes longer.

Store the sautéed vegetables, the grated ginger, minced garlic, and the cut-up sweet potato and cauliflower together in a large airtight container in the refrigerator.

✴ **IN THE MORNING:** Oil the crock of your slow cooker. Combine the sautéed vegetables, ginger, sweet potato, cauliflower, spices, water, bouillon, chickpeas, and salt in the slow cooker.

Cook on low for 7 to 9 hours.

BEFORE SERVING: Taste and adjust the seasonings before serving. Spread half of the cooked rice on a platter, cover with veggie chickpea stew, and top with the rest of the rice.

YIELD: 6 servings
EQUIPMENT: 6-quart slow cooker
COOKING TIME: 7 to 9 hours on low

CHICKPEA CACCIATORE *with* POTATOES

Here's a completely plant-based one-pot meal that will satisfy the hungriest at your table. The potatoes and chickpeas are filling and full of nutrients. The sauce and the rest of the veggies make a sauce that packs a flavor punch.

 GLUTEN-FREE SOY-FREE  NO OIL ADDED

1 bag (24 ounces, or 680 g) baby potatoes, quartered

2 cans (15 ounces, or 425 g each) chickpeas, drained (save liquid to use as aquafaba in other recipes)

1 pound (504 g) mushrooms, sliced (can use all white, baby bella, or a combo)

2 cups (300 g) chopped bell pepper (use multiple colors if you can)

3 carrots, cut into coins

SAUCE INGREDIENTS

1 can (28 ounces, or 784 g) crushed tomatoes

¼ cup (60 ml) red wine (or 2 tablespoons [30 ml] balsamic vinegar)

1 teaspoon minced garlic

1 teaspoon dried marjoram

1 teaspoon dried basil

½ teaspoon salt

¼ teaspoon ground rosemary

SERVING INGREDIENTS

½ cup (50 g) pitted black olives (optional)

☾ THE NIGHT BEFORE: Cut up the veggies. Add veggies and drained chickpeas to a sealable container, and mix. You can mix all the sauce ingredients together now, or wait until morning. Store everything in the fridge.

☀ IN THE MORNING: Mix the sauce and veggie-chickpea mixture together in your slow cooker. Cook on low 7 to 9 hours.

Garnish with pitted black olives, if desired.

YIELD: 6 servings
EQUIPMENT: 5- to 6-quart slow cooker
COOKING TIME: 7 to 9 hours on low

DIANNE'S CANNELLINI BEAN RATATOUILLE

Dianne's Cannellini Bean Ratatouille is a set-it-and-forget-it meal that's filled to the brim with veggies. Dianne is the blogger behind diannesvegankitchen.com. Be sure to visit her site for more vegan recipes.

 GLUTEN-FREE SOY-FREE NO OIL ADDED

1 medium-size eggplant, diced

1 summer squash, sliced

1 zucchini, sliced

1 red bell pepper, diced

1 small red onion, diced

3 cloves of garlic, minced

1½ cup cooked cannellini beans, or 1 can (14 ounces, or 392 g)

1 can (28 ounces, or 784 g) diced tomatoes in their juices

½ cup (120 ml) vegetable broth

1 tablespoon (7 g) herbes de Provence (or 1 teaspoon each of dried thyme, rosemary, and basil)

BEFORE SERVING INGREDIENTS

Sea salt and pepper, to taste

☾ **THE NIGHT BEFORE:** Cut up all the fresh vegetables and place in a container with a lid in the fridge.

☀ **IN THE MORNING:** Add everything but salt and pepper to your slow cooker. Cook on low for 7 to 9 hours.

BEFORE SERVING: Add salt and pepper to taste. Taste and adjust the seasonings. Serve and enjoy!

YIELD: 4 servings
EQUIPMENT: 4-quart slow cooker
COOKING TIME: 7 to 9 hours on low

CHAPTER 5

Casseroles & Loaves

Casseroles are a staple at my house. I love a good one-dish meal that I can whip up in a few minutes. Some of these recipes work for an away-from-home day, and others cook in about 2 hours and fit better in a weekend lunch or dinner menu.

When the weather gets cooler and daylight saving time makes me miss my evening sunshine, I need all the comfort I can get. Although I was never much of a fan of meatloaf growing up, my thirty-five years of living meatless has given me a love of veggie loaves.

They're a good excuse to make mashed potatoes, and the leftovers are great in sandwiches. You can make a loaf right in the slow cooker crock, or you can use a loaf pan that fits into your slow cooker. It will take a little longer in the loaf pan because the end product will be thicker. I have lids for mine though, so it makes it easy to store the leftovers.

Stews that are topped with biscuits or include dumplings are perfect workday dinners because they start their lives as stews and you add the quick-cooking parts right before you are ready to eat.

SOY CURLS *and* DUMPLINGS

It takes a little effort to make the dumplings, but it's well worth it. Gluten and soy intolerant? Try using a can of chickpeas instead. Make it gluten-free by using a gluten-free baking mix instead of flour.

 GLUTEN-FREE OPTION*   SOY-FREE OPTION**   NO OIL ADDED

STEW INGREDIENTS

2 cups (111 g) dry soy curls reconstituted with 2 cups boiling water (** use 2 cups cooked chickpeas or chopped seitan)

6 medium (252 g) carrots cut into coins

2 large stalks celery, minced

4 cups (940 ml) vegan chicken broth (or 4 tablespoons bouillon in 4 cups water or ¼ cup [24 g] nutritional yeast)

1 bay leaf

1 tablespoon dried thyme

1 sprig rosemary or ¼ teaspoon ground rosemary

Salt and pepper, to taste

DUMPLING INGREDIENTS

2 cups (500 g) white or whole-wheat flour (* or use gluten-free baking mix)

1 teaspoon salt (optional)

1 teaspoon dried thyme

¼ teaspoon baking powder

¼ teaspoon black pepper

1 cup (375 ml) plain or unsweetened nondairy milk of choice

☾ **THE NIGHT BEFORE:** Chop veggies and store in the fridge. Reconstitute the soy curls (if using) by pouring the boiling water over the soy curls. Let them soak for about 10 minutes and drain. Store in the fridge

☀ **IN THE MORNING:** Oil the crock. Add all of the stew ingredients to the slow cooker. Add more water if you will cook it over 8 hours, or if your slow cooker runs a little hot. Cook on low for 6 to 10 hours.

30 TO 40 MINUTES BEFORE SERVING: Make dumplings by mixing flour, salt, thyme, baking powder, pepper, and milk in bowl. Turn mixture out on a floured cutting board and roll thin (about the thickness of a thick pie crust). Cut into rectangles, approximately ½ inch by 1 inch (1.3 by 2.5 cm) or to your favorite size. Place the dumplings in the slow cooker, and stir to incorporate the dumplings. Turn the slow cooker to high, and cook 30 minutes more.

The mixture will thicken up as it cooks. Add more broth if needed. Adjust seasonings to taste.

YIELD: 4 servings
EQUIPMENT: 4-quart slow cooker
COOKING TIME: 6 to 10 hours on low

FROM-THE-PANTRY POT PIE

This recipe is a great way to use up what you have on hand. You can also incorporate leftover veggies, sausage, or beans.

 GLUTEN-FREE OPTION* SOY-FREE OPTION ** NO OIL ADDED OPTION***

STEW INGREDIENTS

1 small onion, minced (optional)

2 cloves garlic, minced (optional)

1 large stalk celery, minced (optional)

1½ cups (340 g) **cubed chicken-flavored seitan, store-bought or homemade (page 238), crumbled cooked sausage, *diced tofu, beans, or diced potato

1 pound (454 g) frozen mixed green beans, corn, carrots, and peas (you can use fresh or leftovers instead)

1 cup (235 ml) water, plus more if needed

2 tablespoons (12 g) vegan chicken-flavored bouillon or 4 tablespoons (24 g) DIY Golden Bouillon (page 237)

1 teaspoon dried thyme

Salt and pepper, to taste

2 tablespoons (16 g) flour, if needed

BISCUIT INGREDIENTS

1 cup (120 g) white, whole-wheat, or *gluten-free flour

½ teaspoon salt

½ teaspoon thyme (optional)

1½ teaspoons baking powder

3 tablespoons (45 ml) olive oil ***sub mashed avocado

½ cup (120 ml) plain or unsweetened nondairy milk

☾ THE NIGHT BEFORE: To make the stew: Place the cut-up onion, garlic, celery, and seitan in a large airtight container and store in the refrigerator.

✳ IN THE MORNING: Oil the crock of your slow cooker. Combine all of the ingredients except the flour in the slow cooker. Add 1 to 2 cups (235 to 470 ml) extra water if you will cook it longer than 8 hours, or if your slow cooker runs a little hot. Cook on low for 7 to 9 hours.

ABOUT 30 MINUTES BEFORE SERVING: Add more water if the mixture is too thick, or add the flour if the stew needs to thicken up a bit. Taste and adjust the seasonings.

TO MAKE THE BISCUITS: Combine all the biscuit ingredients in a bowl and work until it comes together into a dough. Turn the mixture out onto a floured cutting board, roll out about ½ inch (1.3 cm) thick, and cut into circles with the rim of a glass. Place in the slow cooker on top of the filling. Turn up the slow cooker to high. Prop open the lid with the handle of a wooden spoon, or place a clean dish towel under the lid to prevent condensation from dripping onto your biscuits. Cook an additional 30 minutes.

YIELD: 4–6 servings

EQUIPMENT: 4-quart slow cooker

COOKING TIME: 7 to 9 hours on low, plus 30 minutes to cook the biscuits

JULIE'S LOADED ENCHILADA CASSEROLE

This is a super-delicious casserole, perfect for game day or a weeknight dinner. If you have a high-powered blender, you won't need to soak the cashews. This casserole has the Cheryl picky eater seal of approval, and it is created by Julie Hasson of juliehasson.com.

 GLUTEN-FREE SOY-FREE ⬡ NO OIL ADDED OPTION*

NACHO SAUCE INGREDIENTS

1½ (355 ml) cups water

½ cup (73 g) raw, unsalted cashews, soaked for several hours

⅓ cup (16 g) nutritional yeast

3 tablespoons (21 g) tapioca starch

1½ teaspoons smoked paprika

1¼ teaspoons sea salt

1 teaspoon granulated onion

1 teaspoon ground cumin

1 canned chipotle in adobo (optional for spiciness; you can freeze the rest of the can)

CASSEROLE INGREDIENTS

1 can (28 ounces, or 784 g) enchilada sauce (mild or spicy for your taste)

14 (6-inch, or 15 cm) corn tortillas

3 cups cooked pinto beans or 2 cans (15 ounces, or 420 g each), rinsed and drained

2 cans (10 ounces, or 280 g each) chopped green roasted chiles, drained

1½ cups (192 g) frozen, thawed corn

1 bag (10 ounces, 280 g) of vegan crumbles (or 2 cups riced cauliflower tossed in)

☾ THE NIGHT BEFORE: Make the nacho sauce. Combine water, cashews, nutritional yeast, tapioca starch, smoked paprika, salt, granulated onion, cumin, and chipotle pepper (if using) in your blender. Blend until the sauce is super smooth. The sauce will be thin, but it will thicken during cooking. Store in the fridge.

If using the cauliflower, you can also rice the cauliflower by pulsing in a food processor until it's small like rice or couscous. Store in the fridge overnight.

☀ IN THE MORNING: Either oil your crock* or line it with parchment paper to keep it oil-free. Add one-third of the enchilada sauce to the bottom.

Cover the sauce with a single layer of corn tortillas. Next add half of the beans, chiles, corn, crumbles or cauliflower. Then follow with another third of the nacho sauce and enchilada sauce. Add a single layer of tortillas.

Next add the last half of the beans, chiles, corn, crumbles or cauliflower. Then follow with another layer of tortillas and the last third of the nacho sauce and enchilada sauce.

Cover with a clean dish towel between the lid and the crock. Cook on low for 3 to 4 hours or high for 2 to 3 hours, or until hot and bubbly and the tortillas are tender when pierced.

Serve with bowls of your favorites from the serving ingredients.

SERVING INGREDIENTS

Sliced scallions

Chopped cilantro

Sliced black olives

Pickled jalapeño slices

Cashew cream

Salsa

Guacamole

YIELD: 6 servings

EQUIPMENT: 6-quart slow cooker

COOKING TIME: 3 to 4 hours on low or 2 to 3 hours on high

ITALIAN EGGPLANT CASSEROLE *with* CASHEW-TOFU RICOTTA

This is my healthy substitute for eggplant parmigiana. Not frying the eggplant saves time and calories, and both of those can be at a premium. It's very saucy and perfect over pasta. Meatless Sausage and Mushroom Ragu (page 100) and Make-Your-Own Marinara Sauce (page 99) are both great sauces to use with this dish.

 GLUTEN-FREE* NO OIL ADDED OPTION**

CASHEW-TOFU RICOTTA INGREDIENTS

½ cup (68 g) cashews

½ cup (48 g) nutritional yeast

3 cloves garlic

1 package (15 ounces, or 420 g) firm tofu

½ cup (120 ml) unsweetened nondairy milk

½ to 1 teaspoon salt (to taste)

Pepper, to taste

1 large eggplant, thinly sliced

1 jar (25 ounces, or 700 g) marinara sauce, store- bought or homemade (page 99)

SERVING INGREDIENTS

Cooked pasta (*use gluten-free pasta)

☾ THE NIGHT BEFORE: To make the ricotta: In a food processor or blender, combine all the ricotta ingredients. Blend until smooth and creamy. Store the ricotta and the sliced eggplant in separate containers in the fridge.

☀ IN THE MORNING: Oil the crock of your slow cooker **or line with parchment paper and pour in one-third of the marinara sauce. Top with half of the eggplant, half of the ricotta, and another one-third of the sauce. Repeat the layers once more, then top with the remaining sauce. Cook on low for 7 to 9 hours. Serve over the pasta.

YIELD: 8 servings
EQUIPMENT: 6-quart slow cooker
COOKING TIME: 7 to 9 hours on low

A Worthy Note

If your slow cooker does not run hot and the final product is too watery, prop up the lid on the handle of a wooden spoon and turn the slow cooker to high. In 30 minutes to 1 hour most of the water will evaporate.

Better-Than-the-Classic SHEPHERD'S PIE

In this recipe, we add some celery root and cauliflower to the usual potato mash.

 GLUTEN-FREE OPTION* SOY-FREE OPTION ** NO OIL ADDED OPTION***

1 package (8 ounces, or 225 g) *tempeh, cut into chunks (or use minced **seitan from page 238)

2 tablespoons (30 ml) olive oil

1 small onion, minced

2 cloves garlic, minced

1½ cups (165 g) sausage crumbles or **Apple Sage Sausage (page 240), or chopped *seitan (page 238)

½ small head of cauliflower

1 small celery root, peeled, roots trimmed, and cut into chunks

2 medium-size potatoes, peeled and cut into chunks

1 tablespoon (6 g) vegan chicken-flavored bouillon or 2 tablespoons (12 g) DIY Golden Bouillon (page 237)

1 to 1½ cups (235 to 355 ml) water

1 teaspoon Cajun seasoning

Salt and pepper, to taste

BEFORE SERVING INGREDIENTS

2 to 4 tablespoons (28 to 56 g) nondairy butter

½ to 1 cup (120 to 235 ml) plain nondairy milk (unsweetened, if possible)

YIELD: 6 servings
EQUIPMENT: 4-quart slow cooker
COOKING TIME: 7 to 9 hours on low

☾ THE NIGHT BEFORE: Steam the tempeh in a steamer basket for 10 minutes. This takes out some of the bitterness. Heat the oil in a skillet over medium heat and sauté the onion until translucent, 3 to 5 minutes. Add the garlic and sauté for 1 minute longer. Add the steamed tempeh and break into crumbles with a spatula.

If you are using a sausage that needs to be precooked (that's not already in crumbles), add it now and cook until done, 10 to 12 minutes. Cut up cauliflower, potatoes, and celery root. Store the tempeh mixture and the cut-up parsnips, celery root, and potatoes in a large airtight container in the refrigerator.

☀ IN THE MORNING: Oil the crock of your slow cooker ***or line with parchment paper. Combine the tempeh mixture, sausage, bouillon, 1 cup (235 ml) water, Cajun seasoning, and salt and pepper in the slow cooker. (If your slow cooker runs hot or you will be gone longer than 8 hours, add the extra ½ cup [120 ml] water.) Top with a piece of parchment paper or aluminum foil and place parsnips, celery root, and potatoes on top of it, so that they are separated from the stew. Cook on low for 7 to 9 hours.

ABOUT 30 MINUTES BEFORE SERVING: Carefully remove the cauliflower, celery root, and potatoes using tongs, and place in a large mixing bowl. Add the butter to taste and ½ cup (120 ml) milk, and mash or purée. Add the remaining ½ cup (120 ml) milk if the mixture is too dry. Season with salt and pepper to taste.

Stir the stew in the slow cooker, then top with the mashed vegetable mixture. Turn up the slow cooker to high and cook until the potato mixture is piping hot, 20 to 40 minutes.

ATOMIC PECAN LOAF

This loaf was inspired by Vegan Lunch Box's Magical Loaf Studio website. I combined about four recipes and added a few things on top of that. You can add almost anything you have on hand, so it's a great way to use up leftovers!

 GLUTEN-FREE OPTION* SOY-FREE ⬡ NO OIL ADDED OPTION**

LOAF INGREDIENTS

1 can (15 ounces, or 425 g) kidney beans, drained but reserve the liquid

1 cup (110 g) rolled oats, pulsed into (*use gluten-free)

½ cup (55 g) pecans

¼ cup (60 ml) liquid from kidney beans (or aquafaba)

1 medium portobello mushrooms with gills removed, minced

2 tablespoons (6 g) nutritional yeast

2 tablespoons (32 g) tomato paste

1 tablespoon (15 ml) vegan Worcestershire sauce

1 teaspoon onion powder

1 teaspoon salt

1 teaspoon thyme

1 teaspoon marjoram

½ teaspoon smoked paprika

½ teaspoon garlic powder

¼ teaspoon ground rosemary

TOPPING INGREDIENTS

½ cup (120 g) ketchup

3 tablespoons (45 g) brown sugar

1 tablespoon (15 ml) balsamic vinegar

1 tablespoon (15 ml) vegan Worcestershire sauce

☾ THE NIGHT BEFORE: Mix all the loaf ingredients together, and store in the fridge until the morning. Also mix together the ingredients for the topping, and store in a separate container in the fridge.

☀ IN THE MORNING: Oil the crock of your slow cooker **or line with parchment paper. Pat the loaf mixture into the slow cooker. Cook on low for 7 to 9 hours.

ABOUT 30 TO 45 MINUTES BEFORE SERVING: Spread the ketchup mixture over the top of the loaf.

YIELD: 6 servings
EQUIPMENT: 4-quart slow cooker
COOKING TIME: 7 to 9 hours on high

HOLIDAY TEMPEH *and* SAGE LOAF

This loaf reminds me a little of Thanksgiving, and in fact I may just serve it as my main course this year. Leftovers make great sandwiches with cranberry sauce.

 GLUTEN-FREE OPTION*　　 NO OIL ADDED OPTION**

1 packages (8 ounces, or 225 g) tempeh (*use plain soy tempeh), cubed

1 small onion

2 cloves garlic

2 stalks celery

1 medium-size carrot

1 cup (70 g) sliced mushrooms

2 tablespoons (30 ml) olive oil (**water sauté)

1 cup (115 g) whole-wheat bread crumbs (*use gluten-free bread crumbs)

2 tablespoons (14 g) ground flaxseed mixed with 2 tablespoons (30 ml) warm water

2 tablespoons (12 g) vegan chicken-flavored bouillon or 4 tablespoons (24 g) DIY Golden Bouillon (page 237)

1 teaspoon thyme

1 teaspoon rubbed sage

½ teaspoon oregano

½ teaspoon dried rosemary or ¼ teaspoon ground

½ teaspoon salt

☾ THE NIGHT BEFORE: Steam the tempeh in a steamer basket for 10 minutes. This takes out some of the bitterness. While the tempeh is cooking, use a food processor to mince the onion, garlic, celery, carrot, and mushrooms. Pulse until you have tiny pieces of veggies, but not so much that it liquefies.

Heat the oil in a skillet over medium heat and sauté the veggies until the onion is translucent, about 3 minutes. Crumble the cooked tempeh into a large bowl, then add the sautéed veggies, bread crumbs, flaxseed mixture, bouillon, thyme, sage, oregano, rosemary, and salt. Store in an airtight container in the refrigerator.

✳ IN THE MORNING: Oil the crock of your slow cooker. Pat the loaf mixture into the slow cooker. Cook on low for 7 to 9 hours. Prop open the lid with a wooden spoon handle or put a clean dish towel underneath the lid to prevent the condensation from dripping onto the loaf during cooking.

YIELD: 6 servings
EQUIPMENT: 4-quart slow cooker
COOKING TIME: 7 to 9 hours on low

CHICK'N *and* MUSHROOM CASSEROLE

This is a comforting retro casserole that you'll wish you had when you were growing up. The creamy cashew sour cream adds richness to the mushroom sauce, while the pasta and seitan make it hearty and filling.

 GLUTEN-FREE OPTION*   SOY-FREE OPTION **   NO OIL ADDED OPTION***

FOR THE CASHEW SOUR CREAM:

½ cup (73 g) cashews

½ cup (120 ml) water

2 teaspoons lemon juice

2 tablespoons (30 ml) olive oil (***water sauté)

1 small onion, minced

2 cloves garlic, minced

1 package (10 ounces, or 280 g) sliced mushrooms

1 tablespoon (6 g) vegan chicken-flavored bouillon or 2 tablespoons (12 g) DIY Golden Bouillon (page 237)

4 cups (940 ml) plain nondairy milk (unsweetened, if possible)

1½ cups (340 g) **cubed chicken-flavored seitan, store-bought or homemade (page 238) (*or reconstituted soy curls)

8 ounces (225 g) dried whole-wheat pasta shells or rotini (*or gluten-free pasta)

½ teaspoon dried thyme

½ teaspoon dried marjoram

Salt and pepper, to taste

2 tablespoons (16 g) flour, if needed

SERVING INGREDIENTS

Bread crumbs, for topping

☾ THE NIGHT BEFORE: To make the cashew sour cream: In a food processor or blender combine the cashews, water, and lemon juice and process until smooth and creamy.

Heat the oil in a skillet over medium heat and sauté the onion until translucent, 3 to 5 minutes. Add the garlic and mushrooms and sauté until the mushrooms reduce in size and are tender, 5 to 10 minutes. Store the sautéed vegetables and the prepared sour cream in separate airtight containers in the fridge.

✳ IN THE MORNING: About 1½ hours before serving: Oil the crock of your slow cooker. Combine the sautéed veggies, cashew sour cream, bouillon, milk, seitan, pasta, thyme, marjoram, and salt and pepper in the slow cooker. Mix thoroughly and cook on high for 1 to 1½ hours, or until the pasta is al dente.

If the pasta is ready but the sauce is not thick enough, add the flour and stir to combine. This should thicken up the mix. Top each serving with the bread crumbs.

YIELD: 4 servings
EQUIPMENT: 4-quart slow cooker
COOKING TIME: 1 to 1½ hours on high

CHAPTER 6

Pasta & Grains

Pasta and grains are the staples of any diet, but they seem to play an even bigger part in the life of a vegan. In this chapter you'll get a few pasta sauces, too. Sauces are another great addition to a weekend cooking rotation. They freeze well and can be used in other recipes.

Pasta can be dressed up in lasagna, which is a perfect dish for introducing non-vegans to vegan food. And people who say they can't be a vegan because they'll miss cheese too much can be introduced to vegan cheesy options in the Mac and Cheese (page 105).

You'll see in the staples chapter that you can make plain rice in the slow cooker, and it's in this chapter that you can really appreciate it. Jambalaya is my favorite dish to bring to a potluck. You cook everything but the rice all day, then add the rice an hour before you want to eat. Quinoa is a perfect grain to cook in the slow cooker as well, and if you haven't tried it before, Spanish Quinoa (page 143) will introduce you to this nutritious and versatile grain.

With all the grain dishes and non-lasagna pastas you will need to stir more frequently, which helps the dish cook more evenly, plus it just feels good to break the old don't-lift-your-slow-cooker-lid rule.

Make-Your-Own MARINARA SAUCE

Sooner or later you'll find yourself wishing you had some marinara sauce on hand. Why not make a big pot of it now and freeze some for later? You can add your favorite veggies, vegan wine, or sun-dried tomatoes and make it just the way you like it.

 GLUTEN-FREE   SOY-FREE ◯ NO OIL ADDED OPTION*

1 teaspoon olive oil (*omit to make it no oil added)

1 large onion, minced

3 cloves garlic, minced

2 cans (28 ounces, or 784 g each) crushed or diced tomatoes or 6 cups (1360 g) Preserve-the-Harvest Diced Tomatoes (page 241)

1 tablespoon (15 ml) agave nectar or (13 g) sugar

1 teaspoon dried basil

1 teaspoon dried oregano

½ teaspoon dried thyme

¼ teaspoon dried rosemary

Salt and pepper, to taste

☾ THE NIGHT BEFORE: Heat the oil (*or water sauté for no oil added) in a skillet over medium heat and sauté the onion until translucent, 3 to 5 minutes. Add the garlic and sauté for 2 minutes longer. Store in an airtight container in the refrigerator.

☀ IN THE MORNING: Combine all the ingredients in your slow cooker (*or line with parchment to make it oil-free). Be sure to adjust the salt if you are using canned tomatoes, because they may already contain salt. Cook on low for 7 to 9 hours.

ABOUT 10 TO 15 MINUTES BEFORE SERVING: Add water if needed. Taste and adjust the seasonings.

Freeze the extra in ice cube trays, resealable plastic bags, or freezer containers.

YIELD: 8 servings
EQUIPMENT: 4-quart slow cooker
COOKING TIME: 7 to 9 hours on low

MEATLESS SAUSAGE *and* MUSHROOM RAGU

This is definitely not the ragu from your supermarket shelves! It's a great way to transition hard-core meat eaters to a meatless meal and makes the perfect topping for grilled polenta. You can just buy a premade tube of polenta and slice it, then crisp it in the oven or on a grill.

SOY-FREE OPTION*   NO OIL ADDED OPTION**

1 teaspoon olive oil (**water sauté)

1 medium-size onion, minced

3 cloves garlic, minced

1 package (14 ounces, or 392 g) vegan Italian sausage, store-bought or *homemade (page 239), sliced into rounds

2 cans (28 ounces, or 784 g each) crushed tomatoes

1 pound (454 g) crimini or button mushrooms, chopped

2 large portobello mushrooms, chopped

Freshly ground black pepper, to taste

1 tablespoon (15 ml) balsamic vinegar

2 to 3 tablespoons (30 to 45 ml) red or port wine

BEFORE SERVING INGREDIENTS

2 tablespoons (5 g) chopped fresh basil

☾ THE NIGHT BEFORE: Heat the oil in a skillet (**or line with parchment to make it oil-free) over medium heat and sauté the onion until translucent, 3 to 5 minutes. Add the garlic and sauté for 1 minute longer. Transfer to a large airtight container.

In the same skillet that you cooked the onions, cook the sausage until brown, 5 to 10 minutes. Break the patties apart with the spatula to make crumbles. Transfer to the same bowl as the onions and store in the fridge.

☀ IN THE MORNING: Combine the sautéed onion, sausage, tomatoes, mushrooms, pepper, vinegar, and wine in the slow cooker. Cook on low for 7 to 9 hours. About 10 minutes before serving, add water if needed, extra seasoning, and the basil.

YIELD: 12 servings

EQUIPMENT: 4-quart slow cooker

COOKING TIME: 7 to 9 hours on low

PUMPKIN WHITE BEAN LASAGNA

This is a perfect dish for introducing nonvegans to vegan food and is much healthier than the traditional, fat-laden lasagna. It's easy to make and hearty. Add a nice spinach salad with a balsamic vinaigrette, and you're all ready to have friends over for dinner.

 NO OIL ADDED OPTION*

PUMPKIN-TOFU RICOTTA INGREDIENTS

1 tablespoon (15 ml) olive oil *use aquafaba

3 sun-dried tomatoes, rehydrated (pour boiling water over them and let them sit for 5 minutes)

1 package (15 ounces, or 420 g) silken, soft, or firm tofu

1 can (15 ounces, or 420 g) cooked pumpkin or 1½ cups (368 g) pureéd cooked fresh

¼ cup (24 g) nutritional yeast

1 tablespoon (3 g) Italian seasoning

1 teaspoon onion powder

2 cloves garlic, crushed

Salt and pepper, to taste

LASAGNA INGREDIENTS

1 jar (24 ounces, or 672 g) marinara sauce, store-bought or homemade (page 99)

About ¾ package (10 ounces, or 280 g) whole-wheat lasagne noodles (the regular kind, not the no-boil noodles)

1 can (14½ ounces, or 406 g) white beans, drained and rinsed, or 1½ cups (340 g) homemade (page 230)

☾ THE NIGHT BEFORE: To make the pumpkin-tofu ricotta: In a food processor, blend the olive oil and the rehydrated sun-dried tomatoes until a paste forms. There may still be some lumps. Add the remaining ricotta ingredients and blend until creamy. Add a little water if the mixture is too thick. Taste and adjust the seasonings. Store in an airtight container in the fridge.

✳ IN THE MORNING: To make the lasagna: Spray the crock with olive oil so you won't have a nightmare cleanup on your hands later on.

Spread a thin layer of sauce over the bottom of the slow cooker. Break off the corners on one side of each noodle so they fit snugly. You can add the corners in as well.

Place a single layer of noodles over the sauce. Spread one-third of the ricotta mixture over the noodles. Spread another thin layer of sauce over the ricotta and sprinkle one-third of the white beans on top of that. Repeat the layers two more times, ending with a last layer of lasagne noodles, and then top that with more sauce.

Cook on low for 3 to 4 hours or on high for 1½ to 2 hours, until a fork will easily go through the middle and the pasta is al dente. Add ½ cup (120 ml) extra sauce or water if you need to leave it an hour or two longer.

YIELD: 6 servings
EQUIPMENT: 4-quart slow cooker
COOKING TIME: 3 to 4 hours on low or 1½ to 2 hours on high

MIX-AND-MATCH JAMBALAYA

Vegans and meat eaters alike love jambalaya. It's an easy dish to make for a dinner party, and it's filling to boot. I like to use Italian sausage and chicken-flavored seitan as proteins, but you can use tempeh, tofu, or even red beans as the center attraction if you want. I usually use white jasmine rice, but any rice will work. Brown rice will require a little more cooking time, but it adds tons of nutrients.

  GLUTEN-FREE OPTION* NO OIL ADDED OPTION**

1 tablespoon (15 ml) olive oil (** water sauté)

1 medium-size onion, minced

2 cloves garlic, minced

2 or 3 large vegan Italian sausage links, cut into half-moons, or steamed tempeh cubes (*use gluten-free)

1 to 2 cups (225 to 450 g) cubed chicken-flavored seitan, store-bought or homemade (page 238), or cubed firm tofu (*gluten-free option) marinated in 2 tablespoons (12 g) vegan chicken-flavored bouillon, or 4 tablespoons (24 g) DIY Golden Bouillon (page 237) and 1 cup (235 ml) water

1 green bell pepper, cored and chopped

1 red or orange bell pepper, cored and chopped

1 can (14½ ounces, or 406 g) diced tomatoes or 1½ cups (340 g) Preserve-the-Harvest Diced Tomatoes (page 241)

1 teaspoon to 1 tablespoon hot pepper sauce (to taste)

2 teaspoons Cajun seasoning

½ teaspoon liquid smoke or smoked paprika

☾ THE NIGHT BEFORE: Heat the oil in a skillet over medium heat and sauté the onion until translucent, 3 to 5 minutes. Add the garlic and sauté for 1 minute longer. Combine the sautéed onion and cut-up sausage, tofu, and bell peppers in a large airtight container and store in the refrigerator.

☀ IN THE MORNING: Combine the sautéed onion, sausage, seitan or tofu, bell peppers, tomatoes, hot sauce, Cajun seasoning, paprika, red pepper flakes, water, bouillon, and salt and pepper in the slow cooker. Cook on low for 7 to 9 hours.

1 HOUR BEFORE SERVING: Add the rice. If the mixture looks dry, add 1 to 2 cups (235 to 470 ml) extra water. Turn up the slow cooker to high and cook for 45 minutes to 1 hour longer. Check occasionally to make sure it doesn't overcook. Taste and adjust the seasonings.

YIELD: 8 servings
EQUIPMENT: 4-quart slow cooker
COOKING TIME: for 7 to 9 hours on low

¼ to 1 teaspoon red pepper flakes or chipotle chile powder (to taste)

3 cups (705 ml) water, plus more as needed

2 tablespoons (12 g) vegan chicken-flavored bouillon or 4 tablespoons (24 g) DIY Golden Bouillon (page 237)

Salt and pepper, to taste

BEFORE SERVING INGREDIENTS

1½ cups (293 g) uncooked rice

CREAMY BUTTERNUT SQUASH RISOTTO

Butternut squash makes the perfect fall risotto. I like to use a combination of herbs in this dish, but you can always just use one if you'd prefer. You can switch out any winter squash for the butternut depending on what you happen to have on hand.

 GLUTEN-FREE SOY-FREE  NO OIL ADDED

2½ cups (588 ml) water

1½ cups (280 g) arborio rice

1 can (15 ounces, or 420 g) cooked butternut squash or 1½ cups (368) puréed cooked fresh or 1½ cups small dice fresh butternut squash

½ cup (48 g) nutritional yeast

1 teaspoon thyme

½ teaspoon rubbed sage

½ teaspoon ground rosemary

½ teaspoon granulated garlic

½ teaspoon onion

Salt and pepper, to taste

✴ IN THE MORNING: Add the water, rice, squash, nutritional yeast, thyme, sage, rosemary, garlic and onion to the slow cooker. Cook on high for 1½ to 2½ hours, until the rice is cooked through but still al dente.

Stir every 20 to 30 minutes, adding extra water if needed. Season with salt and pepper and taste and adjust the herbs as needed.

YIELD: 6 servings
EQUIPMENT: 4-quart slow cooker
COOKING TIME: 1½ to 2½ hours on high

EXTRA CREAMY MAC *and* CHEESE

This is the comfort food you've been looking for! And if you are gluten-free, soy-free, and oil-free, you're in luck. You can use gluten-free pasta. There's no soy naturally. And, if you make the Easy DIY Meltable Vegan Cheese on page 243, it will melt and have no oil added. Try serving this creamy mac and cheese as a side for the Atomic Pecan Loaf on page 95.

 GLUTEN-FREE OPTION* SOY-FREE  NO OIL ADDED OPTION**

4 cups (940 ml) nondairy milk

8 ounces (225 g) dried whole-wheat macaroni (*use brown rice pasta)

2 cups (230 g) shredded vegan cheddar cheese (store-bought or **homemade on page 243)

2 tablespoons (6 g) nutritional yeast

½ teaspoon liquid smoke (optional)

1 teaspoon salt or to taste

Pepper, to taste

You can oil the crock first, or just plan on soaking the pan overnight after you make it. Toss all the ingredients into your 4-quart slow cooker, and stir to combine.

Cook on high for 1 to 1½ hours, or until the pasta is al dente.

You will get the best results if you stir the mixture every 30 minutes. If you don't use whole-wheat pasta it will cook faster, so check it around 45 minutes instead of 1½ hours.

It's important to check this one frequently or you will end up with mushy pasta. And there's only a minute or two between ready-to-eat and mushy.

NOTE: If you hate checking on the pasta, you can just cook the sauce in the slow cooker and add already cooked pasta before serving. Just cut the amount of nondairy milk down to 2 cups (475 ml).

YIELD: 4 servings
EQUIPMENT: 4-quart slow cooker
COOKING TIME: 1½ to 2½ hours on high

SHIITAKE CONGEE *(Rice Porridge)*

The base for the congee gets most of its flavor from the mushrooms, but it's actually a plain congee that's dressed up by the toppings that you choose. This is a great get-well-fast soup and is gentle on your stomach. I like mine with soy sauce, sesame oil, and cilantro.

 GLUTEN-FREE   SOY-FREE OPTION   NO OIL ADDED

CONGEE INGREDIENTS

8 cups (1880 ml) water or broth

4 cups (280 g) thinly sliced fresh shiitake mushrooms

4 cups (280 g) thinly sliced button, baby bella, shiitake mushrooms or combination

1 cup (185 g) brown rice (I used long grain)

3 tablespoons (24 g) grated ginger

SERVING INGREDIENTS (OPTIONAL)

Soy sauce

Scallions

Cilantro

Chopped hot peppers

Extra grated ginger

Leftover cooked veggies

Tofu cubes

☾ THE NIGHT BEFORE: Prepare the mushrooms and ginger, and store in the fridge.

☀ IN THE MORNING: Add the water, mushrooms, rice, and ginger to your slow cooker. Cook on low for 7 to 9 hours.

To serve, place your chosen toppings on the table and let everyone make it their favorite way.

YIELD: 4–6 servings
EQUIPMENT: 4-quart slow cooker
COOKING TIME: for 7 to 9 hours on low

SPAGHETTI SQUASH *with* BALSAMIC TOMATO SAUCE

I am about to blow your mind! In this recipe instead of cooking the squash whole, then scraping out the flesh, we are going to peel out spaghetti squash and remove the seeds after cutting it into rounds. Why? When you're ready for dinner you just press on them with a spoon, and they turn into long strands of veggie pasta.

 GLUTEN-FREE   SOY-FREE   NO OIL ADDED

1 medium spaghetti squash

SAUCE INGREDIENTS

1 can (28 ounces, or 784 g) crushed tomatoes (can be plain or with basil)

2 teaspoons (10 ml) balsamic vinegar

1 teaspoon dried oregano

1 teaspoon dried basil

½ teaspoon minced garlic

¼ teaspoon ground rosemary

2 teaspoons (10 ml) agave nectar or maple syrup

Salt and pepper, to taste

☾ **THE NIGHT BEFORE:** Peel the squash using a potato peeler. If the skin is super hard you can microwave it for a couple of minutes. Then slice into rounds, and use a spoon to remove the stringy parts in the middle along with the seeds. Store in fridge overnight.

If you want, you can mix all the sauce ingredients together and keep in the fridge. They come together quick, so I'll leave that up to you!

☀ **IN THE MORNING:** Add the sauce to the bottom of your slow cooker and stack the squash circles however they will fit. They do not need to be immersed in the sauce to cook well. Cook on low for 7 to 9 hours.

BEFORE SERVING: Mash the squash rounds to create strands and mix with the sauce.

YIELD: *4 servings*
EQUIPMENT: *4-quart slow cooker*
COOKING TIME: *7 to 9 hours*

MUSHROOM LASAGNA *with* CREAMY GARLIC SAUCE

This is a quick and easy dish that is elegant and perfect for last-minute company. For a special treat, add a layer of chanterelle or lobster mushrooms and use one-third less of the regular mushrooms that are called for in the recipe.

 GLUTEN-FREE OPTION*   NO OIL ADDED

BÉCHAMEL SAUCE INGREDIENTS

1 package (15 ounces, or 420 g) silken or soft tofu

Juice of ½ lemon

1 cup (235 ml) water

3 cloves garlic or 1 teaspoon dried

½ to 1 teaspoon salt (to taste)

1½ tablespoons (9 g) vegan chicken-flavored bouillon or 3 tablespoons (18 g) DIY Golden Bouillon (page 237)

¼ cup (24 g) nutritional yeast

MUSHROOM INGREDIENTS

2 tablespoons (30 ml) olive oil (*water sauté)

20 ounces (560 g) mushrooms, sliced

2 sprigs rosemary

½ to ¾ package (10 ounces, or 280 g) whole-wheat lasagne noodles (the regular kind, not the no-boil noodles) *use gluten-free noodles

☾ THE NIGHT BEFORE: To make the béchamel sauce: Pureé all the sauce ingredients in a food processor or blender until smooth.

TO MAKE THE MUSHROOMS: Heat the oil in a skillet over medium heat and sauté the mushrooms with the rosemary until they give off their water and begin to brown, about 10 minutes. Remove and discard the rosemary sprigs. Store the sauce and mushrooms in separate airtight containers in the fridge.

✳ IN THE MORNING: Oil the crock of the slow cooker and spread one-fifth of the sauce on the bottom, then top with a layer of lasagne noodles. Break off the corners on one side of each noodle so they fit snugly in the slow cooker. You can add the corners in as well. Place a layer of noodles over the sauce.

Add a layer of one-third of the mushrooms and top with another one-fifth of the sauce. Repeat the layers two more times, ending with a last layer of lasagne noodles, and then top that with the remaining sauce.

Cook on high for 1½ to 2½ hours, until a fork will easily go through the middle and the pasta is al dente.

YIELD: 4 servings
EQUIPMENT: 4-quart slow cooker
COOKING TIME: 1½ to 2 hours on high

CHAPTER 7

Mains

There's nothing more satisfying than coming home to food you have been craving. If you don't live in a large metropolitan area it can be hard to find vegan restaurants. With this chapter you can make your own Chinese takeout and a few upscale main courses for special dinners at a fraction of the price of going out to eat.

If you don't live in a vegan household, you may get complaints about too many nights of vegetable stews over rice. The recipes in this chapter are hearty enough to satisfy any nonvegan.

KUNG PAO

This Chinese takeout inspired recipe gets its rich flavor from the mushrooms and rice vinegar as well as a great crunch from the water chestnuts.

 GLUTEN-FREE OPTION* SOY-FREE OPTION** NO OIL ADDED OPTION***

SAUCE INGREDIENTS

3 cloves garlic, minced

1 tablespoon (8 g) grated ginger

1½ cups (355 ml) water

¼ cup (60 ml) soy sauce (*use gluten-free **use coconut aminos)

¼ cup (60 ml) seasoned rice vinegar or plain rice vinegar mixed with 1 teaspoon sweetener

2 tablespoons (12 g) vegan chicken-flavored bouillon or 4 tablespoons (24 g) DIY Golden Bouillon (page 237)

¼ to ½ teaspoon red pepper flakes

INGREDIENTS

1 bell pepper, cored and diced

5 ounces (140 g) mushrooms, diced

1 can (8 ounces, or 225 g) water chestnuts, drained and diced

1 package (12 ounces, or 335 g) seitan, store-bought or homemade (page 238), diced (*sub 1½ cups chickpeas, cauliflower florets, or pressed tofu)

BEFORE SERVING INGREDIENTS

2 to 3 tablespoons (16 to 24 g) cornstarch

2 tablespoons (30 ml) sesame oil (*** leave out to make oil-free)

Steamed rice, for serving

Chopped peanuts, for serving

☾ THE NIGHT BEFORE: To make the sauce: Combine all the sauce ingredients and store in an airtight container in the fridge. Store the cut-up bell pepper, mushrooms, water chestnuts, and seitan in an airtight container in the fridge.

IN THE MORNING: Combine the sauce, pepper, mushrooms, water chestnuts, and seitan in the slow cooker. Cook on low for 7 to 9 hours.

30 MINUTES BEFORE SERVING: Turn up slow cooker to high. Make a thickener by mixing the cornstarch with some of the sauce from the slow cooker in a small cup, then add it back to the slow cooker. Right before serving, stir in the sesame oil. Serve over steamed rice, and top with the peanuts.

YIELD: 4 servings
EQUIPMENT: 4-quart slow cooker
COOKING TIME: 7 to 9 hours on low

VEGAN PAD THAI

Thai food is one of my favorite comfort foods. In this recipe I use soy curls and tofu, but you could substitute veggies such as broccoli, cauliflower, kale, onions and more. You can also modify the sweetness and the tanginess to suit your tastes. Try serving it with the Coconut Soup with Mushrooms and Jackfruit on page 65.

 GLUTEN-FREE OPTION* SOY-FREE OPTION**  NO OIL ADDED

3 cups (705 ml) water

2 cups (111 g) dry soy curls

2 cups (300 g) pressed tofu cubes

2 cups (140 g) shredded cabbage

1½ cups (190 g) sliced carrots

1½ cups (105 g) chopped shiitake mushrooms

½ cup (115 g) brown sugar

3 tablespoons (45 ml) soy sauce (* use gluten-free soy or **coconut aminos)

2 to 3 tablespoons (30 to 45 ml) tamarind concentrate, to taste

2 teaspoons (10 ml) rice vinegar

1 teaspoon minced garlic

SERVING INGREDIENTS

1 (8 ounces, 227 g) box brown rice Pad Thai noodles, cooked according to the directions on the box

1 cup (145 g) chopped peanuts

1 cup (16 g) chopped cilantro

3 cups (150 g) beans sprouts

☾ THE NIGHT BEFORE: Prepare the veggies and store in the fridge overnight.

☀ IN THE MORNING: Add the water, soy curls, tofu, cabbage, carrots, mushrooms, brown sugar, soy sauce, tamarind concentrate, rice vinegar, and garlic to your slow cooker. Cook on low for 7 to 9 hours.

TO SERVE: You can either mix the cooked noodles in the slow cooker mixture or ladle the mixture over individual bowls of noodles. Top with peanuts, cilantro, and sprouts.

YIELD: 6 servings
EQUIPMENT: 4-slow cooker
COOKING TIME: for 7 to 9 hours on low

SWEET-AND-SOUR SMOKED TOFU

This dish was inspired by a recipe for sweet-and-sour seitan on Learning Vegan's blog. Save some money and make your Chinese takeout at home. Plus, you know exactly what went in it.

 GLUTEN-FREE OPTION*   SOY-FREE OPTION**   NO OIL ADDED

1 can (20 ounces, or 560 g) pineapple in juice

2 tablespoons (30 ml) low-sodium soy sauce (*use gluten-free or use **coconut aminos)

2 to 3 teaspoons grated fresh ginger

1 package (8 ounces, or 225 g) smoked tofu, cubed

1 medium onion, cut in half and thinly sliced

BEFORE SERVING INGREDIENTS

1 large bell pepper, thinly sliced

2 large carrots, sliced

1 medium-size head broccoli, cut into bite-size pieces

3 tablespoons (24 g) cornstarch

3 tablespoons (45 ml) cold water

☾ THE NIGHT BEFORE: Open the pineapple can and drain the juice into a small bowl. Add the soy sauce and ginger to the juice to make the sauce. Store the sauce, pineapple chunks, and cut-up tofu, onion, pepper, carrots, and broccoli in anfspice airtight container in the fridge.

☀ IN THE MORNING: Combine the sauce, onion, carrots, and tofu in the slow cooker. Cook on low for 7 to 9 hours.

ABOUT 30 TO 45 MINUTES BEFORE SERVING: Turn up slow cooker to high and add the pepper, broccoli, and pineapple chunks. Make a thickener by mixing the cornstarch and water in a small cup, then add it to the slow cooker. It's ready when the sauce has thickened and the broccoli is tender.

YIELD: 4 servings
EQUIPMENT: 4-quart slow cooker
COOKING TIME: 7 to 9 hours on low

MA PO TOFU

This is one of my favorite Chinese dishes. You can make it as mild or spicy as you like.
Silken tofu has a custard-like texture and is the main focus of this dish. If you don't like
that silky texture, feel free to use soft or firm tofu instead. You can usually find black
bean garlic sauce in the international food aisle of most large grocery stores.

 NO OIL ADDED

SAUCE INGREDIENTS

2 tablespoons (30 ml) soy sauce

2 tablespoons (30 ml) rice wine or apple cider vinegar

3 tablespoons (48 g) tomato paste

1½ tablespoons (24 g) black bean garlic sauce

1 to 2 teaspoons sriracha (to taste)

½ teaspoon red pepper flakes (optional)

3 cloves garlic, minced

2 to 3 teaspoons grated fresh ginger

1 teaspoon agave nectar

1 cup (235 ml) water

¼ cup (60 ml) white wine

8 shiitake mushrooms, sliced

2 packages (12 ounces, or 336 g each) silken, soft, or firm tofu, cubed

BEFORE SERVING INGREDIENTS

3 tablespoons (24 g) cornstarch

1 medium-size head broccoli, cut into bite-size pieces

1 tablespoon (15 ml) sesame oil

SERVING INGREDIENTS

Steamed rice, for serving

☾ THE NIGHT BEFORE: To make the sauce: Combine all the sauce ingredients and store in an airtight container in the refrigerator. Store the cut-up mushrooms, tofu, and broccoli in separate airtight containers in the refrigerator.

☀ IN THE MORNING: Combine the sauce, mushrooms, and tofu in the slow cooker. Cook on low for 7 to 9 hours.

ABOUT 45 TO 60 MINUTES BEFORE SERVING: Turn up the slow cooker to high. Make a thickener by mixing the cornstarch with some of the sauce from the slow cooker in a small cup, then add it back to the slow cooker. When the sauce is thickened, add the broccoli and cook until bright green. Right before serving, stir in the sesame oil. Serve over steamed rice.

YIELD: 6 servings
EQUIPMENT: 4-quart slow cooker
COOKING TIME: 7 to 9 hours on low

TEMPEH BRAISED *with* FIGS *and* PORT WINE

Looking for a sophisticated dish? Well, look no further. This recipe combines the complex flavor of port wine with fresh figs and nutty tempeh. Serve over mashed potatoes with roasted asparagus for a meal that will wow the toughest critic.

 GLUTEN-FREE OPTION*   SOY-FREE OPTION**   NO OIL ADDED OPTION***

2 tablespoons (30 ml) olive oil (**water sauté)

1 small onion, minced

2 cloves garlic, minced

1 package (8 ounces, or 225 g) tempeh (*use plain soy tempeh to make this dish gluten-free or use **seitan to make soy-free), cubed

8 fresh figs, each cut into 6 wedges

½ cup (120 ml) water

1 cup (235 ml) port wine

1 tablespoon (15 ml) balsamic vinegar

1 tablespoon (6 g) vegan chicken-flavored bouillon or 2 tablespoons (12 g) DIY Golden Bouillon (page 237)

1 sprig fresh rosemary

1 sprig fresh thyme

Salt and pepper, to taste

☾ THE NIGHT BEFORE: Heat the oil in a skillet over medium heat and sauté the onion until translucent, 3 to 5 minutes. Add the garlic and sauté for 1 minute longer. Combine in an airtight container with the cut-up tempeh and figs and store in the fridge.

☀ IN THE MORNING: Combine all the ingredients in the slow cooker. Cook on low for 7 to 9 hours.

YIELD: 4 servings
EQUIPMENT: 4-quart slow cooker
COOKING TIME: 7 to 9 hours on low

THAI YELLOW CURRY SEITAN *with* PINEAPPLE *and* EDAMAME

Nancie McDermott is the queen of Southern food, but she's also an expert on Thai food. You have to check out her book, Simply Vegetarian Thai Cooking *which has tons of vegan recipes. Nancie suggests that we serve this with rice and sliced cucumbers; or serve over pasta for vibrant and beautiful Asian-style curry-noodle soup. All I have to say is yum!*

 GLUTEN-FREE OPTION*    SOY-FREE OPTION**   NO OIL ADDED

1 medium onion, coarsely chopped

3 carrots, cut into thick half-moons

1 Idaho russet potato, peeled and cut into large chunks

1 package (8 ounces, or 225 g) seitan, drained and each chunk cut in half (*or use tofu to make it gluten-free)

2 cans (8 ounces, or 225 g each) pineapple chunks, drained

2 to 3 tablespoons Thai yellow curry paste (32 to 48 g) (or try Red or Green curry paste)

2 cups (470 ml) water (or broth)

2 teaspoons (10 ml) agave nectar or maple syrup

Salt, to taste

BEFORE SERVING INGREDIENTS

1 can (14 ounces, or 392 g) unsweetened coconut milk

3 scallions, minced/finely chopped

1 cup (118 g) frozen edamame beans (or **frozen green peas)

☾ THE NIGHT BEFORE: Store the cut-up onion, carrots, potato, seitan, and pineapple chunks in an airtight container in the fridge.

✺ IN THE MORNING: Combine the onion, carrots, potato, seitan, pineapple, curry paste, water, agave, and salt in your slow cooker. Cook on low for 6 to 9 hours.

20 MINUTES BEFORE SERVING: Add the coconut milk, scallions, and edamame beans. Stir gently and cook, until edamame beans are tender and curry is hot. Taste and adjust the seasonings.

YIELD: 6 servings
EQUIPMENT: 4-quart slow cooker
COOKING TIME: 6 to 9 hours on low

POTATO STUFFED CHILE RELLENOS

One thing to keep in mind when you make this dish is that some poblanos can be a little spicy. But don't worry, if you have a no-spicy-food eater, just use some of the stuffing in a halved bell pepper instead.

 GLUTEN-FREE SOY-FREE  NO OIL ADDED

4 poblanos, seeds and ribs removed and cut in halves

FILLING INGREDIENTS

5 cups (1125 g) cooked potatoes

⅓ cup (80 ml) unsweetened nondairy milk

2 tablespoons (6 g) nutritional yeast

1 teaspoon salt

1 teaspoon oregano

½ teaspoon chili powder

¼ teaspoon ground cumin

¼ teaspoon jalapeño powder

SAUCE INGREDIENTS

1½ cups (300 g) crushed tomatoes

¼ cup (60 ml) water

1 teaspoon minced garlic

1 teaspoon onion powder

1 teaspoon oregano

¼ teaspoon chili powder

¼ teaspoon salt

¼ teaspoon jalapeño powder

SERVING INGREDIENTS

Steamed rice

Refried beans (see recipe on page 39)

Chopped tomatoes, red onions, cilantro

☾ THE NIGHT BEFORE: Prepare the poblanos. Mix the filling ingredients together and stuff into the peppers. In a separate container, mix the sauce ingredients. Store everything in the fridge overnight.

☀ IN THE MORNING: Spread the sauce over the bottom of your slow cooker. Place the stuffed poblanos in and cook on low 7 to 9 hours.

YIELD: 4 servings
EQUIPMENT: 4-quart slow cooker
COOKING TIME: 7 to 9 hours on low

DILL CABBAGE STEAKS *over* ROASTED RAINBOW POTATOES

This ridiculously easy recipe is sure to be a hit any weeknight dinner. I have to admit that I was skeptical about cabbage steaks, but once I tried them I was hooked. This takes very little effort and makes the perfect stick to your ribs meal. You can double the potatoes if you're extra hungry.

 GLUTEN-FREE   SOY-FREE  NO OIL ADDED OPITON*

4 cups (600 g) quartered baby potatoes (a mix of yellow, red, and purple if possible)

2 tablespoons (30 ml) olive oil (optional) *leave out to make oil-free

4 (½-inch, or 1.3-cm) cabbage slices (green or red)

About 1 tablespoon (15 ml) spray olive oil, (*leave out to make oil-free)

2 teaspoons (2 g) dried dill (or 4-inch [10-cm] sprigs of fresh dill)

BEFORE SERVING INGREDIENTS

Unsweetened vegan yogurt

Fresh dill

Salt and pepper

☾ THE NIGHT BEFORE: Slice 4 cabbage steaks from the thickest part of the cabbage. Coat sides with 1 tablespoon (15 ml) olive oil, if using. Toss the potatoes in 1 tablespoon oil (if using). Store in the fridge overnight.

☀ IN THE MORNING: Either oil your crock* or line with parchment paper. Spread the potatoes out and layer cabbage steaks on top. Sprinkle dill and yogurt over the steaks. Cook on low 7 to 9 hours.

YIELD: 4 servings
EQUIPMENT: 4-quart slow cooker
COOKING TIME: 7 to 9 hours on low

THAI RED CURRY TOFU *and* VEGGIES

Thai curry paste can be found in most groceries, and most are vegan. Use less curry paste if you like milder foods and more if you like it fiery hot.

 GLUTEN-FREE   SOY-FREE OPITON*   NO OIL ADDED

1 large onion, minced

1 bell pepper, julienned

1 can (8 ounces, or 225 g) bamboo shoots, drained and julienned

½ head cauliflower, cut into florets

1½ packages (15 ounces, or 420 g each) extra-firm tofu, cubed (*use jack fruit or seitan)

½ head broccoli, cut into florets

1 to 2 tablespoons (16 to 32 g) red curry paste

2 cups (470 ml) water

Juice of 1 lime

BEFORE SERVING INGREDIENTS

1 can (14 ounces, or 392 g) light coconut milk

SERVING INGREDIENTS

Fresh Thai basil, for serving

1 lime, sliced, for serving

☾ THE NIGHT BEFORE: Store the cut-up onion, bell pepper, bamboo shoots, and cauliflower, and tofu in an airtight container in the fridge. Store the cut-up broccoli in a separate airtight container in the fridge.

☀ IN THE MORNING: Combine the onion, bell pepper, bamboo shoots, cauliflower, tofu, curry paste, water, and lime juice in the slow cooker. Cook on low for 7 to 9 hours.

20 MINUTES BEFORE SERVING: Add the coconut milk and broccoli. Cook until the broccoli is tender. Taste and adjust the seasonings. Serve topped with chopped Thai basil and a slice of lime.

YIELD: 6 servings
EQUIPMENT: 4-quart slow cooker
COOKING TIME: 7 to 9 hours on low

ACORN SQUASH STUFFED *with* CRANBERRY-PECAN RICE

By using your slow cooker instead of an oven, you'll have a dish ready to serve as soon as you get home. Use the recipe below as a jumping-off point. You can use any leftover grains, beans, or chopped stale bread (think Thanksgiving stuffing) to make a filling. Because the acorn squash is a little sweet, I like to add some dried fruit, as well as savory herbs. It's a perfect place to use up that last bit of veggie sausage (cook it first), crumbled baked tofu, or other meat substitute.

 GLUTEN-FREE   SOY-FREE  NO OIL ADDED OPITON*

1 medium-size acorn squash

Olive oil, for rubbing (*leave out to make oil-free)

1 cup (165 g) cooked brown rice or other precooked grain

1 can (15 ounces, or 420 g) lentils, white beans, or kidney beans, drained and rinsed, or 1½ cups (340 g) homemade (page 230)

1 tablespoon (8 g) chopped dried cranberries

1 tablespoon (7 g) chopped pecans

1 clove garlic, minced

2 sprigs fresh thyme, minced

1 teaspoon chopped fresh rosemary

Salt and pepper, to taste

Water or broth, as needed

☾ **THE NIGHT BEFORE:** Cut the acorn squash in half and remove the seeds. Lightly rub the exposed flesh with a little olive oil. Store in an airtight container in the fridge. In a bowl, combine the rice, lentils, cranberries, pecans, garlic, thyme, rosemary, and salt and pepper, stir to mix. Add some water or broth if the mixture is too dry. Cover, and store in the fridge.

☀ **IN THE MORNING:** Pour about ½ inch (1.3 cm) water in the bottom of your slow cooker. Crumple up some aluminum foil and place under the squash halves to keep them from turning over and spilling out the stuffing. No aluminum foil? Cut a little off the bottom side of the squash half to get it to sit straight. Fill the squash with the stuffing and round it over the flesh, if possible. Cook on low for 7 to 9 hours, or until the squash is tender when pierced with a fork.

YIELD: 2 servings
EQUIPMENT: 4-quart slow cooker
COOKING TIME: 7 to 9 hours on low

A Worthy Note
If you have a large, oval slow cooker you can double this recipe and make 4 servings instead of 2.

CHAPTER 8

Sides

———————————————————

I love using my slow cooker for side dishes. It's especially handy when you have an elaborate holiday dinner. Not only will it free up the stove for other dishes, but it will also keep food warm until you can get everyone to sit down to eat.

Making side dishes in slow cookers also makes quick work of setting up a buffet. It's a great reason to have more than one slow cooker on hand.

You can cook most veggies in the slow cooker, but make sure you don't overcook delicate ones, such as asparagus, broccoli, and the like. Root vegetables can cook much longer.

CREAMED CORN *with* TRUFFLE OIL

You can double or triple the recipe and use a larger slow cooker if you like.

Truffle oil is expensive, but a small bottle will last a long time. You can make this recipe without the truffle oil and it will still taste really good. But the truffle oil takes it to a whole other ethereal level, and smells as wonderful as it tastes. You can always drop hints that you'd like some around your birthday like I do!

 GLUTEN-FREE OPTION*  SOY-FREE OPTION**

1 package (16 ounces, or 454 g) frozen corn kernels

½ cup (120 ml) plain or unsweetened nondairy milk

½ teaspoon salt (or to taste)

Pepper, to taste

1 tablespoon (8 g) cornstarch dissolved in 1 tablespoon (15 ml) warm water

1 tablespoon (15 ml) truffle oil

Oil the crock of your slow cooker. Combine the corn, milk, salt, and pepper in the slow cooker. Cook on high for 1 to 1½ hours, stirring every 30 minutes, or until the corn is heated through.

Add the cornstarch mixture and truffle oil and stir to combine. It should thicken up quickly. If not, cook for another 10 to 15 minutes.

YIELD: 2 servings
EQUIPMENT: 1½- to 2-quart slow cooker
COOKING TIME: 1½ to 2½ hours on high

SWEET HERBED BEETS

You can double or triple the recipe and use a larger slow cooker if you like.

I love beets and I always have. To me they are sweet, tasty treats. My other half says they taste like dirt to her, but they just taste nice and earthy to me. The mint complements the natural sweetness of the beets.

 GLUTEN-FREE   SOY-FREE   NO OIL ADDED

4 beets

½ cup (120 ml) water

2 sprigs fresh thyme or 2 teaspoons dried

1 teaspoon crushed mint leaves (fresh or dried)

Salt, to taste

☾ THE NIGHT BEFORE: Peel and dice the beets. Make sure you're not wearing your favorite clothes, because the beet juice will stain. Store in an airtight container in the fridge.

☀ IN THE MORNING: Combine all the ingredients in your small slow cooker. Cook on low for 7 to 9 hours. Remove and discard the thyme sprigs and taste and adjust the seasonings.

YIELD: 4 servings
EQUIPMENT: 1½- to 2-quart slow cooker
COOKING TIME: 7 to 9 hours on low

CREAMY SCALLOPED POTATOES

Creamy, garlicky potatoes are a favorite anytime, but it's a great dish to bring to a holiday dinner. It's also a great side for Atomic Tofu Pecan Loaf (page 95).

 GLUTEN-FREE   SOY-FREE ⬭ NO OIL ADDED OPITON*

SAUCE INGREDIENTS:

1 cup (135 g) cashews

¼ cup (24 g) nutritional yeast

5 cloves garlic

2 cups (475 ml) unsweetened nondairy milk

½ to 1 teaspoon salt (to taste)

½ teaspoon onion powder

2 pounds (910 g) potatoes, peeled (if not organic)

☾ THE NIGHT BEFORE: To make the sauce: In a food processor or blender combine the sauce ingredients. Blend until smooth and creamy. Store in an airtight container in the fridge.

Thinly slice the potatoes and place in a bowl of cold water (to prevent discoloration). Cover and refrigerate.

☀ IN THE MORNING: Oil the crock of your slow cooker *or line with parchment paper. Pour one-third of the sauce on the bottom of the crock. Place half of the potatoes on top, then pour on another one-third of the sauce and repeat the layers one more time, ending with the sauce. Cook on low for 7 to 9 hours.

YIELD: 4 servings
EQUIPMENT: 4-quart slow cooker
COOKING TIME: 7 to 9 hours on low

ASIAN GREENS

Greens are the perfect veggie to eat in the winter. Some people can't deal with the bitterness, and the Asian flavors really help mask it. Getting my other half to eat them was a true feat, one that could have only been done with soy sauce and sesame oil. Mix and match different kinds of greens, such as collards, kale, turnip greens, beet greens, and Swiss chard, to find your perfect blend.

 GLUTEN-FREE OPTION*   SOY-FREE OPTION**   NO OIL ADDED***

1 bunch greens

1 clove garlic, minced

1 teaspoon grated fresh ginger

1 tablespoon (15 ml) soy sauce (*use gluten-free or ** coconut aminos)

1 teaspoon rice wine vinegar

BEFORE SERVING INGREDIENTS

1 tablespoon (15 ml) sesame oil or chili sesame oil (*** leave out)

☾ THE NIGHT BEFORE: Wash and cut up the greens. Combine with the garlic and ginger and store in an airtight container in the fridge.

☀ IN THE MORNING: Oil the crock of your slow cooker. Add the greens, garlic, ginger, soy sauce, and vinegar. Cook on low for 7 to 9 hours. Drizzle each serving with sesame oil, or use chili oil for more of a kick.

YIELD: 6 servings
EQUIPMENT: 4-quart slow cooker
COOKING TIME: 7 to 9 hours on low

SUPER-SIMPLE ROASTED VEGGIES

No matter what size slow cooker you have, you can double or halve this recipe to fit it perfectly.

 GLUTEN-FREE · SOY-FREE

1 medium-size head cauliflower, broken into florets

16 Brussels sprouts

16 baby carrots

16 pearl onions

¼ cup (60 ml) water

2 tablespoons (12 g) vegan chicken-flavored bouillon or 4 tablespoons (24 g) DIY Golden Bouillon (page 237)

1 to 2 tablespoons (15 to 30 ml) olive oil

2 sprigs fresh thyme or 2 teaspoons dried

1 sprig fresh rosemary or 1 teaspoon dried

1 teaspoon rubbed sage

Salt and pepper, to taste

Oil the crock of your slow cooker *or line with parchment paper. Combine all the ingredients in the slow cooker. Cook on low for 4 to 5 hours, or until the veggies are tender. Taste and adjust the seasonings before serving.

YIELD: 6 servings
EQUIPMENT: 4-quart slow cooker
COOKING TIME: 4 to 5 hours on low

CURRIED ROAST CAULIFLOWER

A whole head of cauliflower with a baked-on curry paste makes this recipe into a showstopper! Serve with the Tofu Masala on page 35 or the dal on page 36 and steamed rice for an impressive dinner.

 GLUTEN-FREE SOY-FREE ⬡ NO OIL ADDED OPTION*

1 large head of cauliflower, leaves and stem removed

CURRY PASTE INGREDIENTS

¼ cup (60 ml) mild oil or *aquafaba

2 teaspoons (6 g) grated ginger

1 teaspoon minced garlic

1 teaspoon ground cumin

1 teaspoon ground coriander

½ teaspoon salt

½ teaspoon ground turmeric

¼ teaspoon ground chili such as cayenne (to taste)

¼ teaspoon dry mustard powder

Oil your crock* or line with parchment paper. Place in the prepared cauliflower. Note: if your cauliflower doesn't fit in your slow cooker, you can break it into large pieces.

Mix together all the curry paste ingredients and pour over the cauliflower. Cook on low 7 to 9 hours or on high for 4 hours.

YIELD: 4 servings
EQUIPMENT: 4-quart slow cooker
COOKING TIME: 7 to 9 hours on low

BALSAMIC BRUSSELS SPROUTS

I am a Brussels sprouts lover, and I'm not ashamed to admit it. This is an easy side dish that you can throw in a 1- to 1½-quart (0.9 to 1.4 L) slow cooker while you are making dinner, or better yet, while you relax before dinner!

 GLUTEN-FREE SOY-FREE  NO OIL ADDED

8 ounces (225 g) Brussels sprouts

1 tablespoon (14 ml) balsamic vinegar

2 tablespoons (30 ml) red wine or an extra 1 tablespoon (15 ml) balsamic

4 sprigs fresh thyme or 1 teaspoon dried

½ teaspoon agave nectar or maple syrup

½ cup (120 ml) water

Salt and pepper, to taste

☾ THE NIGHT BEFORE: Cut the Brussels sprouts into quarters and store in an airtight container in the fridge.

2 hours before you want to eat: Combine all the ingredients in the slow cooker. Cook on high for 2 hours. Remove and discard the thyme sprigs. Taste and adjust the seasonings.

YIELD: 4 servings
EQUIPMENT: 1½- to 2-quart slow cooker
COOKING TIME: 2 hours on high or 4 hours on low

A Worthy Note
You can double or triple the recipe and use a larger slow cooker if you like.

SOUTHERN-STYLE GREEN BEANS

In the southern United States, they have a thing called a vegetable plate. Vegans, don't let it fool you. Almost all veggies in the South are traditionally cooked with pork fat. There is nothing less vegan-friendly. But these beans are especially for vegans and get their traditional smoked flavor from liquid smoke. You can easily double this recipe for a holiday side dish.

 GLUTEN-FREE  SOY-FREE ◯ NO OIL ADDED

1 pound (454 g) fresh or frozen green beans, ends cut off

½ cup (120 ml) water

1 teaspoon liquid smoke

½ to 1 teaspoon Cajun seasoning

Salt and pepper, to taste

Oil the crock of your slow cooker and add all the ingredients. Cook on high for 1½ to 2 hours. Taste and adjust the seasonings.

YIELD: 4 servings
EQUIPMENT: 4- to 6-quart slow cooker
COOKING TIME: 1½ to 2½ hours on high

VODKA *and* DILL-GLAZED BABY CARROTS

You can double or triple the recipe and use a larger slow cooker if you like.

Sometimes you need a side dish with a little zip. The vodka, bouillon, and dill cook down into a tasty sauce that isn't plain or overpowering. It's just right.

 GLUTEN-FREE SOY-FREE  NO OIL ADDED

1 pound (454 g) baby carrots

½ cup (120 ml) water

2 tablespoons (30 ml) vodka

2 tablespoons (12 g) vegan chicken-flavored bouillon or 4 tablespoons (24 g) DIY Golden Bouillon (page 237)

2 teaspoons dill

Salt and pepper, to taste

Oil the crock of your slow cooker and add all the ingredients. Cook on low for 7 to 9 hours. Taste and adjust the seasonings.

YIELD: 4 servings
EQUIPMENT: 1½- to 2-quart slow cooker
COOKING TIME: 7 to 9 hours on low

SLOW-COOKED APPLE *and* SAUSAGE STUFFING

This is a perfect side dish to bring to an omnivore holiday dinner. It helps me avoid the hidden meat that could be lurking in other stuffings.

 GLUTEN-FREE OPTION*  SOY-FREE OPTION** NO OIL ADDED OPTION***

2 tablespoons (30 ml) olive oil ***or water sauté

1 small onion, minced

2 cloves garlic, minced

4 stalks celery, minced

2 apples, peeled, cored, and chopped

1 package (10 ounces, or 280 g) organic stuffing or diced stale bread (*use gluten-free)

2 cups (470 ml) water

2 tablespoons (12 g) vegan chicken-flavored bouillon or 4 tablespoons (24 g) DIY Golden Bouillon (page 237)

½ pound (225 g) vegan sausage crumbles, cooked, or **Apple Sage Sausage (page 240)

Salt, to taste

Heat the oil in a skillet over medium heat and sauté the onion until translucent, 3 to 5 minutes. Add the garlic and celery and sauté for 3 to 4 minutes longer, until the celery is soft. Oil the crock of your slow cooker ***or line with parchment paper. Combine the sautéed vegetables with the remaining ingredients in the slow cooker. Cook on high for 2 to 3 hours with the lid propped up on the handle of a wooden spoon, stirring every 20 to 30 minutes.

YIELD: 8 servings
EQUIPMENT: 4- to 6-quart slow cooker
COOKING TIME: 2 to 3 hours on low

SPANISH QUINOA

Spanish rice was one of my favorite side dishes growing up. This recipe uses quinoa instead of rice. It's a nice change of pace and just as tasty.

 GLUTEN-FREE SOY-FREE  NO OIL ADDED OPTION*

2 tablespoons (30 ml) olive oil (*omit for no oil added)

1 small onion, chopped

2 cloves garlic, minced

1 bell pepper, cored and chopped

3 cups (705 g) water

1½ cups (260 g) quinoa

2 tablespoons (12 g) vegan chicken-flavored bouillon or 4 tablespoons (24 g) DIY Golden Bouillon (page 237)

2 tablespoons (32 g) tomato paste

1 teaspoon salt

½ teaspoon chili powder

Heat the oil (* or water sauté for no oil added) in a skillet over medium heat and sauté the onion until translucent, 3 to 5 minutes. Add the garlic and bell pepper and sauté until the pepper is soft, 3 to 5 minutes.

Combine the sautéed veggies, water, quinoa, bouillon, tomato paste, salt, and chili powder in the slow cooker. Stir until the tomato paste and bouillon are mixed in the liquid. Cook on high for 1½ to 2 hours, until the quinoa has unfurled. Taste and adjust the seasonings.

YIELD: 8 servings
EQUIPMENT: 4-quart slow cooker
COOKING TIME: 1½ to 2 hours on high

BEYOND-EASY NOT BAKED POTATOES

Baked potatoes are filling, full of nutrition, and one of my favorite comfort foods! You can cook up some on the spot or cook a batch ahead of time. Eat it as is or serve a stew or chili over it. It's true that you use no water in the slow cooker for this recipe, and no oil is needed to coat the potato. It really is as easy as it seems. You can also cook 1 or 2 potatoes in a 1- to 1½-quart (940 ml to 1.4 L) slow cooker.

 GLUTEN-FREE   SOY-FREE   NO OIL ADDED

---

4 whole "baking" potatoes, washed well

Make a few holes in each potato with a fork. Put them in the slow cooker.

Cook on low for 7 to 9 hours. Enjoy your perfectly baked potato.

MORE POTATO IDEAS:
- Bake the potatoes, then mash them for the perfect side to any dish. Just put into a bowl, and mash with nondairy milk and nondairy butter. Super simple!
- Try cooking some sweet potatoes using the same method. Serve topped with a little brown sugar and cinnamon for a surprise dessert.
- Top with leftover stew or beans to make a hearty meal.

YIELD: 4 servings
EQUIPMENT: 4-quart slow cooker
COOKING TIME: 7 to 9 hours on low

NOT BAKED BEANS

These baked beans have a deep molasses flavor with tang from the apple cider vinegar and mustard. You can also use pinto beans or navy beans in place of Great Northern beans

 GLUTEN-FREE · SOY-FREE · NO OIL ADDED

1 pound (454 g) dry Great Northern beans, soaked overnight

4 cups (940 ml) water for cooking

½ cup blackstrap molasses

¼ cup (60 g) brown sugar

1 tablespoon (15 g) whole-grain Dijon mustard

2 tablespoons (28 ml) apple cider vinegar

1 teaspoon garlic powder

1 teaspoon onion powder

1 teaspoon dried thyme

1 teaspoon liquid smoke

½ teaspoon dry mustard powder

½ teaspoon smoked paprika

BEFORE SERVING INGREDIENTS

2 tablespoons (32 g) tomato paste

Salt, to taste

THE NIGHT BEFORE: Add the dry beans to a large bowl and fill with water until it's about 4 inches (10 cm) over the beans.

IN THE MORNING: the beans and add them to your slow cooker with the blackstrap molasses, brown sugar, mustard, apple cider vinegar, garlic powder, onion powder, thyme, liquid smoke, mustard powder, and smoked paprika. Cook on low 7 to 9 hours.

30 MINUTES BEFORE SERVING: Stir in the tomato paste, and add salt to taste. You can also adjust any of the other seasonings to suit your tastes.

Have leftovers? These freeze great!

YIELD: 10 servings
EQUIPMENT: 4-quart slow cooker
COOKING TIME: 7 to 9 hours

Recipe Ideas & Variations

Want to make this right now, but you don't have any soaked beans? Add the dry beans to a big pot and fill with water about 4 to 5 inches (10 to 13 cm) over the beans and bring to a boil on your stovetop. Remove from heat, cover with lid and let sit for 30 minutes. Now continue with the recipe as written!

HOLIDAY SWEET POTATO CASSEROLE

Every family seems to have a special recipe for sweet potato casserole. This one is less sweet than the sticky sweet casserole of my youth. It skips the caramel and marshmallow that are sometimes included. You could add vegan versions of both if you really want to. After all, any day is a holiday when you get to eat sweet potato casserole!

 GLUTEN-FREE OPTION*   SOY-FREE

TOPPING INGREDIENTS

2 tablespoons (28 g) nondairy butter

3 tablespoons (45 ml) olive oil

¾ cup (170 g) packed brown sugar

¼ cup (30 g) whole-wheat flour (*use gluten-free baking mix)

3 tablespoons (45 ml) nondairy milk or water

8 large sweet potatoes, peeled and cut into chunks

½ cup (55 g) chopped pecans

1½ cups (355 ml) water

BEFORE SERVING INGREDIENTS

¼ to ½ teaspoon cinnamon (to taste)

¼ teaspoon grated nutmeg

⅛ teaspoon allspice

Pinch of ground cloves

¼ to ½ cup (60 to 120 ml) plain or vanilla-flavored nondairy milk

☾ THE NIGHT BEFORE: To make the topping: Combine all the topping ingredients in a large bowl and mix thoroughly. Store the topping and the cut-up sweet potatoes in airtight containers in the fridge. Store the chopped pecans in a covered bowl, unrefrigerated.

☀ IN THE MORNING: Oil the crock of your slow cooker. Add the sweet potatoes and water. Cook on low for 7 to 9 hours.

30 TO 45 MINUTES BEFORE SERVING: Turn up the slow cooker to high. Mash the sweet potatoes in the crock. Add the cinnamon, nutmeg, allspice, cloves, and ¼ cup (60 ml) of the nondairy milk and stir to combine. Add the remaining ¼ cup (60 ml) milk if the potatoes are still too stiff, but leave it out if they are runny.

Drop spoonfuls of the topping onto the sweet potatoes. As the topping begins to melt, spread it evenly with the back of a spoon. Sprinkle on the nuts. Serve once the topping is melted and heated throughout.

YIELD: 8 servings
EQUIPMENT: 4-quart slow cooker
COOKING TIME: 7 to 9 hours on low

Not FRIED PINTO BEANS
with GUAJILLO CHILES

You can't have enough Mexi-style beans, in my opinion. This one is mild and full of flavor from the guajillo chiles. You can get them in most groceries, but they are cheapest at Hispanic markets.

 GLUTEN-FREE SOY-FREE  NO OIL ADDED

5 cups water

1 pound (454 g) dry pinto beans (about 2 cups)

2 to 3 dried guajillo chiles with seeds, stem and ribs removed

2 teaspoons (6 g) minced garlic

BEFORE SERVING INGREDIENTS

1 teaspoon dried oregano

1 teaspoon smoked paprika

1 teaspoon salt, or to taste

✳ IN THE MORNING: Add the water, dry pinto beans, guajillo chiles, and garlic to your slow cooker crock and cook on low for 7 to 9 hours.

If there is extra liquid left, remove and reserve it in case you need it to thin the beans later.

Add the oregano, smoked paprika, and salt. Use your immersion blender and blend until smooth. Alternatively, you can use your blender.

YIELD: 6 servings
EQUIPMENT: 4-quart slow cooker
Cooks 7 to 9 hours

Serving Suggestion
I like to freeze leftovers in one-meal-sized freezer bags or stuffed into tortillas for a grab-and-go freezer lunch!

Recipe Ideas & Variations
No pinto beans? Try using maracoba, cranberry beans, lila beans—really any bean except for kidney beans. (See how to cook kidneys on page 230.)

CREAMY CORN SPOON BREAD

This is in between a soufflé and cornbread. It's moist and delicious, plus it's great as a side or by itself.

 GLUTEN-FREE SOY-FREE ⬤ NO OIL ADDED OPTION*

1 cup (138 g) fine ground cornmeal

½ teaspoon salt

1 can (14.75 ounces, or 397 g) creamed corn (it's vegan!)

¼ cup (60 ml) aquafaba (or 2 tablespoons [14 g] ground flaxseed mixed with ¼ cup [60 ml] warm water)

Mix all the ingredients together. Either oil your crock* or place a piece of parchment paper.

Pour in the batter and spread evenly. Place a clean dish towel between the crock and the lid, pull tight so it doesn't touch the batter. Cook on high for 1½ to 2 hours or until the middle begins to firm up.

YIELD: 6 servings
EQUIPMENT: 4-quart slow cooker
COOKING TIME: 1½ to 2 hours on high

CHAPTER 9

Sandwich & Taco Fillings

Did you know that sandwich, burrito, and taco fillings can all be made in advance in the slow cooker? From the typical sloppy joe–style sandwich to the more unusual pesto winter squash, these recipes let you really add some variety to a midweek dinner or weekend lunch.

Don't forget you can use fillings in some of your vegetables, too. By using your slow cooker instead of an oven, you'll have a dish ready to serve as soon as you get home. You can use any leftover grains, beans, or chopped stale bread (think Thanksgiving stuffing) to make fillings for winter squash, summer squash, bell peppers, or cabbage leaves. Think of these recipes as a jumping-off point, and see what filling experiments you want to try next.

DEBRIS PO'BOY

Po'boys are a staple in New Orleans cuisine, but if you want a vegan one it's time to make your own. The term debris comes from the pieces that are in the bottom of the roasting pan. This recipe recreates that messy po'boy experience. Serve it on a soft French baguette. Add vegan mayo, lettuce, and tomato to make it dressed.

 GLUTEN-FREE OPTION*   SOY-FREE   NO OIL ADDED

3 cups seitan (or 20 ounces [366 g] from recipe on page 238) or *reconstituted soy curls

2 cloves garlic, minced

2 cups water (or broth from homemade seitan)

2 tablespoons vegan chicken-flavored bouillon (or 4 tablespoons DIY Golden Bouillon on page 237)

BEFORE SERVING INGREDIENTS

2 to 4 tablespoons flour (or 1 to 1½ tablespoon cornstarch), as needed

½ teaspoon Cajun seasoning (optional)

Salt and pepper to taste

SERVING INGREDIENTS

French bread, for serving

☾ THE NIGHT BEFORE: Slice ½ the seitan thinly. Take the rest and grate or pulse in a food processor until you have small ragged bits.

☀ IN THE MORNING: Add everything except flour to the slow cooker. Cook on low 7 to 9 hours.

20 MINUTES BEFORE SERVING: Add extra cup of water if the mixture has become dry. Add 2 tablespoons flour or 1 tablespoon cornstarch to the slow cooker and mix well. Cook for 20 more minutes. This should thicken the gravy. If it is not thick enough add the other 2 tablespoons of the flour.

YIELD: 4 servings
EQUIPMENT: 4-quart slow cooker
COOKING TIME: 7 to 9 hours on low

PHILADELPHIA-STYLE CHEESY PORTOBELLO SANDWICH

This is a quick and easy sandwich filling that's ready when you get home. Add a salad or some pasta salad, and you have a casual dinner for friends with almost no work.

 GLUTEN-FREE OPTION*   SOY-FREE   NO OIL ADDED

1 medium-size onion, cut into strips

2 large bell peppers, cut into strips

4 large portobello mushrooms, sliced

2 tablespoons (12 g) vegan beef- or chicken-flavored bouillon or 4 tablespoons (24 g) or DIY Golden Bouillon (page 237)

½ cup (120 ml) water

Salt and pepper, to taste

BEFORE SERVING INGREDIENTS

1 tablespoon (8 g) cornstarch

6 whole-wheat hoagie rolls, toasted, for serving (* use gluten-free bread)

Shredded vegan cheese, for serving (store-bought or recipe on page 243)

☾ THE NIGHT BEFORE: Store the sliced onion, peppers, and mushrooms in an airtight container in the fridge.

☀ IN THE MORNING: Oil the crock of your slow cooker. Mix the bouillon with the water and pour into the slow cooker. Add the onion, bell peppers, mushrooms, and salt and pepper. Cook on low for 7 to 9 hours.

ABOUT 20 MINUTES BEFORE SERVING: Stir the cornstarch into the gravy and mix well. Cook for 20 more minutes. This should thicken the gravy. Taste and adjust the seasonings. Spoon some of the hot sandwich mixture onto each toasted bun and top with the cheddar.

YIELD: 6 servings
EQUIPMENT: 4-quart slow cooker
COOKING TIME: 7 to 9 hours on low

TEMPEH TORNADO

Okay, so this is really just a sloppy joe, Manwich, or whatever they call a meaty sauce inside a sandwich in your part of the world. My friend John thought of this name, and it fits as well as any of the usual ones. This is easy to throw together in the morning before work and can cook all day with no issues.

 GLUTEN-FREE NO OIL ADDED

2 packages (8 ounces, or 227 g) tempeh (*make sure to buy plain soy tempeh to make this dish gluten-free), cubed

3 cloves garlic, minced

½ bell pepper, minced

2 cans (14.5 ounce, or 411 g) diced tomatoes (or 3 cups fresh)

½ (125 ml) cup water

1 tablespoon vegan chicken-flavored bouillon (or 2 tablespoons of my recipe page 237)

1 tablespoon (16 g) tomato paste

1 tablespoon agave nectar or maple syrup

1 tablespoon apple cider vinegar (white is okay too)

1 teaspoon molasses

1 teaspoon Vegan Worcestershire sauce

½ teaspoon liquid smoke

½ teaspoon cumin

½ teaspoon chipotle powder or smoked paprika

½ teaspoon pasilla chili or regular chili powder

½ teaspoon salt

¼ to ½ teaspoon Tabasco, to taste

SERVING INGREDIENTS

Buns

☾ THE NIGHT BEFORE: Cut tempeh into cubes, and steam in a large pot over water for 10 to 15 minutes then drain. This takes out the slight bitter taste from the tempeh. While the tempeh is cooking mince garlic and bell pepper. Mix all the other ingredients together to make the sauce. Store drained tempeh, veggies, and sauce in one container in the fridge overnight.

☀ IN THE MORNING: Add all the ingredients into a slow cooker. Cook on low 7 - 9 hours. Taste and adjust seasonings. Serve inside a bun or as an open-faced sandwich.

YIELD: 8 servings served over buns, about 12 if served inside the bun
EQUIPMENT: 4-quart slow cooker
COOKING TIME: 7 to 9 hours on low

TOFU TACO FILLING

Tex-Mex food is simple, nutritious, and filling. These tacos are easy to throw together, and you can use the filling for burritos, nachos, or any of your favorites. Depending on how much liquid is left, you may want to serve with a slotted spoon so you don't disintegrate your taco.

 GLUTEN-FREE OPTION*   NO OIL ADDED

1 package (15 ounces, or 425 g) firm tofu, cubed

1 clove garlic, minced

Zest of 1 lime

Juice of 1 lime

3 tablespoons salsa

½ teaspoon chili powder

¼ teaspoon chipotle powder or smoked paprika

¼ teaspoon cumin

Hot pepper to taste

Salt to taste

SERVING INGREDIENTS

Hard corn tortilla taco shells (*use gluten-free)

☾ THE NIGHT BEFORE: Cut tofu into cubes, mince garlic, and zest then juice the lime. Store everything in one container in the fridge overnight.

☀ IN THE MORNING: Add all the ingredients into an oiled slow cooker. Cook on low 7 - 9 hours. Taste and adjust seasonings. Serve in warmed corn tortilla shells.

Serve this with Mashed Potato Edamame Burritos (recipe page 37) and Spanish Quinoa (recipe page 143).

YIELD: 6 servings
This recipe requires a small 1- to 1.5-quart slow cooker often know as a Little Dipper. You can double or triple the recipe and use a larger slow cooker.
COOKING TIME: 7 to 9 hours on low

NO-HONEY TOFU LETTUCE WRAPS

Summer is the perfect time to use your slow cooker. It's a great way to make dinner in the morning, it's mostly hands off until you're ready to eat, and it doesn't heat up your kitchen. Cheryl asked me to make a vegan version of honey chicken for her, and this Vegan Slow Cooker No-Honey Tofu was born. If you're allergic to soy, you could make this with hemp tofu, cooked chickpeas, or even cauliflower florets in place of the tofu.

 GLUTEN-FREE OPTION*   NO OIL ADDED

SAUCE INGREDIENTS

½ cup (120 ml) water

¼ cup (60 ml) soy sauce (*use a gluten-free version or coconut aminos)

3 tablespoons (18 g) nutritional yeast

3 tablespoons (45 g) agave nectar or maple syrup

1 tablespoon (8 g) minced ginger

½ tablespoon (8 ml) rice vinegar

1 teaspoon minced garlic

SLOW COOKER INGREDIENTS

¼ cup (32 g) sliced onions

1 cup (130 g) carrot coins

1 package (15 ounces, or 420 g) firm or extra-firm tofu, cut into cubes

BEFORE SERVING INGREDIENTS

1 heaping teaspoon organic corn starch, optional (makes the sauce thicken)

SERVING INGREDIENTS

12 lettuce leaves

☾ THE NIGHT BEFORE: Mix all the sauce ingredients together and set aside. Prepare the veggies and store everything in the fridge overnight.

☀ IN THE MORNING: Layer the onion and carrots on the bottom of the slow cooker, then top with the tofu. Pour the sauce evenly over the tofu. Cook on low 7 to 9 hours.

15 MINITES BEFORE SERVING: If you want to make the sauce thick like the one at your favorite restaurant, mix the cornstarch with about 1 or 2 tablespoons of water to dissolve, then add to the slow cooker and mix well. Turn to high and cook 15 more minutes. The sauce will thicken.

YIELD: 4 servings
EQUIPMENT: 1.5 or 2- quart slow cooker
COOKING TIME: 7 to 9 hours on low

Serving Suggestion

You can garnish with shredded carrots and zucchini to pretty it up, or use chopped green onions.

SAGE WALNUT PESTO SQUASH
Panini Filling

This was inspired by a butternut squash panini that was made for the Bull City Vegan Challenge. Toast is the restaurant that made the original sandwich, make sure to visit them if you are ever in Durham, NC, they always have a vegan soup.

 GLUTEN-FREE OPTION* SOY-FREE  NO OIL ADDED OPTION**

1 medium butternut squash

3 to 4 fresh sage leaves

4 rosemary leaves

Leaves from 1 sprig of thyme

½ cup (56 g) walnuts

2 tablespoons (30 ml) olive oil (** use water instead to make it oil-free)

¼ cup (24 g) nutritional yeast

SERVING INGREDIENTS

Bread, for serving (*use gluten-free bread)

☾ THE NIGHT BEFORE: Get a whole butternut squash that will fit into your slow cooker. Poke holes and put it in the slow cooker on low overnight 7 to 9 hours. (No water or oil is needed.)

☀ IN THE MORNING: Put whole squash in the fridge after letting it cool for about 30 minutes.

BEFORE PANINI MAKING: Take the squash out of the fridge and cut it in half. Scrape out the seeds. Take 1½ to 2 cups of the flesh to use for this recipe, store or freeze the rest for another dish or to remake this one at a later date.

Purée the squash.

Make the pesto by combining the herbs, walnuts, and olive oil in a food processor and pulse until it's grainy but not puréed. Mix the pesto and the nutritional yeast into the squash purée. Use this spread in between 2 slices of bread and cook on the stove top. Use a panini pan if you have one. As an alternative, you can use a pan and a heavy skillet that will fit inside it to press the sandwich or you could use a grill and heavy object of your choice.

YIELD: 6 servings
EQUIPMENT: 4- to 6-quart slow cooker
COOKING TIME: 7 to 9 hours on low

ASIAN LETTUCE WRAPS

In this case iceberg lettuce can be your friend. I love the crunch you get from biting into it, and its mild flavor really lets the Asian filling stand out. This is the perfect food to cook for a summer light dinner because the slow cooker doesn't heat up your house. It's just one more bonus that you can have it ready and waiting for an after-work cocktail party on the deck.

 GLUTEN-FREE OPTION*   SOY-FREE OPTION**   NO OIL ADDED

---

1 package (8 ounces, or 227 g) tempeh, cubed (*make sure to buy plain soy tempeh to make this dish gluten-free, **use minced seitan or shelled edamame beans for soy-free)

1 large stalk celery, minced

2 medium carrots, minced

1 can (8 ounces, or 230 g) water chestnuts, minced

SAUCE INGREDIENTS

2 cloves garlic. minced

1 tablespoon (8 g) grated ginger

1½ cup (375 ml) water

¼ cup (125 ml) soy sauce (*use soy marked gluten-free)

¼ cup (125 ml) seasoned rice vinegar (if you use plain add 1 teaspoon sugar)

¼ teaspoon chili flakes or Sriracha

SERVING INGREDIENTS

Whole iceberg or butter lettuce leaves, for serving

Shredded fresh carrots, for garnish

Scallions, for garnish

☾ THE NIGHT BEFORE: If using tempeh cut into cubes, and steam in a large pot over water for 10 to 15 minutes then drain. (This removes the bitter taste from the tempeh.) While the tempeh is cooking mince water chestnuts, celery and carrot. Mince garlic, grate ginger, and mix all the sauce ingredients together. Store drained tempeh, veggies, and sauce in one container in the fridge overnight.

☀ IN THE MORNING: Add all the ingredients into you slow cooker and smash tempeh with a spoon until it crumbles. Cook on low 7 to 9 hours. Taste and adjust seasonings. Add an additional 1 teaspoon grated ginger if you want to add in a little more. Serve with whole lettuce leaves to wrap filling in.

YIELD: 6 servings
EQUIPMENT: 4-quart slow cooker
COOKING TIME: 7 to 9 hours on low

Recipe Ideas & Variations
Use the same filling and make a Banh Mi sandwich. Serve on a toasted sub roll with fresh bean sprouts, shredded carrots, cilantro, and some jalapeños.

VERDE *almost* ANYTHING!

I love the tangy flavor of tomatillos and the vibrant green color they give stews. This is a cooking sauce that we use with tofu in this recipe. You can substitute cauliflower florets, seitan, chickpeas, or kidney beans.

 GLUTEN-FREE SOY-FREE OPTION* ⬨ NO OIL ADDED

COOKING SALSA INGREDIENTS

1 pound (454 g) tomatillos (about 6–8 large), husks and stems removed and quartered

½ cup (120 ml) water

½ cup (8 g) cilantro (leaves and stems)

1 slice fresh jalapeño or to taste (optional)

2 cloves garlic

1 medium onion, thinly sliced

1 package (16 ounces, or 454 g) extra-firm tofu (*substitute cauliflower florets, seitan, chickpeas, or kidney beans)

BEFORE SERVING INGREDIENTS

Juice of ½ lime

2 tablespoons to ¼ cup (6 g to 24 g) nutritional yeast

Salt, to taste

☾ THE NIGHT BEFORE: Place the tomatillos, water, cilantro, jalapeño and garlic to your blender, and blend until mostly smooth. Cut the tofu into cubes and slice the onion. Store everything in the fridge overnight.

☀ IN THE MORNING: Layer the onion and tofu in your slow cooker, then pour the sauce over them. Cook on low 7 to 9 hours.

RIGHT BEFORE SERVING: Squeeze in the lime juice, and mix in the nutritional yeast. Then add salt to taste.

YIELD: 4 servings
EQUIPMENT: 4-quart slow cooker
COOKING TIME: 7 to 9 hours on low

Recipe Ideas & Variations

Can't find tomatillos near you? Sub store-bought salsa verde for the homemade in the recipe plus ½ cup (120 ml) of water.

MEXICAN SHREDDED JACKFRUIT
for TACOS *and* BOWLS

This spicy jackfruit can be customized to fit your family's tastes. As is, it has a little bite from the chili powder, tang from the green chiles, and a brightness from the lime juice. Try serving it over your favorite grain with some extra sautéed veggies.

 GLUTEN-FREE SOY-FREE NO OIL ADDED

1 can (1 pound 4 ounces, or 567 g) jackfruit in brine (Do not get the kind that's in syrup!!), drained

1 can (15 ounces, or 425 g) black beans, rinsed and drained (or 1½ cups homemade)

1 can (10 ounces, or 283 g) diced tomatoes with green chiles

1 cup (132 g) corn kernels, fresh or frozen

½ cup (80 g) chopped raw onion (use sautéed for a milder flavor)

½ cup (120 ml) water or broth

1½ teaspoon dried oregano

1 teaspoon ground cumin

½ teaspoon chili powder (use chipotle powder to make it spicier)

½ teaspoon jalapeño powder (optional)

½ teaspoon smoked paprika

BEFORE SERVING INGREDIENTS

Juice of ½ a lime

Salt, to taste

✳ IN THE MORNING: Add the jackfruit, black beans, tomatoes, corn, water, oregano, cumin, chili powder, jalapeño powder (if using), and smoked paprika to your slow cooker crock.

Cook on low for 7 to 9 hours.

BEFORE SERVING: Use a spatula to press on the jackfruit chunks and they will begin to shred. Continue until all of it is shredded and mix well.

Add lime and salt, plus any additional seasoning that you feel was cooked out such as a little extra oregano or smoked paprika.

YIELD: 6 servings
EQUIPMENT: 4-quart slow cooker
COOKING TIME: 7 to 9 hours on low

KING MUSHROOM BBQ

King mushrooms might just be the new jackfruit. When you cut them in half you can shred them with a fork and it looks just like jackfruit. You can use your favorite bbq sauce or try my Citrus Rum BBQ Sauce on page 164. In the South, we eat our bbq topped with coleslaw on lightly toasted buns.

 GLUTEN-FREE OPTION*   SOY-FREE   NO OIL ADDED

8 cups (560 g) shredded king mushrooms

1 cup (235 ml) of your favorite vegan bbq sauce (or recipe on page 164)

½ cup (120 ml) water

SERVING INGREDIENTS

Buns (*use gluten-free)

Cole slaw (optional)

☾ THE NIGHT BEFORE: Shred the mushrooms using 2 forks. You can either mash the top or cut them off. Store in the fridge.

☀ IN THE MORNING: Mix the shredded mushrooms, bbq sauce, and water in your slow cooker. Cook on low 7 to 9 hours.

YIELD: 12 servings
EQUIPMENT: 4-quart slow cooker
COOKING TIME: 7 to 9 hours on low

CHAPTER 10

Breads

No one would think a pizza or quick bread could come out of a slow cooker. But basically, a slow cooker is like a small oven, the main difference being the amount of moisture that's present during cooking. The nice thing is that it doesn't heat up the kitchen like an oven, so it's perfect for summer. Plus, it gives you more oven space when you need it for a party.

Keep the moisture from ruining the breads by putting a clean dish towel under the lid to soak up the condensation. You can also place a wooden spoon between the slow cooker and the lid, which will create a space for the condensation to evaporate. The larger the gap, the more it will add to the cooking time, so pick your spoon accordingly.

You can also bake in a loaf pan in your slow cooker. I like the glass ones with no handles. When you are using a pan inside your slow cooker, keep the bottom of the pan slightly elevated from the bottom of the crock. I do this by taking a piece of aluminum foil, rolling it into a rope, and joining the ends into an oval or circle. Then I just place the foil ring in the bottom of the crock and place the pan on top of it. You may need to press just a little to flatten out the foil so your baked goods will be even.

Just like an oven, your slow cooker may have hot spots. I rotate my crock about every hour when I'm baking so one side doesn't cook faster than the other.

SAVORY CHEDDAR SAUSAGE BREAD

This is a savory quick bread that has a nice herb flavor that's complemented by the bite of vegan cheddar cheese.

 GLUTEN-FREE OPTION*  SOY-FREE OPTION** NO OIL ADDED OPTION***

2 cups (240 g) whole-wheat pastry flour (*or gluten-free baking mix)

1 tablespoon (8 g) baking powder

½ teaspoon baking soda

¼ teaspoon salt

Pepper, to taste

2 tablespoons (14 g) ground flaxseed mixed with 2 tablespoons (30 ml) water

2 tablespoons (30 ml) olive oil (use ***aquafaba to make it oil-free)

1 cup (235 ml) unsweetened or plain nondairy milk

1½ cups (153 g) sausage crumbles, cooked, or Apple Sage Sausage (page 240) or chopped Italian sausage links (page 239)

Combine the flour, baking powder, baking soda, salt, and pepper in a large bowl. In another bowl, combine the flaxseed mixture, oil, and milk.

Add the dry mixture to the wet and stir with a wooden spoon until it is just combined. Stir in the sausage and cheese.

Pour the mixture into an oiled crock or into an oiled loaf pan that fits in your slow cooker.

Cook on high, propping up the lid with a wooden spoon to allow the condensation to escape, for 1½ to 2½ hours if cooked in the crock or 3 to 3½ hours if cooked in the loaf pan, or until the middle feels springy when touched.

Remember, if you cook it in a loaf pan, it will continue to cook a little more after you remove it from the slow cooker.

YIELD: 1 loaf

EQUIPMENT: 6-quart oval slow cooker

COOKING TIME: 1½ to 2½ hours on high if cooked in the crock or 3 to 3½ hours on high if cooked in the loaf pan

VEGGIE CORNBREAD

This is a traditional Southern cornbread. It doesn't have any wheat flour in it, only cornmeal. The moisture of the zucchini replaces the oil to make it easy on your waistline, too. Cooking it in the slow cooker will make it extra moist. I like to serve thick and hearty, home-style beans over this for a complete meal.

 GLUTEN-FREE SOY-FREE  NO OIL ADDED OPTION*

1 tablespoon (15 ml) apple cider vinegar

1½ cups (355 ml) nondairy milk

2 cups (275 g) cornmeal

½ teaspoon salt

1½ teaspoons baking powder

½ teaspoon baking soda

3 tablespoons (45 ml) aquafaba

1 cup (132 g) fresh or frozen corn kernels

½ cup (75 g) chopped bell pepper

1½ cup (128 g) broccoli slaw

Add the vinegar to the milk and set aside for 5 minutes. It won't curdle if it's not soymilk, but the vinegar will add a little tang.

In a large bowl, combine the cornmeal, salt, baking powder, and baking soda.

Add the milk mixture, aquafaba, corn, bell pepper, and broccoli slaw to the bowl. Mix until combined. If your mix is not moist enough to combine the mixture, add an extra 1 tablespoon (15 ml) water and mix again.

Pour the mixture into an oiled crock (*or use parchment to keep oil-free). Cook on high for 1½ to 2½ hours if cooking in propping up the lid with a wooden spoon to all the condensation to escape or cover with a clean dish towel between the lid and the crock.

After 2 hours, stick a fork in the center and see if it comes out clean; if not, cook longer and check again. The center will still stay moister than it would if it were oven-baked, but you will see a difference on the fork as it continues to cook.

YIELD: 6 servings
EQUIPMENT: 4-quart slow cooker
COOKING TIME: 1 to 1½ hours on high

FOOLPROOF FOCACCIA

Bread and pizza aren't the first things most people think of when they think of using a slow cooker, but it's perfect for hot summer months, plus you can run errands while the dough is rising or the bread is cooking. This focaccia recipe is easy because it requires no kneading and the dough lasts for 7 days. I make my dough over the weekend and slow cook it throughout the week as I need it.

 SOY-FREE ⬤ NO OIL ADDED OPTION*

1 tablespoon (12 g) or 1 packet dry yeast

1½ cups (355 ml) warm water (105° to 115°F [40.5° to 46°C])

½ teaspoon agave nectar or maple syrup

2 tablespoons (30 ml) olive oil, plus more for drizzling (*or use aquafaba)

2 cups (240 g) whole-wheat flour

1 cup (120 g) white whole-wheat or unbleached white flour

1¼ teaspoons salt

Coarse salt, for sprinkling (optional)

Dried or fresh rosemary, for sprinkling (optional)

YIELD: Dough for 2 focaccias or 4 pizzas
EQUIPMENT: 5½-quart (5 L) oval slow cooker
COOKING TIME: 1 to 1½ hours on high

Combine the yeast, warm water, and agave nectar in a large bowl. Let it sit for 5 to 10 minutes. You should be able to see the difference in the mixture as the yeast grows. The yeast expands and looks almost foamy. When this happens, add the olive oil, flours, and salt and stir with a wooden spoon until combined, or use a mixer with a dough hook. The batter will be very sticky.

Turn the dough out onto a floured cutting board and separate the dough depending on what you plan on making. This recipe makes one thick focaccia, but you can split it in half to make two thinner ones. (You can also make 4 pizzas from this recipe; see page 173.) Store any extra dough in a covered bowl in the fridge for later in the week.

Oil the crock of your slow cooker. Shape the dough to fit the shape of the slow cooker. I like to use a 5½-quart (5 L) oval slow cooker for this, but a round one will work, too. The size and shape of the slow cooker will affect the overall thickness.

Place the shaped dough into the slow cooker.

For focaccia, make indentions with your fingers or a fork, drizzle with more olive oil, and sprinkle with coarse salt and chopped rosemary. Let it rise for about 1 hour with the lid on and the slow cooker turned off.

Place a clean dish towel under the lid while it's cooking to absorb the condensation that will otherwise drip down onto your bread and increase the cooking time. Cook on high for 1½ to 2 hours, or until the middle feels springy.

PERFECT PIZZA *from your* SLOW COOKER

It's really surprising just how much you can do in the slow cooker. Pizza is great in the slow cooker on those blistering hot summer days, when you can't bear to turn on the oven. It's also a great treat when you go camping. I bring premade dough, prechopped veggies, and vegan mozzarella in the cooler. You'll be greeted with lots of oohs and aahs by your camping buddies.

This is a free-form recipe. Use as little or as much sauce as you would typically put on your pizza. The same goes for toppings. If you use fresh onion and bell pepper, cut into a small dice and add them at the beginning so they will be cooked by the end.

 SOY-FREE ◯ NO OIL ADDED OPTION*

¼ recipe Foolproof Focaccia dough

¼ to ½ cup (63 to 125 g) tomato sauce

Chopped veggies of choice, such as onion, green pepper, All-Occasion Roasted Garlic (page 234), Balsamic Onion Marmalade (page 234)

BEFORE SERVING INGREDIENTS

½ to 1 cup (62 to 115 g) shredded vegan mozzarella cheese (*or use homemade cheese on page 243)

Oil the crock of your slow cooker. Shape the dough to fit in the slow cooker. Top with the tomato sauce and then the veggies.

Cook on high for 1½ to 2 hours in a large oval slow cooker, or up to 3½ hours in a round 4-quart (3.8 L) slow cooker, propping up the lid with a wooden spoon to allow the condensation to escape.

ABOUT 15 MINUTES BEFORE SERVING: Sprinkle with the shredded vegan mozzarella. Serve once the cheese is melted (if you are using a vegan cheese that melts, of course).

YIELD: dough for 2 focaccias or 4 pizzas
EQUIPMENT: 5½-quart (5 L) oval slow cooker
COOKING TIME: 1½ to 2 hours in an oval 6-quart on high or 3½ hours in a round 4-quart on high

---

A Worthy Note

This recipe works best in a larger oval slow cooker because the dough will be thinner and cook faster. In a 4-quart (3.8 L) round one it will be more of a thick-crust pizza and will have a longer cooking time.

WHOLE-WHEAT PUMPKIN GINGERBREAD

This gingerbread gets a nutrition boost and fall flavor from the addition of pumpkin. You can use canned organic pumpkin, or make your own purée (page 247). The slow cooker is perfect for gingerbread because things stay moist. You can use regular flour or even a gluten-free baking mix if you don't have whole-wheat pastry flour on hand.

GLUTEN-FREE OPTION* SOY-FREE NO OIL ADDED OPTION**

2 cups (240 g) whole-wheat pastry flour (* use your favorite gluten-free baking blend)

1 tablespoon (8 g) baking powder

½ teaspoon baking soda

1½ tablespoons (8 g) ground ginger

1 teaspoon cinnamon

½ teaspoon ground cloves

½ teaspoon allspice

¼ teaspoon nutmeg

¼ teaspoon salt

2 tablespoons (14 g) ground flaxseed mixed with 2 tablespoons (30 ml) water

1 cup (245 g) pumpkin purée, store-bought or homemade (page 247)

½ cup (170 g) molasses

½ cup (170 g) agave nectar or maple syrup

¼ cup (60 ml) olive oil (** use additional pumpkin or applesauce to make oil-free)

1 teaspoon vanilla extract

In a large bowl, combine the flour, baking powder, baking soda, ginger, cinnamon, cloves, allspice, nutmeg, and salt.

In another bowl, combine the flaxseed mixture, pumpkin, molasses, agave, oil, and vanilla.

Add the dry mixture to the wet and stir with a wooden spoon until just combined.

Pour the mixture into an oiled crock or into an oiled loaf pan that fits in your slow cooker.

Cook on high, propping up the lid with a wooden spoon to allow the condensation to escape, for 1½ to 2½ hours if cooked in the crock or 2½ to 3½ hours if cooked in the loaf pan, or until a knife inserted into the center comes out almost clean.

Remember, if you cook it in a loaf pan, it will continue to cook a little more after you remove it from the slow cooker.

YIELD: 1 loaf

EQUIPMENT: 4- to 6-quart oval slow cooker

COOKING TIME: 1½ to 2½ hours on high if cooked in a 4 to 5-quart crock, 2½ to 3½ hours on high if cooked in a loaf pan in a 6-quart or larger crock

Wholesome CHOCOLATE CHIP BANANA BREAD

This traditional sweet banana bread is full of chocolaty goodness and great for a decadent breakfast or an easy dessert.

 GLUTEN-FREE OPTION* SOY-FREE NO OIL ADDED OPTION**

2 cups (240 g) whole-wheat pastry flour (* or use your favorite gluten-free baking blend to make gluten-free)

1 tablespoon (8 g) baking powder

½ teaspoon baking soda

2 tablespoons (14 g) ground flaxseed mixed with 2 tablespoons (30 ml) water

½ cup (120 g) applesauce

½ cup (100 g) sugar

2 tablespoons (30 ml) olive oil (** use extra applesauce to make oil-free)

1 teaspoon vanilla extract

3 bananas, mashed

1 cup (175 g) chocolate chips (I like to use mini chips)

In a large bowl, combine the flour, baking powder, and baking soda. In another bowl, combine the flaxseed mixture, applesauce, sugar, oil, vanilla, and bananas.

Add the dry mixture to the wet and stir with a wooden spoon until just combined.

Stir in the chocolate chips.

Pour the mixture into an oiled crock or into an oiled loaf pan that fits in your slow cooker.

Cook on high, propping up the lid with a wooden spoon to allow the condensation to escape, for 1½ to 2½ hours if cooked in the crock or 2½ to 3½ hours if cooked in the loaf pan, or until the center feels springy when touched.

Remember, if you cook it in a loaf pan, it will continue to cook a little more after you remove it from the slow cooker.

YIELD: 1 loaf
EQUIPMENT: 4- to 6-quart oval slow cooker
COOKING TIME: 1½ to 2½ hours on high if cooked in a 4 to 5-quart crock, 2½ to 3½ hours on high if cooked in a loaf pan in a 6-quart or larger crock

ROSEMARY WHOLE-WHEAT ROLLS

Ready to hear oohs and aahs from your guests? Make these moist and delicious rolls,
and tell everyone you baked them in your slow cooker. It's great for big holiday meals.

 SOY-FREE NO OIL ADDED OPTION*

SPONGE INGREDIENTS

½ cup (120 ml) water

½ cup (120 ml) nondairy milk

2 teaspoons (9 g) sugar (or you can use maple syrup, agave, or raw sugar)

2¼ teaspoons active dry yeast

DOUGH INGREDIENTS

3 tablespoons (45 ml) olive oil (*or aquafaba)

1 teaspoon salt

3 cups (750 g) whole-wheat flour (or substitute white whole-wheat flour)

Make sure the nondairy milk and water is warm, but not hot enough to kill the yeast. You can test it on your wrist to make sure it's not too hot. You can warm them up on the stove or in the microwave to begin with if they are cold.

Add the sugar and yeast to the bowl of your stand mixer. Mix well with the paddle attachment and let sit for about 10 minutes, or until the yeast begins to bloom and gets foamy. (This make take longer on cold days.)

Add the olive oil or aquafaba, salt, and 1 cup (250 g) flour to the sponge and mix well. Remove the paddle and put on the dough hook, add the other 2 cups (500 g) flour and knead on a low speed for 8 minutes.

If your dough is too wet and doesn't form into a ball, you may need to add extra flour. Add ¼ cup (63 g) at a time until the dough firms up and form a ball around the dough hook.

You can use any slow cooker, though I prefer to use a round one. I made one batch in a 3-quart and another in a 4-quart and both worked fine.

Prepare your slow cooker by lining with parchment paper so the rolls will be easy to lift out.

Sprinkle some flour on a cutting board and put the kneaded dough on it. Divide into 8 even pieces and roll into balls.

Place these in the lined slow cooker. Cover the top of the crock with a clean dish towel or a few paper towels under the lid. This keeps the condensation from dripping on your rolls and making them soggy.

Let rise in the slow cooker by cooking on low for 45 minutes. Then cook on high for 45 minutes to 1 hour.

The tops won't brown like they would in the oven, but you can tell if they are done by looking at how brown the sides and bottom are.

YIELD: 6 servings

EQUIPMENT: 4-quart slow cooker recommended, but larger sizes will work fine

COOKING TIME: 45 minutes on low, then 45 minutes to 1 hour on high

CITRUS ROSEMARY BREAKFAST BREAD

Start the morning with an orangey treat that has a touch of pine from the rosemary. It's made with whole-wheat pastry flour, so it's healthier than your average quick bread. This recipe uses sugar, but you can substitute agave nectar or maple syrup if you prefer. You'll just need to add a few more tablespoons of flour to make up for the extra moisture.

 GLUTEN-FREE OPTION*  SOY-FREE   NO OIL ADDED OPTION**

½ cup (100 g) sugar

2 cups (240 g) whole-wheat pastry flour (*use gluten-free baking mix)

1 tablespoon (8 g) baking powder

½ teaspoon baking soda

1 tablespoon (2 g) minced fresh rosemary

2 tablespoons (14 g) ground flaxseed mixed with 2 tablespoons (30 ml) water

½ cup (120 g) applesauce

2 tablespoons (30 ml) olive oil (** substitute additional applesauce to make oil-free)

½ cup (120 ml) orange juice

Juice of ½ lemon

1 teaspoon vanilla extract

1 teaspoon orange or lemon extract

Combine the sugar, flour, baking powder, baking soda, and rosemary in a large bowl.

In another bowl, combine the flaxseed mixture, applesauce, oil, orange juice, lemon juice, and extracts. Add the wet mixture to the dry and stir with wooden spoon until just combined.

Pour the mixture into an oiled crock or into an oiled loaf pan that fits in your slow cooker.

Cook on high, propping up the lid with a wooden spoon to allow the condensation to escape, for 1½ to 2½ hours if cooked in the crock or 2½ to 3½ hours if cooked in the loaf pan, or until a knife inserted into the center comes out almost clean.

Remember, if you cook it in a loaf pan, it will continue to cook a little more after you remove it from the slow cooker.

YIELD: 1 loaf
EQUIPMENT: 4-to 6-quart oval slow cooker
COOKING TIME: 1½ to 2½ hours on high if cooked in a 4 to 5-quart crock, 2½ to 3½ hours on high if cooked in a loaf pan in a 6-quart or larger crock

CHAPTER 11

Snacks & Appetizers

I love throwing parties. At any party you need to have a few nibbles to serve with drinks while all your guests arrive, especially if your friends are like mine and arrive fashionably late. It's part of being a good host, and it keeps everyone's blood sugar at an acceptable level.

Most of these recipes use a 1½- to 2-quart (1.4 to 1.9 L) slow cooker. You can double or triple the recipes and use a larger slow cooker, but I didn't think you'd really want 4 quarts (3.8 L) of bean dip (even if you can use the leftovers for burrito filling).

BLUEBERRY BALSAMIC MEATBALL SAUCE
with ROSEMARY

The inspiration for this recipe comes from theNoshery.com's blog. This savory sauce has sweet flavors of blueberries and raspberries that are balanced out with rosemary and tangy balsamic. Serve over baked vegan meatballs. (I tried making the meatballs in a larger slow cooker with the sauce, but the meatballs completely lost their shape, so I would not recommend doing it that way.)

Note: This recipe requires a small 1½- to 2-quart (1.4 to 1.9 L) slow cooker or a small ovenproof dish in a larger slow cooker. You can double or triple the recipe and use a larger slow cooker if you like.

 GLUTEN-FREE OPTION*   SOY-FREE OPTION** ⬦ NO OIL ADDED

12 ounces (340 g) fresh or frozen blueberries

2 tablespoons (30 ml) agave nectar or maple syrup

1 tablespoon (16 g) tomato paste

½ cup (120 ml) raspberry or plain balsamic vinegar

½ cup (120 ml) red wine

½ cup (120 ml) water

1 clove garlic, minced

2 sprigs fresh rosemary

BEFORE SERVING INGREDIENTS

1 bag of your favorite frozen vegan Not-meatballs (*use gluten-free **use soy-free)

Add the blueberries, agave, tomato paste, vinegar, wine, water, and garlic to a blender and purée. Oil the crock of your slow cooker. Add the purée and the rosemary and cook on low for 3 to 4 hours, or on high for 1½ to 2 hours. (Many small slow cookers have no temperature control, so they cook everything on low.) Remove and discard the rosemary sprigs. Switch to warm or low to keep the sauce warm for a party.

Serve over vegan meatballs that have just come out of the oven, or keep the sauce in the slow cooker on warm and have the meatballs on the side for dipping.

YIELD: 12 servings
EQUIPMENT: 1½- to 2-quart (1.4 to 1.9 L) slow cooker
COOKING TIME: 3 to 4 hours on low

A Worthy Note
You can make the sauce the day before and keep it in the fridge until you are ready to reheat it for serving.

SPICY MAPLE NUT MIX

You catch a little heat at the end of this nut mix, but it's the sweet that you notice first.

 GLUTEN-FREE   SOY-FREE   ⬤ NO OIL ADDED OPTION*

SAUCE INGREDIENTS

¼ cup (60 ml) apple cider vinegar

2 tablespoons (30 ml) maple syrup

1 tablespoon (15 ml) olive oil (* use aquafaba to make oil-free)

½ teaspoon cayenne pepper

½ teaspoon chipotle chile powder

¼ teaspoon garlic powder

¼ teaspoon paprika (regular or smoked)

4 cups* nuts of choice (I used cashews, pecans, and whole almonds)

You need to measure the nuts by volume because the weight will vary greatly depending on which nuts you choose.

To make the sauce: Oil the crock of your slow cooker *or use parchment paper to keep oil-free. Whisk the sauce ingredients together in the slow cooker until blended. Add the nuts and stir to coat.

Make sure your slow cooker is not more than three-fourths of the way full. Cook on high, uncovered, for 1 to 1½ hours, or until the nuts becomes crunchy, stirring every 10 to 15 minutes to prevent burning.

YIELD: 7 to 9 servings
EQUIPMENT: 4-quart slow cooker
COOKING TIME: 1 to 1½ hours on high

Recipe Ideas & Variations
The recipe as it's written is medium hot. If you like yours fiery, double the amount of chile powder.

Old Fashioned CEREAL SNACK MIX

When I was little one of my favorite things to make with my mom was Chex mix. I think the wheat Chex were the closest thing to health food in my family's pantry. Times change, and my pantry is certainly much healthier than the one I grew up with, but I still love snack mix.

 GLUTEN-FREE OPTION*   SOY-FREE   NO OIL ADDED OPTION**

SAUCE INGREDIENTS

3 tablespoons (42 g) nondairy butter or (45 ml) olive oil (**or use aquafaba)

3 tablespoons (45 ml) vegan Worcestershire sauce

½ teaspoon garlic powder

½ teaspoon dried thyme

½ teaspoon paprika

¼ teaspoon celery seed

¼ teaspoon turmeric

Salt, to taste

6 cups waffled unsweetened cereal, such as Chex (use a mixture of equal parts corn, rice, and wheat cereal, if possible or *your favorite gluten-free cereals)

You need to measure the cereal by volume rather than weight in this recipe. This is because weight will vary greatly depending on the brand's density.

To make the sauce: Oil the crock of your slow cooker **or line with parchment paper. Combine the sauce ingredients in the slow cooker and cook on high, covered, for 15 minutes, until the butter is melted. Add the cereal and stir to combine. Make sure your slow cooker is not more than three-fourths of the way full. The sauce will make the snack mix a little soggy, but the mixture will get crispy again as it cooks.

Cook, uncovered, for 1 to 1½ hours, or until the mixture becomes crunchy again, stirring every 10 to 15 minutes to prevent burning.

YIELD: 8 to 10 servings
EQUIPMENT: 4-quart slow cooker
COOKING TIME: 1 to 1½ hours on high

Recipe Ideas & Variations

Add your favorite extras to personalize your snack mix. My testers used mixed nuts, pretzels, and bagel chips. You can add them during cooking or after if you don't have room for them in your slow cooker.

PIMENTO CHEESE FONDUE

I grew up with sweet tea and grilled pimento cheese sandwiches. This is a way for vegans to enjoy cheesy goodness flecked with sweet, diced pimento. Serve it with veggies and toast points for dipping. Or serve over whole pieces of toast to make an English main dish called rarebit. The recipe is easy to double (or even triple), so it's great for a party.

Note: This recipe requires a 1½- to 2-quart (1.4 to 1.9 L) slow cooker. You can double or triple the recipe and use a larger slow cooker if you like.

 GLUTEN-FREE   SOY-FREE  NO OIL ADDED OPTION*

---

1 can (15 ounces, or 420 g) white beans, drained and rinsed, or 1½ cups (340 g) homemade

¾ cup (180 ml) water

2 tablespoons (12 g) vegan chicken-flavored bouillon or 4 tablespoons (24 g) DIY Golden Bouillon (page 237)

1 jar (2 ounces, or 56 g) diced pimentos, drained

2 cups (225 g) shredded vegan cheddar cheese, store-bought or recipe on page 243

2 tablespoons (28 g) vegan mayonnaise or olive oil *use unsweetened non-dairy milk to make oil-free

½ teaspoon stone-ground mustard

Salt and pepper, to taste

Add the beans and the water to a food processor or blender, and purée until smooth.

Oil the crock of the slow cooker.

Add the purée and the remaining ingredients. Cook on low for 1 to 1½ hours, or until the cheese is fully melted. You will need to stir it a few times (about every 20 minutes) during cooking to fully incorporate the cheese as it melts.

If you prefer a thinner fondue, just add more water until it is the consistency that you desire.

YIELD: 4 servings
EQUIPMENT: 1½- to 2-quart (1.4 to 1.9 L) slow cooker
COOKING TIME: 1 to 1½ hours on low

Serving Suggestion

Use leftovers as a sandwich filling, and grill your sandwich for a traditional Southern treat.

Subtly SPICY PEANUT COCONUT FONDUE

Peanut fondue is a perfect cocktail party dish. Serve with crispy pan-fried tempeh strips, firm tofu cubes, tiny boiled potatoes, and lightly steamed veggies.

Note: Both recipes on this page require a 1½- to 2-quart (1.4 to 1.9 L) slow cooker. You can double or triple the recipe and use a larger slow cooker if you like.

 GLUTEN-FREE OPTION*   SOY-FREE OPTION**   NO OIL ADDED

½ cup (130 g) peanut butter

1 can (14 ounces, or 392 g) light coconut milk

1 clove garlic, minced

1½ tablespoons (12 g) grated ginger

½ to 1 teaspoon soy sauce (to taste)
  *use gluten-free soy sauce, **or use coconut aminos

¼ to ½ teaspoon ground chile

½ to 1 teaspoon garam masala

1 tablespoon (8 g) cornstarch, as needed

Oil the crock of your slow cooker. Combine the peanut butter, coconut milk, garlic, ginger, soy sauce, ground chile, and garam masala in the slow cooker.

Cook on low for 1½ to 2 hours, or until the dip is heated through. If it's too thin, add the cornstarch and cook 15 minutes longer.

YIELD: 4 servings
EQUIPMENT: 1½- to 2-quart (1.4 to 1.9 L) slow cooker
COOKING TIME: 1 to 1½ hours on low

SMOKY BEAN DIP

When you find yourself with an impromptu party, you can make this dip with pantry staples. You control just how spicy this will be by your choice of salsa.

 GLUTEN-FREE OPTION*   SOY-FREE   NO OIL ADDED

1 can (16 ounces, or 454 g) vegan refried beans or 1½ cups (340 g) homemade from page 39

½ cup (130 g) mild or spicy salsa

½ cup (58 g) shredded vegan cheddar cheese

2 to 6 drops liquid smoke (to taste)

½ teaspoon cumin

Salt, to taste

Add all the ingredients and cook on low for 1 to 1½ hours.

YIELD: 4 servings
1½- to 2-quart (1.4 to 1.9 L) slow cooker
COOKING TIME: 1 to 1½ hours on low

SPINACH ARTICHOKE DIP

The cashew sour cream makes this dip thick and rich. This is the traditional spinach artichoke dip that I ate a lot of when I lived in New Orleans, only veganized. Serve with fresh veggies, crackers, or toast points.

 GLUTEN-FREE SOY-FREE  NO OIL ADDED OPTION*

2 tablespoons (30 ml) olive oil (*water sauté)

1 small onion, minced

1 clove garlic, minced

8 cups (10 ounces, or 280 g) fresh baby spinach, washed

1 recipe Cashew Sour Cream (page 53)

Splash of water

1 can (14 ounces, or 392 g) artichoke hearts (packed in water, not marinated)

⅓ cup (37 g) nutritional yeast (*use gluten-free)

¼ teaspoon smoked paprika or plain paprika and a few drops liquid smoke

¼ teaspoon nutmeg (freshly grated, if possible)

Salt and pepper, to taste

Heat the oil in a skillet over medium heat and sauté the onion until translucent, 3 to 5 minutes. Add the garlic and spinach sauté until the spinach is reduced, 5 to 10 minutes.

Oil the crock of your slow cooker. Add the warm spinach mixture, cashew sour cream, water, artichokes, nutritional yeast, paprika, nutmeg, and salt and pepper and mix well.

Cook on high for 30 minutes to 1 hour or on low for 1 to 1½ hours, until thoroughly heated through.

Once hot, turn down the slow cooker to warm or low, and it will stay warm through the party.

(Many small slow cookers have no temperature control, so they cook everything on low.) You may need to stir it every once in a while to prevent the top of the dip from turning brown and drying out.

YIELD: 8 servings
EQUIPMENT: 4-quart slow cooker
COOKING TIME: 1 to 1½ hours on low

CHERRY BOURBON COCKTAIL CARROTS

Everyone needs a good retro snack for a cocktail party. This one uses one of everyone's favorite veggie—the baby carrot. And the sauce is more sophisticated than mixing ketchup with grape jelly—it adds cherry jam and bourbon to premade ketchup. Don't forget you can make your own ketchup, too. Just use the recipe on page 246.

 GLUTEN-FREE SOY-FREE  NO OIL ADDED OPTION*

SAUCE INGREDIENTS

½ cup (120 g) ketchup

½ cup (115 g) brown sugar

½ cup (120 ml) water

2 tablespoons (30 ml) bourbon (or sub whiskey or rum)

2 tablespoons (40 g) cherry jam or preserves

2 teaspoons (10 ml) apple cider vinegar

1 teaspoon toasted sesame oil (optional)
 * leave out to make oil-free

1 teaspoon minced garlic

1 bag (1 pound, or 454 g) baby carrots

☾ **THE NIGHT BEFORE:** Mix together all the sauce ingredients and store overnight in the fridge.

☀ **IN THE MORNING:** Add the carrots and sauce to your small slow cooker, and cook on low for 7 to 9 hours.

YIELD: 8 servings
EQUIPMENT: 1½- to 2-quart (1.4 to 1.9 L) slow cooker
COOKING TIME: 7 to 9 hours on low

Recipe Ideas & Variations
Want to make this for a party tonight? Add everything to your slow cooker and cook on high for 3 hours!

CHAPTER 12

Breakfasts

Every chilly morning, I have a hot breakfast waiting for me in my slow cooker. I'm a Southern girl, so grits are a part of my morning rotation, but oatmeal, quinoa, rice, and polenta work their way in, too.

It's also nice to have a fun, fancy weekend breakfast that can cook in less than 2 hours. Get a head start on your weekend, and put the Weekend Tofu and Hash Brown Casserole (page 206) or the Pear and Cardamom French Toast Casserole (page 207) on to cook.

Many of these recipes call for a 1½- to 2-quart (1.4 to 1.9 L) slow cooker. If you are making breakfast for 2 or 3 people, it's the perfect size. It's inexpensive and you'll use it for dips and fondues, too, so it's worth getting one. You can always double or triple the recipe and use a larger slow cooker. But remember, your cooker needs to be half to three-fourths full.

And don't forget about coffee, tea, and spiced cider. All of them work great in the slow cooker, and are perfect for a large brunch.

LEMON ZUCCHINI WALNUT OATS

This oatmeal is chock-full of zucchini and full of flavor. If you're trying to get rid of your zucchini surplus, or just sneak in some veggies on the kids, this is the oatmeal for you. If you have picky eaters, peel your zucchini and they'll never know! Note: You can double or triple the recipe and use a larger slow cooker if you like.

 GLUTEN-FREE OPTION*   SOY-FREE   NO OIL ADDED OPTION**

½ cup (40 g) steel-cut oats (*use gluten-free)

1½ cups (355 ml) vanilla-flavored nondairy milk

½ small zucchini, grated

Pinch of salt

2 tablespoons (30 g or ml) brown sugar or maple syrup

SERVING INGREDIENTS

2 teaspoons (4 g) grated lemon zest (or 1 teaspoon lemon extract)

¼ cup (28 g) chopped walnuts

☾ THE NIGHT BEFORE: Oil the crock of your slow cooker, **or line with a piece of parchment paper to keep oil-free. Combine the oats, milk, zucchini, salt, and brown sugar in the slow cooker. Cook on low for 7 to 9 hours.

☀ IN THE MORNING: Stir the oatmeal, taste and adjust the seasonings. Add more milk, if needed. Top with the lemon zest and walnuts.

YIELD: 2 servings
EQUIPMENT: 1½- to 2-quart slow cooker
COOKING TIME: 7 to 9 hours on low

VANILLA MAPLE PUMPKIN LATTE

*Fall comes around and hot drinks start seeming better than—or at least as good as—
iced ones. Wake up, throw all the ingredients into the slow cooker, and in 1½ to 2 hours
you have piping hot lattes made with the nondairy milk of your choice. Because you
made this yourself, you can walk around in your comfy sweater and feel slightly smug
as you watch the leaves fall.*

 GLUTEN-FREE SOY-FREE NO OIL ADDED

**1 to 2 cups (250 ml) brewed coffee
or espresso (use more if you like
stronger coffee flavor)**

**2 cups (500 ml) vanilla almond milk (or
nondairy vanilla milk of your choice,
or plain plus 1 teaspoon vanilla
extract)**

**2 to 4 tablespoons (30 to 60 ml) maple
syrup (to taste)**

**3 tablespoons (45 g) pumpkin purée
(store-bought or the recipe on
page 247)**

1 teaspoon cinnamon

¼ teaspoon cloves

¼ teaspoon allspice

⅛ teaspoon nutmeg

Put everything in your blender and blend until smooth. Then
pour into your 2-quart slow cooker (or double or triple the
recipe to use a larger slow cooker).

Cook on high for 1½ to 2 hours. Stir well before serving, the
pumpkin tends to settle at the bottom.

If your small cooker has no heat control, it cooks on low.
Leave yours to cook for about 3 hours, or until hot.

YIELD: 2 to 3 servings
EQUIPMENT: 2-quart slow cooker
COOKING TIME: 1½ to 2 hours on high

CINNAMON SPICE SYRUP

This is a variation on a large coffee chain's syrup. It also goes great in tea, in apple cider, on crêpes, or with the Pear and Cardamom French Toast Casserole on page 207. Note: You can double or triple the recipe and use a larger slow cooker if you like.

 GLUTEN-FREE SOY-FREE  NO OIL ADDED

1 cup (235 ml) water

3 or 4 whole cinnamon sticks

6 whole cloves

¼ teaspoon allspice

⅛ teaspoon nutmeg

1 cup (225 g) packed brown sugar, (235 ml) agave nectar, or (235 ml) maple syrup

Combine the water, cinnamon, cloves, allspice, and nutmeg in the slow cooker.

Whisk to combine.

Cook on low for 5 to 8 hours.

Strain out the cinnamon sticks and spices, stir in the brown sugar, then store in the fridge for 1 to 2 weeks.

YIELD: 6 servings
EQUIPMENT: 1½- to 2-quart (1.4 to 1.9 L) slow cooker
COOKING TIME: 5 to 8 hours on high

Serving Suggestion

Add 1 or 2 tablespoons (15 to 30 ml) to a cup of coffee, tea, or hot apple cider.

Recipe Ideas & Variations

- Make a gingerbread syrup by adding 4 slices fresh ginger and 2 tablespoons (40 g) molasses. Follow the same instructions.
- Want it to taste a little more like the fall drink from the coffee chain? Use brown sugar and increase the amount to 2 cups (450 g). All other ingredients and amounts stay the same.

PUMPKIN SPICE SYRUP
with REAL PUMPKIN

Did you know that Starbuck's pumpkin spice syrup isn't vegan? And there's no pumpkin in it either! This recipe takes care of all your fall cravings, and it's 100% vegan. Now you can drink a pumpkin spice latte anytime you want. You infuse the whole spices in nondairy milk while melting the sugars creating a syrup.

 GLUTEN-FREE   SOY-FREE   NO OIL ADDED

2 cups (475 ml) unsweetened nondairy milk (plain or vanilla)

1 cup (225 g) dark brown sugar or coconut sugar

1 cup (200 g) vegan sugar (white, raw, etc.)

3-inch (7.5-cm) piece of fresh ginger, sliced

4 cinnamon sticks

8 allspice berries

4 whole cloves

BLENDING INGREDIENTS

¼ cup plus 2 tablespoons (92 g) pumpkin purée

¼ to ½ teaspoon salt, to taste (optional)

Add the nondairy milk, sugars, ginger, cinnamon sticks, allspice berries, and cloves to your 2-quart slow cooker crock.

Cook on high for 1 hour, then let cool. Once cool, pour through a fine mesh strainer into your blender.

Add pumpkin and blend on high until smooth. Taste, add salt (if using), and blend again.

Store in the fridge for up to 2 weeks. The pumpkin may settle in the bottom, so stir before using. Note that it will thicken in the fridge.

YIELD: about 3 cups
EQUIPMENT: 2-quart slow cooker
COOKING TIME: 1 hour on high

Serving Suggestion
How to use: Use a few tablespoons in hot or iced coffee to get your vegan pumpkin spice fix. It's also wonderful in hot tea or apple cider, too!

Recipe Ideas & Variations
Sugar-free option: You can make this with the sweetener of your choice, to taste. Just know that it will be much thinner than a syrup made with sugar and may not last as long in the fridge.

Do-It-Yourself CHAI CONCENTRATE

I love chai, but it's getting pricey at coffee shops. It's well worth stocking up on a few spices to make your own, and it's super easy, too. This one is exactly the way I like it, but feel free to add more or less of some spices until it resembles your favorite. If you like licorice, add just one star of anise to get a big flavor punch.

 GLUTEN-FREE   SOY-FREE   NO OIL ADDED

6 cups (1410 ml) water

5 slices fresh ginger

7 whole cinnamon sticks

10 whole cloves

10 whole peppercorns

8 whole allspice berries

¼ teaspoon cardamom seeds

10 tea bags (black, green, or rooibos)

½ to 1 cup (120 to 235 ml) agave nectar or maple syrup (optional) or sweetener of your choice to taste

Combine the water and spices in the slow cooker. Cook on low for 8 to 10 hours.

Add the tea bags to the slow cooker and turn up to high.

Let steep for 5 to 10 minutes, depending on how concentrated you want the flavor to be.

Remove the tea bags and add the agave. Remove the cinnamon sticks.

Pour into a pitcher while straining out the spices through a piece of cheesecloth placed in a funnel.

Store in the fridge for 1 to 2 weeks.

YIELD: 6 servings
EQUIPMENT: 4-quart slow cooker
COOKING TIME: 8 to 10 hours on low

Did You Know?
You can put the spices in a muslin, reusable tea bag, if you have one, and you won't have to strain it later.

Serving Suggestion
Add ½ to 1 cup (120 to 235 ml) of the concentrate to an equal amount nondairy milk. It's great hot or iced!

ANNIE'S MASALA SPICED COFFEE

This is one of Ann Oliverio's creations, and it is delicious. I love the way she spices up coffee with cinnamon, anise, peppercorns, and orange peels. Be sure to check out more of her recipes at her blog, Anunrefinedvegan.com.

 GLUTEN-FREE SOY-FREE  NO OIL ADDED

1¼ cups (295 ml) nondairy milk (I prefer soy)

½ cup (120 ml) freshly-brewed espresso or coffee

2 (2-inch, or 5-cm) slices of orange peel

2 star anise

1 cinnamon stick

4 whole peppercorns (black or white)

6 drops vanilla stevia liquid (or your favorite sweetener, to taste)

Put all the ingredients in a small 1½- to 2-quart slow cooker and set to low. Cook for 3 to 4 hours. You can also cook this on high for 2 to 3 hours. Strain out the solids and discard. Serve with a side of your favorite vegan creamer.

YIELD: 2 to 3 servings
EQUIPMENT: 1½- to 2-quart slow cooker
COOKING TIME: 3 to 4 hours on low

CRANBERRY VANILLA QUINOA

Quinoa is a nice change of pace from plain old oatmeal. And did you know that quinoa is not a grain, but a seed? Plus, it's a complete protein, so it's a perfect way to start your day.

 GLUTEN-FREE ⊛ SOY-FREE

½ cup (86 g) quinoa

2½ cups (588 ml) vanilla-flavored almond milk, plus more as needed

¼ cup (30 g) dried cranberries†

½ cup (123 g) unsweetened applesauce†

½ teaspoon vanilla extract (or scrape ¼ teaspoon vanilla paste from a split whole vanilla bean)

⅛ teaspoon stevia (optional)

SERVING INGREDIENTS

Slivered almonds, for serving

† *Some dried cranberries and applesauces contain ascorbic acid. Ascorbic acid, like lemon juice, will curdle even nondairy milks. If yours contain it, cook with water instead of nondairy milk.*

☾ **THE NIGHT BEFORE:** Rinse the quinoa in a mesh strainer to remove the bitter coating.

Oil the crock of your slow cooker.

Combine the quinoa, milk, cranberries, applesauce, vanilla, and stevia in the slow cooker.

Cook on low for 7 to 9 hours.

⊛ **IN THE MORNING:** Stir the quinoa, and taste and adjust the seasonings, or add more liquid.

Top with the slivered almonds.

YIELD: 2 large servings
EQUIPMENT: 1½- to 2-quart (1.4 to 1.9 L) slow cooker
COOKING TIME: 7 to 9 hours on low

Recipe Ideas & Variations
Try switching out different flavors of apple or pear sauce, or using fruit butters or purées.

Did You Know?
Some quinoa is prerinsed, but some is not. If you are using a new-to-you brand, always assume it is not rinsed, and rinse it yourself. There is nothing worse than throwing away a whole dish because it's too bitter to eat!

PEACH ALMOND BREAKFAST POLENTA

Move over, cream of wheat, it's time to add polenta on the breakfast menu. This recipe has a similar consistency to cream of wheat. Try it the way I've written it (with almond meal and peaches), then make up your own variations. Try cooking up pear and ginger polenta or berries and basil polenta to take advantage of the freshest fruit of the season.

 GLUTEN-FREE SOY-FREE  NO OIL ADDED

½ cup (70 g) polenta

2 cups (470 ml) vanilla-flavored
   nondairy milk

¼ cup (25 g) almond meal

¼ cup (60 g) applesauce†

¼ teaspoon almond extract

2 sprigs thyme (optional)

2 large peaches, peeled, cored, and
   chopped

2 to 4 tablespoons (30 to 60 ml) agave
   nectar or maple syrup

SERVING INGREDIENTS

Minced thyme, for topping (optional)

† *Some applesauces contain ascorbic acid. Ascorbic acid, like lemon juice, will curdle even nondairy milks. If yours contains it, cook with water instead of nondairy milk.*

☾ THE NIGHT BEFORE: Oil the crock of your slow cooker.

Combine the polenta, milk, almond meal, applesauce, almond extract, thyme sprigs, and peaches in the slow cooker.

Cook on low for 7 to 9 hours.

☀ IN THE MORNING: Remove the thyme sprigs. Stir the polenta and add the agave to taste. The amount of sweetener needed will vary with how sweet the peaches are. Top with extra minced thyme.

YIELD: 4 servings
EQUIPMENT: 1½- to 2-quart (1.4 to 1.9 L) slow cooker
COOKING TIME: 7 to 9 hours on low

Recipe Ideas & Variations

Pour leftovers into an oiled pan and chill. Once it has set up, cut into triangles. Grill the triangles until warm. Serve with fresh fruit and additional agave nectar or maple syrup for brunch or dessert.

Big Pot of
GRITS BUFFET

Grits are a staple in any Southern household. Everyone has his or her favorite variation. If you haven't tried grits before, don't be scared. They are very similar to polenta. (In fact, the yellow ones are polenta).

Serve this at a brunch with an assortment of toppings, such as vegan bacon crumbles, vegan cheddar cheese, spicy pickled peppers, and roasted garlic. Everyone loves mix-ins.

 GLUTEN-FREE SOY-FREE  NO OIL ADDED OPTION*

1 cup (140 g) white or yellow grits

4 cups (940 ml) water

2 tablespoons (28 g) nondairy butter or 2 tablespoons (30 ml) olive oil

Salt and pepper, to taste

SERVING INGREDIENTS

Shredded vegan cheddar cheese (optional) store bought or *oil-free recipe on page 243

☾ THE NIGHT BEFORE: Oil the crock of your slow cooker *or line with parchment paper.

Combine the grits, water, butter, and salt and pepper in the slow cooker. Add more water if you will cook it longer the 8 hours or if your slow cooker runs a little hot.

☀ IN THE MORNING: Taste and adjust the seasonings. Top with the vegan cheese.

YIELD: 4 servings
EQUIPMENT: 4-quart slow cooker
COOKING TIME: for 6 to 10 hours on low

PUMPKIN PIE OATMEAL

I am addicted to winter squash. This oatmeal gets a nutritional boost from the pumpkin, but still tastes like dessert for breakfast!

 GLUTEN-FREE OPTION*   SOY-FREE   NO OIL ADDED OPTION*

½ cup (40 g) steel-cut oats (*use gluten-free)

2 cups (470 ml) unsweetened vanilla-flavored almond milk

½ cup (125 g) pumpkin purée, store-bought or homemade (page 247)

½ teaspoon cinnamon

¼ teaspoon allspice

Pinch of ground cloves

SERVING INGREDIENTS

Brown sugar or sweetener of your choice to taste, for serving

Chopped pecans, for serving

☾ THE NIGHT BEFORE: Oil the crock of your slow cooker *or line with parchment paper.

Combine the oats, milk, pumpkin, cinnamon, allspice, and cloves in the slow cooker.

Cook on low for 7 to 9 hours.

☀ IN THE MORNING: Stir the oatmeal to get a consistent texture. Serve in bowls topped with brown sugar and pecans.

YIELD: 2 servings
EQUIPMENT: 1½- to 2-quart (1.4 to 1.9 L) slow cooker
COOKING TIME: for 7 to 9 hours on low

Recipe Ideas & Variations

You can use any winter squash you have on hand in place of the pumpkin. Try acorn or butternut—they are the closest in flavor.

Be-My-Valentine
CHOCOLATE OATMEAL

For Valentine's Day I wasn't sure what to get my other half. We were avoiding white sugar, so no chocolate hearts for us. I got creative and made us bowls of chocolate oatmeal. It tasted divine!

Note: You can double or triple the recipe and use a larger slow cooker if you like.

 GLUTEN-FREE OPTION*   SOY-FREE   NO OIL ADDED OPTION**

½ cup (40 g) steel-cut oats (*use gluten-free)

2 cups (470 ml) water

2 tablespoons (16 g) unsweetened cocoa powder

1 teaspoon vanilla extract

⅛ to ¼ teaspoon stevia (to taste)

½ cup (120 ml) unsweetened vanilla-flavored almond milk

SERVING INGREDIENTS

1 tablespoon (15 ml) agave nectar (optional)

☾ THE NIGHT BEFORE: Oil the crock of your slow cooker **or line with parchment paper.

Combine the oats, water, cocoa, vanilla, and stevia in the slow cooker. If you haven't used stevia before, you may want to start with ⅛ teaspoon and add more later. Stevia gets bitter as soon as you add too much.

Cook on low for 6 to 10 hours.

☀ IN THE MORNING: Stir the oatmeal and add the almond milk. Now you're ready to have some chocolate for breakfast! If you need an extra kick of sweet, go ahead and add the agave.

YIELD: 2 servings
EQUIPMENT: 1½- to 2-quart (1.4 to 1.9 L) slow cooker
COOKING TIME: 7 to 9 hours on low

Recipe Ideas & Variations
Add other favorites to the mix, such as peanut butter, almond butter, chopped walnuts, or anything else you like in your brownies or oatmeal. If you aren't a fan of dark chocolate, try using 1 tablespoon (8 g) of cocoa instead of 2 tablespoons (16 g).

BIG POT *of* OATS

Oatmeal is underestimated in my opinion. It is full of nutrition, inexpensive, and as versatile as your imagination. Give it a little extra respect and feature it at your next brunch. Keep it warm in your slow cooker and add water as necessary to keep it loose. Set out a buffet of toppings, including fresh fruit, maple syrup, vanilla-flavored nondairy milk, chocolate shavings, toasted nuts, and dried fruit. It makes for a beautiful table and will satisfy your guests' appetites.

 GLUTEN-FREE* SOY-FREE** (◌) NO OIL ADDED OPTION***

1 cup (80 g) steel-cut oats (*use gluten-free)

5 cups (1175 ml) water

SERVING INGREDIENTS

Vanilla-flavored nondairy milk (**use almond, rice, hemp, etc.), for serving

Fresh fruit or your favorite topping, for serving

☾ THE NIGHT BEFORE: Oil the crock of your slow cooker ***or line with parchment paper. Add the oats and water to the slow cooker. Add more water if you will cook it longer than 8 hours or if your slow cooker runs a little hot. Cook on low for 6 to 10 hours.

☀ IN THE MORNING: Stir the oatmeal to get a consistent texture. Serve in bowls topped with milk and fresh fruit.

YIELD: 6 servings
EQUIPMENT: 4-quart slow cooker
COOKING TIME: 6 to 10 hours on low

Recipe Ideas & Variations
If your slow cooker is older and cooks at a lower temperature use 4 cups (940 ml) of water instead of 5 cups (1175 ml).

SCRAMBLED TOFU *with* PEPPERS

Scrambled tofu doesn't take long to make on the stove top, so you may be wondering why it's in a slow cooker book. Imagine waking up in the morning and having breakfast waiting for you. That's the real reason to make this dish in the slow cooker. Vary the veggies with onions, broccoli, and carrots for a change of pace.

 GLUTEN-FREE NO OIL ADDED

1 package (15 ounces, or 420 g) tofu, drained and crumbled

½ to 1 cup (120 to 235 ml) water

1 clove garlic, minced

½ bell pepper, chopped

1 teaspoon turmeric

½ teaspoon chili powder

Dash of liquid smoke (optional)

Dash of hot pepper sauce (optional)

SERVING INGREDIENTS

Salt and pepper, to taste

Fresh herbs of choice, minced, for topping (optional)

Salsa, for topping (optional)

☾ THE NIGHT BEFORE: Combine the tofu, water, garlic, bell pepper, turmeric, chili powder, liquid smoke, and hot sauce in the slow cooker. Add more water if you will cook it longer than 8 hours or if your slow cooker runs a little hot.

Cook on low for 6 to 10 hours.

☀ IN THE MORNING: Drain any excess water from the mixture. Season with salt and pepper and top with fresh herbs or salsa.

YIELD: 4 servings
EQUIPMENT: 4-quart slow cooker
COOKING TIME: 6 to 10 hours on low

Recipe Ideas & Variations
Add leftover veggies, black beans and salsa, or even diced onion to make your own variation.

WEEKEND TOFU *and* HASH BROWN BREAKFAST CASSEROLE

This is a breakfast worth waiting for. Go do some yard work, take a walk, or just relax while your breakfast is cooking: cheesy potatoes covered with a light tofu custard.

 GLUTEN-FREE    NO OIL ADDED OPTION*

1 package (16 ounces, or 454 g) frozen hash browns (*no oil added, if possible)

½ cup (58 g) shredded vegan cheddar cheese

1 package (12 ounces, or 340 g) silken tofu

½ cup (120 ml) plain coconut creamer or other nondairy creamer or milk

2 tablespoons (12 g) vegan chicken-flavored bouillon or 4 tablespoons (24 g) DIY Golden Bouillon (page 237)

¼ teaspoon turmeric

⅛ teaspoon garlic powder

½ teaspoon salt

Freshly ground pepper

Paprika, for sprinkling

Oil the crock of your slow cooker *or line with parchment paper. Spread the frozen hash browns over the bottom of the slow cooker, then sprinkle the shredded cheese over them.

Place the tofu, creamer, bouillon, turmeric, garlic powder, and salt in a blender and blend until smooth. Pour the mixture over the hash browns. Sprinkle with freshly ground pepper and paprika.

Cook on high for 1½ to 2 hours. The custard will set up when done, but it will still be a little jiggly in the middle.

YIELD: 4 servings
EQUIPMENT: 4-quart slow cooker
COOKING TIME: 1½ to 2 hours on high

Recipe Ideas & Variations
Try adding a layer of vegan sausage, leftover pesto, or some Italian seasoning to keep it interesting.

PEAR *and* CARDAMOM FRENCH TOAST CASSEROLE

This is similar to bread pudding in texture, but the sausage and fruit add a breakfasty twist. Wake up and throw this together in the slow cooker. You'll have time to take a walk or read the paper while it cooks. It's a perfect weekend treat.

 SOY-FREE OPTION*   NO OIL ADDED OPTION**

4 links vegan breakfast sausages or 1 to 2 cups (110 to 220 g) crumbled precooked Apple Sage Sausage (page 240)

3 medium-size pears

Juice of ½ lemon

½ loaf whole-wheat bread, cubed (approximately 6 cups [300 g])

2 cups (470 ml) nondairy milk (plain, unsweetened, or vanilla-flavored)

3 tablespoons (45 g) unsweetened applesauce †

½ teaspoon cardamom

½ teaspoon cinnamon

SERVING INGREDIENTS

Maple syrup, for serving

† *Some applesauces contain ascorbic acid. Ascorbic acid, like lemon juice, will curdle even nondairy milks. If yours contains it, cook with water instead of nondairy milk.*

☾ THE NIGHT BEFORE: If you are using link sausages, cut them into half-moons. Cook the sausage in a nonstick skillet until done, 10 to 12 minutes.

Peel and core the pears, then chop. Pour the lemon juice over the pears to minimize browning.

Store the pears and sausage in an airtight container in the fridge. Store the cubed bread in a resealable bag.

☀ IN THE MORNING: Oil the crock of your slow cooker **or line with parchment paper. Add the milk, applesauce, cardamom, and cinnamon and stir to combine. Place the bread pears, and sausage on top, then press down into the wet mixture.

Cook on high for 1½ to 2 hours. After 1 hour, press the bread into the wet mixture again to help it cook more thoroughly. Serve drizzled with maple syrup.

YIELD: 4 servings
EQUIPMENT: 4-quart slow cooker
COOKING TIME: 1½ to 2 hours on high

Annie's Multigrain
BREAKFAST PUDDING

Annie adds in the nutrition of whole-grain rice and the creamy texture of arborio rice to your morning steel-cut oats. Be sure to check out more of her recipes on her blog, anunrefinedvegan.com. Note: You can double or triple the recipe and use a larger slow cooker if you like.

 GLUTEN-FREE OPTION*   SOY-FREE NO OIL ADDED

⅔ cup (110 g) brown rice, soaked for 15–30 minutes, rinsed, and drained

⅓ cup (62 g) arborio rice

⅓ cup (28 g) steel-cut oats (* use gluten-free)

⅓ cup (60 g) wild rice blend (I use Lundberg Wild Blend)

1½ (335 ml) cups water

4 cups (940 ml) nondairy milk

1 teaspoon vanilla extract

1½ teaspoon cinnamon

¼ teaspoon cardamom

¼ teaspoon ground ginger

⅛ teaspoon allspice

1 apple, peeled, cored, and chopped

½ cup (75 g) golden raisins (optional)

1 large banana, sliced (optional)

SERVING INGREDIENTS

Toasted nuts (optional)

BEFORE SERVING INGREDIENTS

½ cup (120 ml) full-fat coconut milk (optional)

Your favorite sweetener, to taste

☾ THE NIGHT BEFORE: Lightly coat a slow cooker with cooking oil. Combine all of the ingredients except for the vanilla, spices, apple, raisins, banana, and nuts.

Turn the slow cooker onto low and cook for 7 to 9 hours.

☀ IN THE MORNING: Stir in the vanilla extract, spices, apple, raisins, banana, and nuts.

JUST BEFORE SERVING: Stir in the coconut milk (if using), and add sweetener to taste. Divide the grain pudding among four bowls, and top with toasted nuts.

YIELD: 4 servings
EQUIPMENT: 4-quart slow cooker
COOKING TIME: cooks 7 to 9 hours low

MAPLE PECAN GRANOLA

Tired of burning granola when you make it in the oven? Making it in the slow cooker helps cook it just right. You still need to be around for a few hours to stir it, so it's perfect for a day when you are cooking other staples.

 GLUTEN-FREE*   SOY-FREE   ◊ NO OIL ADDED OPTION**

4 cups (320 g) rolled oats or multigrain rolled cereal (*use gluten-free)

1 cup (110 g) chopped pecans

3 tablespoons (21 g) ground flaxseed

¼ cup (60 ml) maple syrup or agave nectar mixed with 1 teaspoon maple extract

¼ cup (60 ml) olive oil (use aquafaba to make oil-free)**

1 teaspoon vanilla extract

Oil the crock of your slow cooker **or line with parchment paper. Add all the ingredients to the slow cooker and stir to combine. Cook on high, uncovered, for 3 to 4 hours, or until the oats are no longer soft and are a golden brown.

Stir every 15 to 20 minutes. You will need to stir every 10 minutes during the last hour. Let cool before storing or the condensation will make your granola soggy.

It's important to note that you cook this uncovered. I tried cooking it vented, and it took longer than I was willing to wait. Uncovered, it cooks more quickly and is even easier to stir!

YIELD: 4 servings
EQUIPMENT: 4-quart slow cooker
COOKING TIME: 3 to 4 hours on high

MIXED BERRY *and* ALMOND GRANOLA

I love to add sweet, crunchy granola to nondairy yogurt or ice cream. I even eat it plain by the handfuls when I can't be bothered to fix myself a proper breakfast. Use your favorite dried berries or raisins in this recipe.

 GLUTEN-FREE*   SOY-FREE  NO OIL ADDED OPTION**

3 cups (240 g) rolled oats (*use gluten-free)

½ cup (55 g) slivered almonds

½ cup (60 g) dried berry blend

3 tablespoons (21 g) ground flaxseed

¼ cup (60 ml) agave nectar

¼ cup (60 ml) olive oil (**use aquafaba)

1 teaspoon almond or vanilla extract

¼ teaspoon cardamom

¼ teaspoon nutmeg

Oil the crock of your slow cooker **or line with parchment paper. Add all the ingredients to the slow cooker and stir to combine. Cook on high, uncovered, for 3 to 4 hours, or until the oats are no longer soft and are a golden brown.

Stir every 15 to 20 minutes. You will need to stir every 10 minutes for the last hour. Let cool before storing or the condensation will make your granola soggy.

It's important to note that you cook this uncovered. I tried cooking it vented, and it took longer than I was willing to wait. Uncovered, it cooks more quickly and is even easier to stir!

YIELD: *8 servings*
EQUIPMENT: *4-quart slow cooker*
COOKING TIME: *3 to 4 hours on high*

Recipe Ideas & Variations

You can switch the extract to orange, add coconut, and sprinkle with a few mini chocolate chips for a super decadent treat.

CHAPTER 13

Desserts

Desserts aren't the first thing you think of making when you buy a slow cooker, but almost every savvy cook ends up with one or two in his or her repertoire.

Poached pears and other cooked fruit are perfect in the slow cooker, plus they stay warm until you are ready to serve dessert, which is great for a multicourse dinner party. If your dinner party is in the winter, be sure to make Exotic Cardamom Hot Chocolate or Hot, Spiked, and Buttered Spiced Cider, both of which can be made in the slow cooker ahead of time.

Puddings, brownies, and blondies are also slow cooker favorites. Tapioca pudding has never been this easy. Just be sure to make it the night before so you can chill it in the fridge before serving. Try making some of your favorite brownie and blondie recipes in the slow cooker. If it's a fudgy mix, I recommend cooking it in an ovenproof pan that fits in your slow cooker. It's almost impossible to get very moist baked goods directly out of the crock in neat pieces.

The Best
GLUTEN-FREE WALNUT BROWNIES

These are a variation of my favorite gluten-free brownies. I wanted to make a dessert that you can cook in a 4-quart slow cooker and most of the cakes really need a 6-quart cooker to behave properly. I get rave reviews on these all the time. Plus, they are vegan, gluten-free, and have a no oil added option—so you really can please everyone.

 GLUTEN-FREE SOY-FREE  NO OIL ADDED OPTION*

DRY INGREDIENTS

½ cup (65 g) brown teff flour

¼ cup (56 g) brown or coconut sugar

¼ cup (50 g) white or raw sugar

¼ cup (30 g) cocoa or cacao powder

¼ teaspoon salt

WET INGREDIENTS

2 tablespoons (14 g) ground flaxseed mixed with ¼ cup (60 ml) warm water

2 tablespoons (30 ml) avocado oil or other mild flavored oil (*or use mashed avocado to make these no oil added)

1 to 2 tablespoons (15 to 30 ml) nondairy milk, as needed

½ teaspoon vanilla

MIX-INS

¼ cup (28 g) chopped walnuts (Or your favorite nut)

2 tablespoons (14 g) additional chopped walnuts for top of brownies (optional)

Mix the dry ingredients together in a medium-size mixing bowl and the wet ingredients, except for the nondairy milk, in a small bowl.

Combine the two mixtures together. The mix will be very thick, but if you still see dry mixture add 1 to 2 tablespoons (15 to 30 ml) of nondairy milk to get it to combine fully. Stir in the walnuts.

Either spray oil on the crock *or line with parchment paper to make oil-free. Spread the batter out evenly and top with extra walnuts if you want.

Cook on high for 1 to 1½ hours or until firm-ish in the middle. These will be fudgy brownies.

YIELD: 6 servings
EQUIPMENT: 4-quart slow cooker
COOKING TIME: 1½ to 2 hours on high

Have-it-your-way
BROWNIES

I used a 6-quart (5.7 L) oval slow cooker and two small 3-cup (705 ml) rectangular Pyrex dishes to make this recipe. You can use different sizes, but make sure the dishes you plan to use fit in your slow cooker before you start making the batter!

 GLUTEN-FREE OPTION*   SOY-FREE   NO OIL ADDED OPTION**

DRY INGREDIENTS

1 cup (120 g) whole-wheat pastry flour (*use gluten-free baking blend)

1 cup (120 g) unsweetened cocoa powder

½ teaspoon baking powder

¼ teaspoon salt

WET INGREDIENTS

½ cup (112 g) nondairy butter (*use olive oil) **mashed avocado or applesauce

½ cup (115 g) packed brown sugar

2 tablespoons (14 g) ground flaxseed mixed with 2 tablespoons (30 ml) warm water

1 cup (235 ml) plain or unsweetened vanilla-flavored nondairy milk

1 teaspoon vanilla extract

TO PREPARE THE DRY INGREDIENTS: Combine the dry ingredients in a bowl and set aside.

TO PREPARE THE WET INGREDIENTS: In a bowl or mixer, cream the butter with the brown sugar, then add the flaxseed mixture, milk, and vanilla. Mix until combined, then add half of the dry mixture and combine. Add the last of the dry mixture, combine well, and spread into the well-oiled dishes.

Take a piece of aluminum foil, roll it up, make a ring with it, and place on the bottom of the slow cooker. Put the baking dishes on top of the foil ring. (I arranged one dish crisscrossed over the other on top of the aluminum foil ring.) Place a clean dish towel underneath the lid to catch the condensation. Cook on high for 4 to 5 hours, or until a knife inserted into the center comes out almost clean.

YIELD: 12 pieces
EQUIPMENT: 6-quart slow cooker
COOKING TIME: 4 to 5 hours on high

Berrylicious Biscuit-Topped
FRUIT COBBLER

This is one of my favorite slow cooker desserts. You can use any fresh or frozen fruit you have on hand. It's easy to make and a real crowd-pleaser. You can use agave nectar or maple syrup instead of white sugar, if you prefer.

 GLUTEN-FREE OPTION*   SOY-FREE (◯) NO OIL ADDED OPTION**

STEWED FRUIT INGREDIENTS

1 pint (340 g) berries (blueberries, strawberries, raspberries, or blackberries), washed, stemmed, hulled if strawberries, and chopped if large

5 large apples, peeled and cored

1 tablespoon (15 ml) lemon juice

1 teaspoon lemon zest

½ cup (100 g) sugar

1 tablespoon (8 g) cornstarch

Pinch of salt

BISCUIT INGREDIENTS

1½ cups (180 g) flour (white, whole-wheat, or gluten-free baking mix)

½ cup (50 g) oat bran

⅓ cup (67 g) sugar

1½ teaspoons baking powder

Pinch of salt

3 tablespoons (45 ml) olive oil, **or aquafaba

½ cup (120 ml) plain or unsweetened nondairy milk

1 teaspoon vanilla extract

To make the stewed fruit: Combine all of the ingredients in the slow cooker. Add ½ cup (120 ml) water if you will cook it longer than 8 hours or if your slow cooker runs very hot. Cook on low for 7 to 9 hours.

About 30 minutes before serving: Add a little water if the mixture is too thick, or add an additional ½ teaspoon cornstarch if it needs to thicken up a bit.

To make the biscuits: Combine the flour, oat bran, sugar, baking powder, and salt in a bowl. In a separate bowl, combine the oil, milk, and vanilla. Add the dry ingredients to the wet and stir with a wooden spoon to combine. Turn the mixture out onto a floured cutting board, roll out about ½ inch (1.3 cm) thick, and cut into circles with a glass.

Place in the slow cooker on top of the filling, turn up the slow cooker to high, and prop the lid open with a wooden spoon to allow the condensation to evaporate. Cook for 30 minutes longer. Scoop out into bowls for serving.

YIELD: 4–6 servings
EQUIPMENT: 4- to 6-quart slow cooker
COOKING TIME: 7 to 9 hours plus 30 minutes to cook the biscuit crust

BUTTERNUT SQUASH DESSERT PIE
with a KISS *of* MISO

*I wanted to give you a holiday dessert that you can show off to your friends and family.
No plain old pumpkin pie here! The base is a simple whole-grain crust. The middle is a
slightly sweet butternut tofu purée with a hint of miso and lots of spice.*

 GLUTEN-FREE OPTION*  SOY-FREE OPTION**

CRUST INGREDIENTS

2 cups (240 g) whole-wheat pastry
flour (*or use gluten-free baking
blend)

½ teaspoon miso

½ cup (120 ml) cold water

½ cup (112 g) vegan butter (stick is
preferable)

FILLING INGREDIENTS

1 can (15 ounces, or 425 g) butternut
squash purée

1 box (12.3 ounces, or 349 g) silken tofu

¾ cup (168 g) brown or coconut sugar

2 teaspoons (5 g) mild yellow miso

1 teaspoon molasses

1 teaspoon ground cinnamon

¾ teaspoon ground ginger

¼ teaspoon nutmeg

Mix the crust ingredients in your food processor, and pulse
until it begins to form a ball. Line your slow cooker with
parchment to make the pie easier to remove once it's done.

Press the crust in and make it as even as you can and create a
¼-inch lip/crust edge all around.

Rinse the food processor. Add the filling ingredients, and
process until silky smooth. Pour into the crust. Place a clean
dish towel between the lid and the crock.

Cook on high for 1½ to 2½ hours until the middle firms up. It
will still jiggle slightly, but if you notice a lot of steam coming
off the middle you can cook with the lid off to help it firm up
the last 30 minutes of cooking.

YIELD: 8 servings
EQUIPMENT: 6-quart slow cooker
COOKING TIME: 1½ to 2½ hours on high

Recipe Ideas & Variations
If you are oil-free, you can make this without a crust!

MANGO COCONUT RICE PUDDING

This recipe is reminiscent of mango sticky rice. Coconut milk adds creaminess, while the mango adds a burst of fruit flavor to the mix. I like to use light coconut milk, but regular will work fine, too.

 GLUTEN-FREE SOY-FREE  NO OIL ADDED OPTION*

1½ cups (280 g) arborio rice

1 can (14 ounces, or 392 g) light coconut milk

1½ cups (355 ml) vanilla-flavored nondairy milk, plus more as needed

½ cup (100 g) sugar or (120 ml) maple syrup (or sweetener of choice to taste)

SERVING INGREDIENTS

2 mangoes, peeled and diced

Oil the crock of your slow cooker *or line with parchment paper.

Add all the ingredients except for the mango. Cook on high for 1½ to 2 hours.

Add a little more nondairy milk if the mixture is not wet or creamy enough.

Serve topped with fresh mango.

YIELD: 6–8 large servings
EQUIPMENT: 6-quart slow cooker
COOKING TIME: 1½ hours on high

TURKISH DELIGHT TAPIOCA PUDDING

Turkish delight is a gel candy from the Middle East. Although it comes in many flavors, my favorite is rosewater. This pudding has that wonderful sweet floral flavor in a pudding that's textured with tapioca pearls.

Note: This recipe works fine in a 4-quart (3.8 L) slow cooker; however, you should double it if you a using a 6-quart (5.7 L) cooker.

 SOY-FREE · NO OIL ADDED OPTION*

4 cups (940 ml) plain or unsweetened nondairy milk

½ cup (75 g) tapioca pearls (not soaked)

½ cup (100 g) sugar

Pinch of salt

1 teaspoon rosewater (make sure it is labeled food grade)

Oil the crock of your slow cooker *or line with parchment paper. Add the milk, tapioca, sugar, and salt to the slow cooker.

Cook for 3½ hours on low or 2 hours on high.

Stir in the rosewater and transfer to a container to cool for 1 hour, then put in the fridge overnight. The pudding will still seem very runny, but it will set up in the fridge.

YIELD: 2 large servings
EQUIPMENT: 4-quart slow cooker
COOKING TIME: 3½ hours on low or 2 hours on high.

Recipe Ideas & Variations

If you're looking for a more traditional tapioca pudding, just substitute vanilla extract for the rosewater. Almond extract or orange flower water are also excellent. Upon serving, you can always add dried fruit, applesauce, or even a few chocolate chips.

Slightly DRUNKEN APPLES

Sometimes you just need to top off your day with dessert. The rum and liqueur add extra flavor, but if you don't imbibe, feel free to substitute with water or apple juice.

 GLUTEN-FREE SOY-FREE NO OIL ADDED

4 apples, peeled if not organic, cored, and sliced

1 tablespoon (15 g) brown sugar

Juice of 2 or 3 tangerines

Juice of ½ lime or lemon

3 tablespoons (45 ml) rum (optional)

1½ tablespoons (23 ml) Navan, Amaretto, or Triple Sec (optional)

½ teaspoon ground ginger

BEFORE SERVING INGREDIENTS

½ teaspoon dried marjoram or basil (or 1 teaspoon fresh added right before serving)

Place the apples in the slow cooker.

Combine the brown sugar, tangerine and lime juices, rum, Navan, ginger, and marjoram in a small bowl and then pour over the apples.

Cook on low for 7 to 9 hours. (Many small slow cookers have no temperature control, so they cook everything on low.)

YIELD: 4 servings
EQUIPMENT: 1½- to 2-quart slow cooker
COOKING TIME: 7 to 9 on low

Serving Suggestions
Serve by itself, with nondairy creamer poured over the top, over low-fat nondairy vanilla ice cream, or on your oatmeal for a special treat.

EARL GREY POACHED PEARS

I have always admired poached pears, and I always thought of them as the ultimate grown-up dessert. Peeled and left whole, they add a bit of drama to a dinner party. Chopped up, they make a perfect topping for nondairy vanilla ice cream. These are poached in Earl Grey tea sweetened with brown sugar. The flavor is reminiscent of a floral caramel. In fact, you could take the leftover poaching liquid and reduce it on the stove until it's thicker and add it to coffee or tea, or top some other dessert with it.

 GLUTEN-FREE SOY-FREE  NO OIL ADDED

4 pears, peeled, left whole or cored and chopped

1 cup (235 ml) Earl Grey tea (steep 1 tablespoon [4 g] tea in 1 cup [235 ml] hot water for 4 minutes)

½ cup (115 g) brown sugar

½ vanilla bean, scraped, or 1 teaspoon vanilla extract

Pinch of salt

Place the pears in the slow cooker.

Combine the tea, sugar, vanilla, and salt in a bowl and then pour over the pears.

Cook on high for 1½ to 2½ hours. If you are using whole pears place them on their sides and turn them every 30 minutes.

YIELD: 4 servings
EQUIPMENT: 4-quart slow cooker
COOKING TIME: 1½ to 2 hours on high

Recipe Ideas & Variations
If you are avoiding refined sugar, use maple syrup or agave nectar instead of the brown sugar. Another option is to use heated fruit juice instead of water to brew the tea.

THICK CARDAMOM HOT CHOCOLATE

Who needs cake or cookies when all you have to do is ladle yourself a warm mug of extra-thick, sweetly spiced hot chocolate from the slow cooker? Throw this together before dinner and you'll have a sweet treat before you go to bed.

 GLUTEN-FREE  SOY-FREE NO OIL ADDED

4 cups (940 ml) unsweetened vanilla almond milk or plain almond milk mixed with 1 teaspoon vanilla extract

3 ounces (84 g) semisweet chocolate disks or bars, coarsely chopped

¼ to ½ cup (50 to 100 g) sugar

12 whole cardamom pods

2 cinnamon sticks (optional)

SERVING INGREDIENTS

4 to 6 vegan marshmallows, for serving (optional)

Combine the milk, chocolate, sugar, cardamom, and cinnamon in the slow cooker.

Cook on low for 2 to 3 hours, whisking every 30 minutes, or until all the chocolate is melted.

Strain out the cardamom and cinnamon.

Stir well before serving in mugs, topped with a vegan marshmallow.

YIELD: 4 to 6 servings
EQUIPMENT: 1½- to 2-quart (1.4 to 1.9 L) slow cooker
COOKING TIME: 7 to 9 hours on low

Recipe Ideas & Variations

If you are avoiding refined sugar, use unsweetened chocolate instead of the semisweet, and replace the sugar with a natural sweetener of your choice, such as stevia, agave nectar, or maple syrup.

Omit the spices for a traditional hot chocolate. Or add some mint extract or 2 herbal peppermint tea bags for a peppermint chocolate treat.

Not-from-a-Box CAKE MIX

I will not buy cake mix, because it's just simple ingredients that someone premeasured for me. With that said, I tried Julie's Original gluten-free cake mix and kinda fell in love with it. Because I wanted to make a few dump cake recipes, I wanted to give you a gluten-FULL option here!

 GLUTEN-FREE OPTION*   SOY-FREE   NO OIL ADDED

2½ cups (300 g) unbleached white flour (*use gluten-free baking blend)

1¼ cups (250 g) vegan sugar

1 tablespoon (8 g) baking powder

1 teaspoon salt

You can just mix well in a bowl and store in an airtight container if you aren't going to use it immediately.

I like to go a step further and put it in my blender to make the flour and sugar a finer grain. Plus, it mixes them up well.

NOTE: You can make this with a gluten-free baking blend. I've tested some different slow cooker "dump cakes" with Julie's Original Brand gluten-free and vegan cake mixes.

You can also use whole-wheat pastry flour in place of the white flour with no changes. However, if you change the sweetener, you will not get regular cake mix results in the recipes in this book or any recipes online that you veganize.

YIELD: about 3½ cups = to one box store-bought cake mix
EQUIPMENT: Slow cooker not needed

SPICED SWEET POTATO PUDDING CAKE

Because a slow cooker creates wet heat, the cakes you make in it never get a dry crumb.
Instead, they are closer to a pudding cake—moist and delectable.

 SOY-FREE  NO OIL ADDED OPITON*

1 recipe Not-from-a-Box Cake Mix
from page 224 (or store-bought)

1 can (15 ounces, or 425 g) sweet potato
purée, or about 1½ cups

¾ cup (175 ml) nondairy milk

1 tablespoon (15 ml) oil (* or use extra
aquafaba)

1 tablespoon (15 ml) aquafaba (or 1
tablespoon [7 g] ground flaxseed
mixed with 2 tablespoons [30 ml]
warm water)

2 teaspoons (7 g) ground cinnamon

1 teaspoon ground allspice

¾ teaspoons ground ginger

¼ teaspoon ground cloves

*Line the crock with parchment paper or spray with oil. Add the cake mix to a medium mixing bowl. Add in the sweet potato, milk, oil, aquafaba, and spices. Mix well.

Take a clean dish towel, double it and place over the top of the slow cooker, under the lid. This will trap the condensation and keep it from dripping on the cake as it cooks.

Cook 1½ to 2 hours on high, or until most of the cake is firm to the touch. Realize that the heat will continue cooking the middle. YIELD: 8 servings

EQUIPMENT: 6-quart slow cooker

COOKING TIME: 1½ to 2 hours on high

Super Moist

DOUBLE COCONUT CAKE

This moist white cake is easy to whip up and throw in your slow cooker right before you eat. By the time you've eaten and cleaned up, you'll have a treat ready for you. Dress it up with whipped coconut cream and/or a drizzle of sweetened condensed coconut milk.

 SOY-FREE ⬤ NO OIL ADDED OPTION*

1 recipe Not-from-a-Box Cake Mix from page 224 (or store-bought)

1 can (15 ounces, or 425 g) full-fat coconut milk, or about 1½ cups

1 cup (80 g) finely shredded coconut

*Line the crock with parchment paper or spray with oil. Add the cake mix to a medium mixing bowl, and add in the coconut milk and shredded coconut. Mix well.

Take a clean dish towel, double it and place over the top of the slow cooker, under the lid. This will trap the condensation and keep it from dripping on the cake as it cooks.

Cook 1½ to 2 hours or until most of the cake is firm to the touch. Realize that the heat will continue cooking the middle.

YIELD: 8 servings
EQUIPMENT: 6-quart slow cooker
COOKING TIME: 1½ to 2 hours on high

PINEAPPLE UPSIDE DOWN CAKE

This is a fun cake to make. It can be tricky to turn out the cake from your slow cooker, so if that makes you nervous you can just scoop and flip a serving on a plate instead!

 SOY-FREE NO OIL ADDED OPTION*

¼ cup (60 g) brown sugar

1 can (20 ounces, or 567 g) pineapple slices or cubes 100% juice (with juice drained and saved)

1 recipe Not-from-a-Box Cake Mix from page 224 (or store-bought)

1 cup (235 ml) of reserved pineapple juice (or add some water it's not a full cup)

¼ cup (60 ml) oil (* or use extra aquafaba)

2 tablespoons (30 ml) aquafaba (or 1 tablespoon ground flax mixed with 2 tablespoons warm water)

Line the crock with parchment paper and make sure there's enough extra to use as handles to remove the cake after it's cooked. Then sprinkle the brown sugar on the parchment and follow with the pineapple.

In a medium mixing bowl, mix the cake mix, pineapple juice, oil, and aquafaba well. Then pour over the pineapple.

Take a clean dish towel, double it and place over the top of the slow cooker under the lid. This will trap the condensation and keep it from dripping on the cake as it cooks.

Cook 1 to 1½ hours or until most of the cake is firm to the touch. Realize that the heat will continue cooking the middle.

Once the cake is ready, carefully lift it out by the parchment and set it on a cutting board. Flatten the parchment, and place a second cutting board on top of the cake. Flip both boards, righting the pineapple-side of the cake. Carefully peel off the parchment, and your cake is ready to cut!

YIELD: 8 servings
EQUIPMENT: 6-quart slow cooker
COOKING TIME: 1½ to 2 hours on high

CHAPTER 14

Staples

You don't have to make your staples from scratch, but it's good on your budget and often tastes better too. However, don't look at the other recipes in a way where you need to take 3 days to make a dish. You can always use store-bought bouillon, seitan, vegan sausage, vegan cheese in place of homemade.

This chapter is by far my favorite part of the book, because it contains many of the recipes that keep my food budget under control. It allows me to avoid the BPA in canned foods, as well as the ever-rising high prices on vegan staples such as bouillon, sausage, and seitan. These are recipes that you'll find yourself using time and time again.

Make an effort to plan one day a week (or month) to stock your freezer with beans, seitan, and bouillon. That way, you'll always have some on hand, and you'll avoid those extra trips to the grocery. You'll save money, too. For example, one 15-ounce (420-g) can of beans costs three to six times as much as a single 1-pound (455-g) bag of beans. Cooking the 1 pound (454 g) of beans yields the amount of cooked beans you'd get in three or four cans! One 22-ounce (615 g) bag of wheat gluten flour costs about the same as four frozen chicken-style seitan patties. That one bag of flour will make dozens. That's worth part of a quiet Sunday afternoon to me. Happy cooking!

DRY BEANS *from* SCRATCH

If you're picky about what goes into your food, making beans from scratch is perfect for you. You can control how much salt, if any, goes into them. Even better, dry beans cost three to six times less than canned, so you're saving money, too! Use any kind of bean other than lentils or split peas; they cook much quicker, so you will cook them in a dish, not in advance.

 GLUTEN-FREE SOY-FREE  NO OIL ADDED

1 pound (454 g) dry beans

YIELD: 6 servings
EQUIPMENT: 6-quart slow cooker
COOKING TIME: 7 to 9 hours on low

Rinse the beans, and make sure there are no little rocks that might have been missed. Place in the slow cooker and add water to come about 3 inches (7.5 cm) above the beans. Cook on low overnight, or for 7 to 9 hours.

After you cook the beans once in your slow cooker, you'll be able to determine whether you need to use less water (about 2 inches [5 cm], instead of 3 inches [7.5 cm]). It will vary depending on how hot your slow cooker runs. Use a slotted spoon to remove the beans if there is extra water.

A Worthy Note
- Cook extra beans and freeze in bags to use later. I freeze mine in 1½-cup (340 g) portions so that it's easy to switch out a bag for a can of beans.
- Though all dry beans may look alike, beans that have been on the shelf (or in your pantry) a long time can take up to twice as long to cook, so add time if needed.
- Split peas and lentils cook much faster than larger beans such as pinto, black, and white. They are often cooked in a recipe dry, while the larger beans are cooked before they are added to other recipes.
- You can cook any beans in the slow cooker, but be aware that kidney beans can have a toxin called phytohaemagglutinin and need to be brought up to a boiling temperature to destroy the toxin. So boil them for 10 minutes before cooking in the slow cooker.

Linda's Homemade CHICKPEA AQUAFABA

Aquafaba is a fancy name for bean water. You can use chickpea broth in place of eggs or milk in many baking recipes. You can even whip it up like egg whites for meringues! In general, use three tablespoons (45 ml) of aquafaba to replace one whole egg, two egg whites, or 3 tablespoons (45 ml) of milk. This recipe comes from Linda Watson, a wizard at thrifty organic vegan cooking. (cookforgood.com/aquafaba/).

 GLUTEN-FREE SOY-FREE NO OIL ADDED

---

1 pound (454 g) dry chickpeas

5 cups (1175 ml) water

1 teaspoon salt

YIELD: *8 servings aquafaba and 12 servings chickpeas*
EQUIPMENT: *6-quart slow cooker*
COOKING TIME: *8 hours on low*

☾ THE NIGHT BEFORE: Pick through dry beans and rinse very well. Put the beans, water, and salt in a very clean slow cooker. Any trace of oil will nix your chance of whipping up fluffy aquafaba.

☀ IN THE MORNING: Turn the slow cooker on low for 8 hours. Add a little more water if the chickpeas surface during cooking.

When chickpeas are tender, carefully pour cooking liquid (aquafaba!) through a sieve into a container. I put a 2-cup (475-ml) Pyrex measuring cup in a pot, put both in the sink, and aim for the measuring cup. Any splashes go into the pot. If you have more than 1½ cups (355 ml) of aquafaba, pour it into a pot and boil it on medium-high uncovered until you have the right amount.

Recipe Ideas & Variations
Use aquafaba from black beans to make dark, strongly flavored recipes such as brownies. Just don't add any flavorings except salt until after you pour off the broth.

Unwhipped aquafaba keeps refrigerated for 7 days and frozen for a year. Try freezing it in ice cube trays and then popping cubes into a freezer-safe bag.

DIY CAJUN SEASONING BLEND

If you're looking for a salt-free version or just can't find it in your area, this little recipe will keep you in spicy goodness for a while. The best part is you can make it as spicy or mild as you want!

 GLUTEN-FREE SOY-FREE NO OIL ADDED

2 teaspoons (5 g) paprika

2 teaspoons (4 g) thyme

2 teaspoons (3 g) oregano or marjoram

1 teaspoon garlic powder

½ teaspoon onion powder

½ to 1 teaspoon cayenne pepper (depending on heat preference)

¼ teaspoon black pepper

¼ teaspoon allspice

⅛ teaspoon cloves

You can just mix all the ingredients well, and store the seasoning blend in a lidded container. You can also use a spice grinder to make it more like store-bought and to distribute the spices more evenly.

YIELD: about 2½ tablespoons

ITALIAN SPICE BLEND

This is a basic spice blend that I use all the time. It's so much cheaper than buying a bottle of a premade blend.

 GLUTEN-FREE SOY-FREE NO OIL ADDED

1 tablespoon (4 g) dried basil

1 tablespoon (5 g) dried oregano

1 tablespoon (2 g) dried marjoram

1 tablespoon (4 g) dried thyme

1 teaspoon dried rosemary or ½ teaspoon ground

1 teaspoon granulated garlic

½ teaspoon onion powder

Add everything to a food processor and process until uniform. Store in an airtight jar.

YIELD: about ¼ cup

BATCH OF COOKED ONIONS

You may have already noticed, but the onions called for in the recipes are supposed to be precooked. Why? Cooking them really enhances the taste of any dish. Instead of dirtying up 2 pans every time, you can make doing hands off in the slow cooker once every week or two and freeze them in ½ cup increments.

 GLUTEN-FREE SOY-FREE  NO OIL ADDED OPTION*

3 medium onions, or enough to fill your slow cooker ¾ of the way full, minced, diced, or sliced (your choice)

1 to 2 tablespoons (15 to 30 ml) olive oil (*or 2 tablespoons water)

½ teaspoon salt (optional)

Add all the ingredients to your slow cooker and cook on low 7 to 9 hours.

Once cool, put the amount you'll use in the next 5 days in a container in the fridge. Freeze the rest in ½ cup or 1 cup freezer bags.

YIELD: About 3 cups, but will vary on the size of your onions
EQUIPMENT: 2-quart slow cooker
COOKING TIME: 7 to 9 hours on low

A Worthy Note

When you are using freezer bags, add the food, then smash flat as you let the last of the air out. This will make them stackable in a small freezer, and they will thaw faster. That's a win-win we all want!

BALSAMIC ONION MARMALADE

Not for your morning toast, but the sweetness of the cooked onions contrasts nicely with the balsamic vinegar. Use on crostini, or anywhere else it will be appreciated.

 GLUTEN-FREE   SOY-FREE   NO OIL ADDED OPTION*

4 large onions

½ cup (120 ml) water

¼ cup (60 ml) balsamic vinegar

2 tablespoons (30 ml) olive oil (*leave out to make oil-free)

2 tablespoons (25 to 30 g) sugar, agave nectar, or maple syrup

1 sprig fresh rosemary

½ to 1 teaspoon salt (to taste)

☾ THE NIGHT BEFORE: Slice the onions and store in an airtight container in the fridge.

☀ IN THE MORNING: Add all ingredients to the slow cooker. Cook on low for 7 to 9 hours. Remove and discard the rosemary. Let cool completely before using or storing. Store in the fridge for up to a week or freeze for up to 2 months.

YIELD: 2–3 cups
EQUIPMENT: 4-quart slow cooker
COOKING TIME: 7 to 9 hours on low

ALL-OCCASION ROASTED GARLIC

This is a no-fuss treat (it's true, no water) that's good for you and your waistline. Once cooked, just squeeze the cloves, or use a knife to get them out from the skins.

 GLUTEN-FREE   SOY-FREE   NO OIL ADDED

4 to 6 heads garlic

Cut off the top of each garlic head (the pointy side) to expose the cloves. Place in the slow cooker cut side up. Cook on low for 3 to 4 hours. Let cool completely before squeezing the cloves from the skins. Store in the fridge for up to a week.

YIELD: 4–6 servings
EQUIPMENT: 4-quart slow cooker
COOKING TIME: 3 to 4 hours on low

Perfectly Easy Everyday
BROWN RICE

I typically use my rice cooker to make rice, but it's nice to have the slow cooker as an option. It's perfect for camping, or when you've run out of room on the stove. You can make half of this recipe, or store the leftovers in the fridge for eating later in the week.

 GLUTEN-FREE SOY-FREE  NO OIL ADDED OPTION*

2 cups (380 g) brown basmati rice, rinsed

4 cups (940 ml) water

Pinch of salt (optional)

Oil the crock of your slow cooker *or line with parchment paper and add all the ingredients. Cook on high for 1 to 1½ hours. Check it after 45 minutes to make sure it's not cooking too quickly. It's important that you don't let the rice overcook, or it will turn to mush.

YIELD: 8 servings
EQUIPMENT: 4-quart slow cooker
COOKING TIME: 1½ to 2 hours on high

DIY GOLDEN BOUILLON

I use a ton of bouillon in soups, casseroles, stews, and anything else I can think of. I hate buying liquid broth because it is expensive, is in wasteful packaging, and has too much salt. This is easy and inexpensive, plus you can vary the herbs and spices to customize your own flavors.

 GLUTEN-FREE SOY-FREE ◎ NO OIL ADDED

1 large onion, cut into quarters

2 carrots about 8 ounces (225 g), chopped

½ cup (125 ml) water

2 sprigs fresh thyme (or 1 teaspoon dry)

2 stalks of celery, chopped

2 sprigs fresh parsley (or 1 teaspoon dry)

½ teaspoon pepper (or to taste)

1 teaspoon salt (optional or to taste)

½ cup (41 g) nutritional yeast

☾ THE NIGHT BEFORE: Cut veggies and store in the fridge.

☀ IN THE MORNING: Add everything except nutritional yeast to the slow cooker. Cook on low 8 to 12 hours. The water will keep the veggies from sticking to the crock, but you can spray the empty crock with oil before adding your ingredients for extra security.

After cooking remove thyme stems. Add the contents of the crock and the nutritional yeast to a blender or food processor. You can also use an immersion blender if you want, but the texture won't be quite as smooth.

Keep what you think you will use in a week and store it in the fridge. Put the rest in ice cube trays and freeze. Measure at least what you put in one of the cubes so you'll know how many to use in a dish, mine are usually 2 tablespoons. Once the cubes are solid remove them from the trays and put in a re-closable freezer bag.

Use twice as much as you would store-bought bouillon. I typically use 1 to 2 tablespoons of store-bought per recipe, so that works out to 2 to 4. (Aren't you impressed with my math skills?)

YIELD: 2 cups
EQUIPMENT: 4 to 6-quart slow cooker
COOKING TIME: 8 to 12 hours on low

GOLDEN SEITAN

This is not a recipe to try and do on a rushed day or in the morning before you go to work. But trust me, it's wonderful to make your own seitan. First, you control everything that goes into it, and you can customize the spices for the recipe you are going to use it in. It's not as hard as you might think it is, and you will save tons of money making it yourself. It freezes well, and you can use the broth in other dishes if you have some left over.

 SOY-FREE   NO OIL ADDED

BROTH INGREDIENTS

7 cups (1750 ml) water

2 cloves garlic, crushed

2 bay leaves

2 sprigs lovage or 1 celery stalk, minced

1 sprig parsley

3 tablespoons DIY Golden Bouillon (page 237)

SEITAN INGREDIENTS

1½ cups (375 ml) water

1½ cups (180 g) vital wheat gluten

⅓ cup (26 g) nutritional yeast

1 tablespoon (16 g) tomato paste

¼ teaspoon salt

1 tablespoon dried thyme (optional)

1 tablespoon garlic powder(optional)

Combine all the broth ingredients in your slow cooker and turn it on high. Your broth can heat up while you make the actual seitan.

In a large bowl, mix all of the seitan ingredients. Mix until combined, and knead for 5 minutes. (You can "cheat" and use a mixer or put it in a bread machine on the dough cycle for about 5 minutes.) Let the dough rest for about 5 minutes after you have completed kneading it.

Stretch the dough out to the thickness you want and cut into desired sizes. I usually do 4 "chicken breast"–sized pieces and the rest in smaller chunks, but you could so strips, squares, even medallions if you wanted.

Drop seitan pieces into the slow cooker. You know it's done when the pieces float to the top. It may look like they all stuck together, but once you take them out of the broth they will easily come apart.

Store in the fridge submerged in the broth, or freeze extra in the broth to use later. I try to freeze it in recipe-sized portions.

YIELD: 4 large breast-sized pieces and chunks for 1 to 2 other recipes
EQUIPMENT: 4 to 6-quart slow cooker
COOKING TIME: 2 to 3 hours on low

DIY ITALIAN SAUSAGE

I love the flavors of Italian sausage. It's so yummy in things such as soups, pasta, and sandwiches. If you prefer to make staples yourself, then this recipe is for you!

 SOY-FREE NO OIL ADDED

SEITAN INGREDIENTS

¾ (177 ml) cups water

1½ cups drained white beans (about 1 15-ounce [420 g] can)

1½ cups (182 g) vital wheat gluten flour

1 tablespoon (7 g) onion powder

1 tablespoon (7 g) garlic powder

1½ teaspoon dried parsley

1 teaspoon dried oregano

½ teaspoon thyme

¾ teaspoon ground fennel seed

¾ teaspoon black pepper

1 teaspoon salt

FOR COOKING

3 cups (705 ml) water

Add the water and beans to your blender, and blend until smooth. Add the vital wheat gluten flour, onion powder, garlic powder, parsley, oregano, thyme, fennel seed, pepper, and salt to a mixer and mix until the dry ingredients are well incorporated.

Then add the liquid mixture, and knead on a low speed for about 5 minutes. You could also knead in a bread maker or by hand until the dough begins to smooth out or with your hands.

Cut into 8 equal pieces and roll into logs. I wrap mine individually in parchment paper, then use cling wrap.

Add the water and steamer rack to your slow cooker. Place the wrapped sausages in, and cook on high for 4 hours or low for 7 to 9 hours.

YIELD: 8 large links
EQUIPMENT: 4- to 6-quart slow cooker
COOKING TIME: 7 to 9 hours on low or 4 hours on high

Recipe Ideas & Variations
You can make these taste even better if you have a spice grinder. Use 1 teaspoon whole fennel seeds and 1 teaspoon whole black peppercorns in place of the ground that's called for in the recipe. Add those plus the rest of the spices to the grinder. Because it makes everything into a powder, it mixes more thoroughly into the seitan.

APPLE SAGE SAUSAGE PATTIES

This is a great way to make your own vegan sausage to use in other recipes. The crumbles and the cooked patties freeze great, so make a batch once a month.

 GLUTEN-FREE SOY-FREE ⬡ NO OIL ADDED OPTION*

2 cups (330 g) cooked brown rice

1½ cups (165 g) walnuts

2 tablespoons (12 g) nutritional yeast

1 cup (250 g) applesauce

2 tablespoons (14 g) ground flaxseed mixed with 2 tablespoons (30 ml) warm water

1 tablespoon (6 g) vegan chicken-flavored bouillon or 2 tablespoons (12 g) DIY Golden Bouillon (page 237) or

2 tablespoons (4 g) sage

1 teaspoon thyme

1 teaspoon oregano

1 teaspoon Hungarian paprika

½ to 1 teaspoon salt (to taste, use less if your bouillon is salty)

Pepper, to taste

In a food processor, pulse the cooked rice and walnuts until the mixture is coarsely ground but not puréed. Combine the nut mixture with the remaining ingredients in a large mixing bowl.

Oil a baking sheet *or use parchment to make no oil added. Form the mixture into patties. Bake in a 350°F (180°C or gas mark 4) oven for about 15 minutes, then turn them over and cook for 10 to 15 more minutes.

YIELD: 7 to 9 servings
EQUIPMENT: Slow cooker not needed
COOKING TIME: 30 minutes in oven

Preserve-the-Harvest DICED TOMATOES

Here's an easy, free-form recipe. Give it a try and you'll get that satisfied feeling when you use your handiwork in soups and stews later in the year. Try to cook the tomatoes on the same day you buy or pick them, if possible.

 GLUTEN-FREE SOY-FREE  NO OIL ADDED

Tomatoes to fill your crock

YIELD: Depends on the size of your slow
    cooker and how many tomatoes it
    holds
EQUIPMENT: 4- to 6-quart slow cooker
COOKING TIME: 7 to 9 hours on low or 3
    hours on high

Recipe Ideas and Variations

At the farmers' market, select tomatoes that are not overripe or mushy. I try to buy up all the imperfect tomatoes at my market. They are sometimes called "ugly," "seconds," or another creative word to let you know why they cost less per pound than the perfect tomatoes. Many times you can buy these at one-third of the perfect tomato price, making it even more of a bargain.

I do not peel the tomatoes, because I always use organic or at least pesticide-free ones. But if yours aren't organic you can drop them in boiling water for a couple of minutes after making a small X in the bottom of each with a knife. Once they're cool enough to handle, the skins will slide right off. Dice and proceed as indicated.

Rinse the tomatoes. Take the whole tomatoes, and put them in your crock one at a time until they peek out over the rim. This is how many tomatoes you can cook in your slow cooker. Remove the tomatoes, and now you will prep them for cooking.

Peeled or not, dice the tomatoes. Be sure to remove the top of the stem and any bruised or mushy parts. Put the diced tomatoes and their juice in the slow cooker. Cook on low for 7 to 9 hours, or on high for about 3 hours.

Make sure the tomatoes are completely cool before freezing them. Many times, I cool them in the fridge overnight before I pack them.

You can use a freezer-safe container or a resealable plastic bag that says it's for the freezer. Those bags are thicker and help their contents to stay fresh longer. The bags are easy to stack in even the smallest freezer. I put about 1½ cups (270 g, about the size of 1 can of tomatoes) per bag, carefully push the air out, and close. Wipe off the outside of the bag to make sure it's dry, or they will freeze together. Stack them on top of one another, and they will freeze in that thinner shape.

Pull a bag out the night before you need it and thaw it in the fridge. Or, because the bag and its contents were frozen thin, run cold water over the bag in the sink. Most of all, enjoy not going out to the store to buy a can of tomatoes in the middle of a snowstorm!

EASY DIY MELTABLE VEGAN CHEESE

This is so easy to make, and you have Julie Hasson and Kittee Berns to thank for this genius recipe. You will need to invest in a few specialty ingredients, but you can order them from Amazon. Check out julieandkittee.com for more vegan and gluten-free recipes—including more cheese variations!

 GLUTEN-FREE   SOY-FREE   NO OIL ADDED

2 cups (275 ml) water

½ cup (73 g) raw cashews

2 tablespoons (12 g) nutritional yeast flakes

2 teaspoons (11 g) sea salt

1½ teaspoons lactic acid

1 teaspoon granulated onion

3 tablespoons (21 g) tapioca starch

2 tablespoons (10 g) kappa carrageenan

YIELD: about 2 cups
EQUIPMENT: Slow cooker not needed
COOKING TIME: 7 to 9 minutes

In the jar of a strong blender, combine the water, cashews, nutritional yeast, salt, lactic acid, and granulated onion. Blend until super smooth and there aren't any bits of nuts.

Add the tapioca and carrageenan, and blend for 5 to 10 seconds until smooth.

Pour the cashew mixture into a large saucepan, and bring to a simmer over medium heat, whisking continually. Continue cooking, whisking continuously, for about 7 to 9 minutes until the mixture has thickened nicely and is very glossy.

Pour the cheese into a smallish container that can contain a minimum of 2 cups (475 ml) volume. I like small loaf pans or glass bowls.

If properly cooked, the cheese will start to set right away. Allow the cheese to set at room temperature for 30 minutes. Then cover and refrigerate the cheese to finish setting for 3 to 4 hours.

If the cheese doesn't set up properly that means you haven't cooked it long enough, if this happens to you, throw it back into the saucepan and cook for a few minutes more! It'll re-melt and then you can pour it back into the mold for it to solidify.

Remove the cheese from the mold and serve. Store leftovers in the fridge.

FALL HARVEST FRUIT BUTTER

Serve up a bit of fall all winter long by freezing some of this recipe. It's perfect on toast, English muffins, or bagels. This is my friend Faith's favorite recipe.

 GLUTEN-FREE SOY-FREE  NO OIL ADDED

6 large pears, peeled, cored, and chopped

4 large apples (or about 6 medium ones), peeled, cored, and chopped

2 cups (300 g) cubed fresh pumpkin or butternut squash

Juice of 2 lemons

½ cup (115 g) packed brown sugar (you can substitute ½ cup [120 ml] agave nectar or maple syrup)

1 teaspoon cinnamon

½ teaspoon allspice

½ teaspoon cardamom

½ teaspoon ground ginger

¼ teaspoon ground cloves

YIELD: 8 cups
EQUIPMENT: 4-quart slow cooker
COOKING TIME: 8 to 10 hours on low

Oil the crock of your slow cooker. Combine all the ingredients in the slow cooker. Prop the lid open by placing the thin edge of a wooden spoon handle lengthwise across the crock. This will allow the liquid to evaporate. Cook on low for 8 to 10 hours, until most of the liquid has evaporated.

If you need to evaporate more liquid, switch the slow cooker to high, leave the lid propped up, and cook for 1 to 2 hours longer.

Purée the mixture in batches using an immersion blender or a countertop blender. Let cool completely.

Transfer to freezer bags or special freezer containers for preserves. Store in the freezer for 3 to 4 months.

Recipe Ideas & Variations
Want to make a fast and fancy dessert? Combine about 1 cup (320 g) of the fruit butter with 1 container (12 ounces, 336 g) silken tofu in a food processor. Blend until very smooth. Serve chilled in martini glasses as a mousse, or put in a graham cracker crust for a super easy pie.

Recipe Ideas & Variations
No fresh pumpkin on hand? Use 1 can (15 ounces, or 420 g) pumpkin purée or 2 cups (490 g) Perfect Pumpkin Purée (page 247).

CITRUS RUM BBQ SAUCE

Tired of having to read labels with words on them that have little or nothing to do with food? Make your own barbecue sauce at home. This one is slightly sweet from the rum and orange juice, and seasoned with thyme, allspice, and ginger. It makes a mean barbecue tempeh or tofu sandwich. Freeze the leftovers in ice cube trays, and defrost a cube or two the next time you crave a sandwich.

 GLUTEN-FREE SOY-FREE  NO OIL ADDED OPTION*

2 tablespoons (30 ml) olive oil (*water sauté)

1 onion, minced

2 cloves garlic, minced

1 teaspoon grated ginger

1 can (14½ ounces, or 406 g) tomato sauce

1 can (6 ounces, or 170 g) tomato paste

½ cup (120 ml) orange juice

½ lime, juiced

½ cup (120 ml) rum (amber or dark, if possible)

2 tablespoons (30 ml) apple cider vinegar

2 tablespoons (30 ml) agave nectar or maple syrup

3 tablespoons (45 g) brown sugar

1 teaspoon dried thyme

½ teaspoon allspice

½ teaspoon paprika

Pinch of ground cloves

☾ THE NIGHT BEFORE: Heat the oil (*or water) in a skillet over medium heat, add the onion, and cook until translucent, 3 to 5 minutes. Add the garlic and cook for about 1 minute more. Transfer to an airtight container and store in the fridge overnight.

✳ IN THE MORNING: Combine all the ingredients in the slow cooker. Cook on low for 8 to 10 hours. If the sauce is still too thin, turn the slow cooker to high and prop the lid up with the handle of a wooden spoon. This will allow some of the liquid to evaporate. Only keep the amount of sauce you will use in a week in the fridge. Store the rest in the freezer for up to 6 months.

YIELD: 3–4 cups
EQUIPMENT: 4- to 6-quart slow cooker
COOKING TIME: 7 to 9 hours on low

Serving Suggestion
After the sauce has been cooked, add shredded seitan or tofu. Cook on low for 7 to 9 hours. Serve on toasted buns.

HOMEMADE SMOKY KETCHUP

Most people love ketchup and always have it on hand. Try making your own. It's really easy in the slow cooker because it cooks while you're away. This recipe has a smoky flavor, but you can make your own signature ketchup by omitting some or all of the spices in the recipe and adding curry powder or roasted garlic instead. You are only as limited as your imagination.

 GLUTEN-FREE SOY-FREE

2 tablespoons (30 ml) olive oil

½ small onion, minced

2 cloves garlic, minced

1 can (20 ounces, or 560 g) crushed tomatoes (fire-roasted, if possible), drained

2 tablespoons (32 g) tomato paste

½ cup (115 g) packed brown sugar

½ cup (120 ml) apple cider vinegar (you can use white or rice vinegar instead)

½ teaspoon salt (to taste)

¼ teaspoon chipotle chile powder

¼ teaspoon allspice

¼ teaspoon celery seed

⅛ teaspoon dry mustard

⅛ teaspoon ground cloves

⅛ teaspoon ground ginger

☾ THE NIGHT BEFORE: Heat the oil in a skillet over medium heat, add the onion, and cook until translucent, 3 to 5 minutes. Add the garlic and cook for about 1 minute more. Transfer to an airtight container and store in the fridge overnight.

☀ IN THE MORNING: Combine all the ingredients in the slow cooker. Cook on low for 8 to 10 hours. If the ketchup is still too thin, turn the slow cooker to high and prop the lid up with the handle of a wooden spoon. This will allow some of the liquid to evaporate.

YIELD: 2–2½ cups
EQUIPMENT: 4-quart slow cooker
COOKING TIME: 7 to 9 hours on low

Recipe Ideas & Variations

- Only keep the amount of ketchup you will use in a week in the fridge. Store the rest in the freezer for up to 6 months.
- You can use Preserve-the-Harvest Diced Tomatoes (page 241) instead of canned crushed tomatoes. Just purée them first, or purée the batch of ketchup after cooking.

PERFECT PUMPKIN PURÉE

*Never worry about a canned pumpkin shortage again. Each fall, pie pumpkins are
sprinkled in with the larger jack-o'-lantern pumpkins. Pie pumpkins are smaller and
many will even fit in a 1½-quart (1.4 L) slow cooker.*

 GLUTEN-FREE   SOY-FREE   NO OIL ADDED

**1 pie pumpkin that will fit in your slow
cooker**

Wash the pumpkin, and poke holes in it for the steam to
escape. Place it in the slow cooker and cook on low for 7 to 9
hours. When it's ready, a fork should easily slide through the
skin and the flesh.

Let the pumpkin cool until you can touch it without burning
yourself. Move it to a cutting board, and slice it in half.
Remove the seeds and pumpkin guts. Scrape the flesh into a
food processor or blender and purée until smooth.

YIELD: 3–6 cups
EQUIPMENT: 4-quart slow cooker
COOKING TIME: 7 to 9 hours on low

Recipe Ideas & Variations
- Use in any recipe that calls for cooked or canned pumpkin
  in the same portion as called for.
- Freeze in 1½-cup (368-g) portions, so you can thaw the
  same amount that's in one 12-ounce (368-g) can.

Did You Know?
Pie pumpkins are tastier and meant to be used in cooking
because they are fleshier.

BRANDIED CRANBERRY SAUCE

This sophisticated version of a holiday favorite is amazingly easy to make.

Note: This recipe requires a small 1- or 1½-quart (940 ml or 1.4 L) slow cooker. You can double or triple the recipe and use a larger slow cooker if you like.

 GLUTEN-FREE SOY-FREE NO OIL ADDED

1 bag (12 ounces, or 340 g) fresh
   cranberries

½ cup (120 ml) orange juice

½ cup (120 ml) agave nectar or maple
   syrup

¼ cup (63 ml) brandy

Oil the crock of your slow cooker. Add all the ingredients to the slow cooker. Cook on high for 2½ to 3½ hours. After the first hour, prop the lid up on the handle of a wooden spoon to allow the sauce to reduce.

YIELD: ½ to 2 cups
EQUIPMENT: 1- or 1½-quart slow cooker
COOKING TIME: 2½ to 3½ hours on high

Serving Suggestions
Use leftovers to top your morning oatmeal, or purée with silken tofu to make a cranberry pudding.

Appendix

ACCESSORIES

You can cook in your slow cooker just as it is, but there are a few things that can help it out a little.

- I will go ahead and say that I am not a fan of the plastic slow cooker liners, and I know many of you would rather not cook in plastic bags. If you want a super easy clean up, try using parchment paper to line your slow cooker with instead. It will even help you lift out cakes and casseroles!

- Tongs and wooden spoons are a must. Why wooden spoons? Metal can scrape some of the glaze off the crock and leave scratches. Tongs make it easy to get food out while not burning the side of your hand.

- You can use racks to lift up whole potatoes, so they don't get overcooked on the side that's usually directly on the crock.

- I use loaf baking pans in my 6-quart oval slow cookers. You need to measure carefully and make certain the handles on it will fit as well.

FACEBOOK GROUPS AND RESOURCES

You can always find recipes and information on my blog, HealthySlowCooking.com. I also have a private Facebook group called Vegan Cooking with Kathy Hester that you can join for free. (www.facebook.com/groups/vegancookingwithkathy/)

Here are some of my favorite bloggers and FB groups that have good vegan slow cooker recipes.

- Facebook Page, The Vegan Slow Cooker
  (www.facebook.com/veganslowcookerrecipes/)

- Facebook Page, Healthy Slow Cooking
  (www.facebook.com/veganslowcooker/)

- FatFreeVegan.com by Susan Voisin

- FindingVegan.com, a vegan food photo directory with links to the recipes

Be sure to check out my other slow cooker book, *Vegan Slow Cooking for Two or Just You* for great slow cooker recipes in a 1½- to 2-quart slow cooker.

Acknowledgements

This book would not have been possible if not for Amanda Waddell and Sally Ekus.
In fact, this book would have never existed if it weren't for Amanda reaching out to me as a new blogger so many years ago. It's been my pleasure to work with her again on revising and expanding my very first book.

Thanks to Jenna Patton for being so easy to work with and doing a great editing job. I am very grateful to the designer, Laura Klynstra, for creating such an amazing design for this book. The beautiful photography is the work of photographer and food stylist Kate Lewis.

Special thanks to all my testers: Rochelle Arvizo, Brandie Bloggins, Michelle Cardillo, Monica Soria Caruso, Julie Cross, Christina Emery, Faith Hood, Kim Logan, Jenna Patton, Debbie Smith, and Sherrie Thompson for their willingness to cook anything—even if they didn't think it could be done in a slow cooker.

About the Author

Kathy Hester is passionate about making healthy eating easy and delicious. You can find her recipes on her sites www.HealthySlowCooking.com and www.PlantBasedInstantPot.com, and on her private Facebook group, Vegan Recipes: Cooking with Kathy Hester. Her recipes are full of flavor and the meat-eaters in your family will love them, too. Her dishes have been featured in the *Washington Post, Oregonian,* Yoga Journal Online, just to name a few. She is also the author of the best-selling cookbook, *The Ultimate Vegan Cookbook for Your Instant Pot.*

Index